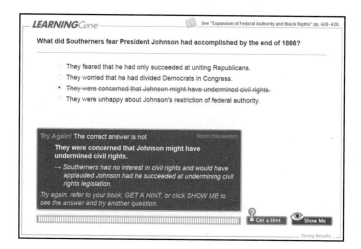

The American Promise

A History of
the United States

The American Promise

A History of the United States

SIXTH EDITION
VOLUME 1: TO 1877

James L. Roark
Emory University

Michael P. Johnson
Johns Hopkins University

Patricia Cline Cohen
University of California, Santa Barbara

Sarah Stage
Arizona State University

Susan M. Hartmann
The Ohio State University

BEDFORD/ST. MARTIN'S

BOSTON ♦ NEW YORK

FOR BEDFORD/ST. MARTIN'S

Vice President, Editorial, Macmillan Higher Education Humanities: Edwin Hill
Publisher for History: Mary V. Dougherty
Senior Executive Editor for History and Technology: William J. Lombardo
Director of Development for History: Jane Knetzger
Senior Developmental Editor: Heidi L. Hood
Production Editor: Kerri A. Cardone
Production Manager: Joe Ford
Executive Marketing Manager: Sandra McGuire
Editorial Assistant: Victoria Royal
Copy Editor: Lisa Wehrle
Indexer: Leoni Z. McVey
Cartography: Mapping Specialists Limited
Photo Researcher: Naomi Kornhauser
Senior Art Director: Anna Palchik
Text Design: Cenveo Publisher Services
Cover Design: William Boardman
Cover Photo: Laying of the cornerstone for the Chicago Water Tower, March 25, 1867.
© Chicago History Museum / Bridgeman Art Library
Composition: Cenveo Publisher Services
Printing and Binding: RR Donnelley and Sons

Manufactured in the United States of America.

9   8   7   6   5
f   e   d   c   b

For information, write: Bedford/St. Martin's, 75 Arlington Street, Boston, MA 02116   (617-399-4000)

ISBN 978-1-4576–6838-8 (Combined Edition)   ISBN 978-1-4576-8887-4 (Loose-leaf Edition)
ISBN 978-1-4576-6841-8 (Volume 1)   ISBN 978-1-4576-8889-8 (Loose-leaf Edition,
ISBN 978-1-4576-6839-5 (Volume 2)   Volume 1)
                                                   ISBN 978-1-4576-8888-1 (Loose-leaf Edition, Volume
                                                       2)

Acknowledgments: Text acknowledgments and copyrights appear at the back of the book on page 525, which constitute an extension of the copyright page. Art acknowledgments and copyrights appear on the same page as the art selections they cover. It is a violation of the law to reproduce these selections by any means whatsoever without the written permission of the copyright holder.

what is truly important. To help students read actively and understand the central idea of the chapter, instructors who use LaunchPad can also assign our **new Guided Reading Exercises**. This new exercise, which appears at the start of each chapter, prompts students to collect information to be used to answer a broad analytic question central to the chapter as a whole.

To further encourage students to read and fully assimilate the text as well as measure how well they do this, instructors can assign the **new multiple-choice summative quizzes** in LaunchPad, where they are automatically graded. These secure tests not only encourage students to study the book, they can be assigned at specific intervals as high stakes testing and thus provide another means for analyzing class performance.

Extra Support

Another big challenge for survey instructors is meeting the needs of a range of students, particularly the students who need the most support. In addition to the formative assessment of LearningCurve, which adapts to the needs of students at any level, *The American Promise* offers a number of tools for the underprepared.

For those who need to know how to sort out what is important, each chapter opener includes **new Content Learning Objectives** to prepare students to read the chapter with purpose.

Once into the heart of the chapter, students are reminded to think about main ideas through **Review Questions** placed at the end of every major section. In print and LaunchPad these questions can be assigned as a chapter review activity.

Some students also have trouble connecting events and ideas, particularly with special boxed features. To address this, we have added a **new Connect to the Big Idea question** to each feature to help students understand the significance of the featured topic to the chapter as a whole. These questions are also available in the print and LaunchPad versions of the book.

Critical Thinking and Analysis

The American Promise also strives to turn students into critical thinkers who read actively and can analyze what they read. We have put this goal at the center of this revision through several activities that invite critical reading, evaluation of primary sources, and geographical literacy.

Critical Reading

To foster not only active reading but critical reading of the narrative, we introduce a **new Reflections assignment** at the end of each major section in LaunchPad, which uses a series of multiple choice and short answer questions to challenge students to think critically about the narrative as historical interpretation. To bring students' critical thinking skills to the next level, the **new Chronological Reasoning Activity** in LaunchPad encourages students to make connections among events and evaluate their importance, while the **new "What's Your Question"** activity, which builds naturally from the Reflections activities, presses students to formulate a solid historical question of their own based on their introspections about the chapter.

To demonstrate and engage students in various methods and perspectives of historical thinking, our 16 **Historical Questions** feature essays pose and interpret specific questions of continuing interest. Perennial favorites brought back in this edition range from "Was the New United States a Christian Country?" and "How Often Were Slaves Whipped?" to "Was There a Sexual Revolution in the 1920s?" and "Why Did the Allies Win World War II?" Short-answer questions at the end of the features prompt students to consider things such as evidence, beliefs and values, and cause and effect as they relate to the historical question at hand. Available both in print and online these features can be easily assigned in LaunchPad, along with multiple choice quizzes that measure student comprehension.

With this edition we also bring back two popular sets of end-of-chapter questions that help widen students' focus as they consider what they have read. **Making Connections** questions ask students to think about broad developments within the chapter, while **Linking to the Past** questions cross-reference developments in earlier chapters, encouraging students to make comparisons, see causality, and understand change over longer periods of time. Both sets of questions are assignable from the print and LaunchPad versions.

Evaluation of Primary Sources

Primary sources form the heart of the feature program in this edition as a means to engage students with history and to actively develop their critical thinking skills. We are pleased to offer **more Documenting the American**

Promise features than ever before—now 23 in all and 7 more than in the last edition. Each of these features juxtaposes two to four primary documents to reveal varying perspectives on a topic or an issue and to provide students with opportunities to build and practice their skills of historical interpretation. Feature introductions and document headnotes contextualize the sources, and short-answer questions at the end of the features promote critical thinking about primary sources. In addition to bringing back some favorites enjoyed in the past, new topics have been added that are rich with human drama and include "Reactions to the Boston Port Act Outside of Massachusetts," "The Gold Rush," "Ida B. Wells and Her Campaign to Stop Lynching," "The Songs of the Knights of Labor," "Americans Encounter the New Deal," and "Ending the War in Vietnam." These features are available both in print and online and they can be easily assigned in LaunchPad, along with multiple choice quizzes that measure student comprehension.

In addition, over 150 documents in the accompanying collection *Reading the American Past* are available free to users who package the documents collection with the main print text, and they are automatically included in the LaunchPad e-book. Not only can the short answers be easily assigned from within LaunchPad, but multiple choice questions are also available for assignment to measure comprehension and hold students accountable for their reading.

LaunchPad for The American Promise also comes with a collection of **over 135 additional primary sources** that instructors can choose to assign. These sources include letters, memoirs, court records, government documents, and more, and they include items by or about such people as John Smith, William Penn, Anne Hutchinson, Jonathan Edwards, Mary Jemison, Black Hawk, John C. Calhoun, Frederick Douglass, Abraham Lincoln, Mary Elizabeth Lease, William Jennings Bryan, Theodore Roosevelt, Nicolo Sacco and Bartolomeo Vanzetti, Huey P. Long, Franklin D. Roosevelt, Harry S. Truman, Paul Robeson, Richard Nixon, Ronald Reagan, and more.

This edition encourages students to think critically about visuals as primary source as well. Because students are so attuned to visuals and instructors deeply value their usefulness as primary sources, we have added 8 **more Visualizing History** features for a total of 20 across the book. A painting of colonial urban life, powder horns, early sketches of the great seal of the United States, a painting of a slave auction, Native American recreation, paintings

with differing viewpoints of Custer's last stand, Marshall Plan posters, and popular art about desegregation enrich this edition as sources for examination. By stressing the importance of historical context in the accompanying essay and, through new short-answer questions prompting critical analysis, each feature shows students how to mine visual documents for evidence about the past. Visualizing History features are available both in print and online and they can be easily assigned in LaunchPad, along with multiple choice quizzes that measure student comprehension.

To give students ample opportunity to practice thinking critically about primary source images, four pictures in each chapter—four times more than in the last edition—include a special **visual activity caption** that reinforces this essential skill. One set of questions in these activities prompts analysis of the image, while a second set of questions helps students connect the images to main points in the narrative. In LaunchPad, the answers to these questions can be submitted directly to the gradebook for convenient assessment.

Geographical Literacy

To help students think critically about the role of geography in American history, with two maps in each chapter we include a **map activity caption**. One set of questions in these activities prompts map analysis, while a second set of questions helps students connect the maps to main points in the narrative. In LaunchPad, the answers to these questions can be submitted directly to the gradebook for convenient assessment.

Acknowledgments

We gratefully acknowledge all of the helpful suggestions from those who have read and taught from previous editions of *The American Promise*, and we hope that our many classroom collaborators will be pleased to see their influence in the sixth edition. In particular, we wish to thank the talented scholars and teachers who gave generously of their time and knowledge to review this book: LeNie Adolphson, *Sauk Valley Community College;* Daniel Anderson, *Cincinnati State Technical and Community College;* Ian Baldwin, *University of Nevada, Las Vegas;* Dustin Black, *El Camino College;* Nawana Britenriker, *Pikes Peak Community College;* Elizabeth Broen, *South Florida State College;* Robert Bush, *Front*

Range Community College; Brian David Collins, *El Centro College;* Alexandra Cornelius, *Florida International University;* Sondra Cosgrove, *College of Southern Nevada;* Rodney E. Dillon, Jr., *Palm Beach State College;* Wayne Drews, *Georgia Institute of Technology;* Edward J. Dudlo, *Brookhaven College;* E. J. Fabyan, *Vincennes University;* Cecilia Gowdy-Wygant, *Front Range Community College;* William Grose, *Wytheville Community College;* Jeff Janowick, *Lansing Community College;* Juneann Klees, *Bay College;* Leonard V. Larsen, *Des Moines Area Community College;* Charles Levine, *Mesa Community College;* Mary Linehan, *University of Texas at Tyler;* Annie Liss, *South Texas College;* Patricia Loughlin, *University of Central Oklahoma;* Walter Miszczenko, *College of Western Idaho;* Rick Murray, *Los Angeles Valley College;* Richard Owens, *West Liberty University;* Stacey Pendleton, *University of Colorado Denver;* Michael J. Pfeifer, *John Jay College of Criminal Justice;* Chris Rasmussen, *Fairleigh Dickinson University;* Robert Sawvel, *University of Northern Colorado;* Benjamin G. Scharff, *West Virginia University;* Christopher Sleeper, *MiraCosta College;* Janet P. Smith, *East Tennessee State University;* John Howard Smith, *Texas A&M University–Commerce;* William Z. Tannenbaum, *Missouri Southern State University;* Ramon C. Veloso, *Palomar College;* and Kenneth A. Watras, *Paradise Valley Community College.*

A project as complex as this requires the talents of many individuals. First, we would like to acknowledge our families for their support, forbearance, and toleration of our textbook responsibilities. Naomi Kornhauser contributed her vast knowledge, tireless energy, and diligent research to make possible the useful and attractive illustration program.

We would also like to thank the many people at Bedford/St. Martin's and Macmillan Education who have been crucial to this project. No one has done more than our friend, senior editor Heidi Hood, who managed the entire revision and supplements program. Heidi, with help from senior editor Leah Strauss and associate editor Jennifer Jovin, guided us through every part of this complex revision, used unfailing good judgment, and saved us from many a misstep. Thanks also go to editorial assistant Victoria Royal for her assistance coordinating the pre-revision review, preparing the manuscript, and for working on the supplements, along with Jennifer Jovin. We are also grateful to Jane Knetzger, director of development for history; William J. Lombardo, senior executive editor for history; and Mary Dougherty, publisher for history, for their support and guidance. For their imaginative and tireless efforts to promote the book, we want to thank Sandi McGuire and Alex Kaufman. With great skill and professionalism, production editor Kerri Cardone pulled together the many pieces related to copyediting, design, and composition, with the guidance of managing editor Michael Granger. Production manager Joe Ford oversaw the manufacturing of the book. Designer Jerilyn Bockorick, copyeditor Lisa Wehrle, and proofreaders Jan Cocker and Nancy Benjamin attended to the myriad details that help make the book shine. Leoni McVey provided an outstanding index. The book's gorgeous cover was designed by William Boardman. Media producer Michelle Camisa managed the process that made sure that *The American Promise* remains at the forefront of technological support for students and instructors. Denise Wydra, vice president of editorial for the humanities, provided helpful advice throughout the course of the project. Finally, Charles H. Christensen, former president of Bedford/St. Martin's, took a personal interest in *The American Promise* from the start, and Joan E. Feinberg, former co-president of Macmillan Higher Education, encouraged us through each edition.

Versions and Supplements

Adopters of *The American Promise* and their students have access to abundant print and digital resources and tools, including documents, assessment and presentation materials, the acclaimed Bedford Series in History and Culture volumes, and much more. And for the first time, the full-featured LaunchPad course space provides access to the narrative with all assignment and assessment opportunities at the ready. See below for more information, visit the book's catalog site at **bedfordstmartins.com/roark/catalog**, or contact your local Bedford/St. Martin's sales representative.

Get the Right Version for Your Class

To accommodate different course lengths and course budgets, *The American Promise* is available in several different formats, including 3-hole punched loose-leaf Budget Books versions and low-priced PDF e-books, which include the *Bedford e-Book to Go for The American Promise* from our Web site and other PDF e-books from other commercial sources. And for the best value of all, package a new print book with LaunchPad at no additional charge to get the best each format offers—a print version for easy portability and reading with a LaunchPad interactive e-book and course space with loads of additional assignment and assessment options.

- **Combined Volume** (Chapters 1–31): available in paperback and e-book formats and in LaunchPad

- **Volume 1, To 1877** (Chapters 1–16): available in paperback, loose-leaf, and e-book formats and in LaunchPad

- **Volume 2, From 1865** (Chapters 16–31): available in paperback, loose-leaf, and e-book formats and in LaunchPad

As noted below, any of these volumes can be packaged with additional titles for a discount. To get ISBNs for discount packages, see the online catalog at **bedfordstmartins.com/roark** /catalog or contact your Bedford/St. Martin's representative.

NEW Assign LaunchPad—A Content-Rich and Assessment-Ready Interactive e-book and Course Space

Available for discount purchase on its own or for packaging with new books at no additional charge, LaunchPad is a breakthrough solution for today's courses. Intuitive and easy-to-use for students and instructors alike, LaunchPad is ready to use as is, and can be edited, customized with your own material, and assigned in seconds. *LaunchPad for The American Promise* includes Bedford/St. Martin's high-quality content all in one place, including the full interactive e-book and the *Reading the American Past* documents collection plus LearningCurve formative quizzing, guided reading activities designed to help students read actively for key concepts, additional primary sources, images, videos, chapter summative quizzes, and more.

Through a wealth of formative and summative assessments, including short answer, essay questions, multiple-choice quizzing, and the adaptive learning program of LearningCurve (see the full description ahead), students gain confidence and get into their reading *before* class. Map and visual activities engage students with visual analysis and critical thinking as they work through each unit, while special boxed features become more meaningful through automatically graded multiple choice exercises and short answer questions that prompt students to analyze their reading.

Best of all, each unit comes with a set of activities specially designed to make critical thinking a part of students' active reading experience. A set of "Reflections" questions at the end of every major section in the chapter exercises students' critical reading skills as they reflect on the narrative as historical interpretation, a "Chronological Reasoning" activity at the end of each chapter prompts students to consider the connections among events and why they are important, and the "What's Your Question?" activity at the end of the unit guides students to formulate their own historical questions.

LaunchPad easily integrates with course management systems and with fast ways to build assignments, rearrange chapters, and add new pages, sections, or links, it lets teachers build the courses they want to teach and hold students accountable. For more information, visit **launchpadworks.com** or to arrange a demo, contact us at **history@bedfordstmartins.com**.

✔ NEW Assign LearningCurve So Your Students Come to Class Prepared

Students using LaunchPad receive access to LearningCurve for *The American Promise*. Assigning LearningCurve in place of reading quizzes is easy for instructors, and the reporting features help instructors track overall class trends and spot topics that are giving students trouble so they can adjust their lectures and class activities. This online learning tool is popular with students because it was designed to help them rehearse content at their own pace in a nonthreatening, game-like environment. The feedback for wrong answers provides instructional coaching and sends students back to the book for review. Students answer as many questions as necessary to reach a target score, with repeated chances to revisit material they haven't mastered. When LearningCurve is assigned, students come to class better prepared.

Take Advantage of Instructor Resources

Bedford/St. Martin's has developed a rich array of teaching resources for this book and for this course. They range from lecture and presentation materials and assessment tools to course management options. Most can be found in LaunchPad or can be downloaded or ordered at **bedfordstmartins.com/roark/catalog**.

Instructor's Resource Manual. The instructor's manual offers both experienced and first-time instructors tools for preparing lectures and running discussions. It includes chapter content learning objectives, annotated chapter outlines, teaching strategies, and a guide to

chapter-specific supplements available for the text, plus research paper topic ideas, suggestions on how to get the most out of LearningCurve, and a survival guide for first-time teaching assistants.

Guide to Changing Editions. Designed to facilitate an instructor's transition from the previous edition of *The American Promise* to the current edition, this guide presents an overview of major changes as well as other changes in each chapter.

Computerized Test Bank. The test bank includes a mix of fresh, carefully crafted multiple-choice, short-answer, and essay questions for each chapter. It also contains volume-wide essay questions. All questions appear in Microsoft Word format and in easy-to-use test bank software that allows instructors to add, edit, re-sequence, and print questions and answers. Instructors can also export questions into a variety of formats, including Blackboard, Desire2Learn, and Moodle.

The Bedford Lecture Kit: PowerPoint Maps and Images. Look good and save time with ***The Bedford Lecture Kit***. These presentation materials are downloadable individually from the Instructor Resources tab at **bedfordstmartins .com/roark/catalog**. They include all maps, figures, and images from the textbook in JPEG and PowerPoint formats.

America in Motion: Video Clips for U.S. History. Set history in motion with *America in Motion*, an instructor DVD containing dozens of short digital movie files of events in twentieth-century American history. From the wreckage of the battleship *Maine* to FDR's fireside chats to Oliver North testifying before Congress, *America in Motion* engages students with dynamic scenes from key events and challenges them to think critically. All files are classroom-ready, edited for brevity, and easily integrated with PowerPoint or other presentation software for electronic lectures or assignments. An accompanying guide provides each clip's historical context, ideas for use, and suggested questions.

Package and Save Your Students Money

For information on free packages and discounts up to 50%, visit **bedfordstmartins.com/roark /catalog**, or contact your local Bedford/St. Martin's sales representative. The products that follow all qualify for discount packaging.

Reading The American Past, **Fifth Edition.** Edited by Michael P. Johnson, one of the authors of *The American Promise*, and designed to complement the textbook, *Reading the American Past* provides a broad selection of over 150 primary source documents, as well as editorial apparatus to help students understand the sources. Available free when packaged with the print text and included in the LaunchPad e-book. Also available on its own as a downloadable PDF e-book.

NEW Bedford Digital Collections at macmillanhighered.com/launchpadsolo /BDC/USHistory/catalog. This source collection provides a flexible and affordable online repository of discovery-oriented primary-source projects that you can easily customize and link to from your course management system or Web site.

The Bedford Series in History and Culture. More than 100 titles in this highly praised series combine first-rate scholarship, historical narrative, and important primary documents for undergraduate courses. Each book is brief, inexpensive, and focused on a specific topic or period. For a complete list of titles, visit **bedfordstmartins .com/history/series**.

Rand McNally Atlas of American History. This collection of over eighty full-color maps illustrates key events and eras from early exploration, settlement, expansion, and immigration to U.S. involvement in wars abroad and on U.S. soil. Introductory pages for each section include a brief overview, timelines, graphs, and photos to quickly establish a historical context.

Maps in Context: A Workbook for American History. Written by historical cartography expert Gerald A. Danzer (University of Illinois at Chicago), this skill-building workbook helps students comprehend essential connections between geographic literacy and historical understanding. Organized to correspond to the typical U.S. history survey course, *Maps in Context* presents a wealth of map-centered projects and convenient pop quizzes that give students hands-on experience working with maps.

The Bedford Glossary for U.S. History. This handy supplement for the survey course gives students historically contextualized definitions for hundreds of terms—from *abolitionism* to *zoot suit*—that they will encounter in lectures, reading, and exams.

U.S. History Matters: A Student Guide to U.S. History Online. This resource, written by Alan Gevinson, Kelly Shrum, and the late Roy Rosenzweig (all of George Mason University), provides an illustrated and annotated guide to 250 of the most useful Web sites for student research in U.S. history as well as advice on evaluating and using Internet sources. This essential guide is based on the acclaimed "History Matters" Web site developed by the American Social History Project and the Center for History and New Media.

Trade Books. Titles published by sister companies Hill and Wang; Farrar, Straus and Giroux; Henry Holt and Company; St. Martin's Press; Picador; and Palgrave Macmillan are available at a 50% discount when packaged with Bedford/ St. Martin's textbooks. For more information, visit **bedfordstmartins.com/tradeup**.

A Pocket Guide to Writing in History. This portable and affordable reference tool by Mary Lynn Rampolla provides reading, writing, and research advice useful to students in all history courses. Concise yet comprehensive advice on approaching typical history assignments, developing critical reading skills, writing effective history papers, conducting research, using and documenting sources, and avoiding plagiarism —enhanced with practical tips and examples throughout—have made this slim reference a best-seller.

A Student's Guide to History. This complete guide to success in any history course provides the practical help students need to be successful. In addition to introducing students to the nature of the discipline, author Jules Benjamin teaches a wide range of skills from preparing for exams to approaching common writing assignments, and explains the research and documentation process with plentiful examples.

Going to the Source: The Bedford Reader in American History. Developed by Victoria Bissell Brown and Timothy J. Shannon, this reader's strong pedagogical framework helps students learn how to ask fruitful questions in order to evaluate documents effectively and develop critical reading skills. The reader's wide variety of chapter topics that complement the survey course and its rich diversity of sources—from personal letters to political cartoons—provoke students' interest as it teaches them the skills they need to successfully interrogate historical sources.

America Firsthand. With its distinctive focus on ordinary people, this primary documents reader, by Anthony Marcus, John M. Giggie, and David Burner, offers a remarkable range of perspectives on America's history from those who lived it. Popular Points of View sections expose students to different perspectives on a specific event or topic, and Visual Portfolios invite analysis of the visual record.

Brief Contents

Contents

CHAPTER 1
Ancient America,
Before 1492   1

CHAPTER 2
Europeans Encounter the
New World, 1492–1600   25

CHAPTER 3
The Southern Colonies in the Seventeenth Century, 1601–1700   51

CHAPTER 4
The Northern Colonies in the Seventeenth Century, 1601–1700   77

CHAPTER 9
The New Nation Takes Form, 1789–1800   225

CHAPTER 10
Republicans in Power, 1800–1824   253

APPENDICES

Maps, Figures, and Tables

Maps

Figures and Tables

Special Features

The American Promise

A History of the United States

Ancient America

Before 1492

CONTENT LEARNING OBJECTIVES

After reading and studying this chapter, you should be able to:

- Distinguish archaeology and history as disciplines, and understand the possibilities and limitations of both.

- Identify the earth's first human inhabitants and what developments allowed them to migrate to the Western Hemisphere.

- Differentiate between Archaic hunter-gatherers and the Paleo-Indians, and identify the main characteristics of their cultures.

- Explain how the Archaic peoples transitioned from being nomadic hunter-gatherers to relying on agriculture and permanent settlements.

- Identify the major Native American cultures that flourished in North America on the eve of Columbus's arrival and the similarities among them.

- Describe the structure, influence, and expanse of the Mexica (Aztec) empire on the eve of Columbus's arrival.

MISSISSIPPIAN WOODEN MASK
Between AD 1200 and 1350, a Mississippian in what is now central Illinois, fashioned this mask. Influenced by the culture of Cahokia, it was probably used in rituals. Photo by John Bigelow Taylor.

NOBODY TODAY KNOWS HIS NAME. BUT ALMOST A THOUSAND years ago, more than four hundred years before Europeans arrived in the Western Hemisphere, many ancient Americans celebrated this man— let's call him Sun Falcon. They buried Sun Falcon during elaborate rituals at Cahokia, the largest residential and ceremonial site in ancient North America, the giant landmass north of present-day Mexico. Located near the eastern shore of the Mississippi River in what is now southwestern Illinois, Cahokia stood at the spiritual and political center of the world of more than 20,000 ancient Americans who lived there and nearby. The way Cahokians buried Sun Falcon suggests that he was a very important person who represented spiritual and political authority.

What we know about Sun Falcon and the Cahokians who buried him has been discovered by archaeologists—scientists who study artifacts, material objects left behind by ancient peoples. Cahokia attracted the attention of archaeologists because of the hundreds of earthen mounds that ancient Americans built in the region. The largest surviving mound, Monks Mound, is a huge pyramid that covers sixteen acres, making it the biggest single structure ever built by ancient North Americans.

Atop Monks Mound, political and religious leaders performed ceremonies watched by thousands of Cahokians who stood on a fifty-acre plaza at the base of the mound. Their ceremonies were probably designed to demonstrate to onlookers the leaders' access to supernatural forces. At the far edge of the plaza, Cahokians buried Sun Falcon in an oblong mound about 6 feet high and 250 feet long.

Before Cahokians lowered Sun Falcon into his grave sometime around AD 1050, they first placed the body of another man facedown in the dirt. On top of that man, Cahokians draped a large cape made of 20,000 shell beads crafted into the likeness of a bird. They then put Sun Falcon faceup on the beaded cape with his head pointing southeast, aligned with the passage of the sun across the sky during the summer solstice. Experts speculate that Cahokians who buried Sun Falcon sought to pay homage not only to him but also to the awe-inspiring forces of darkness and light, of earth and sun, that governed their lives.

To accompany Sun Falcon, Cahokians also buried hundreds of exquisitely crafted artifacts and the bodies of seven other adults who probably were relatives or servants of Sun Falcon. Not far away, archaeologists discovered several astonishing mass graves. One contained 53 women, all but one between the ages of fifteen and twenty-five, who had been sacrificed by poison, strangulation, or having their throats slit. Other graves contained 43 more sacrificed women, and 43 other men and women who had been executed at the burial site. In all, more than 270 people were buried in the mound with Sun Falcon.

Nobody knows exactly who Sun Falcon was or why Cahokians buried him as they did. To date, archaeologists have found no similar burial site in ancient North America. Most likely, Sun Falcon's burial and the human sacrifices that accompanied it were major public rituals that communicated to the many onlookers the fearsome power he wielded, the respect he commanded, and the authority his survivors intended to honor and maintain. Much remains unknown and unknowable about him and his fellow Cahokians, just as it does with other ancient Americans. The history of ancient Americans is therefore necessarily incomplete and controversial. Still, archaeologists have learned enough to understand where ancient Americans came from and many basic features of the complex cultures they created and passed along to their descendants, who dominated the history of America until 1492.

VISUAL ACTIVITY

Cahokia Burial

The excavation of a burial site at Cahokia revealed the remains of a man—presumably a revered leader—whom Cahokians buried atop a large bird-shaped cape covered with shell beads. Nearby in the same mound, excavators found mass graves of scores of other Cahokians, many of them executed just before burial, evidently during ceremonies to honor their leader. Photo courtesy of University of Wisconsin-Milwaukee Archaeological Research Laboratory (ARL image 1967.2.31)

READING THE IMAGE: What does the cape or blanket suggest about patterns of trade and craftsmanship at Cahokia?

CONNECTIONS: Where was Cahokia located and for approximately how many ancient Americans was this an important spiritual and political center?

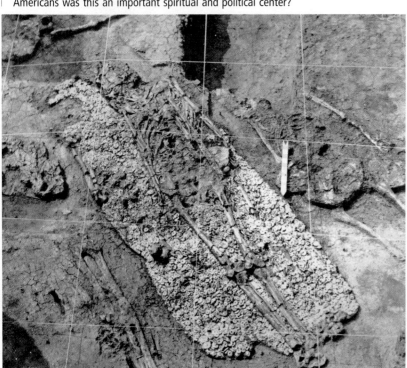

▶ Archaeology and History

Archaeologists and historians share the desire to learn about people who lived in the past, but they usually employ different methods to obtain information. Both archaeologists and historians study artifacts as clues to the activities and ideas of the humans who created them. They concentrate, however, on different kinds of artifacts. Archaeologists tend to focus on physical objects such as bones, spear points, pots, baskets, jewelry, clothing, and buildings. Historians direct their attention mostly to writings, such as letters, diary entries, laws, speeches, newspapers, and court cases. The characteristic concentration of historians on writings and of archaeologists on other physical objects denotes a rough cultural and chronological boundary between the human beings studied by the two groups of scholars, a boundary marked by the use of writing.

Writing is defined as a system of symbols that record spoken language. Writing originated among ancient peoples in China, Egypt, and Central America about eight thousand years ago, within the most recent 2 percent of the four hundred millennia that modern human beings have existed. While the ancient Americans who buried Sun Falcon at Cahokia about AD 1050 and all those who inhabited North America in 1492 possessed many forms of symbolic representation, they did not use writing. Ancient Americans invented hundreds of spoken languages; they learned to survive in almost every natural environment; they chose and honored leaders; they traded, warred, and worshipped; and above all, they learned from and taught one another. However, much of what we would like to know about their experiences and those of other ancient Americans remains unknown because they did not write about it.

Archaeologists specialize in learning about people who did not document their history in writing. They study the millions of artifacts these people created. They also scrutinize geological strata, pollen, and other environmental features to reconstruct as much as possible about the world inhabited by ancient peoples. This chapter relies on studies by archaeologists to sketch a brief overview of ancient America, the long first phase of the history of the United States.

Ancient Americans and their descendants resided in North America for thousands of years before Europeans arrived. While they created societies and cultures of remarkable diversity

CHRONOLOGY

ca. 400,000 BP	• *Homo sapiens* evolve in Africa.
ca. 25,000– 14,000 BP	• Glaciation exposes Beringia land bridge.
ca. 15,000 BP	• Humans arrive in North America.
ca. 13,500– 13,000 BP	• Paleo-Indians use Clovis points.
ca. 11,000 BP	• Extinction of mammoths.
ca. 10,000– 3000 BP	• Archaic hunter-gatherer cultures dominate ancient America.
ca. 5000 BP	• Chumash culture emerges in southern California.
ca. 4000 BP	• Eastern Woodland peoples grow gourds, make pottery.
ca. 3500 BP	• Southwestern cultures cultivate corn.
ca. 2500 BP	• Eastern Woodland cultures build burial mounds, cultivate corn.
ca. 2500– 2100 BP	• Adena culture develops in Ohio.
ca. 2100 BP– AD 400	• Hopewell culture emerges in Ohio and Mississippi valleys.
ca. AD 200– 900	• Mogollon culture develops in New Mexico.
ca. AD 500	• Bows and arrows appear south of Arctic.
ca. AD 500– 1400	• Hohokam culture develops in Arizona.
ca. AD 800– 1500	• Mississippian culture flourishes in Southeast.
ca. AD 1000– 1200	• Anasazi peoples build cliff dwellings and pueblos.
ca. AD 1325– 1500	• Mexica establish Mexican empire.
AD 1492	• Christopher Columbus arrives in New World.

and complexity, their history cannot be reconstructed with the detail and certainty made possible by writing.

> **REVIEW**   Why must historians rely on the work of archaeologists to write the history of ancient America?

▶ The First Americans

The first human beings to arrive in the Western Hemisphere emigrated from Asia. They brought with them hunting skills, weapon- and tool-making techniques, and other forms of human knowledge developed millennia earlier in Africa, Europe, and Asia. These first Americans hunted large mammals, such as the mammoths they had learned in Europe and Asia to kill, butcher, and process for food, clothing, and building materials. Most likely, these first Americans wandered into the Western Hemisphere more or less accidentally in pursuit of prey.

African and Asian Origins

Human beings lived elsewhere in the world for hundreds of thousands of years before they reached the Western Hemisphere. They lacked a way to travel to the Western Hemisphere because millions of years before humans existed anywhere on the globe, North and South America became detached from the gigantic common landmass scientists now call Pangaea. About 240 million years ago, powerful forces deep within the earth fractured Pangaea and slowly pushed continents apart to their present positions (Map 1.1). This process of continental drift encircled the land of the Western Hemisphere with large oceans that isolated it from the other continents long before early human beings (*Homo erectus*) first appeared in Africa about two million years ago.

More than 1.5 million years after *Homo erectus* appeared, or about 400,000 BP, modern humans (*Homo sapiens*) evolved in Africa. (The abbreviation *BP*—for "years before the present"—indicates dates earlier than two thousand years ago; for more recent dates, the common

MAP ACTIVITY

MAP 1.1   Continental Drift

Massive geological forces separated North and South America from other continents eons before human beings evolved in Africa 1.5 million years ago.

READING THE MAP: Which continents separated from Pangaea earliest? Which ones separated from each other last? Which are still closely connected to each other?

CONNECTIONS: How does continental drift explain why human life developed elsewhere on the planet for hundreds of thousands of years before the first person entered the Western Hemisphere 15,000 years ago?

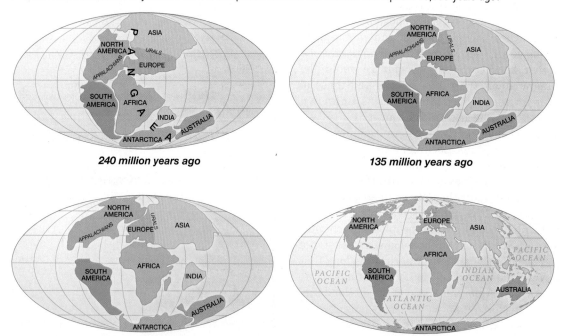

240 million years ago

135 million years ago

65 million years ago

Present day

and familiar notation *AD* is used, as in AD 1492.) All human beings throughout the world today are descendants of these ancient Africans. Their DNA was the template for ours. Slowly, over many millennia, *Homo sapiens* migrated out of Africa and into Europe and Asia, which had retained land connections to Africa, allowing ancient humans to migrate on foot. For roughly 97 percent of the time *Homo sapiens* have been on earth, none migrated across the enormous oceans isolating North and South America from the Eurasian landmass.

Two major developments made it possible for ancient humans to migrate to the Western Hemisphere. First, people successfully adapted to the frigid environment near the Arctic Circle. Second, changes in the earth's climate reconnected North America to Asia.

By about 25,000 BP, *Homo sapiens* had spread from Africa throughout Europe and Asia. People, probably women, had learned to use bone needles to sew animal skins into warm clothing that permitted them to become permanent residents of extremely cold regions such as northeastern Siberia. A few of these ancient Siberians clothed in animal hides walked to North America on land that now lies submerged beneath the sixty miles of water that currently separates easternmost Siberia from westernmost Alaska. A pathway across this watery chasm opened during the last global cold spell—which endured from about 25,000 BP to 14,000 BP—when snow piled up in glaciers, causing the sea level to drop, thereby exposing a land bridge hundreds of miles wide called **Beringia** that connected Asian Siberia and American Alaska.

Siberian hunters roamed Beringia for centuries in search of mammoths, bison, and numerous smaller animals. As the hunters ventured farther east, they eventually became pioneers of human life in the Western Hemisphere. Although they did not know it, their migrations revolutionized the history of the world.

Archaeologists refer to these first migrants and their descendants for the next few millennia as **Paleo-Indians**. They speculate that these Siberian hunters traveled in small bands of no more than twenty-five people. How many such bands arrived in North America before Beringia disappeared beneath the sea will never be known.

When the first migrants came is hotly debated by experts. They

Beringia

Clovis Spear Straightener
Clovis hunters used this bone spear straightener about 11,000 BP at a campsite in Arizona, where archaeologists discovered it lying among the butchered remains of two mammoth carcasses and thirteen ancient bison. Clovis hunters stuck their spear shafts through the opening and then moved the spear straightener back and forth along the length of the spear shaft. Arizona State Museum, University of Arizona.

probably arrived sometime after 15,000 BP. Scattered and inconclusive evidence suggests that they may have arrived several thousand years earlier. (See "Historical Question," page 6.) Certainly, humans who came from Asia—whose ancestors left Africa hundreds of thousands of years earlier—inhabited the Western Hemisphere by 14,000 BP.

Paleo-Indian Hunters

When humans first arrived in the Western Hemisphere, massive glaciers covered most of present-day Canada. Many archaeologists believe that Paleo-Indians probably migrated along an ice-free passageway on the eastern side of Canada's Rocky Mountains in pursuit of game. Other Paleo-Indians may have traveled along the Pacific coast in small boats, hunting marine life and hopscotching from one desirable landing spot to another. At the southern edge of the glaciers, Paleo-Indians entered a hunters' paradise teeming with wildlife that had never before confronted human predators armed with razor-sharp spears. The abundance of game presumably made hunting relatively easy. Ample food permitted the Paleo-Indian population to grow. Within a thousand years or so, Paleo-Indians had migrated throughout the Western Hemisphere.

Early Paleo-Indians used a distinctively shaped spearhead

Who Were the First Americans?

To learn who the first Americans were and when they arrived requires following a trail that has grown very cold during the past 15,000 or 20,000 years.

After millennia of erosion and environmental change, much of the land they walked, hunted, and camped on is now submerged and inaccessible beneath the Bering Sea and along the Atlantic and Pacific coasts, where rising sea levels have flooded wide, previously exposed coastal plains. Most of the numerous Paleo-Indian sites archaeologists have excavated were occupied more than a hundred centuries after the first migrants arrived. These sites often yield spear points and large animal bones, but Paleo-Indian human skeletal remains are very rare. And yet evidence that Paleo-Indians inhabited the Western Hemisphere is overwhelming and indisputable. Human craftsmanship is the only credible explanation for Clovis points, and carbon dating establishes that the oldest Clovis sites are about 13,500 years old.

Scattered and controversial evidence suggests, however, that Clovis peoples were not the first arrivals. The Monte Verde excavation in Chile has persuaded many archaeologists that the first Americans resided in South America sometime between 14,750 BP and 14,000 BP. This site and a few other likely pre-Clovis sites in North America, most notably Meadowcroft in Pennsylvania, contain no Clovis-era artifacts, suggesting that their inhabitants arrived earlier and differed from the later Clovis peoples. But if the first Americans already lived in Chile and Pennsylvania 14,000 or more years ago, when did they first arrive and from where?

Some experts hypothesize that pre-Clovis peoples sailed or floated across the Pacific from Australia or Antarctica. Most scholars consider those ideas far-fetched. The Pacific is too wide and tempestuous for these ancient peoples and their small boats to have survived a long trans-oceanic trip.

Ancient Siberians had the means (hunting skills and adaptation to the frigid climate), motive (pursuit of game animals), and opportunity (the Beringian land bridge) to become the first humans to arrive in America, and most archaeologists believe they did just that. But when they came is difficult to determine since the Beringian land bridge existed for thousands of years. The extreme rarity of the earliest archaeological sites in North America also makes it difficult to estimate with confidence when pre-Clovis hunters arrived. A rough guess is 15,000 BP, although it might have been earlier. The scarcity of pre-Clovis sites discovered so far strongly suggests that these ancient Americans were few in number (compared to the much more numerous Clovis-era Paleo-Indians), very widely scattered, and ultimately unsuccessful in establishing permanent residence in the hemisphere. Although they and their descendants may have survived in America for a millennium or more, pre-Clovis peoples appear to have died out. The sparse archaeological evidence discovered to date does not suggest that they evolved into Clovis peoples. Although Clovis peoples evidently were not the first humans to arrive in the Western Hemisphere, they probably represent the first Paleo-Indians to establish a permanent American presence.

To investigate where the mysterious first Americans came from, experts have supplemented archaeological evidence with careful study of modern-day Native Americans. Although many millennia separate today's Native Americans from those ancient hunters, most scholars agree known as a **Clovis point**, named for the place in New Mexico where it was first excavated. Archaeologists' discovery of abundant Clovis points throughout North and Central America in sites occupied between 13,500 BP and 13,000 BP provides evidence that these nomadic hunters shared a common ancestry and way of life. At a few isolated sites, archaeologists have found still-controversial evidence of pre-Clovis artifacts that suggest the people who used Clovis spear points may have been preceded by several hundred years by a few non-Clovis pioneers. Paleo-Indians hunted mammoths and bison, but they probably also killed smaller animals. Concentration on large animals, when possible, made sense because just one mammoth could supply meat for months. Some Paleo-Indians even refrigerated killed mammoths by filling their body cavities with stones and submerging the carcasses in icy lakes for later use. In addition to food, mammoths provided Paleo-Indians with hides and bones for clothing, shelter, tools, and much more.

About 11,000 BP, Paleo-Indians confronted a major crisis. The mammoths and other large mammals they hunted became extinct. The extinction was gradual, stretching over several hundred years. Scientists are not completely certain why

Clovis Point
This spear point excavated along the Columbia River in what is now Washington state was crafted by Clovis people around 11,000 BP. It illustrates how small fragments of stone were chipped away to create the point used for killing animals—a feature common to Clovis points throughout the hemisphere. Archaeologists believe that such commonalities document a widely shared Clovis culture practiced for many generations.
Washington State Historical Society.

that telltale clues to the identity of the first Americans can be gleaned from dental, linguistic, and genetic evidence collected from their descendants who still live throughout the hemisphere.

Detailed scientific analyses of the teeth of thousands of ancient and modern Native Americans have identified distinctive dental shapes—such as incisors with a scooped-out inner surface—commonly found among ancient Siberians, ancient Americans, and modern Native Americans, but rare elsewhere. This dental evidence strongly supports the Asian origins and Beringian migration route of the first Americans.

Linguistic analysis of more than a thousand modern Native American languages demonstrates that Native Americans throughout the hemisphere speak some form of Amerind, the consequence (presumably) of its arrival with the earliest wave of ancient migrants around 13,000 BP. This migration chronology and linguistic analysis remain controversial among experts, but they suggest that Clovis peoples spoke some ancient form of Amerind.

Genetic research into the mutation rate of DNA reveals that many modern Native Americans share genetic characteristics commonly found among Asians. Estimates of the evolutionary time required to produce the subtle differences between Asian and Native American DNA suggest a migration from Asia as early as 25,000

BP or before. But like the other high-tech evidence, this genetic evidence is sharply disputed by experts.

Fascinating as the genetic, linguistic, and dental studies are, they are unlikely to win widespread support among experts until they can be corroborated by archaeological evidence that, so far, has not been found. Until then, specialists will continue to debate when the first Americans arrived and how they were related to subsequent generations of ancient Americans.

Thinking about Evidence

1. What evidence supports the hypothesis that the first Americans came from Asia? Do you find the evidence persuasive?

2. If pre-Clovis peoples were the first Americans, what evidence suggests when they arrived and what happened to them?

3. Can you imagine archaeological evidence that, if found, would conclusively identify the first Americans and when they arrived?

Connect to the Big Idea

⊙ In what ways were the first Americans related to their ancestors elsewhere in the world?

it occurred, although environmental change probably contributed to it. About this time, the earth's climate warmed, glaciers melted, and sea levels rose. Mammoths and other large mammals probably had difficulty adapting to the warmer climate. Many archaeologists also believe, however, that Paleo-Indians probably contributed to the extinctions in the Western Hemisphere by killing large animals more rapidly than the animals could reproduce. Some experts dispute this overkill interpretation, but similar environmental changes had occurred for millions of years before the arrival of Paleo-Indians without triggering the extinction of large animals—the presence of

skilled hunters seems to have made a decisive difference. Whatever the causes, after the extinction of large mammals, Paleo-Indians literally inhabited a new world.

Paleo-Indians adapted to this drastic environmental change by making at least two important changes in their way of life. First, hunters began to prey more intensively on smaller animals. Second, Paleo-Indians devoted more energy to foraging—that is, to collecting wild plant foods such as roots, seeds, nuts, berries, and fruits. When Paleo-Indians made these changes, they replaced the apparent uniformity of the big-game-oriented Clovis culture with great cultural diversity adapted to the many natural environments throughout the hemisphere.

These post-Clovis adaptations to local environments resulted in the astounding variety of Native American cultures that existed when Europeans arrived in AD 1492. By then, more than three hundred major tribes and hundreds of lesser groups inhabited North America alone. Hundreds more lived in Central and South America. Hundreds of other ancient American cultures had disappeared or transformed as their people constantly adapted to environmental and other challenges.

> **REVIEW**   Why and how did Paleo-Indians adapt to environmental change?

▶ Archaic Hunters and Gatherers

Archaeologists use the term *Archaic* to describe the many different hunting and gathering cultures that descended from Paleo-Indians and the long period of time when those cultures dominated the history of ancient America—roughly from 10,000 BP to somewhere between 4000 BP and 3000 BP. The term describes the era in the history of ancient America that followed the Paleo-Indian big-game hunters and preceded the development of agriculture. It denotes a **hunter-gatherer** way of life that persisted in North America long after European colonization.

Like their Paleo-Indian ancestors, **Archaic Indians** hunted with spears, but they also took smaller game with traps, nets, and hooks. Unlike their Paleo-Indian predecessors, many Archaic peoples became excellent basket makers in order to collect and store seeds, roots, nuts, and berries they gathered from wild plants. They prepared food from these plants by using a variety of stone tools. A characteristic Archaic artifact is a grinding stone used to pulverize seeds into edible form. Most Archaic Indians migrated from place to place to harvest plants and hunt animals. They usually did not establish permanent villages, although they often returned to the same river valley or fertile meadow year after year. In regions with especially rich resources—such as present-day California and the Pacific Northwest—they developed permanent settlements. Archaic peoples followed these practices in distinctive ways in the different environmental regions of North America (Map 1.2).

Great Plains Bison Hunters

After the extinction of large game animals, some hunters began to concentrate on bison in the huge herds that grazed the plains stretching hundreds of miles east of the Rocky Mountains. For almost a thousand years after the big-game extinctions, Archaic Indians hunted bison with Folsom points, named after a site near Folsom, New Mexico. In 1908, George McJunkin, an African American cowboy, discovered this site, which contained a deposit of large fossilized bones. In 1926, archaeologists excavated this site and found evidence that proved conclusively for the first time that ancient Americans were contemporaries of giant bison—which were known to have been extinct for at least ten thousand years. One Folsom point remained stuck between two ribs of a giant bison, where a Stone Age hunter had plunged it more than ten thousand years earlier. Until this discovery, leading experts had believed that ancient Americans had arrived in the New World fairly recently, some three thousand years ago. Since the 1920s, thanks to McJunkin's discovery, archaeologists and historians came to understand that the history of ancient Americans was far more ancient than experts previously imagined.

Like their nomadic predecessors, Folsom hunters moved constantly to maintain contact with their prey. Great Plains hunters often stampeded bison herds over cliffs and then slaughtered the animals that plunged to their deaths. At the Folsom site McJunkin discovered, hunters drove bison into a narrow gulch and then speared twenty-three of the trapped animals.

Bows and arrows reached Great Plains hunters from the north about AD 500. They largely replaced spears, which had been the hunters' weapons of choice for millennia. Bows permitted hunters to wound animals from farther away, arrows made it possible to shoot repeatedly, and arrowheads were easier to make and therefore less costly to lose than the larger, heavier spear points. These new weapons did not otherwise alter age-old ways of hunting. Although we often imagine bison hunters on horseback, in reality ancient Great Plains people hunted on foot. Horses did not arrive on the Great Plains until decades after 1492, when Europeans imported them. Only then did Great Plains bison hunters obtain horses and become expert riders.

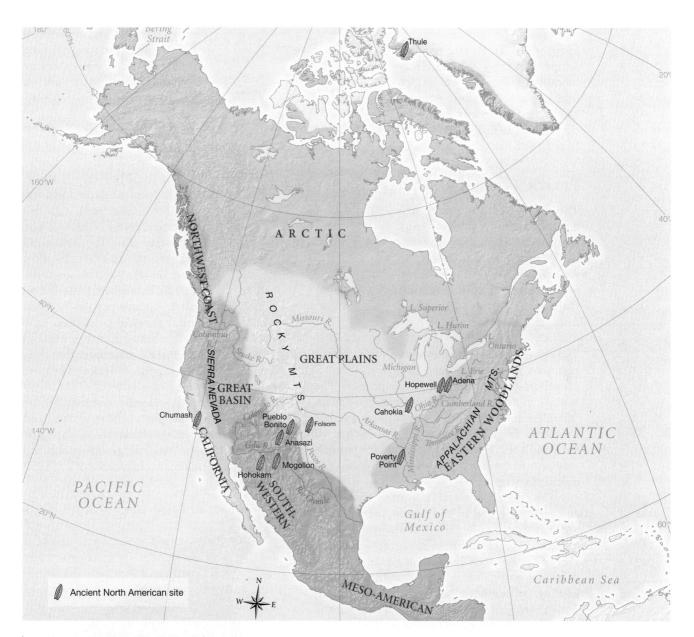

Ancient North American site

MAP ACTIVITY

Map 1.2 Native North American Cultures
Environmental conditions defined the boundaries of the broad zones of cultural similarity among ancient North Americans.

READING THE MAP: What crucial environmental features set the boundaries of each cultural region? (The topography indicated on Map 1.3, "Native North Americans about 1500," may be helpful.)
CONNECTIONS: How did environmental factors and variations affect the development of different groups of Native American cultures? Why do you think historians and archaeologists group cultures together by their regional positions?

Great Basin Cultures

Archaic peoples in the Great Basin between the Rocky Mountains and the Sierra Nevada inhabited a region of great environmental diversity defined largely by the amount of rain. While some lived on the shores of lakes and marshes fed by the rain and ate fish, others hunted deer, antelope, bison, and smaller game. To protect against shortages in fish and game caused by the fickle rainfall, Great Basin Indians relied on plants as their most important food. Unlike meat and fish, plant food could be collected and stored for long periods. Many Great Basin peoples gathered piñon nuts as a dietary staple. Great Basin peoples adapted to the severe environmental challenges of the region and maintained their Archaic hunter-gatherer way of life for centuries after Europeans arrived in AD 1492.

Pacific Coast Cultures

The richness of the natural environment made present-day California the most densely settled area in all of ancient North America. The land and ocean offered such ample food that California peoples remained hunters and gatherers for hundreds of years after AD 1492. The diversity of California's environment also encouraged corresponding variety among native peoples. The mosaic of Archaic settlements in California included about five hundred separate tribes speaking some ninety languages, each with local dialects. No other region of comparable size in ancient North America exhibited such cultural variety.

The Chumash, one of the many California cultures, emerged in the region surrounding what is now Santa Barbara about 5000 BP. Comparatively plentiful food resources—especially acorns—permitted Chumash people to establish relatively permanent villages. Conflict, probably caused by competition for valuable acorn-gathering territory, often broke out among the villages, as documented by Chumash skeletons that display unmistakable signs of violence. Although few other California cultures achieved the population density and village settlements of the Chumash, all shared the hunter-gatherer way of life and reliance on acorns as a major food source.

Another rich natural environment lay along the Pacific Northwest coast. Like the Chumash, Northwest peoples built more or less permanent villages. After about 5500 BP, they concentrated on catching whales and large quantities of salmon, halibut, and other fish, which they dried to last throughout the year. They also traded with people who lived hundreds of miles from the coast. Fishing freed Northwest peoples to develop sophisticated woodworking skills. They fashioned elaborate wood carvings that denoted wealth and status, as well as huge canoes for

Ancient California Peoples

fishing, hunting, and conducting warfare against neighboring tribes. Archaic northwesterners often fought with one another over access to prime fishing sites.

Eastern Woodland Cultures

East of the Mississippi River, Archaic peoples adapted to a forest environment that included the major river valleys of the Mississippi, Ohio, Tennessee, and Cumberland; the Great Lakes region; and the Atlantic coast (see Map 1.2). Throughout these diverse locales, Archaic peoples pursued similar survival strategies.

Woodland hunters stalked deer as their most important prey. Deer supplied Woodland peoples with food as well as hides and bones that they crafted into clothing, weapons, and many other tools. Like Archaic peoples elsewhere, Woodland Indians gathered edible plants, seeds, and nuts. About 6000 BP, some Woodland groups established more or less permanent settlements of 25 to 150

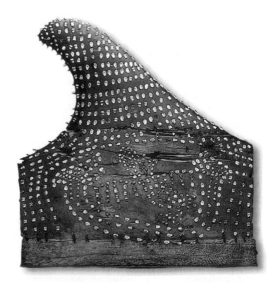

Ozette Whale Effigy
This carving of a whale fin decorated with hundreds of sea otter teeth was discovered along with thousands of other artifacts of daily life at Ozette, an ancient village on the tip of the Olympic Peninsula in present-day Washington that was inundated by a catastrophic mud slide about five hundred years ago. The fin illustrates the importance of whale hunting to the residents of Ozette.
Richard Alexander Cooke III.

people, usually near a river or lake that offered a wide variety of plant and animal resources. Woodland burial sites suggest that life expectancy was about eighteen years, a relatively short time to learn all the skills necessary to survive, reproduce, and adapt to change.

Around 4000 BP, Woodland cultures added two important features to their basic hunter-gatherer lifestyle: agriculture and pottery. Trade and migration from Mexico brought gourds and pumpkins to Woodland peoples, who also began to cultivate sunflowers and small quantities of tobacco. Corn, which had been grown in Mexico and South America since about 7000 BP, also traveled north and became a significant food crop among Eastern Woodland peoples around 2500 BP. Most likely, women learned how to plant, grow, and harvest these crops as an outgrowth of their work gathering edible wild plants. Cultivated crops did not alter Woodland peoples' dependence on gathering wild plants, seeds, and nuts.

Like agriculture, pottery probably originated in Mexico. Pots were more durable than baskets for cooking and the storage of food and water, but they were also much heavier and therefore were shunned by nomadic peoples. The permanent settlements of Woodland peoples made the heavy weight of pots much less important than their advantages compared to leaky and fragile baskets. While pottery and agriculture introduced changes in Woodland cultures, ancient Woodland Americans retained the other basic features of their Archaic hunter-gatherer lifestyle until 1492 and beyond.

REVIEW Why did Archaic Native Americans shift from big-game hunting to foraging and hunting smaller animals?

▶ Agricultural Settlements and Chiefdoms

Among Eastern Woodland peoples and most other Archaic cultures, agriculture supplemented but did not replace hunter-gatherer subsistence strategies. Reliance on wild animals and plants required most Archaic groups to remain small and mobile. But beginning about 4000 BP, distinctive southwestern cultures began to *depend* on agriculture and to build permanent settlements. Later, around 2500 BP, Woodland peoples in the vast Mississippi valley began to construct burial mounds and other earthworks that suggest the existence of social and political hierarchies that archaeologists term *chiefdoms*. Although the hunter-gatherer lifestyle never entirely disappeared, the development of agricultural settlements and chiefdoms represented important innovations to the Archaic way of life.

Southwestern Cultures

Ancient Americans in present-day Arizona, New Mexico, and southern portions of Utah and Colorado developed cultures characterized by agricultural settlements and multiunit dwellings called **pueblos**. All southwestern peoples confronted the challenge of a dry climate and unpredictable fluctuations in rainfall that made the supply of wild plant food very unreliable. These ancient Americans probably adopted agriculture in response to this basic environmental uncertainty.

About 3500 BP, southwestern hunters and gatherers began to cultivate corn, their signature food crop. (See "Beyond America's Borders," page 12.) The demands of corn cultivation encouraged hunter-gatherers to restrict their migratory habits in order to tend the crop. A vital consideration was access to water. Southwestern Indians became irrigation experts, conserving water from streams, springs, and rainfall and distributing it to thirsty crops.

About AD 200, small farming settlements began to appear throughout southern New Mexico, marking the emergence of the Mogollon culture. Typically, a Mogollon settlement included a dozen pit houses, each made by digging out a pit about fifteen feet in diameter and a foot or two deep and then erecting poles to support a roof of branches or dirt. Larger villages usually had one or two bigger pit houses that may have been the predecessors of the circular kivas, the ceremonial rooms that became a characteristic of nearly all southwestern settlements. About AD 900, Mogollon culture began to decline, for reasons that remain obscure.

Around AD 500, while the Mogollon culture prevailed in New Mexico, other ancient people migrated from Mexico to southern Arizona and established the distinctive Hohokam culture. Hohokam settlements used sophisticated grids of irrigation canals to plant and harvest crops twice a year. Hohokam settlements reflected Mexican cultural practices that northbound migrants brought with them, including the building of sizable platform mounds and ball courts. About AD 1400, Hohokam culture declined for

Corn: An Ancient American Legacy

Corn on the cob slathered with butter, salted popcorn, corn chips—Americans consume and produce more corn than any other nation on earth. Today, each American eats an average of 52 quarts of popped corn a year. Popcorn grown in the United States is also munched in Mexico City, Tokyo, Seoul, Beijing, and London, and corn on the cob is even sold at Moscow's famed Gorky Park. Yet popcorn and corn on the cob account for a miniscule fraction of the gigantic mountain of 34 billion bushels of corn produced across the globe each year, one-third of it in the United States. All of that corn is descended from a plant domesticated and cultivated by ancient Americans beginning about ten thousand years ago.

The ancient ancestor of what we know today as corn is a grass called *teosinte*. Ancient people in central Mexico, probably women, selected desirable seeds from *teosinte* and over many generations managed to transform the small grass seeds into rows of corn kernels arrayed around a central cob. Slowly, during thousands of years, ancient agriculturalists developed many varieties of corn adapted to different growing conditions, with different nutritional qualities, and varying productivity (the number of kernels grown from one corn seed). The remarkable adaptability of the corn plant and the high food value of the corn kernels caused the crop to spread among ancient Americans throughout the Western Hemisphere.

Entirely unknown to Europeans when they arrived in the New World in 1492, corn acquired the name by which it is known in most of the world today: *maize*, which is derived from *mahiz* ("life-giver"), the word for corn Christopher Columbus learned from the Taino Indians he first encountered. It is no wonder ancient Americans worshiped maize gods, given how important corn was to their survival. Columbus and other Spaniards carried corn back to Europe in 1493, and within a generation corn seeds had sprouted for the first time not only in Europe but also in the Middle East, Africa, India, and China.

At first, people outside the Americas did not find corn an appetizing food. An English botanist in the seventeenth century spoke for many others when he declared corn a food of the "barbarous Indians which know no better." He pronounced corn "a more convenient food for swine than for man." But Europeans in the New World, following Native American foodways, soon learned to eat corn ground into meal, often mixed with vegetables or meat, moistened, and served as a kind of mush they called samp or hominy or grits. Or they made a cornmeal dough that they baked in the coals of a fire or on an iron griddle to produce corn bread, which they also called hoecake, johnnycake, or corn pone—all of them adaptations of ancient American tortillas. Corn helped sustain Euro-Americans in the New World for centuries after 1492, just as it had ancient Americans for thousands of years before Europeans arrived.

Today corn is grown throughout the world and is a major commodity in global trade. The United States produces more than half of global corn exports, while Argentina, Brazil, and Ukraine account for another third. This exported corn goes to countries all around the world. Japan takes about a fifth of the global corn imports, and another third of corn imports go to South Korea, Mexico, Egypt, and Taiwan.

reasons that remain a mystery, although the rising salinity of the soil brought about by centuries of irrigation probably caused declining crop yields and growing food shortages.

North of the Hohokam and Mogollon cultures, in a region that encompassed southern Utah and Colorado and northern Arizona and New Mexico, the Anasazi culture began to flourish about AD 100. The early Anasazi built pit houses on mesa tops and used irrigation much as their neighbors did to the south. Beginning around AD 1000, some Anasazi began to move to large, multistory cliff dwellings whose spectacular ruins still exist at Mesa Verde, Colorado, and elsewhere. Other Anasazi communities—like the one known as **Pueblo Bonito** whose impressive ruins can be visited at Chaco Canyon, New Mexico—erected huge stone-walled pueblos with enough rooms to house everyone in the settlement. (See "Visualizing History," page 16.) Anasazi pueblos and cliff dwellings typically included one or more kivas used for secret ceremonies, restricted to

Florida Woman

This sixteenth-century drawing with watercolor of a Native American woman in Florida shows her extending a gift of hospitality with ears of corn in one hand and a basket of corn mush in the other. The watercolor captures the gift of corn ancient Americans bestowed on people throughout the world today.

Of Florida.

chicken, pork, and dairy products in American supermarkets came from animals that ate corn. And the United States exports billions of dollars' worth of corn-fed meat and dairy products to the rest of the world every year. A similar pattern prevails in many of the other products corn is used to create, such as corn sugar used to sweeten hundreds of processed foods and corn byproducts used, for example, in products as varied as skateboards, toothpaste, tires, batteries, and lipstick. Even pulling into a gas station for a fill-up often means pumping gasoline mixed with ethanol made from corn into your gas tank—about a fourth of the American corn crop is used to make ethanol fuel, a product that reduces American dependence on foreign sources of oil.

America in Global Context

1. How did ancient Americans contribute to what we know today as corn?

2. In what ways does corn connect the United States to the rest of the world?

3. How is corn used today compared to its use by ancient Americans?

Connect to the Big Idea

⊙ How did the cultivation of corn change the habits of archaic southwestern hunter-gatherers?

Corn connects the United States to the rest of the world in many more ways than the export of millions of bushels of corn kernels. Only about a fifth of the U.S. corn crop is exported annually. The rest is used in dozens of products that Americans consume themselves as well as export to countries around the globe. The seventeenth-century English botanist was correct that corn is an excellent food for animals. Today, about half of the American corn crop is fed to livestock. Chances are that the beef,

men, that sought to communicate with the supernatural world. The alignment of Chaco buildings with solar and lunar events (such as the summer and winter solstices) also suggest that the Anasazi studied the sky carefully, probably because they believed supernatural celestial powers influenced their lives in every way. Pueblo Bonito stood at the center of thousands of smaller pueblos that sent food and other goods to support Bonito's spiritual and political elites. Exactly how the Pueblo Bonito elites exercised power over the satellite pueblos is not known, but it probably involved a combination of violence and spiritual ceremonies performed in the kivas. Drought began to plague the region about AD 1130, and it lasted for more than half a century, triggering the disappearance of the Anasazi culture. By AD 1200, the large Anasazi pueblos had been abandoned. The prolonged drought probably intensified conflict among the pueblos and made it impossible to depend on the techniques of irrigated agriculture that had worked for centuries. Some

VISUAL ACTIVITY

Ancient Agriculture

Dropping seeds into holes punched in cleared ground by a pointed stick known as a "dibble," this ancient American farmer sows a new crop while previously planted seeds—including the corn and beans immediately opposite him—bear fruit for harvest. Created by a sixteenth-century European artist, the drawing misrepresents who did the agricultural work in many ancient American cultures—namely, women rather than men. The Pierpont Morgan Library/Art Resource, NY.

READING THE IMAGE: In what ways has this ancient farmer modified and taken advantage of the natural environment?

CONNECTIONS: What were the advantages and disadvantages of agriculture compared to hunting and gathering?

Anasazi migrated toward regions with more reliable rainfall and settled in Hopi, Zuñi, and Acoma pueblos that their descendants in Arizona and New Mexico have occupied ever since.

Woodland Burial Mounds and Chiefdoms

No other ancient Americans created dwellings similar to pueblos, but around 2500 BP, Woodland cultures throughout the Mississippi River watershed began to build **burial mounds**. The size of the mounds, the labor and organization required to erect them, and differences in the artifacts buried with certain individuals suggest the existence of a social and political hierarchy that archaeologists term a **chiefdom**. Experts do not know the name of a single chief, nor do they understand the organizations chiefs headed. But the only way archae-

Mexican Ball Court Model

The Mexica and other Mesoamerican peoples commonly built special courts (or playing fields) for their intensely competitive ball games. This rare model of a Mexican ball court, made between 2200 BP and AD 250, shows a game in progress, complete with players and spectators. A few ball courts have been excavated in North America, compelling evidence of the many connections to Mexico. Yale University Art Gallery, Stephen Carlton Clark, B.A. 1903, Fund. 1973.88.26/Art Resource, NY.

VISUAL ACTIVITY

Ancient Petroglyph
More than a thousand years ago one or more members of the Fremont people crafted this hunting scene on a sandstone surface in Cottonwood Canyon in northeastern Utah. Four hunters aim their arrows into a flock of big horn sheep. Other human-like forms appear in the image—perhaps shamans or decoys to move the flock toward the hunters. Cave Art Gallery/Getty Images.
READING THE IMAGE: What techniques might have allowed the hunters to concentrate the flock in the way depicted?
CONNECTIONS: What weapons did earlier Paleo-Indians and Archaic Indians use for killing and capturing game?

ologists can account for the complex and labor-intensive burial mounds is to assume that one person—whom scholars term a *chief*—commanded the labor and obedience of very large numbers of other people, who made up the chief's chiefdom.

Between 2500 BP and 2100 BP, Adena people built hundreds of burial mounds radiating from central Ohio. In the mounds, the Adena usually included grave goods such as spear points and stone pipes as well as thin sheets of mica (a glasslike mineral) crafted into animal or human shapes. Sometimes burial mounds were constructed all at once, but often they were built up slowly over many years.

About 2100 BP, Adena culture evolved into the more elaborate Hopewell culture, which lasted about five hundred years. Centered in Ohio, Hopewell culture extended throughout the enormous drainage of the Ohio and Mississippi rivers. Hopewell people built larger mounds than did their Adena predecessors and filled them with more magnificent grave goods. Burial was probably reserved for the most important members of Hopewell groups. Most people were cremated, not buried. Burial rituals appear to have brought many people together to honor the dead person and to help build the mound. Hopewell mounds were often one hundred feet high and thirty feet in diameter. Grave goods at Hopewell sites testify to the high quality of Hopewell crafts and to a thriving trade network that ranged from present-day Wyoming to Florida.

Hopewell culture declined about AD 400 for reasons that are obscure. Archaeologists speculate that bows and arrows, along with increasing reliance on agriculture, made small settlements more self-sufficient and therefore less dependent on the central authority of the Hopewell chiefs who were responsible for the burial mounds.

Four hundred years later, another mound-building culture flourished. The Mississippian culture emerged in the floodplains of the major southeastern river systems about AD 800 and lasted until about AD 1500. Major Mississippian sites, such as the one at **Cahokia**, included huge mounds with platforms on top for ceremonies and for the residences of great chiefs. Most likely, the ceremonial mounds and ritual practices were influenced by Mexican cultural expressions brought north by traders and migrants. At Cahokia, skilled farmers supported the large population with ample crops of corn. In addition to mounds, Cahokians erected what archaeologists call woodhenges (after the famous Stonehenge in England)—long wooden poles set upright in the ground and carefully arranged in huge circles. Experts believe that Cahokians probably built woodhenges partly for ceremonies linked to celestial observations. The large plazas at Cahokia were used for religious and political ceremonies as well as for playing the Cahokians' signature game of chunkey, which involved rolling a concave stone disk and trying to throw a spear that landed as close as possible to where the stone stopped.

Daily Life in Chaco Canyon

Pueblo Bonito, Chaco Canyon, New Mexico

About AD 1000, Pueblo Bonito stood at the center of Chacoan culture in the arid region at the intersection of present-day Utah, Colorado, Arizona, and New Mexico. The largest site in Chaco Canyon, Pueblo Bonito originally stood four or five stories tall and housed more than 600 rooms, including 35 kivas, the circular structures visible around the perimeter of the large plazas. Chaco residents covered each kiva with a roof, creating a darkened underground space for ceremonial rituals.

The exact nature of Chacoan ceremonies remains a mystery, but less mysterious are the routines of daily life that sustained the people at Pueblo Bonito for centuries. Imagine a woman setting out from the pueblo on a spring day to plant corn, the most important food crop. She might first strap on sandals, like the one shown here, woven from fibers of the yucca plant. To dig

Sandal

The game of chunkey spread throughout the region of Cahokians' cultural influence, and chunkey stones are commonly found in Mississippian graves, signifying the importance Cahokians attached to chunkey in the hereafter as well as the here and now.

Cahokia and other Mississippian cultures dwindled by AD 1500. When Europeans arrived, most of the descendants of Mississippian cultures, like those of the Hopewell culture, lived in small dispersed villages supported by hunting and gathering, supplemented by agriculture. Clearly, the conditions that caused large chiefdoms to emerge—whatever they were—had changed, and chiefs no longer commanded the sweeping powers they had once enjoyed.

REVIEW How and why did the societies of the Southwest differ from eastern societies?

a hole for planting corn seeds, our imagined woman might use a digging stick like the one shown here, tipped by the horn of a mountain sheep, tightly bound with sinew to a sturdy cottonwood branch, and covered with animal hide to protect the binding.

Ladle

Digging Stick

Once harvested and dried, corn needed to be ground in order to be cooked and eaten. By looking at the small flat stone (the *mano*) and the larger stone slab (the *metate*) shown here, can you imagine how our Chacoan woman used these tools? Some rooms at Pueblo Bonito held numerous grinding stones like the ones shown here.

To cook the cornmeal she had ground, our imagined woman needed

to mix it with water. She might use a ceramic ladle like the one shown here—crafted and decorated by a pottery maker at Chaco—to dip some fresh water from a storage pot. Why do you think the decoration at the end of ladle's handle is blurred? To make a fire, she could use the Chacoan fire starter kit shown here. After kindling a cooking fire, she could heat the cornmeal gruel in a ceramic pot and use the ladle again to transfer servings into small bowls for eating.

Chacoans flourished at Pueblo Bonito by using their knowledge and skills to grow and cook corn and to craft vital items such as ceramics and footwear.

SOURCES: Pueblo Bonito, Chaco Canyon, New Mexico: © Richard A. Cooke/CORBIS; sandal, mano and metate, fire starter kit, ladle, digging stick: Courtesy National Park Service, Chaco Culture National Historical Park.

Mano and Metate

Questions for Analysis

1. Why might kivas have been built below ground and separated from the other rooms of the pueblo?

2. What do the sandal and digging stick suggest about the interdependence of hunting and agriculture in the daily lives of Chacoans?

3. Can you imagine each step in the creation of the artifacts shown here as well as the organization and scheduling of daily tasks required to use them?

Connect to the Big Idea

G How does the lifestyle of Chaco Canyon society compare to indigenous societies in other regions?

Fire Starter Kit

► Native Americans in the 1490s

On the eve of European colonization in the 1490s, Native Americans lived throughout North and South America, but their total population is uncertain. Some experts claim that Native Americans inhabiting what are now the United States and Canada numbered 18 million to 20 million, while others place the population at no more than 1 million. A prudent estimate is about 4 million, or about the same as the number of people living on the small island nation of England at that time. The vastness of the territory meant that the overall population density of North America was low, just 60 people per 100 square miles, compared to more than 8,000 in England. Native Americans were spread thin across the land

Cahokia Pipe
This pipe bowl excavated at Cahokia depicts a chunkey player preparing to roll the concave chunkey stone with his right hand. Chunkey stones are frequently found in Cahokian and other Mississippian burials, suggesting the importance of the chunkey game in their culture. The man shown here also wears the characteristic skull cap of chunkey players. © Ira Block/National Geographic Society/Corbis.

because of their survival strategies of hunting, gathering, and agriculture, but regional populations varied (Figure 1.1).

Eastern and Great Plains Peoples

About one-third of native North Americans inhabited the enormous Woodland region east of the Mississippi River; their population density approximated the average for North America as a whole. Eastern Woodland peoples clustered into three broad linguistic and cultural groups: Algonquian, Iroquoian, and Muskogean.

Algonquian tribes inhabited the Atlantic seaboard, the Great Lakes region, and much of the upper Midwest (Map 1.3). The relatively mild climate along the Atlantic permitted the coastal Algonquians to grow corn and other crops as well as to hunt and fish. Around the Great Lakes and in northern New England,

however, cool summers and severe winters made agriculture impractical. Instead, the Abenaki, Penobscot, Chippewa, and other tribes concentrated on hunting and fishing, using canoes both for transportation and for gathering wild rice.

Inland from the Algonquian region, Iroquoian tribes occupied territories centered in Pennsylvania and upstate New York, as well as the hilly upland regions of the Carolinas and Georgia. Three features distinguished Iroquoian tribes from their neighbors. First, their success in cultivating corn and other crops allowed them to build permanent settlements, usually consisting of several longhouses housing five to ten families. Second, Iroquoian societies adhered to matrilineal rules of descent. Property of all sorts belonged to women. Women headed family clans and even selected the chiefs (normally men) who governed the tribes. Third, for purposes of war and diplomacy, an Iroquoian confederation—

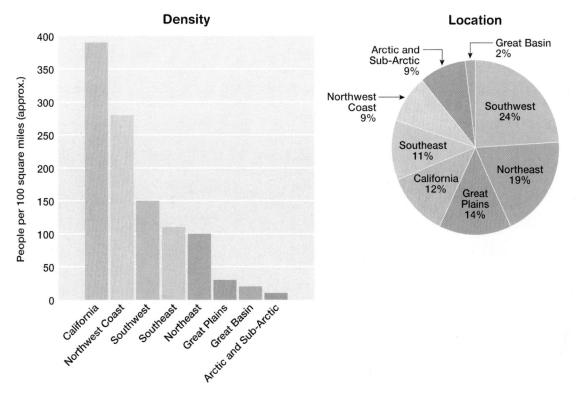

FIGURE 1.1   Native American Population In North America About 1492 (Estimated)
Just before Europeans arrived, Native American population density varied widely, depending in large part on the availability of natural resources. The Pacific coast, with its rich marine resources, had the highest concentration of people. Overall, the population density of North America was less than 1 percent that of England, which helps explain why Europeans viewed North America as a relatively empty wilderness.

including the Seneca, Onondaga, Mohawk, Oneida, and Cayuga tribes—formed the League of Five Nations, which remained powerful well into the eighteenth century.

Muskogean peoples spread throughout the woodlands of the Southeast, south of the Ohio River and east of the Mississippi. Including the Creek, Choctaw, Chickasaw, and Natchez tribes, Muskogeans inhabited a bountiful natural environment that provided abundant food from hunting, gathering, and agriculture. Remnants of the earlier Mississippian culture still existed in Muskogean religion. The Natchez, for example, worshiped the sun and built temple mounds modeled after those of their Mississippian ancestors, including Cahokia.

Great Plains peoples accounted for about one out of seven native North Americans. Inhabiting the huge region west of the Eastern Woodland people and east of the Rocky Mountains, many tribes had migrated to the Great Plains within the century or two before the 1490s, forced westward by Iroquoian and Algonquian

tribes. Some Great Plains tribes—especially the Mandan and Pawnee—farmed successfully, growing both corn and sunflowers. But the Teton Sioux, Blackfeet, Comanche, Cheyenne, and Crow on the northern plains and the Apache and other nomadic tribes on the southern plains depended on buffalo (American bison) for their subsistence.

Southwestern and Western Peoples

Southwestern cultures included about a quarter of all native North Americans. These descendants of the Mogollon, Hohokam, and Anasazi cultures lived in settled agricultural communities, many of them pueblos. They continued to grow corn, beans, and squash using methods they had refined for centuries.

However, their communities came under attack by a large number of warlike Athapascans who invaded the Southwest beginning around AD 1300. The Athapascans—principally Apache

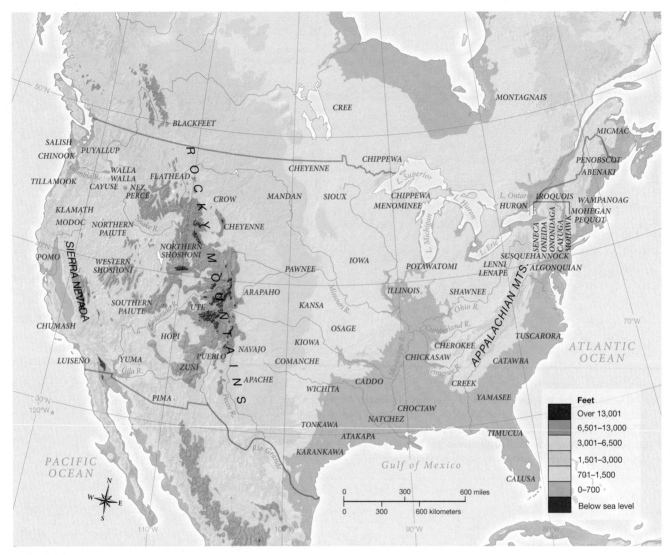

MAP 1.3

Native North Americans About 1500

Distinctive Native American peoples resided throughout the area that, centuries later, became the United States. This map indicates the approximate location of some of the larger tribes about 1500. In the interest of legibility, many other peoples who inhabited North America at the time are omitted from the map.

and Navajo—were skillful warriors who preyed on the sedentary pueblo Indians, reaping the fruits of agriculture without the work of farming.

About a fifth of all native North Americans resided along the Pacific coast. In California, abundant acorns and nutritious marine life continued to support high population densities, but this abundance retarded the development of agriculture. Similar dependence on hunting and gathering persisted along the Northwest coast, where fishing reigned supreme. Salmon were so plentiful at The Dalles, a prime fishing site on the Columbia River on the border of present-day Oregon and California, that

Northwest peoples caught enough to use themselves as well as to trade dried fish as far away as California and the Great Plains. It is likely that The Dalles was the largest Native American trading center in ancient North America, although other ancient trading centers, such as Pueblo Bonito and Cahokia, also existed.

Cultural Similarities

While trading was common, all native North Americans in the 1490s still depended on hunting and gathering for a major portion of their food. Most of them also practiced agriculture.

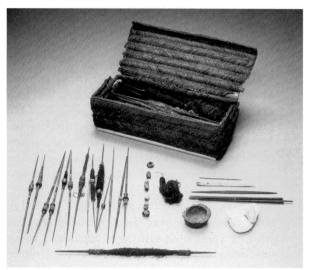

VISUAL ACTIVITY

Ancient American Weaving
This workbasket of a master weaver illustrates the technology of ancient American textile production. Found in a woman's grave in the Andes dating from one thousand years ago, the workbasket contains tools and thread for every stage of textile production. Weaving—like cooking, hunting, and worship—depended on human knowledge that survived only when passed from an experienced person to a novice. Museum of Fine Arts, Boston, Massachusetts, USA/Gift of Charles H. White/The Bridgeman Art Library.
READING THE IMAGE: What human activities were required to produce the tools in the workbasket?
CONNECTIONS: The production of woven materials such as baskets and textiles was common in the North American cultures of the 1490s; what other similarities did these cultures hold?

Some used agriculture to supplement hunting and gathering; for others, the balance was reversed. People throughout North America used bows, arrows, and other weapons for hunting and warfare. To express themselves, they drew on stones, wood, and animal skins; wove baskets and textiles; crafted pottery, beads, and carvings; and created songs, dances, and rituals.

North American life did not include features common in Europe during the 1490s. Native North Americans did not use writing, wheels, or sailing ships; they had no large domesticated animals such as horses or cows; their only metal was copper. However, the absence of these European conveniences mattered less than Native Americans' adaptations to local natural environments and to the social environment among neighboring peoples, adaptations that all native North Americans held in common.

It would be a mistake, however, to conclude that native North Americans lived in blissful harmony. Archaeological sites provide ample evidence of violent conflict. Warfare was common, making violence and fear typical features of ancient American life. Warfare not only killed people and destroyed their settlements, but victors often took captives, especially women and children, and often treated them as slaves. Skeletons, like those at Cahokia, not only bear the marks of wounds but also exhibit clear signs of ritualistic human sacrifice. Religious, ethnic, economic, and familial conflicts must have occurred, but they remain in obscurity because they left few archaeo-

logical traces. In general, anxiety and instability must have been at least as common among ancient North Americans as feelings of peace and security.

Native North Americans not only adapted to the natural environment but also changed it in many ways. They built thousands of structures, from small dwellings to massive pueblos and enormous mounds, permanently altering the landscape. Their gathering techniques selected productive and nutritious varieties of plants, thereby shifting the balance of local plants toward useful varieties. The first stages of North American agriculture, for example, probably involved Native Americans gathering wild seeds and then sowing them in a meadow for later harvest. To clear land for planting seeds, native North Americans set fires that burned off thousands of acres of forest.

Ancient North Americans also used fires for hunting. Hunters often started fires to frighten and force together deer, buffalo, and other animals and make them easy to slaughter. Indians also started fires along the edges of woods to burn off shrubby undergrowth, encouraging the growth of tender young plants that attracted deer and other game, bringing them within convenient range of hunters' weapons. The burns also encouraged the growth of sun-loving food plants that Indians relished, such as blackberries, strawberries, and raspberries.

Because the fires set by native North Americans usually burned until they ran out of fuel or were extinguished by rain or wind, enormous regions of North America were burned over. In the long run, fires created and maintained a diverse and productive natural environment. Fires, like other activities of native North Americans, shaped the landscape of North America long before Europeans arrived in 1492.

> REVIEW   What cultural similarities did native peoples of the Western Hemisphere share in the 1490s, and why?

▶ The Mexica: A Mesoamerican Culture

The vast majority of the 80 million people who lived in the Western Hemisphere in the 1490s inhabited Mesoamerica and South America, where the population approximately equaled that of Europe. Like their much less numerous counterparts north of the Rio Grande, these people lived in a natural environment of tremendous diversity. Among all these cultures, the Mexica stood out. Their empire stretched from coast to coast across central Mexico, encompassing between 8 million and 25 million

people (experts disagree about the total population). Their significance in the history of the New World after 1492 dictates a brief survey of their culture and society.

The Mexica began their rise to prominence about 1325, when small bands settled on a marshy island in Lake Texcoco, the site of the future city of Tenochtitlán, the capital of the Mexican empire. Resourceful, courageous, and cold-blooded warriors, the Mexica were often hired out as mercenaries for richer, more settled tribes.

By 1430, the Mexica succeeded in asserting their dominance over their former allies and leading their own military campaigns in an ever-widening arc of empire building. Despite pockets of resistance, by the 1490s the Mexica ruled an empire that covered more land than Spain and Portugal combined and contained almost three times as many people.

The empire exemplified the central values of Mexican society. The Mexica worshipped the war god Huitzilopochtli. Warriors held the most exalted positions in the social hierarchy, even above the priests who performed the sacred ceremonies that won Huitzilopochtli's favor. In the almost constant battles necessary to defend and extend the empire, young Mexican men exhibited the courage and daring that

Mexican Human Sacrifice
This graphic portrayal of human sacrifice drawn by a Mexican artist in the sixteenth century shows the typical routine of human sacrifice. The victim climbed the temple steps and then was stretched over a stone pillar to make it easier for the priest to plunge a stone knife into the victim's chest, cut out the still-beating heart, and offer it to the bloodthirsty gods.
Scala/Art Resource, NY

would allow them to rise in the carefully graduated ranks of warriors. The Mexica considered capturing prisoners the ultimate act of bravery. Warriors usually turned over the captives to Mexican priests, who sacrificed them to Huitzilopochtli by cutting out their hearts. The Mexica believed that human sacrifice fed the sun's craving for blood, which kept the sun aflame and prevented the fatal descent of everlasting darkness and chaos.

The empire contributed far more to Mexican society than victims for sacrifice. At the most basic level, the empire functioned as a military and political system that collected **tribute** from subject peoples. The Mexica forced conquered tribes to pay tribute in goods, not money. Tribute redistributed to the Mexica was as much as one-third of the goods produced by conquered tribes. It included everything from candidates for human sacrifice to textiles and basic food products as well as exotic luxury items such as gold, turquoise, and rare bird feathers.

Tribute reflected the fundamental relations of power and wealth that pervaded the Mexican empire. The relatively small nobility of Mexican warriors, supported by a still smaller priesthood, possessed the military and religious power to command the obedience of thousands of non-noble Mexicans and of millions of non-Mexicans in subjugated colonies. The Mexican elite exercised their power to obtain tribute and thereby to redistribute wealth from the conquered to the conquerors, from the commoners to the nobility, from the poor to the rich. This redistribution of wealth made possible the achievements of Mexican society that amazed the Spaniards after AD 1492: the huge cities, teeming markets, productive gardens, and the storehouses stuffed with gold and other treasures.

On the whole, the Mexica did not interfere much with the internal government of conquered regions. Instead, they usually permitted the traditional ruling elite to stay in power—so long as they paid tribute. Subjugated communities felt exploited by the constant payment of tribute to the Mexica. The high level of discontent among subject peoples constituted the soft, vulnerable underbelly of the Mexican empire, a fact that Spanish intruders exploited after 1492 to conquer the Mexica.

REVIEW How did the conquest and creation of an empire exemplify the central values of Mexican society?

▶ Conclusion: The World of Ancient Americans

Ancient Americans shaped the history of human beings in the New World for more than thirteen thousand years. They established continuous human habitation in the Western Hemisphere from the time the first big-game hunters crossed Beringia until 1492 and beyond. Much of their history remains lost because they relied on oral rather than written communication. But much can be pieced together from artifacts they left behind at camps, kill sites, and ceremonial and residential centers such as Cahokia and Pueblo Bonito. Ancient Americans achieved their success through resourceful adaptation to the hemisphere's many and changing natural environments. They also adapted to social and cultural changes caused by human beings—such as marriages and deaths, as well as political struggles and warfare among chiefdoms. Their creativity and artistry are unmistakably documented in their numerous artifacts. Those material objects sketch the only likenesses of ancient Americans we will ever have—blurred, shadowy images that are indisputably human but forever silent.

When European intruders began arriving in the Western Hemisphere in 1492, their attitudes about the promise of the New World were heavily influenced by the diverse peoples they encountered. Europeans coveted Native Americans' wealth, labor, and land, and Christian missionaries sought to save their souls. Likewise, Native Americans marveled at such European technological novelties as sailing ships, steel weapons, gunpowder, and horses, while often reserving judgment about Europeans' Christian religion.

In the centuries following 1492, as the trickle of European strangers became a flood of newcomers from both Europe and Africa, Native Americans and settlers continued to encounter one another. Peaceful negotiations as well as violent conflicts over both land and trading rights resulted in chronic fear and mistrust. While the era of European colonization marked the beginning of the end of ancient America, the ideas, subsistence strategies, and cultural beliefs of native North Americans remained powerful among their descendants for generations and continue to persist to the present.

See the Selected Bibliography for this chapter in the Appendix.

1 Chapter Review

MAKE IT STICK

 LearningCurve

Go online and use LearningCurve to see what you know. Then review the key terms and answer the questions.

KEY TERMS

Beringia (p. 5)
Paleo-Indians (p. 5)
Clovis point (p. 6)
hunter-gatherer (p. 8)
Archaic Indians (p. 8)
pueblos (p. 11)
Pueblo Bonito (p. 12)
burial mounds (p. 14)
chiefdom (p. 14)
Cahokia (p. 15)
Mexica (p. 22)
tribute (p. 23)

REVIEW QUESTIONS

1. Why must historians rely on the work of archaeologists to write the history of ancient America? (pp. 3–4)

2. Why and how did Paleo-Indians adapt to environmental change? (pp. 5–8)

3. Why did Archaic Native Americans shift from big-game hunting to foraging and hunting smaller animals? (pp. 8–11)

4. How and why did the societies of the Southwest differ from eastern societies? (pp. 11–16)

5. What common characteristic underlay Native American diversity in the 1490s? (pp. 17–22)

6. How did the conquest and creation of an empire exemplify the central values of Mexican society? (pp. 22–23)

MAKING CONNECTIONS

1. How did ancient peoples' different approaches to survival contribute to the diversity of Native American cultures?

2. Native Americans both adapted to environmental changes in North America and produced changes in the environments around them. Discuss specific examples of such changes.

3. How did the Mexica establish and maintain their expansive empire?

LINKING TO THE PAST

1. Did the history of ancient Americans make them unusually vulnerable to eventual conquest by European colonizers? Why or why not?

2. Do you think that ancient American history would have been significantly different if North and South America had never separated from the Eurasian landmass? If so, how and why? If not, why not?

2 Europeans Encounter the New World

1492–1600

SPANISH GOLD COIN
This gold coin celebrates Queen Isabella and King Ferdinand, who patronized the voyages of Christopher Columbus. Minted around 1500, the coin illustrates the use of gold as European currency. Erich Lessing/Art Resource, NY.

CONTENT LEARNING OBJECTIVES

After reading and studying this chapter, you should be able to:

- Recognize the demographic shifts and technological innovations of the fifteenth century that allowed Europeans to explore regions outside their own continent.

- Follow the Columbian exchange, including its costs and benefits to Europeans and Indians.

- Understand how Spain created its empire in the Caribbean and in Central and South America, including the costs of Spanish conquest and colonization.

- Explain how Spain's New World colonies affected its political ambitions in Europe.

TWO BABIES WERE BORN IN SOUTHERN EUROPE IN 1451, SEPARATED by about seven hundred miles and a chasm of social, economic, and political power. The baby girl, Isabella, was born in a king's castle in what is now Spain. The baby boy, Christopher, was born in the humble dwelling of a weaver near Genoa in what is now Italy. Forty-one years later, the lives and aspirations of these two people intersected in southern Spain and permanently changed the history of the world.

Isabella was named for her mother, the wife of the king of Castile, whose monarchy encompassed the large central region of present-day Spain. As a young girl, Isabella was well educated, and she became a strong, resolute woman. When her half-brother Henry became king and tried to arrange her marriage, Isabella refused to accept Henry's choices and maneuvered to marry Ferdinand, the king of Aragon, a region of northeastern Spain. The couple married in 1469, and Isabella became queen when Henry died in 1474.

Queen Isabella and King Ferdinand battled to unite the monarchies of Spain under their rule, to complete the long campaign known as the reconquest to eliminate Muslim strongholds on the Iberian Peninsula, and to purify Christianity. In their intense efforts to defend Christianity, persecute Jews, and defeat Muslims, Isabella and Ferdinand traveled throughout their realm, meeting local notables, hearing appeals and complaints, and impressing all with their regal splendor.

Tagging along in the royal cavalcade of advisers, servants, and hangers-on that moved around Spain in 1485 was Christopher Columbus, a deeply religious man obsessed with obtaining support for his scheme to sail west across the Atlantic Ocean to reach China and Japan. An experienced sailor, Columbus had become convinced that it was possible to reach the riches of the East by sailing west. Columbus finally won an audience with the monarchs in January 1486. They rejected his plan. The earth was too big, the ocean between Europe and China was too wide, and no sailors or ships could possibly withstand such a long voyage. Doggedly, year after year, Columbus kept trying to interest Isabella until mid-April 1492, when she summoned him and agreed to support his risky scheme, hoping to expand the wealth and influence of her monarchy.

Columbus hurriedly organized his expedition, and just before sunrise on August 3, 1492, three ships under his command caught the tide out of a harbor in southern Spain and sailed west. Barely two months later, in the predawn moonlight of October 12, 1492, he glimpsed an island on the western horizon. At daybreak, Columbus rowed ashore, and as the curious islanders crowded around, he claimed possession of the land for Isabella and Ferdinand.

Columbus's encounters with Isabella and those islanders in 1492 transformed the history of the world and unexpectedly made Spain the most important European power in the Western Hemisphere for more than a century. Long before 1492, other Europeans had restlessly expanded the limits of the world known to them, and their efforts helped make possible Columbus's voyage. But without Isabella's sponsorship, it is doubtful that Columbus could have made his voyage. With her support and his own unflagging determination, Columbus blazed a watery trail to a world that neither he nor anyone else in Europe knew existed. As Isabella, Ferdinand, and subsequent Spanish monarchs sought to reap the rewards of what they considered their emerging empire in the West, they created a distinctively Spanish colonial society that conquered and killed Native Americans, built new institutions, and extracted great wealth that enriched the Spanish monarchy and made Spain the envy of other Europeans.

SPANISH TAPESTRY
This detail from a lavish sixteenth-century tapestry depicts Columbus (kneeling) receiving a box of jewels from Queen Isabella (whose husband, King Ferdinand, stands slightly behind her) in appreciation for his voyages to the New World. © Julio Donoso/Sygma/Corbis

► Europe in the Age of Exploration

Historically, the East—not the West—attracted Europeans. Europeans did not venture across the North Atlantic until around AD 1000, when Norsemen founded a small fishing village at L'Anse aux Meadows on the tip of Newfoundland that lasted only a decade or so. When the world's climate cooled, choking the North Atlantic with ice, the Norse left and other Europeans remained unaware of North America. Instead of looking to the West, wealthy Europeans developed tastes for luxury goods from Asia and Africa, and merchants competed to satisfy those desires. As Europeans traded with the East and with one another, they acquired new information about the world they inhabited. A few people—sailors, merchants, and aristocrats—took the risks of exploring beyond the limits of the world known to Europeans. Those risks could be deadly, but sometimes they paid off in new information, new opportunities, and eventually the discovery of a world entirely new to Europeans.

Mediterranean Trade and European Expansion

From the twelfth through the fifteenth centuries, spices, silk, carpets, ivory, and gold traveled overland from Persia, Asia Minor, India, and Africa and then funneled into continental Europe through Mediterranean trade routes (Map 2.1). Dominated primarily by the Italian cities of Venice, Genoa, and Pisa, this lucrative trade enriched Italian merchants and bankers, who fiercely defended their near monopoly of access to Eastern luxuries. The vitality of the Mediterranean trade offered merchants few incentives to look for alternatives. New routes to the East and the discovery of new lands were the stuff of fantasy.

Preconditions for turning fantasy into reality developed in fifteenth-century Europe. In the mid-fourteenth century, a catastrophic epidemic of bubonic plague (or the **Black Death**, as it was called) killed at least a third of the European population. This devastating pestilence had major long-term consequences. By drastically reducing the population, it made Europe's limited supply of food more plentiful for survivors. Many survivors inherited property from plague victims, giving them new chances for advancement.

Understandably, most Europeans perceived the world as a place of alarming risks where the delicate balance of health, harvests, and peace

CHRONOLOGY

1480	• Portuguese ships reach Congo.
1488	• Bartolomeu Dias rounds Cape of Good Hope.
1492	• Christopher Columbus lands in the Caribbean.
1493	• Columbus's second voyage to New World.
1494	• Treaty of Tordesillas.
1497	• John Cabot searches for Northwest Passage.
1498	• Vasco da Gama sails to India.
1513	• Vasco Núñez de Balboa crosses Isthmus of Panama.
1517	• Protestant Reformation begins in Germany.
1519	• Hernán Cortés searches for wealth in Mexico. • Ferdinand Magellan sets out to sail around the world.
1520	• Mexica in Tenochtitlán revolt against Spaniards.
1521	• Cortés conquers Mexica.
1532	• Francisco Pizarro begins conquest of Peru.
1535	• Jacques Cartier explores St. Lawrence River.
1539	• Hernando de Soto explores southeastern North America.
1540	• Francisco Vásquez de Coronado starts to explore Southwest and Great Plains.
1542	• Juan Rodríguez Cabrillo explores California coast.
1549	• Repartimiento reforms replace encomienda.
1565	• St. Augustine, Florida, settled.
1576	• Martin Frobisher explores northern Canadian waters.
1587	• English settle Roanoke Island.
1598	• Juan de Oñate explores New Mexico.
1599	• Acoma pueblos revolt against Oñate.

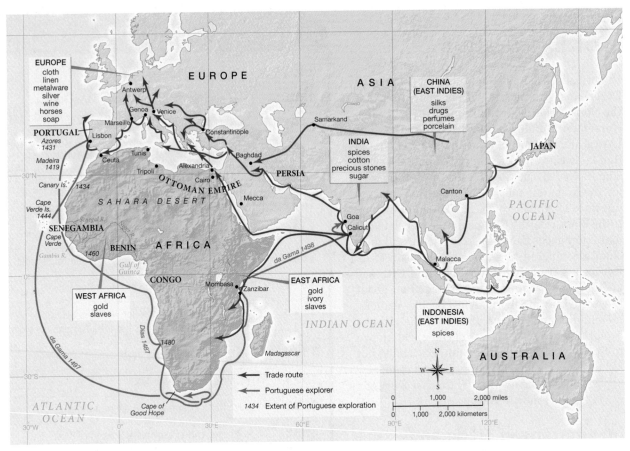

MAP 2.1

European Trade Routes and Portuguese Exploration in the Fifteenth Century

The trade of Italian cities from Asia was slowly undermined during the fifteenth century by Portuguese explorers who hop-scotched along the coast of Africa and eventually found a sea route that opened the rich trade of the East to Portuguese merchants.

could quickly be tipped toward disaster by epidemics, famine, and violence. Most people protected themselves from the constant threat of calamity by worshipping the supernatural, by living amid kinfolk and friends, and by maintaining good relations with the rich and powerful. But the insecurity and uncertainty of fifteenth-century European life also encouraged a few people to take greater risks, such as embarking on dangerous sea voyages through uncharted waters to points unknown.

In European societies, exploration promised fame and fortune to those who succeeded, whether they were kings or commoners. Monarchs such as Isabella hoped to enlarge their realms and enrich their dynasties by sponsoring journeys of exploration. More territory meant more subjects who could pay more taxes, provide more soldiers, and participate in more commerce, magnifying the monarch's power and prestige. Voyages of exploration also could stabilize the monarch's

regime by diverting unruly noblemen toward distant lands. Some explorers, such as Columbus, were commoners who hoped to be elevated to the aristocracy as a reward for their daring achievements.

Scientific and technological advances also helped set the stage for exploration. The invention of movable type by Johannes Gutenberg around 1450 in Germany made printing easier and cheaper, stimulating the diffusion of information, including news of discoveries, among literate Europeans such as Isabella and Columbus. By 1400, crucial navigational aids employed by maritime explorers like Columbus were already available: compasses; hourglasses; and the astrolabe and quadrant, which were devices for determining latitude. Although many people throughout fifteenth-century Europe knew about such technological advances, the Portuguese were the first to use them in a campaign to sail beyond the limits of the world known to Europeans.

A Century of Portuguese Exploration

With only 2 percent of the population of Christian Europe, Portugal devoted far more energy and wealth to the geographic exploration of the world between 1415 and 1460 than all other European countries combined. As a Christian kingdom, Portugal cooperated with Spain in the **Reconquest**, the centuries-long drive to expel the Muslims from the Iberian Peninsula. The religious zeal that propelled the Reconquest also justified expansion into what the Portuguese considered heathen lands. A key victory came in 1415 when Portuguese forces conquered Ceuta, the Muslim bastion at the mouth of the Strait of Gibraltar that had previously blocked Portugal's access to the Atlantic coast of Africa.

The most influential advocate of Portuguese exploration was Prince Henry the Navigator, son of the Portuguese king. From 1415 until his death in 1460, Henry collected the latest information about sailing techniques and geography, supported new crusades against the Muslims, sought fresh sources of trade to fatten Portuguese pocketbooks, and pushed explorers to go farther still. Expeditions to Africa promised to capture wheat fields from their Moroccan owners and to obtain gold for currency, which had become scarce due to the quickening pace of European commerce and the luxury trade in Eastern goods.

Neither the Portuguese nor anybody else in Europe knew the immensity of Africa or the length of its coastline, which fronted the Atlantic for more than seven thousand miles. At first, Portuguese mariners cautiously hugged the west coast of Africa, seldom venturing beyond sight of land. By 1434, they had reached the northern edge of the Sahara Desert, where they learned to ride strong westerly currents before catching favorable easterly winds that turned them back toward land, which allowed them to reach Cape Verde by 1444.

To stow the supplies necessary for long sea voyages and to withstand the battering of waves in the open ocean, the Portuguese developed the caravel, a fast, sturdy ship that became explorers' vessel of choice. In caravels, Portuguese mariners sailed into and around the Gulf of Guinea and as far south as the Congo by 1480.

Fierce African resistance confined Portuguese expeditions to coastal trading posts, where they bartered successfully for gold, slaves, and ivory. Powerful African kingdoms welcomed Portuguese

Ivory Saltcellar
This exquisitely carved sixteenth-century ivory saltcellar combines African materials, craftsmanship, and imagery in an artifact for Portuguese tables. Designed to hold table salt in the central globe, the saltcellar dramatized African brutality and quietly suggested the beneficial influence of Portuguese in Africa. Photo: akg-images

trading ships loaded with iron goods, weapons, textiles, and ornamental shells. Portuguese merchants learned that establishing relatively peaceful trading posts on the coast offered more

Sixteenth-Century Pomander

This jewel-encrusted pomander was designed to hold expensive aromatic spices brought to Europe through the Mediterranean trade routes dominated by Italians or through the Indian Ocean trade route around Africa dominated by the Portuguese. A wealthy European wore the pomander on a chain at the neck or waist and sniffed it to overcome noxious stenches common in daily life. © Burghley House Collection, Lincolnshire, UK/The Bridgeman Art Library.

lished a network of Portuguese outposts in Africa and Asia, and developed methods of sailing the high seas that Columbus employed on his revolutionary voyage west.

> **REVIEW**   Why did European exploration expand dramatically in the fifteenth century?

▶ A Surprising New World in the Western Atlantic

The Portuguese and other experts believed that sailing west across the Atlantic to Asia was literally impossible. The European discovery of America required someone bold enough to believe that the experts were wrong. That person was Christopher Columbus. His explorations inaugurated a geographic revolution that forever altered Europeans' understanding of the world and its peoples, including themselves. Columbus's landfall in the Caribbean initiated a thriving exchange between the people, ideas, cultures, and institutions of the Old and New Worlds that continues to this day.

The Explorations of Columbus

Columbus went to sea when he was about fourteen and eventually made his way to Lisbon, where he married Felipa Moniz, whose father had been raised in the household of Prince Henry the Navigator. Through Felipa, Columbus gained access to explorers' maps and information about sailing in the tricky currents and winds of the Atlantic. Like other educated Europeans, Columbus believed that the earth was a sphere and that theoretically it was possible to reach the East Indies by sailing west. With flawed calculations, he estimated that Asia was only about 2,500 miles away, a shorter distance than Portuguese ships routinely sailed between Lisbon and the Congo. In fact, the shortest distance to Japan from Europe's jumping-off point was nearly 11,000 miles. Convinced by his erroneous calculations, Columbus became obsessed with a scheme to prove he was right.

In 1492, after years of unsuccessful lobbying in Portugal, Spain, England, and France, Columbus finally won financing for his journey from the Spanish monarchs, Queen Isabella and King Ferdinand. They saw Columbus's venture

profit than attempting violent conquest and colonization of inland regions. In the 1460s, the Portuguese used African slaves to develop sugar plantations on the Cape Verde Islands, inaugurating an association between enslaved Africans and plantation labor that would be transplanted to the New World in the centuries to come.

About 1480, Portuguese explorers, eager to bypass the Mediterranean merchants, began a conscious search for a sea route to Asia. In 1488, Bartolomeu Dias sailed around the Cape of Good Hope at the southern tip of Africa and hurried back to Lisbon with the exciting news that it appeared to be possible to sail on to India and China. In 1498, after ten years of careful preparation, Vasco da Gama commanded the first Portuguese fleet to sail to India. Portugal quickly capitalized on the commercial potential of da Gama's new sea route. By the early sixteenth century, the Portuguese controlled a far-flung commercial empire in India, Indonesia, and China (collectively referred to as the East Indies). Their new sea route to the East eliminated overland travel and allowed Portuguese merchants to charge much lower prices for the Eastern goods they imported.

Portugal's African explorations during the fifteenth century broke the monopoly of the old Mediterranean trade with the East, dramatically expanded the world known to Europeans, estabas an inexpensive gamble: The potential loss was small, but the potential gain was huge. They gave Columbus a letter of introduction to China's Grand Khan, the ruler they hoped he would meet on the other side of the Atlantic.

After frantic preparation, Columbus and his small fleet—the *Niña* and *Pinta*, both caravels, and the *Santa María*, a larger merchant vessel—headed west. Six weeks after leaving the Canary Islands, Columbus landed on a tiny Caribbean island about three hundred miles north of the eastern tip of Cuba.

Columbus claimed possession of the island for Spain and named it San Salvador, in honor of the Savior, Jesus Christ. He called the islanders "Indians," assuming that they inhabited the East Indies somewhere near Japan or China. The islanders called themselves **Tainos**, which in their language meant "good" or "noble." An agricultural people, the Tainos grew cassava, corn, cotton, tobacco, and other crops. Instead of dressing in the finery Columbus had expected to find in the East Indies, the Tainos "all . . . go around as naked as their mothers bore them," Columbus wrote. Although Columbus concluded that the Tainos "had no religion," in reality they worshipped gods they called *zemis*, ancestral spirits who inhabited natural objects such as trees and stones. The Tainos had no riches. "It seemed to me that they were a people very poor in everything," Columbus wrote.

What the Tainos thought about Columbus and his sailors we can only surmise since they left no written documents. At first, Columbus got the impression that the Tainos believed the Spaniards came from heaven. But after six weeks of encounters, Columbus decided that "the people of these lands do not understand me nor do I, nor anyone else that I have with me, [understand] them." The confused communication between the Spaniards and the Tainos suggests how strange each group

Columbus's First Voyage to the New World, 1492–1493

12 Oct. 1492
First landing on
San Salvador I.

seemed to the other. Columbus's perceptions of the Tainos were shaped by European attitudes, ideas, and expectations, just as the Tainos' perceptions of the Europeans were no doubt colored by their own culture.

Columbus and his men understood that they had made a momentous discovery. In 1493, when Queen Isabella and King Ferdinand learned Columbus's news, they were overjoyed. With a voyage that had lasted barely eight months, Columbus appeared to have catapulted Spain into a serious challenger to Portugal, whose explorers had not yet sailed to India or China. Columbus was elevated to the nobility, given the title "Admiral of the Ocean Sea," and the seven Tainos he brought to Spain were baptized as Christians and King Ferdinand became their godfather. Soon after Columbus returned to Spain, the Spanish monarchs rushed to obtain the pope's support for their claim to the new lands in the West. When the pope, a Spaniard, complied, the Portuguese feared that their own claims to recently discovered territories were in jeopardy. To protect their claims, the Portuguese and Spanish monarchs negotiated the **Treaty of Tordesillas** in 1494. The treaty drew an imaginary line eleven hundred miles west of the Canary Islands (Map 2.2). Land discovered west of the line (namely, the islands that Columbus discovered and any additional land that might be found) belonged to Spain; Portugal claimed land to the east (namely, its African and East Indian trading empire).

Isabella and Ferdinand moved quickly to realize the promise of their new claims. In the fall of 1493, they dispatched Columbus once again, this time with a fleet of seventeen

Taino Zemi Effigy
This sixteenth-century carving of a manatee bone depicts a Taino zemi in the form of a pipe-like container for inhaling cohoba, a psychedelic substance the Taino smoked to induce trances that revealed the supernatural world. Holes barely visible here in the feet placed behind the head of the zemi allowed the user to inhale with both nostrils simultaneously. Fundacion Garcia Arevalo, Dominican Republic/Photo © Dirk Bakker/The Bridgeman Art Library.

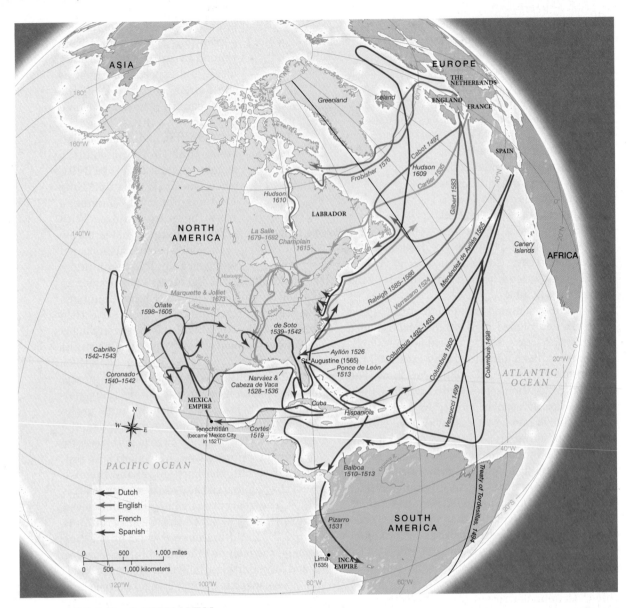

MAP ACTIVITY

Map 2.2   European Exploration in Sixteenth-Century America
This map illustrates the approximate routes of early European explorations of the New World.

READING THE MAP: Which countries were most actively exploring the New World? Which countries were exploring later than others?

CONNECTIONS: What were the motivations behind the explorations? What were the motivations for colonization?

ships and more than a thousand men who planned to locate the Asian mainland, find gold, and get rich. Before Columbus died in 1506, he returned to the New World two more times (in 1498 and 1502) without relinquishing his belief that the East Indies were there, someplace. Other explorers continued to search for a passage to the East or some other source of profit. Before long, however, prospects of beating the Portuguese to Asia began

to dim along with the hope of finding vast hoards of gold.

Nonetheless, Columbus's discoveries forced sixteenth-century Europeans to think about the world in new ways. He proved it was possible to sail from Europe to the western rim of the Atlantic and return to Europe. Most important, Columbus's voyages demonstrated that lands and peoples entirely unknown to Europeans lay across the Atlantic.

The Geographic Revolution and the Columbian Exchange

Within thirty years of Columbus's initial discovery, Europeans' understanding of world geography underwent a revolution. An elite of perhaps twenty thousand people with access to Europe's royal courts and trading centers learned the exciting news about global geography. But it took a generation of additional exploration before they could comprehend the larger contours of Columbus's discoveries.

European monarchs hurried to stake their claims to the newly discovered lands. In 1497, King Henry VII of England sent John Cabot to look for a Northwest Passage to the Indies across the North Atlantic (see Map 2.2). Cabot reached the tip of Newfoundland, which he believed was part of Asia, and hurried back to England, where he assembled a small fleet and sailed west in 1498. But he was never heard from again.

Three thousand miles to the south, a Spanish expedition landed on the northern coast of South America in 1499 accompanied by Amerigo Vespucci, an Italian businessman. In 1500, Pedro Álvars Cabral commanded a Portuguese fleet bound for the Indian Ocean that accidentally made landfall on the east coast of Brazil as it looped westward into the Atlantic.

By 1500, European experts knew that several large chunks of land cluttered the western Atlantic. A few cartographers speculated that these chunks were connected to one another in a landmass that was not Asia. In 1507, Martin Waldseemüller, a German cartographer, published the first map that showed the New World separate from Asia; he named the land America, in honor of Amerigo Vespucci.

Two additional discoveries confirmed Waldseemüller's speculation. In 1513, Vasco Núñez de Balboa crossed the Isthmus of Panama and reached the Pacific Ocean. Clearly, more water lay between the New World and Asia. Ferdinand Magellan discovered just how much water when he led an expedition to circumnavigate the globe in 1519. Sponsored by Spain, Magellan's voyage took him first to the New World, around the southern tip of South America, and into the Pacific. Crossing the Pacific took almost four months, decimating his crew with hunger and thirst. Magellan himself was killed by Philippine tribesmen. A remnant of his expedition continued on to the Indian Ocean and managed to transport a cargo of spices back to Spain in 1522.

In most ways, Magellan's voyage was a disaster. One ship and 18 men crawled back from an expedition that had begun with five ships and more than 250 men. But the geographic information it provided left no doubt that America was a continent separated from Asia by the enormous Pacific Ocean. Magellan's voyage made clear that it was possible to sail west to reach the East Indies, but that was a terrible way to go. After Magellan, most Europeans who sailed west set their sights on the New World, not on Asia.

Columbus's arrival in the Caribbean anchored the western end of what might be imagined as a sea bridge that spanned the Atlantic, connecting the Western Hemisphere to Europe. Somewhat like the Beringian land bridge traversed by the first Americans millennia earlier (see "African and Asian Origins" in chapter 1), the new sea bridge reestablished a connection between the Eastern and Western Hemispheres. The Atlantic Ocean, which had previously isolated America from Europe, became an aquatic highway, thanks to sailing technology, intrepid seamen, and their European sponsors. This new sea bridge launched the **Columbian exchange**, a transatlantic trade of goods, people, and ideas that has continued ever since.

Spaniards brought novelties to the New World that were commonplace in Europe, including Christianity, iron technology, sailing ships, firearms, wheeled vehicles, and horses. Unknowingly, they also carried many Old World microorganisms that caused devastating epidemics of smallpox, measles, and other diseases that killed the vast majority of Indians during the sixteenth century and continued to decimate survivors in later centuries. European diseases made the Columbian exchange catastrophic for Native Americans. In the long term, these diseases helped transform the dominant

Maize Goddess
In 1493, Columbus told Spaniards about an amazingly productive New World plant he called *maize*, his version of the Taino word *mahiz*, which means "life-giver." This maize, or corn, goddess was crafted in Peru about a thousand years before Columbus arrived in the New World. bpk, Berlin/Ethnologisches Museum/Waltraud Schneider-Schuetz/Art Resource, NY

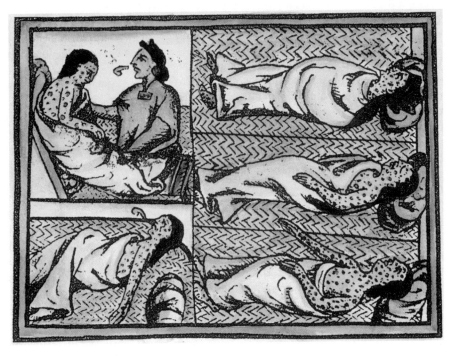

Smallpox Victims
This sixteenth-century picture shows four Mexican smallpox victims lying on woven mats while a fifth victim is treated by a Mexican healer. In reality, there were no known remedies for smallpox, which the Spaniards brought to Mexico. Millions died from smallpox, and those who survived were often greatly disfigured and demoralized. The Granger Collection, New York.

peoples of the New World from descendants of Asians, who had inhabited the hemisphere for millennia, to descendants of Europeans and Africans, the recent arrivals from the Old World.

Ancient American goods, people, and ideas made the return trip across the Atlantic. Europeans were introduced to New World foods such as corn and potatoes that became important staples in European diets, especially for poor people. Columbus's sailors became infected with syphilis in sexual encounters with New World women and unwittingly carried the deadly bacteria back to Europe. New World tobacco created a European fashion for smoking that ignited quickly and has yet to be extinguished. But for almost a generation after 1492, this Columbian exchange did not reward the Spaniards with the riches they yearned to find.

REVIEW   How did Columbus's discoveries help revolutionize Europeans' understanding of global geography?

▶ Spanish Exploration and Conquest

During the sixteenth century, the New World helped Spain become the most powerful monarchy in both Europe and the Americas. Initially, Spaniards enslaved Caribbean tribes and put them to work growing crops and mining gold. But the profits from these early ventures barely

covered the costs of maintaining the settlers. After almost thirty years of exploration, the promise of Columbus's discovery seemed illusory.

In 1519, however, that promise was spectacularly fulfilled by Hernán Cortés's march into Mexico. By about 1545, Spanish conquests extended from northern Mexico to southern Chile, and New World riches filled Spanish treasure chests. Cortés's expedition served as the model for Spaniards' and other Europeans' expectations that the New World could yield bonanza profits for its conquerors while forced labor and deadly epidemics decimated native populations.

The Conquest of Mexico

Hernán Cortés, an obscure nineteen-year-old Spaniard, arrived in the New World in 1504. Throughout his twenties, he fought in the conquest of Cuba and elsewhere in the Caribbean. In 1519, the governor of Cuba authorized Cortés to organize an expedition of about six hundred men and eleven ships to investigate rumors of a fabulously wealthy kingdom somewhere in the interior of the mainland.

A charismatic and confident man, Cortés could not speak any Native American language. Landing first on the Yucatán peninsula with his ragtag army, he had the good fortune to receive from a local Tobascan chief the gift of a young girl named Malinali. She spoke several native languages, including Nahuatl, the language of the Mexica, the most powerful people in what is now Mexico and Central America (see "The Mexica:

A Mesoamerican Culture" in chapter 1). Malinali, whom the Spaniards called Marina, had acquired her linguistic skills painfully. Born into a family of Mexican nobility, she learned Nahuatl as a child. After her father died and her mother remarried, her stepfather sold her as a slave to Mayan-speaking Indians, who subsequently gave her to the Tobascans, who in turn presented her to Cortés. She soon learned Spanish, became Cortés's interpreter, one of his several mistresses, and the mother of his son. Malinali was the Spaniards' lifeline of communication with the Indians. "Without her help," wrote one of the Spaniards who accompanied Cortés, "we would not have understood the language of New Spain and Mexico."

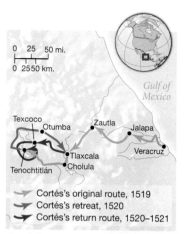

Cortés's Invasion of Tenochtitlán, 1519–1521

In Tenochtitlán, the capital of the Mexican empire, the emperor Montezuma heard about some strange creatures sighted along the coast. (Montezuma and his people called themselves Mexica.) The emperor sent representatives to bring the strangers large quantities of food. But along with the food, the Mexica also brought the Spaniards another gift, a "disk in the shape of a sun, as big as a cartwheel and made of very fine gold," as a Mexican recalled. Here was conclusive evidence that the rumors of fabulous riches heard by Cortés had some basis in fact.

In August 1519, Cortés marched inland to find Montezuma. Leading about 350 men, Cortés had to live off the land, establishing peaceful relations with indigenous tribes when he could and killing them when he thought it necessary. On Novem-

ber 8, 1519, Cortés reached Tenochtitlán, where Montezuma welcomed him and showered the Spaniards with lavish hospitality. Quickly, Cortés took Montezuma hostage and held him under house arrest, hoping to make him a puppet through whom the Spaniards could rule the Mexican empire. This uneasy peace existed for several months until one of Cortés's men led a brutal massacre of many Mexican nobles, causing the people of Tenochtitlán to revolt. Montezuma was killed, and the Mexica mounted a ferocious assault on the Spaniards. On June 30, 1520, Cortés and about a hundred other Spaniards fought their way out of Tenochtitlán (losing much of the gold they had confiscated since it proved too heavy to carry away in haste) and retreated about one hundred miles to Tlaxcala, a stronghold of bitter enemies of the Mexica. The Tlaxcalans—who had long resented Mexican power—allowed Cortés to regroup, obtain reinforcements, and plan a strategy to conquer Tenochtitlán.

In the spring of 1521, Cortés and thousands of Indian allies laid siege to the Mexican capital. With a relentless, scorched-earth strategy, Cortés finally defeated the last Mexican defenders on August 13, 1521. The great capital of the Mexican empire "looked as if it had been ploughed up," one of Cortés's soldiers remembered.

How did a few hundred Spaniards so far away from home defeat millions of Indians fighting on their home turf? For one thing, the Spaniards had superior military technology that partially offset the Mexicans' numerical advantages. (See "Visualizing History," page 36.) They fought with weapons of iron and steel against the Mexicans'

VISUAL ACTIVITY

Cortés Arrives in Tenochtitlán

In this portrayal of Cortés and his army arriving in the Mexican capital, Malinali stands at the front of the procession, serving as the Spaniards' translator and intermediary with Montezuma (not pictured). Painted by a Mexican artist after the conquest, the work displays the choices the Mexica faced: accept the peaceful overtures of Cortés (doffing his hat) or face his battle-ready soldiers. Bibliotheque Nationale, Paris, France/The Bridgeman Art Library.

READING THE IMAGE: How did each of the different kinds of people illustrated in the portrait contribute to the Spanish conquest of Tenochtitlán?

CONNECTIONS: How did Cortés's conquest of Tenochtitlán compare to Mexicans' conquest of the numerous people in their empire?

Weapons of Conquest

Mexican Warriors Battle Spanish Conquistadors
This sixteenth-century painting illustrates the war clubs, spears, and feather shields Mexican warriors deployed against the steel swords and armor of attacking Spaniards.

For centuries, Spanish soldiers and Mexican warriors wielded weapons that had proven to be effective in their respective military cultures and dominated their lands. When the Spanish conquistadors traveled to the New World during the sixteenth century, the battles of conquest revealed the deadly limitations of weaponry that the Mexica had used to build their mighty empire.

The Mexica fought with offensive weapons similar to the wooden club shown here. Razor-sharp fragments of obsidian, a glasslike mineral, studded the edges of the club, allowing Mexican warriors, like those pictured here, to deliver lacerating, even lethal, blows against an enemy at close range. The Mexica and their enemies used shields made of hides, wood, and feathers, as shown here to defend themselves against wood and stone weapons.

In Europe, Spaniards had gone to battle for centuries with offensive weapons made of steel, like the sword shown here. Like the Mexican club, the steel sword was effective only at close range; the sword shown here, for example, is three feet long. (The effective range of a modern military rifle is nearly a mile.) This sword is inscribed with Latin mottoes that read on one side, "Turn away these

Spanish Shield

stone, wood, and copper. The muscles of Mexican warriors could not match the power of cannons and muskets fueled by gunpowder.

European viruses proved to be even more powerful weapons. Smallpox arrived in Mexico with Cortés, and in the ensuing epidemic thousands of Mexicans died and many others became too sick to fight. The sickness spread along the network of trade and tribute feeding Tenochtitlán, causing many to fear that their gods had abandoned them. "Cut us loose," one Mexican pleaded, "because the gods have died."

The Spaniards' concept of war also favored them. Mexicans tended to consider war a way to impose their tribute system on conquered people and to take captives for sacrifice. They believed that the high cost of continuing to fight would cause their adversaries to surrender and pay tribute. In contrast, Spaniards sought total victory by destroying their enemy's ability to fight.

Politics proved decisive in Cortés's victory over the Mexicans. Cortés shrewdly exploited the tensions between the Mexica and the people they ruled in their empire (see chapter 1). Cortés reinforced his small army with thousands of Indian allies who were eager to seek revenge against the Mexica. Hundreds of thousands of other Indians aided Cortés by failing to come to the Mexicans' defense. In the end, the political tensions created by the Mexican empire proved to be its crippling weakness.

troubles from us," and on the other side, "With God we achieve lofty goals but nothing by ourselves." Why might these inscriptions have been meaningful to a Spanish soldier who slashed and stabbed enemies with this sword?

On the battlefields of sixteenth-century Europe, Spanish soldiers defended themselves against the steel weapons of their enemies

Mexican War Club

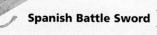

Spanish Battle Sword

Mexican Warrior's Shield

with steel or iron shields, as shown here, and steel body armor. In Mexico, the wood and stone weapons of Mexican warriors tended to bounce off the Spaniards' shields and armor, in effect disarming Mexicans' major offensive weaponry. Likewise, Spaniards' sword blows, which might have clanked off a European enemy's steel shield, slashed through Mexican warriors' shields of hide and feathers, leaving them defenseless.

Horses were unknown in Mexico until Spaniards imported them. What offensive and defensive advantages did horses provide for mounted Spanish soldiers when in combat against Mexican foot soldiers? Did horses have any disadvantages for Spaniards or any advantages for the Mexica?

While the Mexica wounded and killed many Spaniards, in the end Spaniards prevailed and conquered Mexico. Although Spaniards' superior

weaponry contributed to their success, can you imagine tactics that the Mexica might have used to delay, subvert, or even defeat Spanish conquest?

Questions for Analysis

1. Why might Mexican warriors have considered bright designs made with feathers useful for offense or defense?

2. Looking at the Mexican war club and the Spanish battle sword, what does each weapon's design suggest about the fighter's ultimate goal in combat?

3. What does the relatively short effective range of the Spanish sword and the Mexican club suggest about combat during the conquest?

Connect to the Big Idea

⊙ While combat was an important part of Spanish conquest, what else contributed to Spaniards' conquest of Mexicans?

The Search for Other Mexicos

Lured by their insatiable appetite for gold, Spanish **conquistadors** (soldiers who fought in conquests) quickly fanned out from Tenochtitlán in search of other sources of treasure. The most spectacular prize fell to Francisco Pizarro, who conquered the **Incan empire** in Peru. The Incas controlled a vast, complex region that contained more than nine million people and stretched along the western coast of South America for more than two thousand miles. In 1532, Pizarro and his army of fewer than two hundred men captured the Incan emperor Atahualpa and held him hostage. As ransom, the Incas gave Pizarro the largest treasure yet produced by the conquests: gold and

silver equivalent to half a century's worth of precious-metal production in Europe. With the ransom safely in their hands, the Spaniards murdered Atahualpa. The Incan treasure proved that at least one other Mexico did indeed exist, and it spurred the Spaniards' search for others.

Juan Ponce de León sailed to Florida in 1521 to find riches, only to be killed in battle with Calusa Indians. A few years later, Lucas Vázquez de Ayllón explored the Atlantic coast north of Florida to present-day South Carolina. In 1526, he established a small settlement on the Georgia coast that he named San Miguel de Gualdape, the first Spanish attempt to establish a foothold in what is now the United States. This settlement was soon swept away by sickness and hostile Indians. In 1528, Pánfilo de Narváez surveyed the Gulf coast from Florida to Texas, but his expedition ended disastrously with a shipwreck near present-day Galveston, Texas.

In 1539, Hernando de Soto, a seasoned conquistador, set out with more than six hundred men to find another Peru in North America. Landing in Florida, de Soto slashed his way through much of southeastern North America for three years. After the brutal slaughter of many Native Americans and much hardship, de Soto died in 1542. His men buried him in the Mississippi River and turned back to Mexico, disappointed.

VISUAL ACTIVITY

Zuñi Defend Pueblo Against Coronado

This sixteenth-century drawing by a Mexican artist shows Zuñi bowmen fighting back against Coronado's men and the entreaties of Christian missionaries. The drawing depicts a Zuñi defender aiming his arrow at a Mexican missionary armed with a crucifix, a rosary, and the Bible.
© Glasgow University Library, Scotland/The Bridgeman Art Library.

READING THE IMAGE: How did this picture convey Spaniards' point of view about Zuñi opposition to Coronado and his men?

CONNECTIONS: Why did missionaries seek to convert Native Americans to Christianity, and why did many Native Americans resist the missionaries' efforts?

Tales of the fabulous wealth of the mythical Seven Cities of Cíbola also lured Francisco Vásquez de Coronado to search the Southwest and Great Plains of North America. In 1540, Coronado left northern Mexico with more than three hundred Spaniards, a thousand Indians, and a priest who claimed to know the way to what he called "the greatest and best of the discoveries." Cíbola turned out to be a small Zuñi pueblo of about a hundred families. When the Zuñi shot arrows at the Spaniards, Coronado attacked the pueblo and routed the defenders after a hard battle. Convinced that the rich cities must lie somewhere over the horizon, Coronado kept moving all the way to central Kansas before deciding in 1542 that the rumors he had pursued were just that.

The same year Coronado abandoned his search for Cíbola, Juan Rodríguez Cabrillo's maritime expedition sought to find wealth along the coast of California. Cabrillo died on Santa Catalina Island, offshore from present-day Los Angeles, but his men sailed on to Oregon, where a ferocious storm forced them to turn back toward Mexico.

These probes into North America by de Soto, Coronado, and Cabrillo persuaded other Spaniards that although enormous territories stretched northward from Mexico, their inhabitants had little to loot or exploit. After a generation of vigorous exploration, the Spaniards concluded that there was only one Mexico and one Peru.

Spanish Outposts in Florida and New Mexico

Disappointed by the explorers' failure to discover riches in North America, the Spanish monarchy insisted that a few settlements be established in Florida and New Mexico to give a token of reality to Spain's territorial claims. Settlements in Florida would have the additional benefit of protecting Spanish ships from pirates and privateers who lurked along the southeastern coast, waiting for the Spanish treasure fleet sailing toward Spain.

In 1565, the Spanish king sent Pedro Menéndez de Avilés to found St. Augustine in Florida, the first permanent European settlement within what became the United States. By 1600, St. Augustine had a population of about five hundred, the only remaining Spanish beachhead on North America's vast Atlantic shoreline.

More than sixteen hundred miles west of St. Augustine, the Spaniards founded another outpost in 1598. Juan de Oñate led an expedition of about five hundred people to settle northern Mexico, now called New Mexico, and claim the booty rumored to exist there. Oñate had impeccable credentials for both conquest and mining. His father helped to discover the bonanza silver mines of Zacatecas in central Mexico, and his wife Isabel Tolsa Cortés Montezuma was the granddaughter of Cortés and the great-granddaughter of Montezuma. When Oñate and his companions reached pueblos near present-day Albuquerque and Santa Fe, he sent out scouting parties to find the legendary treasures of the region. Meanwhile, many of his soldiers planned to mutiny, and relations with the Indians deteriorated. When Indians in the Acoma pueblo revolted against the Spaniards, Oñate ruthlessly suppressed the uprising, killing eight hundred men, women, and children. Although Oñate's response to the **Acoma pueblo revolt** reconfirmed the Spaniards' military superiority, he did not bring peace or stability to the region.

After another pueblo revolt occurred in 1599, many of Oñate's settlers returned to Mexico, leaving New Mexico a small, dusty assertion of Spanish claims to the North American Southwest.

New Spain in the Sixteenth Century

For all practical purposes, Spain was the dominant European power in the Western Hemisphere during the sixteenth century (Map 2.3). Portugal claimed the giant territory of Brazil under the Tordesillas Treaty but was far more concerned with exploiting its hard-won trade with the East Indies than with colonizing the New World. England and France were absorbed by domestic and diplomatic concerns in Europe and largely

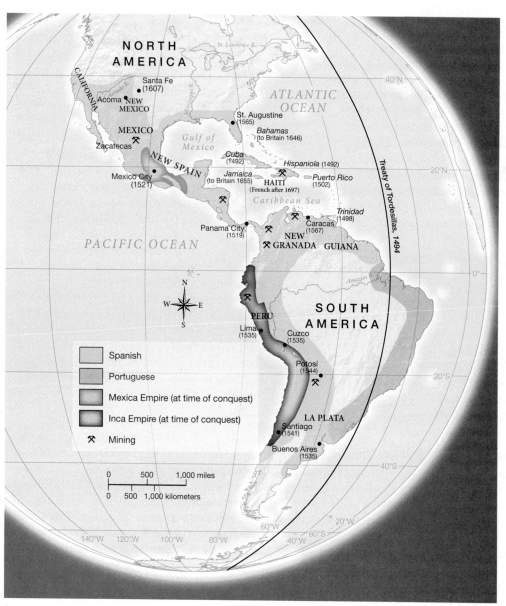

MAP ACTIVITY

Map 2.3 Sixteenth-Century European Colonies in the New World

Spanish control spread throughout Central and South America during the sixteenth century, with the important exception of Portuguese Brazil. North America, though claimed by Spain under the Treaty of Tordesillas, remained peripheral to Spain's New World empire.

READING THE MAP: Track Spain's efforts at colonization by date. How did political holdings, the physical layout of the land, and natural resources influence where the Spaniards directed their energies?

CONNECTIONS: What was the purpose of the Treaty of Tordesillas? How might the location of silver and gold mines have affected Spain's desire to assert its claims over regions still held by Portugal after 1494, and Spain's interest in California, New Mexico, and Florida?

Justifying Conquest

The immense riches Spain reaped from its New World empire came largely at the expense of Native Americans. A few individual Spaniards raised their voices against the brutal exploitation of the Indians. Their criticisms prompted the Spanish monarchy to formulate an official justification of conquest that, in effect, blamed the Indians for resisting Spanish dominion.

DOCUMENT 1
Montecino's 1511 Sermon

In 1511, a Dominican friar named Antón Montecino delivered a blistering sermon that astonished the Spaniards gathered in the church in Santo Domingo, headquarters of the Spanish Caribbean.

Your greed for gold is blind. Your pride, your lust, your anger, your envy, your sloth, all blind. . . . You are in mortal sin. And you are heading for damnation. . . . For you are destroying an innocent people. For they are God's people, these innocents, whom you destroyed. By what right do you make them die? Mining gold for you in your mines or working for you in your fields, by what right do you unleash enslaving wars upon them? They have lived in peace in this land before you came, in peace in their own homes. They did nothing to harm you to cause you to slaughter them wholesale. . . .

Are you not under God's command to love them as you love yourselves?

Are you out of your souls, out of your minds? Yes. And that will bring you to damnation.

Source: Zvi Dor-Ner, *Columbus and the Age of Discovery* (New York: William Morrow, 1991), 220–21.

DOCUMENT 2
The Requerimiento

In 1512 and 1513, King Ferdinand met with philosophers and theologians, and concluded that the holy duty to

spread Christianity justified conquest. To buttress this claim, the king had his advisers prepare the requerimiento.

According to the requerimiento, Indians who failed to welcome Spanish conquest and all its blessings deserved to die. Conquistadors were commanded to read the requerimiento to the Indians before any act of conquest.

On the part of the King . . . [and] queen of [Spain], subduers of the barbarous nations, we their servants notify and make known to you, as best we can, that the Lord our God, living and eternal, created the heaven and the earth, and one man and one woman, of whom you and we, and all the men of the world, were and are descendants. . . .

God our lord gave charge to one man called St. Peter, that he should be lord and superior to all the men in the world, that all should obey him, and that he should be the head of the whole human race, wherever men should live . . . and he gave him the world for his kingdom and jurisdiction. . . .

[The Pope] who succeeded that St. Peter as lord of the world . . . made donation of these islands and mainland to the . . . king and queen [of Spain] . . . .

So their highnesses are kings and lords of these islands and mainland by virtue of this donation; and . . . almost all those to whom this has been notified, have received and served their highnesses, as lords and kings, in the way that subjects ought to do, with good will, without any resistance, immediately, without

lost interest in America until late in the century. In the decades after 1519, the Spaniards created the distinctive colonial society of **New Spain**, which showed other Europeans how the New World could be made to serve the purposes of the Old.

The Spanish monarchy gave the conquistadors permission to explore and plunder what they found. (See "Documenting the American Promise," above.) The crown took one-fifth, called

the "royal fifth," of any loot confiscated and allowed the conquerors to divide the rest. In the end, most conquistadors received very little after the plunder was divided among leaders such as Cortés and his favorite officers. To compensate his disappointed, battle-hardened soldiers, Cortés gave them towns the Spaniards had subdued.

The distribution of conquered towns institutionalized the system of *encomienda*, which empowered the conquistadors to rule the Indians delay, when they were informed of the aforesaid facts. And also they received and obeyed the priests whom their highnesses sent to preach to them and to teach them our holy faith; and all these, of their own free will, without any reward or condition have become Christians, and are so, and their highnesses have joyfully and graciously received them, and they have also commanded them to be treated as their subjects and vassals; and you too are held and obliged to do the same. Wherefore, as best we can, we ask and require that you consider what we have said to you, and that you take the time that shall be necessary to understand and deliberate upon it, and that you acknowledge the Church as the ruler and superior of the whole world, and the high priest called Pope, and in his name the king and queen [of Spain] our lords, in his place, as superiors and lords and kings of these islands and this mainland . . . and that you consent and permit that these religious fathers declare and preach to you. . . .

If you do so . . . we . . . shall receive you in all love and charity, and shall leave you your wives and your children and your lands free without servitude, that you may do with them and with yourselves freely what you like and think best, and they shall not compel you to turn to Christians unless you yourselves, when informed of the truth, should wish to be converted to our holy Catholic faith. . . . And besides this, their highnesses award you many privileges and exemptions and will grant you many benefits.

But if you do not do this or if you maliciously delay in doing it, I certify to you that with the help of God we shall forcefully enter into your country and shall make war against you in all ways and manners that we can, and shall subject you to the yoke and obedience of the Church and of their highnesses; we shall take you and your wives and your children and shall make slaves of them, and as such shall sell and dispose of them as their highnesses may command; and we shall take away your goods and shall do to you all the harm and damage that we can, as to vassals who do not obey and refuse to receive their lord and resist and contradict him; and we protest that the deaths and losses which shall accrue from this are your fault, and not that of their highnesses, or ours, or of these soldiers who come with us.

The Indians who heard the requerimiento could not understand Spanish, of course. No native documents survive to record the Indians' thoughts upon hearing the Spaniards' official justification for conquest, even when it was translated into a language they recognized. But one conquistador reported that when the requerimiento was translated for two chiefs in Colombia, they responded that if the pope gave the king so much territory that belonged to other people, "the Pope must have been drunk."

Source: Adapted from A. Helps and M. Oppenheim, eds., *The Spanish Conquest in America and Its Relation to the History of Slavery and to the Government of the Colonies*, 4 vols. (London, 1900–1904), 1:264–67.

Questions for Analysis and Debate

1. How did the requerimiento address the criticisms of Montecino? According to the requerimiento, why was conquest justified? What was the source of the Indians' resistance to conquest?

2. What arguments might a critic like Montecino have used to respond to the requerimiento's justification of conquest? What arguments might the Mexican leader Montezuma have made against those of the requerimiento?

3. Was the requerimiento a faithful expression or a cynical violation of the Spaniards' Christian faith?

Connect to the Big Idea

⊙ How did the Spanish view the conquest of the Americas?

empowered the conquistadors to rule the Indians and the lands in and around their towns. Encomienda transferred to the Spanish *enco-mendero* (the man who "owned" the town) the tribute that the town had previously paid to the Mexican empire. In theory, the encomendero was supposed to guarantee order and justice, be responsible for the Indians' material welfare, and encourage them to become Christians.

Catholic missionaries worked hard to convert the Indians. They fervently believed that God expected them to save the Indians' souls by convincing them to abandon their old sinful beliefs and to embrace the one true Christian faith. (See "Seeking the American Promise," page 42.) But after baptizing tens of thousands of Indians, the missionaries learned that many Indians continued to worship their own gods. Most priests came to believe that the Indians were lesser beings

Spreading Christianity in New Spain

Spanish officials aspired to accompany the military and political conquest of the New World with spiritual conquest. With royal support, priests flocked to New Spain to save the millions of souls unexpectedly disclosed by the voyages of Columbus. In 1529, a young priest named Bernardino de Sahagún sailed to New Spain, where he spent the remaining sixty-one years of his life seeking to realize the promise of spreading Christianity to people who had never heard of it.

Sahagún believed that preaching the gospel in the New World was a heaven-sent opportunity to revitalize global Christianity. In Asia, he wrote, "there are nothing but Turks and Moors"; in Africa, "there are no longer any Christians"; in Germany, "there are nothing but heretics"; and in Europe, "in most places there is no obedience to the Church." Now, Sahagún wrote, "Our Lord [ordained] the Spanish people to traverse the Ocean Sea to make discoveries in the West" and to "bring into the embrace of the Church that multitude of peoples, kingdoms, and nations." In pursuit of his goal to rescue Christianity by converting the New World Indians, Sahagún compiled the most important collection of information in existence about the lives and beliefs of sixteenth-century Mexicans.

Sahagún and other Spaniards considered Christianity the one true faith. When Cortés and his men marched into Mexico a decade before Sahagún arrived, they went out of their way to destroy effigies of Mexican gods and to replace them with crosses, the icons of Christianity. "It was necessary," Sahagún wrote, "to destroy the idolatrous things, and all the idolatrous buildings, and even the customs of the [Mexicans] . . . that were intertwined with idolatrous rites and accompanied by idolatrous ceremonies."

What Sahagún considered idolatry was rooted in individual Mexicans' belief in what he called their own "innumerable insanities and gods without number." Sahagún and other priests set out to persuade the Indians to reject belief in traditional deities and to have faith instead in the divinity of Jesus Christ and in the Catholic Church as Christ's representative on earth.

At first, the conversion campaign seemed amazingly successful. One priest claimed that more than nine million Mexicans had been baptized by 1539. But after a few years, Sahagún and other priests realized that many Indians simply "took [Jesus Christ] as yet another god . . . without . . . relinquishing their ancient gods." Adopting some of the outward rituals of Christianity while maintaining belief in what Spaniards considered pagan idols was a "twisted perversity," Sahagún wrote, one that caused the New World church "to be founded on falsehood."

Unlike many other Spaniards, Sahagún believed that in order to purge Mexicans' idolatries, church leaders needed to become familiar with Mexicans' traditional religious ideas. To diagnose what he called the Mexicans' "spiritual illnesses," Sahagún set out to record everything he could learn about the Indians' beliefs.

As a first step, Sahagún learned Nahuatl, the Mexicans' unwritten language. Next, he and other priests started schools to teach Latin and eventually Spanish to young Indian students, usually drawn from elite families. These "trilinguals," as Sahagún called them, could translate religious texts into Nahuatl, which the priests could use in their missionary efforts.

Beginning in 1558, Sahagún used his trilinguals to undertake a systematic investigation of every facet of Mexican life. Sahagún and his assistants interviewed Mexican

Connections between Spanish Christianity and Mexican Traditional Religions
Spanish missionaries struggled to eradicate all forms of Mexicans' traditional religion. The painting portrays a Catholic priest instructing two Mexican children while another priest shelters a group of children and wields a cross to protect them from the diabolical creatures seeking to tempt them to embrace evil. Even Mexicans who converted to Christianity continued to express their spirituality in traditional ways. The Granger Collection, New York.

Montezuma Receiving Tribute
In this drawing, Montezuma (seated at left) is receiving a rich array of featherwork, ritualistic costumes, battle shields, and other luxuries from one of his subjects. Made by a Mexican artist in the mid-sixteenth century, the drawing illustrates the enormous power and respect that Montezuma commanded. By the time the drawing was made, the Spaniards, not Montezuma's descendants, collected tribute (mostly labor) from the Indians. Biblioteca Medicea-Laurenziana, Florence, Italy/The Bridgeman Art Library.

them immediately to Spain for destruction. The Spanish monarchy and most church officials wanted to stamp out the Mexicans' beliefs, not preserve them. Sahagún dutifully sent his volumes to Spain, but he was still working on a final copy, which he later gave to a priest friend, who saved it, and it survives to this day. Unbeknownst to him, Sahagún's masterwork preserved for posterity an unrivaled account of the hearts and souls of sixteenth-century Mexicans in their own words.

Questions for Consideration

1. In what ways did Sahagún's work contribute to the conquest of Mexico?

2. What did Sahagún believe about the global significance of his missionary work? How might his "trilinguals" and Mexican informants have interpreted his efforts?

Connect to the Big Idea

◐ What ideas about the Mexicans did Sahagún hold in common with the Spanish monarchy, royal officials, and other Catholic missionaries? To what extent did his ideas conflict with those held by other Spaniards?

elders, asking them not only about gods and religious ceremonies but also about farming, family life, education, poetry, songs, and even their conquest by the Spaniards. Sahagún developed great admiration for both the Mexicans and their language. "They are quick to learn," he wrote. "There is no art for which they do not have the talent to learn and use it." In fact, Sahagún declared, the Mexicans "are held to be barbarians and a people of little worth, yet in truth, in matters of culture, they are a step ahead of many nations that presume to be civilized."

For years, Sahagún edited and organized this massive treasure trove of information about Mexican life and beliefs, all in the hope that it would ultimately help priests make converts to Christianity. When church officials heard about Sahagún's great work, they obtained a royal order in 1577 to collect all copies and send

inherently incapable of fully understanding Christianity.

In practice, encomenderos were far more interested in what the Indians could do for them than in what they or the missionaries could do for the Indians. Encomenderos subjected the Indians to chronic overwork, mistreatment, and abuse. According to one Spaniard, "Everything [the Indians] do is slowly done and by compulsion. They are malicious, lying, [and] thievish." Economically, however, encomienda recognized a fundamental reality of New Spain: The most important treasure the Spaniards could plunder from the New World was not gold but uncompensated Indian labor.

The practice of coerced labor in New Spain grew directly out of the Spaniards' assumption that they were superior to the Indians. As one missionary put it, the Indians "are more stupid than asses and refuse to improve in anything." Therefore, most Spaniards assumed, Indians' labor should be organized by and for their conquerors. Spaniards seldom hesitated to use violence to punish and intimidate recalcitrant Indians.

Encomienda engendered two groups of influential critics. A few missionaries were horrified at the brutal mistreatment of the Indians. "What will [the Indians] think about the God of the

Christians," Friar Bartolomé de Las Casas asked, when they see their friends "with their heads split, their hands amputated, their intestines torn open? . . . Would they want to come to Christ's sheepfold after their homes had been destroyed, their children imprisoned, their wives raped, their cities devastated, their maidens deflowered, and their provinces laid waste?" Las Casas and other outspoken missionaries softened few hearts among the encomenderos, but they did win some sympathy for the Indians from the Spanish monarchy and royal bureaucracy. The Spanish monarchy moved to abolish encomienda in an effort to replace swashbuckling old conquistadors with royal bureaucrats as the rulers of New Spain.

In 1549, a reform called the *repartimiento* began to replace encomienda. It limited the labor an encomendero could command from his Indians to forty-five days per year from each adult male. The repartimiento, however, did not challenge the principle of forced labor, nor did it prevent encomenderos from continuing to cheat, mistreat, and overwork their Indians, many of whom were put to work in silver mines. Mining was grueling and dangerous work. One Spaniard claimed that ten Indians died for every peso earned in the mines, an exaggeration. But the mines were fabulously profitable for the Spaniards. During the entire sixteenth century, precious-metal exports from New Spain to Spain were worth twenty-five times more than the next most important export, leather hides (Figure 2.1).

For Spaniards, life in New Spain after the conquests was relatively easy. As one colonist wrote to his brother in Spain, "Don't hesitate [to come]. . . . This land [New Spain] is as good as ours [in Spain], for God has given us more here than there, and we shall be better off." During the century after 1492, about 225,000 Spaniards settled in the colonies. Virtually all of them were poor young men of common (non-noble) lineage who came directly from Spain. Laborers and artisans made up the largest proportion, but soldiers and sailors were also numerous. Men vastly outnumbered women.

The gender and number of Spanish settlers shaped two fundamental features of the society of New Spain. First, Europeans never made up more than 1 or 2 percent of the total population. Although Spaniards ruled New Spain, the population was almost wholly Indian. Second, the shortage of Spanish women meant that Spanish men frequently married Indian women or used them as concubines. The relatively few women from Spain usually married Spanish men, contributing to a tiny elite defined by European origins.

The small number of Spaniards, the masses of Indians, and the frequency of intermarriage created a steep social hierarchy defined by perceptions of national origin and race. Natives of Spain—*peninsulares* (people born on the Iberian Peninsula)—enjoyed the highest social status in New Spain. Below them but still within the white elite were **creoles**, the children born in the New

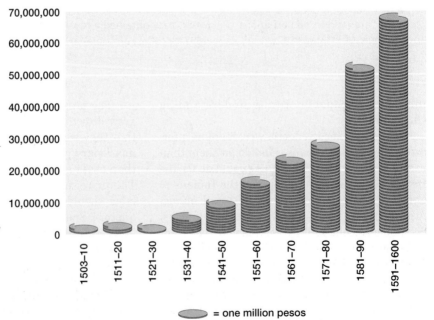

FIGURE 2.1   New World Gold and Silver Imported into Spain during the Sixteenth Century, in Pesos
Spain imported more gold than silver during the first three decades of the sixteenth century, but the total value of this treasure was quickly eclipsed during the 1530s and 1540s, when rich silver mines were developed. Silver accounted for most of the enormous growth in Spain's precious-metal imports from the New World.

= one million pesos

Español con India.
Mestizo.

Mestizo con Españolo
Castizo.

Castizo con Española
Español.

Español con Mora
Mulato.

5

6

Mulato con Española.
Morisco.

Morisco con Española
Chino.

7

Chino con India.
Salta atras.

Salta atras con Mulata.
Lobo.

VISUAL ACTIVITY

Mixed Races

These eighteenth-century paintings illustrate forms of racial mixture common in the sixteenth century. In the first painting, a Spanish man and an Indian woman have a mestizo son; in the fourth, a Spanish man and a woman of African descent have a mulatto son. Can you detect any meanings of racial categories in the clothing? © Bob Schalkwijk.

READING THE IMAGE: What do these paintings reveal about social status in New Spain?

CONNECTIONS: How do the paintings illustrate the power the Spaniards exercised in their New World colonies? What were some other aspects of colonial society that demonstrated Spanish domination?

tion. Some mestizos worked as artisans and labor overseers and lived well, and a few rose into the ranks of the elite, especially if their Indian ancestry was not obvious from their skin color. Most mestizos, however, were lumped with the Indians, the enormous bottom slab of the social pyramid.

The society of New Spain established the precedent for what would become a pronounced pattern in the European colonies of the New World: a society stratified sharply by social origin and race. All Europeans of whatever social origin considered themselves superior to Native Americans; in New Spain, they were a dominant minority in both power and status.

The Toll of Spanish Conquest and Colonization

By 1560, the major centers of Indian civilization had been conquered, their leaders overthrown, their religion held in contempt, and their people forced to work for the Spaniards. Profound demoralization pervaded Indian society. A Mexican poet wrote:

> Nothing but flowers and songs of sorrow are left in Mexico . . .
>
> Where once we saw warriors and wise men . . .
>
> We are crushed to the ground; we lie in ruins.
>
> There is nothing but grief and suffering in Mexico.

World to Spanish men and women. Together, peninsulares and creoles made up barely 1 or 2 percent of the population. Below them on the social pyramid was a larger group of *mestizos*, the offspring of Spanish men and Indian women, who accounted for 4 or 5 percent of the popula-

Adding to the culture shock of conquest and colonization was the deadly toll of European diseases. As conquest spread, the Indians succumbed to epidemics of measles, smallpox, and respiratory illnesses. They had no immunity to these diseases because they had not been exposed to them before the arrival of Europeans. By 1570 the Indian population of New Spain had fallen about 90 percent from what it was when Columbus arrived, a catastrophe unequaled in human history. A Mayan Indian recalled that when sickness struck his village, "The dogs and vultures devoured the bodies. The mortality was terrible. . . . So it was that we became orphans. . . . We were born to die." For most Indians, New Spain was a graveyard.

For the Spaniards, Indian deaths meant that the most valuable resource of New Spain—Indian labor—dwindled rapidly. By the last quarter of the sixteenth century, Spanish colonists began to import African slaves. Some Africans had come to Mexico with the conquistadors. One Mexican recalled that among Cortés's men were "some black-skinned one[s] with kink[y] hair." In the years before 1550, while Indian labor was still adequate, only 15,000 slaves were imported from Africa. The relatively high cost of African slaves kept imports low, totaling approximately 36,000 from 1550 to the end of the century. During the sixteenth century, New Spain continued to rely primarily on a shrinking number of Indians.

> REVIEW   How did New Spain's distinctive colonial population shape its economy and society?

▶ The New World and Sixteenth-Century Europe

The riches of New Spain helped make the sixteenth century the Golden Age of Spain. After Queen Isabella and King Ferdinand died, their sixteen-year-old grandson became King Charles I of Spain in 1516. Three years later, just as Cortés ventured into Mexico, King Charles became Holy Roman Emperor Charles V. His empire encompassed more territory than that of any other European monarch. He used the wealth of New Spain to promote his interests in sixteenth-century Europe. He also sought to defend orthodox Christianity from the insurgent heresy of the Protestant Reformation. The power of the Spanish monarchy spread the message throughout sixteenth-century Europe that a New World empire could bankroll Old World ambitions.

The Protestant Reformation and the Spanish Response

In 1517, Martin Luther, an obscure Catholic priest in central Germany, initiated the **Protestant Reformation** by publicizing his criticisms of the Catholic Church. Luther's ideas won the sympathy of many Catholics, but they were considered extremely dangerous by church officials and by monarchs such as Charles V, who believed that just as the church spoke for God, they ruled for God.

Luther preached a doctrine known as "justification by faith": Individual Christians could obtain salvation and life everlasting only by having faith that God would save them. Giving monetary offerings to the church, following the orders of priests, or participating in church rituals would not bring believers closer to heaven. The only true source of information about God's will was the Bible, not the church. By reading the Bible, any Christian could learn as much about God's commandments as any priest. Indeed, Luther called for a "priesthood of all believers."

In effect, Luther charged that the Catholic Church was in many respects fraudulent. Luther declared that the church had neglected its true purpose of helping individual Christians understand the spiritual realm revealed in the Bible and had wasted its resources in worldly conflicts of politics and wars. Luther hoped his ideas would reform the Catholic Church, but instead they ruptured forever the unity of Christianity in western Europe.

Charles V pledged to exterminate Luther's Protestant heresies. The wealth pouring into Spain from the New World fueled his efforts to defend orthodox Catholic faith against Protestants, as well as against any other challenge to Spain's supremacy. As the most powerful monarch in Europe, Charles V, followed by his son and successor Philip II, assumed responsibility for upholding the existing order of sixteenth-century Europe.

American wealth, particularly Mexican silver, fueled Spanish ambitions, but Charles V's and Philip II's expenses for constant warfare far outstripped the revenues arriving from New Spain. To help meet military expenditures, both kings raised taxes in Spain more than fivefold during the sixteenth century. Since the wealthy nobility were exempted from taxation, the tax burden fell mostly on poor peasants. The monarchy's ambitions impoverished the vast majority of Spain's population and brought the nation to the brink of bankruptcy. When taxes failed to produce enough revenue to fight its wars, the monarchy borrowed heavily from European bankers. By the end of the sixteenth century, interest payments on royal debts swallowed two-thirds of the crown's annual revenues. In retrospect, the riches from New Spain proved a short-term blessing but a long-term curse.

Most Spaniards, however, looked upon New Spain as a glorious national achievement that displayed Spain's superiority over Native Americans and other Europeans. They had added enormously to their own knowledge and wealth. They had built mines, cities, Catholic churches, and even universities on the other side of the Atlantic. These military, religious, and economic achievements gave them great pride and confidence.

Europe and the Spanish Example

The lessons of sixteenth-century Spain were not lost on Spain's European rivals. Spain proudly displayed the fruits of its New World conquests. In 1520, for example, the German artist Albrecht Dürer wrote in his diary that he "marveled over the subtle ingenuity of the men in these distant lands [of New Spain]" who created such things as "a sun entirely of gold, a whole fathom [six feet] broad." But the most exciting news about "the men in these distant lands" was that they could serve the interests of Europeans, as Spain had shown. With a few notable exceptions, Europeans saw the New World as a place for the expansion of European influence, a place where, as one Spaniard wrote, Europeans could "give to those strange lands the form of our own."

France and England tried to follow Spain's example. Both nations warred with Spain in Europe, preyed on Spanish treasure fleets, and ventured to the New World, where they too hoped to find an undiscovered passageway to the East Indies or another Mexico or Peru.

In 1524, France sent Giovanni da Verrazano to scout the Atlantic coast of North America from North Carolina to Canada, looking for a Northwest Passage (see Map 2.2). Eleven years later, France probed farther north with Jacques Cartier's voyage up the St. Lawrence River. Encouraged, Cartier returned to the region with a group of settlers in 1541, but the colony they established— like the search for a Northwest Passage—came to nothing.

English attempts to follow Spain's lead were slower but equally ill fated. Not until 1576, almost eighty years after John Cabot's voyages, did the English try again to find a Northwest Passage. This time Martin Frobisher sailed into the frigid waters of northern Canada (Map 2.2). Like many other explorers mesmerized by the Spanish example, Frobisher believed he had found gold. But the tons of "ore" he hauled back to England proved worthless, and English interests shifted southward to the giant region on the northern margins of New Spain.

English explorers' attempts to establish North American settlements were no more fruitful than their search for a northern route to China. Sir Humphrey Gilbert led expeditions in 1578 and 1583 that made feeble efforts to found colonies in Newfoundland until Gilbert vanished at sea. Sir Walter Raleigh organized an expedition in 1585 to settle Roanoke Island off the coast of present-day North Carolina. The first group of explorers left no colonists on the island, but in 1587 Raleigh sent a contingent of more than one hundred settlers to Roanoke under John White's leadership. White went back to England for supplies, and when he returned to Roanoke in 1590, the colonists had disappeared. Roanoke colonists most likely died from a combination of natural causes and unfriendly Indians. Neither mines nor a route to Asia were found, and the colony was abandoned. By the end of the century, England had failed to secure a New World beachhead.

Roanoke Settlement, 1585–1590

REVIEW How did Spain's conquests in the New World shape Spanish influence in Europe?

VISUAL ACTIVITY

Algonquian Ceremonial Dance
When English artist John White visited the coast of present-day North Carolina in 1585 as part of Raleigh's expedition, he painted this Algonquian ceremonial dance. This is one of the only likenesses of sixteenth-century North American Indians that were drawn from direct observation. British Museum, London, UK/The Bridge-man Art Library.
READING THE IMAGE: What features of Algonquian life does the image show?
CONNECTIONS: How did this Algonquian dance compare with common Mexican rituals?

▶ Conclusion: The Promise of the New World for Europeans

The sixteenth century in the New World belonged to the Spaniards who employed Columbus and to the Indians who greeted him as he stepped ashore. The Portuguese, whose voyages to Africa and Asia set the stage for Columbus's voyages, won the important consolation prize of Brazil, but Spain hit the jackpot. Isabella of Spain helped initiate the Columbian exchange between the New World and the Old, which massively benefited first Spain and later other Europeans and which continues to this day. The exchange also subjected Native Americans to the ravages of European diseases and Spanish conquest. Spanish explorers, conquistadors, and colonists forced the Indians to serve the interests of Spanish settlers and the Spanish monarchy. The exchange illustrated one of the most important lessons of the sixteenth century: After millions of years, the Atlantic no longer was an impermeable barrier separating the Eastern and Western Hemispheres. After the voyages of Columbus, European sailing ships regularly bridged the Atlantic and carried people, products, diseases, and ideas from one shore to the other.

No European monarch could forget the seductive lesson taught by Spain's example: The New World could vastly enrich the Old. Spain remained a New World power for almost four centuries, and its language, religion, culture, and institutions left a permanent imprint. By the end of the sixteenth century, however, other European monarchies had begun to contest Spain's dominion in Europe and to make forays into the northern fringes of Spain's New World preserve. To reap the benefits the Spaniards enjoyed from their New World domain,

the others had to learn a difficult lesson: how to deviate from Spain's example. That discovery lay ahead.

While England's rulers eyed the huge North American hinterland of New Spain, they realized that it lacked the two main attractions of Mexico and Peru: incredible material wealth and large populations of Indians to use as workers. In the absence of gold and silver booty and plentiful native labor in North America, England would need to find some way to attract colonizers to a region that—compared to New Spain—did not appear very promising. During the next century, England's leaders overcame these dilemmas by developing a distinctive colonial model, one that encouraged land-hungry settlers from England and Europe to engage in agriculture and that depended on other sources of unfree labor: indentured servants from Europe and slaves from Africa.

See the Selected Bibliography for this chapter in the Appendix.

2 Chapter Review

MAKE IT STICK

 LearningCurve

Go online and use LearningCurve to see what you know. Then review the key terms and answer the questions.

KEY TERMS

Black Death (p. 27)
Reconquest (p. 29)
Tainos (p. 31)
Treaty of Tordesillas (p. 31)
Columbian exchange (p. 33)
conquistadors (p. 37)
Incan empire (p. 37)
Acoma pueblo revolt (p. 39)
New Spain (p. 40)
encomienda (p. 40)
creoles (p. 44)
Protestant Reformation (p. 46)

REVIEW QUESTIONS

1. Why did European exploration expand dramatically in the fifteenth century? (pp. 27–30)

2. How did Columbus's discoveries help revolutionize Europeans' understanding of global geography? (pp. 30–34)

3. How did New Spain's distinctive colonial population shape its economy and society? (pp. 34–46)

4. How did Spain's conquests in the New World shape Spanish influence in Europe? (pp. 46–47)

MAKING CONNECTIONS

1. How did the Columbian exchange lead to redistributions of power and population? Discuss these changes, being sure to cite examples from both contexts.

2. Why did the Spanish conquest of the Mexica succeed, and how did the Spaniards govern the conquered territory to maintain their dominance?

3. How did the Spaniards' and Indians' perceptions of each other shape their interactions? How did perceptions change over time?

4. How did the wealth generated by the Spanish conquest of the New World influence interest in European colonial exploration throughout the sixteenth century?

LINKING TO THE PAST

1. How did the legacy of ancient Americans influence their descendants' initial encounters and subsequent economic, social, and military relations with Europeans in the sixteenth century? (See chapter 1.)

2. Before the arrival of Europeans, Native Americans in the New World had no knowledge of Christianity, just as Europeans had no knowledge of Native American religions. To what extent did contrasting religious beliefs and assumptions influence relations among Europeans and Native Americans in the New World in the sixteenth century? (See chapter 1.)

3

The Southern Colonies in the Seventeenth Century

1601–1700

CONTENT LEARNING OBJECTIVES

After reading and studying this chapter, you should be able to:

- Explain why England decided to establish colonies in the New World and what challenges the early colonists faced.

- Recognize how the introduction of tobacco into the Chesapeake region shaped the Virginia colony.

- Define the social, political, and economic inequalities that led to Bacon's Rebellion.

- Differentiate the Spanish colonies in New Mexico and Florida from the Chesapeake, and explain why the Pueblo Indians in New Mexico revolted against Spanish rule in the late seventeenth century.

- Describe how the British developed a slave labor system in the West Indies, Carolina, and the Chesapeake. Identify the similarities and differences between the systems in each of these colonies.

IN DECEMBER 1607, AFTER ARRIVING AT JAMESTOWN with the first English colonists, Captain John Smith was captured by warriors of Powhatan, the supreme chief of about fourteen thousand Algonquian Indians who inhabited the coastal plain of present-day Virginia. According to Smith, Powhatan "feasted him after their best barbarous manner." Then, Smith recalled, "two great stones were brought before Powhatan: then as many [Indians] as could layd hands on [Smith], dragged him to [the stones], and thereon laid his head, and being ready with their clubs, to beate out his braines." At that moment, Pocahontas, Powhatan's eleven-year-old daughter, rushed forward and "got [Smith's] head in her armes, and laid her owne upon his to save him from death." Pocahontas, Smith wrote, "hazarded the beating out of her owne braines to save mine, and . . . so prevailed with her father, that I was safely conducted [back] to James towne."

Historians believe that this episode happened more or less as Smith described it. But Smith did not understand why Pocahontas acted as she did. Most likely, what Smith interpreted as Pocahontas's saving him from certain death was instead a ritual enacting Powhatan's willingness to

ALGONQUIAN POUCH
This dazzling pouch belonged to an important Algonquian Indian, possibly chief Powhatan. Decorated with nearly 6,000 beads made from shells, it was probably used to carry tobacco and ritualistic objects that symbolized his authority. Ashmolean Museum, University of Oxford, UK/The Bridgeman Art Library.

Ætatis suæ 21. Aº. 1616.

Matoaks als Rebecka daughter to the mighty Prince Powhatan Emperour of Attanoughkomouck als Virginia converted and baptized in the Christian faith, and Wife to the worlⁿ Mᵗ Tho: Rolff.

Pocahontas in England
Shortly after Pocahontas and her husband, John Rolfe, arrived in England in 1616, she posed for this portrait dressed in English clothing. The portrait captures the dual novelty of England for Pocahontas and of Pocahontas for the English. The mutability of Pocahontas's identity is displayed in the identification of her as "Matoaks" or "Rebecka." National Portrait Gallery, Smithsonian Institution/Art Resource, NY.

incorporate Smith and the white strangers at Jamestown into Powhatan's empire. By appearing to save Smith, Pocahontas was probably acting out Smith's new status as an adopted member of Powhatan's extended family.

After Smith returned to England about two years later, relations between Powhatan and the English colonists deteriorated into bloody raids. In 1613, the colonists captured Pocahontas and held her hostage at Jamestown. Within a year, she converted to Christianity and married a colonist named John Rolfe. After giving birth to a son named Thomas, Pocahontas, her husband, and the new baby sailed for England in the spring of 1616. There, promoters of the Virginia colony dressed her as a proper Englishwoman and arranged for her to go to a ball attended by the king and queen.

Pocahontas died in England in 1617. Her son, Thomas, ultimately returned to Virginia, but the world he and his descendants inhabited was shaped by a reversal of the power ritualized when his mother "saved" John Smith. By the end of the seventeenth century, Native Americans no longer dominated the newcomers who arrived in the Chesapeake with John Smith.

During the seventeenth century, English colonists learned how to deviate from the example of New Spain (see "Europe and the Spanish Example" in chapter 2) by growing tobacco, a crop Native Americans had cultivated in small quantities for centuries. The new settlers grew enormous quantities of tobacco and exported most of it to England. Instead of incorporating Powhatan's people into their emerging society, the settlers encroached on Indian land and built new societies on the foundation of tobacco and transatlantic trade.

Producing large crop surpluses for export required hard labor and people who were willing—or could be forced—to do it. While New Spain took advantage of Native American labor, for the most part the Native Americans in British North America refused to be conscripted into the English colonists' fields. Instead, the settlers depended on the labor of family members, indentured servants, and, by the last third of the seventeenth century, African slaves.

By the end of the century, the southern colonies had become sharply different both from the world dominated by Powhatan when the Jamestown settlers first arrived and from seventeenth-century English society. In ways unimaginable to Powhatan, Pocahontas, and John Smith, the colonists paid homage to the international market and the English monarch by working mightily to make a good living growing crops for sale to the Old World.

▶ An English Colony on Chesapeake Bay

In 1606, England's King James I granted the Virginia Company more than six million acres in North America in hopes of establishing the English equivalent of Spain's New World empire. Enthusiastic reports from the Roanoke voyages twenty years earlier (see "Europe and the Spanish Example" in chapter 2) claimed that in Virginia "the earth bringeth foorth all things in aboundance ... without toile or labour." Investors hoped to profit by growing some valuable exotic crop, finding gold or silver, or raiding Spanish treasure ships. Their hopes failed to confront the difficulties of adapting English desires and expectations to the New World already inhabited by Native Americans. The Jamestown settlement struggled to survive for nearly two decades, until the royal government replaced the private Virginia Company, which never earned a profit for its investors.

The Fragile Jamestown Settlement

Although Spain claimed all of North America under the 1494 Treaty of Tordesillas (see "The Explorations of Columbus" in chapter 2), King James believed that England could encroach on the outskirts of Spain's New World empire. An influential proponent of colonization claimed that "God hath reserved" the lands "lying north of Florida" to be brought "unto Christian civility by the English nation." In effect, the king acted upon this claim by granting to the **Virginia Company**, a joint-stock company, a royal license to poach on both Spanish claims and Powhatan's chiefdom.

English merchants had pooled their capital and shared risks for many years by using joint-stock companies for trading voyages to Europe, Asia, and Africa. The London investors of the Virginia Company, however, had larger ambitions: They hoped to found an empire that would strengthen England both overseas and at home. Richard Hakluyt, a strong proponent of colonization, claimed that a colony would provide work for swarms of poor "valiant youths rusting and hurtfull by lack of employment" in England. Colonists could buy English goods and supply products that England now had to import from other nations.

In December 1606, the ships *Susan Constant*, *Discovery*, and *Godspeed* carried 144 Englishmen toward Virginia. A few weeks after they arrived

CHRONOLOGY

1606	• Virginia Company receives royal charter.
1607	• English colonists found Jamestown; Pocahontas "rescues" John Smith.
1607–1610	• Starvation plagues Jamestown.
1612	• John Rolfe begins to plant tobacco in Virginia.
1617	• First commercial tobacco shipment to England. • Pocahontas dies in England.
1618	• Powhatan dies; Opechancanough becomes Algonquian chief.
1619	• First Africans arrive in Virginia. • House of Burgesses begins to meet.
1622	• Opechancanough leads first uprising in Virginia.
1624	• Virginia becomes royal colony.
1630s	• Barbados colonized by English.
1632	• Colony of Maryland founded.
1634	• Colonists begin to arrive in Maryland.
1640s	• Barbados colonists grow sugarcane with slave labor.
1644	• Opechancanough leads second uprising.
1660	• Navigation Act requires colonial products be shipped only to English ports. • Virginia law defines slavery as inherited, lifelong servitude.
1663	• Carolina colony founded.
1670	• Charles Towne, South Carolina, founded.
1670–1700	• Slave labor system emerges in Carolina and Chesapeake colonies.
1676	• Bacon's Rebellion.
1680	• Pueblo Revolt.

VISUAL ACTIVITY

Secotan Village

This engraving was copied from an original drawing John White made in 1585 when he visited the village of Secotan on the coast of North Carolina. The drawing shows daily life in the village, which may have resembled one of Powhatan's settlements. This drawing conveys the message that Secotan was orderly, settled, religious, harmonious, and peaceful, and very different from English villages. Service Historique de la Marine, Vincennes, France/Giraudon/The Bridgeman Art Library.

READING THE IMAGE: What does this image say about Indian life in Secotan?

CONNECTIONS: How did Indian society differ from the English tobacco society that emerged later?

at the mouth of Chesapeake Bay on April 26, 1607, they went ashore on a small peninsula in the midst of the territory ruled by Powhatan and quickly built a fort, the first building in **Jamestown.** The fort showed the colonists' awareness that they needed to protect themselves from Indians and Spaniards. Spanish plans to wipe out Jamestown were never carried out. Powhatan's people, however, defended Virginia as their own. For weeks, the settlers and Powhatan's **Algonquian** warriors skirmished repeatedly. English firearms repelled Indian attacks, but the Indians' superior numbers and knowledge of the wilderness made it risky for settlers to venture far beyond the fort.

The settlers soon confronted invisible dangers: disease and starvation. Saltwater and freshwater mixed in the swampy marshland surrounding Jamestown, creating an ecological zone where

diseases thrived, especially since the colonists neglected careful sanitary habits. During the summer, many of the Englishmen lay "night and day groaning in every corner of the Fort most pittiful to heare," wrote George Percy, one of the settlers. The colonists increased their misery by bickering among themselves, leaving crops unplanted and food supplies shrinking. "For the most part [the settlers] died of meere famine," Percy wrote; "there were never Englishmen left in a forreigne Countrey in such miserie as wee were in this new discovered Virginia."

Powhatan's people came to the rescue of the weakened and demoralized Englishmen. Early in September 1607, they began to bring corn to the colony for barter. Accustomed to eating food derived from wheat, English people considered corn the food "of the barbarous Indians which know no better . . . a more convenient food for

Chief Powhatan

In 1612, John Smith published a map of early Virginia that included this drawing of Powhatan, surrounded by some of his many wives, smoking a pipe, and adorned with a feathered headdress. The illustration was almost certainly made by an English artist who had never been to Virginia or seen Powhatan but who tried to imagine the scene as described by John Smith. Newberry Library/SuperStock.

Cooperation and Conflict between Natives and Newcomers

Powhatan's people stayed in contact with the English settlers but maintained their distance. The Virginia Company boasted that the settlers bought from the Indians "the pearles of earth [corn] and [sold] to them the pearles of heaven [Christianity]." In fact, few Indians converted to Christianity, and the English devoted scant effort to proselytizing. Marriage between Indian women and English men also was rare, despite the acute shortage of English women in Virginia in the early years. Few settlers other than John Smith bothered to learn the Indians' language.

Powhatan's people regarded the English with suspicion, for good reason. Although the settlers often made friendly overtures to the Indians, they did not hesitate to use their guns and swords to enforce English notions of proper Indian behavior. When Indians refused to trade their corn to the settlers, the English pillaged their villages and confiscated their corn.

The Indians retaliated against English violence, but for fifteen years they did not organize an all-out assault on the European intruders, probably for several reasons. Although Christianity held few attractions for the Indians, the power of the settlers' God impressed them. One chief told John Smith that "he did believe that our [English] God as much exceeded theirs as our guns did their bows and arrows." Powhatan probably concluded that these powerful strangers would make better allies than enemies. As allies, the English strengthened Powhatan's dominion over the tribes in the region.

The colonists also traded with Powhatan's people, usually exchanging European goods for corn. Native Virginians quickly recognized the superiority of the intruders' iron and steel knives, axes, and pots, and they eagerly traded corn for them.

But why were the settlers unable to feed themselves for more than a decade? First, as the staggering death rate suggests, many settlers were too sick to be productive. Second, very few farmers came to Virginia in the early years. Instead, most of the newcomers were gentlemen and their servants who, in John Smith's words, "never did know what a day's work was." The proportion of gentlemen in Virginia in the early years was six times greater than in England, a reflection of the Virginia Company's urgent need for investors and settlers. Smith declared repeatedly that in Virginia "there is no country to pillage [as in New Spain]. . . . All you can expect from [Virginia]

swine than for man." The famished colonists soon overcame their prejudice against corn. Jamestown leader Captain John Smith recalled that the settlers were so hungry that "they would have sould their soules" for half a basket of Powhatan's corn. Indians' corn acquired by both trade and plunder managed to keep 38 of the original settlers alive until a fresh supply of food and 120 more colonists arrived from England in January 1608.

It is difficult to exaggerate the fragility of the early Jamestown settlement. One colonist lamented that "this place [is] a meere plantacion of sorrowes and Cropp of trobles, having been plentifull in nothing but want and wanting nothing but plenty." When a new group of colonists arrived in 1610, they found only 60 of the 500 previous settlers still alive. The Virginia Company sent hundreds of new settlers to Jamestown each year, each of them eager to find the paradise promised by the company. But most settlers went instead to early graves.

must be by labor." For years, however, colonists clung to English notions that gentlemen should not work with their hands and that tradesmen should work only in trades for which they had been trained, ideas that made more sense in labor-rich England than in labor-poor Virginia.

The persistence of the Virginia colony created difficulties for Powhatan's chiefdom. Steady contact between natives and newcomers spread European diseases among the Indians, who suffered deadly epidemics. To produce enough corn for trade with the English required the Indian women to spend more time and effort growing crops. But from the Indians' viewpoint, the most important fact about the always-hungry English colonists was that they were not going away.

Powhatan died in 1618, and his brother Opechancanough replaced him as supreme chief. In 1622, Opechancanough organized an all-out assault on the English settlers. As an English colonist observed, "When the day appointed for the massacre arrived [March 22], a number of savages visited many of our people in their dwellings, and while partaking with them of their meal[,] the savages, at a given signal, drew their weapons and fell upon us murdering and killing everybody they could reach[,] sparing neither women nor children." In all, the Indians killed 347 colonists, nearly a third of the English population. But the attack failed to dislodge the colonists. Instead, in the years to come the settlers unleashed a murderous campaign of Indian extermination that pushed the Indians beyond the small circumference of white settlement. After 1622, most colonists considered Indians their perpetual enemies. As an Englishman declared, the "murdered carcasses" of the colonists "speak, proclaim, and cry, *This our earth is truly English, and therefore this Land [of Virginia] is justly yours O English.*"

From Private Company to Royal Government

In the immediate aftermath of the 1622 uprising, the survivors became demoralized because, as one explained, the "massacre killed all our Countrie ... [and] burst the heart of all the rest." The disaster prompted a royal investigation of affairs in Virginia. The investigators discovered that the appalling mortality among the colonists was caused more by disease and mismanagement than by Indian raids. In 1624, King James revoked the charter of the Virginia Company and made Virginia a **royal colony**, subject to the direction of the royal government rather than to the company's private investors, an arrangement that lasted until 1776.

The king now appointed the governor of Virginia and his council, but most other features of local government established under the Virginia Company remained intact. In 1619, for example, the company had inaugurated the **House of Burgesses**, an assembly of representatives (called burgesses) elected by the colony's inhabitants. Under the new royal government, laws passed by the burgesses had to be approved by the king's bureaucrats in England rather than by the company. Otherwise, the House of Burgesses continued as before, acquiring distinction as the oldest representative legislative assembly in the English

VISUAL ACTIVITY

Jamestown Trade Goods
Jamestown colonists used these objects to trade with Powhatan's people. The bead (upper right) was made in Venice, Italy, while Jamestown settlers crafted the triangular copper pendant, and the incised bone pendant. Courtesy of Preservation Virginia.
READING THE IMAGE: What do these trade goods suggest about the needs and desires of the settlers and the Native Americans?
CONNECTIONS: Why was trade between settlers and Indians important to each group?

colonies. Under the new royal government, all free adult men in Virginia could vote for the House of Burgesses, giving it a far broader and more representative constituency than the English House of Commons.

The demise of the Virginia Company marked the end of the first phase of colonization of the Chesapeake region. From the first 105 adventurers in 1607, the population had grown to about 1,200 by 1624. Despite mortality rates higher than during the worst epidemics in London, new settlers still came. Their arrival and King James's willingness to take over the struggling colony reflected a fundamental change in Virginia. After years of fruitless experimentation, it was becoming clear that English settlers could make a fortune in Virginia by growing tobacco.

REVIEW   Why did Powhatan behave as he did toward the English colonists?

▶ A Tobacco Society

Tobacco grew wild in the New World, and Native Americans used it for thousands of years before Europeans arrived. Many sixteenth-century European explorers noticed the Indians' habit of "drinking smoke." During the sixteenth century, tobacco was an expensive luxury used sparingly by a few in Europe. During the next century, English colonists in North America sent so much

tobacco to European markets that it became an affordable indulgence used often by many people. (See "Beyond America's Borders," page 58.)

By 1700, nearly 100,000 colonists lived in the Chesapeake region, encompassing Virginia, Maryland, and northern North Carolina (Map 3.1). Although they differed in wealth, landholding, access to labor, and religion, they shared a dedication to growing tobacco. They exported more than 35 million pounds of tobacco in 1700, a fivefold increase in per capita production since 1620. Chesapeake colonists mastered the demands of tobacco agriculture, and the "Stinkinge Weede" (a seventeenth-century Marylander's term for tobacco) also mastered the colonists. Settlers lived by the rhythms of tobacco agriculture, and their endless need for labor attracted droves of English indentured servants to grueling work in tobacco fields.

Tobacco Agriculture

Initially, the Virginia Company had no plans to grow and sell tobacco. "As for tobacco," John Smith wrote, "we never then dreamt of it." John Rolfe—future husband of Pocahontas—planted West Indian tobacco seeds in 1612 and learned that they flourished in Virginia. By 1617, the colonists had grown enough tobacco to send the first commercial shipment to England, where it sold for a high price. After that, Virginia pivoted from a colony of rather aimless adventurers to a society of dedicated tobacco planters.

A demanding crop, tobacco required close attention and a great deal of hand labor

Tobacco Plantation
This print illustrates the processing of tobacco on a seventeenth-century plantation. Workers cut the mature plants and put the leaves in piles to wilt (left foreground). After the leaves dried somewhat, they were suspended from poles in a drying barn (right foreground), where they were seasoned before being packed in casks for shipping. The New York Public Library/Art Resource, NY

American Tobacco and European Consumers

English colonies in the Chesapeake were "wholly built upon smoke," King Charles I observed during the second quarter of the seventeenth century. The king's shrewd observation highlighted the fundamental reason the seventeenth-century Chesapeake colonies prospered by growing ever-larger crops of tobacco: namely, because people on the eastern side of the Atlantic were willing to buy ever-greater quantities of tobacco to smoke—and to sniff and chew. Europeans' desire for tobacco was the only reason it had commercial value.

Some Europeans hated tobacco, most notably England's King James I (who preceded Charles I). In *A Counterblaste to Tobacco*, a pamphlet published in 1611, James declared that smoking was "A custome lothsome to the eye, hatefull to the Nose, harmefull to the braine, [and] dangerous to the Lungs." He reviled the "filthy smoke," the "stinking Suffumigation," the "spitting," the "lust," the "shameful imbecilitie," and the "sin" of tobacco. James's fulminations acknowledged that "the generall use of Tobacco" was "daily practiced . . . by all sorts and complexions of people." He noted, "The publike use [of tobacco], at all times,

Tobacco Cutter
Planters in the southern colonies of British North America shipped tobacco to England where tobacconists used machines like the one shown here to chop the leaves into small pieces for smoking. Tobacco merchants often flavored the chopped leaves with oils, herbs, and spices. The illustration on the side of the cutter refers to the Native American origins of tobacco. Historisch Museum Haarlem.

year-round. Like the Indians, the colonists "cleared" fields by cutting a ring of bark from each tree (a procedure known as "girdling"), thereby killing the tree. Girdling brought sunlight to clearings but left fields studded with tree stumps, requiring colonists to use heavy hoes to till their tobacco fields. To plant, a visitor observed, they "just make holes [with

a stick] into which they drop the seeds," much as the Indians did. Colonists young and old enjoyed the fruits of their labor. "Everyone smokes while working or idling," a traveler observed, including "men, women, girls, and boys, from the age of seven years."

English settlers worked hard because their labor promised greater rewards in the Chesapeake and in all places, hath now so farre prevailed that a man cannot heartily welcome his friend now, but straight they must bee in hand with Tobacco." Clearly, James championed a lost cause.

When the Spaniards first brought tobacco to Europe during the sixteenth century, physicians praised it as a wonder drug. One proclaimed that "this precious herb is so general a human need [that it is] not only for the sick but for the healthy." Such strong recommendations from learned men were reinforced by everyday experiences of commoners. Sailors returning from the New World "suck in as much smoke as they can," one Spaniard observed, "[and] in this way they say that their hunger and thirst are allayed, their strength is restored and their spirits are refreshed; [and] . . . their brains are lulled by a joyous intoxication." That joyous intoxication—"a bewitching quality," King James called it—made tobacco irresistible to most Europeans.

At the beginning of the seventeenth century, tobacco was scarce and therefore expensive. In 1603, for example, England imported only about 25,000 pounds of tobacco, all from New Spain. By 1700, England imported nearly 40 million pounds of tobacco, almost all from the Chesapeake colonies. The huge increase in the tobacco supply caused prices to plummet. A quantity of tobacco that sold for a dollar in 1600 cost less than two and a half cents by 1700.

The low prices made possible by bumper crops harvested by planters in the Chesapeake transformed tobacco consumption in England and elsewhere in Europe. Annual per capita tobacco use in England grew more than 200-fold during the seventeenth century. American tobacco became the first colonial product of mass consumption by Europeans, blazing a trail followed by New World sugar, coffee, and chocolate.

Tobacco altered European culture. It spawned new industries, new habits, and new forms of social life. Smoking was the most common form of tobacco consumption in the seventeenth century, and smokers also needed pipes, boxes, or tins to hold their tobacco; a flint and steel to strike sparks; pipe cleaners; and spittoons, if they were smoking in a respectable place that disapproved of spitting on the floor. European merchants and manufacturers supplied all these needs, along with the tobacco itself, which had to be graded, chopped, flavored, packaged, stored, advertised, and sold. Men and women smoked in taverns, in smoking clubs, around dinner tables, and in bed.

The somewhat cumbersome paraphernalia of smoking caused many tobacco users to shift to snuff, which became common in the eighteenth century. Snuff use eliminated smoke, fire, and spitting, replacing them with the more refined gesture of taking a pinch of powdered, flavored tobacco from a snuffbox and sniffing it into one or both nostrils, which produced a fashionable sneeze followed by a genteel wipe with a dainty handkerchief. One snuff taker explained the health benefits of such a sneeze: "by its gently pricking and stimulating the membranes, [snuff] causes Sneezing or Contractions, whereby the Glands like so many squeezed Sponges, dismiss their Seriosities and Filth."

Whether consumed by sniffing, smoking, or in other ways, tobacco profoundly changed European habits, economies, and societies. And its popularity turned the Chesapeake colonies into invaluable assets for England.

America in a Global Context

1. Why did European demand for tobacco grow so dramatically during the seventeenth century?

2. How did Europeans use tobacco, and why? Why did some people object to tobacco use?

3. What were the consequences of the transatlantic tobacco market both in the Chesapeake and in Europe?

Connect to the Big Idea

C In what ways did tobacco shape America's colonial history?

region than in England. One colonist proclaimed that "the dirt of this Province affords as great a profit to the general Inhabitant, as the Gold of Peru doth to . . . the Spaniard." Although he exaggerated, it was true that a hired man could expect to earn two or three times more in Virginia's tobacco fields than in England. Better still, in Virginia land was so abundant that it was extremely cheap compared with land in England.

By the mid-seventeenth century, common laborers could buy a hundred acres for less than their annual wages—an impossibility in England. New settlers who paid their own transportation to the Chesapeake received a grant of fifty acres of free land (termed a **headright**). The Virginia

MAP ACTIVITY

Map 3.1 Chesapeake Colonies in the Seventeenth Century

This map illustrates the intimate association between land and water in the settlement of the Chesapeake in the seventeenth century. The fall line indicates the limit of navigable water, where rapids and falls prevented travel farther upstream.

READING THE MAP: Using the notations on the map, create a chronology of the establishment of towns and settlements. What physical features correspond to the earliest habitation by English settlers?

CONNECTIONS: Why was access to navigable water so important? Given the settlers' need for defense against native tribes, what explains the distance between settlements?

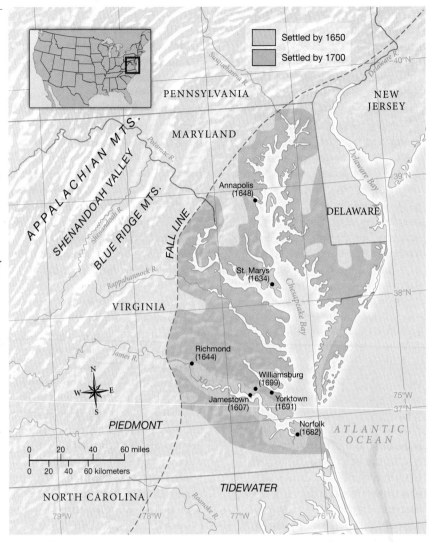

A Servant Labor System

Company granted headrights to encourage settlement, and the royal government continued them for the same reason.

Headrights, cheap land, and high wages gave poor English folk powerful incentives to immigrate to the New World. Yet many potential immigrants could not scrape together the money to pay for a trip across the Atlantic. Their poverty and the colonists' crying need for labor formed the basic context for the creation of a servant labor system.

About 80 percent of the immigrants to the Chesapeake during the seventeenth century came as **indentured servants**. Instead of a slave society, the seventeenth-century Chesapeake region was fundamentally a society of white servants and ex-servants.

Relatively few African slaves were brought to the Chesapeake in the first half century after settlement. The first known Africans arrived in Virginia in 1619 aboard the *White Lion*, an English privateer that had seized them from a Portuguese slave ship bound for South America. The "20. And odd Negroes," as John Rolfe called them, were slaves captured in Angola in west-central Africa. A few more slaves trickled into the Chesapeake region during the next several decades. Until the 1670s, however, only a small number of slaves labored in Chesapeake tobacco fields. Men and women of African descent occasionally became indentured servants, served out their terms of servitude, and became free. A few slaves purchased their way out of bondage and lived as free people. These people were exceptions, however. Almost all people of African descent were slaves and remained enslaved for life.

The overwhelming majority of indentured servants were white immigrants from England. To buy passage aboard a ship bound for the Chesapeake, an English immigrant had to come up with about a year's wages for an English servant or laborer. Earning wages at all was difficult in England since job opportunities were shrinking. Many country landowners needed fewer farmhands because they shifted from growing crops to raising sheep in newly enclosed fields. Unemployed people drifted into seaports such as Bristol, Liverpool, and London, where they learned about the plentiful jobs in North America. Unable to pay for their trip across the Atlantic, poor immigrants agreed to a contract called an indenture, which functioned as a form of credit. By signing an indenture, an immigrant borrowed the cost of transportation to the Chesapeake from a merchant or ship captain in England. To repay this loan, the indentured person agreed to work as a servant for four to seven years in North America.

Once the indentured person arrived in the colonies, the merchant or ship captain sold his right to the immigrant's labor to a local tobacco planter. To obtain the servant's labor, the planter paid about twice the cost of transportation and agreed to provide the servant with food and shelter during the term of the indenture. When the indenture expired, the planter owed the former servant "freedom dues," usually a few barrels of corn and a suit of clothes.

Ideally, indentures allowed poor immigrants to trade their most valuable assets—their freedom and their ability to work—for a trip to the New World and a period of servitude followed by freedom in a land of opportunity. Planters reaped more immediate benefits. Servants meant more hands to grow more tobacco. A planter expected a servant to grow enough tobacco in one year to cover the price the planter paid for the indenture. Servants' labor during the remaining three to six years of the indenture promised a handsome profit for the planter. No wonder one Virginian declared, "Our principall wealth . . . consisteth in servants." Although many servants died before their indentures expired, planters still profited because they received a headright of fifty acres of land from the colonial government for every newly purchased servant.

About three out of four servants were young men between the ages of fifteen and twenty-five when they arrived in the Chesapeake. Typically, they shared the desperation of sixteen-year-old Francis Haires, who indentured himself for seven years because, according to his contract, "his father and mother and All friends [are] dead and he [is] a miserable wandering boy." Like Francis, most servants had no special training or skills, although the majority had some experience with agricultural work. "Hunger and fear of prisons bring to us onely such servants as have been brought up to no Art of Trade," one Virginia planter complained. A skilled craftsman could obtain a shorter indenture, but few risked coming to the colonies since their prospects were better in England.

Women were almost as rare as skilled craftsmen in the Chesapeake and more ardently desired. In the early days of the tobacco boom, the Virginia Company shipped young single women servants to the colony as prospective wives for male settlers willing to pay "120 weight [pounds] of the best leaf tobacco for each of them," in effect getting both a wife and a servant. The company reasoned that, as one official wrote in 1622, "the plantation can never flourish till families be planted, and the respect of wives and children fix the people on the soil." Nonetheless, women remained a small minority of the Chesapeake population until late in the seventeenth century.

The servant labor system perpetuated the gender imbalance. Although female servants cost about the same as males and generally served for the same length of time, planters preferred male servants, as one explained, because they were "the mor[e] excellent and yousefull Cretuers," especially for field work. Although many servant women hoed and harvested tobacco fields, most also did household chores such as cooking, washing, cleaning, gardening, and milking.

The Rigors of Servitude

Servants—whether men or women, whites or blacks, English or African—tended to work together and socialize together. During the first half century of settlement, racial intermingling occurred, although the small number of blacks

VISUAL ACTIVITY

Bristol Docks

This painting of the docks in Bristol, England, portrays a scene common at ports throughout the seventeenth-century Atlantic world. Tobacco flooded into Bristol in the seventeenth century while Bristol merchants also became active in the African slave trade, trading British goods on the west African coast for slaves, who were then taken to the New World to be sold to eager sugar and tobacco planters.
©Bristol City Museum and Art Gallery UK/The Bridgeman Art Library.

READING THE IMAGE: What kinds of work are being done by the people shown on the dock?

CONNECTIONS: Why was transatlantic commerce important to settlers in the seventeenth-century Chesapeake region?

made it infrequent. In general, the commonalities of servitude caused servants—regardless of their race and gender—to consider themselves apart from free people, whose ranks they longed to join eventually.

Servant life was harsh by the standards of seventeenth-century England and even by the frontier standards of the Chesapeake. Unlike servants in England, Chesapeake servants had no control over who purchased their labor—and thus them—for the period of their indenture. They were "sold here upp and downe like horses,"

one observer reported. A Virginia servant complained in 1623 that his master "hath sold me for £150 sterling like a damnd slave." But tobacco planters' need for labor muffled complaints about treating servants as property.

For servants, the promise of indentured servitude in the Chesapeake often withered when they confronted the rigors of labor in the tobacco fields. Severe laws aimed to keep servants in their place. James Revel, an eighteen-year old thief punished by being indentured to a Virginia tobacco planter, declared he was a "slave" sent to hoe "tobacco plants all day" from dawn to dusk. Punishments for petty crimes stretched servitude far beyond the original terms of indenture. Richard Higby, for example, received six extra years of servitude for killing three hogs. After midcentury, the Virginia legislature added three or more years to the indentures of most servants by requiring them to serve until they were twenty-four years old.

Settlement Patterns along the James River

Women servants were subject to special restrictions and risks. They were prohibited from marrying until their servitude had expired. A servant woman, the law assumed, could not serve two masters at the same time: one who owned her indentured labor and another who was her husband. As a rule, if a woman servant gave birth to a child, she had to serve two extra years and pay a fine. Inevitably, the predominance of men in the colonial population pressured servant women to engage in sexual relations, and about a third of immigrant women were pregnant when they married. (See "Seeking the American Promise," page 64.)

Harsh punishments reflected four fundamental realities of the servant labor system. First, planters' hunger for labor caused them to demand as much labor as they could get from their servants. Second, servants hoped to survive their servitude and use their freedom to obtain land and start a family. Third, since servants saw themselves as free people in a temporary status of servitude, they often made grudging, halfhearted workers. Finally, planters put up with this contentious arrangement because the alternatives were less desirable.

Planters could not easily hire free men and women because land was readily available and free people preferred to work for themselves on their own land. Nor could planters depend on much labor from family members because families were few, were started late, and thus had few children. And, until the 1680s and 1690s, slaves were expensive and hard to come by. Before then, masters who wanted to grow more tobacco had few alternatives to buying indentured servants.

Cultivating Land and Faith

Villages and small towns dotted the rural landscape of seventeenth-century England, but in the Chesapeake towns were few and far between. Instead, tobacco farms occupied small clearings surrounded by hundreds of acres of wilderness. Since tobacco was a labor-intensive crop that quickly exhausted the fertility of the soil, each farmer cultivated only 5 or 10 percent of his land at any one time. Tobacco planters sought land that fronted a navigable river in order to minimize the work of transporting the heavy barrels of tobacco onto ships. A settled region thus resembled a lacework of farms stitched around waterways.

Most Chesapeake colonists were nominally Protestants. Attendance at Sunday services and conformity to the doctrines of the Church of England were required of all English men and women. Few clergymen migrated to the Chesapeake, however, and too few of those who did were models of piety. Certainly, some colonists

Jamestown Church Tower
This modern-day photograph shows the remains of the tower of the Anglican church that colonists constructed in Jamestown beginning in 1639. Nearby is the foundation of an older church, built in 1617. The churches illustrate the importance Virginia's leaders attached to maintaining the central British institution of worship and spiritual order in the fledgling colony. Courtesy of Preservation Virginia.

The Gamble of Indentured Servitude

Anne Orthwood sailed out of her native Bristol, England, in September 1662, shortly after her twenty-third birthday. Her mother, Mary, had moved there in 1640 to escape the humiliation of giving birth to Anne out of wedlock, and in Bristol she had a second daughter, also illegitimate. Mary never married. Anne and her sister grew up with the stigma of being bastards, a shameful and degraded status at a time when the vast majority of children were born to married couples.

Bristol was a thriving seaport, second only to London in its overseas trade, but poor unmarried women— especially those like Mary, with two illegitimate daughters—had little hope to share in the city's commercial prosperity. Instead, they usually worked at menial jobs such as domestic servant or washerwoman. The continual arrival and departure of ships, sailors, merchants, passengers, and cargoes of all kinds from throughout the Atlantic world made Bristol a hub of information and gossip that Anne could not have avoided. She probably heard that in Virginia jobs were plentiful and workers were few. Hundreds of people sailed from Bristol to Virginia every year, five hundred in 1662

alone, most of them poor young men who agreed to become indentured servants. Anne probably also heard about the shortage of women in Virginia, along with the tantalizing news that, as one promoter declared, if women "come of an honest stock and have a good repute, they may pick and chuse their Husbands out of the better sort of people." The promise of both work and matrimony proved irresistible to Anne, especially compared to the gloomy prospect of staying in Bristol. In August 1662, Anne signed an indenture to a ship's surgeon who agreed to pay her way to Virginia in exchange for her consent to work for four years as a servant.

Anne arrived in Virginia late in the fall of 1662, and the surgeon quickly sold her indenture—and thus her—to William Kendall, a wealthy planter and prominent official on Virginia's Eastern Shore. Kendall himself had come to Virginia as a servant in 1650, but unlike Anne, he was from a respectable family and had received a valuable education as a merchant's clerk. When he became free in 1654, he prospered, thanks in large part to his good fortune in marriage. Kendall married a wealthy widow in

Virginia, and after she died, he married another wealthy widow, helping him amass more than 25,000 acres of land. When Anne joined Kendall's household, some twenty people lived there, including seven or eight servants, two slaves, a free black man, and numerous relatives, among them a nephew, John Kendall.

Like Anne, John Kendall had recently arrived in Virginia from England, was in his early twenties, and was unmarried. We cannot know whether Anne thought John was one of the "better sort of people" she might marry, but it appears that she and John felt a mutual attraction. William Kendall had no intention of allowing his nephew to get mixed up with a lowly servant woman, and a bastard at that. His own experience confirmed that marrying upward was the path to prosperity in Virginia. About eight months after Anne became his servant, William Kendall decided to separate her and John by selling Anne's indenture—and thus her—to a tenant farmer named Jacob Bishop, who lived several miles away.

As young people will, Anne and John found a way to get together. Anne accompanied Bishop when he

took their religion seriously. Church courts punished fornicators, censured blasphemers, and served notice on parishioners who spent Sundays "goeing a fishing." But on the whole, religion did not awaken the zeal of Chesapeake settlers, certainly not as it did the zeal of New England settlers in these same years (as discussed in "Church, Covenant, and Conformity" in chapter 4). The religion of the Chesapeake colonists

was Anglican, but their faith lay in the turbulent, competitive, high-stakes gamble of survival as tobacco planters.

The situation was similar in the Catholic colony of Maryland. In 1632, England's King Charles I granted his Catholic friend Lord Baltimore about six and a half million acres in the northern Chesapeake region. Lord Baltimore intended to create a refuge for Catholics, who

English Servants
This collective portrait of English servants painted by William Hogarth in the mid-eighteenth century features three young women who perhaps somewhat resembled indentured servant Anne Orthwood, who had immigrated to Virginia nearly a century earlier. No likeness of Orthwood exists. Unlike Orthwood, most servants who came to the Chesapeake during the seventeenth century were young boys, like the boy depicted here at top center. Tate Gallery, London/Art Resource, NY.

identified John as the father when a midwife quizzed her during the rigors of giving birth to twin boys. One baby died shortly after birth, as did Anne. Her other son, whom she named Jasper, was indentured as an infant to a Virginia planter and, after twenty-two years of servitude, became a free man. John Kendall never acknowledged Jasper as his son, but he did follow his uncle William's advice and married a wealthy widow.

Like so many other Virginia colonists, Anne found an early grave rather than the work, marriage, and respectability she craved. She gambled her freedom for the promise of a better life in Virginia, and she lost. Other former servants gambled and won, grandly like William Kendall or modestly like Anne's son Jasper.

Questions for Consideration

1. How did family relationships and popular assumptions about them influence Anne Orthwood? How did they influence John Kendall?

2. How did Anne Orthwood's experiences reflect the risks and opportunities confronted by other female and male servants?

Connect to the Big Idea

◐ What laws and practices governed the lives of indentured servants in the Chesapeake?

went to conduct legal business at court, held at a local tavern, as was customary at the time. While there, on Saturday night and Sunday, November 28 and 29, 1663, she met John Kendall, and they had sex. "Three tymes She thought hee had to doe with her," Anne later testified, "but twice She was Certaine."

John impregnated Anne. We do not know whether Anne hoped that John would buy her indenture, free her, and marry her, but she probably did. She refused to say who was responsible for her condition; her silence suggests that she hoped John Kendall would step forward and rescue her. But he did not. She finally

suffered severe discrimination in England. He fitted out two ships, the *Ark* and the *Dove*; gathered about 150 settlers; and sent them to the new colony, where they arrived on March 25, 1634. However, Maryland failed to live up to Baltimore's hopes. The colony's population grew very slowly for twenty years, and most settlers were Protestants rather than Catholics. The religious turmoil of the Puritan Revolution in England (see "Religious Controversies and Economic Changes" in chapter 4) spilled across the Atlantic, creating conflict between Maryland's few Catholics—most of them wealthy and prominent—and the Protestant majority, most of them neither wealthy nor prominent. Maryland's leaders hoped to attract decent people as servants, unlike those in Virginia who were described by one Marylander as "the scumme of the people,

. . . vagrants and runnewayes from their m[aste]rs, deabauched, idle, lazie squanderers, [and] jaylbirds." During the 1660s, however, Maryland began to attract settlers very much like Virginia, and most of them were Protestants. Although Catholics and the Catholic faith continued to exert influence in Maryland, the colony's society, economy, politics, and culture became nearly indistinguishable from Virginia's. Both colonies shared a devotion to tobacco, the true faith of the Chesapeake.

REVIEW   Why did the vast majority of European immigrants to the Chesapeake come as indentured servants?

▶ Hierarchy and Inequality in the Chesapeake

The system of indentured servitude sharpened inequality in Chesapeake society by the mid-seventeenth century, propelling social and political polarization that culminated in 1676 with Bacon's Rebellion. The rebellion prompted reforms that stabilized relations between elite planters and their lesser neighbors and paved the way for a social hierarchy that muted differences of landholding and wealth and amplified racial differences. Amid this social and political evolution, Chesapeake colonists' dedication to growing tobacco did not change.

Social and Economic Polarization

The first half of the seventeenth century in the Chesapeake was the era of the yeoman—a farmer who owned a small plot of land sufficient to support a family and tilled largely by servants and a few family members. A small number of elite planters had larger estates and commanded ten or more servants. But for the first several decades, few men lived long enough to accumulate fortunes sufficient to set them much apart from their neighbors.

Until midcentury, the principal division in Chesapeake society was less between rich and poor planters than between free farmers and unfree servants. Although these two groups contrasted sharply in their legal and economic status, their daily lives had many similarities. Servants looked forward to the time when their indentures would expire and they, too, would become free and eventually own land.

Three major developments splintered this rough frontier equality during the third quarter of the century. First, as planters grew more and more tobacco, the ample supply depressed tobacco prices in European markets. Cheap tobacco reduced planters' profits and made saving enough to become landowners more difficult for freed servants. Second, because the mortality rate in the Chesapeake colonies declined, more and more servants survived their indentures, and landless freemen became more numerous and grew more discontented. Third, declining mortality also encouraged the formation of a planter elite. By living longer, the most successful planters compounded their success. The wealthiest planters also began to buy slaves as well as to serve as merchants.

By the 1670s, the society of the Chesapeake had become polarized. Landowners—the planter elite and the more numerous yeoman planters—clustered around one pole. Landless colonists, mainly freed servants, gathered at the other. Each group eyed the other with suspicion and mistrust. For the most part, planters saw landless freemen as a dangerous rabble rather than as fellow colonists with legitimate grievances. Governor William Berkeley feared the political threat to the governing elite posed by "six parts in seven [of Virginia colonists who] . . . are poor, indebted, discontented, and armed."

Government Policies and Political Conflict

In general, government enforced the distinction separating servants and masters with an iron fist. Poor men complained that "nether the Governor nor Counsell could or would doe any poore men right, but that they would shew favor to great men and wronge the poore." Most Chesapeake colonists, like most Europeans, assumed that "great men" should bear the responsibilities of government. Until 1670, all freemen could vote, and they routinely elected prosperous planters to the legislature. No former servant served in either the governor's council or the House of Burgesses after 1640. Yet poor Virginians believed that the "great men" used their government offices to promote their selfish personal interests rather than governing impartially.

As discontent mounted among the poor during the 1660s and 1670s, colonial officials tried to keep political power in safe hands. Beginning in 1661, for example, Governor William Berkeley did not call an election for the House of Burgesses for fifteen years. In 1670, the House of Burgesses outlawed

Governor William Berkeley
This portrait illustrates the distance that separated Governor Berkeley and the other Chesapeake grandees from poor planters, landless freemen, servants, and slaves. Berkeley's clothing suited the genteel homes of Jamestown, not the rustic dwellings of lesser Virginians. His haughty, satisfied demeanor suggests his lack of sympathy for poor Virginians, who, he was certain, deserved their lot. National Gallery of Art, Washington, D.C., USA/SuperStock.

voting by poor men, permitting only men who were landowners and headed households to vote.

The king also began to tighten the royal government's control of trade and to collect substantial revenue from the Chesapeake colonies. A series of English laws funneled the colonial trade exclusively into the hands of English merchants and shippers. The **Navigation Acts** of 1650 and 1651 specified that colonial goods had to be transported in English ships with predominantly English crews. A 1660 act required colonial products to be sent only to English ports, and a 1663 law stipulated further that all goods sent to the colonies must pass through English ports and be carried on English ships manned by English sailors. Taken together, these navigation acts reflected the English government's mercantilist assumption that what was good for England (channeling all trade though English hands) should determine colonial policy.

Assumptions about mercantilism also underlay the import duty on tobacco inaugurated by the Navigation Act of 1660. The law assessed an import tax of two pence on every pound of colonial

tobacco brought into England, about the price a Chesapeake tobacco farmer received. The tax gave the king a major financial interest in the size of the tobacco crop, which yielded about a quarter of all English customs revenues during the 1660s.

Bacon's Rebellion

Colonists, like residents of European monarchies, accepted class divisions and inequality as long as they believed that government officials ruled for the general good. When rulers violated that precept, ordinary people felt justified in rebelling. In 1676, **Bacon's Rebellion** erupted as a dispute over Virginia's Indian policy. Before it was over, the rebellion convulsed Chesapeake politics and society, leaving in its wake death, destruction, and a legacy of hostility between the great planters and their poorer neighbors.

Opechancanough, the Algonquian chief who had led the Indian uprising of 1622 in Virginia, mounted another surprise attack in 1644 and killed about five hundred Virginia colonists in two days. During the next two years of bitter fighting, the colonists eventually gained the upper hand, capturing and murdering the old chief. After the war, the Indians relinquished all claims to land already settled by the English. Wilderness land beyond the fringe of English settlement was supposed to be reserved exclusively for Indian use. The colonial government hoped this arrangement would minimize contact between settlers and Indians and thereby maintain the peace.

If the Chesapeake population had not grown, the policy might have worked. But the number of land-hungry colonists multiplied. In their quest for land, they encroached steadily on Indian land. During the 1660s and 1670s, violence between colonists and Indians repeatedly flared along the frontier. The government, headquartered in the tidewater region near the coast, far from the danger of Indian raids, tried to calm the disputes and reestablish the peace.

Frontier settlers thirsted for revenge against what their leader, Nathaniel Bacon, termed "the protected and Darling Indians." Bacon proclaimed his "Design not only to ruine and extirpate all Indians in Generall but all Manner of Trade and Commerce with them." Bacon also urged the colonists to "see what spounges have suckt up the Publique Treasure." He charged that grandees, or elite planters, operated the government for their private gain, a charge that made sense to many colonists. In fact, officeholders had profited enough to buy slaves to replace their servants; by the 1660s, they owned about 70 percent of all the colony's slaves. Bacon crystallized the grievances of the

Why Did English Colonists Consider Themselves Superior to Indians and Africans?

Were seeds of the racial prejudice that has been such a powerful force in American history planted in the seventeenth-century Chesapeake? To answer that question, historians have paid close attention to the language colonists used to describe Indians, Africans, and themselves.

In the mid-1500s, the English adopted the words *Indian* and *Negro* from Spanish, where they had come to mean, respectively, an aboriginal inhabitant of the New World and a black person of African ancestry. Both terms were generic, homogenizing an enormous diversity of tribal affiliations, languages, and cultures. Neither term originated with the people to whom it referred. The New England minister Roger Williams, who published a book on Indian languages in 1643, reported, "They have often asked mee, why we call them Indians," a poignant question that reveals the European origins of the term, dating back to Columbus.

After *Indians*, the word the settlers used most frequently to describe Native Americans was *savages*. The Indians were savages in the colonists' eyes because they lacked the traits of English civilization. As one Englishman put it in 1625, the natives of Virginia were "so bad a people, having little of humanitie but shape, ignorant of Civilitie, of Arts, of

Religion; more brutish than the beasts they hunt, more wild and unmanly than that unmanned wild countrey, which they range rather than inhabite; captivated also to Satans tyranny in foolish pieties, mad impieties, wicked idlenesse, busie and bloudy wickednesse." Some English colonists counterbalanced this harsh indictment with admiration for certain features of Indian behavior. They praised Indians' calm dignity and poise, their tender love and care for family members, and their simple, independent way of life in apparent harmony with nature.

Color was not a feature of the Indians' savagery. During the seventeenth century, colonists never referred to Indians as "red." Instead, they saw Indians' skin color as tawny or tanned, the "Sun's livery," as one settler wrote. To the English, tanned skin denoted a member of the working class who spent his or her days toiling under the sun; pale skin was the fashion. Many settlers held the view that Indians were innately white like the English but in other ways woefully un-English.

Despite their savagery in English eyes, Indians controlled two things colonists desperately wanted: land and peace. Early in the seventeenth century, when English settlements were small and weak, peace with the Indians was a higher priority than land. In this period, English

comments on Indian savagery noted the obvious differences between settlers and Indians, but the colonists' need for peace kept them attuned to ways to coexist with the Indians. By the middle of the seventeenth century, as colonial settlements grew and the desire for land increased, violent conflict with Indians erupted repeatedly. The violence convinced settlers that the only way to achieve both land and peace was to eliminate the Indians, by either killing them or pushing them far away from colonial settlements. English assumptions of their superiority to savage Indians provided justification and a gloss of respectability to the colonists' violent and relentless grab of Indian land.

The colonists identified Africans quite differently. Their most common term for Africans was *Negroes*, but the other was not *savage* or *heathen* but *black*. What struck English colonists most forcefully about Africans was not their un-English ways but their un-English skin color.

Black was not a neutral color to the colonists. According to the *Oxford English Dictionary* (which catalogs the changing meaning of words), *black* meant to the English people who settled the Chesapeake "deeply stained with dirt; soiled, dirty, foul . . . having dark or deadly purposes, malignant; pertaining to or involving death, deadly; baneful, disastrous, sinister . . .

small planters and poor farmers against both the Indians and the colonial rulers in Jamestown.

Hoping to maintain the fragile peace on the frontier in 1676, Governor Berkeley pronounced Bacon a rebel, threatened to punish him for treason, and called for new elections of burgesses

who, Berkeley believed, would endorse his get-tough policy. To Berkeley's surprise, the elections backfired. Almost all the old burgesses were voted out of office and replaced by local leaders, including Bacon, who chafed at the rule of the elite planters.

European Attitudes toward Africans
This lavish portrait of two seventeenth-century aristocratic ladies illustrates common European attitudes toward Africans. Both ladies appear completely at ease with the black servant boy. They gaze confidently at the viewer while the boy stares at the black lapdog, whose color and protruding eyes he shares, along with an ornamental collar. The portrait suggests that the ladies consider the African boy akin to the dog—an inferior pet. © RMN-Grand Palais/Art Resource, NY.

foul, iniquitous, atrocious, horrible, wicked." Black was the opposite of white, which connoted purity, beauty, and goodness—attributes the colonists identified with themselves. By the middle of the seventeenth century, the colonists referred to themselves not only as English but also as free, hinting that they believed that people who were not English were not free. After about 1680, colonists often referred to themselves as white, acknowledging the color of free people. By the end of the seventeenth century, blacks were triply cursed in English eyes: un-English, un-white, and un-free.

Virginians did not legally define slavery as permanent, lifelong, inherited bondage until 1660. The sparse surviving evidence demonstrates, however, that colonists practiced slavery from the start. The debasements of slavery strengthened the colonists' prejudice toward blacks, while racial prejudices buttressed slavery.

Colonists' attitudes toward Indians and Africans exaggerated and hardened English notions about social hierarchy, about superiority and inferiority. Colonists' convictions of their own superiority to Indians and Africans justified, they believed, their exploitation of Indians' land and Africans' labor. Those justifications planted the seeds of pernicious racial prejudices that flourished in America for centuries.

Thinking about Beliefs and Attitudes

1. How did the words colonists used to describe Indians and Africans indicate their beliefs?

2. To what extent did colonists' ideas about themselves shape their attitudes toward Indians and Africans?

Connect to the Big Idea

C What were the consequences of English colonists' belief in their own superiority?

In June 1676, the new legislature passed a series of reform measures known as Bacon's Laws. Among other changes, the laws gave local settlers a voice in setting tax levies, forbade officeholders from demanding bribes or other extra fees for carrying out their duties, placed limits on holding multiple offices, and restored the vote to all freemen. But elite planters soon convinced Berkeley that Bacon and his men were a greater threat than Indians.

When Bacon learned that Berkeley had once again branded him a traitor, he declared war against Berkeley and the other grandees. For three months, Bacon's forces fought the Indians, sacked the grandees' plantations, and attacked Jamestown. Berkeley's loyalists retaliated by plundering the homes of Bacon's supporters. The fighting continued until Bacon unexpectedly died, most likely from dysentery, and several English ships arrived to bolster Berkeley's strength. With the rebellion crushed, Berkeley hanged several of Bacon's allies and destroyed farms that belonged to Bacon's supporters.

The rebellion did nothing to dislodge the grandees from their positions of power. If anything, it strengthened them. When the king learned of the turmoil in the Chesapeake and its devastating effect on tobacco exports and customs duties, he ordered an investigation. Royal officials replaced Berkeley with a governor more attentive to the king's interests, nullified Bacon's Laws, and instituted an export tax on tobacco as a way to pay the expenses of the colony's government without having to obtain the consent of the tightfisted House of Burgesses.

In the aftermath of Bacon's Rebellion, tensions between great planters and small farmers moderated. Bacon's Rebellion showed, a governor of Virginia said, that it was necessary "to steer between . . . either an Indian or a civil war." The ruling elite concluded that it was safer for the colonists to fight the Indians than to fight each other, and the government made little effort to restrict settlers' encroachment on Indian land. Tax cuts also were welcomed by all freemen. The export duty on tobacco imposed by the king allowed the colonial government to reduce taxes by 75 percent between 1660 and 1700. In the long run, however, the most important contribution to political stability was the declining importance of the servant labor system. During the 1680s and 1690s, fewer servants arrived in the Chesapeake, partly because of improving economic conditions in England. Accordingly, the number of poor, newly freed servants also declined, reducing the size of the lowest stratum of free society. In 1700, when about one-third of the free colonists still worked as tenants on land owned by others, the Chesapeake was in the midst of transitioning to a slave labor system that minimized the differences between poor farmers and rich planters and magnified the differences between whites and blacks.

REVIEW Why did Chesapeake colonial society become increasingly polarized between 1650 and 1670?

► Toward a Slave Labor System

Although forced native labor was common practice in New Spain, English colonists were unsuccessful in conscripting Indian labor. They looked instead to another source of workers used by the Spaniards and Portuguese: enslaved Africans. On this foundation, European colonizers built African **slavery** into the most important form of coerced labor in the New World.

During the seventeenth century, English colonies in the West Indies followed the Spanish and Portuguese examples and developed sugar plantations with slave labor. In the English North American colonies, however, a slave labor system did not emerge until the last quarter of the seventeenth century. During the 1670s, settlers from Barbados brought slavery to the new English mainland colony of Carolina, where the imprint of the West Indies remained strong for decades. In Chesapeake tobacco fields at about the same time, slave labor began to replace servant labor, marking the transition toward a society of freedom for whites and slavery for Africans.

Religion and Revolt in the Spanish Borderland

While English colonies in the Chesapeake grew and prospered with the tobacco trade, the northern outposts of the Spanish empire in New Mexico and Florida stagnated. Only about fifteen hundred Spaniards lived in Florida, and roughly twice as many inhabited New Mexico, yet both colonies required regular deliveries of goods and large subsidies. One royal governor complained that "no [Spaniard] comes . . . to plow and sow [crops], but only to eat and loaf."

Instead of attracting settlers and growing crops for export, New Mexico and Florida appealed to Spanish missionaries seeking to convert Indians to Christianity. In both colonies, Indians outnumbered Spaniards ten or twenty to one. Royal officials hoped that the missionaries' efforts would pacify the Indians and be a relatively cheap way to preserve Spanish footholds in North America. The missionaries baptized thousands of Indians in Spanish North America during the seventeenth century, but they also planted the seeds of Indian uprisings against Spanish rule.

Dozens of missionaries came to Florida and New Mexico, as one announced, to free the Indians "from the miserable slavery of the demon and from the obscure darkness of their idolatry." The missionaries followed royal instructions that

VISUAL ACTIVITY

Spanish Missionary in Florida
This sixteenth-century picture illustrates the methods Spanish missionaries used to teach Christianity to Native Americans. The picture shows the importance of reading and the punishment for students who did not measure up to the missionary's expectations.
The Granger Collection, New York.
READING THE IMAGE: Aside from the doctrines of Christianity, what are the Native Americans students being taught by these methods of instruction?
CONNECTIONS: How did missionary activity among the English colonists in the seventeenth-century southern colonies differ from that among the Spanish colonies?

Indians should be taught "to live in a civilized manner, clothed and wearing shoes . . . [and] given the use of . . . bread, linen, horses, cattle, tools, and weapons, and all the rest that Spain has had." In effect, the missionaries sought to convert the Indians not just into Christians but also into surrogate Spaniards.

The missionaries supervised the building of scores of Catholic churches across Florida and New Mexico. Adopting practices common elsewhere in New Spain, they forced the Indians both to construct these churches and to pay tribute in the form of food, blankets, and other goods. Although the missionaries congratulated themselves on the many Indians they converted, their coercive methods subverted their goals. A missionary reported that an Indian in New Mexico asked him, "If we [missionaries] who are Christians caused so much harm and violence [to Indians], why should they become Christians?"

The Indians retaliated repeatedly against Spanish exploitation, but the Spaniards suppressed the violent uprisings by taking advantage of the disunity among the Indians, much as Cortés did in the conquest of Mexico (see "The Conquest of Mexico" in chapter 2). In 1680, however, the native leader Popé organized the **Pueblo Revolt**, ordering his followers, as one recounted, to "break up and burn the images of the holy Christ, the

Virgin Mary, and the other saints, the crosses, and everything pertaining to Christianity." During the revolt, Indians desecrated churches, killed two-thirds of the Spanish missionaries, and drove the Spaniards out of New Mexico to present-day El Paso, Texas. The Spaniards managed to return to New Mexico by the end of the seventeenth century, but only by curtailing the missionaries and reducing labor exploitation. Florida Indians never mounted a unified attack on Spanish rule, but they too organized sporadic uprisings and resisted conversion, causing a Spanish official to report by the end of the seventeenth century that "the law of God and the preaching of the Holy Gospel have now ceased."

The West Indies: Sugar and Slavery

The most profitable part of the English New World empire in the seventeenth century lay in the Caribbean (Map 3.2). The tiny island of **Barbados**, colonized in the 1630s, was the jewel of the English West Indies. During the 1640s, a colonial official proclaimed Barbados "the most flourishing Island in all those American parts, and I verily believe in all the world for the production of sugar." Sugar commanded high prices in England, and planters rushed to grow

MAP ACTIVITY

Map 3.2 The West Indies and Carolina in the Seventeenth Century

Although Carolina was geographically close to the Chesapeake colonies, it was culturally closer to the West Indies in the seventeenth century because its early settlers—both blacks and whites—came from Barbados. South Carolina maintained strong ties to the West Indies for more than a century.

READING THE MAP: Locate English colonies in America and English holdings in the Caribbean. Which European country controlled most of the mainland bordering the Caribbean? Where was the closest mainland English territory?

CONNECTIONS: Why were colonists in Carolina so interested in Barbados? What goods did they export? Describe the relationship between Carolina and Barbados in 1700.

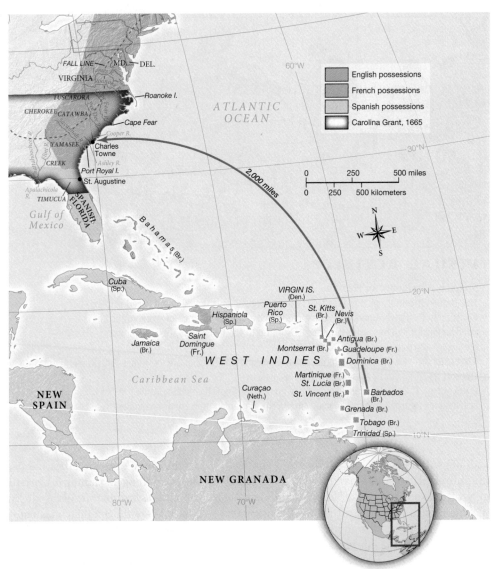

as much as they could. By midcentury, annual sugar exports from the English Caribbean totaled about 150,000 pounds; by 1700, exports reached nearly 50 million pounds.

Sugar transformed Barbados and other West Indian islands. Poor farmers could not afford the expensive machinery that extracted and refined sugarcane juice, but planters with enough capital to grow sugar got rich. By 1680, the wealthiest Barbadian sugar planters were, on average, four times richer than tobacco grandees in the Chesapeake. The sugar grandees differed from their Chesapeake counterparts in another crucial way: The average sugar baron in Barbados owned 115 slaves in 1680.

African slaves planted, cultivated, and harvested the sugarcane that made West Indian planters wealthy. Beginning in the 1640s, Barbadian planters purchased thousands of slaves to work their plantations, and the African popu-

lation on the island mushroomed. During the 1650s, when blacks made up only 3 percent of the Chesapeake population, they had already become the majority in Barbados. By 1700, slaves constituted more than three-fourths of the island's population (Figure 3.1).

For slaves, work on a sugar plantation was a life sentence to brutal, unremitting labor. Slaves suffered high death rates. Since slave men outnumbered slave women two to one, few slaves could form families and have children. These grim realities meant that in Barbados and elsewhere in the West Indies, the slave population did not grow by natural reproduction. Instead, planters continually purchased enslaved Africans. Although sugar plantations did not gain a foothold in North America in the seventeenth century, the West Indies nonetheless exerted a powerful influence on the development of slavery in the mainland colonies.

Carolina: A West Indian Frontier

The early settlers of what became South Carolina were immigrants from Barbados. In 1663, a Barbadian planter named John Colleton and a group of seven other men obtained a charter from England's King Charles II to establish a colony north of the Spanish territories in Florida. The men, known as "proprietors," hoped to siphon settlers from Barbados and other colonies and encourage them to develop a profitable export crop comparable to West Indian sugar and Chesapeake tobacco. The proprietors enlisted the English philosopher John Locke to help draft the *Fundamental Constitutions of Carolina*, which provided for religious liberty and political rights for small property holders while envisioning a landed aristocracy supported by bound laborers and slaves. Following the Chesapeake example, the proprietors also offered headrights of up to 150 acres of land for each settler, a provision that eventually undermined the *Constitutions'* goal of a titled aristocracy. In 1670, the proprietors established the colony's first permanent English settlement, Charles Towne, later spelled Charleston (see Map 3.2).

As the proprietors had planned, most of the early settlers were from Barbados, and they brought their slaves with them. More than a fourth of the early settlers were slaves, and by 1700 slaves made up about half the Carolina population. The new colony's close association with Barbados caused English officials to refer routinely to "Carolina in ye West Indies."

The Carolinians experimented unsuccessfully to match their semitropical climate with profitable export crops of tobacco, cotton, indigo, and olives. In the mid-1690s, colonists identified a hardy strain of rice and took advantage of the knowledge of rice cultivation among their many African slaves to build rice plantations. Settlers also sold livestock and timber to the West Indies, as well as another "natural resource": They captured and enslaved several thousand local Indians and sold them to Caribbean planters. Both economically and socially, seventeenth-century Carolina was a frontier outpost of the West Indian sugar economy.

Slave Labor Emerges in the Chesapeake

By 1700, more than eight out of ten people in the southern colonies of English North America lived in the Chesapeake. Until the 1670s, almost all Chesapeake colonists were white people from England. By 1700, however, one out of eight people in the region was a black person from Africa. A few black people had lived in the

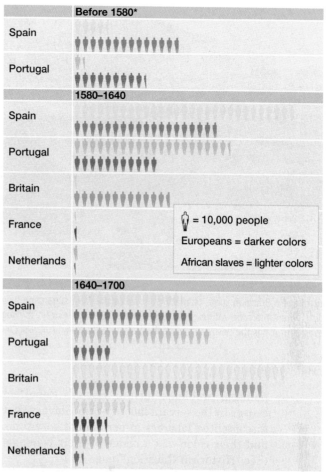

*Note: Before 1580, migration from Britain, France, and the Netherlands was negligible.

FIGURE 3.1 Global Comparison: Migration to the New World From Europe and Africa, 1492–1700
Before 1640, Spain and Portugal sent four out of five European migrants to the New World, virtually all of them bound for New Spain or Brazil. But from 1640 to 1700, nearly as many migrants came from England as from all other European nations combined, a measure of the growing significance of England's colonies. From 1492 to 1700, more enslaved Africans than Europeans arrived in the New World. What might explain the shifts in the destinations of enslaved Africans? Were those shifts comparable to shifts among European immigrants?

Chesapeake since the 1620s, but the black population grew fivefold between 1670 and 1700 as hundreds of tobacco planters made the transition from servant to slave labor.

Planters saw several advantages to purchasing slaves rather than servants. Although slaves cost three to five times more than servants, slaves never became free. Because the mortality rate had declined by the 1680s, planters could reasonably expect a slave to live longer than a servant's period of indenture. Slaves also promised to be a perpetual labor force since children of slave mothers inherited the status of slavery. And unlike servants, they could be controlled politically. A slave labor system promised to avoid the

Sugar Plantation
This portrait of a Brazilian sugar plantation shows cartloads of sugarcane being hauled to the mill, which is powered by a waterwheel (far right), where the cane will be squeezed between rollers to extract the sugary juice. The juice will then be distilled over a fire tended by the slaves until it has the desired consistency and purity. Courtesy of the John Carter Brown Library at Brown University.

political problems such as Bacon's Rebellion caused by the servant labor system. Slavery kept discontented laborers in permanent servitude, and their color was a badge of their bondage. (See "Historical Question," page 68.)

The slave labor system polarized Chesapeake society along lines of race and status: All slaves were black, and nearly all blacks were slaves; almost all free people were white, and all whites were free or only temporarily bound in indentured servitude. Unlike Barbados, however, the Chesapeake retained a vast white majority. Among whites, huge differences of wealth and status still existed. By 1700, more than three-quarters of white families had neither servants nor slaves. Nonetheless, poor white farmers enjoyed the privileges of free status. They could own property, get married, have families, and bequeath their property and their freedom to their descendants; they could move when and where they wanted; they could associate freely with other people; they could serve on juries, vote, and hold political office; and they could work, loaf, and sleep as they chose. These privileges of freedom—none of them possessed by slaves—made lesser white folk feel they had a genuine stake in the existence of slavery, even if they did not own a single slave. By emphasizing the privileges of freedom shared by all white people, the slave labor system reduced the tensions between poor folk and grandees that had plagued the Chesapeake region in the 1670s.

In contrast to slaves in Barbados, most slaves in the seventeenth-century Chesapeake colonies had frequent and close contact with white people. Slaves and white servants performed the same tasks on tobacco plantations, often working side by side in the fields. Slaves took advantage of every opportunity to slip away from white supervision and seek out the company of other slaves. Planters often feared that slaves would turn such seemingly innocent social pleasures to political ends, either to run away or to conspire to strike against their masters. Slaves often did run away, but they were usually captured or returned after a brief absence. Despite planters' nightmares, slave insurrections did not occur.

Although slavery resolved the political unrest caused by the servant labor system, it created new political problems. By 1700, the bedrock political issue in the southern colonies was keeping slaves in their place, at the end of a hoe. The slave labor system in the southern colonies stood roughly midway between the sugar plantations and black majority of Barbados to the south and the small farms and homogeneous villages that developed in seventeenth-century New England to the north (see "Religious Controversies and Economic Changes" in chapter 4).

REVIEW   Why had slave labor largely displaced indentured servant labor by 1700 in Chesapeake tobacco production?

Tobacco Wrapper
This wrapper labeled a container of tobacco from the English colonies sold at Reighly's shop in Essex. The wrapper was much like a brand, promising consumers consistency in quality and taste. The wrapper illustrates tobacco growing in a field and harvested leaves ready to be packed into a barrel, ferried to the ships waiting off-shore, and transported to Reighly's and other tobacco-nists in England. The Granger Collection, New York.

▶ Conclusion: The Growth of English Colonies Based on Export Crops and Slave Labor

By 1700, the colonies of Virginia, Maryland, and Carolina were firmly established. The staple crops they grew for export provided a livelihood for many, a fortune for a few, and valuable revenues for shippers, merchants, and the English monarchy. Their societies differed markedly from English society in most respects, yet the colonists considered themselves English people who happened to live in North America. They claimed the same rights and privileges as English men and women, while they denied those rights and privileges to Native Americans and African slaves.

The English colonies also differed from the example of New Spain. Settlers and servants flocked to English colonies, in contrast to Spaniards who trickled into New Spain. Few English missionaries sought to convert Indians to Protestant Christianity, unlike the numerous Catholic missionaries in the Spanish settlements in New Mexico and Florida. Large quantities of gold and silver never materialized in English North America. English colonists never adopted the system of encomienda (see "New Spain in the Sixteenth Century" in chapter 2). Yet important forms of coerced labor and racial distinction that developed in New Spain had North American counterparts, as English colonists employed servants and slaves and defined themselves as superior to Indians and Africans.

By 1700, the remnants of Powhatan's people still survived. As English settlement pushed north, west, and south of Chesapeake Bay, the Indians faced the new colonial world that Powhatan and Pocahontas had encountered when John Smith and the first colonists had arrived at Jamestown. By 1700, the many descendants of Pocahontas's son, Thomas, as well as other colonists and Native Americans, understood that the English had come to stay.

Economically, the southern colonies developed during the seventeenth century from the struggling Jamestown settlement that could not feed itself into a major source of profits for England. The European fashion for tobacco provided livelihoods for numerous white families and riches for elite planters. But after 1700, enslaved Africans were conscripted in growing numbers to grow tobacco in the Chesapeake and rice in Carolina. The slave society that dominated the eighteenth-century southern colonies was firmly rooted in the developments of the seventeenth century.

A desire for land, a hope for profit, and a dream for security motivated southern white colonists. Realizing these aspirations involved great risks, considerable suffering, and frequent disappointment, as well as seizing Indian lands and coercing labor from servants and slaves. By 1700, despite huge disparities in individual colonists' success in achieving their goals, tens of thousands of white colonists who were immigrants or descendants of immigrants now considered the southern colonies their home, shaping the history of the region and of the nation as a whole for centuries to come.

See the Selected Bibliography for this chapter in the Appendix.

3 Chapter Review

MAKE IT STICK

 LearningCurve

Go online and use LearningCurve to see what you know. Then review the key terms and answer the questions.

KEY TERMS

Virginia Company (p. 53)
Jamestown (p. 54)
Algonquian Indians (p. 54)
royal colony (p. 56)
House of Burgesses (p. 56)
headright (p. 59)
indentured servants (p. 60)
Navigation Acts (p. 67)
Bacon's Rebellion (p. 67)
slavery (p. 70)
Pueblo Revolt (p. 71)
Barbados (p. 71)

REVIEW QUESTIONS

1. Why did Powhatan behave as he did toward the English colonists? (pp. 53–57)

2. Why did the vast majority of European immigrants to the Chesapeake come as indentured servants? (pp. 57–66)

3. Why did Chesapeake colonial society become increasingly polarized between 1650 and 1670? (pp. 66–70)

4. Why had slave labor largely displaced indentured servant labor by 1700 in Chesapeake tobacco production? (pp. 70–74)

MAKING CONNECTIONS

1. Given the vulnerability of the Jamestown settlement in its first two decades, why did its sponsors and settlers not abandon it?

2. How did tobacco agriculture shape the Chesapeake region's development? In your answer, be sure to address the demographic and geographic features of the colony.

3. Bacon's Rebellion highlighted significant tensions within Chesapeake society. What provoked the rebellion, and what did it accomplish?

4. How did European colonists' relations with Native Americans and enslaved Africans contribute to political friction and harmony within the colony?

LINKING TO THE PAST

1. How did England's colonization efforts in the Chesapeake and Carolina during the seventeenth century compare with Spain's conquest and colonization of Mexico? (See chapter 2.)

2. How did the development of the transatlantic tobacco trade exemplify the Columbian exchange? (See chapter 2.)

4 The Northern Colonies in the Seventeenth Century

1601–1700

CONTENT LEARNING OBJECTIVES

After reading and studying this chapter, you should be able to:

- Explain why England became a Protestant nation and who the Puritans were.
- Understand how the Puritans came to dominate New England society.
- Recognize how Puritanism influenced the development of New England.
- Describe how the middle colonies were founded and how the founding and settlement of New York, New Jersey, and Pennsylvania differed from the founding and settlement of the New England colonies.
- Explain how the English monarchy consolidated its authority over the American colonies.

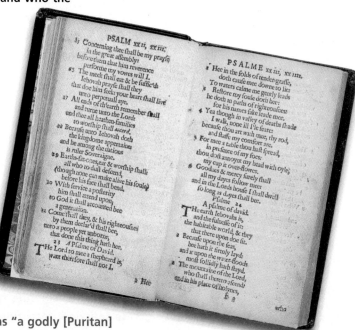

AMERICA'S FIRST BOOK
Published in Cambridge, Massachusetts, in 1640, this copy of *The Whole Book of Psalmes Faithfully Translated into English Metre* was used by worshippers to sing psalms, celebrating God's truth. AP Photo/ Sotheby's.

ROGER WILLIAMS AND HIS WIFE, MARY, arrived in Massachusetts in February 1631. Fresh from a superb education at Cambridge University, the twenty-eight-year-old Williams was "a godly [Puritan] minister," noted Governor John Winthrop, whose Boston church asked Williams to become its minister. But Williams refused the invitation because the church had not openly rejected the corrupt Church of England. New England's premier Puritan church was not pure enough for Roger Williams.

Williams and his wife moved to Plymouth colony, where he spent a great deal of time among the Narragansett Indians. Williams believed that "Nature knows no difference between Europeans and [Native] Americans in blood, birth, [or] bodies . . . God having made of one blood all mankind." He insisted that the colonists respect the Indians' religion and culture since all human beings—Christians and non-Christians alike—should live according to their consciences as revealed to them by God.

Williams condemned English colonists for their "sin of unjust usurpation" of Indian land. He believed that English claims were legally, morally, and spiritually invalid. In contrast, Massachusetts officials defended colonists' settlement on Indian land. Governor Winthrop declared, "if we leave [the Indians] sufficient [land] for their use, we may lawfully take the rest, there being more than enough for them and us." Winthrop's arguments prevailed, but Williams refused to knuckle under. "God Land," he said, "[is] as great a God with us English as God Gold was with the Spaniards."

In 1633, Williams believed that the Bible shrouded the Word of God in "mist and fog." That observation led him to denounce the emerging New England order as impure, ungodly, and tyrannical. He disagreed with the New England government's requirement that everyone attend church services. He argued that forcing people who were not Christians to attend church was "False Worshipping" that only promoted "spiritual drunkenness and whoredom." He believed that to regulate religious behavior would be "spiritual rape"; that governments should tolerate all religious beliefs because only God knows the Truth. "I commend that man," Williams wrote, "whether Jew, or Turk, or Papist, or whoever, that steers no otherwise than his conscience dares."

New England's leaders denounced Williams's arguments and banished him for his "extreme and dangerous" opinions. In January 1636, he fled south to Narragansett Bay, where he and his followers established the colony of Rhode Island, which enshrined "Liberty of Conscience" as a fundamental ideal and became a refuge for other dissenters. Although New England's leaders expelled Williams from their holy commonwealth, his dissenting ideas arose from orthodox Puritan doctrines. Puritanism inspired believers such as Roger Williams to draw their own conclusions and stick to them.

During the seventeenth century, New England's Puritan zeal cooled, and the promise of a holy New England faded. Late in the century, the new "middle" colonies of New York, New Jersey, and Pennsylvania were founded, featuring greater religious and ethnic diversity than New England. Religion remained important throughout all the colonies, but it competed with the growing faith that a better life required less focus on salvation and more attention to worldly concerns of family, work, and trade.

Throughout the English mainland colonies, settlements encroached on Indian land, causing violent conflict to flare up repeatedly. Political conflict also arose among colonists, particularly in response to major political upheavals in England. By the end of the seventeenth century, the English monarchy exerted greater control over North America and the rest of its Atlantic empire, but the products, people, and ideas that pulsed between England and the colonies energized both.

► Puritans and the Settlement of New England

Puritans who emigrated to North America aspired to escape the turmoil and persecution they suffered in England, a long-term consequence of the English Reformation. They also sought to build a new, orderly, Puritan version of England. Puritans established the first small settlement in New England in 1620, followed a few years later by additional, larger settlements by the Massachusetts Bay Company. Allowed self-government through royal charter, these Puritans were in a unique position to direct the new colonies according to their faith. Although many New England colonists were not Puritans, Puritanism remained a paramount influence in New England's religion, politics, and community life during the seventeenth century.

Puritan Origins: The English Reformation

The religious roots of the Puritans who founded New England reached back to the Protestant Reformation, which arose in Germany in 1517 (see "The Protestant Reformation and the Spanish Response" in chapter 2). The English church initially remained within the Catholic fold. Henry VIII, who reigned from 1509 to 1547, saw that the Reformation offered him an opportunity to break with Rome and take control of the church in England. In 1534, Henry formally initiated the **English Reformation**. At his insistence, Parliament outlawed the Catholic Church and proclaimed the king "the only supreme head on earth of the Church of England." Henry seized the vast properties of the Catholic Church in England as well as the privilege of appointing bishops and others in the church hierarchy.

In the short run, the English Reformation allowed Henry VIII to achieve his political goal of controlling the church. In the long run, however, the Reformation brought to England the political and religious turmoil that Henry had hoped to avoid. Henry himself sought no more than a halfway Reformation. Protestant doctrines held no attraction for him; in almost all matters of religious belief and practice he remained an orthodox Catholic. Many English Catholics wanted to revoke the English Reformation; they hoped to return the Church of England to the pope and to restore Catholic doctrines and ceremonies. But many other English people insisted on a

CHRONOLOGY

1534	• English Reformation begins.
1609	• Henry Hudson searches for Northwest Passage.
1620	• Plymouth colony founded.
1626	• Manhattan Island purchased; New Amsterdam founded.
1629	• Massachusetts Bay Company receives royal charter.
1630	• John Winthrop leads Puritan settlers to Massachusetts Bay.
1636	• Rhode Island colony established. • Connecticut colony founded.
1636–1637	• Pequot War.
1638	• Anne Hutchinson excommunicated.
1642	• Puritan Revolution inflames England.
1649	• English Puritans win civil war.
1656	• Quakers arrive in Massachusetts and are persecuted.
1660	• Monarchy restored in England.
1662	• Many Puritan congregations adopt Halfway Covenant.
1664	• English seize Dutch colony, rename it New York. • Colony of New Jersey created.
1675–1676	• King Philip's War.
1681	• Colony of Pennsylvania founded.
1686	• Dominion of New England created.
1688	• England's Glorious Revolution.
1689–1697	• King William's War.
1692	• Salem witch trials.

Queen Elizabeth
This sixteenth-century portrait of Queen Elizabeth celebrates English victory over the Spanish Armada in 1588 (shown in the panels on either side of Elizabeth's head) that resulted in England's empire reaching North America (notice her right hand covering North America on the globe). © Bettmann/Corbis.

genuine, thoroughgoing Reformation; these people came to be called **Puritans**.

During the sixteenth century, Puritanism was less an organized movement than a set of ideas and religious principles that appealed strongly to many dissenting members of the Church of England. They sought to eliminate what they considered the offensive features of Catholicism that remained in the religious doctrines and practices of the Church of England. For example, they wanted to do away with the rituals of Catholic worship and instead emphasize that an individual Christian's relationship with God developed through Bible study, prayer, and introspection. All Puritans shared a desire to make the English church thoroughly Protestant.

The fate of Protestantism waxed and waned under the monarchs who succeeded Henry VIII.

English Monarchy and the Protestant Reformation

1509–1547	Henry VIII	Leads the English Reformation, outlawing the Catholic Church in England and establishing the English monarch as supreme head of the Church of England.
1547–1553	Edward VI	Moves religious reform in a Protestant direction.
1553–1558	Mary I	Outlaws Protestantism and strives to reestablish the Catholic Church in England.
1558–1603	Elizabeth I	Tries to position the Church of England between extremes of Catholicism and Protestantism.
1603–1625	James I	Authorizes a new, Protestant translation of the Bible but is unsympathetic to Puritan reformers.
1625–1649	Charles I	Continues move away from Puritan reformers. Beheaded during the Puritan Revolution.
1642		Puritan Revolution (English Civil War) begins.
1644–1660	Oliver Cromwell	Leads Puritan side to victory in the English Civil War. Parliament proclaims England a Puritan republic (1649) and declares Cromwell the nation's "Lord Protector" (1653).
1660–1685	Charles II	Restored to the monarchy by Parliament and attempts to enforce religious toleration of Catholics and Protestant dissenters from the Church of England.
1685–1688	James II	Ousted by Parliament for pro-Catholic policies and replaced by his Protestant son-in-law, William, and his daughter (William's wife) in the "Glorious Revolution" (1688).
1689–1694	William III and Mary II	Reassert Protestant influence in England and its empire.

In 1558 Elizabeth I, the daughter of Henry and his second wife, Anne Boleyn, became queen. During her long reign, Elizabeth reaffirmed the English Reformation and tried to position the English church between the extremes of Catholicism and Puritanism. Like her father, she desired a church that would strengthen the monarchy and the nation. By the time Elizabeth died in 1603, many people in England looked on Protestantism as a defining feature of national identity.

When Elizabeth's successor, James I, became king, English Puritans petitioned for further reform of the Church of England. James authorized a new translation of the Bible, known ever since as the King James Version. However, neither James I nor his son Charles I, who became king in 1625, was receptive to the ideas of Puritan reformers. James and Charles moved the Church of England away from Puritanism. They enforced conformity to the Church of England and punished dissenters. In 1629, Charles I dissolved Parliament—where Puritans were well represented—and initiated aggressive anti-Puritan policies. Many Puritans despaired about continuing to defend their faith in England and made plans to emigrate to Europe, the West Indies, or America.

The Pilgrims and Plymouth Colony

One of the first Protestant groups to emigrate, later known as Pilgrims, professed an unortho-dox view known as separatism. These **Separatists** sought to withdraw—or separate—from the Church of England, which they considered hopelessly corrupt. In 1608 they moved to Holland; by 1620 they realized that they could not live and worship there as they had hoped. William Bradford, a leader of the Separatists, recalled that "many of their children, by . . . the great licentiousness of youth [in Holland], and the manifold temptations of the place, were drawn away by evil examples." Bradford and other Separatists believed that America promised to better protect and preserve their children and their community. Separatists obtained permission to settle in the extensive territory granted to the Virginia Company (see "The Fragile Jamestown Settlement" in chapter 3). In August 1620, the Pilgrim families boarded the *Mayflower*, and after eleven weeks at sea all but one of the 102 immigrants arrived at the outermost tip of Cape Cod in present-day Massachusetts.

The Pilgrims realized immediately that they had landed far north of the Virginia grants and had no legal authority to settle in the area. To provide order, security, and a claim to legitimacy, they drew up the Mayflower Compact on the day they arrived. They pledged to "covenant and combine ourselves together into a civil Body Politick, for our better Ordering and Preservation." The signers (all men) agreed to enact and obey necessary and just laws.

The Pilgrims settled at Plymouth and elected William Bradford their governor. That first win-

VISUAL ACTIVITY

Plymouth Village
This historically accurate modern-day reconstruction of the Plymouth settlement depicts the simple dwellings the Pilgrims built with materials readily at hand. Even the chimneys were built with wood. Notice that the buildings are huddled together rather than scattered across the landscape, all the better to promote community cohesion and protection against Indians. Plus One Pix/Alamy.
READING THE IMAGE: What kinds of work were required to erect these buildings?
CONNECTIONS: How did New England settlements reflect Puritan religious ideas?

Seal of Massachusetts Bay Colony
In 1629, the Massachusetts Bay Company designed this seal depicting an Indian man inviting English settlers to "come over and help us." Of course, such an invitation was never issued. The seal was an attempt to lend an aura of altruism to the Massachusetts Bay Company's colonization efforts. What does the seal suggest about English views of Indians? Private Collection/Peter Newark American Pictures/The Bridgeman Art Library.

ter, which they spent aboard their ship, "was most sad and lamentable," Bradford wrote later. "In two or three months' time half of [our] company died . . . being the depth of winter, and wanting houses . . . [and] being infected with scurvy and other diseases."

In the spring, Indians rescued the floundering Plymouth settlement. First Samoset and then Squanto befriended the settlers. Samoset had learned English from previous contacts with sailors and fishermen who had visited the coast to dry fish before the Plymouth settlers arrived. Squanto had been kidnapped by an English trader in 1614 and taken as a slave to Spain, where he escaped to London and learned English before finally making his way back home. Samoset arranged for the Pilgrims to meet and establish good relations with Massasoit, the chief of the Wampanoag Indians, whose territory included Plymouth. Squanto, Bradford wrote, "was a special instrument sent of God for their [the Pilgrims'] good. . . . He directed them how to set their corn, where to take fish, and to procure other commodities." With the Indians' guidance, the Pilgrims managed to harvest enough food to guarantee their survival through the coming winter, an occasion they celebrated in the fall of 1621 with a feast of thanksgiving attended by Massasoit and other Wampanoags.

Plymouth colony remained precarious for years, but the Pilgrims persisted, living simply and coexisting in relative peace with the Indians. By 1630, Plymouth had become a small permanent settlement, but it failed to attract many other English Puritans.

The Founding of Massachusetts Bay Colony

In 1629, shortly before Charles I dissolved Parliament, a group of Puritans obtained a royal charter for the Massachusetts Bay Company. The charter provided the usual privileges granted to joint-stock companies, including land for colonization that spanned present-day Massachusetts, New Hampshire, Vermont, Maine, and upstate New York. A unique provision of the charter permitted the government of the Massachusetts Bay Company to be located in the colony rather than in England. This provision allowed Puritans to exchange their status as a harassed minority in England for self-government in Massachusetts.

To lead the emigrants, the Massachusetts Bay Company selected John Winthrop, a prosperous lawyer and landowner, to serve as governor. In March 1630, eleven ships crammed with seven hundred passengers sailed for Massachusetts; six more ships and another five hundred emigrants followed a few months later. Unlike the

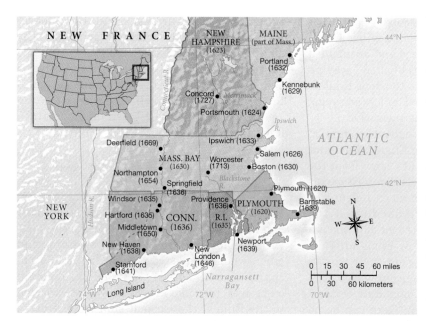

MAP ACTIVITY

Map 4.1 New England Colonies in the Seventeenth Century
New Englanders spread across the landscape town by town during the seventeenth century. (For the sake of legibility, only a few of the more important towns are shown on the map.)

READING THE MAP: Using the dates on the map, create a chronology of the establishment of New England towns. What physical features correspond to the earliest habitation by English settlers?

CONNECTIONS: Why were towns so much more a feature of seventeenth-century New England than of the Chesapeake (see also "Cultivating Land and Faith" in chapter 3)? How did Puritan dissent influence the settlement of New England colonies?

Separatists, Winthrop's Puritans aspired to reform the corrupt Church of England (rather than separate from it) by setting an example of godliness in the New World. Winthrop and a small group chose to settle on the peninsula that became Boston, and other settlers clustered at promising locations nearby (Map 4.1).

In a sermon to his companions aboard the *Arbella* while they were still at sea—probably the most famous sermon in American history—Winthrop proclaimed the cosmic significance of their journey. The Puritans had "entered into a covenant" with God to "work out our salvation under the power and purity of his holy ordinances," Winthrop declared. This sanctified agreement with God meant that the Puritans had to make "extraordinary" efforts to "bring into familiar and constant practice" religious principles that most people in England merely preached. To achieve their pious goals, the Puritans had to subordinate their individual interests to the common good. "We must be knit together in this work as one man," Winthrop preached. "We must delight in each other, make others' conditions our own, rejoice together, mourn together, labor and suffer together." The stakes could not be higher, Winthrop told his listeners: "We must consider that we shall be as a city upon a hill. The eyes of all people are upon us."

That belief shaped seventeenth-century New England as profoundly as tobacco shaped the Chesapeake. Winthrop's vision of a city on a hill fired the Puritans' fierce determination to keep their covenant and live according to God's laws,

unlike the backsliders and compromisers who accommodated to the Church of England. Their resolve to adhere strictly to God's plan charged nearly every feature of life in seventeenth-century New England with a distinctive, high-voltage piety.

The new colonists had "all things to do, as in the beginning of the world," as Winthrop's son wrote later. Unlike the early Chesapeake settlers, the first Massachusetts Bay colonists encountered few Indians because the local population had been almost entirely exterminated by an epidemic. Still, many of the colonists succumbed to diseases. During the first year, more than two hundred settlers died, including one of Winthrop's sons and eleven of his servants. Winthrop himself remained confident and optimistic. He wrote to his wife that "I like so well to be heer as I do not repent my comminge.... I would not have altered my course, though I had forseene all these Afflictions." And each year from 1630 to 1640, ship after ship followed in the wake of Winthrop's fleet, bringing more than twenty thousand new settlers.

Often, when the Church of England cracked down on a Puritan minister in England, he and many of his followers moved together to New England. Smaller groups of English Puritans moved to the Chesapeake and elsewhere in the colonies, including New Amsterdam (present-day New York). By 1640, New England had one of the highest ratios of preachers to population in all of Christendom. Several ministers sought to carry the message of Christianity to the Indians in order to replace what missionary John Eliot termed the Indians' "unfixed, confused, and ungoverned . . . life, uncivilized and unsubdued to labor and order" and established "praying towns" to encourage Indians to adopt English ways. But the colonists focused far less on saving Indians' souls than on saving their own.

The occupations of New England immigrants reflected the social origins of English Puritans. On the whole, the immigrants came from the middle ranks of English society. The vast majority were either farmers or tradesmen. Indentured servants, whose numbers dominated the Chesapeake settlers, accounted for only about a fifth of those headed for New England. Most New England immigrants paid their way to Massachusetts. They were encouraged by the promise of bounty in New England reported in Winthrop's letter to his son: "Here can be no want of anything to those who bring means to raise [it] out of the earth and sea."

In contrast to Chesapeake newcomers, New England immigrants usually arrived as families. In fact, more Puritans came with family members than did any other group of immigrants in all of American history. Unlike immigrants to the Chesapeake, women and children made up a solid majority in New England.

As Winthrop reminded the first settlers in his *Arbella* sermon, each family was a "little commonwealth" that mirrored the hierarchy among all God's creatures. Just as humankind was subordinate to God, so young people were subordinate to their elders, children to their parents, and wives to their husbands. The immigrants' family ties reinforced their religious beliefs with the interlocking institutions of family, church, and community.

> **REVIEW**   What was a "little commonwealth," and why was it so important to New England settlement?

▶ The Evolution of New England Society

The New England colonists, unlike their counterparts in the Chesapeake, settled in small towns, usually located on the coast or by a river (see Map 4.1). Massachusetts Bay colonists founded 133 towns during the seventeenth century, each with one or more churches. Church members' fervent piety, buttressed by the insti-

tutions of local government, enforced remarkable religious and social conformity in the small New England settlements. During the century, tensions within the Puritan faith and changes in New England communities splintered religious orthodoxy and weakened Puritan zeal. By 1700, however, Puritanism retained a distinctive influence in New England.

Church, Covenant, and Conformity

Puritans believed that a church consisted of men and women who had entered a solemn covenant with one another and with God. Winthrop and others who signed the covenant of the first Boston church in 1630 agreed to "Promisse, and bind our selves, to walke in all our wayes according to the Rule of the Gospell, and in all sincere Conformity to His holy Ordinaunces." Each new member of the covenant had to persuade existing members that she or he had fully experienced conversion.

Puritans embraced a distinctive version of Protestantism derived from **Calvinism**, the doctrines of John Calvin, who insisted that Christians strictly discipline their behavior to conform to God's commandments announced in the Bible. Like Calvin, Puritans believed in **predestination**—the idea that the all-powerful God, before the creation of the world, decided which few human souls would receive eternal life. Only God knows the identity of these fortunate predestined individuals—the "elect" or "saints." Nothing a person did in his or her lifetime could alter God's choice or provide assurance that the person was predestined for salvation with the elect or damned to hell with the doomed multitude.

Despite the looming uncertainty about God's choice of the elect, Puritans believed that if a person lived a rigorously godly life—constantly winning the daily battle against sin—his or her behavior was likely to be a hint, a visible sign, that he or she was one of God's chosen few. Puritans thought that "sainthood" would become visible in individuals' behavior, especially if they were privileged to know God's Word as revealed in the Bible.

The connection between sainthood and saintly behavior, however, was far from certain. Some members of the elect, Puritans believed, had not heard God's Word. One reason Puritans required all town residents to attend church services was to enlighten anyone who was ignorant of God's Truth. The slippery relationship between saintly behavior and God's predestined election caused

THE
World turn'd upfide down:
OR
A briefe defcription of the ridiculous Fafhions of thefe duftacted Times.

By T. J. a well-willer to King, Parliament and Kingdom.

Puritans to worry constantly that individuals who acted like saints were fooling themselves and others. Nevertheless, Puritans thought that **visible saints**—persons who passed their demanding tests of conversion and church membership—probably were among God's elect.

Members of Puritan churches ardently hoped that God had chosen them to receive eternal life and tried to demonstrate saintly behavior. Their covenant bound them to help one another attain salvation and to discipline the entire community by saintly standards. Church members kept an eye on the behavior of everybody in town. By overseeing every aspect of life, the visible saints enforced a remarkable degree of righteous conformity in Puritan communities. Total conformity, however, was never achieved. Ardent Puritans differed among themselves, and non-Puritans shirked orthodox rules, such as the Roxbury servant who declared that "if hell were ten times hotter, [I] would rather be there than [I] would serve [my] master."

Despite the central importance of religion, churches played no direct role in the civil government of New England communities. Puritans did not want to mimic the Church of England, which they considered a puppet of the king rather than an independent body that served the Lord. They were determined to insulate New England churches from the contaminating influence of the civil state and its merely human laws. Ministers were prohibited from holding government office.

Puritans had no qualms, however, about their religious beliefs influencing New England governments. As much as possible, the Puritans tried to bring public life into conformity with their view of God's law. For example, fines were issued for Sabbath-breaking activities such as working, traveling, playing a flute, smoking a pipe, and visiting neighbors.

Puritans mandated other purifications of what they considered corrupt English practices. (See "Visualizing History," page 86.) They refused to celebrate Christmas or Easter because the Bible did not mention either one. They outlawed religious wedding ceremonies; couples were married by a magistrate in a civil ceremony. They banned cards, dice, shuffleboard, and other games

Targets of Puritan Reform

Since medieval times, Christian churches throughout Europe used magnificent architecture and stained glass to display the majesty of the Almighty, as illustrated by the photo from the interior of Canterbury Cathedral in England.

Stained glass images like the one from Canterbury of Adam shown here, illustrated Bible passages for the multitude of illiterate worshipers. Adam, for example, dramatizes the story of God's creation of man and, after Adam sinned, God's consignment of Adam to toil to bring forth abundance from the earth.

Originally a Catholic church, Canterbury Cathedral became the headquarters of the protestant Church of England when King Henry VIII—shown at the left of the panel of three figures —launched the English Reformation and declared the Archbishop of Canterbury the religious head of the Church of England. Henry appointed Thomas Cranmer—the second of the three figures in the panel—Archbishop of Canterbury in 1532, and Cranmer led the new Church of England to create distinctive non-Catholic doctrines and religious rituals, such as reading from the Book of Common Prayer. Queen Mary, a Catholic, had Cranmer burnt at the stake for heresy in 1556.

Almost eighty years later, King Charles I sought to repress the Puritan challenge to the Church of England, and in 1633 appointed William Laud—the figure on the right of the panel—Archbishop of Canterbury. Laud persecuted Puritans for deviating from the orthodox forms of worship of the Church of England, which the Puritans protested as heretical.

Puritans believed the awe-inspiring architecture of churches like Canterbury Cathedral celebrated the handiwork of mankind, not God, and represented an unholy false pride in human achievement. Puritans favored plain churches with virtually no ornamentation that would divert the attention of worshippers. According to the Puritans, images of Bible stories drew people away from reading the Bible for themselves, which was the only way

Partial Interior View of Canterbury Cathedral

to learn about God's Word. In addition, images like Adam or the panel of king and archbishops encouraged idolatry, which the Bible prohibits, and stained glass panels of leaders like King Henry VIII embodied the state sponsorship of the Church of England which the Puritans hated.

of chance, as well as music and dancing. "Mixt or Promiscuous Dancing . . . of Men and Women" could not be tolerated since "the unchaste Touches and Gesticulations used by Dancers have a palpable tendency to that which is evil."

Government by Puritans for Puritanism

It is only a slight exaggeration to say that seventeenth-century New England was governed by Puritans for Puritanism. The charter of the Massachusetts Bay Company empowered the company's stockholders, known as freemen, to meet as a body known as the General Court and make the laws needed to govern the company's affairs. The colonists transformed this arrangement for running a joint-stock company into a structure for governing the colony. Hoping to ensure that godly men would decide government policies, the General Court expanded the number of freemen in 1631 to include all male church members. Only freemen had the right to vote for governor and other officials. When the size of the General Court grew too large to meet conveniently, the freemen agreed in 1634 that each town would send two deputies to the General Court to act as the colony's legislative assembly. All other men were classified as "inhabitants," who had the right to vote, hold office, and participate fully in town government.

A "town meeting," composed of a town's inhabitants and freemen, chose the selectmen who administered local affairs. New England town meetings routinely practiced a level of popular participation in political life that was unprecedented elsewhere in the world during the seventeenth

Puritans' rejection of common forms of worship practiced by the Church of England made them targets for persecution in England and prompted thousands to emigrate to New England during the 1630s.

SOURCE: Canterbury Cathedral interior: Dan Kitwood/ Getty Images; Adam: Canterbury Cathedral, Kent, UK/ The Bridgeman Art Library; Stained Glass Panel: Art Directors & TRIP/Alamy.

Stained Glass Panel Depicting (left to right) Henry VIII, Thomas Cranmer, and William Laud

Adam

Questions for Analysis

1. What would the image of Adam have told illiterate worshippers about the Bible story of God's creation of mankind?

2. What religious attitudes are suggested by the architecture and ornamentation shown in the photo of an interior of Canterbury Cathedral?

3. How did the images of Henry VIII and Archbishops Cranmer and Laud signify religious doctrines that Puritans rejected?

Connect to the Big Idea

C How did Puritans' religious ideas shape their desire to reform the Church of England and to build a new, holy, city on the hill in New England?

century. Almost every adult man could speak out and vote in town meetings, but all women—even church members—were prohibited from voting. This widespread political participation tended to reinforce conformity to Puritan ideals.

The General Court granted land for town sites to pious petitioners, once the Indians agreed to relinquish their claim to the land, usually in exchange for manufactured goods. William Pynchon, for example, purchased the site of Springfield, Massachusetts, from the Agawam Indians for "eighteen fathams [arm's lengths] of Wampum [strings of shell-beads used in trade], eighteen coates, 18 hatchets, 18 hoes, [and] 18 knives." Town founders then apportioned land among themselves and any newcomers they approved. Most family plots clustered between roughly fifty to one hundred acres, resulting in a more nearly equal distri-

bution of land in New England than in the Chesapeake.

The physical layout of New England towns encouraged settlers to look inward toward their neighbors, multiplying the opportunities for godly vigilance. Most people considered the forest that lay just beyond every settler's house an alien environment. Footpaths connecting one town to another were so rudimentary that even John Winthrop once got lost and spent a sleepless night in the forest only a half mile from his house.

The Splintering of Puritanism

Almost from the beginning, John Winthrop and other leaders had difficulty enforcing their views of Puritan orthodoxy. In England, persecution as a dissenting minority had unified Puritan

Old Ship Meeting House
Built in Hingham, Massachusetts, in 1681, this meeting house is one of the oldest surviving buildings used for church services in English North America. The unadorned walls and windows reflect the austere religious aesthetic of New England Puritanism. The family pews mark boundaries of kinship and piety visible to all. The elevated pulpit signals the superiority of God's word as preached by the minister. Photo © Steve Dunwell.

voices in opposition to the Church of England. In New England, the promise of a godly society and the Puritans' emphasis on individual Bible study led toward different visions of godliness. Puritan leaders, however, interpreted dissent as an error caused either by a misguided believer or by the malevolent power of Satan. As one Puritan minister proclaimed, "The Scripture saith . . . there is no Truth but one."

Shortly after banishing Roger Williams, Winthrop confronted another dissenter, this time a devout Puritan woman steeped in Scripture and absorbed by religious questions: Anne Hutchinson. The mother of fourteen children, Hutchinson served her neighbors as a midwife and in 1634 began to give weekly lectures on recent sermons attended by women who gathered at her home. Hutchinson lectured on the "covenant of grace"—the idea that individuals could be saved only by God's grace in choosing them to be members of the elect. This familiar Puritan doctrine contrasted with the covenant of works, the erroneous belief that a person's behavior—one's works—could win God's favor and ultimately earn a person salvation.

The meetings at Hutchinson's house alarmed her nearest neighbor, Governor John Winthrop, who believed that she was subverting the good order of the colony. In 1637, Winthrop had formal charges brought against Hutchinson and denounced her lectures as "not tolerable nor comely in the sight of God nor fitting for your sex." He told her, "You have stept out of your place, you have rather bine a Husband than a Wife and a preacher than a Hearer; and a Magistrate than a Subject."

Winthrop and other Puritan elders referred to Hutchinson and her followers as **antinomians**, people who believed that Christians could be saved by faith alone and did not need to act in accordance with God's law as set forth in the Bible and as interpreted by the colony's leaders. Hutchinson nimbly defended herself against the accusation of antinomianism. Yes, she acknowledged, she believed that men and women were saved by faith alone; but no, she did not deny the need to obey God's law. "The Lord hath let me see which was the clear ministry and which the wrong," she said. How could she tell, Winthrop asked, which ministry was which? "By an immediate revelation," she replied, "by the voice of [God's] own spirit to my soul." Winthrop seized this statement as the heresy of prophecy, the view that God revealed his will directly to a believer instead of exclusively through the Bible, as every right-minded Puritan knew.

In 1638, the Boston church formally excommunicated Hutchinson. The minister decreed, "I doe cast you out and . . . deliver you up to Satan." Banished, Hutchinson and her family moved first to Roger Williams's Rhode Island and then to present-day New York, where she and most of her family were killed by Indians.

The strains within Puritanism exemplified by Anne Hutchinson and Roger Williams caused communities to splinter repeatedly during the seventeenth century. Thomas Hooker, a prominent minister, clashed with Winthrop and other leaders over the composition of the church. Hooker argued that men and women who lived godly lives should be admitted to church membership even if they had not experienced conversion. In 1636, Hooker led an exodus of more than eight hundred colonists from Massachusetts to the Connecticut River valley, where they founded Hartford and neighboring towns. In 1639, the towns adopted the Fundamental Orders of Connecticut, a quasi-constitution that could be altered by the vote of freemen, who did not have to be church members, though nearly all of them were.

Other Puritan churches divided and subdivided throughout the seventeenth century as acrimony developed over doctrine and church government. Sometimes churches split over the appointment of a controversial minister. These schisms arose from ambiguities and tensions within Puritan belief. As the colonies matured, other tensions developed as well.

Religious Controversies and Economic Changes

A revolutionary transformation in the fortunes of Puritans in England had profound consequences in New England. Disputes between King Charles I and Parliament, which was dominated by Puritans, escalated in 1642 to civil war in England, a conflict known as the **Puritan Revolution**. Parliamentary forces led by the staunch Puritan Oliver Cromwell were victorious, executing Charles I in 1649 and proclaiming England a Puritan republic. From 1649 to 1660, England's rulers were not monarchs who suppressed Puritanism but believers who championed it.

When the Puritan Revolution began, the stream of immigrants to New England dwindled to a trickle, creating hard times for the colonists. They could no longer consider themselves a city on a hill setting a godly example for humankind. Puritans in England, not New England, were reforming English society. Furthermore, when immigrant ships became rare, the colonists faced sky-high prices for scarce English goods and few customers for their own colonial products. As they searched to find new products and markets, they established the enduring patterns of New England's economy.

New England's rocky soil and short growing season ruled out cultivating the southern colonies' crops of tobacco and rice that found ready markets in Atlantic ports. Exports that New Englanders could not get from the soil they took instead from the forest and the sea. By the 1640s, furbearing animals had become scarce unless traders ventured far beyond the frontiers of English settlement. Trees from the seemingly limitless forests of New England proved a longer-lasting resource. Masts for ships and staves for barrels of Spanish wine and West Indian sugar were crafted from New England timber.

The most important New England export was fish. Dried, salted codfish from the rich North Atlantic fishing grounds found markets in southern Europe and the West Indies. The fish trade also stimulated colonial shipbuilding and trained generations of fishermen, sailors, and merchants. But the lives of most New England colonists revolved around their farms, churches, and families.

Although immigration came to a standstill in the 1640s, the colonial population continued to boom, doubling every twenty years. In New England, almost everyone married, and women often had eight or nine children. Long, cold winters minimized the presence of warm-weather ailments such as malaria and yellow fever, so the mortality rate was lower than in the South. By the end of the seventeenth century, the New England population roughly equaled that of the southern colonies (over 100,000 colonists).

During the second half of the seventeenth century, under the pressures of steady population growth (Figure 4.1) and integration into the Atlantic economy, the red-hot piety of the founders cooled. After 1640, the population grew faster than church membership. Boston's churches in 1650 could house only about a third of the city's residents. By the 1680s, women were the majority of church members throughout New England. In some towns, only 15 percent of the adult men were members. A growing fraction of New Englanders, especially men, practiced what one historian has called "horse-shed Christianity." They attended sermons but afterward loitered outside near the horse shed, gossiping about the weather, fishing, their crops, or the scandalous behavior of neighbors. This slackening of piety led the Puritan minister Michael Wigglesworth to ask, in verse:

> How is it that
> I find In stead of holiness Carnality;
> In stead of heavenly frames an Earthly mind,
> For burning zeal luke-warm Indifferency,
> For flaming love, key-cold Dead-heartedness. . . .
> Whence cometh it, that Pride, and Luxurie
> Debate, Deceit, Contention and Strife,

False-dealing, Covetousness, Hypocrisie
   . . . amongst them are so rife,
   . . . that an honest man can hardly
   Trust his Brother?

Most alarming to Puritan leaders, many of the children of the visible saints of Winthrop's generation failed to experience conversion and attain full church membership. Puritans tended to assume that sainthood was inherited—that the children of visible saints were probably also among the elect. As these children grew up during the 1640s and 1650s, however, they seldom experienced the inward transformation that signaled conversion and qualification for church membership. The problem of declining church membership and the watering-down of Puritan orthodoxy became urgent during the 1650s when the children of saints, who had grown to adulthood in New England but had not experienced conversion, began to have children themselves. Their sons and daughters—the grandchildren of the founders of the colony—could not receive the protection that baptism afforded against the terrors of death because their parents had not experienced conversion.

FIGURE 4.1   **Population of the English North American Colonies in the Seventeenth Century**

The colonial population grew at a steadily accelerating rate during the seventeenth century. New England and the southern colonies each accounted for about half the total colonial population until after 1680, when growth in Pennsylvania and New York contributed to a surge in the population of the middle colonies.

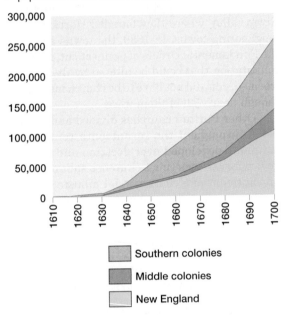

Southern colonies

Middle colonies

New England

VISUAL ACTIVITY

New England Mother and Child

This seventeenth-century painting of Elizabeth Freake and her baby Mary illustrates the evolution of New England society away from the Puritan austerity of the founders and toward worldly elegance and display. Both mother and daughter appear prosperous, healthy, and somewhat proud. Worcester Art Museum, Massachusetts, USA/The Bridgeman Art Library.

READING THE IMAGE: What does the clothing of Elizabeth and Mary suggest about their religion?

CONNECTIONS: Why did New England's Puritan zeal diminish in the latter third of the seventeenth century?

Puritan churches debated what to do. To allow anyone, even the child of a saint, to become a church member without conversion was an unthinkable retreat from fundamental Puritan doctrine. In 1662, a synod of Massachusetts ministers reached a compromise known as the **Halfway Covenant**. Unconverted children of saints would be permitted to become "halfway" church members. Like regular church members, they could baptize their infants. But unlike full church members, they could not participate in communion or have the voting privileges of church membership. The Halfway Covenant generated a controversy that sputtered through Puritan churches for the remainder of the century. With the Halfway Covenant, Puritan churches came to terms with the lukewarm piety that had replaced the founders' burning zeal.

Nonetheless, New England communities continued to enforce piety with holy rigor. Beginning in 1656, small bands of **Quakers**—members of the Society of Friends, as they called themselves—began to arrive in Massachusetts. Quakers believed that God spoke directly to each individual through an "inner light" and that individuals needed neither a preacher nor the Bible to discover God's Word. Maintaining that all human beings were equal in God's eyes, Quakers refused to conform to mere temporal powers such as laws and governments unless God requested otherwise. Women often took a leading role in Quaker meetings, in contrast to Puritan congregations, where women usually outnumbered men but remained subordinate.

New England communities treated Quakers with ruthless severity. Some Quakers were branded on the face "with a red-hot iron with [an] H. for heresie." When Quakers refused to leave Massachusetts, Boston officials hanged four of them between 1659 and 1661.

New Englanders' partial success in realizing the promise of a godly society ultimately undermined the intense appeal of Puritanism. In the pious Puritan communities of New England, leaders tried to eliminate sin. In the process, they diminished the sense of utter human depravity that was the wellspring of Puritanism. By 1700, New Englanders did not doubt that human beings sinned, but they were more concerned with the sins of others than with their own.

Witch trials held in Salem, Massachusetts, signaled the erosion of religious confidence and assurance. From the beginning of English settlement in the New World, more than 95 percent of all legal accusations of witchcraft occurred in New England, a hint of the Puritans' preoccupation with sin and evil. The most notorious witchcraft trials took place in Salem in 1692, when witnesses accused more than one hundred people of witchcraft, a capital crime. (See

Witches Show Their Love for Satan
Witches debased themselves by standing in line to kiss Satan's buttocks—or so it was popularly believed. This seventeenth-century print portrays Satan with clawlike hands and feet, the tail of a rodent, the wings of a bat, and the head of a lustful ram attached to the torso of a man. Notice that women predominate among the witches eager to express their devotion to Satan. The Granger Collection, New York.

Hunting Witches in Salem, Massachusetts

In the summer of 1692, many people in and around Salem, Massachusetts, accused dozens of their neighbors and kinfolk of being witches. Officials convened a special court to hear the testimony of the accusers and to examine the accused. In the end, nineteen convicted witches were hanged, and more than 150 accused witches crammed the jails before the trials were finally called off.

DOCUMENT 1
Witnesses against Accused Witch Susanna Martin, 1692

Neighbors lined up to give testimony that, in their minds, proved that the accused were witches. Like many other accused people, Susanna Martin pleaded not guilty to witchcraft. The court, persuaded by the testimony of witnesses, sentenced her to death, and she was executed on July 19, 1692.

Bernard Peache testify'd, That being in Bed on a Lords-day Night, he heard a scrabbling at the Window, whereat he then saw, *Susanna Martin* come in, and jump down upon the Floor. She took hold of this Deponents Feet, and drawing his Body up into an Heap, she lay upon him, near Two Hours; in all which time he could neither speak nor stirr. At length, when he could begin to move, he laid hold on her Hand, and pulling it up to his mouth, he bit three of her Fingers, as he judged, unto the Bone. Whereupon she went from the Chamber, down the Stairs, out at the Door. . . .

John Kembal . . . Being desirous to furnish himself with a Dog, he applied himself to buy one of this Martin. . . . But she not letting him have his Choice [Kembal went to another neighbor to get a puppy]. Within a few days after, [when] this *Kembal* . . . came below the Meeting-House, there appeared unto him, a little thing like a *Puppy*, of a Darkish Colour; and it shot Backwards and forwards between his Leggs. He had the Courage to use all possible Endeavors of Cutting it, with his Axe; but he could not Hit it. . . . Going a little further, there appeared unto him a Black Puppy, somewhat bigger than the first; but Black as Cole. Its motions were quicker than those of his Ax; it Flew at his Belly and away; then at his Throat, also over his Shoulder. . . . His heart now began to fail him, and he thought the Dog would have Tore his Throat out. But he recovered himself, and called upon God in his Distress; and Naming the Name of JESUS CHRIST, it Vanished away at once. . . . [The next day, Susanna Martin told other people that he had been frightened by puppies, although] Kembal [said he] had mentioned the Matter to no Creature Living.

Joseph Ring . . . has been strangely carried about by *Demons*, from one *Witch-Meeting* to another, for near two years together. . . . Afterwards . . . this poor man would be visited with unknown shapes . . . which would force him away with them, unto unknown Places, where he saw

"Documenting the American Promise.") Bewitched young girls shrieked in pain, their limbs twisted into strange contortions, as they pointed out the witches who tortured them. According to the trial court record, the bewitched girls declared that "the shape of [one accused witch] did oftentimes very grievously pinch them, choke them, bite them, and afflict them; urging them to write their names in a book"— the devil's book. Most of the accused witches were older women, and virtually all of them were well known to their accusers. The Salem court hanged nineteen accused witches and pressed one to death, signaling enduring belief in the supernatural origins of evil and gnawing doubt about the strength of Puritan New Englanders' faith. Why else, after all, had so many New Englanders succumbed to what their accusers and the judges believed were the temptations of Satan?

REVIEW Why did Massachusetts Puritans adopt the Halfway Covenant?

meetings, Feastings, Dancings. . . . When he was brought into these Hellish meetings, one of the First things they still did unto him, was to give him a knock on the Back, where-upon he was . . . as if Bound with chains, uncapable of Stirring out of the place, till they should Release him. . . . There often came to him a man, who presented him a Book, whereto he would have him set his Hand; promising to him, that he should then have even what he would; and presenting him with all the delectable Things, persons, and places that he could imagine. But he refusing to subscribe, the business would end with dreadful Shapes, Noises and Screechings, which almost scared him out of his witts. . . . He saw the Prisoner [Susanna Martin], at several of those Hellish Randezvouzes. Note, This Woman was one of the most Impudent, Scurrilous, wicked creatures in the world & she did now throughout her whole Trial, discover herself to be such an one. Yet when she was asked what she had to say for her self, her Cheef Plea was, *That she had Led a most virtuous and Holy Life.*

Source: Cotton Mather, *The Wonders of the Invisible World* (Boston, 1692), 115–26.

Document 2
Robert Calef, *More Wonders of the Invisible World*, 1700

A few New Englanders spoke out against the witch-hunt as the persecution of innocent people. Robert Calef, a Boston merchant, wrote a scathing criticism of the witch trials and their supporters.

And now to sum up all in a few words, we have seen a biggotted zeal, stirring up a blind, and most bloody rage, not against enemies, or irreligious, profligate persons—but . . . against as virtuous and religious as any they have left behind them in this country . . . and this by the testimony of vile varlets, as not only were known before, but have been further apparent since, by their manifest lives, whoredoms, incest &c. The accusations of these, from their spectral sight, being the chief evidence against those that suffered; in which accusations they were upheld by both magistrates and ministers, so long as they apprehended themselves in no danger. And then, tho' they could defend neither the doctrine nor the practice, yet none of them have in such a publick manner as the case requires, testified against either; tho', at the same time they could not but be sensible what a stain and lasting infamy they have brought upon the whole country, to the indangering of the future welfare not only of this but of other places, induced by their example . . . occasioning the great dishonour and blasphemy of the name of God . . . and as a natural effect thereof, to the great increase of Atheism.

Source: Robert Calef, *More Wonders of the Invisible World* (London, 1700), unpaginated "Epistle to the Reader."

Questions for Analysis and Debate

1. What persuaded witnesses against Susanna Martin that she was a witch? How might a critic such as Robert Calef have responded to the testimony of these witnesses? How might the witnesses have explained Martin's claim that she led "a most virtuous and Holy Life"?

2. What do these documents suggest about the status of Christianity in New England in the late seventeenth century? Why did witch-hunters believe that the devil was such a threat, when Calef believed that the witch-hunters themselves were the greater danger?

Connect to the Big Idea

C Why did some Puritans accuse their friends and neighbors of being witches?

▶ The Founding of the Middle Colonies

South of New England and north of the Chesapeake, a group of middle colonies were founded in the last third of the seventeenth century. Before the 1670s, few Europeans settled in the region. For the first two-thirds of the seventeenth century, the most important European outpost in the area was the relatively small Dutch colony of New Netherland. By 1700, however, the English monarchy had seized New Netherland, renamed it New York, and encouraged the creation of a Quaker colony in Pennsylvania led by William Penn. Unlike the New England colonies, the middle colonies of New York, New Jersey, and Pennsylvania originated as land grants by the English monarch to one or more proprietors, who then possessed both the land and the extensive, almost monarchical, powers of government (Map 4.2). These middle colonies attracted settlers of more diverse European origins and religious faiths than were found in New England.

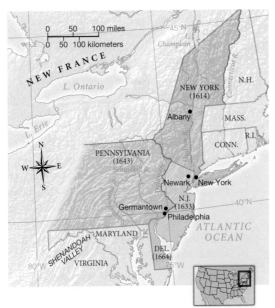

MAP 4.2

Middle Colonies in the Seventeenth Century

For the most part, settlers in the middle colonies in the seventeenth century clustered along the Hudson and Delaware rivers. The geographic extent of the colonies shown in this map reflects land grants authorized in England. Most of this area was inhabited by Native Americans rather than colonists.

From New Netherland to New York

In 1609, the Dutch East India Company dispatched Henry Hudson to search for a Northwest Passage to the Orient. Hudson ventured up the large river that now bears his name until it dwindled to a stream that obviously did not lead to China. A decade later, the Dutch government granted the West India Company—a group of Dutch merchants and shippers—exclusive rights to trade with the Western Hemisphere. In 1626, Peter Minuit, the resident director of the company, purchased Manhattan Island from the Manhate Indians for trade goods worth the equivalent of a dozen beaver pelts. New Amsterdam, the small settlement established at the southern tip of Manhattan Island, became the principal trading center in **New Netherland** and the colony's headquarters.

Unlike the English colonies, New Netherland did not attract many European immigrants. Like New England and the Chesapeake colonies, New Netherland never realized its sponsors' dreams of great profits. The company tried to stimulate immigration by granting patroonships—allotments of eighteen miles of land along the Hudson River—to wealthy stockholders who would bring fifty families to the colony and settle them as serflike tenants on their huge domains. Only one patroonship succeeded; the others failed to attract settlers, and the company eventually recovered much of the land.

Though few in number, New Netherlanders were remarkably diverse, especially compared with the homogeneous English settlers to the north and south. Religious dissenters and immigrants from Holland, Sweden, France, Germany, and elsewhere made their way to the colony. A minister of the Dutch Reformed Church complained to his superiors in Holland that several groups of Jews had recently arrived, adding to the religious mixture of "Papists, Mennonites and Lutherans among the Dutch [and] many Puritans . . . and many other atheists . . . who conceal themselves under the name of Christians."

The West India Company struggled to govern the motley colonists. Peter Stuyvesant, governor from 1647 to 1664, pointed out to company officials in Holland that "the *English* and *French* colonies are continued and populated by their own nation and countrymen and consequently [are] bound together more firmly and united," while the "colonies in *New-Netherland* are only gradually and slowly peopled by the scrapings of all sorts of nationalities (few excepted), who consequently have the least interest in the welfare and maintenance of the commonwealth." Stuyvesant tried to enforce conformity to the Dutch Reformed Church, but the company—eager for more immigrants—declared that "the consciences of men should be free and unshackled," making a virtue of New Netherland necessity. The company never permitted the colony's settlers to form a representative government. Instead, the company appointed government officials who established policies, including taxes, that many colonists deeply resented.

In 1664, New Netherland became New York. Charles II, who became king of England in 1660 when Parliament restored the monarchy, gave his brother James, the Duke of York, an enormous grant of land that included New Netherland. The duke quickly organized a small fleet of warships, which appeared off Manhattan Island in late summer 1664, and demanded that Stuyvesant surrender. With little choice, he did.

N. AMSTERDAM, ou N.IORK
in Amerig.

VISUAL ACTIVITY

New Amsterdam

The settlement on Manhattan Island appears in the background of this 1673 Dutch portrait of New Amsterdam. In the foreground, the Dutch artist placed native inhabitants of the mainland, drawing them to resemble Africans rather than Lenni Lenape (Delaware) Indians. The portrait contrasts orderly, efficient, businesslike New Amsterdam with the exotic natural environment of America. © Collection of the New-York Historical Society, USA/The Bridgeman Art Library.

READING THE IMAGE: What features of New Amsterdam contrast with the natural environment of Native Americans?

CONNECTIONS: How did New Amsterdam differ from New England?

As the new proprietor of the colony, the Duke of York exercised almost the same unlimited authority over the colony as had the West India Company, although the duke never set foot in the colony. Like the Dutch, the duke permitted "all persons of what Religion soever, quietly to inhabit . . . provided they give no disturbance to the publique peace, nor doe molest or disquiet others in the free exercise of their religion." This policy of religious toleration was less an affirmation of liberty of conscience than a recognition of the reality of the most heterogeneous colony in seventeenth-century North America.

New Jersey and Pennsylvania

The creation of New York led indirectly to the founding of two other middle colonies, New Jersey and Pennsylvania. In 1664, the Duke of York subdivided his grant and gave the portion between the Hudson and Delaware rivers to two of his friends. The proprietors of this new colony, New Jersey, quarreled and called in a prominent English Quaker, William Penn, to arbitrate their dispute. Penn eventually worked out a settlement that continued New Jersey's proprietary government. In the process, Penn became intensely interested in what he termed

Quaker Couple
This seventeenth-century picture of a Quaker couple illustrates their plain clothing and modest habits. The woman and man do not appear poor; their clothing fits them and is well made, but the colors in their clothing are somber and muted, unlike the richly ornamented and brightly colored clothes worn by prosperous non-Quakers. Private Collection/The Stapleton Collection/The Bridgeman Art Library.

a "holy experiment" of establishing a genuinely Quaker colony in America.

Unlike most Quakers, William Penn came from an eminent family. His father had served both Cromwell and Charles II and had been knighted. Born in 1644, the younger Penn trained for a military career, but the ideas of dissenters from the reestablished Church of England appealed to him, and he became a devout Quaker. By 1680 Penn had published fifty books and spoken at countless public meetings, but he had failed to win public toleration for Quakers in England.

The Quakers' concept of an open, generous God who made his love equally available to all people continually brought them into conflict with the English government. Quaker leaders were ordinary men and women, not specially trained preachers. Quakers allowed women to assume positions of religious leadership. "In souls there is no sex," they said. Since all people were equal in the spiritual realm, Quakers considered social hierarchy false and evil. They called everyone "friend" and shook hands instead of curtsying or removing their hats—even when meeting the king. These customs enraged many non-Quakers and provoked innumerable beatings and worse. Penn was jailed four times for such offenses, once for nine months.

Despite his many run-ins with the government, Penn remained on good terms with Charles II. Partly to rid England of the troublesome Quakers, in 1681 Charles made Penn the proprietor of a new colony of some 45,000 square miles called Pennsylvania.

Toleration and Diversity in Pennsylvania

Quakers flocked to Pennsylvania in numbers exceeded only by the great Puritan migration to New England fifty years earlier. Between 1682 and 1685, nearly eight thousand immigrants arrived. Penn wrote in 1685 that the settlers were "a collection of divers nations in Europe: as, French, Dutch, Germans, Swedes, Danes, Finns, Scotch-Irish, and English; and of the last equal to all the rest." The settlers represented a cross section of the artisans, farmers, and laborers who predominated among English Quakers.

Quaker missionaries also encouraged immigrants from the European continent, and many came, giving Pennsylvania greater ethnic diversity than any other English colony except New York. The Quaker colony prospered, and the capital city, Philadelphia, soon rivaled New York as a center of commerce. By 1700, the city's five thousand inhabitants participated in a thriving trade exporting flour and other food products to the West Indies and importing English textiles and manufactured goods.

Penn was determined to live in peace with the Indians who inhabited the region. His Indian policy expressed his Quaker ideals and contrasted sharply with the hostile policies of the other English colonies. As he explained to the chief of the Lenni Lenape (Delaware) Indians, "God has written his law in our hearts, by which we are taught and commanded to love and help and do good to one another . . . [and] I desire to enjoy [Pennsylvania lands] with your love and consent." Penn instructed his agents to obtain the Indians' consent by purchasing their land, respecting their claims, and dealing with them fairly.

Penn declared that the first principle of government was that every settler would "enjoy the free possession of his or her faith and exercise of worship towards God." Accordingly, Pennsylvania tolerated Protestant sects of all kinds as well as Roman Catholicism. All voters and officeholders had to be Christians, but the government did not compel settlers to attend religious services, as in Massachusetts, or to pay taxes to maintain a state-supported church, as in Virginia.

Despite its toleration and diversity, Pennsylvania was as much a Quaker colony as New England was a stronghold of Puritanism. "Government seems to me a part of religion itself," Penn wrote, "for there is no power but of God. The powers that be, are ordained of God: whosoever therefore resists the power [of government] resists the ordinance of God." Penn believed that government had two basic purposes: "to terrify evildoers . . . [and] to cherish those that do well." Penn had no hesitation about using civil government to enforce religious morality. One of the colony's first laws provided severe punishment for "all such offenses against God, as swearing, cursing, lying, profane talking, [and] drunkenness . . . which excite the people to rudeness, cruelty, looseness, and irreligion."

As proprietor, Penn had extensive powers subject only to review by the king. He appointed a governor, who maintained the proprietor's power to veto any laws passed by the colonial council, which was elected by property owners who possessed at least one hundred acres of land or who paid taxes. The council had the power to originate laws and administer all the affairs of government. A popularly elected assembly served as a check on the council; its members had the authority to reject or approve laws framed by the council.

Penn stressed that the exact form of government mattered less than the men who served in it. In Penn's eyes, "good men" staffed Pennsylvania's government because Quakers dominated elective and appointive offices. Quakers, of course, differed among themselves. Members of the assembly struggled to win the right to debate and amend laws, especially tax laws. They finally won the battle in 1701 when a new Charter of Privileges gave the proprietor the power to appoint the council and in turn stripped the council of all its former powers and gave them to the assembly, which became the only single-house legislature in all the English colonies.

REVIEW   How did Quaker ideals shape the colony of Pennsylvania?

▶ The Colonies and the English Empire

Proprietary grants to faraway lands were a cheap way for the king to reward friends. As the colonies grew, however, the grants became more valuable. After 1660, the king took initiatives to channel colonial trade through English hands and to consolidate royal authority over colonial governments. Occasioned by such economic and political considerations and triggered by King Philip's War between colonists and Native Americans, these initiatives defined the basic relationship between the colonies and England that endured until the American Revolution (Map 4.3).

Royal Regulation of Colonial Trade

English economic policies toward the colonies were designed to yield customs revenues for the monarchy and profitable business for English

MAP ACTIVITY

Map 4.3 American Colonies at the End of the Seventeenth Century

By the end of the seventeenth century, settlers inhabited a narrow band of land that stretched from Boston to Norfolk, with pockets of settlement farther south. The colonies' claims to enormous tracts of land to the west were contested by Native Americans as well as by France and Spain.

READING THE MAP: What geographic feature acted as the western boundary for colonial territorial claims? Which colonies were the most settled and which the least?

CONNECTIONS: The map divides the colonies into four regions. Can you think of an alternative organization? On what criteria would it be based?

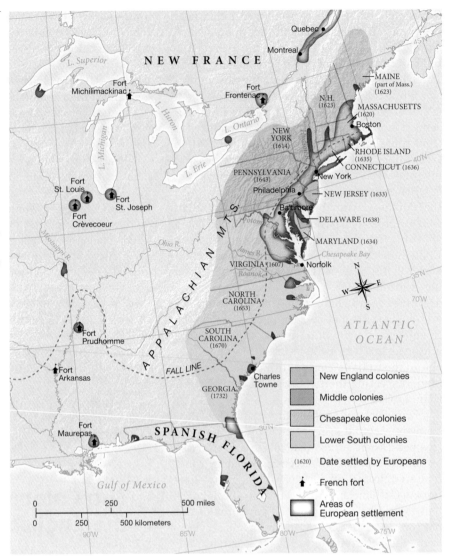

merchants and shippers. Also, the policies were intended to divert the colonies' trade from England's enemies, especially the Dutch and the French.

The Navigation Acts of 1650, 1651, 1660, and 1663 (see "Government Policies and Political Conflict" in chapter 3) set forth two fundamental rules governing colonial trade. First, goods shipped to and from the colonies had to be transported in English ships using primarily English crews. Second, the Navigation Acts listed colonial products that could be shipped only to England or to other English colonies. While these regulations prevented Chesapeake planters from shipping their tobacco directly to the European continent, they interfered less with the commerce of New England and the middle colonies, whose principal exports—fish, lumber, and flour—could legally be sent directly to their most important markets in the West Indies.

By the end of the seventeenth century, colonial commerce was defined by regulations that subjected merchants and shippers to royal supervision and gave them access to markets throughout the English empire. In addition, colonial commerce received protection from the English navy. By 1700, colonial goods (including those from the West Indies) accounted for one-fifth of all English imports and for two-thirds of all goods re-exported from England to the European continent. In turn, the colonies absorbed more than one-tenth of English exports. The commercial regulations gave economic value to England's proprietorship of the American colonies.

King Philip's War and the Consolidation of Royal Authority

The monarchy also took steps to exercise greater control over colonial governments. Virginia had been a royal colony since 1624; Maryland, South Carolina, and the middle colonies were proprietary colonies with close ties to the crown. The New England colonies possessed royal charters, but they had developed their own distinctively Puritan governments. Charles II, whose father, Charles I, had been executed by Puritans in England, took a particular interest in harnessing the New England

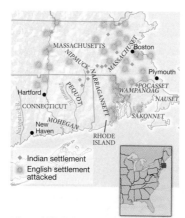

- ◆ Indian settlement
- ● English settlement attacked

King Philip's War, 1675

colonies more firmly to the English empire. The occasion was a royal investigation following **King Philip's War**.

A series of skirmishes in the Connecticut River valley between 1636 and 1637 culminated in the Pequot War when colonists massacred hundreds of Pequot Indians. In the decades that followed, New Englanders established relatively peaceful relations with the more potent Wampanoags, but they steadily encroached on Indian land. In 1642, a native leader urged warring tribes to band together against the English. "We [must] be one as they [the English] are," he said; "otherwise we shall be gone shortly, for . . . these English having gotten our land, they with scythes cut down the grass, and with axes fell the trees, and their cows and horses eat the grass, and their hogs spoil our clam banks, and we shall all be starved."

Such grievances accumulated until 1675, when the Wampanoags led by their chief Metacomet—whom the colonists called King Philip—attacked English settlements in western Massachusetts. Militias from Massachusetts and other New England colonies counterattacked the Wampanoags, Nipmucks, and Narragansetts in a deadly sequence of battles that killed more than a thousand colonists and thousands more Indians. The Indians destroyed thirteen English settlements and partially burned another half dozen. Mary Rowlandson, a minister's wife in Lancaster, Massachusetts, who was captured by Indians, recalled later that it was a "solemn sight to see so many Christians lying in their blood . . . like a company of sheep torn by wolves. All of them stripped naked by a company of hell-hounds, roaring, singing, ranting and insulting, as if they would have torn our very hearts out."

By the spring of 1676, Indian warriors ranged freely within seventeen miles of Boston. The

Wampanoag War Club

This seventeenth-century war club was used to kill King Philip, according to the Anglican missionary who obtained it from Indians early in the eighteenth century. Although the tale is probably a legend, the club is certainly a seventeenth-century Wampanoag weapon that could have been used in King Philip's War. The heavy ball carved into the head of the club could deliver a fatal blow. Courtesy of the Fruitlands Museums, Harvard, Massachusetts.

John Sheldon's Snowshoes

John Sheldon, a resident of Deerfield, Massachusetts—first settled by colonists in 1669—wore these snowshoes to rescue more than one hundred colonists taken hostage by the French and their Indian allies during the Deerfield Raid of 1704. The design of snowshoes, which colonists in 1666 called "a Rackett tyed to each foote," was adopted from the Native Americans, who had used them for centuries.
Photograph courtesy of the Pocumtuck Valley Memorial Association, Memorial Hall Museum Deerfield, Massachusetts.

New France and the Indians: The English Colonies' Northern Borderlands

North of New England, French explorers, traders, and missionaries carved out a distinctive North American colony that contrasted, competed, and periodically fought with the English colonies to the south.

The explorer Jacques Cartier sailed into the St. Lawrence River in 1535 and claimed the region for France. Cartier's attempts to found a permanent colony failed, but French ships followed in his wake and began to trade with Native Americans for wild animal pelts. By the time King Louis XIV made New France a royal colony in 1663, the fur trade had become the colony's economic foundation.

The French monarchy hoped to channel the fur trade through French hands into the broader European market and to compete against rival Dutch traders, whose headquarters at Albany (in what is now New York) funneled North American furs down the Hudson River to markets in the Netherlands. The crown also hoped the fur trade would allow the creation of a North American colony on the cheap.

The fur trade required little investment other than the construction and staffing of trading outposts at Quebec, Montreal, and elsewhere. In exchange for textiles and various metal trade goods, the Iroquois, Huron, Ottawa, Ojibwa, and other Native Americans did the arduous, time-consuming, and labor-intensive work of tracking, trapping, and skinning the animals and transporting the pelts—usually by canoe—to French traders. Unlike the English colonies, which attracted numerous settlers to engage in agriculture and produce food as well as valuable export crops, New France needed only a few colonists to keep the trading posts open and to maintain friendly relations with their Indian suppliers. By 1660, English colonists in North America outnumbered their French counterparts by more than twenty to one.

After England seized control of New York in 1664, English fur traders replaced the Dutch at Albany and eagerly competed to divert the northern fur trade away from New France. By then, the Iroquois—strategically located between the supply of furs to the north and west, New France to the east, and New York to the south—had become middlemen, collecting pelts from Huron, Ottawa, and other Indians and swapping them with French or English traders, depending on who offered the better deal. Able to mobilize scores of fierce warriors to threaten European traders as well as their Indian suppliers, the Iroquois managed to play the French and English off against each other and to maintain a near choke hold on the supply of furs.

Native Americans preferred English trade goods, which tended to be of higher quality and less expensive than those available at French outposts, but New France cultivated better relationships with the Indians. When English colonists had the required military strength, they seldom hesitated to kill Indians, especially those who occupied land the colonists craved. The small number of colonists in New France never had as much military power as the English colonists; hence, they sought to stay on relatively peaceful and friendly terms with the Indians. French men commonly married or cohabited with Indian women, an outgrowth of both the shortage of French women among the colonists and the acceptance of such couplings, compared with the strong taboo prevalent in the English colonies.

Jesuit missionaries led the spiritual colonization of New France. Zealous enemies of what they considered Protestant heresies and stout defenders of Catholicism, the Jesuits fanned out to Indian villages

colonists finally defeated the Indians, principally with a scorched-earth policy of burning their food supplies. But King Philip's War left the New England colonists with a large war debt, a devastated frontier, and an enduring hatred of Indians. "A Swarm of Flies, they may arise, a Nation to Annoy," a colonial officer wrote in justification of destroying the Indians; "Yea Rats and Mice, or Swarms of Lice a Nation may destroy."

In 1676, an agent of the king arrived to investigate whether New England was abiding by English laws. Not surprisingly, the king's agent found all sorts of deviations from English rules, and the monarchy decided to govern New England more directly. In 1684, an English court revoked the Massachusetts charter, the foundation of the distinctive Puritan government. Two years later, royal officials incorporated Massachusetts and

Indians in New France
Native Americans used canoes for efficient transportation. Heavy furs, for example, were carried long distances from remote trapping regions to trading posts in canoes. This seventeenth-century drawing from New France illustrates Native Americans' skills in handling a canoe, in this case by standing up while netting and spearing fish. The figure on the right appears to be playing a flute, perhaps to attract fish.
De Agostini Picture Library/The Bridgeman Art Library.

a colored patch on European maps. The dominant military power in New France remained the Iroquois, not the French.

England and France clashed repeatedly in North America over the fur trade and in a colonial extension of their rivalry at home. European conflict between France and England spread to North America during King William's War (1689–1697), when the colonists and their Indian allies carried out numerous deadly raids, marking the contested boundary between New France and the English colonies as a bloody zone controlled by none of its claimants or inhabitants.

America in a Global Context

1. In what ways did New France reflect the colonial objectives of the French monarchy?

2. How did New France differ from the English colonies in seventeenth-century North America?

3. How did European rivalries influence the encounters of Indians with French and English colonists?

Connect to the Big Idea

⊙ Why was New France important to the seventeenth-century English colonists?

throughout New France, determined to convert the Native Americans and to preserve the colony as a Catholic stronghold. Unwittingly, the missionaries also spread European diseases among the Native Americans, repeatedly causing deadly epidemics. Above all, the missionaries worked hand in hand with the fur traders and royal officials to make New France a low-cost Catholic colony on the thinly defended borders of the predominantly Protestant English colonies.

To extend the boundaries of New France far to the west and south, almost encircling the English colonies along the Atlantic coast, royal officials in 1673 sponsored a voyage by the explorer Louis Jolliet and the priest Jacques Marquette to explore the vast interior of the North American continent by canoeing down the Mississippi River to what is now Arkansas. Jolliet and Marquette made grandiose claims to the Mississippi valley, but in reality these claims amounted to little more than

the other colonies north of Maryland into the Dominion of New England. To govern the dominion, the English sent Sir Edmund Andros to Boston. Some New England merchants cooperated with Andros, but most colonists were offended by his flagrant disregard of such Puritan traditions as keeping the Sabbath. Worst of all, the Dominion of New England invalidated all land titles, confronting every landowner in New

England with the horrifying prospect of losing his or her land.

Events in England, however, permitted Massachusetts colonists to overthrow Andros and retain title to their property. When Charles II died in 1685, he was succeeded by his brother James II, a zealous Catholic. James's aggressive campaign to appoint Catholics to government posts engendered such unrest that in 1688 a group of Protestant noblemen in Parliament invited the Dutch ruler William III of Orange, James's son-in-law, to claim the English throne.

When William III landed in England at the head of a large army, James fled to France, and William III and his wife, Mary II (James's daughter), became corulers in the relatively bloodless "Glorious Revolution," reasserting Protestant influence in England and its empire. Rumors of the revolution raced across the Atlantic and emboldened colonial uprisings against royal authority in Massachusetts, New York, and Maryland.

In Boston in 1689, rebels tossed Andros and other English officials in jail, destroyed the Dominion of New England, and reestablished the former charter government. New Yorkers followed the Massachusetts example. Under the leadership of Jacob Leisler, rebels seized the royal governor in 1689 and ruled the colony for more than a year. That same year in Maryland, the Protestant Association, led by John Coode, overthrew the colony's pro-Catholic government, fearing it would not recognize the new Protestant king.

But these rebel governments did not last. When King William III's governor of New York arrived in 1691, he executed Leisler for treason. Coode's men ruled Maryland until the new royal governor arrived in 1692 and ended both Coode's rebellion and Lord Baltimore's proprietary government. In Massachusetts, John Winthrop's city on a hill became another royal colony in 1691. The new charter said that the governor of the colony would be appointed by the king rather than elected by the colonists' representatives. But perhaps the most unsettling change was the new qualification for voting. Possession of property replaced church membership as a prerequisite for voting in colony-wide elections. Wealth replaced God's grace as the defining characteristic of Massachusetts citizenship.

Much as colonists chafed under increasing royal control, they still valued English protection from hostile neighbors. Colonists worried that the Catholic colony of New France menaced frontier regions by encouraging Indian raids and by competing for the lucrative fur trade. (See "Beyond America's Borders," page 100.) Although French leaders tried to buttress the military strength of New France during the last third of the seventeenth century to block the expansion of the English colonies, most of the military efforts mustered by New France focused on defending against attacks by the powerful Iroquois. However, when the English colonies were distracted by the Glorious Revolution, French forces from the fur-trading regions along the Great Lakes and in Canada attacked villages in New England and New York. Known as King William's War, the conflict with the French was a colonial outgrowth of William's war against France in Europe. The war dragged on until 1697 and ended inconclusively in both Europe and the colonies. But it made clear to many colonists that along with English royal government came a welcome measure of military security.

> **REVIEW** Why did the Glorious Revolution in England lead to uprisings in the American colonies?

▶ Conclusion: An English Model of Colonization in North America

By 1700, the northern English colonies of North America had developed along lines quite different from the example set by their southern counterparts. Emigrants came with their families and created settlements unlike the scattered plantations and largely male environment of early Virginia. Puritans in New England built towns and governments around their churches and placed worship of God, not tobacco, at the center of their society. They depended chiefly on the labor of family members rather than on that of servants and slaves.

The convictions of Puritanism that motivated John Winthrop and others to reinvent England in the colonies became muted, however, as New England matured and dissenters such as Roger Williams multiplied. Catholics, Quakers, Anglicans (members of the Church of England), Jews, and others settled in the middle and southern colonies, creating considerable religious toleration, especially in Pennsylvania and New York. At the same time, northern colonists, like their southern counterparts, developed an ever-increasing need for land that inevitably led to bloody conflict with the Indians who were displaced. By the closing years of the seventeenth century, the royal government in England intervened to try to moderate those conflicts and to govern the colonies more directly for the benefit of the monarchy. Assertions of royal control triggered colonial resistance that was ultimately suppressed, resulting in Massachusetts losing its special charter status and becoming a royal colony much like the other British North American colonies.

During the next century, the English colonial world would undergo surprising new developments built on the achievements of the seventeenth century. Immigrants from Scotland, Ireland, and Germany streamed into North America, and unprecedented numbers of African slaves poured into the southern colonies. On average, white colonists attained a relatively comfortable standard of living, especially compared with most people in England and continental Europe. While religion remained important, the intensity of religious concern that characterized the seventeenth century waned during the eighteenth century. Colonists worried more about prosperity than about providence, and their societies grew increasingly secular, worldly, and diverse.

See the Selected Bibliography for this chapter in the Appendix.

4 Chapter Review

MAKE IT STICK

 LearningCurve

Go online and use LearningCurve to see what you know. Then review the key terms and answer the questions.

KEY TERMS

English Reformation (p. 79)
Puritans (p. 80)
Separatists (p. 81)
Calvinism (p. 84)
predestination (p. 84)
visible saints (p. 85)
antinomians (p. 88)
Puritan Revolution (p. 89)
Halfway Covenant (p. 91)
Quakers (p. 91)
New Netherland (p. 94)
King Philip's War (p. 99)

REVIEW QUESTIONS

1. What was a "little commonwealth," and why was it so important to New England settlement? (pp. 79–84)

2. Why did Massachusetts Puritans adopt the Halfway Covenant? (pp. 84–92)

3. How did Quaker ideals shape the colony of Pennsylvania? (pp. 93–97)

4. Why did the Glorious Revolution in England lead to uprisings in the American colonies? (pp. 99–102)

MAKING CONNECTIONS

1. How did the religious dissenters who flooded into the northern colonies address the question of religious dissent in their new homes? Comparing two colonies, discuss their different approaches.

2. John Winthrop spoke of the Massachusetts Bay Colony as "a city upon a hill." What did he mean? How did this expectation influence life in New England during the seventeenth century?

3. How did religious and political turmoil in seventeenth-century England affect life in the colonies? In your answer, consider the establishment of the colonies and the crown's attempts to exercise authority over them.

4. To what extent did the New England and middle colonies become more alike during the seventeenth century? To what extent did they remain distinctive?

LINKING TO THE PAST

1. How did the communal goals of New England settlers compare with the aspirations of the tobacco and rice planters of the southern colonies? (See chapter 3.)

2. To what degree did religious intolerance shape events in the New World colonies of Spain, France, and England? (See chapters 2 and 3.)

5 Colonial America in the Eighteenth Century

1701–1770

CONTENT LEARNING OBJECTIVES

After reading and studying this chapter, you should be able to:

- Understand the link between eighteenth-century colonial population growth and economic growth.

- Explain how the market economy developed in New England and in what ways Puritanism was weakened.

- Discern how the population growth of the middle colonies differed from that of New England and the South.

- Recognize how the large influx of slaves into the southern colonies shaped the region's economy, society, and politics.

- Identify the shared experiences that unified the culture of the colonies of British North America.

- Understand how the policies of the British Empire provided a common framework of political expectations and experiences for American colonists, including their relations with Native Americans throughout North America.

TEXTILE SAMPLE BOOK
These cloth samples assembled by an English textile manufacturer, allowed North American colonial merchants to choose from a wide range of designs, textures, and fibers that they believed customers would purchase. Norfolk Museums Service.

THE BROTHERS AMBOE ROBIN JOHN AND LITTLE EPHRAIM ROBIN JOHN lived in Old Calabar on the Bight of Biafra in West Africa. The Robin Johns were part of a slave-trading dynasty headed by their kinsman Grandy King George, one of the most powerful leaders of the Efik people. Grandy King George owned hundreds of slaves whom he employed to capture still more slaves in the African interior. He sold these captives to captains of European slave ships for transport to the sugar, tobacco, and rice fields in the New World.

British slave ship captains and Grandy King George's African rivals conspired in 1767 to destroy the king's monopoly. In a bloody battle, Little Ephraim and Ancona Robin John were enslaved and transported across the Atlantic to the West Indies.

Unlike most slaves, the Robin Johns spoke and wrote English, a skill they had learned as slave traders in Old Calabar. The Robin Johns escaped

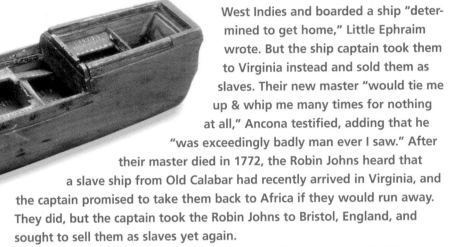

Model of a Slave Ship
Jammed into the holds of slave ships, enslaved Africans made the dreaded Middle Passage to the New World. This model slave ship was used in parliamentary debates by antislavery leaders in Britain to demonstrate the inhumanity of shipping people like cargo. The model does not show another typical feature of slave ships: weapons. Slaves vastly outnumbered the crews, and crew members justifiably feared slave uprisings. © Wilberforce House, Hull City Museums and Art Galleries, UK/The Bridgeman Art Library.

from the man who bought them in the West Indies and boarded a ship "determined to get home," Little Ephraim wrote. But the ship captain took them to Virginia instead and sold them as slaves. Their new master "would tie me up & whip me many times for nothing at all," Ancona testified, adding that he "was exceedingly badly man ever I saw." After their master died in 1772, the Robin Johns heard that a slave ship from Old Calabar had recently arrived in Virginia, and the captain promised to take them back to Africa if they would run away. They did, but the captain took the Robin Johns to Bristol, England, and sought to sell them as slaves yet again.

While imprisoned in Bristol harbor, the Robin Johns smuggled letters to a Bristol slave trader they had known in Old Calabar. With his help, the Robin Johns appealed to the chief justice of England for their freedom on the grounds that they were unjustly enslaved because they "were free people . . . [who] had not done anything to forfeit our liberty." After complex negotiations, they won their freedom.

As free Africans in Bristol, the Robin Johns converted to Christianity, but they longed to return to Africa. In 1774, they left Bristol as free men on a slave ship bound for Old Calabar, where they resumed their careers as slave traders.

The Robin Johns' quest to escape enslavement and redeem their freedom was shared but not realized by millions of Africans who were victims of slave traders such as Grandy King George and numberless merchants, ship captains, and colonists. In contrast, tens of thousands of Europeans voluntarily crossed the Atlantic to seek opportunities in North America—often by agreeing to several years of contractual servitude. Both groups illustrate the undertow of violence and deceit beneath the surface of the eighteenth-century Atlantic commerce linking Britain, Africa, the West Indies, and British North America. Many people, like the Robin Johns, turned to the consolations of religious faith as a source of meaning and hope in an often cruel and unforgiving society.

The flood of free and unfree migrants crossing the Atlantic contributed to unprecedented population growth in eighteenth-century British North America. In contrast, Spanish and French colonies in North America remained thinly populated outposts of European empires interested principally in maintaining a toehold in the vast continent. While the New England, middle, and southern colonies retained regional distinctions, commercial, cultural, and political trends built unifying experiences and assumptions among British North American colonists.

▶ A Growing Population and Expanding Economy in British North America

The most important fact about eighteenth-century British America is its phenomenal population growth: from about 250,000 in 1700 to more than two million by 1770. The eightfold growth of the colonial population signaled the maturation of a distinctive colonial society. A sign of the emerging significance of colonial North America is that in 1700 there were nineteen people in England for every American colonist, while by 1770 there were only three. Colonists of different ethnic groups, races, and religions lived in varied environments under thirteen different colonial governments, all of them part of the British empire.

In general, the growth and diversity of the eighteenth-century colonial population derived from two sources: immigration and **natural increase** (growth through reproduction). Natural increase contributed about three-fourths of the population growth, immigration about one-fourth. Immigration shifted the ethnic and racial balance among the colonists, making them by 1770 less English and less white than ever before. Fewer than 10 percent of eighteenth-century immigrants came from England; about 36 percent were Scots-Irish, mostly from northern Ireland; 33 percent arrived from Africa, almost all of them slaves; nearly 15 percent had left the many German-language principalities (the nation of Germany did not exist until 1871); and almost 10 percent came from Scotland. In 1670, more than 9 out of 10 colonists were of English ancestry, and only 1 out of 25 was of African ancestry. By 1770, only about half of the colonists were of English descent, while more than 20 percent descended from Africans. Thus, by 1770, the people of the colonies had a distinctive colonial—rather than English—profile (Map 5.1).

The booming population of the colonies hints at a second major feature of eighteenth-century colonial society: an expanding economy. The nearly limitless wilderness stretching westward made land relatively cheap compared with its price in the Old World. The abundance of land made labor precious, and the colonists always needed more. The insatiable demand for labor

CHRONOLOGY

1711	• North Carolina founded.
1730s	• Jonathan Edwards promotes Great Awakening.
1732	• Georgia founded.
1733	• Benjamin Franklin publishes *Poor Richard's Almanack*.
1739	• Stono Rebellion.
1740s	• George Whitefield preaches religious revival.
1745	• Olaudah Equiano born.
1750s	• Colonists move down Shenandoah Valley.
1754	• Seven Years' War begins.
1769	• First California mission established.
1770	• Mission and presidio established at Monterey, California. • British North American colonists number more than two million.
1775	• Indians destroy San Diego mission.

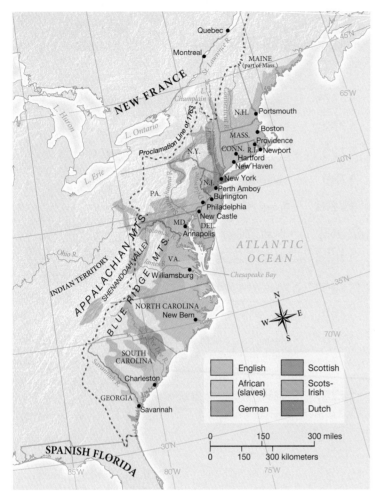

MAP 5.1

Europeans and Africans in the Eighteenth Century

This map illustrates regions where Africans and certain immigrant groups clustered. It is important to avoid misreading the map. Predominantly English and German regions, for example, also contained colonists from other places. Likewise, regions where African slaves resided in large numbers also included many whites, slave masters among them. The map suggests the diversity of eighteenth-century colonial society.

► New England: From Puritan Settlers to Yankee Traders

The New England population grew sixfold during the eighteenth century but lagged behind the growth in the other colonies. Most immigrants chose other destinations because of New England's relatively densely settled land and because Puritan orthodoxy made these colonies comparatively inhospitable to those of other faiths and those indifferent to religion. As the population grew, many settlers in search of farmland dispersed from towns, and Puritan communities lost much of their cohesion. Nonetheless, networks of economic exchange laced New Englanders to their neighbors, to Boston merchants, and to the broad currents of Atlantic commerce. In many ways, trade became a faith that competed strongly with the traditions of Puritanism.

Natural Increase and Land Distribution

The New England population grew mostly by natural increase, much as it had during the seventeenth century. The perils of childbirth gave wives a shorter life expectancy than husbands, but wives often lived to have six, seven, or eight babies. Anne Franklin and her husband Josiah, a soap and candle maker in Boston, had seven children before Anne died. Josiah quickly remarried his second wife, Abiah, and the couple had ten more children, including their son Benjamin, who became one of the most prominent colonial leaders of the eighteenth century. Like many other New Englanders, Benjamin Franklin felt hemmed in by family pressures and lack of opportunity and moved away from Boston when he was seventeen to "assert my freedom," as he put it, first in New York and then in Philadelphia.

The growing New England population pressed against a limited amount of land (see Map 5.1). Moreover, as the northernmost group of British colonies, New England had contested frontiers where powerful Native Americans, especially the Iroquois and Mahicans, jealously guarded their territory. The French (and Catholic) colony of New France also menaced the British (and mostly Protestant) New England colonies when provoked by colonial or European disputes.

was the fundamental economic environment that sustained the mushrooming population. Economic historians estimate that free colonists (those who were not indentured servants or slaves) had a higher standard of living than the majority of people elsewhere in the Atlantic world.

> **REVIEW** How did the North American colonies achieve the remarkable population growth of the eighteenth century?

During the seventeenth century, New England towns parceled out land to individual families. In most cases, the original settlers practiced **partible inheritance**—that is, they subdivided land more or less equally among sons. By the eighteenth century, the original land allotments had to be further subdivided, and many plots of land became too small to support a family. Sons who could not hope to inherit sufficient land had to move away from the town where they were born.

During the eighteenth century, colonial governments in New England abandoned the seventeenth-century policy of granting land to towns. Needing revenue, the governments of both Connecticut and Massachusetts sold land directly to individuals, including speculators. Now money, rather than membership in a community bound by a church covenant, determined whether a person could obtain land. The new land policy eroded the seventeenth-century pattern of settlement. As colonists spread north and west, they tended to settle on individual farms rather than in the towns and villages that characterized the

seventeenth century. Far more than in the seventeenth century, eighteenth-century New Englanders regulated their behavior by their own individual choices.

Farms, Fish, and Atlantic Trade

A New England farm was a place to get by, not to get rich. New England farmers grew food for their families, but their fields did not produce huge marketable surpluses. Instead of one big crop, a farmer grew many small ones. If farmers had extra, they sold to or traded with neighbors. Poor roads made travel difficult, time-consuming, and expensive, especially with bulky and heavy agricultural goods. The one major agricultural product the New England colonies exported—livestock— walked to market on its own legs. By 1770, New Englanders had only one-fourth as much wealth per capita as free colonists in the southern colonies.

As consumers, New England farmers participated in a diversified commercial economy that linked remote farms to markets throughout

VISUAL ACTIVITY

New York Harbor

This portrait of New York harbor about 1756 illustrates the importance of Atlantic commerce to the prosperous city in the background. The painting emphasizes a variety of ocean-going ships in the foreground. During its busiest seasons, the harbor commonly had ten times as many ships at anchor, which was nearly impossible for the artist to depict. © Collection of the New-York Historical Society, USA/The Bridgeman Art Library.

READING THE IMAGE: How does the painting reflect New York's participation in Atlantic commerce?

CONNECTIONS: Why were the largest and most prosperous cities in eighteenth-century America port cities?

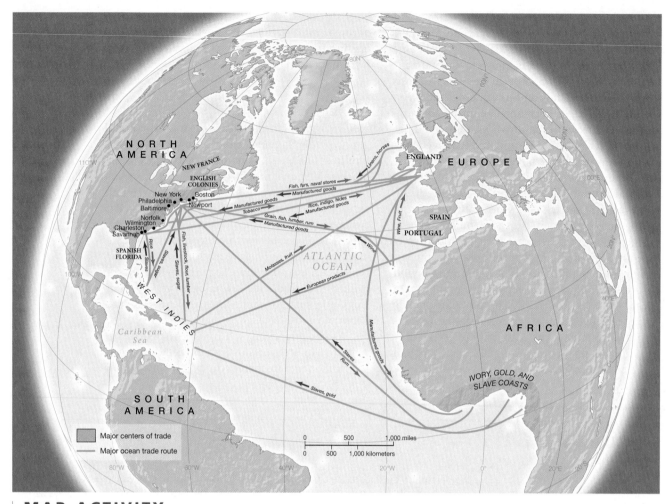

MAP ACTIVITY

Map 5.2 Atlantic Trade in the Eighteenth Century

This map illustrates the economic outlook of the colonies in the eighteenth century—east toward the Atlantic world rather than west toward the interior of North America. The long distances involved in the Atlantic trade and the uncertainties of ocean travel suggest the difficulties Britain experienced governing the colonies and regulating colonial commerce.

READING THE MAP: What were the major markets for trade coming out of Europe? What goods did the British colonies import and export?

CONNECTIONS: In what ways did the flow of raw materials from the colonies affect British industry? How did British colonial trade policies influence the Atlantic trade?

the Atlantic world. Merchants large and small stocked imported goods—British textiles, ceramics, and metal goods; Chinese tea; West Indian sugar; and Chesapeake tobacco. Farmers' needs supported local shoemakers, tailors, wheelwrights, and carpenters. Larger towns, especially Boston, housed skilled tradesmen such as cabinetmakers, silversmiths, and printers. Shipbuilders were among the many New Englanders who made their fortunes at sea.

Fish accounted for more than a third of New England's eighteenth-century exports; livestock and timber made up another third. The West Indies absorbed two-thirds of all New England's

exports. Slaves on Caribbean sugar plantations ate dried, salted codfish caught by New England fishermen, filled barrels crafted from New England timber with molasses and refined sugar, and loaded those barrels aboard ships bound ultimately for Europeans with a taste for rum (made from molasses) and sweets. Almost all of the rest of New England's exports went to Britain and continental Europe (Map 5.2). This Atlantic commerce benefited the entire New England economy, providing jobs for laborers and tradesmen as well as for ship captains, clerks, merchants, and sailors. (See "Seeking the American Promise," page 112.)

Merchants dominated Atlantic commerce. The largest and most successful New England merchants lived in Boston at the hub of trade between local folk and the international market. The magnificence of a wealthy Boston merchant's home stunned John Adams, who termed it a house seemed fit "for a noble Man, a Prince." Such luxurious Boston homes contrasted with the modest dwellings of Adams and other New Englanders, a measure of the polarization of wealth that developed in Boston and other seaports during the eighteenth century.

By 1770, the richest 5 percent of Bostonians owned about half the city's wealth; the poorest two-thirds of the population owned less than one-tenth. Still, the incidence of genuine poverty did not change much. About 5 percent of New Englanders qualified for poor relief throughout the eighteenth century. Overall, colonists were better off than most people in England.

New England was more homogeneously English than any other colonial region. People of African ancestry (almost all of them slaves) numbered more than fifteen thousand by 1770, but they barely diversified the region's 97 percent white majority. Most New Englanders had little use for slaves on their family farms. Instead, the few slaves concentrated in towns, especially Boston, where most of them worked as domestic servants and laborers.

By 1770, the population, wealth, and commercial activity of New England differed from what they had been in 1700. Ministers still enjoyed high status, but Yankee traders had

VISUAL ACTIVITY

Boston Common in Needlework

Hannah Otis embroidered this portrait of Boston Common in 1750 when she was eighteen years old. The house belonged to the Hancock family. John Hancock, who later signed the Declaration of Independence, is shown on horseback. The needlework reveals that eighteenth-century Bostonians owned slaves.
Museum of Fine Arts, Boston/The Bridgeman Art Library.

READING THE IMAGE: What features of the portrait would communicate to an eighteenth-century viewer that it portrays a city?

CONNECTIONS: How did life in Boston differ from that on rural farms in New England?

A Sailor's Life in the Eighteenth-Century Atlantic World

Although most eighteenth-century North American colonists made their living on farms, tens of thousands manned the vessels that ferried people, animals, commodities, consumer goods, ideas, and microorganisms from port to port throughout the Atlantic world. Built almost entirely from wood and fiber, ships were the most complex machines in the eighteenth century. Seamen needed to learn how to handle the intricacies of a vessel's working parts quickly, smoothly, and reliably. The ship, the cargo, and their own lives depended on their knowledge and dexterity. They had to endure hard physical labor for weeks or months on end in a cramped space packed with cargo and crew. Sailors followed "one of the hardest and dangerousest callings," one old salt declared.

Despite the certainty of strenuous work and spartan accommodations, young men like Ashley Bowen made their way to wharves in small ports such as Marblehead, Massachusetts—Bowen's hometown—or large commercial centers such as Boston, Philadelphia, New York, and Charleston. There they boarded vessels and launched a life of seafaring, seeking the promise of a future wafting on the surface of the deep rather than rooted below the surface of the soil.

Born in 1728, Bowen grew up in Marblehead, one of the most important fishing ports in North America. Like other boys who lived in or near ports, Bowen probably watched ships come and go; heard tales of adventure, disaster, and intrigue; and learned from neighbors and pals how to maneuver small, shallow-draft boats within sight of land. Young girls sometimes learned to handle a small boat, but they almost never worked as sailors aboard Atlantic vessels. When Bowen was only eleven years old, he sailed as a ship's boy aboard a vessel captained by the father of a friend to pick up a load of tar bound for Bristol, England. The ship then loaded a cargo of coal in Wales and carried it to Boston, where Bowen, now twelve, arrived with a yearlong seafaring education under his belt.

Most commonly, young men first went to sea when they were fifteen to eighteen years old. Like Bowen, they were single, living with their parents, and casting about for work. They usually sailed with friends, neighbors, or kinfolk, and they sought an education in the ways of the sea. Also like Bowen, they aspired to earn some wages, to rise in the ranks eventually from seaman to mate and possibly to master (the common term for captain), to save enough to marry and support a family, and after twenty years or so to retire from the rigors of the seafaring life with a "competency"—that is, enough money to live modestly.

It typically took about four years at sea to become a fully competent seaman. Shortly after Bowen returned from his first voyage, his father apprenticed him to a sea captain for seven years. In return for a hefty payment, the captain agreed to tutor young Bowen in the art of seafaring, which ideally promised to ease his path to become a captain himself. In reality, the captain employed him as a cabin boy, taught him little except to obey, and beat him for trivial mistakes, causing Bowen to run away after four years of servitude.

Now seventeen years old, Bowen had already sailed to dozens of ports in North America, the West Indies, the British Isles, and Europe. For the next eighteen years, he shipped out as a common seaman on scores of vessels carrying nearly every kind of cargo afloat on the Atlantic. He sailed mostly aboard merchant freighters, but he also worked on whalers, fishing boats, privateers, and warships. He survived sickness, imprisonment, foul weather, accidents, and innumerable close calls. But when he retired from seafaring at age thirty-five, he still had not managed to attain command. In twenty-four years at sea, he had worked as either a common seaman or a mate. For

replaced Puritan saints as the symbolic New Englanders. Atlantic commerce competed with religious convictions in ordering New Englanders' daily lives.

REVIEW Why did settlement patterns in New England change from the seventeenth to the eighteenth century?

► The Middle Colonies: Immigrants, Wheat, and Work

In 1700, the middle colonies of Pennsylvania, New York, New Jersey, and Delaware had only half the population of New England. But by 1770,

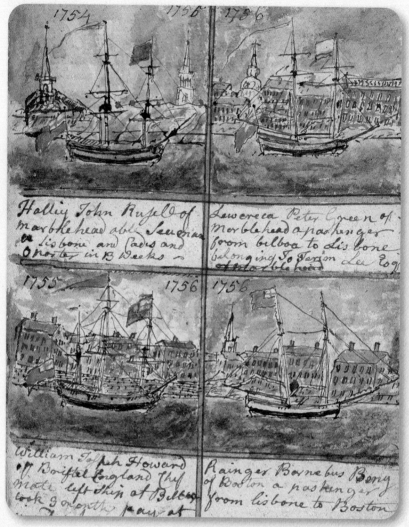

Ashley Bowen's Journal
Ashley Bowen painted these watercolors of ships he sailed aboard in 1754, 1755, and 1756. He paid attention to the distinctive rigging and flags of each vessel, and he kept notes about the vessels' owners, masters, mates, passengers, and destinations. The vessels dwarf the buildings of Marblehead, Massachusetts, in the background. Why might the differences among ships be important to Bowen? Photo courtesy of The Marblehead Museum & Historical Society, Marblehead, MA.

whatever reason, when most ship-owners eyed Bowen, they did not see a man they would trust to command their vessels.

Like Bowen, about three out of ten seamen spent their entire seafaring lives as seamen or mates, earning five dollars or so a month in wages, roughly comparable to the wages of farm laborers. Another three out of ten seamen died at sea, many by drowning or as a result of injuries or, most commonly, from tropical diseases usually picked up in the West Indies. Bowen lived to the age of eighty-five, working as a rigger, crafting nautical fittings for sailing vessels. When Bowen, like thousands of other seafarers, looked at the world, his gaze did not turn west toward the farms and forests of the interior but rather turned east, toward the promise of the Atlantic deep beyond.

Questions for Consideration

1. What attracted Ashley Bowen to a seafaring life? How successful was he?

2. How did Bowen's experiences as a seaman compare to those of farmers in the colonies?

3. How might Bowen's outlook on the world compare to that of the vast majority of colonists who seldom or never went to sea?

Connect to the Big Idea

C How did the lives of farmers and merchants in eighteenth-century North America compare with the lives of sailors?

the population of the middle colonies had multiplied tenfold and nearly equaled the population of New England. Immigrants—mainly German, Irish, Scottish—made the middle colonies a uniquely diverse society. By 1800, barely one-third of Pennsylvanians and less than half the total population of the middle colonies traced their ancestry to England. New white settlers, both free and in servitude, poured into the middle colonies because they perceived unparalleled opportunities.

German and Scots-Irish Immigrants

Germans made up the largest contingent of migrants from the European continent to the middle colonies. By 1770, about 85,000 Germans had arrived in the colonies. Their fellow colonists often referred to them as **Pennsylvania Dutch**, an English corruption of *Deutsch*, the word the immigrants used to describe themselves.

Most German immigrants came from what is now southwestern Germany, where, one observer noted, peasants were "not as well off as cattle elsewhere." German immigrants included numerous artisans and a few merchants, but the great majority were farmers and laborers. Economically, they represented "middling folk," neither the poorest (who could not afford the trip) nor the better-off (who did not want to leave).

By the 1720s, Germans who had established themselves in the colonies wrote back to their friends and relatives, as one reported, "of the civil and religious liberties [and] privileges, and of all the goodness I have heard and seen." Such letters prompted still more Germans to pull up stakes and embark for the middle colonies.

Similar motives propelled the **Scots-Irish**, who considerably outnumbered German immigrants. The "Scots-Irish" actually hailed from northern Ireland, Scotland, and northern England. Like the Germans, the Scots-Irish were Protestants, but with a difference. Most German immigrants worshipped in Lutheran or German Reformed churches; many others belonged to dissenting sects such as the Mennonites, Moravians, and Amish, whose adherents sought relief from persecution they had suffered in Europe for their refusal to bear arms and to swear oaths, practices they shared with the Quakers. In contrast, the Scots-Irish tended to be militant Presbyterians who seldom hesitated to bear arms or swear oaths. Like German settlers, however, Scots-Irish immigrants were clannish, residing when they could among relatives or neighbors from the old country.

In the eighteenth century, wave after wave of Scots-Irish immigrants arrived, culminating in a flood of immigration in the years just before the American Revolution. Deteriorating economic conditions in northern Ireland, Scotland, and England pushed many toward America. One Ulster Scot remarked that "oppression has brought us" to the "deplorable state . . . [that] the very marrow is screwed out of our bones." Most of the immigrants were farm laborers or tenant farmers fleeing droughts, crop failures, high food prices, or rising rents. They came, they told British officials, because of "poverty," the "tyranny of landlords," and their desire to "do better in America."

Both Scots-Irish and Germans probably heard the common saying "Pennsylvania is heaven for farmers [and] paradise for artisans," but they almost certainly did not fully understand the risks of their decision to leave their native lands. Ship captains, aware of the hunger for labor in the colonies, eagerly signed up the penniless German emigrants as **redemptioners**, a variant of indentured servants. A captain would agree to provide transportation to Philadelphia, where redemptioners would obtain the money to pay for their passage by borrowing it from a friend or relative who was already in the colonies or, as most did, by selling themselves as servants. Many redemptioners traveled in family groups, unlike impoverished Scots-Irish emigrants, who usually traveled alone and paid for their passage by contracting as indentured servants before they sailed to the colonies.

Redemptioners and indentured servants were packed aboard ships "as closely as herring," one migrant observed. Seasickness compounded by exhaustion, poverty, poor food, bad water, inadequate sanitation, and tight quarters encouraged the spread of disease. When one ship finally approached land, a passenger wrote, "everyone crawls from below to the deck . . . and people cry for joy, pray, and sing praises and thanks to God." Unfortunately, their troubles were far from over. Unlike indentured servants, redemptioners negotiated independently with their purchasers about their period of servitude. Typically, a healthy adult redemptioner agreed to four years of labor. Indentured servants commonly served five, six, or seven years.

"God Gives All Things to Industry": Urban and Rural Labor

An indentured servant in 1743 wrote that Pennsylvania was "the best poor Man's Country in the World." Although the servant reported that "the Condition of bought Servants is very hard" and masters often failed to live up to their promise to provide decent food and clothing, opportunity abounded in the middle colonies because there was more work to be done than workers to do it.

Most servants toiled in Philadelphia, New York City, or one of the smaller towns or villages. (See "Visualizing History," page 116.) Artisans, small manufacturers, and shopkeepers prized the labor of male servants. Female servants made valuable additions to households, where nearly all of them cleaned, washed, cooked, or minded children. From the masters' viewpoint, servants were a bargain. A master could purchase five or six years of a servant's labor for approximately the wages a common laborer would earn in four months.

Since a slave cost at least three times as much as a servant, only affluent colonists could afford the long-term investment in slave labor. Most farmers in the middle colonies used family labor, not slaves. Wheat, the most widely grown crop, did not require more labor than farmers could typically muster from relatives, neighbors, and a hired hand or two. Consequently, although people of African ancestry (almost all slaves) increased to more than thirty thousand in the middle colonies by 1770, they accounted for only about 7 percent of the total population and much less outside the cities.

Most slaves came to the middle colonies and New England after a stopover in the West Indies, as the Robin Johns did. Very few came directly from Africa. Slaves—unlike servants—could not charge masters with violating the terms of their contracts. Colonial laws punished slaves much more severely than servants for the same offense. A master's commands, not a written contract, set the terms of a slave's bondage. Small numbers of slaves managed to obtain their freedom, but no African Americans escaped whites' firm convictions about black inferiority.

Whites' racism and blacks' lowly social status made African Americans scapegoats for European Americans' suspicions and anxieties. In 1741, when arson and several unexplained thefts plagued New York City, officials suspected a murderous slave conspiracy and executed thirty-one slaves. On the basis of little evidence other than the slaves' "insolence" (refusal to conform fully to whites' expectations of servile behavior), city authorities burned thirteen slaves at the stake and hanged eighteen others. Although slaves were certifiably impoverished, they were not among the poor for whom the middle colonies were reputed to be the best country in the world.

Immigrants swarmed to the middle colonies because of the availability of land. The Penn family (see "New Jersey and Pennsylvania" in chapter 4) encouraged immigration to bring in potential buyers for their enormous tracts of land in Pennsylvania. From the beginning, Pennsylvania followed a policy of negotiating with Indian tribes to purchase additional land. This policy reduced the violent frontier clashes more common elsewhere in the colonies. Few colonists drifted beyond the northern boundaries of Pennsylvania. Owners of the huge estates in New York's Hudson valley preferred to rent rather than sell their land, and therefore they attracted fewer immigrants. The Iroquois Indians dominated the lucrative fur trade of the St. Lawrence valley and eastern Great Lakes, and they vigorously defended their territory from colonial encroachment, causing most settlers to prefer the comparatively safe environs of Pennsylvania.

Since the cheapest land always lay at the margin of settlement, would-be farmers tended to migrate to promising areas just beyond already improved farms. By midcentury, settlement had reached the eastern slopes of the Appalachian Mountains, and newcomers spilled south down the fertile valley of the Shenandoah River into western Virginia and the Carolinas. Thousands of settlers migrated from the middle colonies through this back door to the South. Abraham Lincoln's great-grandfather, John Lincoln—whose own grandfather, Mordecai, had migrated from England to Puritan Massachusetts in the 1630s— moved his family in the 1760s from Pennsylvania down the Shenandoah Valley into Virginia, where the future president's grandfather, also named Abraham, raised his family, including the future president's father, Thomas Lincoln.

Farmers like the Lincolns made the middle colonies the breadbasket of North America. They planted a wide variety of crops to feed their families, but they grew wheat in abundance. Flour milling was the number one industry and flour the number one export, constituting nearly three-fourths of all exports from the middle colonies. Farmers profited from the grain market in the Atlantic world. By 1770 a bushel of wheat was worth twice as much (adjusted for inflation) as it had been in 1720. The steady rise of grain prices after 1720 helped make the standard of living in rural Pennsylvania higher than in any other agricultural region of the eighteenth-century world. The comparatively widespread prosperity of all the middle colonies permitted residents to indulge in a half-century shopping spree for British imports. The middle colonies' per capita consumption of imported goods from Britain more than doubled between 1720 and 1770, far outstripping the per capita consumption of British goods in New England and the southern colonies.

Philadelphia stood at the crossroads of trade in wheat exports and British imports. Merchants

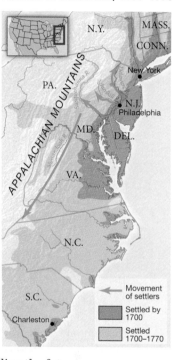

Patterns of Settlement, 1700–1770

Movement of settlers

Settled by 1700

Settled 1700–1770

A View of Urban Life

John Street, New York City, 1768

This painting depicts John Street, a residential neighborhood of New York City, in 1768, as recalled by the artist Joseph B. Smith early in the nineteenth century. The painting highlights the urbane pleasures of casual encounters and friendly conversations on the street. Unlike many urban streets today, John Street appears quiet. People could talk casually while a horseman rode past and dogs romped.

occupied the top stratum of Philadelphia society. In a city where only 2 percent of the residents owned enough property to qualify to vote, merchants built grand homes and dominated local government. Many of Philadelphia's wealthiest merchants were Quakers. Quaker traits of industry, thrift, honesty, and sobriety encouraged the accumulation of wealth. A colonist complained that a Quaker "prays for his neighbors on First Days [Sabbaths] and then preys on him the other six."

The lower ranks of merchants included aspiring tradesmen such as Benjamin Franklin. In 1728, Franklin opened a small shop, run mostly by his wife Deborah, that sold a little of everything: cheese, codfish, coffee, goose feathers, soap, and occasionally a slave. In 1733, Franklin began to publish *Poor Richard's Almanack*, which preached the likelihood of long-term rewards for tireless labor and quickly became Franklin's

most profitable product. The popularity of *Poor Richard's Almanack* suggests that many Pennsylvanians thought less about the pearly gates of heaven than about their pocketbooks. Poor Richard's advice that "God gives all Things to Industry" might be considered the motto for the middle colonies. The promise of a worldly payoff made work a secular faith. Poor Richard advised, "Work as if you were to live 100 years, Pray as if you were to die Tomorrow."

Although Quakers remained influential in Pennsylvania, Franklin spoke for most colonists with his aphorisms of work, discipline, and thrift that celebrated the spark of ambition and the promise of worldly gain.

REVIEW Why did immigrants flood into Pennsylvania during the eighteenth century?

The street also appears safe and secure. Men, women, and children show no sign of caution about theft or assault. People sit on their porches, doors ajar. Modest dwellings adjoin more elaborate homes, suggesting a mix of wealth and taste among John Street residents. Notice that fences separate house yards from the street, rather than houses from one another, hinting of friendly relations among neighbors. Few of the people depicted are alone. Most people accompany one or more other people, suggesting the importance of the street as a place to socialize, to nod to strangers, chat with friends, or even to conduct business.

The large building is the John Street Methodist Church. The church is not set apart from the houses of the neighborhood but mingled among them with a minimum of ostentation or display.

Overall, the street appears orderly and prosperous, not a place of disorder or poverty. People appear to be well dressed and purposeful. Ragged paupers, staggering drunks, or disreputable people appear nowhere. The street is spacious and smooth, not muddy, rutted, or choked with garbage and filth. Broad sidewalks offer room for leisurely strolling. Yet the street itself is portrayed as more of a sidewalk than an avenue for the traffic of wheeled vehicles or horseback riders.

The painting depicts an idealized and sanitized version of mid-eighteenth century urban life. In New York and other cities, streets were typically dirty and unpleasant, dusty when dry and swampy when wet. Sidewalks were often little more than wooden planks plopped unsteadily onto the ground. Households routinely emptied human waste into the street, along with bones, animal carcasses, and rotting vegetable matter. Horses and oxen that carried people and goods through the streets made their own contributions to the stinky muck. The reeking streets often contaminated water supplies (which typically were shallow private wells located in the backs of houses or public wells positioned in the streets), making waterborne diseases common. In sum, the density of housing and human habitation that made mid-eighteenth century cities places of urban pleasures depicted in the painting also made cities unhealthy and even dangerous, compared to life on more isolated rural farms.

SOURCE: John Street United Methodist Church (New York, NY).

Questions for Analysis

1. What pleasures of urban life does the painting depict?

2. What kinds of social interactions does the painting portray?

3. What common features of mid-eighteenth-century city life are missing from the painting?

Connect to the Big Idea

C How did rural life differ from that in cities like New York?

▶ The Southern Colonies: Land of Slavery

Between 1700 and 1770, the population of the southern colonies of Virginia, Maryland, North Carolina, South Carolina, and Georgia grew almost ninefold. By 1770, about twice as many people lived in the South as in either the middle colonies or New England. As elsewhere, natural increase and immigration accounted for the rapid population growth. Many Scots-Irish and German immigrants funneled from the middle colonies into the southern backcountry. Other immigrants were indentured servants (mostly English and Scots-Irish). But slaves made the most striking contribution to the booming southern colonies, transforming the racial composition of the population. Slavery became the defining characteristic of the southern colonies during the eighteenth century, shaping the region's economy, society, and politics.

The Atlantic Slave Trade and the Growth of Slavery

The number of southerners of African ancestry (nearly all of them slaves) rocketed from just over 20,000 in 1700 to well over 400,000 in 1770. The black population increased nearly three times faster than the South's briskly growing white population. Consequently, the proportion of southerners of African ancestry grew from 20 percent in 1700 to 40 percent in 1770.

Southern colonists clustered into two distinct geographic and agricultural zones. The colonies in the upper South, surrounding the Chesapeake Bay, specialized in growing tobacco, as they had

VISUAL ACTIVITY

Bethlehem, Pennsylvania
This view of Bethlehem, Pennsylvania, in 1757 dramatizes the profound transformation of the natural land-scape humans wrought in the eighteenth century. In less than twenty years, precisely laid-out orchards and fields replaced forests and glades. By carefully penning their livestock (lower center right) and fencing their fields (lower left), farmers safeguarded their livelihoods from the risks and disorders of untamed nature. Individual farmsteads (lower center) and brick town buildings (upper center) integrated the bounty of the land with community life. Few eighteenth-century communities were as orderly as Bethlehem, but many effected a comparable transformation of the environment. The New York Public Library/Art Resource, NY.
READING THE IMAGE: What does this painting indicate about the colonists' priorities?
CONNECTIONS: Why might Pennsylvanians have been so concerned about maintaining order?

since the early seventeenth century. Throughout the eighteenth century, nine out of ten southern whites and eight out of ten southern blacks lived in the Chesapeake region. The upper South retained a white majority during the eighteenth century.

In the lower South, a much smaller cluster of colonists inhabited the coastal region and specialized in the production of rice and indigo (a plant used to make blue dye). Lower South colonists made up only 5 percent of the total population of the southern colonies in 1700 but inched upward to 15 percent by 1770. South Carolina was the sole British colony along the southern Atlantic coast until 1732. (North Carolina, founded in 1711, was largely an

TABLE 5.1	SLAVE IMPORTS, 1451–1870
Estimated Slave Imports to the Western Hemisphere	
1451–1600	275,000
1601–1700	1,341,000
1701–1810	6,100,000
1811–1870	1,900,000

extension of the Chesapeake region.) Georgia was founded in 1732 as a refuge for poor people from England. Georgia's leaders banned slaves from 1735 to 1750, but few settlers arrived until after 1750, when the prohibition on slavery was lifted and slaves flooded in. In South Carolina, in contrast to Georgia and every other British mainland colony, slaves outnumbered whites almost two to one; in some low-country districts, the ratio of blacks to whites exceeded ten to one.

The enormous growth in the South's slave population occurred through natural increase and the flourishing Atlantic slave trade (Table 5.1 and Map 5.3). Slave ships brought almost 300,000 Africans to British North America between 1619 and 1780. Of these Africans, 95 percent arrived in the South and 96 percent arrived during the eighteenth century. Unlike indentured servants and redemptioners, these Africans did not choose to come to the colonies. Like the Robin Johns, most of them had been born into free families in villages located within a few hundred miles of the West African coast. Although they shared

African origins, they came from many different African cultures, such as Akan, Angolan, Asante, Bambara, Gambian, Igbo, Mandinga, among others. They spoke different languages, worshipped different deities, observed different rules of kinship, grew different crops, and recognized different rulers. The most important experience they had in common was enslavement.

Captured in war, kidnapped, or sold into slavery by other Africans, they were brought to the coast, sold to African traders like the Robin Johns who assembled slaves for resale, and sold again to European or colonial slave traders or ship captains, who packed two hundred to three hundred or more aboard ships that carried them on the **Middle Passage** across the Atlantic and then sold them yet again to colonial slave merchants or southern planters.

Olaudah Equiano published an account of his enslavement that hints at the common experiences of millions of other Africans swept up in the slave trade. In 1756 when he was eleven years old, Equiano was kidnapped by Africans in what is now Nigeria, who sold him to other Africans, who in turn eventually sold him to a slave ship on the coast. Equiano wrote that he "had never heard of white men or Europeans, nor of the sea," and he feared that he was "going to be killed" and "eaten by those white men with horrible looks, red faces, and loose hair." Once the ship set sail, many of the slaves, crowded together in suffocating heat fouled by filth of all descriptions, died from sickness. "The shrieks of the women and the groans of the dying rendered the whole a scene of horror almost inconceivable," Equiano recalled. Most of the slaves on the ship were sold in Barbados, but Equiano and other leftovers were shipped off to Virginia, where he "saw few or none of our native Africans and not one soul who could talk to me." Equiano felt isolated and "exceedingly miserable" because he "had no person to speak to that I could understand." Finally, the captain of a tobacco ship bound for England purchased Equiano, and he traveled as a slave between North America, England,

Olaudah Equiano
Painted after he had bought his freedom, this portrait evokes Equiano's successful acculturation to eighteenth-century English customs. In his *Interesting Narrative,* Equiano wrote that he "looked upon [the English] . . . as men superior to us [Africans], and therefore I had the stronger desire to resemble them, to imbibe their spirit and imitate their manners." Library of Congress.

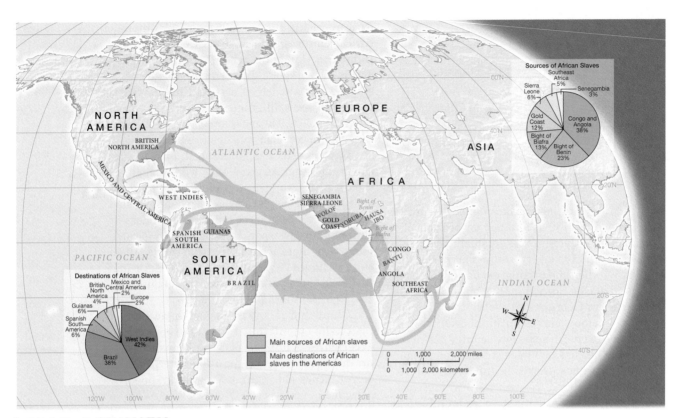

MAP ACTIVITY

Map 5.3   The Atlantic Slave Trade

Although the Atlantic slave trade lasted from about 1450 to 1870, it peaked during the eighteenth century, when more than six million African slaves were imported to the New World. Only a small fraction of these slaves were taken to British North America. Most went to sugar plantations in Brazil and the Caribbean.

READING THE MAP: Where in Africa did most slaves originate? Approximately how far was the trip from the busiest ports of origin to the two most common New World destinations?

CONNECTIONS: Why were so many more African slaves sent to the West Indies and Brazil than to British North America?

and the West Indies for ten years until he succeeded in buying his freedom in 1766.

Only about 15 percent of the slaves brought into the southern colonies came aboard ships from the West Indies, as Equiano and the Robin Johns did. All the other slaves brought into the southern colonies came directly from Africa, and almost all the ships that brought them (roughly 90 percent) belonged to British merchants. Most of the slaves on board were young adults, with men usually outnumbering women two to one. Children under the age of fourteen, like Equiano, typically accounted for no more than 10 to 15 percent of a cargo.

Mortality during the Middle Passage varied considerably from ship to ship. On average, about 15 percent of the slaves died, but sometimes half or more perished. The average mortality among the white crew of slave ships was often nearly as bad. In general, the longer the voyage lasted, the

more people died. Slaves and crew succumbed not only to epidemic diseases such as smallpox and dysentery but also to acute dehydration caused by fluid loss from perspiration, vomiting, and diarrhea combined with severe shortage of drinking water.

Normally, an individual planter purchased at any one time a relatively small number of newly arrived Africans, or **new Negroes**, as they were called. New Negroes were often profoundly depressed, demoralized, and disoriented. Planters expected their other slaves—either those born into slavery in the colonies (often called country-born or creole slaves) or Africans who had arrived earlier—to help new Negroes become accustomed to their strange new surroundings. Planters' preferences for slaves from specific regions of Africa aided slaves' acculturation (or seasoning, as it was called) to the routine of bondage in the southern colonies. Chesapeake planters preferred slaves from Senegambia, the Gold Coast, or—like Equiano and the Robin Johns—the Bight of Biafra, which combined accounted for about 40 percent of Africans imported to the Chesapeake. South Carolina planters favored slaves from the central African Congo and Angola regions, the origin of about 40 percent of the slaves they imported. Although slaves spoke many different languages, enough linguistic and cultural similarities existed that they could usually communicate with other Africans from the same region.

New Africans had to adjust to the physical as well as the cultural environment of the southern colonies. Slaves who had just endured the Middle Passage were poorly nourished, weak, and sick. In this vulnerable state, they encountered the alien diseases of North America without having developed a biological arsenal of acquired immunities. As many as 10 to 15 percent of newly arrived Africans died during their first year in the southern colonies. Nonetheless, the large number of newly enslaved Africans made the influence of African culture in the South stronger in the eighteenth century than ever before—or since.

While newly enslaved Africans poured into the southern colonies, slave mothers bore children, which caused the slave population in the South to grow rapidly. Slave owners encouraged these births. Thomas Jefferson explained, "I consider the labor of a breeding [slave] woman as no object, that a [slave] child raised every 2 years is of more profit than the crop of the best laboring [slave] man." Although slave mothers loved and nurtured their children, the mortality rate among slave children was high, and the ever-present risk of being separated by sale brought grief to many slave families. Nonetheless, the growing number of slave babies set the southern colonies apart from other New World slave societies, where mortality rates were so high that deaths exceeded births. The high rate of natural increase in the southern colonies meant that by the 1740s the majority of southern slaves were country-born.

Slave Labor and African American Culture

Southern planters expected slaves to work from sunup to sundown and beyond. George Washington wrote that his slaves should "be at their work as soon as it is light, work til it is dark, and be diligent while they are at it." The conflict between the masters' desire for maximum labor and the slaves' reluctance to do more than necessary made the threat of physical punishment a constant for eighteenth-century slaves. Masters

preferred black slaves to white indentured servants, not just because slaves served for life but also because colonial laws did not limit the force masters could use against slaves. Slaves often resisted their masters' demands, one traveler noted, because of their "greatness of soul"—their stubborn unwillingness to conform to their masters' definition of them as merely slaves.

Some slaves escalated their acts of resistance to direct physical confrontation with the master, the mistress, or an overseer. But a hoe raised in anger, a punch in the face, or a desperate swipe with a knife led to swift and predictable retaliation by whites. Throughout the southern colonies, the balance of physical power rested securely in the hands of whites.

Rebellion occurred, however, at Stono, South Carolina, in 1739. A group of about twenty slaves attacked a country store, killed the two storekeepers, and confiscated the store's guns, ammunition, and powder. Enticing other slaves to join, the group plundered and burned more than half a dozen plantations and killed more than twenty white men, women, and children. A mounted force of whites quickly suppressed the rebellion. They placed the rebels' heads atop mileposts along the main road, grim reminders of the consequences of rebellion. The South Carolina legislature enacted a draconian slave code in 1740 to punish with the utmost severity enslaved "negroes from the coast of Africa who are generally of a barbarous and savage disposition." The **Stono Rebellion** illustrated that eighteenth-century slaves had no chance of overturning slavery and very little chance of defending themselves in any bold strike for freedom. No other similar uprisings occurred during the colonial period.

Slaves maneuvered constantly to protect themselves and to gain a measure of autonomy within the boundaries of slavery. In Chesapeake tobacco fields, most slaves were subject to close supervision by whites. In the lower South, the **task system** gave slaves some control over the pace of their work and some discretion in the use of the rest of their time. A "task" was typically defined as a certain area of ground to be cultivated or a specific job to be completed. A slave who completed the assigned task might use the remainder of the day, if any, to work in a garden, fish, hunt, spin, weave, sew, or cook. When masters sought to boost productivity by increasing tasks, slaves did what they could to defend their customary work assignments.

Eighteenth-century slaves also planted the roots of African American lineages that branch out to the present. Slaves valued family ties, and, as in West African societies, kinship structured slaves' relations with one another. Slave parents often gave a child the name of a grandparent, aunt, or uncle. In West Africa, kinship identified a person's place among living relatives and linked the person to ancestors in the past and to descendants in the future. Newly imported African slaves usually arrived alone, like Equiano, without kin. Often slaves who had traversed the Middle Passage on the same ship adopted one another as "brothers" and "sisters." Likewise, as new Negroes were seasoned and incorporated into existing slave communities, established families often adopted them as fictive kin.

When possible, slaves expressed many other features of their West African origins in their lives on New World plantations. They gave their children African names such as Cudjo or Quash, Minda, or Fuladi. They grew food crops they had known in Africa, such as yams and okra. They constructed huts with mud walls and thatched roofs similar to African residences. They fashioned banjos, drums, and other musical instruments, held dances, and observed funeral rites that echoed African practices. In these and many other ways, slaves drew upon their African heritages as much as the oppressive circumstances of slavery permitted.

Tobacco, Rice, and Prosperity

Slaves' labor bestowed prosperity on their masters, British merchants, and the monarchy. Slavery was so important and valuable that one minister claimed in 1757 that "to live in Virginia without slaves is morally impossible." The southern colonies supplied 90 percent of all North American exports to Britain. Rice exports from the lower South exploded from less than half a million pounds in 1700 to eighty million pounds in 1770, nearly all of it grown by slaves. Exports of indigo also boomed. Together, rice and indigo made up three-fourths of lower South exports, nearly two-thirds of them going to Britain and most of the rest to the West Indies, where sugar-growing slaves ate slave-grown rice.

Tobacco was by far the most important export from British North America; by 1770, it represented almost one-third of all colonial exports and three-fourths of all Chesapeake exports. Under the provisions of the Navigation Acts (see "Royal Regulation of Colonial Trade" in chapter 4), nearly all of it went to Britain, where the monarchy collected a lucrative tax on each pound. British merchants then reexported more than 80 percent of the tobacco to the European continent, pocketing a nice markup for their troubles.

Colonial Slave Drum
An African in Virginia made this drum sometime around the beginning of the eighteenth century. The drum combines deerskin and cedarwood from North America with African workmanship and designs. During rare moments of respite from their work, slaves played drums to accompany dances learned in Africa. They also drummed out messages from plantation to plantation. ©The Trustees of the British Museum/Art Resource, NY.

These products of slave labor made the southern colonies by far the richest in North America. The per capita wealth of free whites in the South was four times greater than that in New England and three times that in the middle colonies. At the top of the wealth pyramid stood the rice grandees of the lower South and the tobacco gentry of the Chesapeake. These elite families commonly resided on large estates in handsome mansions adorned by luxurious gardens, all maintained and supported by slaves.

The vast differences in wealth among white southerners engendered envy and occasional tension between rich and poor, but remarkably little open hostility. In private, the planter elite spoke disparagingly of humble whites, but in public the planters acknowledged their lesser neighbors as equals, at least in belonging to the superior—in their minds—white race. Looking upward, white yeomen and tenants (who owned neither land nor slaves) sensed the gentry's condescension and veiled contempt. But they also appreciated the gentry for granting favors, upholding white supremacy, and keeping slaves in their place. Although racial slavery made a few whites much richer than others, it also gave those who did not get rich a powerful reason to feel similar (in race) to those who were so different (in wealth).

The slaveholding gentry dominated the politics and economy of the southern colonies. In Virginia, only adult white men who owned at least one hundred acres of unimproved land or twenty-five acres of land with a house could vote. This property-holding requirement prevented about 40 percent of white men in Virginia from voting for representatives to the House of Burgesses. In South Carolina, the property requirement was only fifty acres of land, and therefore most adult white men qualified to vote. In both colonies, voters elected members of the gentry to serve in the colonial legislature. The gentry passed elected political offices from generation to generation, almost as if they were hereditary. Politically, the gentry built a self-perpetuating oligarchy—rule by the elite few—with the votes of their many humble neighbors.

The gentry also set the cultural standard in the southern colonies. They entertained lavishly, gambled regularly, and attended Anglican (Church of England) services more for social than for religious reasons. Above all, they cultivated the leisurely pursuit of happiness. They did not condone idleness, however. Their many pleasures and responsibilities as plantation owners kept them busy. Thomas Jefferson, a phenomenally productive member of the gentry, recalled that his earliest childhood memory was of being carried on a pillow by a family slave—a powerful image of the slave hands supporting the gentry's leisure and achievement.

REVIEW How did slavery influence the society and economy of the southern colonies?

▶ Unifying Experiences

The societies of New England, the middle colonies, and the southern colonies became more sharply differentiated during the eighteenth century, but colonists throughout British North America also shared unifying experiences that eluded settlers in the Spanish and French colonies. The first was economic. All three British colonial regions had their economic roots in agriculture. Colonists sold their distinctive products in markets that, in turn, offered a more or

Eliza Lucas Pinckney's Gown
When Eliza Lucas was sixteen years old in 1738, she took over day-to-day management of her father's rice plantations. Highly educated, independent, and energetic, Lucas introduced numerous innovations on the plantations, including the cultivation of indigo—which became a major export crop in South Carolina—and silkworms. The gown shown here was made for her out of silk produced on her plantation. Division of Home and Community Life, National Museum of American History, Smithsonian Institution.

less uniform array of goods to consumers throughout British North America. Another unifying experience was a decline in the importance of religion. Some settlers called for a revival of religious intensity, but most people focused less on religion and more on the affairs of the world than they had in the seventeenth century. Also, white inhabitants throughout British North America became aware that they shared a distinctive identity as *British* colonists. Thirteen different governments presided over these North American colonies, but all of them answered to the British monarchy. British policies governed not only trade but also military and diplomatic relations with the Indians, French, and Spanish arrayed along colonial borderlands. Royal officials who expected loyalty from the colonists often had difficulty obtaining obedience. The British colonists asserted their prerogatives as British subjects to defend their special colonial interests.

Commerce and Consumption

Eighteenth-century commerce whetted colonists' appetites to consume. Colonial products spurred the development of mass markets throughout the Atlantic world (Figure 5.1). Huge increases in the supply of colonial tobacco and sugar brought the price of these small luxuries within the reach of most free whites. Colonial goods brought into focus an important lesson of eighteenth-century commerce: Ordinary people, not just the wealthy elite, would buy the things that they desired in addition to what they absolutely needed. Even news, formerly restricted mostly to a few people through face-to-face conversations or private letters, became an object of public consumption through the innovation of newspapers and the rise in literacy among whites. With the appropriate stimulus, market demand seemed unlimited.

The Atlantic commerce that took colonial goods to markets in Britain brought objects of consumer desire back to the colonies. British merchants and manufacturers recognized that colonists made excellent customers, and the Navigation Acts gave British exporters privileged access to the colonial market. By midcentury, export-oriented industries in Britain were growing ten times faster than firms attuned to the home market.

When the colonists' eagerness to consume exceeded their ability to pay, British exporters willingly extended credit, and colonial debts soared. Imported mirrors, silver plates, spices, bed and table linens, clocks, tea services, wigs, books, and more infiltrated parlors, kitchens, and bedrooms throughout the colonies. Despite the many differences among the colonists, the consumption of British exports built a certain material uniformity across region, religion, class, and status.

The dazzling variety of imported consumer goods also presented women and men with a novel array of choices. In many respects, the choices might appear trivial: whether to buy knives and forks, teacups, a mirror, or a clock. But such small choices confronted eighteenth-century consumers with a big question: What do you want? As colonial consumers defined and expressed their desires with greater frequency during the eighteenth century, they became accustomed to thinking of themselves as individuals who had the power to make decisions that influenced the quality of their lives.

Religion, Enlightenment, and Revival

Eighteenth-century colonists could choose from almost as many religions as consumer goods. Virtually all of the many religious denominations represented some form of Christianity, almost all of them Protestant. Slaves made up the largest group of non-Christians. A few slaves converted to Christianity in Africa or after they arrived in North America, but most continued to embrace elements of indigenous African religions. Roman Catholics concentrated in Maryland as they had since the seventeenth century, but even there they were far outnumbered by Protestants.

The varieties of Protestant faith and practice ranged across a broad spectrum. The middle colonies and the southern backcountry included militant Baptists and Presbyterians. Huguenots who had fled persecution in Catholic France peopled congregations in several cities. In New England, old-style Puritanism splintered into strands of Congregationalism that differed over fine points of theological doctrine. The Congregational Church was the official established church in New England, and all residents paid taxes for its support. Throughout the plantation South and in urban centers such as Charleston, New York, and Philadelphia, prominent colonists belonged to the Anglican Church, which received tax support in the South. But dissenting faiths grew everywhere, and in most colonies their adherents won the right to worship publicly, although the established churches retained official support.

Many educated colonists became deists, looking for God's plan in nature more than in the Bible. Deism shared the ideas of eighteenth-

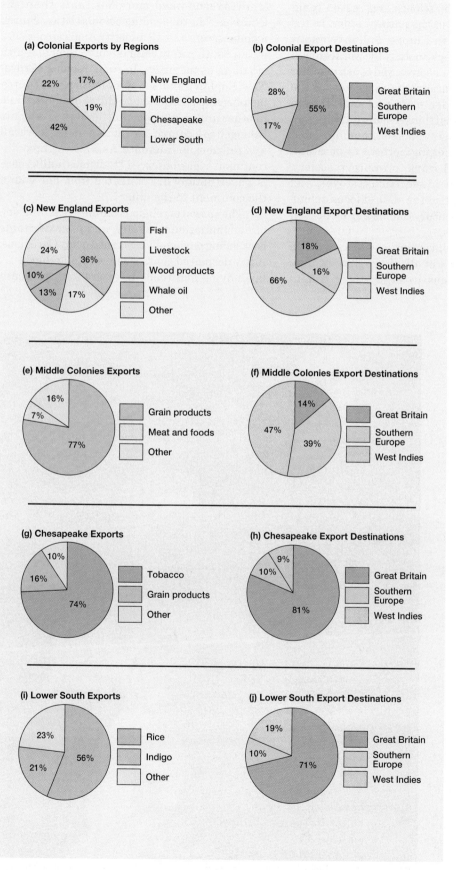

(a) Colonial Exports by Regions
- 17% New England
- 19% Middle colonies
- 42% Chesapeake
- 22% Lower South

(b) Colonial Export Destinations
- 55% Great Britain
- 17% Southern Europe
- 28% West Indies

(c) New England Exports
- 36% Fish
- 17% Livestock
- 13% Wood products
- 10% Whale oil
- 24% Other

(d) New England Export Destinations
- 18% Great Britain
- 16% Southern Europe
- 66% West Indies

(e) Middle Colonies Exports
- 77% Grain products
- 7% Meat and foods
- 16% Other

(f) Middle Colonies Export Destinations
- 14% Great Britain
- 39% Southern Europe
- 47% West Indies

(g) Chesapeake Exports
- 74% Tobacco
- 16% Grain products
- 10% Other

(h) Chesapeake Export Destinations
- 81% Great Britain
- 10% Southern Europe
- 9% West Indies

(i) Lower South Exports
- 56% Rice
- 21% Indigo
- 23% Other

(j) Lower South Export Destinations
- 71% Great Britain
- 10% Southern Europe
- 19% West Indies

FIGURE 5.1   Colonial Exports, 1768–1772

These pie charts provide an overview of the colonial export economy in the 1760s. The first two show that almost two-thirds of colonial exports came from the South and that the majority of the colonies' exports went to Great Britain. The remaining charts illustrate the distinctive patterns of exports in each colonial region. What do these patterns reveal about regional variations in Britain's North American colonies? What do they suggest about Britain's economic interest in the colonies?

century European Enlightenment thinkers, who tended to agree that science and reason could disclose God's laws in the natural order. In the colonies as well as in Europe, **Enlightenment** ideas encouraged people to study the world around them, to think for themselves, and to ask whether the disorderly appearance of things masked the principles of a deeper, more profound natural order. Leading colonial thinkers such as Benjamin Franklin and Thomas Jefferson communicated with each other seeking both to understand nature and to find ways to improve society. Franklin's interest in electricity, stoves, and eyeglasses exemplified the shift of focus among many eighteenth-century colonists from heaven to the here and now.

Most eighteenth-century colonists went to church seldom or not at all, although they probably considered themselves Christians. A min-ister in Charleston observed that on the Sabbath "the Taverns have more Visitants than the Churches." In the leading colonial cities, church members were a small minority. Anglican parishes in the South rarely claimed more than one-fifth of adults as members. In some regions of rural New England and the middle colonies, church membership embraced two-thirds of adults, while in other areas only one-quarter of the residents belonged to a church. The dominant faith overall was religious indifference. As a late-eighteenth-century traveler observed, "Religious indifference is imperceptibly disseminated from one end of the continent to the other."

The spread of religious indifference, of deism, of denominational rivalry, and of comfortable backsliding profoundly concerned many Christians. A few despaired that, as one wrote, "religion . . . lay a-dying and ready to expire its last breath

George Whitefield

An anonymous artist portrayed George White-field preaching, emphasizing the power of his sermons to transport his audience to a revived awareness of divine spirituality. The woman below his hands appears transfixed. Her eyes and Whitefield's do not meet, yet the artist's use of light suggests that she and Whitefield see the same core of holy Truth.

National Portrait Gallery/SuperStock.

of life." To combat what one preacher called the "dead formality" of church services, some ministers set out to convert nonbelievers and to revive the piety of the faithful with a new style of preaching that appealed more to the heart than to the head. Historians have termed this wave of revivals the **Great Awakening**. In Massachusetts during the mid-1730s, the fiery Puritan minister Jonathan Edwards reaped a harvest of souls by reemphasizing traditional Puritan doctrines of humanity's utter depravity and God's vengeful omnipotence. A member of Edwards's church noted that his sermons caused "great moaning and crying through the whole [church]—What shall I do to be saved—oh I am going to Hell . . . the shrieks and cries were piercing and amazing." In Pennsylvania and New Jersey, William Tennent led revivals that dramatized spiritual rebirth with accounts of God's miraculous powers. The most famous revivalist in the eighteenth-century Atlantic world was George Whitefield. An Anglican, Whitefield preached well-worn messages of sin and salvation to large audiences in England using his spellbinding, unforgettable voice. Whitefield visited the North American colonies seven times, staying for more than three years during the mid-1740s and attracting tens of thousands to his sermons, including Benjamin Franklin and Olaudah Equiano. Whitefield's preaching transported many in his audience to emotion-choked states of religious ecstasy, as he wrote, with "most lifting their eyes to heaven, and crying to God for mercy."

Whitefield's successful revivals spawned many lesser imitations. Itinerant preachers, many of them poorly educated, roamed the colonial backcountry after midcentury. Bathsheba Kingsley, a member of Jonathan Edwards's flock, preached the revival message informally—as did an unprecedented number of other women throughout the colonies—causing Edwards's congregation to brand her a "brawling woman" who had "gone quite out of her place."

The revivals awakened and refreshed the spiritual energies of thousands of colonists struggling with the uncertainties and anxieties of eighteenth-century America. The conversions at revivals did not substantially boost the total number of church members, however. After the revivalists moved on, the routines and pressures of everyday existence reasserted their primacy in the lives of many converts. But the revivals communicated the important message that every soul mattered, that men and women could choose to be saved, that individuals had the power to make a decision for everlasting life or death. Colonial revivals expressed in religious terms many of the same democratic and egalitarian values expressed in economic terms by colonists' patterns of consumption. One colonist noted the analogy by referring to itinerant revivalists as "Pedlars in divinity." Like consumption, revivals contributed to a set of common experiences that bridged colonial divides of faith, region, class, and status.

Trade and Conflict in the North American Borderlands

British power defended the diverse inhabitants of its colonies from Indian, French, and Spanish enemies on their borders—as well as from foreign powers abroad. Royal officials warily eyed the small North American settlements of New France and New Spain for signs of threats to the colonies.

Alone, neither New France nor New Spain jeopardized British North America, but with Indian allies they could become a potent force that kept colonists on their guard (Map 5.4). Native Americans' impulse to defend their territory from colonial incursions competed with their desire for trade, which tugged them toward the settlers. As a colonial official observed in 1761, "A modern Indian cannot subsist without Europeans. . . . [The European goods that were] only conveniency at first [have] now become necessity." To obtain such necessities as guns, ammunition, clothing, and sewing utensils manufactured largely by the British, Indians trapped beavers, deer, and other furbearing animals.

British, French, Spanish, and Dutch officials competed for the fur trade. Indians took advantage of this competition to improve their own prospects, playing one trader and empire off another. Indian tribes and confederacies also competed among themselves for favored trading rights with one colony or another, a competition colonists encouraged.

The shifting alliances and complex dynamics of the fur trade struck a fragile balance along the frontier. The threat of violence from all sides was ever present, and the threat became reality often enough for all parties to be prepared for the worst. In the Yamasee War of 1715, for example, the Yamasee and Creek Indians—with French encouragement—mounted a coordinated attack against colonial settlements in South Carolina. The Cherokee Indians, traditional enemies of the Creeks, refused to join the attack. Instead, they protected their access to British trade goods by allying with the colonists and turning the tide of battle, triggering a murderous rampage of revenge by the colonists against the Creeks and Yamasee.

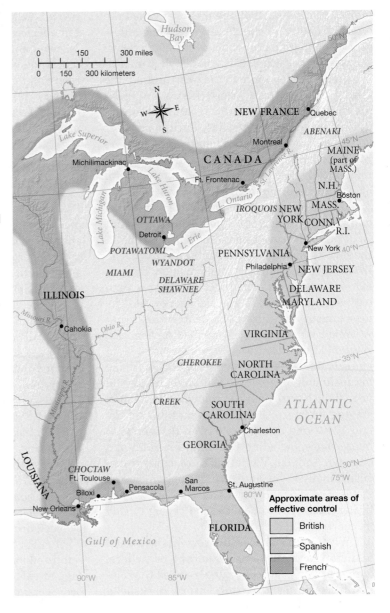

MAP 5.4

Zones of Empire in Eastern North America

The British zone, extending west from the Atlantic coast, was much more densely settled than the zones under French, Spanish, and Indian control. The comparatively large number of British colonists made them more secure than the relatively few colonists in the vast regions claimed by France and Spain or the settlers living among the many Indian peoples in the huge area between the Mississippi River and the Appalachian Mountains. Yet the British colonists were not powerful enough to dominate the French, Spanish, or Indians. Instead, they had to guard against attacks by powerful Indian groups allied with the French or Spanish.

Relations between Indians and colonists differed from colony to colony and from year to year. But the British colonists' nagging perceptions of menace on the frontier kept them continually hoping for help from the British to keep the Indians at bay and to maintain the essential flow of trade. In 1754, the British colonists' endemic competition with the French flared into the Seven Years' War (also known as the French and Indian War), which would inflame the frontier for years (see "French-British Rivalry in the Ohio Country" in chapter 6). Colonists agreed that Indians made deadly enemies, profitable trading partners, and powerful allies.

The Spanish kept an eye on the Pacific coast, where Russian hunters in search of seals and sea otters threatened to become a permanent presence on New Spain's northern frontier. To block Russian access to present-day California, officials in New Spain mounted a campaign to build forts (called **presidios**) and missions there. In 1769, an expedition headed by a military man, Gaspar de Portolá, and a Catholic priest, Junípero Serra, traveled north from Mexico to present-day San Diego, where they founded the first California mission, San Diego de Alcalá. They soon journeyed all the way to Monterey, which became the capital of Spanish California. There Portolá established a presidio in 1770 "to defend us from attacks by the Russians," he wrote. The same year, Serra founded Mission San Carlos Borroméo de Carmelo in Monterey to convert the Indians and recruit them to work to support the soldiers and other Spaniards in the presidio.

By 1772, Serra had founded other missions along the path from San Diego to Monterey.

One Spanish soldier praised the work of the missionaries, writing that "with flattery and presents [the missionaries] attract the savage Indians and persuade them to adhere to life in society and to receive instruction for a knowledge of the Catholic faith, the cultivation of the land, and the arts necessary for making the instruments most needed for farming." Yet for the Indians, the Spaniards' California missions had horrendous consequences, as they had elsewhere in the Spanish borderlands. European diseases decimated Indian populations, Spanish soldiers raped Indian women, and missionaries beat Indians and subjected them to near slavery. Indian uprisings against the Spaniards occurred repeatedly (see "Documenting the American Promise," page 130), but the presidios and missions endured as feeble projections of the Spanish empire along the Pacific coast.

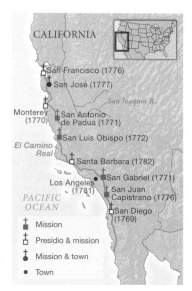

Spanish Missions in California

Colonial Politics in the British Empire

The plurality of peoples, faiths, and communities that characterized the North American colonies arose from the somewhat haphazard policies of the eighteenth-century British empire. Unlike Spain and France—whose policies of excluding Protestants and foreigners kept the population of their North American colonial territories tiny—Britain kept the door to its colonies open to anyone, and tens of thousands of non-British immigrants settled in the North American colonies and raised families. The open door did not extend to trade, however, as the seventeenth-century Navigation Acts restricted colonial trade to British ships and traders. These policies evolved because they served the interests of the monarchy and of influential groups in Britain and the colonies. The policies also gave the colonists a common framework of political expectations and experiences.

British attempts to exercise political power in their colonial governments met with success so long as British officials were on or very near the sea. Colonists acknowledged—although they did not always readily comply with—British authority to collect customs duties, inspect cargoes, and enforce trade regulations. But when royal officials tried to wield their authority in the internal affairs of the colonies on land, they invariably encountered colonial resistance. A governor appointed by the king in each of the nine royal colonies (Rhode Island and Connecticut selected their own governors) or by the proprietors in Maryland and Pennsylvania headed the government of each colony. The British envisioned colonial governors

VISUAL ACTIVITY

Mission Carmel

This eighteenth-century drawing portrays a reception for a Spanish visitor at Mission Carmel in what is now Carmel, California. Lines of mission Indians dressed in robes flank the entrance to the chapel where a priest and his assistants await the visitor. The Granger Collection, New York.

READING THE IMAGE: How does the reception ritual illustrate the relations among Indians, missionaries and Spanish officials?

CONNECTIONS: How did policies toward Indians in Spanish North American colonies differ from those in eighteenth-century English colonies?

Spanish Priests Report on California Missions

Catholic missionaries sent regular reports to their superiors in Mexico City, New Spain's capital city. The reports described what the missionaries considered their successes in converting pagan Indians—whom they called gentiles—as well as the difficulties caused by the behavior of both Spaniards and Indians.

DOCUMENT 1
Father Luís Jayme Describes Conditions at Mission San Diego de Alcalá, 1772

Father Luís Jayme, a Franciscan missionary, reported on the deplorable behavior of some of the Spanish soldiers at Mission San Diego de Alcalá, who frequently raped Indian women, causing many Indians to resist the efforts of the missionaries.

With reference to the Indians, I wish to say that great progress [in converting Indians] would be made if there was anything to eat and the soldiers would set a good example. . . . As for the example set by the soldiers, no doubt some of them are good exemplars and deserve to be treated accordingly, but very many of them deserve to be hanged on account of the continuous outrages which they are committing in seizing and raping the women. There is not a single mission where all the gentiles have not been scandalized, and even on the roads. . . . Surely, as the gentiles themselves state, they [the soldiers] are committing a thousand evils, particularly of a sexual nature. . . .

At one of these Indian villages near this mission of San Diego . . . the gentiles therein many times have been on the point of coming here to kill us all, and the reason for this is that some soldiers went there and raped their women, and other soldiers who were carrying the mail to Monterey turned their animals into their fields and they ate up their crops. Three other Indian villages . . . [near] here have reported the same thing to me several times. For this reason on several occasions when . . . I have gone to see these Indian villages, as soon as they saw us they fled from their villages and fled to the woods or other remote places. . . . They do this so that the soldiers will not rape their women as they have already done so many times in the past. . . .

Now [the Indians] all want to be Christians because they know that there is a God who created the heavens and earth and all things, that there is a Hell and Glory, that they have souls, etc. . . . [Now] they . . . do not have idols; they do not go on drinking sprees; they do not marry relatives; and they have but one wife. The married men sleep with their wives only. . . . Some of the first adults whom we baptized, when we pointed out to them that it was wrong to have sexual intercourse with a woman to whom they were not married, told me that they already knew that, and that among them it was considered to be very bad, and so they do not do so at all. "The soldiers," they told me, "are Christians and, although they know that God will punish them in Hell, do so,

as mini-monarchs able to exert influence in the colonies much as the king did in Britain. But colonial governors were not kings, and the colonies were not Britain.

Even the best-intentioned colonial governors had difficulty developing relations of trust and respect with influential colonists because their terms of office averaged just five years and could be terminated at any time. Colonial governors controlled few patronage positions to secure political friendships in the colonies. Obedient and loyal to their superiors in Britain, colonial governors fought incessantly with the colonists' assemblies. They battled over issues such as governors' vetoes of colonial legislation, removal of colonial judges, and dismissal of the representative assemblies. But during the eighteenth century, the assemblies gained the upper hand.

Since British policies did not clearly define the colonists' legal powers, colonial assemblies seized the opportunity to make their own rules. Gradually, the assemblies established a strong tradition of representative government analogous, having sexual intercourse with our wives." . . . When I heard this, I burst into tears to see how these gentiles were setting an example for us Christians.

Source: Maynard Geiger, trans. and ed., *The Letter of Luís Jayme, O.F.M.: San Diego, October 17, 1772* (Los Angeles, 1970), 38–42.

DOCUMENT 2
Father Junípero Serra Describes the Indian Revolt at Mission San Diego de Alcalá, 1775

Father Junípero Serra, the founder of many of the California missions, reported to his superiors in Mexico City that an Indian uprising had destroyed Mission San Diego de Alcalá. He recommended rebuilding and urged officials to provide additional soldiers to defend the missions, but not to punish the rebellious Indians.

I have just received [news] of the total destruction of the San Diego Mission, and of the death of the senior of its two religious ministers, called Father Luís Jayme, at the hand of the rebellious gentiles and of the Christian neophytes [Indians who lived in the mission]. All this happened . . . about one or two o'clock at night. The gentiles came together from forty rancherías [settlements] . . . and set fire to the church, after sacking it. They then went to the storehouse, the house where the Fathers lived, the soldiers' barracks, and all the rest of the buildings. They killed a carpenter . . . and a blacksmith. . . . They wounded with their arrows the four soldiers, who alone were on guard at the . . . mission. . . .

And now, after the Father has been killed, the Mission burned, its many and valuable furnishings destroyed, together with the sacred vessels, its paintings, its baptismal, marriage, and funeral records, and all the furnishings for the sacristy, the house, and the farm implements—now the forces [of soldiers] of both presidios [nearby] come together to set things right. . . . What happened was that before they set about reestablishing the Mission, they wanted to . . . lay hands on the guilty ones who were responsible for the burning of the Mission, and the death of the Fathers, and chastise them. The harassed Indians rebelled anew and became more enraged. . . . And so the soldiers there are gathered together in their presidios, and the Indians in their state of heathenism. . . .

But . . . what can be gained by campaigns [against the rebellious Indians]? Some will say to frighten them and prevent them from killing others. What I say is that, in order to prevent them from killing others, keep better guard over them than they did over the one who has been killed; and, as to the murderer, let him live, in order that he should be saved—which is the very purpose of our coming here, and the reason which justifies it.

Source: Antonine Tibesar, O.F.M., ed., *The Writings of Junípero Serra* (Washington, DC, 1956), 2:401–7. Reprinted by permission of the American Academy of Franciscan History.

Questions for Analysis and Debate

1. In what ways did Jayme and Serra agree or disagree about the motivations of Indians in and around Mission San Diego de Alcalá?

2. How did the goals and activities of the Spanish soldiers compare with those of the Catholic missionaries?

3. What might Spanish soldiers or Indians have said about these events? What might they have said about missionaries like Jayme and Serra?

Connect to the Big Idea

© How did Indian resistance to the British and French in the fur trade differ from Indian resistance to the Spanish in missions?

in their eyes, to the British Parliament. Voters often returned the same representatives to the assemblies year after year, building continuity in power and leadership that far exceeded that of the governor.

By 1720, colonial assemblies had won the power to initiate legislation, including tax laws and authorizations to spend public funds. Although all laws passed by the assemblies (except in Maryland, Rhode Island, and Connecticut) had to be approved by the governor and then by the Board of Trade in Britain, the difficulties in communication about complex subjects over long distances effectively ratified the assemblies' decisions. Years often passed before colonial laws were repealed by British authorities, and in the meantime the assemblies' laws prevailed.

The heated political struggles between royal governors and colonial assemblies that occurred throughout the eighteenth century taught colonists a common set of political lessons. They learned to employ traditionally British ideas of representative government to defend their own

Ambush of Spanish Expedition
In 1720, the New Mexico governor sent forty-three Spanish soldiers and sixty Pueblo Indians to expel French intruders from New Spain's northern borderlands. The French and their Indian allies ambushed the expedition killing thirty-three Spaniards and twelve Pueblos. Shortly afterward, an unknown artist recorded the event in this hide painting. Shown in the center of the painting is Father Juan Minguez of Albuquerque, and the Indian directly in front of him is Joseph Naranjo, leader of the Spaniards' Pueblo allies; both were killed in the ambush. MPI/Getty Images.

colonial interests. More important, they learned that power in the British colonies rarely belonged to the British government.

> REVIEW   How did culture, commerce, and consumption shape the collective identity of Britain's North American colonists in the eighteenth century?

▶ Conclusion: The Dual Identity of British North American Colonists

During the eighteenth century, a society that was both distinctively colonial and distinctively British emerged in British North America. Tens of thousands of immigrants and slaves gave the colonies an unmistakably colonial complexion and contributed to the colonies' growing population and expanding economy. People of different ethnicities and faiths sought their fortunes in the colonies, where land was cheap, labor was dear, and work promised to be rewarding.

Indentured servants and redemptioners risked temporary periods of bondage for the potential reward of better opportunities in the colonies than on the Atlantic's eastern shore. Slaves arrived in unprecedented numbers and endured lifelong servitude, which they neither chose nor desired but from which their masters greatly benefited.

None of the European colonies could claim complete dominance of North America. The desire to expand and defend their current claims meant that the English, French, and Spanish colonies were drawn into regular conflict with one another, as well as with the Indians upon whose land they encroached. In varying degrees, all sought control of the Native Americans and their land, their military power, their trade, and even their souls. Spanish missionaries and soldiers sought to convert Indians on the West Coast and exploit their labor; French alliances with Indian tribes posed a formidable barrier to westward expansion of the British empire.

Yet despite their attempts to tame their New World holdings, Spanish and French colonists did not develop societies that began to rival the European empires that sponsored and supported them. They did not participate in the cultural, economic, social, and religious changes experienced by their counterparts in British North America, nor did they share in the emerging political identity of the British colonists.

Identifiably colonial products from New England, the middle colonies, and the southern colonies flowed to the West Indies and across the Atlantic. Back came unquestionably British consumer goods along with fashions in ideas, faith, and politics. The bonds of the British empire required colonists to think of themselves as British subjects and, at the same time, encouraged them to consider their status as colonists. By 1750, British colonists in North America could not imagine that their distinctively dual identity—as British and as colonists—would soon become a source of intense conflict.

See the Selected Bibliography for this chapter in the Appendix.

5 Chapter Review

MAKE IT STICK

 **LearningCurve**

Go online and use LearningCurve to see what you know. Then review the key terms and answer the questions.

KEY TERMS

natural increase (p. 107)
partible inheritance (p. 109)
Pennsylvania Dutch (p. 114)
Scots-Irish (p. 114)
redemptioners (p. 114)
Middle Passage (p. 119)
new Negroes (p. 120)
Stono Rebellion (p. 121)
task system (p. 121)
Enlightenment (p. 126)
Great Awakening (p. 127)
presidios (p. 128)

REVIEW QUESTIONS

1. How did the North American colonies achieve the remarkable population growth of the eighteenth century? (pp. 107–108)

2. Why did settlement patterns in New England change from the seventeenth to the eighteenth century? (pp. 108–112)

3. Why did immigrants flood into Pennsylvania during the eighteenth century? (pp. 112–117)

4. How did slavery influence the society and economy of the southern colonies? (pp. 117–123)

5. How did culture, commerce, and consumption shape the collective identity of Britain's North American colonists in the eighteenth century? (pp. 123–127)

MAKING CONNECTIONS

1. How did consumption influence the relationship between the American colonies and Britain in the eighteenth century?

2. Why did the importance of religion decline throughout the colonies from the seventeenth to the eighteenth century?

3. How did colonists and Indians manage relationships with each other?

4. Compare patterns of immigration to the middle and southern colonies. Who came, and how did they get there? How did they shape the economic, cultural, and political character of each colony?

LINKING TO THE PAST

1. How did the British North American colonies in 1750 differ politically and economically from those in 1650? Were there important continuities? (See chapters 3 and 4.)

2. Is there persuasive evidence that colonists' outlook on the world shifted from the seventeenth to the eighteenth century? Why or why not? (See chapters 3 and 4.)

6

The British Empire and the Colonial Crisis

1754–1775

After reading and studying this chapter, you should be able to:

- Recognize how the American colonies fit into the British Empire's campaigns against other European powers and how the Seven Years' War laid the groundwork for the imperial crisis of the 1760s in British North America.

- Define the Sugar and Stamp Acts, and explain why and how American colonists opposed them.

- Explain how the British government responded to colonists' growing opposition to royal authority.

- Identify the events that escalated tensions between British leaders and the colonists.

- Explain the Intolerable Acts and the purposes and goals of the First Continental Congress.

- Identify the origins of the battles of Lexington and Concord.

PATRICK HENRY'S MAP DESK
This map table with pullout extensions supported large maps and larger dreams of wealth. Patrick Henry, like many Virginia planters, bought thousands of acres of land west of the Appalachian Mountains, hoping to resell later at a higher price to settlers. Yet his acreage was occupied by the Cherokee. To avoid frontier war, the British in 1763 prohibited speculation and settlement west of the mountains.
Courtesy of Preservation Virginia.

IN 1771, THOMAS HUTCHINSON BECAME THE ROYAL GOVERNOR OF THE colony of Massachusetts. Most royal governors were British aristocrats sent over by the king for short tours of duty, but Hutchinson was a fifth-generation American with a long record of public service in local institutions. He lived in the finest mansion in Boston; wealth, power, and influence were his in abundance. He was proud of his connection to the British empire and loyal to his king.

Hutchinson had the misfortune to be a loyal colonial leader during the two tumultuous decades leading up to the American Revolution. He worked hard to keep the British and colonists aligned in interests, even promoting a plan to unify the colonies with a limited government (the Albany Plan of Union) to deal with Indian policy. His plan of union ultimately failed, however, and a major war—the Seven Years' War—ensued, pitting the British and colonists against the French and their Indian allies in the backcountry of the American colonies. When the war ended and the British government proposed to tax colonists to help pay for it, Hutchinson was certain that the new British taxation policies were legitimate—unwise, perhaps, but legitimate.

Not everyone in Boston shared his opinion. Enthusiastic crowds protested a succession of taxation policies enacted after 1763, from the Sugar Act to the Tea Act. But Hutchinson maintained his steadfast loyalty to Britain. His love of order and tradition inclined him to unconditional support of the British empire, and by nature he was a measured and cautious man. "My temper does not incline to enthusiasm," he once wrote.

Privately, he lamented the stupidity of the British acts that provoked trouble, but his rigid sense of duty always prevailed, making him an inspiring villain to the emerging revolutionary movement. The man not inclined to enthusiasm unleashed popular enthusiasm all around him. He never appreciated that irony.

In another irony, Thomas Hutchinson early recognized the difficulties of maintaining full rights and privileges for colonists so far from their supreme government, the king and Parliament in Britain. At a crisis point in 1769, when British troops occupied Boston, he wrote privately to a friend in England, "There must be an abridgement of what are called English liberties. . . . I doubt whether it is possible to project a system of government in which a colony three thousand miles distant from the parent state shall enjoy all the liberty of the parent state." He could not imagine the colonies without a parent state, existing independently.

Thomas Hutchinson was a loyalist, as were most English-speaking colonists in the 1750s. But the Seven Years' War, in which Britain and its colonies were allies, shook that affection, and imperial policies in the decade following the war shattered it completely. Over the course of 1763 to 1773, Americans insistently raised serious questions about Britain's governance of its colonies. Many came to believe what Thomas Hutchinson could never accept—that a tyrannical Britain had embarked on a course to enslave the colonists by depriving them of their traditional English liberties.

The opposite of liberty was slavery, a coerced condition of nonfreedom. Political rhetoric about liberty, tyranny, and slavery heated up the emotions of white colonists during the many crises of the 1760s and 1770s. But this rhetoric turned out to be a two-edged sword. The call for an end to tyrannical slavery meant one thing when sounded by Boston merchants whose commercial shipping rights had been curtailed, but the same call meant something quite different in 1775 when sounded by black Americans locked in the bondage of slavery.

Thomas Hutchinson
The only formal portrait of Thomas Hutchinson still in existence shows an assured young man in ruffles. Doubtless he sat for other portraits, but none survive. One portrait in his summer house outside Boston was mutilated by a revolutionary crowd. In 1775, Hutchinson fled to Britain, the country he regarded as his cultural home, only to realize how very American he was.
© Massachusetts Historical Society, Boston, MA/The Bridgeman Art Library.

▶ The Seven Years' War, 1754–1763

For the first half of the eighteenth century, Britain was at war intermittently with France or Spain. Often the colonists in America experienced reverberations from these conflicts, most acutely along the frontier of New France in northern New England. In 1754, international tensions returned, this time sparked by events in America's Ohio Valley. The land—variously claimed by Virginians, Pennsylvanians, and the French—was actually inhabited by more than a dozen Indian tribes. The result was the costly **Seven Years' War** (its British name—Americans called it the French and Indian War), which spread in 1756 to encompass much of Europe, the Caribbean, and even India. The British and their colonial allies won the war, but the immense costs of the conflict—in money, death, and desire for revenge by losers and even winners—laid the groundwork for the imperial crisis of the 1760s between the British and Americans.

French-British Rivalry in the Ohio Country

For several decades, French traders had cultivated alliances with the Indian tribes in the Ohio Country, a frontier region they regarded as part of New France, establishing a profitable exchange of manufactured goods for beaver furs (Map 6.1). But in the 1740s, aggressive Pennsylvania traders began to infringe on the territory. Adding to the tensions, a group of enterprising Virginians, including the brothers Lawrence and Augustine Washington, formed the Ohio Company in 1747 and advanced on the same land. Their hope for profit lay not in the fur trade but in land speculation, fueled by American population expansion.

In response to these incursions, the French sent soldiers to build a series of military forts to secure their trade routes and to create a western barrier to American expansion. In 1753, the royal governor of Virginia, Robert Dinwiddie, himself a shareholder in the Ohio Company, dispatched a messenger to warn the French that they were trespassing on Virginia land. For this dangerous mission, he chose the twenty-one-year-old George Washington, half-brother of the Ohio Company leaders, who did not disappoint. Washington returned with crucial intelligence confirming French military intentions. Impressed, Dinwiddie appointed the youth to lead a small military expedition west to assert Virginia's claim

CHRONOLOGY

1754	• Seven Years' War begins. • Albany Congress.
1755	• Braddock defeated in western Pennsylvania.
1757	• William Pitt fully commits to war.
1760	• Montreal falls to British. • George III becomes British king.
1763	• Treaty of Paris ends Seven Years' War. • Pontiac's Rebellion. • Proclamation of 1763. • Paxton Boys massacre friendly Indians.
1764	• Parliament enacts Sugar Act.
1765	• Parliament enacts Stamp Act. • Virginia Resolves challenge Stamp Act. • Sons of Liberty stage crowd actions. • Stamp Act Congress meets.
1766	• Parliament repeals Stamp Act, passes Declaratory Act.
1767	• Parliament enacts Townshend duties.
1768	• British station troops in Boston.
1768–1769	• Merchants sign nonimportation agreements.
1770	• Boston Massacre. • Parliament repeals Townshend duties.
1772	• British navy ship *Gaspée* burned.
1773	• Parliament passes Tea Act. • Tea dumped in Boston harbor.
1774	• Parliament passes Coercive Acts. • Powder Alarm shows colonists' readiness. • First Continental Congress meets.
1775	• Battles of Lexington and Concord. • Lord Dunmore promises freedom to defecting slaves.

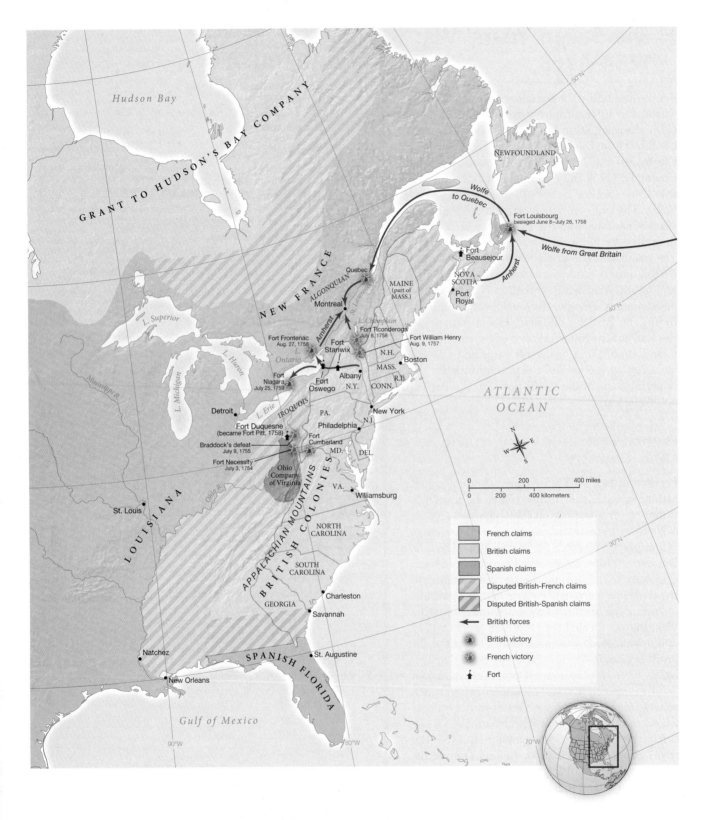

MAP 6.1 European Areas of Influence and the Seven Years' War, 1754–1763

In 1750, the French and Spanish empires had relatively few people on the ground, compared to the exploding population of the Anglo-American colonies. The disputed lands shown here, contested by the imperial powers, were inhabited by a variety of Native American tribes.

and chase the French away—but without attacking them.

In the spring of 1754, Washington set out with 160 Virginians and a small contingent of Mingo Indians equally concerned about the French military presence in the Ohio Country. Early one morning the Mingo chief Tanaghrisson led a detachment of Washington's soldiers to a small French encampment in the woods. Who fired first was in dispute, but fourteen Frenchmen (and no Virginians) were wounded. While Washington, lacking a translator, struggled to communicate with the injured French commander, Tanaghrisson and his men intervened to kill and then scalp the wounded soldiers, including the commander, probably with the aim of inflam-

Ohio River Valley, 1753

Washington's Journal, 1754

When George Washington returned from his first mission to the French, he presented Governor Dinwiddie with a military intelligence report full of his own dangerous exploits: traveling in deep snow, falling off a raft into an icy river, and being shot at by a lone Indian. The printed report circulated in London, bringing Washington notice as a young man of resolute and rugged courage. This item is reproduced by permission of the Huntington Library, San Marino, California.

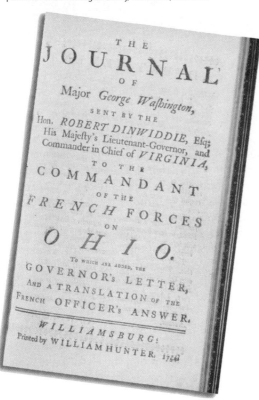

ing hostilities between the French and the colonists.

This sudden massacre violated Dinwiddie's instructions to Washington and raised the stakes considerably. Fearing retaliation, Washington ordered his men to throw together a makeshift "Fort Necessity." Several hundred Virginia reinforcements arrived, but the Mingos, sensing disaster and displeased by Washington's style of command, fled. (Tanaghrisson later said, "The Colonel was a good-natured man, but had no experience; he took upon him to command the Indians as his slaves, [and] would by no means take advice from the Indians.") Retaliation arrived in the form of six hundred French soldiers aided by one hundred Shawnee and Delaware warriors, who attacked Fort Necessity, killing or wounding a third of Washington's men. The message was clear: The French would not depart from the disputed territory.

The Albany Congress

British imperial leaders hoped to prevent the conflict in the Ohio Country from leading to a larger war. One obvious strategy was to strengthen an old partnership with the Mohawks of New York's Iroquois Confederacy, who since 1692 had joined with New York fur merchants in an alliance called the Covenant Chain. Yet unsavory land speculators caused the Mohawks to doubt British friendship. Authorities in London directed New York's royal governor to convene a colonial conference to repair trade relations and secure the Indians' help—or at least their neutrality—against the looming French threat. The conference convened at Albany, in June and July 1754. All six tribes of the Iroquois Confederacy attended, along with twenty-four delegates from seven colonies, making this an unprecedented pan-colony gathering. The elderly Mohawk chief Hendrick gave a powerful and widely reprinted speech, asserting that recent British neglect would inevitably reorient Indian trade relations to the French. "Look at the French, they are men; they are fortifying every where; but we are ashamed to say it; you are like women, bare and open, without any fortifications." Hendrick urged the assembled colonists to prepare for defense against the French. (See "Visualizing History," page 140.)

Cultural Cross-Dressing in Eighteenth-Century Portraits

CHIEF HENDRICK

JOHN CALDWELL

Two delegates at the congress seized the occasion to present an ambitious plan. Benjamin Franklin of Pennsylvania and Thomas Hutchinson of Massachusetts, both rising political stars, coauthored the Albany Plan of Union, a proposal for a unified but limited government to exercise sole authority over questions of war, peace, and trade with the Indians. Delegates at the Albany Congress, alarmed by news of the defeat of Virginians at Fort Necessity, agreed to present the plan to their respective assemblies. To Franklin's surprise, not a single colony approved the Albany Plan. The Massachusetts assembly feared it was "a Design of gaining power over the Colonies," especially the power of taxation. Others objected that it would be impossible to agree on unified policies toward scores of quite different Indian tribes. The British government never backed the Albany Plan; instead, it appointed two superintendents of Indian affairs, one for the northern and another for the southern colonies, each with exclusive powers to negotiate treaties, trade, and land sales with all tribes.

The Indians at the Albany Congress were not impressed with the Albany Plan either. The Covenant Chain alliance with the Mohawk tribe was reaffirmed, but the other nations left without pledging to help the British battle the French. Some of the Iroquois figured that the French military presence around the Great Lakes would discourage the westward push of American colonists and therefore better serve the Indians' interests.

Having one's portrait painted was a mark of distinction in the eighteenth century, usually available only to the wealthy or newsworthy. Rarer still were portraits of sitters dressed in clothes from other cultures. Here, Chief Hendrick, the Mohawk leader at the 1754 Albany Congress, appears in fine British clothing in a 1755 engraving, while John Caldwell, a titled Irishman and a British army officer, sports colorful Indian dress in a 1780 British painting.

Soon after the Albany Congress, Hendrick traveled to Philadelphia, where an elite men's club paid for a professional portrait. When Hendrick met death in the first northern battle in the Seven Years' War, great public mourning erupted both in America and in Britain. Two taverns and three sailing vessels in Philadelphia were named in his honor. Prints of this engraving, based on the portrait, were sold in British and American bookshops.

Hendrick's gold-braided coat, ruffled shirt, and three-cornered hat are all signs of a well-dressed English gentleman. Why might he have chosen this outfit for the Philadelphia portrait? What statement might it have made to London purchasers about Hendrick's political allegiance? What marks his Indianness in the engraving? Note the facial tattoos—a starburst over his ear, the two lines under the eye—and the long scar on his left cheek. Do they suggest a generic Indian image, or is this a picture of a particular man?

John Caldwell, of an Irish aristocratic family, spent the Revolutionary War (see "The War in the West: Indian Country" chapter 7) at Fort Detroit, a British garrison supporting the Great Lakes tribes battling Americans. The Ojibwas of that region honored Caldwell by giving him an Indian name in a ceremony, and it was likely that he then acquired the clothing and accessories shown in this portrait. Notice the headdress, breechcloth, beaded pouch, knife and sheath, tomahawk, wampum belt, red leggings and garters (showing an expanse of thigh, immodest by British standards). Why might Caldwell have posed in this garb? Was he trying to channel the power of Indian men, doubtless seen as exotic by British viewers of the painting? Did Caldwell "go native"? Or was this his way to display manly courage?

Consider the differences in these images. Hendrick's portrait of 1755 was engraved and publicly disseminated to memorialize the leader of one of the few tribes loyal to Britain during the Seven Years' War. The taverns and sailing ships named for him further mark his celebrated status. Caldwell's portrait was a private possession, commissioned after the Revolutionary War when much of Britain's North American land claims had fallen to the colonies. What attitude do you think Hendrick and Caldwell intended to convey regarding the other's culture?

Questions for Analysis

1. Why was Chief Hendrick so celebrated by the Anglo-Americans after his death, and why did his fame spread to England?

2. In receiving an Indian name and wearing Indian clothing, had Caldwell in some sense been adopted by the Ojibwa?

3. How might Hendrick and Caldwell have reacted to the other's portrait?

Connect to the Big Idea

C How did Native Americans participate in the Seven Years' War?

The War and Its Consequences

By 1755, George Washington's frontier skirmish had turned into a major war. The British expected quick victories on three fronts. General Edward Braddock, recently arrived from England, marched his army toward Fort Duquesne in western Pennsylvania. Farther north, British troops moved toward Fort Niagara, critically located between Lakes Erie and Ontario. And William Johnson, a New Yorker recently appointed superintendent of northern Indian affairs, led forces north toward Lake Champlain, intending to defend the border against the French in Canada (see Map 6.1).

Unfortunately for the British, the French were prepared to fight and had enlisted many Indian tribes in their cause. When Braddock's army of 2,000 British soldiers marched west toward Fort Duquesne, a mere eight Oneida warriors came as guides. They were ambushed by 250 French soldiers joined by 640 Indian warriors. Surviving soldiers reported that they never saw more than a half dozen Indians at a time, so hidden were they in the woods. But the soldiers could hear them. One soldier wrote weeks later that "the yell of the Indians is fresh on my ear, and the terrific sound will haunt me until the hour of my dissolution." The disciplined British troops stood their ground, making them easy targets. In the bloody battle nearly a thousand on the British side were killed or wounded, including General Braddock.

For the next two years, British leaders stumbled badly, deploying inadequate numbers of undersupplied troops. What finally turned the war around was the rise to power in 1757 of William Pitt, Britain's prime minister, a man ready to commit massive resources to fight France and Spain worldwide. In America, British troops aided by American provincial soldiers at last captured Forts Duquesne, Niagara, and Ticonderoga, followed by the French cities of Quebec and finally Montreal, all from 1758 to 1760. By 1761, the war subsided in America but expanded globally, with battles in the Caribbean, Austria, Prussia, and India. The British captured the French sugar islands Martinique and Guadeloupe and then invaded Spanish Cuba with an army of some four thousand provincial soldiers from New York and New England. By the end of 1762, France and Spain capitulated, and the Treaty of Paris was signed in 1763.

In the complex peace negotiations that followed, Britain gained control of Canada, eliminating the French threat from the north. British and American title to the eastern half of North America was confirmed. But French territory west of the Mississippi River, including New Orleans, was transferred to Spain as compensation for Spain's assistance during the war. Strangely, Cuba was returned to Spain, and Martinique and Guadeloupe were returned to France (Map 6.2).

The British credited their army for their victory and criticized the colonists for inadequate support. William Pitt was convinced that colonial smuggling—beaver pelts from French fur traders and illegal molasses in the French Caribbean—"principally, if not alone, enabled France to sustain and protract this long and expensive war."

Colonists read the lessons of the war differently. American soldiers had turned out in force, they claimed, but had been relegated to grunt work by British commanders and subjected to harsh military discipline, including floggings and executions. They bristled at British arrogance, as when Benjamin Franklin heard General Braddock brag that "these savages may, indeed, be a formidable enemy to your raw American militia, but upon the king's regular and disciplined troops, sir, it is impossible they should make any impression." Braddock's crushing defeat "gave us Americans," Franklin wrote, "the first suspicion that our

MAP ACTIVITY

MAP 6.2   Europe Redraws the Map of North America, 1763

In 1763, France ceded to Britain its interior territory from Quebec to New Orleans, retaining fishing rights in the north and sugar islands in the Caribbean. France transferred to Spain its claim to extensive territory west of the Mississippi River.

READING THE MAP: Who actually lived on and controlled the lands ceded by France? In what sense, if any, did Britain or Spain own these large territories?

CONNECTIONS: What was the goal of the Proclamation of 1763? (See page 143.) Could it ever have worked?

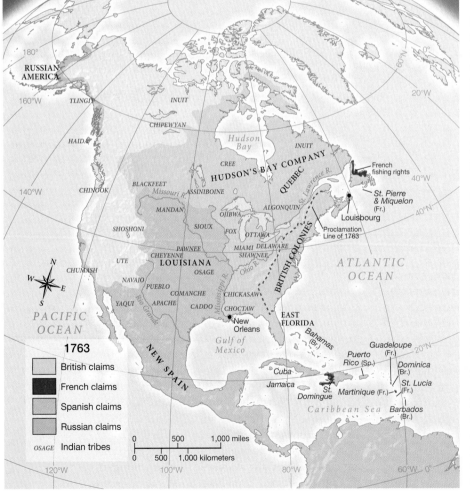

exalted ideas of the prowess of British regulars had not been well founded."

Perhaps most important, the enormous expense of the war cast a huge shadow over the victory. By 1763, Britain's national debt, double what it had been when Pitt took office, posed a formidable challenge to the next decade of leadership in Britain.

Pontiac's Rebellion and the Proclamation of 1763

One glaring omission marred the Treaty of Paris: The major powers at the treaty table failed to include or consult the Indians. Minavavana, an Ojibwa chief of the Great Lakes region, put it succinctly to an English trader: "Englishman, although you have conquered the French, you have not yet conquered us! We are not your slaves. These lakes, these woods and mountains were left to us by our ancestors. . .; and we will part with them to none." Furthermore, Minavavana pointedly noted, "your king has never sent us any presents, nor entered into any treaty with us, wherefore he and we are still at war."

Minavavana's complaint about the absence of British presents was significant. To Indians, gifts cemented social relationships, symbolizing honor and establishing obligation. Over many decades, the French had mastered the subtleties of gift exchange, distributing textiles and hats and receiving calumets (ceremonial pipes) in return. British military leaders, new to the practice, often discarded the calumets as trivial trinkets, thereby insulting the givers. From the British view, a generous gift might signify tribute (thus demeaning the giver), or it might be positioned as a bribe. "It is not my intention ever to attempt to gain the friendship of Indians by presents," Major General Jeffery Amherst declared. The Indian view was the opposite: Generous givers expressed dominance and protection, not subordination, in the ceremonial practices of giving.

Despite Minavavana's confident words, Indians north of the Ohio River had cause for concern. Old French trading posts all over the Northwest were beefed up by the British into military bases. Fort Duquesne, renamed Fort Pitt to honor the victorious leader, gained new walls sixty feet thick at their base, announcing that this was no fur trading post. Tensions between the British and the Indians in this area ran high.

The Seven Years' War

1692–1750s	English and Iroquois create and affirm the Covenant Chain alliance in western New York.
1700–1740s	French settlers enjoy exclusive trade with Indians in Ohio Valley.
1747	Ohio Company receives land grant from British king.
1753	Mohawk chief Hendrick accuses English of breaking Covenant Chain.
	French soldiers advance from Canada into Ohio Country.
	George Washington delivers message telling French they are trespassing.
1754	French build Fort Duquesne.
	Washington returns to Ohio Country with troops and Mingo allies.
	May. Washington, guided by Mingo chief Tanaghrisson, attacks French.
	June–July. Albany Congress convenes.
	July. French and Indian soldiers defeat Washington at Fort Necessity.
1755	British authorities appoint two superintendents of Indian affairs.
	July. Braddock defeated at Monongahela.
1756	William Pitt becomes British prime minister.
1758	British capture Fort Duquesne.
1759	British capture Forts Niagara and Ticonderoga.
1760	British capture Montreal.
1762	British capture Cuba.
1763	Treaty of Paris signed.

A religious revival among the Indians magnified feelings of antagonism toward the British. In 1763, the renewal of commitment to Indian ways and the formation of tribal alliances led to open warfare, which the British called **Pontiac's Rebellion**, named for the chief of the Ottawas. In mid-May, Ottawa, Potawatomi, and Huron warriors attacked Fort Detroit. Six more attacks on forts

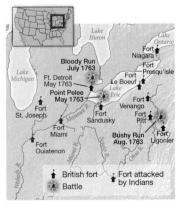

Pontiac's Uprising, 1763

followed within weeks, and frontier settlements were raided by tribes from western New York, the Ohio Valley, and the Great Lakes region. By fall, Indians had captured every fort west of Detroit. More than four hundred British soldiers were dead and another two thousand colonists killed or taken captive.

Some Americans exacted revenge. The worst violent aggression occurred in late 1763, when some fifty Pennsylvania vigilantes known as the Paxton Boys descended on a peaceful village of friendly Conestoga Indians, murdering twenty. The vigilantes, now numbering five hundred, marched on Philadelphia to try to capture and murder some Christian Indians held in protective custody there. British troops prevented that, but the Paxton Boys escaped punishment for their murderous attack on the Conestoga village.

In early 1764, the uprising faded. The Indians were short on ammunition, and the British were tired and broke. The British government recalled the imperious general Amherst, blaming him for mishandling the conflict, and his own soldiers toasted his departure. A new military leader, Thomas Gage, took command and began distributing gifts profusely among the Indians.

To minimize violence, the British government issued the Proclamation of 1763, forbidding colonists to settle west of the Appalachian Mountains in order to protect Indian territory. But the Proclamation's language also took care not to identify western lands as belonging to the Indians. Instead, it spoke of lands that "are reserved to [Indians], as their Hunting Grounds."

Other parts of the Proclamation of 1763 referred to American and even French colonists in Canada as "our loving subjects," entitled to English rights and privileges. In contrast, the Indians were rejected as British subjects and described more vaguely as "Tribes of Indians with whom We are connected." Of course, the British were not really well connected with any Indians, nor did they wish connections to form among the tribes. As William Johnson, the superintendent of northern Indian affairs, advised in 1764, "It will be expedient to treat with each nation separately . . . for could they arrive at a perfect union, they must prove very dangerous Neighbours."

The 1763 boundary was a further provocation to American settlers and also to land speculators who (like Virginia's Patrick Henry or the men of the Ohio Company) had already staked claims to huge tracts of western lands in hopes of profitable resale. Yet the boundary proved impossible to enforce. Surging population growth had already sent many hundreds of settlers, many of them squatters, west of the Appalachians. Periodic bloodshed continued and left the settlers fearful, uncertain about their futures, and increasingly wary of British claims to be a protective mother country.

> **REVIEW** How did the Seven Years' War erode relations between colonists and British authorities?

Silver Medal to Present to Indians
After Pontiac's uprising, the British distributed gifts to foster peace. This 1766 silver medal shows King George III on the front and an Indian and a Briton smoking a peace pipe on the back. How would an English translator explain what HAPPY WHILE UNITED might mean? Courtesy of the American Numismatic Society.

▶ The Sugar and Stamp Acts, 1763–1765

In 1760, George III, twenty-two years old, became king of England. Timid and insecure, George struggled to gain his footing in his new job. He rotated through a succession of leaders, searching for a prime minister he could trust. A half dozen ministers in seven years took turns dealing with one basic underlying British reality: A huge war debt needed to be serviced, and the colonists, as British subjects, should help pay it off. To many American colonists, however, that proposition seemed in deep violation of what they perceived to be their rights and liberties as British subjects, and it created resentment that eventually erupted in large-scale street protests.

VISUAL ACTIVITY

Tea and Sugar in the 1760s
In the mid-eighteenth century, rising sugarcane production in the West Indies transformed sugar into a commonplace commodity in the English-speaking world. It became a desired taste indulged in by the elite classes (as pictured here) and by non-elites. At the center of this 1764 painting, titled "The Honeymoon," a young woman delicately drops a sugar cube into her husband's cup of tea. The Colonial Williamsburg Foundation. Museum Purchase

READING THE IMAGE: How does the artist convey the relationship between the two people? How does the sugar contribute to the theme of youthful romance?

CONNECTIONS: Why did sugar and molasses—newly popular and exotic stimulants—become politicized in the 1760s?

The first provocative revenue acts were the work of Sir George Grenville, prime minister from 1763 to 1765.

Grenville's Sugar Act

To find revenue, George Grenville scrutinized the customs service, which monitored the shipping trade and collected all import and export duties. Grenville found that the salaries of customs officers cost the government four times what was collected in revenue. The shortfall was due in part to bribery and smuggling, so Grenville began to insist on rigorous attention to paperwork and a strict accounting of collected duties. The hardest duty to enforce was the one imposed by the Molasses Act of 1733—a stiff tax of six pence per gallon on any molasses imported to British colonies from non-British sources. Rum-loving Americans, however, were eager to buy molasses from French Caribbean islands—cheap because

the French scorned rum, preferring wines and brandy. Americans had ignored the Molasses Act for decades.

Grenville's inspired solution was the **Revenue Act** of 1764, popularly dubbed the **Sugar Act**. It lowered the duty on French molasses to three pence, making it more attractive for shippers to obey the law, and at the same time raised penalties for smuggling. The act appeared to be in the tradition of navigation acts meant to regulate trade (see "Royal Regulation of Colonial Trade" in chapter 4), but Grenville's actual intent was to raise revenue. The Sugar Act toughened enforcement policies. From now on, all British naval crews could act as impromptu customs officers, boarding suspicious ships and seizing cargoes found to be in violation. Smugglers caught without proper paperwork would be prosecuted, not in a local court with a friendly jury but in a vice-admiralty court located in Nova Scotia, where a crown judge presided.

The implication was that justice would be sure and severe. Grenville's hopes for the Sugar Act did not materialize. The small decrease in duty did not offset the attractions of smuggling, while the increased vigilance in enforcement led to several ugly confrontations in port cities. Reaction to the Sugar Act foreshadowed questions about Britain's right to tax Americans, but in 1764 objections to the act came principally from the small numbers of Americans engaged in the shipping trades. From the British point of view, the Sugar Act seemed to be a reasonable effort to administer the colonies. To Americans, however, the British supervision appeared to be a disturbing intrusion on colonial practices of self-taxation by elected colonial assemblies. Benjamin Franklin, Pennsylvania's lobbyist in London, warned that "two distinct Jurisdictions or Powers of Taxing cannot well subsist together in the same country."

The Stamp Act

In February 1765, Grenville escalated his revenue program with the **Stamp Act**, precipitating a major conflict between Britain and the colonies over Parliament's right to tax. The Stamp Act imposed a tax on all paper used for official documents—newspapers, pamphlets, court documents, licenses, wills, ships' cargo lists—and required an affixed stamp as proof that the tax had been paid. Unlike the Sugar Act, which regulated trade, the Stamp Act was designed plainly and simply to raise money. It affected nearly everyone who used any taxed paper but, most of all, users of official documents in the business and legal communities. Anticipating that the stamp tax would be unpopular—Thomas Hutchinson had forewarned him—Grenville delegated the administration of the act to Americans to avoid taxpayer hostility toward British enforcers. In each colony, local stamp distributors would be hired at a handsome salary of 8 percent of the revenue collected.

English tradition held that taxes were a gift of the people to their monarch, granted by the people's representatives. This view of taxes as a freely given gift preserved an essential concept of English political theory: the idea that citizens have the liberty to enjoy and use their property without fear of confiscation. The king could not demand taxes; only the House of Commons could grant it. Grenville agreed with the notion of taxation by consent, but he argued that the colonists were already "virtually" represented in Parliament. The House of Commons, he insisted, represented all British subjects, wherever they were.

Colonial leaders emphatically rejected this view, arguing that **virtual representation** could not withstand the stretch across the Atlantic. Colonists willingly paid local and provincial taxes, levied by their town, county, or colonial assemblies, to fund government administrative expenses and shared necessities like local roads, schools, and poor relief. In contrast, the stamp tax was a clear departure as a fee-per-document tax, levied by a distant Parliament on unwilling colonies.

Resistance Strategies and Crowd Politics

News of the Stamp Act arrived in the colonies in April 1765, seven months before it was to take effect. There was time, therefore, to object. Governors were unlikely to challenge the law, for most of them owed their offices to the king. Instead, the colonial assemblies took the lead; eight of them held discussions on the Stamp Act.

Virginia's assembly, the House of Burgesses, was the first. At the end of its May session, after two-thirds of the members had left, Patrick Henry, a young political newcomer, presented a series of resolutions on the Stamp Act that were debated and passed, one by one. They became known as the Virginia Resolves. Henry's resolutions inched the assembly toward radical opposition to the Stamp Act. The first three stated the obvious: that Virginians were British citizens, that they enjoyed the same rights and privileges as Britons, and that self-taxation was one of those rights. The fourth resolution noted that Virginians had always taxed themselves, through their representatives in the House of Burgesses. The fifth took a radical leap by pushing the other four unexceptional statements to one logical conclusion—that the Virginia assembly alone had the right to tax Virginians.

Two more fiery resolutions were debated as Henry pressed the logic of his case to the extreme. The sixth resolution denied legitimacy to any tax law originating outside Virginia, and the seventh boldly called anyone who disagreed with these propositions an enemy of Virginia. This was too much for the other representatives. They voted down resolutions six and seven and later rescinded their vote on number five as well.

Their caution hardly mattered, however, because newspapers in other colonies printed all seven Virginia Resolves, creating the impression that a daring first challenge to the Stamp Act had occurred. Consequently, other assemblies were willing to consider even more radical ques-

Symbolic Death to Stamp Agents
Protesters in many towns staged threatening demonstrations designed to make any stamp distributor reconsider selling the hated stamps. In this contemporary cartoon, a dummy wearing a hat and waistcoat is being led to destruction. One protester carries a hangman's gallows, another a large bundle of sticks to burn the dummy. Do you think the cartoonist was in sympathy with the demonstrators? The Granger Collection, New York.

tions, such as this: By what authority could Parliament legislate for the colonies without also taxing them? No one disagreed, in 1765, that Parliament had legislative power over the colonists, who were, after all, British subjects. Several assemblies advanced the argument that there was a distinction between *external taxes*, imposed to regulate trade, and *internal taxes*, such as a stamp tax or a property tax, which could only be self-imposed.

Reaction to the Stamp Act ran far deeper than political debate in assemblies. Every person whose livelihood required official paper had to decide whether to comply with the act. The first organized resistance to the Stamp Act began in Boston in August 1765 under the direction of town leaders, chief among them Samuel Adams, John Hancock, and Ebenezer Mackintosh. Adams and Hancock, both Harvard graduates, were town officers. Adams, in his forties, had shrewd political instincts and a gift for organizing. Hancock, not yet thirty, had inherited an uncle's shipping business and was one of the wealthiest men in Massachusetts. Mackintosh, also a young man, was a shoemaker and highly experienced street activist. (See "Seeking the American Promise," page 148.) Many other artisans, tradesmen, printers, tavern keepers, dockworkers, and sailors—the middling and lower orders—mobilized to oppose the Stamp Act, taking the name "Sons of Liberty."

The plan hatched in Boston called for a large street demonstration highlighting a mock execution designed to convince Andrew Oliver, the designated stamp distributor, to resign. On August 14, 1765, a crowd of two thousand to three thousand demonstrators, led by Mackintosh, hung an effigy of Oliver in a tree and then paraded it around town before finally beheading and burning it. In hopes of calming tensions, the royal governor Francis Bernard took no action. The next day Oliver resigned his office in a well-publicized announcement.

The demonstration provided lessons for everyone. Oliver learned that stamp distributors would be very unpopular people. Governor Bernard, with no police force to call on, learned the limitations of his power to govern. The demonstration's leaders learned that street action was effective. And hundreds of ordinary men not only learned what the Stamp Act was all about but also gained pride in their ability to have a decisive impact on politics.

Pursuing Liberty, Protesting Tyranny

In August 1765, a little-known Boston shoemaker gained sudden prominence as the leader of crowd actions opposing the Stamp Act. Ebenezer Mackintosh boldly encouraged thousands of ordinary men in Massachusetts to assert a claim to liberty against what they identified as British tyranny. Mackintosh's story offers a glimpse into the political thinking of the man in the street during the decade of pre-Revolutionary turmoil. By 1776, this quest for liberty would be a defining feature of the fledgling United States.

Born in poverty in 1737, Ebenezer Mackintosh lacked family resources to ease his way in the world. His ancestors arrived in the Puritan migration of the 1630s; a century later, his family was quite poor. Ebenezer's father, an orphan, struggled against bad fortune. He owned no land and lacked a trade; he married and buried wives at least three times. The best he could do for young Ebenezer was to apprentice him to a shoemaker. During the Seven Years' War, Ebenezer joined the army to secure a signing bonus. He saw brief action and returned to Boston in 1758 to resume shoemaking. He was twenty-one.

A major fire in Boston in 1760 marked a dramatic change in direction for Mackintosh. In the aftermath of the fire, the city looked to young, able-bodied men to reinvigorate its volunteer fire companies and picked Ebenezer to join a select firemen's association in the city's South End. Fighting fires demonstrated one's sense of civic duty and manly responsibility. Fire clubs also generated fraternal sociability, with firemen regularly meeting in taverns over pitchers of beer, cementing the team spirit so critical to successful firefighting. Mackintosh proved to be a leader of men in times of emergency; he soon became head of the South End gang, which staged a mock battle once a year against the rival North End gang. In this traditional street festival, Mackintosh gained direct experience managing rowdy crowds.

Expertise in fire and crowd control paved the way for Mackintosh's transition from community leader to community activist in 1765. Stamp Act protests erupted twice in August of that year. In the first event, Mackintosh presided over the mock hanging of a dummy representing Andrew Oliver, the stamp distributor, at a century-old elm tree known as the Liberty Tree. The shoemaker led several thousand protesters in a march on the new stamp office, which was pulled down and burned. Twelve days later, a smaller but far more destructive demonstration almost certainly led by Mackintosh demolished the mansion of Governor Thomas Hutchinson. Hutchinson ordered Mackintosh arrested, but no witnesses cared to identify him. Hours later, the sheriff—a member of Mackintosh's fire company—released him, predicting worse trouble if he was kept in jail.

The shoemaker continued to lead large demonstrations in November and December, forcing Andrew Oliver to repudiate his stamp distributor duties. Ordinary people like Mackintosh exerted a new authority and confidence, commanding their social betters to do their bidding.

In 1766, the Stamp Act was repealed, and Mackintosh went back to shoemaking. He married Elizabeth Maverick and had two children by 1769. Perhaps he took a break from activism; no record links him to protest activities when British troops came to town in 1769–1770, nor was his presence recorded at the Boston Massacre in March 1770. In 1773, he was apparently back at it, bragging later in life that he helped throw tea into Boston harbor.

A well-publicized rumor spread in 1774 that a ship en route from London carried official orders to arrest four rebellious subjects, most notably Samuel Adams and Mackintosh. Adams stayed put, but Mackintosh, still lacking resources and at a low moment in life—his young wife had recently died—decided that flight was his best option. Carrying his two young

Twelve days later, a second crowd action showed how well these lessons had been learned. On August 26, a crowd visited the houses of three detested customs and court officials, breaking windows and raiding wine cellars. A fourth target was the finest dwelling in Massachusetts, owned by Thomas Hutchinson, lieutenant governor of Massachusetts and the chief justice of the colony's highest court. Rumors abounded that Hutchinson had urged Grenville to adopt the Stamp Act. Although he had actually done the opposite, Hutchinson refused to set the record straight, saying curtly, "I am not obliged to give an answer to all the questions that may be put me by every lawless person." The crowd attacked his house, and by daybreak only the exterior walls were standing. Governor Bernard gave orders to call out the militia, but

Mackintosh the Fireman

Skilled Boston firemen tapped water from underground water mains made from hollowed logs and pumped it vigorously by hand to douse fires. Demolition to halt the spread of fires was also essential work. Mackintosh's fire-control skills transferred easily to anti–Stamp Act actions, whether burning effigies and small buildings or pulling down Hutchinson's house. The Granger Collection, New York.

children and his meager belongings, he walked 150 miles to a village in northern New Hampshire, where he set up shop as a shoemaker. He served locally and briefly as a soldier in the Revolution and then remarried and fathered four more children.

An especially telling clue to Mackintosh's idealization of liberty appears in the unusual name he gave his son born in 1769: Paschal Paoli Mackintosh, named in honor of Pasquale Paoli of Corsica, an anti-monarchical freedom fighter who battled Italian foes and who won approving coverage in American newspapers in 1767–1769. (In those years, some scores of babies through-out the colonies were named

Paschal.) Mackintosh enjoyed his brief moment of fame, and he lived to see liberty defined and enshrined in the foundational documents of the United States. Although his life ended in 1816 in obscurity, as it had begun, Mackintosh's activism in 1765 helped ensure that the thousands of people he mobilized learned a new political language of rights and liberties—a language that still resonates loudly today.

Questions for Consideration

1. Why would a twenty-eight-year-old shoemaker of low social status get upset about Britain's passage of the Stamp Act?

2. How likely was it that Mackintosh's wife, Elizabeth Maverick Mackintosh, participated in any of the crowd actions led by her husband?

3. What was at stake for Mackintosh in the American Revolution? What did he gain? What stayed the same?

Connect to the Big Idea

C How did many ordinary Americans of limited means, limited tax liabilities, limited political experience, and limited literacy get drawn into the developing political crisis with Britain?

he was told that many militiamen were among the crowd.

The destruction of Hutchinson's house brought a temporary halt to protest activities in Boston. The town meeting issued a statement of sympathy for Hutchinson, but a large reward for the arrest and conviction of rioters failed to produce a single lead. Hutchinson believed that Adams commanded Mackintosh, but Adams denied involvement and professed shock at the "truly mobbish Nature" of the violence. Essentially, the opponents of the Stamp Act in Boston had triumphed; no one replaced Oliver as distributor. When the act took effect on November 1, ships without stamped permits continued to clear the harbor. Since he could not bring the lawbreakers to court, Hutchinson, ever principled, felt obliged to resign his office as chief justice. He remained lieutenant governor, however, and within five years he became the royal governor.

Liberty and Property

Boston's crowd actions of August sparked similar eruptions by groups calling themselves Sons of Liberty in nearly fifty towns throughout the colonies, and stamp distributors everywhere hastened to resign. A crowd forced one Connecticut distributor to throw his hat and powdered wig in the air while shouting a cheer for "Liberty and property!" This man fared better than another Connecticut stamp agent who was nearly buried alive by Sons of Liberty. Only when the thuds of dirt sounded on his coffin did he have a sudden change of heart, shouting out his resignation to the crowd above. Luckily, he was heard. In Charleston, South Carolina, the stamp distributor resigned after crowds burned effigies and chanted "Liberty! Liberty!"

Some colonial leaders, disturbed by the riots, sought a more moderate challenge to parliamentary authority. In October 1765, twenty-seven delegates representing nine colonial assemblies met in New York City as the Stamp Act Congress. For two weeks, the men hammered out a petition about taxation addressed to the king and Parliament. Their statement closely resembled the first five Virginia Resolves, claiming that taxes were "free gifts of the people," which only the people's representatives could give. They dismissed virtual representation: "The people of these colonies are not, and from their local circumstances, cannot be represented in the House of Commons." At the same time, the delegates carefully affirmed their subordination to Parliament and monarch in deferential language. Nevertheless, the Stamp Act Congress, by the mere fact of its meeting, advanced a radical potential—the notion of intercolonial political action.

The rallying cry of "Liberty and property" made perfect sense to many white Americans of all social ranks, who feared that the Stamp Act threatened their traditional rights to liberty as British subjects. The liberty in question was the right to be taxed only by representative government. "Liberty and property" came from a trinity of concepts—"life, liberty, property"—that had come to be regarded as the birthright of freeborn British subjects since at least the seventeenth century. A powerful tradition of British political thought invested representative government with the duty to protect individual lives, liberties, and property against potential abuse by royal authority. Up to 1765, Americans had consented to accept

Parliament as a body that represented them. But now, in this matter of taxation via stamps, Parliament seemed a distant body that had failed to protect Americans' liberty and property against royal authority.

Alarmed, some Americans began to speak and write about a plot by British leaders to enslave them. A Maryland writer warned that if the colonies lost "the right of exemption from all taxes without their consent," that loss would "deprive them of every privilege distinguishing freemen from slaves." In Virginia, a group of planters headed by Richard Henry Lee issued a document called the Westmoreland Resolves, claiming that the Stamp Act was an attempt "to reduce the people of this country to a state of abject and detestable slavery." The opposite meanings of *liberty* and *slavery* were utterly clear to white Americans, but they stopped short of applying similar logic to the half million black Americans they held in bondage. Many blacks, however, could see the contradiction. When a crowd of Charleston blacks paraded with shouts of "Liberty!" just a few months after white Sons of Liberty had done the same, the town militia turned out to break up the demonstration.

Politicians and merchants in Britain reacted with distress to the American demonstrations and petitions. Merchants particularly feared trade disruptions and pressured Parliament to repeal the Stamp Act. By late 1765, yet another new minister, the Marquess of Rockingham, headed the king's cabinet and sought a way to repeal the act without losing face. The solution came in March 1766: The Stamp Act was repealed, but with the repeal came the **Declaratory Act**, which asserted Parliament's right to legislate for the colonies "in all cases whatsoever." Perhaps the stamp tax had been inexpedient, and indeed a failure, but the power to tax—one prime case of a legislative power—was stoutly upheld.

REVIEW   Why did the Sugar Act and the Stamp Act draw fierce opposition from colonists?

▶ The Townshend Acts and Economic Retaliation, 1767–1770

Rockingham did not last long as prime minister. By the summer of 1766, George III had persuaded William Pitt to resume that position. Pitt appointed Charles Townshend to be chancellor of the exchequer, the chief financial minister. Facing both the old war debt and the cost of the British troops in America, Townshend turned again to taxation, but his plan to raise revenue touched off coordinated boycotts of British goods in 1768 and 1769. Even women were politicized as self-styled "Daughters of Liberty." Boston led the uproar, causing the British to send peacekeeping soldiers to assist the royal governor. The stage was thus set for the first fatalities in the brewing revolution.

The Townshend Duties

Townshend proposed new taxes in the old form of a navigation act. Officially called the Revenue Act of 1767, it established new duties on tea, glass, lead, paper, and painters' colors imported into the colonies, to be paid by the importer but passed on to consumers in the retail price. A recent further reduction in the duty on French molasses had persuaded some American shippers to quit smuggling, and finally Britain was deriving a moderate revenue stream from its colonies. Townshend naively concluded that Americans accepted external taxes.

The **Townshend duties** were not especially burdensome, but the principle they embodied—taxation through trade duties—looked different to the colonists in the wake of the Stamp Act crisis. Although Americans once distinguished between external and internal taxes, accepting external duties as a means to direct the flow of trade, that distinction was wiped out by an external tax meant only to raise money. John Dickinson, a Philadelphia lawyer, articulated this view in an essay titled *Letters from a Farmer in Pennsylvania*, widely circulated in late 1767. "We are taxed without our consent. . . . We are therefore—SLAVES," Dickinson wrote, calling for "a total denial of the power of Parliament to lay upon these colonies any 'tax' whatever."

A controversial provision of the Townshend duties directed that some of the revenue generated would pay the salaries of royal governors. Before 1767, local assemblies set the salaries of their own officials, giving them significant influence over crown-appointed officeholders. Through his new provision, Townshend aimed to strengthen the governors' position as well as to curb what he perceived to be the growing independence of the assemblies.

Massachusetts again took the lead in protesting the Townshend duties. Samuel Adams, now an elected member of the provincial assembly, argued that any form of parliamentary taxation was unjust because Americans were not represented in Parliament. Further, he argued that the new way to pay governors' salaries subverted the proper relationship between the people and their rulers. The assembly circulated a letter with Adams's arguments to other colonial assemblies for their endorsement. As with the Stamp Act Congress of 1765, colonial assemblies were starting to coordinate their protests.

In response to Adams's letter, Lord Hillsborough, the new man in charge of colonial affairs in Britain, instructed Massachusetts governor Bernard to dissolve the assembly if it refused to repudiate the letter. The assembly refused, by a vote of 92 to 17, and Bernard carried out his instruction. In the summer of 1768, Boston was in an uproar.

Nonconsumption and the Daughters of Liberty

The Boston town meeting led the way with nonconsumption agreements calling for a boycott of all British-made goods. Dozens of other towns passed similar resolutions in 1767 and 1768. For example, prohibited purchases in the town of New Haven, Connecticut, included carriages, furniture, hats, clothing, lace, clocks, and textiles. The idea was to encourage home manufacture and to hurt trade, causing London merchants to pressure Parliament for repeal of the duties.

Nonconsumption agreements were very hard to enforce. With the Stamp Act, there was one hated item, a stamp, and a limited number of official distributors. In contrast, an agreement to boycott all British goods required serious personal sacrifice, which not everyone was prepared to make. A more direct blow to trade came from nonimportation agreements, but getting merchants to agree to these proved more difficult, because of fears that merchants in other colonies might continue to import goods and make handsome profits. Not until late 1768 could Boston merchants agree to suspend trade through a nonimportation agreement lasting one year starting January 1, 1769. Sixty signed the agreement. New York merchants soon followed suit, as did Philadelphia and Charleston merchants in 1769.

Many of the British products specified in nonconsumption agreements were household goods traditionally under the control of the "ladies." By 1769, male leaders in the patriot cause clearly understood that women's cooperation in nonconsumption and home manufacture was beneficial to their cause. The Townshend duties thus provided an unparalleled opportunity for encouraging female patriotism. During the Stamp Act crisis, Sons of

Edenton Tea Ladies
Patriotic women in Edenton, North Carolina, pledged to renounce British tea and were satirized in this British cartoon, which shows brazen women shedding their femininity. Neglected babies, urinating dogs, wanton sexuality, and mean-looking women were the consequences, according to the artist. The cartoon was humorous to the British because of the gender reversals it predicts and because of the insult it directs at American men. Library of Congress.

Liberty took to the streets in protest. During the difficulties of 1768 and 1769, the concept of Daughters of Liberty emerged to give shape to a new idea—that women might play a role in public affairs. Any woman could express affiliation with the colonial protest through conspicuous boycotts of British-made goods. In Boston, more than three hundred women signed a petition to abstain from tea, "sickness excepted," in order to "save this abused Country from Ruin and Slavery."

Homespun cloth became a prominent symbol of patriotism. A young Boston girl learning to spin called herself "a daughter of liberty," noting that "I chuse to wear as much of our own manufactory as pocible." In the boycott period of 1768 to 1770, newspapers reported on spinning matches, or bees, in some sixty New England towns, in which women came together in public to make yarn. Newspaper accounts variously called the spinners "Daughters of Liberty" or "Daughters of Industry."

This surge of public spinning was related to the politics of the boycott, which infused traditional women's work with new political purpose.

But the women spinners were not equivalents of the Sons of Liberty. The Sons marched in streets, burned effigies, threatened hated officials, and celebrated anniversaries of their successes with raucous drinking in taverns. The Daughters manifested their patriotism quietly, in ways marked by piety, industry, and charity. The difference was due in part to cultural ideals of gender, which prized masculine self-assertion and feminine selflessness. It also was due to class. The Sons were a cross-class alliance, with leaders from the middling orders reliant on men and boys of the lower ranks to fuel their crowds. The Daughters dusting off spinning wheels and shelving their teapots were genteel ladies accustomed to buying British goods. The difference between the Sons and the Daughters also speaks to two views of how best to challenge authority: violent threats and street actions, or the self-disciplined, self-sacrificing boycott of goods?

On the whole, the anti-British boycotts were a success. Imports fell by more than 40 percent; British merchants felt the pinch and let Parliament know it. In Boston, the extended Hutchinson family—whose fortune rested on British trade—also endured losses, but even more alarming to the lieutenant governor, Boston seemed overrun with anti-British sentiment. The Sons of Liberty staged rollicking annual celebrations of the Stamp Act riot, and both Hutchinson and Governor Bernard concluded that British troops were necessary to restore order.

Military Occupation and "Massacre" in Boston

In the fall of 1768, three thousand uniformed troops arrived to occupy Boston. The soldiers drilled conspicuously on the town Common, played loud music on the Sabbath, and in general grated on the nerves of Bostonians. Although the situation was frequently tense, no major troubles occurred that winter and through most of 1769. But as January 1, 1770, approached, marking the end of the nonimportation agreement, it was clear that some merchants—such as Thomas Hutchinson's two sons, both importers—were ready to break the boycott.

Trouble began in January, when a crowd smeared the door of the Hutchinson brothers' shop with excrement. In February, a crowd surrounded the house of a confrontational customs official who panicked and fired a musket, accidentally killing a young boy passing on the street. The Sons of Liberty mounted a massive funeral procession to mark this first instance of violent death in the struggle with Britain.

For the next week, tension gripped Boston. The climax came on Monday evening, March 5, 1770, when a crowd taunted eight British soldiers guarding the customs house. Onlookers threw snowballs and rocks and dared the soldiers to fire; finally one did. After a short pause, someone yelled "Fire!" and the other soldiers shot into the crowd, hitting eleven men, killing five of them.

The **Boston Massacre**, as the event was quickly labeled, was over in minutes. Hutchinson, now acting governor of the colony, showed courage in addressing the crowd from the balcony of the statehouse. He immediately removed the regiments to an island in the harbor to prevent further bloodshed, and he jailed Captain Thomas Preston and his eight soldiers for their own protection, promising they would be held for trial.

The Sons of Liberty staged elaborate martyrs' funerals for the five victims. Significantly, the one nonwhite victim shared equally in the

VISUAL ACTIVITY

The Bloody Massacre Perpetrated in King Street, Boston, on March 5, 1770
Paul Revere's mass-produced engraving shows the patriot version of events. Soldiers appear as a firing squad, shooting simultaneously at an unarmed and bewigged crowd; more likely the shooting was chaotic and the fatalities were from lower classes who were not the sort to wear wigs. Crispus Attucks, an African-Indian dockworker, was killed, but Revere depicts only whites among the injured. Anne S. K. Brown Military Collection, Brown University Library

READING THE IMAGE: How does this picture attempt to enlist its viewers' sympathies?
CONNECTIONS: Does this picture accurately represent the events of the Boston Massacre? What might account for its biases?

public's veneration. Crispus Attucks, a sailor and rope maker in his forties, was the son of an African man and a Natick Indian woman. A slave in his youth, he was at the time of his death a free laborer at the Boston docks. Attucks was one of the first American partisans to die in the revolutionary struggle with Britain, and certainly the first African American.

At trial in the fall of 1770, the eight soldiers were ably defended by two Boston attorneys, John Adams and Josiah Quincy. While both had direct ties to the leadership of the Sons of Liberty, Adams was deeply committed to the principle that even unpopular defendants deserved a fair trial. Samuel Adams respected his cousin's decision to take the case, for there was a tactical benefit as well. It showed that the Boston leadership was not lawless but could be seen as defenders of British liberty and law. The five-day trial resulted in acquittal for Preston and for all but two of the soldiers, who were convicted of manslaughter, branded on the thumbs, and released.

> **REVIEW** Why did British authorities send troops to occupy Boston in the fall of 1768?

▶ The Destruction of the Tea and the Coercive Acts, 1770–1774

In the same week as the Boston Massacre, yet another new British prime minister, Frederick North, acknowledged the harmful impact of the boycott on trade and recommended repeal of the Townshend duties. A skillful politician, Lord North took office in 1770 and kept it for twelve years; at last King George had stability at the helm. Seeking peace with the colonies and prosperity for British merchants, Lord North persuaded Parliament to remove all the duties except the tax on tea, kept as a symbol of Parliament's power. For nearly two years following repeal of the Townshend duties, peace seemed possible, but tense incidents in 1772, followed by a renewed struggle over the tea tax in 1773, precipitated a full-scale crisis in the summer and fall of 1774. In response, men from nearly all the colonies came together in a special "Continental Congress" to debate the crisis.

The Calm before the Storm

Repeal of the Townshend duties brought an end to nonimportation. Trade boomed in 1770 and 1771, driven by pent-up demand. Moreover, the leaders of the popular movement seemed to be losing their power. Samuel Adams, for example, ran for a minor local office and lost to a conservative merchant. Then in 1772, several incidents again brought the conflict with Britain into sharp focus. One was the burning of the *Gaspée*, a Royal Navy ship pursuing suspected smugglers near Rhode Island. A British investigating commission failed to arrest anyone but announced that it would send suspects, if any were found, to Britain for trial on charges of high treason. This ruling seemed to fly in the face of the traditional English right to trial by a jury of one's peers.

When news of the *Gaspée* investigation spread, it was greeted with disbelief in other colonies. Patrick Henry, Thomas Jefferson, and Richard Henry Lee in the Virginia House of Burgesses proposed that a network of standing committees be established to link the colonies and pass along alarming news. By mid-1773, all but one colonial assembly had set up a "committee of correspondence."

Massachusetts, the continuing hotspot of the conflict, developed its own rapid communications network, with urgency provided by a new proposal by Lord North to pay the salaries of county court justices out of the tea revenue, reminiscent of Townshend's plan for paying royal governors. By spring 1773, more than half the towns in Massachusetts had set up **committees of correspondence** to receive, discuss, distribute, and act on political news. The first message to circulate came from Boston; it framed North's salary plan for judges as the latest proof of a British conspiracy to undermine traditional liberties: first taxation without consent, then military occupation and a massacre, and now a plot to subvert the justice system. Express riders swiftly distributed the message, which sparked ordinary townspeople to embrace a revolutionary language of rights and constitutional duties. Eventually the committees of correspondence would foster rapid mobilization to defend a countryside feeling under literal attack.

The paramount incident shattering the relative calm of the early 1770s was the **Tea Act of 1773**. After nonimportation ended, Americans had resumed buying the taxed British tea, but they were also smuggling much larger quantities of tea obtained from Dutch sources, greatly undercutting the sales of Britain's East India Company.

To reverse this trend, Parliament lowered the colonists' tax on East India Company tea and, at the same time, allowed the Company to sell its product directly to a few selected merchants in four colonial cities, cutting out British middlemen. The combined effect was to lower the retail price of the East India tea well below that of smuggled Dutch tea, thus motivating Americans to obey the law.

Tea in Boston Harbor

In the fall of 1773, news of the Tea Act reached the colonies. Parliamentary legislation to make tea inexpensive struck many colonists as an insidious plot to trick Americans into buying the dutied tea. The real goal, some argued, was the increased revenue that would pay the salaries of royal governors and judges and the reassertion of Britain's right to tax the colonists.

But how to resist the Tea Act? Nonimportation was not viable because the tea trade was too lucrative to expect merchants to give it up willingly. Consumer boycotts seemed ineffective because it was impossible to distinguish between dutied tea and smuggled tea once it was in the teapot. The appointment of official tea agents, parallel to the Stamp Act distributors, suggested one solution. In every port city, revived Sons of Liberty pressured tea agents to resign. Without agents, governors yielded, and tea cargoes either landed duty-free or were sent home.

Governor Hutchinson, however, would not bend any rules. Three ships bearing tea arrived in Boston in November 1773. The ships cleared customs, and the crews, sensing the town's extreme tension, unloaded all cargo except the tea. Picking up on the tension on the town, the captains wished to return to England, but Hutchinson would not grant them clearance to leave without paying the tea duty. To add to the difficulties, another long-standing law imposed a twenty-day limit for the payment of duties after which time cargo would be confiscated. Hutchinson made it clear he planned to enforce that law.

For the full twenty days, crowds swelled by concerned people from surrounding towns kept the pressure high. On the final day, December 16, a large crowd gathered at Old South Church to debate a course of action. No solution emerged at that meeting, but immediately after, 100 to 150 men disguised as Mohawk Indians, with soot-darkened faces and blankets wrapped around them, boarded the ships and dumped over 90,000 pounds of tea into the harbor. Their disguises served to distinguish them from the Boston

Hutchinson the Traitor Faces Death
This hideous engraving enlivened the cover of a Boston almanac published during the high drama over tea. The devil taunts Thomas Hutchinson while a skeleton representing death spears him. On page 2, readers of this anti-Hutchinson diatribe were invited to think about "the Horrors that Man must endure, who owes his Greatness to his Country's Ruin." The Granger Collection, New York.

townsmen at Old South Church, whose leaders did not join the crowd of 2,000 bystanders watching the near-silent and efficient destruction of the tea. In admiration, John Adams wrote in his diary, "This Destruction of the Tea is so bold, so daring, so firm, intrepid and inflexible, and it must have so important Consequences."

The Coercive Acts

Lord North's response was swift and stern: He persuaded Parliament to issue the **Coercive Acts,** four laws meant to punish Massachusetts for destroying the tea. In America, those laws, along with a fifth one, the Quebec Act, were soon known as the **Intolerable Acts.** The first act, the Boston Port Act, closed Boston harbor to all shipping as of June 1, 1774, until the destroyed tea was paid for. Britain's objective was to halt the commercial life of the city. The second act, called the Massachusetts Government Act, greatly altered the colony's charter, underscoring Parliament's claim to supremacy over Massachusetts. The royal governor's powers were augmented, and the governor's council became an appointive, rather than elective, body. Further, the governor could now appoint all judges, sheriffs, and officers of the court. No town meeting beyond the annual spring election of town selectmen could be held without the governor's approval, and every agenda item required prior approval. Every Massachusetts town was affected.

The third Coercive Act, the Impartial Administration of Justice Act, stipulated that any royal official accused of a capital crime—for example, Captain Preston and his soldiers at the Boston Massacre—would be tried in a court in Britain. It did not matter that Preston had received a fair trial in Boston. What this act ominously suggested was that down the road, more Captain Prestons and soldiers might be firing into unruly crowds. The fourth act amended the 1765 Quartering Act and permitted military commanders to lodge soldiers wherever necessary, even in private households. In a related move, Lord North appointed General Thomas Gage, the commander of the Royal Army in New York, to be governor of Massachusetts. Thomas Hutchinson was out, relieved at long last of his duties. Military rule, including soldiers, returned once more to Boston.

The fifth act, concerning Quebec, now part of the British Empire, was unrelated to the four Coercive Acts, but it magnified American fears. It confirmed the continuation of French civil law as well as Catholicism for Quebec—an affront to Protestant New Englanders who had recently been denied their own representative government. It also awarded Quebec land (and the lucrative fur trade) in the Ohio Valley, an area also claimed by Virginia, Pennsylvania, and a number of Indian tribes.

The five Intolerable Acts spread alarm in all the colonies (see "Documenting the American Promise," page 158). If Britain could squelch Massachusetts—change its charter, suspend local government, inaugurate military rule, and on top of that give Ohio to Catholic Quebec—what liberties were secure? Fearful royal governors in a half dozen colonies dismissed the sitting assemblies, adding to the sense of urgency. A few of the assemblies defiantly continued to meet in new locations. Via the committees of correspondence, colonial leaders arranged to convene in Philadelphia in September 1774 to respond to the crisis.

Beyond Boston: Rural New England

The Coercive Acts fired up all of New England to open insubordination. With a British general occupying the Massachusetts governorship and some three thousand troops controlling Boston, the revolutionary momentum shifted from urban radicals to rural farmers who protested in dozens of spontaneous, dramatic showdowns. Some towns found creative ways to get around the Massachusetts Government Act's prohibition on town meetings, and others just ignored the law. Governor Gage's call for elections for a new provincial assembly under his control sparked the formation of a competing unauthorized assembly that met in defiance of his orders. In all Massachusetts counties outside Boston, crowds of thousands of armed men converged to prevent the opening of county courts run by crown-appointed jurists. No judges were physically harmed, but they were forced to resign and made to doff their judicial wigs or run a humiliating gauntlet. By August 1774, farmers and artisans all over Massachusetts had effectively taken full control of their local institutions.

Unfettered by the crown, ordinary citizens throughout New England began serious planning for the showdown everyone assumed would come. Town militias stockpiled gunpowder "in case of invasion." Militia officers repudiated their official chain of command to the governor and stepped up drills of their units. Town after town withheld its tax money from the royal governor and diverted it to military supplies. Governor Gage felt under heavy threat, but he could do little. He wrote London begging for troop reinforcements, and he beefed up fortifications around Boston. But without more soldiers, his options were limited. Seizing the stockpiles of gunpowder was his best move.

The Powder Alarm of September 1 showed just how ready the defiant Americans were to take up arms against Britain. Gage sent troops to a town just outside Boston reported to have a hidden powder storehouse, and in the surprise and scramble of the attack, false news spread that the troops had fired on men defending the powder, killing six. Within twenty-four hours, several thousand armed men from Massachusetts, New Hampshire, and Connecticut streamed on foot to Boston to avenge what they thought was the first bloodshed of war. At this moment, ordinary men became insurgents, willing to kill or be killed in the face of the British clampdown. Once the error was corrected and the crisis defused, the men returned home peaceably. But Gage could no longer doubt the speed, numbers, and deadly determination of the rebellious subjects.

No. X   Engraved for Royal American Magazine.   · Vol. I.

The able Doctor, or America Swallowing the Bitter Draught.

VISUAL ACTIVITY

The Able Doctor, or America Swallowing the Bitter Draught, 1774, Engraved by Paul Revere

Revere's cartoon, a response to the Boston Port Act, shows Lord North forcing tea down the throat of America, depicted as an Indian maiden. The older woman is Britannia (known by her shield), who averts her eyes from the attack. Two British lords hold America down, while two other men to the left, representing France and Spain, look on with amusement and pleasure. Private Collection/The Bridgeman Art Library.

READING THE IMAGE: How does this cartoon rely on widely shared stereotypes of gender and sexual danger to express power relations in the masculine world of politics? What is gained by representing the country of Britain as a woman, in contrast to the male political figures?

CONNECTIONS: According to the Americans, in what sense was Britain forcing them to purchase and drink tea in 1773? Was that sense of coercion still in play in 1774, at the time of this cartoon?

All this had occurred without orchestration by Boston radicals, Gage reported. But British leaders found it hard to believe, as one put it, that "a tumultuous Rabble, without any Appearance of general Concert, or without any Head to advise, or Leader to conduct" could pull off such effective resistance. Repeatedly in the years to come, the British would seriously underestimate their opponents.

The First Continental Congress

Every colony except Georgia sent delegates to Philadelphia in September 1774 to discuss the looming crisis at the **First Continental Congress**. The gathering included notables such as Samuel Adams and John Adams from Massachusetts and George Washington and Patrick Henry from Virginia. A few colonies purposely sent men who opposed provoking Britain, such as Pennsylvania's Joseph Galloway, to keep the congress from becoming too radical.

Delegates sought to articulate their liberties as British subjects and the powers Parliament held over them, and they debated possible responses to the Coercive Acts. Some wanted a total ban on trade with Britain to force repeal,

Reactions to the Boston Port Act outside of Massachusetts

As punishment for the destruction of the tea in Boston, Parliament closed Boston's port by naval blockade as of June 1, 1774, until the tea was paid for. News of Parliament's action spurred discussion and action all around the American colonies.

DOCUMENT 1
George Washington Writes to George William Fairfax, 1774

Washington describes the transformation of the Virginia Assembly, shut down by the royal governor, into a new legislative body meeting at a tavern. In one long, breathless sentence he voices his concerns about the Boston Port Act and the threats facing Virginia.

Williamsburg, June 10, 1774 . . . [The Assembly] Members convend themselves at the Raleigh Tavern & enterd into the Inclosd Association which being followed two days after by an Express from Boston accompanied by the Sentiments of some Meetings in our Sister Colonies to the Northwd the proceedings mentiond in the Inclos'd Papers were had thereupon & a general meeting requested of all the late Representatives in this City on the first of August when it is hopd, & expected that some vigorous measures will be effectually adopted to obtain that justice which is denied to our Petitions & Remonstrances; in short the Ministry may rely on it that Americans will never be tax'd without their own consent that the cause of Boston the despotick Measures in respect to it I mean now is and ever will be considerd as the cause of America (not that we approve their cond[uc]t in destroyg the Tea) & that we shall not suffer ourselves to be sacrificed by piecemeal though god only knows what is to become of us, threatned as we are with so many hoverg evils as hang over us at present; having a cruel & blood thirsty Enemy upon our Backs, the Indians, between whom & our Frontier Inhabitants many Skirmishes have happend, & with who(m) a general

War is inevitable whilst those from whom we have a right to Seek protection are endeavouring by every piece of Art & despotism to fix the Shackles of Slavry upon us.

Source: "George Washington to George William Fairfax 10-15 June 1774," The Papers of George Washington, The University Press of Virginia. Copyright © 1995 by the Rector and Visitors of the University of Virginia.

DOCUMENT 2
An Anonymous Philadelphian Implores Boston to Pay for the Tea, 1774

A self-described "friend to the cause of America" argues that paying for the tea is in the best interests of justice and liberty, using repetition for effect.

To the Inhabitants on the Town of BOSTON, and Province of MASSACHUSETTS-BAY.

My Dear BRETHREN,

IN Messi'rs Mills and Hick's Gazette of the 20th of June, I observed with great concern a paragraph with the signature of "Consideration," calculated to deter you from paying for the tea, a measure at this alarming juncture highly necessary and what every REAL friend to the cause of America must think your indispensible duty. While we contend for liberty, let us not destroy the idea of justice. A trespass has been committed on private property in consequence of the Resolves of your town. Restore to the sufferers the most ample compensation for the injury they have received—convince your enemies that their property is secure in every Port on the British Continent—Convince

while others, especially southerners dependent on tobacco and rice exports, opposed halting trade. Samuel Adams and Patrick Henry were eager for a ringing denunciation of all parliamentary control. The conservative Joseph Galloway proposed a plan (quickly defeated) to create a secondary parliament in America to assist the British Parliament in ruling the colonies.

The congress met for seven weeks and produced a declaration of rights couched in traditional language: "We ask only for peace, liberty and security. We wish no diminution of royal prerogatives, we demand no new rights." But from them that you do not regard the value of the article destroyed—that you only deny the right of taxation. Let not the annals of your history be sullied by a refusal—pay for the tea—it will rejoice your friends—it will convince your adversaries that the cause you are attach'd to is a righteous and just cause. Convince them that you regard honesty as much as liberty, and that you detest libertinism and licentiousness. . . . Then can you with a degree of confidence call on your friends to stand by and protect you—your enemies, if any there be, you may defy to prejudice you. I beseech you, by every thing you hold dear—I conjure you, as you value a union of the colonies, pay for the tea; it is but justice, pay for it, let nothing retard it; it is an expedient, which ought to have been effected e'er this; we lament that it yet remains undone. . . .

These are the sentiments of the Pennsylvanians, and the anxious prayer of a A PHILADELPHIAN.

Source: *The Massachusetts Gazette and the Boston Weekly News-Letter*, 14 July 1774, p. 2. Also at http://www.masshist.org /revolution/image-viewer.php?item_id=691&mode=large&img_ step=2&tpc=#page2

DOCUMENT 3
A New Hampshire Town Offers Sympathy and Support to Boston, 1774

Kingston, New Hampshire, was one of hundreds of towns to pledge assistance to Boston.

Sept. 14, 1774
Gentlemen,
The inhabitants of Kingston, in the Province of New Hampshire, see with deep concern the unhappy misunderstanding and disagreement that now subsists between Great Britain and these American Colonies, being fully sensible that the happiness of both countries depend on an union, harmony, and agreement to be established between them on a just, equitable, and permanent foundation. But when we consider the new, arbitrary, and unjust claims of our brethren in Great Britain, to levy taxes upon us at their sovereign will and pleasure, and to make laws to bind us in all cases, whatsoever, we view and consider ourselves and our posterity under the operations of these claims, as absolute slaves: for what is a slave, but one who

is bound in all cases whatsoever by the will and command of another. And we look on the late unjust, cruel, hostile, and tyrannical Acts of the British Parliament, respecting the Massachusetts Bay in general, and the Town of Boston in particular, as consequences of these unrighteous claims, and from them clearly see what the whole continent has to expect under their operation.

But when we consider the military forces, both by sea and land, sent in an hostile manner to enforce, with the point of the sword, and mouths of cannon, those acts and claims, we esteem it an high infringement of your rights and privileges, and an insult upon all North America, and are fully persuaded that unless there is a speedy alteration of those measures, a total disaffection will soon take place, and Britain, instead of being our best friend, will be looked upon as an enemy; and then a final separation in all respects will no doubt soon follow, the thoughts of which fill our minds with trouble, anxiety, and concern.

Source: "Correspondence in 1774 and 1775, Between a Committee of the Town of Boston and Contributors of Donations for the Relief of the Sufferers by the Boston Port Bill," in *Collections of the Massachusetts Historical Society*, vol. 4, 4th ser. (1858), pp. 74–76.

Questions for Analysis and Debate

1. What are the "hovering evils" Washington fears at this moment in 1774? Do the Philadelphia and New Hampshire writers have similar concerns?

2. Why does the Philadelphia correspondent urge that the tea must be paid for? How does his position on the destruction of the tea compare to Washington's?

3. Both Washington and the townsmen of Kingston invoke slavery. What do they mean?

4. Which of these three documents most clearly anticipates that a separation from Britain might lie in the future? Why?

Connect to the Big Idea

C Could it be said that the Boston Port Act was the most radicalizing British action in the entire run-up to the American Revolution? Why or why not?

Britain's point of view, the rights assumed already to exist were radical. Chief among them was the claim that Americans were not represented in Parliament and so each colonial government had the sole right to govern and tax its own people. The one slight concession to Britain was a carefully worded agreement that the colonists would "cheerfully consent" to trade regulations for the larger good of the empire, so long as trade regulation was not a covert means of raising revenue.

To put pressure on Britain, the delegates agreed to a staggered and limited boycott of trade: imports prohibited this year, exports the following,

MAP 6.3 Lexington and Concord, April 1775

Two Americans slipped out of Boston to warn of a surprise British attack on Concord. Paul Revere went by boat to Charlestown and then by horse to Lexington, while William Dawes casually rode past British sentries and then galloped at full speed through Lexington to Concord.

READING THE MAP: How did Dawes's route differ from Revere's? What kinds of terrain and potential dangers did each man face during his ride, according to the map?

CONNECTIONS: Why send two men on the same mission? Why not send four or more?

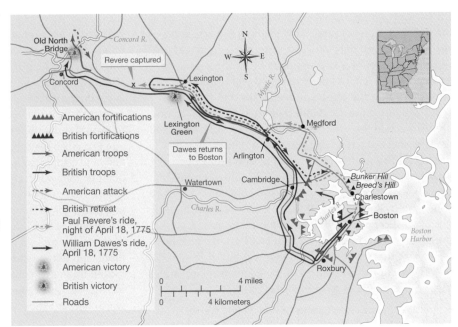

and rice totally exempted (to keep South Carolinians happy). To enforce the boycott, they called for a Continental Association, with chapters in each town variously called committees of public safety or of inspection, to monitor all commerce and punish suspected violators of the boycott (sometimes with a bucket of tar and a bag of feathers). Its work done in a month, the congress disbanded with agreement to reconvene in May.

The committees of public safety, the committees of correspondence, the regrouped colonial assemblies, and the Continental Congress were all political bodies functioning defiantly without any constitutional authority. British officials did not recognize them as legitimate, but many Americans who supported the patriot cause instantly accepted them. A key reason for the stability of such unauthorized governing bodies was that they were composed of many of the same men who had held elective office before.

Britain's severe reaction to Boston's destruction of the tea finally succeeded in making many colonists from New Hampshire to Georgia realize that the problems of British rule went far beyond questions of nonconsensual taxation. The Coercive Acts infringed on liberty and denied self-government; they could not be ignored. With one colony already subordinated to military rule and a British army camped in Boston, the threat of a general war was very real.

> **REVIEW** Why did Parliament pass the Coercive Acts in 1774?

▶ Domestic Insurrections, 1774–1775

Before the Second Continental Congress could meet, violence and bloodshed came to Massachusetts in the towns of Lexington and Concord. Fearing domestic insurrection, General Thomas Gage sent his soldiers there to capture an ammunition depot, but New England farmers mobilized against an intrusive power they feared would enslave them. To the south, a different and inverted version of the same story began to unfold, as thousands of enslaved black men and women seized an unprecedented opportunity to mount a different kind of insurrection—against planter-patriots who looked over their shoulders uneasily whenever they called out for liberty from the British.

Lexington and Concord

During the winter of 1774–75, Americans pressed on with boycotts. Optimists hoped to effect a repeal of the Coercive Acts; pessimists stockpiled arms and ammunition. In Massachusetts, militia units known as minutemen prepared to respond at a minute's notice to any threat from the British troops in Boston.

Thomas Gage realized how desperate the British position was. The people, Gage wrote Lord North, were "numerous, worked up to a fury, and not a Boston rabble but the freeholders and farmers of the country." Gage requested twenty thousand reinforcements. He also strongly advised repeal

VISUAL ACTIVITY

The British Retreat from Lexington and Concord, April 19, 1775

Two self-trained artists—Ralph Earle, eighteen, and Amos Doolittle, twenty-one—hustled to Concord and Lexington ten days after April 19 to interview witnesses and create engravings for mass production. This scene depicts the British retreat to Boston, with the redcoats under ambush by American insurgents. On route, the British set fire to several houses. The Granger Collection, New York.

READING THE IMAGE: Who is firing from behind the stone wall? Which side is inflicting the most damage, as depicted in this picture?

CONNECTIONS: In 1774 and 1775, were American militia units up to the task of defending their country against an invasion by Britain?

of the Coercive Acts, but leaders in Britain could not admit failure. Instead, in mid-April 1775, they ordered Gage to arrest the troublemakers immediately, before the Americans got better organized.

Gage quickly planned a surprise attack on a suspected ammunition storage site at Concord, a village eighteen miles west of Boston (Map 6.3). Near midnight on April 18, British soldiers moved west across the Charles River. Paul Revere and William Dawes raced ahead to alert the minutemen. When the soldiers got to Lexington, five miles east of Concord, they were met by some seventy armed men. The British commander barked out, "Lay down your arms, you damned rebels, and disperse." The militiamen hesitated and began to comply, but then someone—nobody knows who—fired. Within two minutes, eight Americans were dead and ten were wounded.

The British units continued their march to Concord, any pretense of surprise gone. Three companies of minutemen nervously occupied the town center but offered no challenge to the British as they searched in vain for the ammunition. Finally, at Old North Bridge in Concord, British troops and minutemen exchanged shots, killing two Americans and three British soldiers. As the British returned to Boston, militia units ambushed them, bringing the bloodiest fighting of the day. In the end, 273 British soldiers were wounded or dead; the toll for the Americans stood at about 95. It was April 19, 1775, and the war had begun.

Rebelling against Slavery

News of the battles of Lexington and Concord spread within days. In Virginia, Thomas Jefferson observed that "a phrenzy of revenge seems to have seized all ranks of people," causing the royal governor of Virginia, Lord Dunmore, to remove all gunpowder from the Williamsburg powder house to a ship, out of reach of angry Virginians. He also threatened to arm slaves, if necessary, to ward off attacks by colonists. This threat proved effective for several months.

In November 1775, as the crisis deepened, Dunmore issued an official proclamation promising freedom to defecting able-bodied slaves who would fight for the British. Dunmore had no intention of liberating all slaves, and astute blacks noticed that Dunmore neglected to free his own slaves. A Virginia barber named Caesar declared that "he did not know any one foolish enough to believe him [Dunmore], for if he intended to do so, he ought first to set his own free." Within a month some fifteen hundred slaves had joined Dunmore's "Ethiopian Regiment." Camp diseases quickly set in: dysentery, typhoid fever, and smallpox. When Dunmore sailed for England in mid-1776, he took three hundred black survivors with him. But the association of freedom with the British authorities had been established, and throughout the war thousands more southern slaves

Phillis Wheatley
African-born Phillis became the slave of John Wheatley in Boston at age seven. Remarkably gifted in English, she read the Bible and learned to write elegant poetry and essays. She traveled to London in 1773 and published a book of poems, gaining notice in British literary circles. Once freed, she briefly married and then worked in a Boston boarding house. She died in 1784. ©Corbis.

fled their masters whenever the British army was close enough to offer safe refuge.

In the northern colonies as well, slaves clearly recognized the evolving political struggle with Britain as an ideal moment to bid for freedom. A twenty-one-year-old Boston domestic slave employed biting sarcasm in a 1774 newspaper essay to call attention to the hypocrisy of local slave owners: "How well the Cry for Liberty, and the reverse Disposition for exercise of oppressive Power over others agree,— I humbly think it does not require the Penetration of a Philosopher to Determine." This extraordinary young woman, Phillis Wheatley, had already gained international recognition through a book of poems published in London in 1773. Wheatley's poems spoke of "Fair Freedom" as the "Goddess long desir'd" by Africans enslaved in America. Wheatley's master freed the young poet in 1775.

From north to south, groups of slaves pressed their case. Several Boston blacks offered to fight for the British in exchange for freedom, but General Gage turned them down. In Maryland, a planter complained that blacks impatient for freedom had to be disarmed of about eighty guns along with some swords. In North Carolina, white suspicions about a planned slave uprising led to the arrest of scores of African Americans who were ordered to be whipped by the revolutionary committee of public safety.

By 1783, when the Revolutionary War ended, as many as twenty thousand blacks had voted against slavery with their feet by seeking refuge with the British army. About half failed to achieve the liberation they were seeking, instead succumbing to disease, especially smallpox, in refugee camps. But some eight thousand to ten thousand persisted through the war and later, under the protection of the British army, left America to start new lives of freedom in Canada's Nova Scotia or Africa's Sierra Leone.

REVIEW How did enslaved people in the colonies react to the stirrings of revolution?

▶ Conclusion: The Long Road to Revolution

In the aftermath of the Seven Years' War, neither losers nor victors came away satisfied. France lost vast amounts of North American land claims, and Indian land rights were increasingly violated or ignored. Britain's huge war debt and subsequent revenue-generating policies distressed Americans and set the stage for the imperial crisis of the 1760s and 1770s. The years 1763 to 1775 brought repeated attempts by the British government to subordinate the colonies into contributing partners in the larger scheme of empire.

American resistance to British policies grew slowly but steadily. In 1765, both loyalist Thomas Hutchinson and patriot Samuel Adams agreed that it was unwise for Britain to assert a right to taxation because Parliament did not adequately represent Americans. As a royal official, Hutchinson was obliged to uphold policy, while Adams protested and made political activists out of thousands in the process.

By 1775, events propelled many Americans to the conclusion that a concerted effort was afoot to deprive them of all their liberties, the most important of which were the right to self-rule and the right to live free of an occupying army. Prepared to die for those liberties, hundreds of minutemen converged on Concord. April 19 marked the start of their rebellion.

Another rebellion under way in 1775 was doomed to be short-circuited. Black Americans who had experienced actual slavery listened to shouts of "Liberty!" from white crowds and appropriated the language of revolution to their own circumstances. Defiance of authority was indeed contagious.

Despite the military conflict at the battles of Lexington and Concord, a war with Britain seemed far from inevitable to colonists outside New England. In the months ahead, American colonial leaders pursued peaceful as well as military solutions to the question of who actually had authority over them. By the end of 1775, however, reconciliation with the crown would be unattainable.

See the Selected Bibliography for this chapter in the Appendix.

6 Chapter Review

MAKE IT STICK

 LearningCurve

Go online and use LearningCurve to see what you know. Then review the key terms and answer the questions.

KEY TERMS

Seven Years' War (p. 137)
Pontiac's Rebellion (p. 143)
Sugar (Revenue) Act (p. 145)
Stamp Act (p. 146)
virtual representation (p. 146)
Declaratory Act (p. 150)
Townshend duties (p. 151)
Boston Massacre (p. 153)
committees of correspondence (p. 154)
Tea Act of 1773 (p. 154)
Coercive (Intolerable) Acts (p. 155)
First Continental Congress (p. 157)

REVIEW QUESTIONS

1. How did the Seven Years' War erode relations between colonists and British authorities? (pp. 137–144)

2. Why did the Sugar Act and the Stamp Act draw fierce opposition from colonists? (pp. 144–150)

3. Why did British authorities send troops to occupy Boston in the fall of 1768? (pp. 150–154)

4. Why did Parliament pass the Coercive Acts in 1774? (pp. 154–160)

5. How did enslaved people in the colonies react to the stirrings of revolution? (pp. 160–163)

MAKING CONNECTIONS

1. In the mid-eighteenth century, how did Native Americans influence relations between European nations? Between Britain and the colonies?

2. What other grievances, besides taxation, led colonists by 1775 to openly rebel against Britain?

3. How did the colonists organize to oppose British power so effectively? In your answer, discuss the role of communication in facilitating the colonial resistance, being sure to cite specific examples.

LINKING TO THE PAST

1. In Bacon's Rebellion in Virginia in 1676, backcountry farmers protested the rule of a royal governor who did not seem to have the economic interests of many Virginians at heart. Compare the administration of Sir William Berkeley of Virginia with that of Thomas Hutchinson of Massachusetts in the 1760s. Are there more differences than similarities? (See chapter 3.)

2. How does the growing ethnic and religious diversity of the mid-eighteenth-century colonies help explain the evolution of anti-British feeling that culminated in insurrection in 1775? (See chapter 5.)

7

The War for America
1775–1783

CONTENT LEARNING OBJECTIVES

After reading and studying this chapter, you should be able to:

- Define the objectives of the Second Continental Congress.

- Characterize the British and the American armies' strengths and weaknesses during the first year of the Revolutionary War.

- Explain how conflicts between patriots and loyalists played out on the local level.

- Understand how the war proceeded in the North and West, and the roles Native Americans played in the war.

- Consider King George III's southern strategy from 1778 to 1781, including what went wrong for the British, and what were the terms of the peace.

ROBERT SHURTLIFF WAS A LATECOMER TO THE AMERICAN Revolution, enlisting in the Continental army after the last decisive battle at Yorktown had been fought. The army still needed fresh recruits to counter the British army occupying New York City. The standoff would last nearly two years before the peace treaty was finalized in Paris.

New recruits were scarce in a country exhausted by war. Attracted by cash bounties, beardless boys who had been children in 1775 now stepped forward, Shurtliff among them. Reportedly eighteen, the youth was single, poor, and at loose ends. With a muscular physique and proficiency with a musket, Shurtliff won assignment to an elite light infantry unit, part of Washington's army of 10,000 men stationed north of New York City.

That is, 10,000 men and 1 woman. "Robert Shurtliff" was actually Deborah Sampson, age twenty-three, from Middleborough, Massachusetts. For seventeen months, Sampson masqueraded as a man, marching through woods, skirmishing with the enemy, and enduring the boredom of camp. Understating her age enabled her to blend in with the beardless boys, as did her competence as a soldier. With privacy at a minimum, she faced constant risk of discovery. Why did she run this risk?

A hard-luck childhood had left Sampson both impoverished and unusually plucky. Placed in foster care at age five, Deborah became a servant in a succession of families. Along the way, she learned to plow a field and to read and write, uncommon skills for a female servant. Next she worked

CONTINENTAL ARMY UNIFORM
The Continental Army issued dark blue coats for officers' uniforms, using shoulder stripes and facings in varied colors to establish rank. As an officer rose in the ranks, he changed stripes, not coats. Armed Forces History Division, National Museum of American History, Smithsonian Institution.

as a weaver and then a teacher, low-wage jobs but also ones without supervising bosses. Marriage was the usual next step, but probably the wartime shortage of men kept Deborah "masterless," rare for an eighteenth-century woman. Masterless, but also poor; the cash bounty enticed her to enlist.

When Sampson's true sex was finally discovered, she was discharged immediately. What eventually made Sampson famous was not her war service alone but her success in selling her story to the public. In 1797, she told her life story (a blend of fact and fiction) in a short book and then went on tour reenacting her wartime masquerade. Once again, she was crossing gender boundaries since women normally did not speak from public stages.

Except for her disguised sex, Sampson's Revolutionary War experience was similar to that of most Americans. Disruptions affected everyone's life, whether in military service or on the home front. Wartime shortages caused women to do male jobs. Soldiers fought for ideas, but they also fought to earn money. Hardship was widely endured. And Sampson's quest for personal independence—a freedom from the constraints of being female—was echoed in the general quest for political independence that many Americans identified as a major goal of the war.

Political independence was not everyone's primary goal at first. For more than a year after fighting began, the Continental Congress resisted declaring independence. Some delegates cautiously hoped for reconciliation with Britain. The congress raised an army, financed it, and sought alliances with foreign countries—all the while exploring diplomatic channels for peace.

Once King George III rejected all peace overtures, Americans loudly declared their independence, and the war moved into high gear. In part a classic war with professional armies, the Revolutionary War was also a civil war between committed rebels and loyalists. It had complex ethnic dimensions, pitting Indian tribes allied with the British against others allied with the Americans, and international involvement as well from France and Spain. It also provided an unprecedented opportunity for some enslaved African Americans to win freedom, by joining either the British or the Continental army and state militias, fighting alongside white Americans.

Deborah Sampson

Deborah Sampson opted for this small portrait to illustrate *The Female Review*, a short book about her unusual military career published in 1797. By then a wife and mother, she displays femininity here: long curly hair, necklace, and stylish low-cut gown. Sampson the soldier had used a cloth band to compress her breasts; Sampson the matron wore a satin band to define her bustline. Getty Images.

DEBORAH SAMPSON.
Published by H. Mann. 1797.

► The Second Continental Congress

On May 10, 1775, nearly one month after the fighting at Lexington and Concord, the **Second Continental Congress** assembled in Philadelphia. The congress immediately set to work on two crucial but contradictory tasks: to raise and supply an army and to explore reconciliation with Britain. To do the former, they needed soldiers and a commander, they needed money, and they needed to work out a declaration of war. To do the latter, they needed diplomacy to approach the king. But the king was not receptive, and by 1776, as the war progressed and hopes of reconciliation faded, delegates at the congress began to ponder the treasonous act of declaring independence.

Assuming Political and Military Authority

The delegates to the Second Continental Congress were prominent figures at home, but they now had to learn to know and trust one another. Moreover, they did not always agree. The Adams cousins John and Samuel defined the radical end of the spectrum, favoring independence. John Dickinson of Pennsylvania, who in 1767 critiqued British tax policy in *Letters from a Farmer*, was now a moderate, seeking reconciliation with Britain. Benjamin Franklin, fresh off a ship from an eleven-year residence in London, was feared by some to be a British spy. Mutual suspicions flourished easily when the undertaking was so dangerous, opinions were so varied, and a misstep could spell disaster.

Most of the delegates were not yet prepared to break with Britain. Some felt that government without a king was unworkable, while others feared it might be suicidal to lose Britain's protection against its traditional enemies, France and Spain. Colonies that traded actively with Britain feared undermining their economies. Probably the vast majority of ordinary Americans were unable to envision complete independence. From the Stamp Act of 1765 to the Coercive Acts of 1774 (see chapter 6), the constitutional struggle with Britain had focused on the issue of parliamentary power, but almost no one had questioned the legitimacy of the monarchy.

The few men at the Continental Congress who did think that independence was desirable were, not surprisingly, from Massachusetts, the target of the Coercive Acts and the scene of

CHRONOLOGY

1775
- Second Continental Congress convenes.
- Battle of Bunker Hill.
- Olive Branch Petition.
- Battle of Quebec.

1776
- *Common Sense* published.
- British evacuate Boston.
- Declaration of Independence.
- British take Manhattan.

1777
- British Parliament suspends habeas corpus.
- Ambush at Oriskany; Americans hold Fort Stanwix.
- British occupy Philadelphia.
- British surrender at Saratoga.

1777–1778
- Continental army winters at Valley Forge.

1778
- France signs treaty with America.
- British take Savannah, Georgia.

1779
- Militias attack Cherokee in North Carolina.
- Americans destroy Iroquois villages in New York.
- Americans take Forts Kaskaskia and Vincennes.

1780
- Philadelphia Ladies Association raises money for soldiers.
- The siege of Charleston, South Carolina.
- French army arrives in Newport, Rhode Island.
- British win battle of Camden.
- Benedict Arnold exposed as traitor.
- Americans win battle of King's Mountain.

1781
- British forces invade Virginia.
- French blockade Chesapeake Bay.
- Cornwallis surrenders at Yorktown.

1783
- Treaty of Paris ends war.

bloodshed at Lexington and Concord. Even so, those men knew that it was premature to push for a break with Britain. John Adams wrote his wife, Abigail, in June 1775: "America is a great, unwieldy body. Its progress must be slow. It is like a large fleet sailing under convoy. The fleetest sailors must wait for the dullest and slowest."

Yet swift action was needed, for the Massachusetts countryside was under threat of further attack. Even the hesitant moderates in the congress agreed that a military buildup was necessary. Around the country, militia units from New York to Georgia collected arms and trained on village greens in anticipation. On June 14, the congress voted to create the **Continental army**, choosing a Virginian, George Washington, as commander in chief. This sent the clear message that there was widespread commitment to war beyond New England.

Next the congress drew up a document titled "A Declaration on the Causes and Necessity of Taking Up Arms," which rehearsed familiar arguments about the tyranny of Parliament and the need to defend English liberties. This declaration was first drafted by a young Virginia planter, Thomas Jefferson, a radical on the question of independence. The moderate John Dickinson, fearing that the declaration would offend Britain, was allowed to rewrite it. However, he left intact much of Jefferson's highly charged language about choosing "to die freemen rather than to live slaves." Even a moderate like Dickinson understood the necessity of military defense against an invading army.

To pay for the military buildup, the congress authorized a currency issue of $2 million. The Continental dollars were merely paper; they were not backed by gold or silver. The delegates somewhat naively expected that the currency would be accepted as valuable on trust as it spread in the population through the hands of soldiers, farmers, munitions suppliers, and beyond.

In just two months, the Second Continental Congress had created an army, declared war, and issued its own currency. It had taken on the major functions of a legitimate government, both military and financial, without any legal basis for its authority, for it had not yet declared independence from the king.

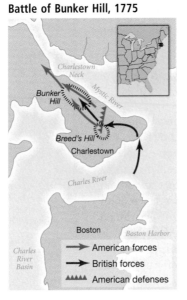

Battle of Bunker Hill, 1775

Charlestown Neck

Mystic River

Bunker Hill

Breed's Hill

Charlestown

Charles River

Boston

Boston Harbor

Charles River Basin

→ American forces

→ British forces

▲▲▲▲▲ American defenses

Pursuing Both War and Peace

The second battle of the Revolution occurred on June 16 in Boston. New England militia units had fortified the hilly terrain of the peninsula of Charlestown, which faced the city, and Thomas Gage, still commander in Boston, prepared to attack, aided by the arrival of new troops and three talented generals, William Howe, John Burgoyne, and Henry Clinton.

General William Howe insisted on a bold frontal assault, sending 2,500 soldiers across the water and up Bunker Hill in an intimidating but potentially costly attack. Three bloody assaults were needed before the British took the hill, the third succeeding mainly because the American ammunition supply gave out, and the defenders quickly retreated. The **battle of Bunker Hill** was thus a British victory, but an expensive one. The dead numbered 226 on the British side, with more than 800 wounded; the Americans suffered 140 dead, 271 wounded, and 30 captured. As General Clinton later remarked, "It was a dear bought victory; another such would have ruined us."

Instead of pursuing the fleeing Americans, Howe retreated to Boston, unwilling to risk more raids into the countryside. If the British had had any grasp of the basic instability of the American units around Boston, they might have decisively defeated the Continental army in its infancy. Instead, they lingered in Boston, abandoning it without a fight nine months later.

Howe used the time in Boston to inoculate his army against smallpox because a new epidemic of the deadly disease was spreading in port cities along the Atlantic. Inoculation worked by producing a mild but real (and therefore risky) case of smallpox, followed by lifelong immunity. Howe's instinct was right: During the American Revolution, some 130,000 people on the American continent, most of them Indians, died of smallpox.

A week after Bunker Hill, when General Washington arrived to take charge of the new Continental army, he found enthusiastic but undisciplined troops. Sanitation was an unknown concept, with inadequate latrines fouling the campground. Washington attributed the disarray to the New England custom of letting militia units elect their

VISUAL ACTIVITY

An Exact View of the Late Battle at Charlestown, June 17th 1775
This engraving was for sale within weeks of the battle of Bunker Hill. British and American soldiers in fixed formation fire muskets at one another, while Charlestown is in flames in the background. The Americans, to the left, are dug in along the crest of the hill; British casualties have begun to mount up. Who would buy this picture? The Colonial Williamsburg Foundation. Museum Purchase.
READING THE IMAGE: In the end, the British won the battle by taking the hill, but is that the story told in this picture?
CONNECTIONS: In what significant ways did the battle of Bunker Hill differ from the battles of Lexington and Concord two months earlier?

own officers, which he felt undermined deference. Washington spotted a militia captain, a barber in civilian life, shaving an ordinary soldier, and he moved quickly to impose more hierarchy and authority. "Be easy," he advised his newly appointed officers, "but not too familiar, lest you subject yourself to a want of that respect, which is necessary to support a proper command."

While military plans moved forward, the Second Continental Congress pursued its contradictory objective: reconciliation with Britain. Delegates from the middle colonies (Pennsylvania, Delaware, and New York), whose merchants depended on trade with Britain, urged that channels for negotiation remain open. In July 1775, congressional moderates led by John Dickinson engineered an appeal to the king called the Olive Branch Petition, affirming loyalty to the monarchy and blaming all the troubles on the king's ministers and on Parliament. It proposed that the American colonial assemblies be recognized as individual parliaments under the umbrella of the monarchy. King George III rejected the Olive Branch Petition and heatedly condemned the Americans as traitors.

Thomas Paine, Abigail Adams, and the Case for Independence

Pressure for independence started to mount in January 1776, when a pamphlet titled *Common Sense* appeared in Philadelphia. Thomas Paine, its author, was an English artisan and coffeehouse intellectual who had come to America in the fall of 1774. With the encouragement of members of the Second Continental Congress, he wrote *Common Sense* to lay out a lively and compelling case for complete independence.

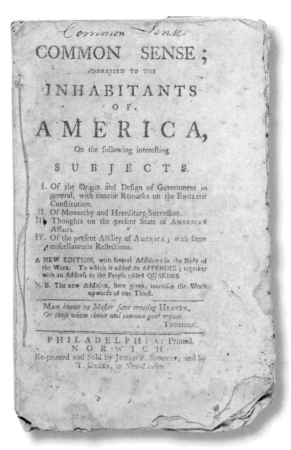

Common Sense

Thomas Paine's sensational pamphlet *Common Sense* advanced the popular debate on independence. Paine remained a provocative pamphleteer, writing *The Rights of Man* in revolutionary France, followed by *The Age of Reason*, which to many seemed to avow atheism. In 1802, he returned to the United States; although welcomed by Thomas Jefferson, Paine was spurned by nearly everyone else for his irreligiosity. He died in obscurity in 1809. Private Collection/Photo © Christie's Images/The Bridgeman Art Library.

In simple yet forceful language, Paine elaborated on the absurdities of the British monarchy. Why should one man, by accident of birth, claim extensive power over others? he asked. A king might be foolish or wicked. "One of the strongest natural proofs of the folly of hereditary right in kings," Paine wrote, "is that nature disapproves it; otherwise she would not so frequently turn it into ridicule by giving mankind *an ass for a lion*." Calling the British king an ass broke through the automatic deference most Americans still had for the monarchy. To replace monarchy, Paine advocated republican government based on the consent of the people. Rulers, according to Paine, were only representatives of the people, and the best form of government relied on frequent elections to achieve the most direct democracy possible.

Paine's pamphlet sold more than 150,000 copies in a matter of weeks. Newspapers reprinted it; men read it aloud in taverns and coffeehouses; John Adams sent a copy to his wife, Abigail, who passed it around to neighbors in Braintree, Massachusetts. New Englanders desired independence, but other colonies, under no immediate threat of violence, remained cautious.

Abigail Adams was impatient not only for independence but also for other legal changes that would revolutionize the new country. In a series of astute letters to her husband, she outlined obstacles and gave advice. She worried that southern slave owners might shrink from a war in the name of liberty: "I have sometimes been ready to think that the passion for Liberty cannot be Equally strong in the Breasts of those who have been accustomed to deprive their fellow Creatures of theirs." And in March 1776, she expressed her hope that women's legal status would improve under the new government: "In the new Code of Laws which I suppose it will be necessary for you to make I desire you would Remember the Ladies, and be more generous and favourable to them than your ancestors." Her chief concern was husbands' legal dominion over wives: "Do not put such unlimited power into the hands of the Husbands," she advised. "Remember all Men would be tyrants if they could." Abigail Adams anticipated a more radical end to tyranny than did Thomas Paine.

John Adams dismissed his wife's concerns. But to a male politician, Adams privately rehearsed the reasons why women (and men who were free blacks, or young, or propertyless) should remain excluded from political participation. Even though he concluded that nothing should change, at least Abigail's letter had forced him to ponder the exclusion, something few men—or women—did in 1776. Urgent talk of political independence was as radical as most could imagine.

The Declaration of Independence

In addition to Paine's *Common Sense*, another factor hastening independence was the prospect of an alliance with France, Britain's archrival. France was willing to provide military supplies and naval power only if assured that the Americans would separate from Britain. News that the British were negotiating to hire German mercenary soldiers further solidified support for independence. By May 1776, all but four colonies were agitating for a declaration. The holdouts

were Pennsylvania, Maryland, New York, and South Carolina, the latter two containing large loyalist populations. An exasperated Virginian wrote to his friend in the congress, "For God's sake, why do you dawdle in the Congress so strangely? Why do you not at once declare yourself a separate independent state?"

In early June, the Virginia delegation introduced a resolution calling for independence. The moderates still commanded enough support to postpone a vote on the measure until July. In the meantime, the congress appointed a committee, with Thomas Jefferson and others, to draft a longer document setting out the case for independence.

On July 2, after intense politicking, all but one state voted for independence; New York abstained. The congress then turned to the document drafted by Jefferson and his committee. Jefferson began with a preamble that articulated philosophical principles about natural rights, equality, the right of revolution, and the consent of the governed as the only true basis for government. He then listed more than two dozen specific grievances against King George. The congress passed over the preamble with little comment and instead wrangled over the list of grievances, especially the issue of slavery. Jefferson had included an impassioned statement blaming the king for slavery, which delegates from Georgia and South Carolina struck out, not wishing to denounce their labor system. But the congress let stand another of Jefferson's grievances, blaming the king for mobilizing "the merciless Indian Savages" into bloody frontier warfare, a reference to Pontiac's Rebellion (see "Pontiac's Rebellion and the Proclamation of 1763" in chapter 6).

On July 4, the amendments to Jefferson's text were complete, and the congress formally adopted the **Declaration of Independence**, with New York switching from abstention to approval ten days later, making the vote unanimous. In August, the delegates gathered to sign the official parchment copy. Four men, including John Dickinson, declined to sign; several others "signed with regret . . . and with many doubts," according to John Adams. The document was then printed, widely distributed, and read aloud in celebrations everywhere.

Printed copies did not include the signers' names, for they had committed treason, a crime punishable by death. On the day of signing, they indulged in gallows humor. When Benjamin Franklin paused before signing, John Hancock of Massachusetts teased him, "Come, come, sir. We must be unanimous. No pulling different ways. We must all hang together." Franklin replied, "Indeed we must all hang together. Otherwise we shall most assuredly hang separately."

REVIEW Why were many Americans initially reluctant to pursue independence from Britain?

▶ The First Year of War, 1775–1776

Both sides approached the war for America with uneasiness. The Americans, with inexperienced militias, were opposing the mightiest military power in the world. Also, their country was not

THE FEMALE COMBATANTS

OR WHO SHALL

Publish'd according to Act Jan.ʳ 26. 1776. Price 6.ᵈ

VISUAL ACTIVITY

Female Combatants, 1776

This British cartoon of January 1776 follows a long tradition of representing countries as female characters: a fancy-dressed matron as Britain and a near-naked Indian maiden as Britain's North American colonies, pummeling each other with fists. The British matron calls out "I'll force you to Obedience, you Rebellious Slut," while the Indian maiden replies "Liberty, Liberty forever, Mother, while I exist."
Courtesy of the Yale University Library

READING THE IMAGE: Does this cartoon express sympathy with one side over the other in the brewing Revolutionary War? What is your evidence?

CONNECTIONS: Does the message of this cartoon, of a struggle over obedience versus liberty, well capture the essence of the Revolutionary struggle as of January 1776?

unified; many people remained loyal to Britain. The British faced serious obstacles as well. Their disdain for the fighting abilities of the Americans required reassessment in light of the Bunker Hill battle. The logistics of supplying an army with food across three thousand miles of water were daunting. And since the British goal was to regain allegiance, not to destroy and conquer, the army was often constrained in its actions. These patterns—undertrained American troops and British troops strangely unwilling to press their advantage—played out repeatedly in the first year of war.

The American Military Forces

Americans claimed that the initial months of war were purely defensive, triggered by the British invasion. But the war also quickly became a rebellion, an overthrowing of long-established authority. As both defenders and rebels, many Americans were highly motivated to fight, and the potential manpower that could be mobilized was, in theory, very great.

Local defense in the colonies had long rested with a militia composed of all able-bodied men over age sixteen. Militias, however, were best suited for local and limited engagements, responding to conflict with Indians or slave rebellions, both relatively infrequent events. In forming the Continental army, the congress set enlistment at one year, which proved inadequate as the war progressed. Incentives produced longer commitments: a $20 bonus for three years of service, a hundred acres of land for enlistment for the duration of the war—a reward good only if the Americans won the war. Over the course of the war, some 230,000 men enlisted, about one-quarter of the white male adult population. Women also served in the Continental army, cooking, washing, and nursing the wounded. The British army established a ratio of one woman to every ten men; in the Continental army, the ratio was set at one woman to fifteen men. Close to 20,000 "camp followers," as they were called, served during the war, many of them wives of men in service. Some 12,000 children also tagged along, and babies were born in the camps. Some women helped during battles, supplying drinking water or ammunition to soldiers.

Black Americans at first were excluded from the Continental army. But as manpower needs increased, northern states welcomed free blacks into service; slaves in some states could serve with their masters' permission. About 5,000 black men served in the Revolutionary War on the rebel side, nearly all from the northern states. Black soldiers sometimes were segregated into separate units, and while some of these men were draftees, others were clearly inspired by ideals of freedom in a war against tyranny. For example, twenty-three blacks gave "Liberty," "Freedom," and "Freeman" as their surnames at the time of enlistment.

Military service helped politicize Americans during the early stages of the war (see "Visualizing History," page 174). In early 1776, independence was a risky, potentially treasonous idea. But as the war heated up and recruiters demanded commitment, some Americans discovered that apathy had its dangers as well. Anyone who refused to serve ran the risk of being called a traitor to the cause. Military service became a prime way of demonstrating political allegiance.

The American army was at times raw and inexperienced, and often woefully undermanned. It never had the precision and discipline of European professional armies. But it was never as bad as the British continually assumed. The British would learn that it was a serious mistake to underrate the enemy.

The British Strategy

The American strategy was straightforward—to repulse and defeat an invading army. The British strategy was not as clear. Britain wanted to put down a rebellion and restore monarchical power in the colonies, but the question was how to accomplish this. A decisive defeat of the Continental army was essential but not sufficient to end the rebellion, for the British would still have to contend with an armed and motivated insurgent population. Furthermore, there was no single political nerve center whose capture would spell certain victory. The Continental Congress moved from place to place, staying just out of reach of the British. During the course of the war, the British captured and occupied every major port city, but that brought no serious loss to the Americans, 95 percent of whom lived in the countryside.

Britain's delicate task was to restore the old governments, not to destroy an enemy country. British generals were at first reluctant to ravage the countryside, confiscate food, or burn villages. There were thirteen distinct political entities to capture, pacify, and then restore to the crown, and they stretched in a long line from New Hampshire to Georgia. Clearly, a large land army was required for the job. Without the willingness to seize food from the locals, the British needed hundreds of supply ships—hence their desire to capture the ports. The British strategy also assumed that many Americans remained loyal to the king and would come to the British military's aid.

The overall British plan was a divide-and-conquer approach, focusing first on New York, the state judged to have the greatest number of loyal subjects. New York offered a geographic advantage as well: Control of the Hudson River would allow the British to isolate New England. British armies could descend from Canada and move north from New York City along the Hudson River. Squeezed between a naval blockade on the eastern coast and army raids in the west, Massachusetts could be driven to surrender. New Jersey and Pennsylvania would fall in line, the British thought, because of loyalist strength. Virginia was a problem, like Massachusetts, but the British were confident that the Carolinas would help them isolate and subdue Virginia.

Quebec, New York, and New Jersey

In late 1775, an American expedition was launched to capture the cities of Montreal and Quebec before British reinforcements could arrive (Map 7.1). This offensive was a clear sign that the war was not purely a reaction to the invasion of Massachusetts. A force of New York Continentals commanded by General Richard Montgomery took Montreal easily in September 1775 and then advanced on Quebec. Meanwhile, a second contingent of Continentals led by Colonel Benedict Arnold moved north through Maine to Quebec, a punishing trek through freezing rain with woefully inadequate supplies. Arnold showed heroic determination, but close to half of his men either died or turned back during the march. Arnold and Montgomery jointly attacked Quebec in December but failed to take the city. Worse yet, they encountered smallpox, which killed more men than had the battle for Quebec.

The main action of the first year of the war came not in Canada, however, but in New York. In August 1776, some 45,000 British troops (including 8,000 German mercenaries, called Hessians) under the command of General Howe landed south of New York City. General Washington had anticipated this move and had relocated his army of 20,000 south from Massachusetts. The **battle of Long Island** in late August pitted the well-trained British "redcoats" (slang referring to their red uniforms) against a very green Continental army. Howe attacked, inflicting many casualties and taking 1,000 prisoners. A British general crowed, "If a good bleeding can bring those Bible-faced Yankees to their senses, the fever of independency should soon abate." Howe failed to press forward, however, perhaps remembering the costly victory of Bunker Hill, and Washington evacuated his troops to Manhattan Island.

Washington knew it would be hard to hold Manhattan, so he withdrew farther north to two forts on either side of the Hudson River. For two months, the armies engaged in limited skirmishing, but in November Howe finally captured Fort Washington and Fort Lee, taking another 3,000

Keeping Powder Dry

Musket-toting soldiers needed a ready-at-hand, moisture-tight container for gunpowder. The eighteenth-century solution to this packaging problem was the powder horn, made from the horn of an ox or cow and carried on a shoulder strap. Tight wooden plugs sealed both ends. A soldier filled the large end with explosive powder and dispensed it through the small end into the firing pan of the musket. Experienced soldiers took a total of 45 to 90 seconds to reload and fire.

During the considerable down-time of military life, soldiers personalized their horns with carved or engraved words and pictures, sometimes hiring skilled artisans or possibly doing it themselves. Hundreds of surviving horns from the Revolutionary War bear their owners' names and often a precise date. Popular choices for pictures included sailing ships, soldiers in battle formation, and animals real and fictive. Some horns depicted maps while others celebrated victories the soldier had witnessed.

The two powder horns shown here are emblazoned with patriotic rhetoric about liberty. William Waller joined a Virginia militia unit in 1775 and defended New York against the British invasion in August 1776. He chose two slogans: "LIBERTY or DEATH" and, on the other side, "KILL or be KILLD." The first had become something of a popular catchphrase in 1775; it graced the masthead of a fiery Massachusetts newspaper, and it also appeared in occasional personal correspondence. (Its usage did not originate with a March 1775 speech by Patrick Henry, alleged to end with the stirring words "Give me Liberty or Give me Death." Henry's speech was nowhere reported in the press of his day, nor did he speak from a written copy. A biographer in 1816 crafted the famous lines, based on a recollection of an old man present that day.) Waller carried his powder horn into a November 1776 battle defending Fort Washington, just north of New York City. The fort fell, and Waller was one of 3,000 men captured by the British that day. Most of those captives were herded into prison ships in the waters off New York City, and almost none of them survived.

SOURCES: Waller Powder Horn: Image courtesy of the Museum of the American Revolution; Sherburne Powder Horn and Detail: Photo by David Wesbrook. Reprinted courtesy of the Honourable Company of Horners.

Waller's Powder Horn

prisoners. Washington retreated quickly across New Jersey into Pennsylvania. Again Howe unaccountably failed to press his advantage. Instead, he parked his German troops in winter quarters along the Delaware River. Perhaps he knew that many of the Continental soldiers' enlistment periods ended on December 31, making him confident that the Americans would not attack him. He was wrong.

On December 25, in an icy rain, Washington stealthily moved his army across the Delaware River and at dawn made a quick capture of the unsuspecting German soldiers. This impressive victory lifted the sagging morale of the patriot side. For the next two weeks, Washington remained on the offensive, capturing supplies in a clever attack on British units at Princeton. Soon he was safe in Morristown, in northern New Jersey, where he settled his army for the winter. Washington finally had time to administer mass smallpox inoculations and see his men through the abbreviated course of the disease.

All in all, in the first year of declared war, the rebellious Americans had a few proud moments but also many worries. The inexperienced Continental army had barely hung on in the New York campaign. Washington had shown exceptional daring and admirable restraint, but what really saved the Americans was the repeated reluctance of the British to follow through militarily when they had the advantage.

REVIEW Why did the British initially exercise restraint in their efforts to defeat the rebellious colonies?

Sherburne's Powder Horn

Edward Sherburne from New Hampshire joined the Continental army in January 1776. His bold name on his seventeen-inch horn ensured that no one might mistake it for another. To the left are the words "Success to" followed by "Liberty," inscribed in a heart. A rabbit and a lion sit atop the banner "Liberty," joined by a bust possibly of George Washington. The inset enlarges the carving above Sherburne's name, showing eight soldiers firing at one another. Sherburne rose to be a major, but his career was cut short; he died in battle at Germantown, Pennsylvania, in October 1777.

Detail of Sherburne's Powder Horn

Questions for Analysis

1. Why would soldiers put their names on their powder horns? How were the horns similar to military dog tags?

2. What might the date on a powder horn signify about a soldier's participation in the war? Why might it be important or useful to carry dated equipment?

3. These two horns and many others carry military motifs and themes. Is it in any way surprising to find a lack of pictorial references to civilian life or loved ones back home?

Connect to the Big Idea

⊙ The scores of existing powder horns show us an intricate and often beautiful form of folk art. What can they also show us about the political beliefs and personally felt allegiances of the common soldier in the Revolutionary War?

▶ The Home Front

Battlefields alone did not determine the outcome of the war. Struggles on the home front were equally important. Men who joined the army often left wives to manage on their own. Some men did not join because they were loyal to Britain and did not welcome war, and many others were undecided about independence. In many communities, both persuasion and force were used to gain the allegiance of the many neutrals. A major factor pushing neutrals to side with the revolution was the harsh British treatment of prisoners of war. Adding to the turbulence of the times was a very shaky wartime economy. The creative financing of the fledgling government brought hardships as well as opportunities, forcing Americans to confront new manifestations of virtue and corruption.

Patriotism at the Local Level

Committees of correspondence, of public safety, and of inspection dominated the political landscape in patriot communities. These committees took on more than customary local governance; they enforced boycotts, picked army draftees, and policed suspected traitors. They sometimes invaded homes to search for contraband goods such as British tea or textiles.

Loyalists were dismayed by the increasing show of power by patriots. A man in Westchester, New York, described his response to intrusions by committees: "Choose your committee or suffer it to be chosen by a half dozen fools in your

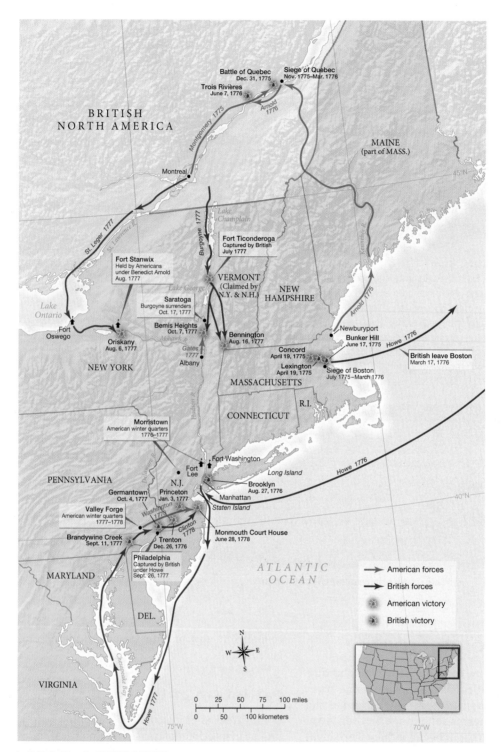

MAP ACTIVITY

Map 7.1   The War in the North, 1775–1778

After battles in Massachusetts in 1775, rebel forces invaded Canada but failed to capture Quebec. The British army landed in New York in 1776, causing turmoil in New Jersey in 1777 and 1778. Burgoyne attempted to isolate New England, but he was stopped at Saratoga in 1777 in the decisive battle of the early war.

READING THE MAP: Which general's troops traveled the farthest in each of these years: 1775, 1776, and 1777? How did the availability of water routes affect British and American strategy?

CONNECTIONS: Why did the French wait until early 1778 to join American forces against the British? What did France hope to gain from participating in the war?

neighborhood—open your doors to them—let them examine your tea-cannisters and molasses-jugs, and your wives' and daughters' petty coats—bow and cringe and tremble and quake—fall down and worship our sovereign lord the mob. . . . Should any pragmatical committee-gentleman come to my house and give himself airs, I shall show him the door." Oppressive or not, the local committees were rarely challenged. Their persuasive powers convinced many middle-of-the-road citizens that neutrality was not a comfortable option.

Another group new to political life—white women—increasingly demonstrated a capacity for patriotism as wartime hardships dramatically altered their work routines. Many wives whose husbands were away on military or political service took on masculine duties. Their competence to manage farms and make business decisions encouraged some to assert interest in politics as well, as Abigail Adams did while John Adams served in the Continental Congress in Philadelphia. Eliza Wilkinson managed a South Carolina plantation and talked revolutionary politics with women friends. "None were greater politicians than the several knots of ladies who met together," she remarked, alert to the unusual turn female conversations had taken.

Women from prominent Philadelphia families took more direct action, forming the **Ladies Association** to collect money for Continental soldiers. Mrs. Esther DeBerdt Reed, wife of Pennsylvania's governor, published a broadside in 1780 titled "The Sentiments of an American Woman" to defend their female activism: "The time is arrived to display the same sentiments which animated us at the beginning of the Revolution, when we renounced the use of teas [and] when our republican and laborious hands spun the flax."

The Loyalists

Around one-fifth of the American population remained loyal to the crown in 1776, and another two-fifths tried to stay neutral, providing a strong base for the British. In general, **loyalists** believed that social stability depended on a government anchored by monarchy and aristocracy. They feared that democratic tyranny was emergent among the self-styled patriots who appeared to be unscrupulous, violent men grabbing power for themselves.

Pockets of loyalism existed everywhere (Map 7.2). The most visible loyalists (called Tories by their enemies) were royal officials, not

Abigail Adams
Abigail Smith Adams, twenty-two, wears feminine pearls and a lace collar along with a facial expression projecting confidence and maturity not often credited to young women of the 1760s. A decade later, she was running the family's Massachusetts farm while her husband, John, attended the Continental Congress in Philadelphia. Her frequent letters gave him the benefit of her sage advice on politics and the war. © Massachusetts Historical Society, Boston, MA, USA/The Bridgeman Art Library.

only governors but also local judges and customs officers. Wealthy merchants gravitated toward loyalism to maintain the trade protections of navigation acts and the British navy. Conservative urban lawyers admired the stability of British law and order. Some colonists chose loyalism simply to oppose traditional adversaries, for example many backcountry Carolina farmers who resented the power of the pro-revolution gentry. Southern slaves had their own resentments against the white slave-owning class and looked to Britain in hope of freedom. Even New England towns at the heart of the turmoil, such as Concord, Massachusetts, had a small and increasingly silenced core of loyalists. On occasion, husbands and wives, fathers and sons disagreed completely on the war. (See "Documenting the American Promise," page 180.)

TEUCRO DUCE NIL DESPERANDOM.

Firſt Battalion of PENNSYLVANIA LOYALISTS, commanded by His Excellency Sir WILLIAM HOWE, K.B.

ALL INTREPID ABLE-BODIED

HEROES,

WHO are willing to ſerve His MAJESTY KING GEORGE the Third, in Defence of their Country, Laws and Conſtitution, againſt the arbitrary Uſurpations of a tyrannical Congreſs, have now not only an Opportunity of manifeſting their Spirit, by aſſiſting in reducing to Obedience their too-long deluded Countrymen, but alſo of acquiring the polite Accompliſhments of a Soldier, by ſerving only two Years, or during the preſent Rebellion in America.

Such ſpirited Fellows, who are willing to engage, will be rewarded at the End of the War, beſides their Laurels, with 50 Acres of Land, where every gallant Hero may retire. . . . .

Each Volunteer will receive, as a Bounty, FIVE DOLLARS, beſides Arms, Cloathing and Accoutrements, and every other Requiſite proper to accommodate a Gentleman Soldier, by applying to Lieutenant Colonel ALLEN, or at Captain KEARNY's Rendezvous, at PATRICK TONRY's, three Doors above Market-ſtreet, in Second-ſtreet.

Loyalist Recruiting Poster, 1777
The British army invites a few good men to restore obedience to their "deluded countrymen." A five dollar signing bonus and a promise of free land await each new recruit, who will also be trained in "the polite Accomplishments of a soldier." Notice the Latin phrase heading the poster, referencing a military leader in the ancient battle of Troy. What subtle message did that send?
The Granger Collection, New York.

Many Indian tribes chose neutrality at the war's start, seeing the conflict as a civil war between the English and Americans. Eventually, however, they were drawn in, most taking the British side. The powerful Iroquois Confederacy divided: The Mohawk, Cayuga, Seneca, and Onondaga peoples lined up with the British; the Oneida and Tuscarora tribes aided Americans. One young Mohawk leader, Thayendanegea (known also by his English name, Joseph Brant), traveled to England in 1775 to complain to King George about land-hungry New York settlers. "It is very hard when we have let the King's subjects have so much of our lands for so little value," he wrote, "they should want to cheat us in this manner of the small spots we have left for our

women and children to live on." Brant pledged Indian support for the king in exchange for protection from encroaching settlers. In the Ohio Country, parts of the Shawnee and Delaware tribes started out pro-American but shifted to the British side by 1779 in the face of repeated betrayals by American settlers and soldiers.

Loyalists were most vocal between 1774 and 1776, when the possibility of a full-scale rebellion against Britain was still uncertain. They challenged the emerging patriot side in pamphlets and newspapers. In 1776 in New York City, 547 loyalists signed and circulated a broadside titled "A Declaration of Dependence" in rebuttal to the congress's July 4 declaration, denouncing the "most unnatural, unprovoked Rebellion that ever disgraced the annals of Time."

Who Is a Traitor?

In June 1775, the Second Continental Congress declared all loyalists to be traitors. Over the next year, state laws defined as treason acts such as provisioning the British army, saying anything that undermined patriot morale, and discouraging men from enlisting in the Continental army. Punishments ranged from house arrest and suspension of voting privileges to confiscation of property and deportation. Sometimes self-appointed committees of Tory hunters bypassed the judicial niceties and terrorized loyalists, raiding their houses or tarring and feathering them.

Were wives of loyalists also traitors? When loyalist families fled the country, their property was typically confiscated. But if the wife stayed, courts usually allowed her to keep one-third of the property, the amount due her if widowed, and confiscated the rest. Yet a wife who fled with her husband might have little choice in the matter. After the Revolution, descendants of refugee loyalists filed several lawsuits to regain property that had entered the family through the mother's inheritance. In one well-publicized Massachusetts case in 1805, the American son of loyalist refugee Anna Martin recovered her dowry property on the grounds that she had no independent will to be a loyalist.

Tarring and feathering, property confiscation, deportation, terrorism—to the loyalists, such denials of liberty of conscience and of freedom to own private property proved that democratic tyranny was more to be feared than the monarchical variety. A Boston loyalist named Mather Byles aptly expressed this point: "They call me a brainless Tory, but tell me . . . which

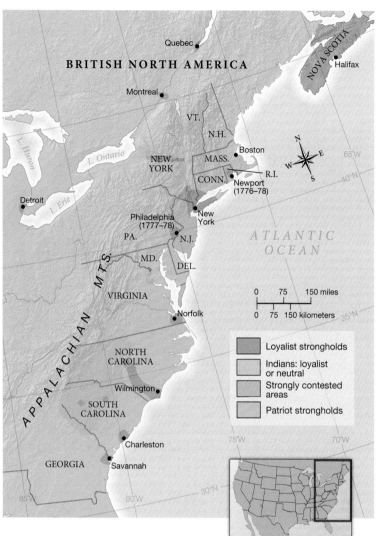

MAP ACTIVITY

Map 7.2 Loyalist Strength and Rebel Support

The exact number of loyalists can never be known. No one could have made an accurate count at the time, and political allegiance often shifted with the wind. This map shows the regions of loyalist strength on which the British relied—most significantly, the lower Hudson valley and the Carolina Piedmont.

READING THE MAP: Which forces were stronger, those loyal to Britain or those rebelling? (Consider the size of their respective areas, centers of population, and vital port locations.) What areas were contested? If the contested areas ultimately had sided with the British, how would the balance of power have changed?

CONNECTIONS: Who was more likely to be a loyalist and why? How many loyalists left the United States? Where did they go?

is better—to be ruled by one tyrant three thousand miles away, or by three thousand tyrants not a mile away?" Byles was soon sentenced to deportation.

Throughout the war, probably 7,000 to 8,000 loyalists fled to England, and 28,000 eventually found haven in Canada. Many stayed put while the war's outcome was unknown. In New Jersey, for example, 3,000 Jerseyites felt protected (or scared) enough by the occupying British army in 1776 to swear an oath of allegiance to the king. But then the British drew back to New York City, leaving them at the mercy of local patriot committees. Despite the staunch backing of loyalists in 1776, the British found it difficult to build a winning strategy on their support.

Prisoners of War

The poor handling of loyalists as traitors paled in comparison to the handling of American prisoners of war by the British. Among European military powers, humane treatment of captured soldiers was the custom, including adequate provisions (paid for by the captives' own government) and the possibility of prisoner exchanges. But British leaders refused to see American captives as foot soldiers employed by a sovereign nation. Instead they were traitors, to be treated worse than common criminals.

The 4,000 American prisoners taken in the fall of 1776 were crowded onto two dozen vessels anchored in the river between Manhattan and

Families Divide over the Revolution

Generalizing about rebels versus loyalists is a complex historical task. Sometimes categorizing by class, race, and geographic descriptors helps explain the split. But beyond economic interests or cultural politics, sometimes the loyalist-patriot divide cut across families—and cut deeply. These documents reveal people pitted against loved ones over wartime allegiance.

DOCUMENT 1
Patriot Benjamin Franklin and Loyalist Son William Correspond, 1784

Benjamin Franklin, a keen advocate of the Revolution, had a son who stayed loyal to the crown. William was Benjamin's illegitimate son, resulting from a youthful indiscretion. Benjamin raised him and took him to England in 1757 during his extended service as Pennsylvania's colonial agent. William thus acquired connections at court, and in 1762, he was appointed royal governor of New Jersey, a post he held until 1776. When the war began, he was placed under house arrest as a traitor to the patriot cause. Father and son did not communicate for the next nine years, even when William was confined in a Connecticut prison for eight months. During this time, Benjamin took charge of William's oldest son, an illegitimate child born before William's legal marriage. After the war, William moved to England, and in 1784 he wrote to his father, then in Paris, asking for a meeting of reconciliation. He did not apologize for his loyalism.

Dear and honored Father,
Ever since the termination of the unhappy contest between Great Britain and America, I have been anxious to write to you. . . . There are narrow illiberal Minds in all Parties. In that which I took, and on whose Account I have

so much suffered, there have not been wanting some who have insinuated that my Conduct has been founded on Collusion with you, that one of us might succeed whichever Party should prevail. . . . The Falsity of such Insinuation in our Case you well know, and I am happy that I can with Confidence appeal not only to you but to my God, that I have uniformly acted from a strong Sense of what I conceived my Duty to my King, and Regard to my Country, required. If I have been mistaken, I cannot help it. It is an Error of Judgment what the maturest Reflection I am capable of cannot rectify; and I verily believe were the same Circumstances to occur again Tomorrow, my Conduct would be exactly similar to what it was heretofore.

The father replied:
Dear Son,
I . . . am glad to find that you desire to revive the affectionate Intercourse, that formerly existed between us. It will be very agreeable to me; indeed nothing has ever hurt me so much and affected me with such keen Sensations, as to find myself deserted in my old age by my only Son; and not only deserted, but to find him taking up Arms against me, in a Cause, wherein my good Fame, Fortune and Life were all at Stake. You conceived, you say, that your Duty to your King and regard for your Country requir'd this. I ought not to blame you for differing in

Brooklyn. The largest ship, the HMS *Jersey*, was a broken-down hull built to house a crew of 400 but now packed with more than 1,100 prisoners. Survivors described the dark, stinking space below decks where more than half a dozen men died daily. A twenty-year-old captive seaman described his first view of the hold: "Here was a motley crew, covered with rags and filth; visages pallid with disease, emaciated with hunger and anxiety, . . . and surrounded with

the horrors of sickness and death." The Continental Congress sent food to the prisoners, but most was diverted to British use, leaving General Washington fuming.

Treating the captives as criminals potentially triggered the Anglo-American right of habeas corpus, a thirteenth-century British liberty that guaranteed every prisoner the right to challenge his detention before a judge and to learn the charges against him. To remove

Sentiment with me in Public Affairs. We are Men, all subject to errors. Our opinions are not in our own Power; they are form'd and govern'd much by Circumstances, that are often as inexplicable as they are irresistible. Your Situation was such that few would have censured your remaining Neuter, *tho' there are Natural Duties which preceded political ones, and cannot be extinguish'd by them.*

This is a disagreeable Subject. I drop it. And we will endeavor, as you propose mutually to forget what has happened relating to it, as well as we can. I send your Son over to pay his Duty to you. . . . He is greatly esteem'd and belov'd in this Country, and will make his Way anywhere. . . . Wishing you Health, and more happiness than it seems you have lately experienced, I remain your affectionate father, B. Franklin

Source: Courtesy of the American Philosophical Society, http://www.amphilsoc.org.

DOCUMENT 2
Two Oneida Brothers Confront Their Different Allegiances, 1779

Mary Jemison was captured as a girl during the Seven Years' War and adopted into the Seneca tribe of western New York, where she remained for life. When she was eighty, her narrative was taken down and published. In this story from her narrative, she relates how some Oneida warriors siding with the British captured two Indians guiding General Sullivan's 1779 campaign of terror in central New York. One of the captors recognized his own brother.

Envy and revenge glared in the features of the conquering savage, as he advanced to his brother (the prisoner) in all the haughtiness of Indian pride, heightened by a sense of power, and addressed him in the following manner:

"Brother, you have merited death! The hatchet or the war-club shall finish your career! When I begged of you to follow me in the fortunes of war, you was deaf to my cries—you spurned my entreaties!

"Brother! You have merited death and shall have your deserts! When the rebels raised their hatchets to fight their good master, you sharpened your knife, you brightened your rifle and led on our foes to the fields of our fathers! You have merited death and shall die by our hands! When those rebels had drove us from the fields of our fathers to seek out new homes, it was you who could dare to step forth as their pilot, and conduct them even to the doors of our wigwams, to butcher our children and put us to death! No crime can be greater! But though you have merited death and shall die on this spot, my hands shall not be stained in the blood of a brother! *Who will strike?"*

Little Beard, who was standing by, as soon as the speech was ended, struck the prisoner on the head with his tomahawk, and dispatched him at once.

Source: James E. Seaver, *A narrative of the life of Mrs. Mary Jemison, who was taken by the Indians, in the year 1755, when only about twelve years of age, and has continued to reside amongst them to the present time* (1824), chapter VII, Project Gutenberg, http://www.gutenberg.org/ebooks/6960 (accessed August 2, 2013).

Questions for Analysis and Debate

1. What did Benjamin Franklin mean by the emphasized words *"Natural Duties"*? Do you think Franklin really believed that his son was entitled to his own political opinions on the Revolutionary War? What factors help explain why William remained loyal to the crown?

2. Why did the Oneida warrior believe that his brother merited death?

Connect to the Big Idea

C To what extent was the American Revolution a civil war, that is, a war between inhabitants of the same country?

that possibility, Parliament voted in early 1777 to suspend habeas corpus specifically for "persons taken in the act of high treason" in any of the colonies.

Despite the prison-ship horrors, Washington insisted that captured British soldiers be treated humanely. From the initial group of Hessians taken on Christmas 1776 to the several thousands more soldiers captured in American victories by 1778, America's prisoners of war were gathered in rural encampments. Guarded by local townsmen, the captives typically could cultivate small gardens, move about freely during the day, and even hire themselves out to farmers suffering wartime labor shortages. Officers with money could purchase lodging with local families and mix socially with Americans. Many officers were even allowed to keep their guns as they waited for prisoner exchanges to release them.

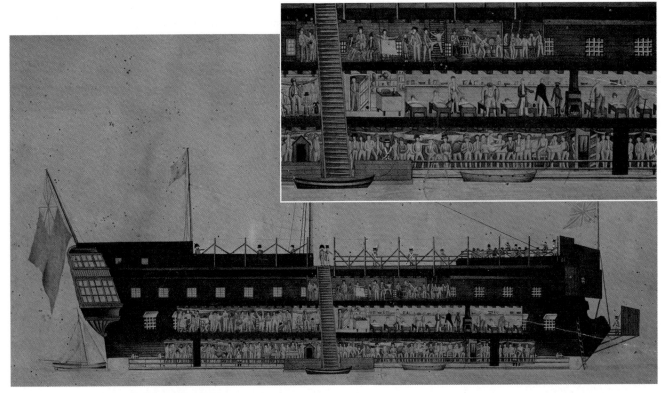

A British Prison Ship
A carefully executed cutaway drawing of a prison ship shows scores of American POWs below decks being guarded by redcoats. The degree of crowding and of care—note the infirmary on the middle level to the right of the gangplank (see inset)—is represented as more humane than was actually the case. The artist added these words in French beside the drawing: "My God, Have you forgotten me?"   Museum of the City of New York/The Art Archive at Art Resource, NY

Such exchanges were negotiated when the British became desperate to regain valued officers and thus freed American officers. Death was the most common fate of ordinary American soldiers and seamen. More than 15,000 men endured captivity in the prison ships, and two-thirds of them died, a number double those who died in battle (estimated to be around 5,000). News of the horrors of the British death ships increased the revolutionaries' resolve and convinced some neutrals of the necessity of the war.

Financial Instability and Corruption

Wars cost money—for arms and ammunition, for food and uniforms, for soldiers' pay, for provisions for prisoners. The Continental Congress printed money, but its value quickly deteriorated because the congress held no precious metals to back the currency. The dollar eventually bottomed out at one-fortieth of its face value. States, too, were printing paper money to pay for wartime expenses, further complicating the economy.

As the currency depreciated, the congress turned to other means to procure supplies and labor. One method was to borrow hard money (gold or silver coins) from wealthy men in exchange for certificates of debt (public securities) promising repayment with interest. The certificates of debt were similar to present-day government bonds. To pay soldiers, the congress issued land grant certificates, written promises of acreage usually located in frontier areas such as central Maine or eastern Ohio. Both the public securities and the land grant certificates quickly became forms of negotiable currency, and they too soon depreciated.

Depreciating currency inevitably led to rising prices, as sellers compensated for the falling value of the money. The wartime economy of the late 1770s, with its unreliable currency and price inflation, was extremely demoralizing to Americans everywhere. In 1778, in an effort to impose stability, local committees of public safety began to fix prices on essential goods such as flour. Inevitably, some turned this unstable situation to their advantage. Money that fell fast in value needed to be spent quickly; being in debt was suddenly advantageous because the debt could be repaid in devalued currency. A brisk black market sprang up in prohibited luxury imports, such as tea, sugar, textiles, and wines, even though these items came from Britain. A New Hampshire delegate to the Continental Congress denounced the trade: "We are a crooked and perverse generation, longing for the fineries and follies of those Egyptian task masters from whom we have so lately freed ourselves."

REVIEW   How did the patriots promote support for their cause in the colonies?

▶ The Campaigns of 1777–1779: The North and West

In early 1777, the Continental army faced bleak choices. General Washington had skillfully avoided defeat, but the minor victories in New Jersey lent only faint optimism to the American side. Meanwhile, British troops moved south from Quebec, aiming to isolate New England by taking control of the Hudson River. Their presence drew the Continental army up into central New York, turning the Mohawk Valley into a bloody war zone and polarizing the tribes of the ancient Iroquois Confederacy. By 1779, rival tribes in the Ohio Valley were fully involved in the Revolutionary War. Despite an important victory at Saratoga, the increasing involvement of pro-British Indians and the continuing strength of the British forced the American government to look to France for help.

Burgoyne's Army and the Battle of Saratoga

In 1777, British general John Burgoyne commanding a considerable army began the northern squeeze on the Hudson River valley.

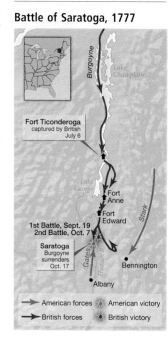

Battle of Saratoga, 1777

Fort Ticonderoga captured by British July 6

Fort Anne

Fort Edward

1st Battle, Sept. 19
2nd Battle, Oct. 7

Saratoga
Burgoyne surrenders
Oct. 17

Bennington

Albany

→ American forces   ⚔ American victory
→ British forces   ⚔ British victory

Coming from Canada, he marched south hoping to capture Albany, near the intersection of the Hudson and Mohawk rivers (see Map 7.1, page 176). Accompanied by 1,000 "camp followers" (cooks, laundresses, musicians) and some 400 Indian warriors, mostly Mohawks, Burgoyne's army of 7,800 men did not travel light. Food had to be packed in, not only for people but for 400 horses hauling heavy artillery.

In July, Burgoyne captured Fort Ticonderoga with ease. American troops stationed there spotted the approaching British and abandoned the fort without a fight. The British continued to move south, but they lost a month hacking their way through dense forests. Supply lines back to Canada were severely stretched, and soldiers sent out to forage for food were beaten back by local militia units.

The logical second step in isolating New England should have been to advance troops up the Hudson from New York City to meet Burgoyne. American surveillance indicated that General Howe in Manhattan was readying his men for a major move in August 1777. But Howe surprised everyone by sailing south to attack Philadelphia.

To reinforce Burgoyne, British and Hessian troops from Montreal came from the west along the Mohawk River, aided by some thousand Mohawks and Senecas of the Iroquois Confederacy. A hundred miles west of Albany, the British encountered American Continental soldiers at Fort Stanwix and laid siege, causing hundreds of local patriot German militiamen and a number of Oneida Indians to rush to the Continentals' support. On August 6, 1777, Mohawk chief Joseph Brant led his large force of warriors in an ambush on the patriot fighters in a narrow ravine called Oriskany. The result was the bloodiest battle of the entire war. By the end of the day, some thousand men were dead, wounded, or missing. Nearly 500 out of 840 of the local militiamen were killed in the carnage, while on Brant's side, some 90 warriors died. The defenders of Fort Stanwix ultimately repelled their attackers, who retreated north to Canada. The deadly **battle of Oriskany** and battle of Fort Stanwix were complexly multiethnic, pitting

***The Death of Jane McCrea* by John Vanderlyn**
Jane McCrea, a patriot's daughter in love with a loyalist in Burgoyne's army, gained fame as a martyr in 1777. She met death on her way to join her fiancé—either shot in the crossfire of battle (the British claim) or murdered by Indians (the patriots' version). American leaders used the story of the vulnerable maiden as propaganda to inspire the American drive for victory at Saratoga. Wadsworth Atheneum Museum of Art, Hartford/Art Resource, NY.

but at the great cost of 600 dead or wounded. Three weeks later, an American attack on Burgoyne's forces in the second stage of the **battle of Saratoga** cost the British another 600 men and most of their cannons. General Burgoyne finally surrendered to the American forces on October 17, 1777. It was the first decisive victory for the American Continentals, touching off great celebration throughout the colonies.

General Howe, meanwhile, had succeeded in occupying Philadelphia in September 1777. Figuring that the Saratoga loss was balanced by the capture of Philadelphia, the British government proposed a negotiated settlement—not including independence—to end the war. The American side refused.

Patriot optimism was not well founded. Spirits ran high, but supplies of arms and food ran precariously low. Washington moved his troops into winter quarters at Valley Forge, just west of Philadelphia. Quartered in drafty huts, the men lacked blankets, boots, stockings, and food. Some 2,000 men at Valley Forge died of disease; another 2,000 deserted over the bitter six-month encampment.

Washington blamed the citizenry for lack of support; indeed, evidence of corruption and profiteering was abundant. Army suppliers too often provided defective food, clothing, and gunpowder. One shipment of bedding arrived with blankets one-quarter their customary size. Food supplies arrived rotten. As one Continental officer said, "The people at home are destroying the Army by their conduct much faster than Howe and all his army can possibly do by fighting us."

The War in the West: Indian Country

Between the fall of 1777 and the summer of 1778, the fighting on the Atlantic coast slowed. But in the interior western areas—the Mohawk Valley, the Ohio Valley, and Kentucky—the war of Indians against the American rebels heated up. Native Americans fought to protect their sovereignty, their independence, and their traditional culture, in a near mirror image to the Americans' quest for "life, liberty, and the pursuit of happiness."

The ambush and slaughter at Oriskany in August 1777 marked the beginning of three years of terror for the inhabitants of the Mohawk Valley. Loyalists and Indians engaged in many raids throughout 1778, capturing or killing

German Americans against Hessian mercenaries, New York patriots against New York loyalists, English Americans against British soldiers, and Indians against Indians. They marked the beginning of the end of the Iroquois Confederacy, ruptured by lethal violence between members of the constituent tribes. By January 1779, the eternal flame of the council fire at Onondaga, which had symbolized the unity of the six confederated tribes of Iroquoia, was extinguished.

The British retreat at Fort Stanwix deprived General Burgoyne of the additional troops he expected. Camped at a small village called Saratoga, he was isolated, with food supplies dwindling and men deserting. His adversary at Albany, General Horatio Gates, began moving his army toward Saratoga. Burgoyne decided to attack first, and the British prevailed,

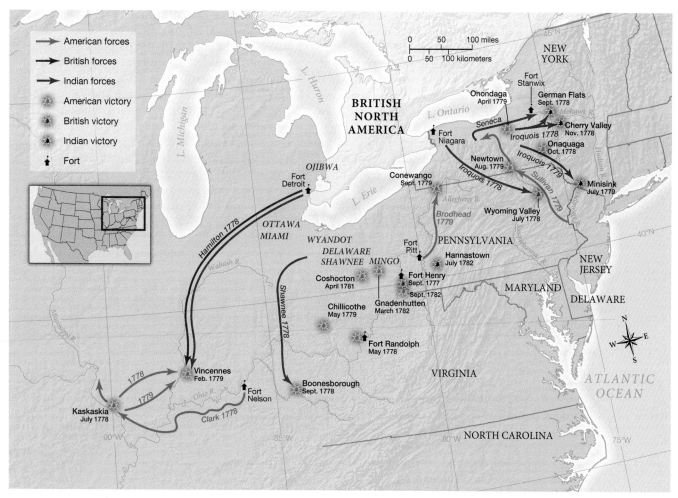

MAP 7.3

The Indian War in the West, 1777–1782

Most Indian tribes supported the British. Iroquois Indians attacked New York's Mohawk Valley throughout 1778, causing the Continental army to destroy Iroquois villages throughout central New York. Shawnee and Delaware in western Pennsylvania tangled with American militiamen in 1779, while tribes near Fort Detroit conducted raids on Kentucky settlers. Sporadic frontier fighting continued through 1782.

inhabitants. In retaliation, American militiamen destroyed Joseph Brant's village, killing several children. A month later, Brant's warriors attacked the town of Cherry Valley, killing 16 soldiers and 32 civilians.

The following summer, General Washington authorized a campaign to wreak "total destruction and devastation" on all the Iroquois villages of central New York. Some 4,500 troops commanded by General John Sullivan implemented a campaign of terror in the fall of 1779. Forty Indian towns met with total obliteration; the soldiers torched dwellings, cornfields, and orchards. In a few towns, women and children were slaughtered, but in most, the inhabitants managed to escape, fleeing to

the British at Fort Niagara. Thousands of Indian refugees, sick and starving, camped around the fort in one of the most miserable winters on record.

Much farther to the west, beyond Fort Pitt, another complex story of alliances and betrayals between American militiamen and Indians unfolded. Some 150,000 native people lived between the Appalachian Mountains and the Mississippi River, and by 1779 neutrality was no longer an option. Most sided with the British, but a portion of the Shawnee and Delaware at first sought peace with the Americans. In mid-1778, the Delaware chief White Eyes negotiated a treaty at Fort Pitt, pledging Indian support for the Americans in exchange for supplies and trade goods. But escalating violence undermined the agreement. That fall, when American soldiers killed two friendly Shawnee chiefs, Cornstalk and Red Hawk, the Continental Congress hastened to apologize, as did the governors of Pennsylvania and Virginia, but the soldiers who stood trial for the murders were acquitted. Two months later, White Eyes died under mysterious circumstances, almost certainly murdered by militiamen, who repeatedly had trouble honoring distinctions between allied and enemy Indians.

West of North Carolina (today's Tennessee), militias attacked Cherokee settlements in 1779, destroying thirty-six villages, while Indian raiders repeatedly attacked white settlements such as Boonesborough (in present-day Kentucky) (Map 7.3). In retaliation, a young Virginian named George Rogers Clark led Kentucky militiamen into what is now Illinois, attacking and taking the British fort at Kaskaskia. Clark's men wore native clothing—hunting shirts and breechcloths—but their dress was not a sign of solidarity with the Indians. When they attacked British-held Fort Vincennes in 1779, Clark's troops tomahawked Indian captives and threw their still-live bodies into the river in a gory spectacle witnessed by the redcoats. "To excel them in barbarity is the only way to make war upon Indians," Clark announced.

By 1780, very few Indians remained neutral. Violent raids by Americans drove Indians into the arms of the British at Forts Detroit and Niagara, or into the arms of the Spaniards, west of the Mississippi River. Said one officer on the Sullivan campaign, "Their nests are destroyed but the birds are still on the wing." For those who stayed near their native lands, chaos and confusion prevailed. Rare as it was, Indian support for the American side occasionally emerged out of a strategic sense that the Americans were unstoppable in their westward pressure and that it was better to work out an alliance than to lose in a war. But American treatment of even friendly Indians showed that there was no winning strategy for them.

The French Alliance

On their own, the Americans could not have defeated Britain, especially as pressure from hostile Indians increased. Essential help arrived as a result of the victory at Saratoga, which convinced the French to enter the war; a formal alliance was signed in February 1778. France recognized the United States as an independent nation and promised full military and commercial support. Most crucial was the French navy, which could challenge British supplies and troops at sea and aid the Americans in taking and holding prisoners of war.

Well before 1778, however, the French had been covertly providing cannons, muskets, gunpowder, and highly trained military advisers to the Americans. From the French monarchy's view, the main attraction of an alliance was the opportunity it provided to defeat archrival Britain. A victory would also open pathways to trade and perhaps result in France's acquiring the coveted British West Indies. Even an American defeat would not be a disaster for France if the war lasted many years and drained Britain of men and money.

French support materialized slowly. The navy arrived off the Virginia coast in July 1778 but then sailed south to the West Indies to defend the French sugar-producing islands. French help would prove indispensable to the American cause in 1780 and 1781, but the alliance's first months brought no dramatic changes, and some Americans grumbled that the partnership would prove worthless.

REVIEW   Why did the Americans need assistance from the French to ensure victory?

► The Southern Strategy and the End of the War

When France joined the war, some British officials favored abandoning the fight. As one troop commander shrewdly observed, "we are far from an anticipated peace, because the bitterness of the rebels is too widespread, and in regions where we are masters the rebellious spirit is still in them. The land is too large, and there are too many people. The more land we win, the weaker our army gets in the field." The commander of the British navy agreed, as did Lord North, the prime minister. But the king was determined to crush the rebellion, and he encouraged a new strategy for victory focusing on the southern colonies, thought to be more reliably loyalist. He had little idea of the depth of anger that would produce deadly guerrilla warfare between loyalists and patriots. The king's plan was brilliant but desperate, and ultimately unsuccessful.

VISUAL ACTIVITY

"The Balance of Power," 1780

This English cartoon mocks the alliance of Spain and the Netherlands with France in support of the American war. On the left, the female figure Britannia cannot be moved by all the lightweights on the right. France and Spain embrace while a Dutch boy hops on, saying "I'll do anything for Money." The forlorn Indian maiden, representing America, wails, "My Ingratitude is Justly punished." The New York Public Library/Art Resource, NY.

READING THE IMAGE: What does this cartoon reveal about British perceptions of the American Revolution?

CONNECTIONS: How did British attitudes toward the colonies contribute to the British defeat in the war?

Georgia and South Carolina

The new strategy called for British forces to abandon New England and focus on the South, with its valuable crops and its large slave population, a destabilizing factor that might keep rebellious white southerners in line. Georgia and the Carolinas appeared to hold large numbers of loyalists, providing a base for the British to recapture the southern colonies one by one, before moving north to the more problematic middle colonies and New England.

Georgia, the first target, fell easily at the end of December 1778 (Map 7.4). Most of the Continental army was in the North, keeping an eye on the British occupation of New York; the French were still in the West Indies. A small army of British soldiers occupied Savannah and Augusta, and a new royal governor and loyalist assembly were quickly installed. The British quickly organized twenty loyal militia units, and 1,400 Georgians swore an oath of allegiance to the king. So far, the southern strategy looked as if it might work.

Next came South Carolina. The Continental army put ten regiments into the port city of Charleston to defend it from attack by British troops shipped south from New York under the command of General Clinton, Howe's replacement as commander in chief. For five weeks in early spring 1780, the British laid siege to the city and took it in May 1780, capturing 3,300 American soldiers.

Clinton next announced that slaves owned by rebel masters were welcome to seek refuge with his army, and several thousand escaped to the coastal city. Untrained in formal warfare, they were of use to the British as knowledgeable guides to the countryside and as laborers building defensive

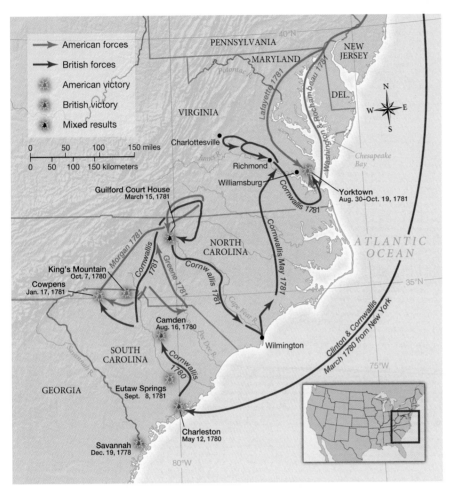

MAP 7.4
The War in the South, 1780–1781
After taking Charleston in May 1780, the British advanced into South and North Carolina, touching off a bloody civil war. An American loss at Camden was followed by victories at King's Mountain and Cowpens. The British next invaded Virginia but got trapped and overpowered at Yorktown in the fall of 1781.

Carolina, on August 16 (see Map 7.4). The militiamen panicked at the sight of the approaching British cavalry, however, and fled. When regiment leaders tried to regroup the next day, only 700 soldiers showed up. The battle of Camden was a devastating defeat, the worst of the entire war, and prospects seemed very grim for the Americans.

Treason and Guerrilla Warfare

Britain's southern strategy succeeded in 1780 in part because of information about American troop movements secretly conveyed by an American officer, Benedict Arnold. The hero of several American battles, Arnold was a deeply insecure man who never felt he got his due. Sometime in 1779, he opened secret negotiations with General Clinton in New York, trading information for money and hinting that he could deliver far more of value. When General Washington made him commander of West Point, a new fort on the Hudson River sixty miles north of New York City, Arnold's plan crystallized. West Point controlled the Hudson; its capture by the British might well have meant victory in the war.

Arnold's plot to sell a West Point victory to the British was foiled in the fall of 1780 when Americans captured the man carrying plans of the fort's defense from Arnold to Clinton. News of Arnold's treason created shock waves. Arnold represented all of the patriots' worst fears about themselves: greedy self-interest, like that of the war profiteers; the unprincipled abandonment of war aims, like that of turncoat southern Tories; panic, like that of the terrified soldiers at Camden. But instead of demoralizing the Americans, Arnold's treachery revived their commitment to the patriot cause. Vilifying Arnold allowed Americans to stake out a wide distance between themselves and dastardly conduct. It inspired a renewal of patriotism at a particularly low moment.

Shock over Gates's defeat at Camden and Arnold's treason revitalized rebel support in western South Carolina, an area that Cornwallis thought was pacified and loyal. The backcountry of the South soon became the site of guerrilla

fortifications. Escaped slaves with boat-piloting skills were particularly valuable for crucial aid in navigating the inland rivers of the southern colonies.

Clinton returned to New York, leaving the task of pacifying the rest of South Carolina to General Charles Cornwallis and 4,000 troops. A bold commander, Lord Cornwallis quickly chased out the remaining Continentals and established military rule of South Carolina by midsummer. He purged rebels from government office and disarmed rebel militias. Exports of rice, South Carolina's main crop, resumed, and pardons were offered to Carolinians willing to prove their loyalty by taking up arms for the British.

By August, American troops arrived from the North to strike back at Cornwallis. General Gates, the hero of Saratoga, led 3,000 troops, many of them newly recruited militiamen, into battle against Cornwallis at Camden, South

A Shaming Ritual Targeting the Great Traitor
In late 1780, Philadelphians staged a ritual humiliation of Benedict Arnold, represented by a two-faced effigy. Behind him stands the devil, prodding him with a pitchfork and shaking a bag of coins near his ear, reminding all that Arnold sold out for money. To the beat of a fife and drums, soldiers and onlookers march to a bonfire, where the effigy was burned to ashes. Library of Congress.

warfare. In hit-and-run attacks, both sides burned and ravaged not only opponents' property but also the property of anyone claiming to be neutral. Loyalist militia units organized by the British were met by fierce rebel militia units. In South Carolina, some 6,000 men became active partisan fighters, and they entered into at least twenty-six engagements. Guerrilla warfare soon spread to Georgia and North Carolina. Both sides committed atrocities and plundered property, clear deviations from standard military practice.

The British southern strategy depended on sufficient loyalist strength to hold reconquered territory as Cornwallis's army moved north. The backcountry civil war proved this assumption false. The Americans won few major battles in the South, but they ultimately succeeded by harassing the British forces and preventing them from foraging for food. Cornwallis moved the war into North Carolina in the fall of 1780 because the North Carolinians were supplying the South Carolina rebels with arms and men (see Map 7.4). Then news of a massacre of loyalist units by 1,400 frontier riflemen at the battle of King's Mountain, in western South Carolina, sent him hurrying back. The British were stretched too thin to hold even two colonies.

Surrender at Yorktown

By early 1781, the war was going very badly for the British. Their defeat at King's Mountain was quickly followed by a second major defeat at the battle of

Cowpens in South Carolina in January 1781. Cornwallis retreated to North Carolina and thence to Virginia, where he captured Williamsburg in June. A raiding party proceeded to Charlottesville, the seat of government, capturing members of the Virginia assembly but not Governor Thomas Jefferson, who escaped the soldiers by a mere ten minutes. (The slaves at Monticello, Jefferson's home, stood their ground and saved his house from plundering, but more than a dozen at two other plantations he owned sought refuge with the British.) These minor victories allowed Cornwallis to imagine he was succeeding in Virginia. His army, now swelled by some 4,000 escaped slaves, marched to Yorktown, near the Chesapeake Bay area. As the general waited for backup troops by ship from British headquarters in New York City, smallpox and typhus began to set in among the black recruits.

At this juncture, the French-American alliance came into play. French regiments commanded by the Comte de Rochambeau had joined General Washington in Newport, Rhode Island, in mid-1780, and in early 1781 warships under the Comte de Grasse had sailed from France to the West Indies. Washington, Rochambeau, and de Grasse now fixed their attention on Chesapeake Bay. The French fleet got there ahead of the British troop ships from New York; a five-day naval battle left the French navy in clear control of the Virginia coast. This proved to be the decisive factor in ending the war because the French ships prevented any rescue of Cornwallis's army.

On land, General Cornwallis and his 7,500 troops faced a combined French and American army of 16,000. For twelve days, the Americans and French bombarded the British fortifications at Yorktown; Cornwallis ran low on food and ammunition. He also began to expel the black recruits, some of them sick and dying. A Hessian officer serving under Cornwallis later criticized this British action as disgraceful: "We had used them to good advantage, and set them free, and now, with fear and trembling, they had to face the reward of their cruel masters." The twelve-day siege brought Cornwallis to the realization that neither victory nor escape was possible. He surrendered on October 19, 1781.

What began as a promising southern strategy in 1778 had turned into a discouraging defeat. British attacks in the South had energized American resistance, as did the timely exposure of Benedict Arnold's treason. The arrival of the French fleet sealed the fate of Cornwallis at the **battle of Yorktown**, and major military operations came to a halt.

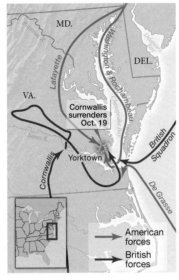

Siege of Yorktown, 1781

The Losers and the Winners

The surrender at Yorktown spelled the end for the British, but two more years of skirmishes ensued. Frontier areas in Kentucky, Ohio, and Illinois blazed with battles pitting Americans against various Indian tribes. The British army still occupied three coastal cities, including New York, and in response, an augmented Continental army stayed at the ready, north of New York City. Occasional clashes occurred, like the ones in which Deborah Sampson saw action while cross-dressing as a male soldier.

The **Treaty of Paris**, also called the **Peace of Paris**, was two years in the making. (See "Beyond America's Borders," page 192.) Commissioners from America and Britain worked out the ten articles of peace, while a side treaty signed by Britain, France, Spain, and the Netherlands sealed related deals. The first article went to the heart of the matter: "His Britannic Majesty acknowledges the said United States to be free Sovereign and independent States." Other articles set the western

VISUAL ACTIVITY

Lafayette at Yorktown, with James

In 1781, French officer Lafayette met and borrowed James, slave of a Virginia owner. At the siege of Yorktown, James infiltrated the British command by pretending to be an escaped slave. James fed the British misinformation and brought crucial intelligence back to Lafayette. At the surrender, British leaders spotted James with Lafayette and realized they'd been had. Lafayette was instrumental in obtaining James's freedom in 1786. Lafayette College Easton, PA. Gift of Helen Fahnstock Hubbard in memory of her husband, John Hubbard, Harvard (class of 1892).

READING THE IMAGE: Lafayette posed for this picture in France in 1783. Do you think James also personally posed for the artist? Why or why not?

CONNECTIONS: Why did many enslaved people side with the British? Why would some (like James) help out the American cause?

boundary at the Mississippi River and guaranteed that creditors on both sides would be paid in sterling money, a provision important to British merchants. Britain agreed to withdraw its troops quickly, but more than a decade later this promise still had not been fully kept. Another agreement prohibited the British from "carrying away any Negroes or other property of the American inhabitants." The treaty was signed on September 3, 1783.

News of the treaty signing was cause for celebration among most Americans, but not among the thousands of self-liberated blacks who had joined the British under promise of freedom. South Carolinian Boston King, a refugee in New York City, recalled that the provision prohibiting evacuation of black refugees "filled us with inexpressible anguish and terror." King and others pressed the British commander in New York, Sir Guy Carleton, to honor pre-treaty British promises. Carleton obliged: For all refugees under British protection for more than a year, he issued certificates of freedom—making them no longer "property" to be returned. More than 4,000 blacks sailed out of New York for Nova Scotia, Boston King and his family among them. As Carleton coolly explained to a protesting George Washington, "the Negroes in question . . . I found free when I arrived at New York, I had therefore no right, as I thought, to prevent their going to any part of the world they thought proper." British commanders in Savannah and Charleston followed Carleton's lead and aided the exit of perhaps 10,000 blacks from the United States.

The emancipation of slaves had never been a war goal of the British; destabilizing patriot planters and gaining manpower were their initial reasons for promises of freedom. Had the British won the war, they might well have reenslaved insurgent blacks to restore the profitable plantation economy of the South. For their part, blacks viewed British army camps as sites of refuge (not figuring on the devastations of epidemic diseases and food shortages) and had no reason to revere the British monarchy. In fact, some runaways had headed for Indian country instead.

The Treaty of Paris had nothing to say about the Indian participants in the Revolutionary War. As one American told the Shawnee people, "Your Fathers the English have made Peace with us for themselves, but forgot you their Children, who Fought with them, and neglected you like Bastards." Indian lands were assigned to the victors as though they were uninhabited. Some Indian refugees fled west into present-day

Missouri and Arkansas, and others, such as Joseph Brant's Mohawks, relocated to Canada. But significant numbers remained within the new United States, occupying their traditional homelands in areas west and north of the Ohio River. For them, the Treaty of Paris brought no peace at all; their longer war against the Americans would extend at least until 1795 and for some until 1813. Their ally, Britain, conceded defeat, but the Indians did not.

With the treaty finally signed, the British began their evacuation of New York, Charleston, and Savannah, a process complicated by the sheer numbers involved—soldiers, fearful loyalists, and refugees from slavery by the thousands. In New York City, more than 27,000 soldiers and 30,000 loyalists sailed on hundreds of ships for England in the late fall of 1783. In a final act of mischief, on the November day when the last ships left, the losing side raised the British flag at the southern tip of Manhattan, cut away the ropes used to hoist it, and greased the flagpole.

REVIEW Why did the British southern strategy ultimately fail?

▶ Conclusion: Why the British Lost

The British began the war for America convinced that they could not lose. They had the best-trained army and navy in the world; they were familiar with the landscape from the Seven Years' War; they had the willing warrior-power of most of the native tribes of the backcountry; and they easily captured every port city of consequence in America. A majority of colonists were either neutral or loyal to the crown. Why, then, did the British lose?

One continuing problem the British faced was the uncertainty of supplies. The army depended on a steady stream of supply ships from home, and insecurity about food helps explain their reluctance to pursue the Continental army aggressively. A further obstacle was their continual misuse of loyalist energies. Any plan to repacify the colonies required the cooperation of the loyalists, but the British repeatedly left them to the mercy of vengeful rebels. French aid also helps explain the British defeat. Even before the formal alliance, French artillery and

European Nations and the Peace of Paris, 1783

News of the decisive British defeat at Yorktown in late 1781 caused Britain's prime minister, Lord North, to stagger as though wounded and exclaim, "Oh, God, it is all over!" But in truth, it was far from over. A full year elapsed before the elements of a formal peace treaty could be worked out, and an additional year passed before the treaty was signed and Britain finally ended its occupation of New York City. The delay occurred in part because several European countries besides Britain had stakes in the war that had nothing to do with the chief American goal of political independence.

France had entered the war mainly to thwart and damage Britain. Certainly the French monarchy had no real sympathy for a democratic revolution in the British colonies. Indeed, for months before the victory at Yorktown, French leaders conferred covertly with the British about a plan to divide the colonies among the key European powers, with Britain to retain New York City and the rice and tobacco colonies of the South, while France and Spain would carve up the rest.

The stubbornness of Britain's George III prevented such a deal. Even after receiving news of the defeat at Yorktown, the delusional king still imagined he could retain

all thirteen rebellious colonies. After a series of antiwar votes in Parliament and the resignation of Lord North, George III briefly considered abdicating his throne. Instead, he replaced North with a new minister, Lord Shelburne, who approached the peace talks with the view that independence for America was still up for debate.

Spain's interest in the war stemmed from a secret alliance with France in 1779. The Spanish king wanted to oust the British from Gibraltar, a tiny three-square-mile territory dominated by a massive rock and situated at the southern end of the Iberian Peninsula. From this strategic location, Britain controlled the passage between the Atlantic and the Mediterranean, disrupting Spanish trade. Spain launched a siege that lasted more than three years and tied up scores of British ships and thousands of troops, military assets that were thus not available for the war in America. Another important interest for Spain was control of navigation rights on the Mississippi River. Since 1763, Spain had held the lands west of the river, and it hoped to gain the eastern bank—and thus fully control all navigation of that major river—as a prize for its contribution to defeating Britain.

At various times, Russia, Austria, and even Poland had agents in Paris offering to mediate peace talks in order to adjust the balance of power in Europe. None of these countries viewed American independence as a priority. Only Holland offered formal diplomatic recognition of the new country, an act of faith quickly followed up by a sizable loan of money to the new government. No other country was so supportive.

The Continental Congress entrusted three Americans of great distinction to handle the treaty negotiations. Benjamin Franklin, John Adams, and John Jay considered independence as the precondition for the talks to begin, so they were taken aback when the British negotiator showed up with credentials that pointedly addressed them as "the Commissioners of the Colonies." A month later, updated credentials referenced the three as representatives "of the Thirteen United States of America," a far more satisfactory acknowledgment of their new standing. In September 1782, peace talks began in earnest. Shelburne conceded on independence and set his goal as the maintenance of favored trading status with the new country. He saw, perhaps more clearly than did his king, that although Britain's political dominance over its colonies had now

ammunition proved vital to the Continental army. After 1780, the French army fought alongside the Americans, and the French navy made the Yorktown victory possible. Finally, the British abdicated civil power in the colonies in 1775 and 1776, when royal officials fled to safety, and they never really regained it. The

basic British goal—to turn back the clock to imperial rule—receded into impossibility as the war dragged on.

The Revolution profoundly disrupted the lives of Americans everywhere. It was a war for independence from Britain, but it was more. It was a war that required men and women to think about

The General P—s, or Peace.

Say what they will, I call this an honourable P—.

I call this a free and Independent P—.

Jack English we confess your exceeding good nature, tho' we have wrangled you out of America you freely make P— with us.

"The P—s of Paris"

A British broadside of 1783 satirizes the diplomats who negotiated the Peace of Paris. The Indian declares "I call this a Free and Independent P—s" while the Frenchman (far right) gloats that "tho' we have wrangled you out of America, you freely make P—s with us." Who does the Indian figure represent? What is the point of view of this cartoon?
Library of Congress.

sidestepped their instructions and negotiated with Britain in secret, producing an acceptable draft treaty in just a few weeks.

By January 1783, France, Britain, and Spain had produced their own treaties, involving deals with lands in India, Africa, and the Mediterranean, and in September of that year all the treaties were officially approved and signed. Franklin wrote to a friend in Massachusetts, "We are now Friends with England and with all Mankind. May we never see another War! for in my Opinion, there never was a good War, or a bad Peace."

America in a Global Context

1. Why would the monarchies of France and Spain spend vast sums to help the rebellious American colonies in their fight against Britain?

2. A 1976 book about the Treaty of Paris is titled *The Virgin Diplomats*. Does anyone in this story fit that title? Why or why not?

Connect to the Big Idea

C Many Indian tribes fought boldly with their British allies in the Revolution, so why did they not participate in the treaty making in Paris? Did Britain represent any of the tribes' interests in the diplomatic agreements?

ended, economic dominance might nicely replace it.

The congress also instructed its three diplomats to consult France at every step of the negotiation with Britain, a condition insisted on by the French minister to the United States. But Jay and Adams had deep suspicions of the motives of the French foreign minister, the Count of Vergennes. They feared, with justice, that Vergennes planned on placing their nation's western boundary some distance east of the Mississippi River, to meet the demands of Spain. So the Americans

politics and the legitimacy of authority. The rhetoric employed to justify the revolution against Britain put the words *liberty, tyranny, slavery, independence,* and *equality* into common usage. These words carried far deeper meanings than a mere complaint over taxation without representation. The Revolution unleashed a dynamic of equality and liberty that was largely unintended and unwanted by many of the political leaders of 1776. But that dynamic emerged as a potent force in American life in the decades to come.

See the Selected Bibliography for this chapter in the Appendix.

7 | Chapter Review

MAKE IT STICK

 LearningCurve

Go online and use LearningCurve to see what you know. Then review the key terms and answer the questions.

KEY TERMS

Second Continental Congress (p. 167)
Continental army (p. 168)
battle of Bunker Hill (p. 168)
Common Sense (p. 169)
Declaration of Independence (p. 171)
battle of Long Island (p. 173)
Ladies Association (p. 177)
loyalists (p. 177)
battle of Oriskany (p. 183)
battle of Saratoga (p. 184)
battle of Yorktown (p. 190)
Treaty (Peace) of Paris, 1783 (p. 190)

REVIEW QUESTIONS

1. Why were many Americans initially reluctant to pursue independence from Britain? (pp. 167–171)

2. Why did the British initially exercise restraint in their efforts to defeat the rebellious colonies? (pp. 171–174)

3. How did the patriots promote support for their cause in the colonies? (pp. 175–183)

4. Why did the Americans need assistance from the French to ensure victory? (pp. 183–186)

5. Why did the British southern strategy ultimately fail? (pp. 186–191)

MAKING CONNECTIONS

1. How did the colonists mobilize for war? Discuss specific challenges they faced, noting the unintended consequences of their solutions.

2. Discuss the importance of loyalism for British strategy in the Revolutionary War. In your answer, consider both military and political strategy.

3. How did Native Americans shape the Revolutionary War? What role did African Americans play? What benefits did these two groups hope to gain?

LINKING TO THE PAST

1. Most Indian tribes joined with the French and opposed the British in the Seven Years' War; yet in the American Revolution, most tribes sided with the British and opposed the Americans. What accounts for this apparent shift in alliances? (See chapter 6.)

2. Consider the leading roles of Massachusetts and Virginia in the coming of the American Revolution. With such very different origins and such very different economic, demographic, and religious histories, how could these two so readily join in partnership in the break from British rule? (See chapters 3, 4, and 5.)

8 Building a Republic
1775–1789

After reading and studying this chapter, you should be able to:

- Articulate the concerns of the Second Continental Congress about sovereignty, representation, taxation, and citizenship; recognize how these concerns shaped the Articles of Confederation.

- Explain the role state governments played under the Articles of Confederation. Identify how the differing state governments defined citizenship and handled slavery.

- Explain the major issues confronting the new United States to 1788, including how the Articles of Confederation limited the government's ability to solve these problems.

- Understand how the U.S. Constitution was debated and created, and understand the Constitution's position on slavery.

- Distinguish the Federalists and the Antifederalists, and explain their visions for the federal and state governments.

- Follow the process by which the U.S. Constitution was ratified, how its proponents secured ratification, and why some people opposed ratification.

A CHAIR FOR THE NEW NATION
The golden Sun on George Washington's chair at the Constitutional Convention in Philadelphia worried Benjamin Franklin. Was it setting, thus symbolizing failure, or rising, signaling a new beginning for the nation? Courtesy of Independence National Historic Park.

JAMES MADISON GRADUATED FROM PRINCETON COLLEGE IN New Jersey in 1771, undecided about his next move. Returning to his wealthy father's plantation in Virginia held little appeal. He much preferred the pleasures of books to farming. Fluent in Greek, Latin, French, and mathematics, he enjoyed reading and discussing the great thinkers, both ancient and modern. So he stayed in Princeton as long as he could.

In 1772, he returned home, still adrift. He studied law, but his unimpressive oratorical talents discouraged him. Instead, he swapped reading lists and ideas about political theory by letter with a Princeton classmate. While Madison struggled for direction, the powerful winds before the storm of the American Revolution swirled through the colonies. A trip north to deliver his brother to boarding school put Madison in Philadelphia just as news broke that Britain had shut down the port of Boston. Turbulent protests over the Coercive Acts turned the young man into a committed revolutionary.

Back in Virginia, Madison joined his father on the committee of public safety. He took up musket practice, but he proved a poor shot. Realizing

James Madison, by Charles Willson Peale

Philadelphia artist Charles Willson Peale painted this miniature portrait of Madison in 1783, paired with one of Madison's fiancée, Kitty Floyd, the sixteen-year-old daughter of a New York congressman. Meant to be worn like jewelry (note the pin on the right), miniatures were tokens of mutual affection. After Floyd broke off the engagement, Madison waited eleven more years before finding a wife. Library of Congress.

that his keen study of political theory was useful, he gained election in 1776 to the Virginia Convention, a new Revolutionary assembly. The convention's main task was to hammer out a state constitution with innovations such as frequent elections and limited executive power. Shy and still learning the ropes, Madison stayed on the sidelines, but Virginia's elder statesmen noted his thoughtful contributions. When his county failed to reelect him, he was appointed to the governor's council and spent the next two years rapidly gaining political experience.

In 1780, Madison represented Virginia in the Continental Congress. Twenty-eight, single, and supported by family money, he was free of the burdens that made distant political service difficult for older married men. Three years in Philadelphia acquainted him with a network of leading revolutionaries and a thorny bundle of governance problems arising from the chaotic economy and the precarious war effort. In one crisis, Madison's negotiating skills proved crucial: He broke the deadlock over the ratification of the Articles of Confederation by arranging for the cession of Virginia's vast western lands, soon called the Northwest Territory. But more often, service in the congress frustrated Madison because the central government seemed to lack essential powers, chief among them the power to tax.

Madison returned to the Virginia assembly in 1784. But he did not retreat to a local point of view held by other state politicians. The economic hardships created by heavy state taxation—which in Massachusetts led to a full-fledged rebellion against state government—spurred Madison to pursue means to strengthen the new national government.

Madison helped organize a convention in May 1787, where delegates completely rewrote the structure of the national government, investing it with considerably greater powers. True to form, Madison spent the months before that Philadelphia meeting in feverish study of the great thinkers he had read in college, seeking the best way to constitute a government on republican principles. His lifelong passion for scholarly study, seasoned by a dozen years of energetic political experience, paid off handsomely. The United States Constitution was the result.

By the end of the 1780s, James Madison had had his finger in every kind of political pie on the local, state, confederation, and finally national levels. He even managed to observe the first U.S.—Indian treaty negotiations carried out in 1784. He had transformed himself from a directionless and solitary youth into one of the leading political thinkers of the Revolutionary period. His personal history over the 1780s was deeply entwined with the path of the emerging United States.

▶ The Articles of Confederation

Creating and approving a written plan of government for the new confederation took five years, as delegates and states sought agreement on fundamental principles. With monarchy gone, where would sovereignty lie? What would be the nature of representation? Who would hold the power of taxation? The resulting plan, called the **Articles of Confederation**, proved to be surprisingly difficult to implement, mainly because the thirteen states disagreed over boundaries in the land to the west of the states. Once the Articles were ratified and the active phase of the war had drawn to a close, the congress faded in importance compared with politics in the individual states.

Confederation and Taxation

Only after declaring independence did the Continental Congress turn its attention to creating a written document that would specify what powers the congress had and by what authority it existed. There was widespread agreement on key government powers: pursuing war and peace, conducting foreign relations, regulating trade, and running a postal service. Because the congress's attention was fixed on the war, it took another year of tinkering to reach agreement on the Articles of Confederation, defining the union as a loose confederation of states existing mainly to foster a common defense. Much like the existing Continental Congress, there was no national executive (that is, no president) and no judiciary. The Congress, consisting of delegates selected annually by their state legislatures, was the sole governing agency.

Delegates faced term limits of three years, to ensure rotation in office. Anywhere from two to seven delegates could represent each state, with each delegation casting a single vote. Routine decisions required a simple majority of seven states, whereas momentous decisions, such as declaring war, required nine. To approve or amend the Articles required the unanimous consent both of the thirteen state delegations and of the thirteen state legislatures—giving any state a crippling veto power. Most crucially, the Articles gave the national government no power of direct taxation.

Yet taxation was a necessity since all governments require money. To finance the Revolutionary War, the confederation congress issued

CHRONOLOGY

1775	• Second Continental Congress opens.
1776	• Declaration of Independence adopted. • Virginia adopts state bill of rights.
1777	• Articles of Confederation sent to states.
1778	• State constitutions completed.
1780	• Pennsylvania institutes gradual emancipation.
1781	• Articles of Confederation ratified. • Creation of executive departments. • Massachusetts slaves sue for freedom.
1782	• Virginia relaxes state manumission law.
1783	• Newburgh Conspiracy exposed. • Treaty of Paris ends the war. • Massachusetts enfranchises taxpaying free blacks.
1784	• Gradual emancipation laws passed in Rhode Island and Connecticut. • Treaty of Fort Stanwix.
1785	• Treaty of Fort McIntosh. • Congress calls for large requisition.
1786	• Shays's Rebellion begins.
1787	• Shays's Rebellion crushed. • Northwest Ordinance. • Delaware provides manumission law. • Constitutional convention meets in Philadelphia. • *The Federalist Papers* begin to publish.
1788	• U.S. Constitution ratified.
1790	• Maryland provides manumission law.
1799	• Gradual emancipation law passed in New York.
1804	• Gradual emancipation law passed in New Jersey.

Revolutionary War Flag Used on a Naval Ship
In 1777, Congress called for a flag with thirteen red and white stripes and thirteen white stars in a field of blue, "representing a new Constellation," a powerful metaphor that anchored the fragile union in the vast and timeless expanse of the heavens. Early American flags were strictly military banners; not for another half century would they become ever-present symbols of nonmilitary patriotism. © 1998 Veninga-Zaricor Family, Zaricor Flag Collection (ZFC) & Fog Kist of Santa Cruz LLC.

interest-bearing bonds purchased by French and Dutch bankers as well as middling to wealthy Americans, and revenue was necessary to repay these loans. Other routine government functions required money: Trade regulation required salaried customs officers; a postal system required postmen, horses and wagons, and well-maintained postal roads; the western lands required surveyors; and Indian diplomacy (or war) added further large costs. Article 8 of the confederation document declared that taxes were needed to support "the common defence or general welfare" of the country, yet the congress also had to be sensitive to the rhetoric of the Revolution, which denounced taxation by a nonrepresentative power.

The Articles of Confederation posed a delicate two-step solution. The congress would requisition (that is, request) money to be paid into the common treasury, and each state legislature would then levy taxes within its borders to pay the requisition. The Articles called for state contributions assessed in proportion to the improved property value of the state's land, so that populous states paid more than did sparsely populated states. Requiring that the actual tax bill be passed by the state legislatures preserved the Revolution's principle of taxation only by direct representation. However, no mechanism compelled states to pay.

The lack of authority in the confederation government was exactly what many state leaders wanted in the late 1770s. A league of states

with rotating personnel, no executive branch, no power of direct taxation, and a requirement of unanimity for any major change seemed to be a good way to keep government in check. The catch was that ratification itself required unanimous agreement, and that proved difficult to secure.

The Problem of Western Lands

The most serious disagreement delaying ratification of the Articles concerned the absence of any plan for the lands to the west of the thirteen original states. This absence was deliberate: Virginia and Connecticut had old colonial charters that located their western boundaries at the Mississippi River, and six other states also claimed parts of that land. But five states without extensive land claims insisted on redrawing those colonial boundaries to create a national domain to be sold to settlers (Map 8.1). As one Rhode Island delegate put it, "the western world opens an amazing prospect as a national fund; it is equal to our debt."

The eight land-claiming states were ready to sign the Articles of Confederation in 1777 since it protected their interests. Three states without claims—Rhode Island, Pennsylvania, and New Jersey—eventually capitulated and signed, "not from a Conviction of the Equality and Justness of it," said a New Jersey delegate, "but merely from an absolute Necessity there was of complying to save the Continent." But Delaware and Maryland continued to hold out, insisting on a national domain policy. In 1779, the disputants finally compromised: Any land a state volunteered to relinquish would become the national domain. When James Madison and Thomas Jefferson ceded Virginia's huge land claim in 1781, the Articles of Confederation were at last unanimously approved.

The western lands issue demonstrated that powerful interests divided the thirteen new states. The apparent unity of purpose inspired by fighting the war against Britain papered over sizable cracks in the new confederation.

Running the New Government

No fanfare greeted the long-awaited inauguration of the new government in 1781. The congress continued to sputter along, its problems far from solved by the signing of the Articles. Lack of a quorum—defined as two men from seven states, or fourteen men—often hampered day-to-day activities. The search for the government's

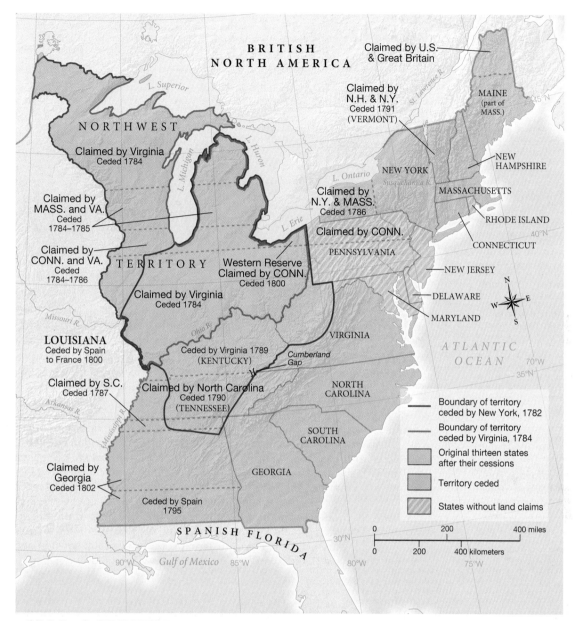

MAP ACTIVITY

Map 8.1   Cession of Western Lands, 1782–1802

The thirteen new states found it hard to ratify the Articles of Confederation without settling their conflicting land claims in the West, a vast area occupied by Indian tribes. The five states objecting to the Articles' silence over western lands policy were Maryland, Delaware, New Jersey, Rhode Island, and Pennsylvania.

READING THE MAP: Which state had the largest claims on western territory?

CONNECTIONS: In what context did the first dispute regarding western lands arise? How was it resolved? Does the map suggest a reason why Pennsylvania, a large state, joined the four much smaller states on this issue?

official seal stretched out over six years. (See "Visualizing History," page 200.) State legislatures were slow to select delegates, and many politicians preferred to devote their energies to state governments, especially when the congress

seemed deadlocked or, worse, irrelevant. Some had difficulty learning the art of formal debate. A Pennsylvanian reflected that "I find there is a great deal of difference between sporting a sentiment in a letter, or over a glass of wine

The Great Seal of the United States

In 1776, Congress sought to produce an official "seal" or logo for the United States, just like all European monarchies had. Metal seals pressed into sealing wax were used to authenticate official documents and treaties.

The first entry, submitted by a French artist in Philadelphia, featured a decorated shield like a European coat of arms. A goddess of liberty and a rifleman in buckskin flank the shield, which depicts thirteen mini-shields, one per state, encircling six central shields honoring the European countries that contributed (white) people to the United States. Do you recognize the single eye in a triangle? By old convention, an eye radiating lines of vision represented the watchful eye of God. The phrase *E Pluribus Unum*, or Out of many, One, was this Latin motto's first appearance in the United States. The entire design was a nonstarter; can you suggest several reasons why?

Pierre Eugene Du Simitiere's Design for the Great Seal, 1776

Francis Hopkinson's Design, 1780

Four years later another artist prepared this crowded emblem with the Latin motto "For War or For Peace" at the bottom. In an earlier draft, the artist sketched an Indian warrior on the left, but a second draft changed this figure to a Roman centurion brandishing a sword, paired with a female figure holding an olive branch to signify peace. As before, a shield domi-nates the center but now carries thirteen diagonal stripes set underneath a cloud of randomly placed stars. Clearly the number thirteen had symbolic importance. Did they not anticipate there would be more states, and soon?

In 1782, Congress considered a third variation on the theme of war and peace: a classically gowned and crowned woman holds a dove; a

upon politics, and discharging properly the duties of a senator."

It did not help that the congress had no permanent home. During the war, when the British army threatened Philadelphia, the congress relocated to small Pennsylvania towns such as Lancaster and York and then to Baltimore. After hostilities ceased, the congress moved from Trenton to Princeton to Annapolis to New York City. Many delegates were reluctant to travel far from home, especially if they had wives and children. Consequently, some of the most committed delegates were young bachelors, such as James Madison, and men in their fifties and sixties whose families were grown, such as Samuel Adams.

To address the difficulties of an inefficient congress, executive departments of war, finance, and foreign affairs were created in 1781 to handle purely administrative functions. When the department heads were ambitious—as was Robert Morris, a wealthy Philadelphia merchant who served as superintendent of finance—they could exercise considerable executive power. The Articles of Confederation had deliberately refrained from setting up an executive branch, but a modest one was being invented by necessity.

REVIEW Why was the confederation government's authority so limited?

William Barton's Design, 1782

Charles Thomson's Design, 1782

Questions for Analysis

1. How do the various Latin mottos stack up as aspirational slogans for the new nation? Why did the congress choose Latin instead of English?

2. Why did every proposal emphasize the twinned themes of war and peace? Can you suggest alternative themes?

3. How was gender mobilized to embody specific themes? How did the male figures change over time? Did the female figures?

4. The current version of the Great Seal likely sits in your wallet; check the $1 bill. Notice any changes?

Connect to the Big Idea

⊙ In addition to the Great Seal, in what other ways did the fledgling U.S. government engage in nation-building activities that encouraged citizens to feel increased patriotism and allegiance to the new country?

soldier in a contemporary uniform wears a sword. The Latin mottoes read "In Defense of Liberty" (top) and "Only Virtue Unconquered" (bottom). A spread-winged eagle makes its first appearance, clutching a sword and a flag. Reportedly the artist first placed a rooster here but switched. Why might an eagle be more appealing than a rooster? Not everyone loved the eagle. Benjamin Franklin later wrote his daughter that he preferred the turkey as the nation's preeminent symbol. Eagles were "of bad moral character," he wrote, taking food from hard-working birds. The turkey was smarter, more respectable, and more courageous, he claimed,

and "a true original Native of America." This effort was set aside.

In June 1782, the congress knew that the peace treaty would soon require the seal. After dithering for years, they commissioned and approved the winning seal in just one week. The designer, a member of congress, combined several elements from the first three plans; can you identify them? How did the eagle change from its appearance in image 3? How are the themes of war and peace differently represented?

SOURCES: Pierre Eugene du Simitiere's Design for the Great Seal, 1776: Library of Congress; Francis Hopkinson's Design, 1780: National Archives; William Barton's Design, 1782: National Archives; Charles Thomson's Design, 1782: National Archives.

▶ The Sovereign States

In the first decade of independence, the states were sovereign and all-powerful. Only a few functions, such as declaring war and peace, had been transferred to the confederation government. Familiar and close to home, state governments claimed the allegiance of citizens and became the arena in which the Revolution's innovations would first be tried. Each state implemented a constitution and determined voter qualifications, and many states grappled with the issue of squaring slavery with Revolutionary ideals, with varying outcomes.

The State Constitutions

In May 1776, the congress recommended that all states draw up constitutions based on "the authority of the people." By 1778, ten states had done so, and three more (Connecticut, Massachusetts, and Rhode Island) had adopted and updated their original colonial charters. A shared feature of all the state constitutions was the conviction that government ultimately rests on the consent of the governed. Political writers in the late 1770s embraced the concept of **republicanism** as the underpinning of the new governments. Republicanism meant more than popular elections and representative institutions. For some, republicanism stood for leaders who were autonomous, virtuous citizens putting civic values above private interests. For others, it suggested direct democracy, with nothing standing in the way of the will of the people. For all, it meant government that promoted the people's welfare.

Widespread agreement about the virtues of republicanism went hand in hand with the idea that republics could succeed only in relatively small units, where people could make sure their interests were being served. Eleven states continued the colonial practice of a two-chamber assembly but greatly augmented the powers of the lower house. Pennsylvania and Georgia abolished the more elite upper house altogether, and most states severely limited the powers of the governor. Real power thus resided with the lower houses, responsive to popular majorities due to annual elections and guaranteed rotation in office (term limits). If a representative displeased his constituents, he could be out of office in a matter of months. James Madison learned about such political turnover when he lost reelection to the Virginia assembly in 1777. Ever shy, he attributed the loss to his reluctance to socialize at taverns and glad-hand his constituents in the traditional Virginia style. His series of increasingly significant political posts from 1778 to 1787 all came as a result of appointment, not popular election.

Six of the state constitutions included bills of rights—lists of individual liberties that government could not abridge. Virginia's bill was the first. Passed in June 1776, it asserted that "all men are by nature equally free and independent, and have certain inherent rights, of which, when they enter into a state of society, they cannot by any compact deprive or divest their posterity; namely, the enjoyment of life and liberty, with the means of acquiring and possessing property, and pursuing and obtaining happiness and safety." Along with these inherent rights went more specific rights to freedom of speech, freedom of the press, and trial by jury.

Who Are "the People"?

When the Continental Congress called for state constitutions based on "the authority of the people," and when the Virginia bill of rights granted "all men" certain rights, who was meant by "the people"? Who exactly were the citizens of this new country, and how far would the principle of democratic government extend? Different people answered these questions differently, but in the 1770s certain limits to political participation were widely agreed on.

One limit was defined by property. In nearly every state, voters and political candidates had to meet varying property qualifications. In Maryland, candidates for governor had to be worth the large sum of £5,000, while voters had to own fifty acres of land or £30. In the most democratic state, Pennsylvania, voters and candidates simply needed to be property tax payers, large or small. Only property owners were presumed to possess the necessary independence of mind to make wise political choices. Are not propertyless men, asked John Adams, "too little acquainted with public affairs to form a right judgment, and too dependent upon other men to have a will of their own?" Property qualifications probably disfranchised from one-quarter to one-half of adult white males in all the states. Not all of them took their nonvoter status quietly. One Maryland man wondered what was so special about being worth £30, his state's threshold for voting: "Every poor man has a life, a personal liberty, and a right to his earnings; and is in danger of being injured by government in a variety of ways." Others noted that propertyless men were fighting and dying in the Revolutionary War; surely they had legitimate political concerns. A few radical voices challenged the notion that wealth was correlated with good citizenship; maybe the opposite was true. But ideas like this were outside the mainstream. The writers of the new constitutions, themselves men of property, viewed the right to own and preserve property as a central principle of the Revolution.

Another exclusion from voting—women—was so ingrained that few stopped to question it. Yet the logic of allowing propertied females to vote did occur to a handful of well-placed women. Abigail Adams wrote to her husband, John, in 1782, "Even in the freest countrys our property is subject to the controul and disposal of our partners, to whom the Laws have given a sovereign Authority. Deprived of a voice in Legislation, obliged to submit to those Laws which are imposed upon us, is it not sufficient to make us indifferent to the publick Welfare?"

Only three states specified that voters had to be male, so powerful was the unspoken assumption that only men could vote. Yet in New Jersey, small numbers of women began to go to the polls in the 1780s. The state's constitution of 1776 enfranchised all free inhabitants worth more than £50, language that in theory opened the door to free blacks and unmarried women who met the property requirement. (Married women owned no property, for by law their husbands held title to everything.) Little fanfare accompanied this radical shift, and some historians have inferred that the inclusion of unmarried women and blacks was an oversight. Yet other parts of the suffrage clause pertaining to residency and property were extensively debated when the clause was put in the state constitution, and no objections were raised at that time to its gender- and race-free language. Thus other historians have concluded that the law was intentionally inclusive. In 1790, a revised election law used the words *he* or *she* in reference to voters, making woman suffrage explicit. As one New Jersey legislator declared, "Our Constitution gives this right to maids or widows *black* or *white*." However, that legislator was complaining, not bragging, so his words do not mean that egalitarian suffrage was a fact accepted by all.

In 1790, only about 1,000 free black adults of both sexes lived in New Jersey, a state with a population of 184,000. The number of unmarried adult white women was probably also small and comprised mainly widows. In view of the property requirement, the voter blocs enfranchised under this law were minuscule. Still, this highly unusual situation lasted until 1807, when a new state law specifically disfranchised both blacks and women. Henceforth, independence of mind, held essential for voting, was redefined to be sex- and race-specific.

In the 1780s, voting everywhere was class-specific because of property restrictions. John Adams urged the framers of the Massachusetts constitution to stick with traditional property qualifications. If suffrage is brought up for debate, he warned, "there will be no end of it. New claims will arise; women will demand a vote; lads from twelve to twenty-one will think their rights not enough attended to; and every man who has not a farthing, will demand an equal voice with any other."

Equality and Slavery

Restrictions on political participation did not mean that propertyless people enjoyed no civil rights and liberties. The various state bills of rights applied to all individuals who were free; unfree people were another matter.

The author of the Virginia bill of rights was George Mason, a planter who owned 118 slaves. When he wrote that "all men are by nature equally free and independent," Mason did not

A Potential Voter in New Jersey
Mrs. Annis Boudinot Stockton of Princeton, New Jersey, was married to Richard Stockton, a delegate to the Continental Congress and signer of the Declaration of Independence in 1776. Widowed in 1782, she would have been eligible to vote in state elections according to New Jersey's unique enfranchisement of property-holding women. The widow Stockton died in 1801, before suffrage was redefined to be the exclusive right of males. Princeton University Art Museum/Art Resource, NY.

have slaves in mind; he instead was asserting that white Americans were the equals of the British and entitled to equal liberties. Other Virginia legislators, worried about misinterpretations, added a qualifying phrase: that all men "when they enter into a state of society" have inherent rights. As one legislator wrote, with relief, "Slaves, not being constituent members of our society, could never pretend to any benefit from such a maxim."

One month later, the Declaration of Independence used essentially the same phrase about equality, this time without the modifying clause about entering society. Two state constitutions, Pennsylvania and Massachusetts, also picked it up. In Massachusetts, one town suggested rewording the draft constitution to read "All men, whites and blacks, are born free and equal." The suggestion was not implemented.

Nevertheless, after 1776, the ideals of the Revolution about natural equality and liberty

A Slave Sues for Her Freedom

Stirring language about liberty, equality, and freedom that inspired revolutionaries in the 1770s appeared in many state constitutions in the 1780s. Yet unfree people, held as property, had little recourse to challenge their status.

Massachusetts law, however, had long recognized slaves as persons with legal standing to bring lawsuits against whites. Less than 2 percent of the state's population consisted of slaves, who numbered under four thousand. Before 1780, some thirty Massachusetts slaves had sued for freedom, but their cases had turned on individual circumstances, such as an owner's unfulfilled promise to emancipate. In 1780, a new state constitution boldly declared that "all men are born free and equal," opening the door to lawsuits based on a broad right to freedom. The first such case was brought by Bett, a slave living in the Massachusetts town of Sheffield.

Born of African parents in the early 1740s, Bett and her sister Lizzie grew up as slaves in Claverack, New York, in the wealthy Dutch American family of Pieter Hogeboom. When Hogeboom died, Bett and Lizzie were transported twenty-four miles east into Massachusetts, where Hogeboom's daughter lived with her husband, Colonel John Ashley. A town tax list of 1771 shows Ashley as the richest man in Sheffield and owner of five slaves. He was known as a kind and gentle man, but as one account suggests, his wife was "a shrew untamable" and "the most despotic of mistresses." One day, Mrs. Ashley became enraged with Lizzie and heaved a hot kitchen shovel at her. Bett interceded and sustained a burn on her arm that left a lifelong scar.

On another occasion, in 1773, Bett was, in her own words, "keepin' still and mindin' things" while she served refreshments to a dozen men meeting with Colonel Ashley to draft anti-British resolutions. The first read, "Resolved, That mankind in a state of nature are equal, free, and independent of each other, and have a right to the undisturbed enjoyment of their lives, their liberty and property." Bett well noted the import of their discussion.

In the fall of 1780, Bett overheard conversations at the Ashleys' about the new Massachusetts state constitution proclaiming equality and reasonably concluded that they applied to her. So she contacted Theodore Sedgwick, Sheffield's representative in the state legislature, who filed a writ in April 1781 requesting the recovery of unlawfully held property—in this case, the human property of Bett and a second plaintiff owned by Ashley, a man identified only as Brom. Ashley contested the writ, and the case, officially called *Brom and Bett v. J. Ashley, Esq.*, went to trial. The jury agreed that Bett and Brom were entitled to freedom and ordered Ashley to pay each plaintiff damages as well as court costs. The brief court records do not reveal the legal arguments presented, but Sedgwick descendants later boasted that Theodore Sedgwick invoked the Massachusetts constitution to argue that slavery could not exist in the state.

Bett chose a new name to go with her new status: Elizabeth Freeman. She left Colonel Ashley's and became a paid housekeeper in the Sedgwick family, raising the children when their mother became incapacitated by illness. "Her spirit spurned slavery," a Sedgwick daughter wrote, offering this quotation from Bett as evidence: "Anytime, anytime while I was a

began to erode the institution of slavery. Often, enslaved blacks led the challenge. In 1777, several Massachusetts slaves petitioned for their "natural & unalienable right to that freedom which the great Parent of the Universe hath bestowed equally on all mankind." They modestly asked for freedom for their children at age twenty-one and were turned down. In 1779, similar petitions in Connecticut and New Hampshire met with no success. Seven Massachusetts free men, including the mariner brothers Paul and John Cuffe, refused to pay taxes on the grounds that they could not vote and so were not represented. The Cuffe brothers landed in jail in 1780 for tax evasion, but their petition to the Massachusetts legislature spurred the extension of suffrage to taxpaying free blacks in 1783.

Another way to bring the issue before lawmakers was to sue in court. In 1781, a woman called Elizabeth Freeman (Mum Bett) was the first to win freedom in a Massachusetts court, basing her case on the just-passed state constitution that declared "all men are born free and equal." (See "Seeking the American Promise," above.) Another Massachusetts slave, Quok Walker, charged his master with assault and battery, arguing that he was a free man under that same constitutional phrase. Walker won slave, if one minute's freedom had been offered to me, and I had been told I must die at the end of that minute, I would have taken it—just to stand one minute on God's earth a free woman—I would."

The Sedgwicks were especially grateful to Freeman for her commanding presence of mind during Shays's Rebellion in 1786 (see page 213). Because Sedgwick represented the legal elite of the county, he was a target of hostile crowd action. Freeman was home alone when insurgents, searching for Sedgwick and for valuables to plunder, demanded entry. Unable to block them, Freeman let the dissidents in but followed them around with a large shovel, threatening to flatten anyone who damaged property. When Freeman died in 1829, she was buried in the Sedgwick family plot, with a gravestone inscription supplied by the Sedgwicks that ended "Good mother, farewell."

Freeman's lawsuit of 1781 inspired others to sue, and in a case in 1783 the judge of the Massachusetts Supreme Court declared that "slavery is in my judgment as effectively abolished as it can be by the granting of rights and privileges" in the state constitution. It took several more legal challenges and additional time for that news to trickle out, but the erosion of slavery in Massachusetts gradually picked up

Elizabeth Freeman in 1811
In freedom, "Mum Bett" found secure employment with the family of her lawyer, Theodore Sedgwick. A Sedgwick son later wrote, "If there could be a practical refutation of the imagined superiority of our race to hers, the life and character of this woman would afford that refutation. She had, when occasion required it, an air of command which conferred a degree of dignity." © Massachusetts Historical Society, Boston, MA, USA/The Bridgeman Art Library.

speed as blacks demanded manumission or wages for work, or simply walked away from their masters. In 1790, the federal census listed 5,369 "other free persons" (that is, nonwhites) in the state and not a single slave.

Questions for Consideration

1. What events encouraged the slave Bett to take her master to court to sue for freedom?

2. How would you characterize Mum Bett's status in the Sedgwick household? Was she merely a hired servant, or something more?

Connect to the Big Idea

⊙ In what way was Elizabeth Freeman's desire for freedom similar to and different from those of white revolutionaries who sought freedom from being "enslaved" by Britain?

and was set free, a decision confirmed in an appeal to the state's superior court in 1783. Several similar cases followed, and by 1789 slavery had been effectively abolished by a series of judicial decisions in Massachusetts.

State legislatures acted more slowly. Pennsylvania enacted a gradual emancipation law in 1780, providing that infants born to a slave mother on or after March 1, 1780, would be freed at age twenty-eight. Not until 1847 did Pennsylvania fully abolish slavery, but slaves did not wait for such slow implementation. Untold numbers in Pennsylvania simply ran away and asserted their freedom. One estimate holds that

more than half of young slave men in Philadelphia joined the ranks of free blacks, and by 1790, free blacks outnumbered slaves in Pennsylvania two to one.

Rhode Island and Connecticut adopted gradual emancipation laws in 1784; New York waited until 1799 and New Jersey until 1804 to enact theirs. These last were the two northern states with the largest number of slaves: New York in 1800 with 20,000, New Jersey with more than 12,000, whereas in Pennsylvania the number was just 1,700. Gradual emancipation illustrates the tension between radical and conservative implications of republican ideology. Republican

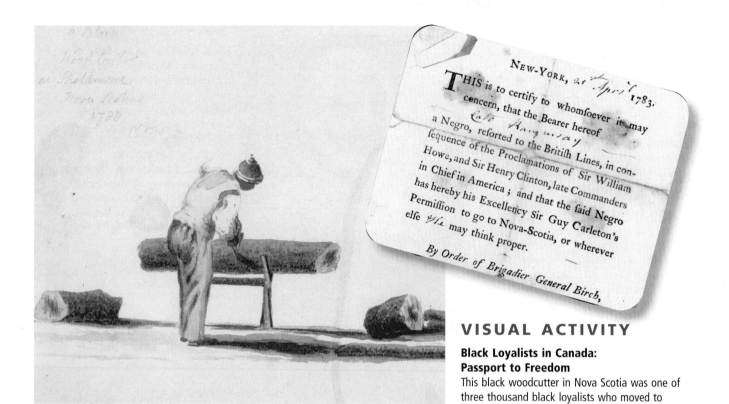

New-York, 21 April 1783.

THIS is to certify to whomsoever it may concern, that the Bearer hereof Cato Rammsay a Negro, resorted to the British Lines, in consequence of the Proclamations of Sir William Howe, and Sir Henry Clinton, late Commanders in Chief in America; and that the said Negro has hereby his Excellency Sir Guy Carleton's Permission to go to Nova-Scotia, or wherever else he may think proper.

By Order of Brigadier General Birch,

VISUAL ACTIVITY

Black Loyalists in Canada: Passport to Freedom

This black woodcutter in Nova Scotia was one of three thousand black loyalists who moved to Canada between 1783 and 1785. The inset shows a passport issued by the British high command to Cato Rammsay, permitting him to leave New York in 1783. Very few of the Nova Scotia refugees were able to acquire land, forcing most to become laborers for whites. Low wages created dissatisfaction, and in 1791–1792, nearly a third left for Sierra Leone in West Africa. Sketch: Library and Archives Canada, Acc. No. 1970-188-1090 W.H. Coverdale Collection of Canadiana; passport: Nova Scotia Archives (Halifax, NS)

READING THE IMAGE: On what specific grounds did Sir Guy Carleton, British commander in New York City, authorize freedom of passage on this passport?

CONNECTIONS: Thousands of white and black loyalists fled the United States during and after the Revolution. What did they need to start life over in a new location?

government protected people's liberties and property, yet slaves were both people and property. Gradual emancipation balanced the civil rights of blacks and the property rights of their owners by promising delayed freedom.

South of Pennsylvania, in Delaware, Maryland, and Virginia, where slavery was critical to the economy, emancipation bills were rejected. All three states, however, eased legal restrictions and allowed individual acts of emancipation for adult slaves below the age of forty-five under new manumission laws passed in 1782 (Virginia), 1787 (Delaware), and 1790 (Maryland). By 1790, close to 10,000 newly freed Virginia slaves had formed local free black communities complete with schools and churches.

Legal Changes to Slavery, 1777–1804

BRITISH NORTH AMERICA

MAINE (part of MASS.)

L. Ontario

VT. 1777
N.H. 1783
N.Y. 1799
MASS. 1783
CONN. 1784
Hudson R.
R.I. 1784
PA. 1780
N.J. 1804
MD. 1790
DEL. 1787
VA. 1782
ATLANTIC OCEAN
N.C.

Abolished slavery

Gradual emancipation

Individual cases of emancipation

In the deep South—the Carolinas and Georgia—freedom for slaves was unthinkable among most whites. Yet several thousand slaves had defected to the British during the war, and between 3,000 and 4,000 left with the British at the war's conclusion. Adding northern blacks evacuated from New York City in 1783, the probable total of emancipated blacks who left the United States was between 8,000 and 10,000. Some went to Canada, some to England, and some to Sierra Leone on the west coast of Africa. Many hundreds took refuge with the Seminole and Creek Indians, becoming permanent members of their communities in Spanish Florida and western Georgia.

Although all these instances of emancipation were gradual, small, and certainly incomplete, their symbolic importance was enormous. Every state from Pennsylvania north acknowledged that slavery was fundamentally inconsistent with Revolutionary ideology; "all men are created equal" was beginning to acquire real force as a basic principle.

> **REVIEW** What were the limits of citizenship, rights, and freedom within the various states?

▶ The Confederation's Problems

In 1783, the confederation government faced three interrelated concerns: paying down the large war debt, making formal peace with the Indians, and dealing with western settlement. Lacking the power to enforce its tax requisitions, the congress faced added debt pressures when army officers suddenly demanded secure pensions. Revenue from sales of western lands seemed to be a promising solution, but Indian inhabitants of those lands had different ideas.

From 1784 to 1786, the congress struggled mightily with these three issues. Some leaders were gripped by a sense of crisis, fearing that the Articles of Confederation were too weak. Others defended the Articles as the best guarantee of liberty because real governance occurred at the state level, closer to the people. A major outbreak of civil disorder in western Massachusetts quickly crystallized the debate and propelled the critics of the Articles into decisive and far-reaching action.

The War Debt and the Newburgh Conspiracy

For nearly two years, the Continental army camped at Newburgh, north of the British-occupied city of New York, awaiting news of a peace treaty. The soldiers were bored, restless, and upset about military payrolls that were far in arrears. An earlier promise to officers of generous pensions (half pay for life), made in 1780 in a desperate effort to retain them, seemed unlikely to be honored. In December 1782, officers petitioned the congress for immediate back pay for their men so that when peace arrived, no one would go home penniless. The petition darkly hinted that failure to pay the men "may have fatal effects."

Instead of rejecting the petition outright for lack of money, several members of the congress saw an opportunity to pressure the states to approve taxation powers. One of these was Robert Morris, a Philadelphia merchant with a gift for financial dealings. As the congress's superintendent of finance, Morris kept the books and wheedled loans from European bankers using his own substantial fortune as collateral. To forestall total insolvency, Morris led efforts in 1781 and again in 1786 to amend the Articles to allow collection of a 5 percent impost (an import tax). Each time it failed by one vote, illustrating the difficulties of achieving unanimity. Now the officers' petition offered new prospects to make the case for taxation.

The result was a plot called the **Newburgh Conspiracy**. Morris and several other congressmen

Lucky Man in Massachusetts?
This New Englander posed for a formal portrait around 1790, proudly holding a lottery ticket. Has this man just won the lottery, or is he merely hopeful? State taxes and confederation requisitions often proved hard to collect in the 1780s. Lotteries became a common way to raise supplementary state financing for schools and public works in the earliest years of the Republic. American, *Man Holding a (Massachusetts) Lottery Ticket*, ca 1790. Oil on canvas, 29 5/8 x 24 5/8 in. (75.25 x 62.55cm). Milwaukee Art Museum, Layton Art Collection, Purchase L1964.1. Photographer credit: Larry Sanders. Lottery ticket: © Massachusetts Historical Society, Boston, MA, USA/The Bridgeman Art Library.

Maſſachuſetts LOTTERY. (Nº 702)
THIS TICKET entitles the Poſſeſſor to ſuch Prize as may be drawn againſt its Number, agreeable to an Act of the General Aſſembly of this State, paſſed *February* 19th, 1781.

B

Saml Barrett

encouraged the officers to march the army on the congress to demand its pay. No actual coup was envisioned; both sides shared the goal of wanting to augment the congress's power of taxation. Yet the risks were great, for not everyone would understand that this was a ruse. What if the soldiers, incited by their grievances, could not be held in check?

General George Washington, sympathetic to the plight of unpaid soldiers and officers, had approved the initial petition. But the plotters, knowing of his reputation for integrity, did not inform him of their collusion with congressional leaders. In March 1783, when the general learned of these developments, he delivered an emotional speech to a meeting of five hundred officers, reminding them in stirring language of honor, heroism, and sacrifice. He urged them to put their faith in the congress, and he denounced the plotters as "subversive of all order and discipline." His audience was left speechless and tearful, and the plot was immediately defused.

Morris continued to work to find money to pay the soldiers. But in the end, a trickle of money from a few states was too little and too late, coming after the army began to disband. For its part, the congress voted to endorse a plan to commute, or transform, the lifetime pension promised the officers into a lump-sum payment of full pay for five years. But no lump sum of money was available. Instead, the officers were issued "commutation certificates," promising future payment with interest, which quickly depreciated in value.

In 1783, the soldiers' pay and officers' pensions added some $5 million to the rising public debt, forcing the congress to press for larger requisitions from the states. The confederation, however, had one new source of enormous untapped wealth: the extensive western territories, attractive to the fast-growing white population but currently inhabited by Indians.

The Treaty of Fort Stanwix

Since the Indians had not participated in the Treaty of Paris of 1783, the confederation government hoped to formalize treaties ending ongoing hostilities between Indians and settlers and securing land cessions. The most pressing problem was the land inhabited by the Iroquois Confederacy, a league of six tribes,

now claimed by the states of New York and Massachusetts based on their colonial charters (see Map 8.1).

At issue was the revenue stream that land sales would generate: Which government would get it? The congress summoned the Iroquois to a meeting in October 1784 at Fort Stanwix, on the upper Mohawk River. The Articles of Confederation gave the congress (as opposed to individual states) the right to manage diplomacy, war, and "all affairs with the Indians, not members of any of the States." But New York's governor seized on that ambiguous language, claiming that the Iroquois were in fact "members" of his state, and called his own meeting at Fort Stanwix in September. Suspecting that New York might be superseded by the congress, the most important chiefs declined to come and instead sent deputies without authority to negotiate. The Mohawk leader Joseph Brant shrewdly identified the problem of divided authority that afflicted the confederation government: "Here lies some Difficulty in our Minds, that there should be two separate bodies to manage these Affairs." No deal was struck with New York.

Three weeks later, U.S. commissioners opened proceedings at Fort Stanwix with the Seneca chief Cornplanter and Captain Aaron Hill, a Mohawk leader, accompanied by six hundred Iroquois. (James Madison, by chance traveling up the Mohawk River on a trip with a friend, witnessed the opening ceremonies.)

The Americans (accompanied by their own security detail of New Jersey militiamen) demanded a return of prisoners of war; recognition of the confederation's (and not states') authority to negotiate; and an all-important cession of a strip of land from Fort Niagara due south, which established U.S.-held territory adjacent to the border with Canada. This crucial change enclosed the Iroquois land within the United States and made it impossible for the Indians to claim to be between the United States and Canada. When the tribal leaders balked, one of the commissioners sternly replied, "You are mistaken in supposing that, having been excluded from the treaty between the United States and the King of England, you are become a free and independent nation and may make what terms you please. It is not so. You are a subdued people."

In the end, the treaty was signed, gifts were given, and

Treaty of Fort Stanwix, 1784

Lake Ontario

BRITISH NORTH AMERICA

Fort Niagara

Lake Erie

NEW YORK

IROQUOIS LANDS

Ceded to U.S., 1784

PENNSYLVANIA

VISUAL ACTIVITY

Cornplanter

Cornplanter, whose Indian name was Kaintwakon ("what one plants"), headed the Seneca delegation at Fort Stanwix in 1784. Raised fully Indian, he was the son of a highborn Seneca woman of the Wolf Clan and a traveling Dutch fur trader he barely knew. During the Revolution, when his father faced capture by Indians, Cornplanter recognized him by his name and released him. © Collection of the New-York Historical Society, USA/ The Bridgeman Art Library

READING THE IMAGE: Does this portrait, painted in 1796 by an Italian artist in New York City, convey any clue of Cornplanter's mixed-race heritage?

CONNECTIONS: When the U.S. commissioners met with Cornplanter at the Treaty of Fort Stanwix, do you think his mixed-race background might have had any bearing on the outcome of the negotiations? Why or why not?

six high-level Indian hostages were kept at the fort awaiting the release of the American prisoners taken during the Revolutionary War, mostly women and children. In addition, a significant side deal sealed the release of much of the Seneca tribe's claim to the Ohio Valley to the United States. This move was a major surprise to the Delaware, Mingo, and Shawnee Indians who lived there. In the months to come, tribes not at the meeting tried to disavow the **Treaty of Fort Stanwix** as a document signed under coercion by virtual hostages. But the confederation government ignored those complaints and made plans to survey and develop the Ohio Territory.

New York's governor astutely figured that the congress's power to implement the treaty terms was limited. The confederation's financial coffers were nearly empty, and its leadership was stretched. So New York quietly began surveying and then selling the very land it had failed to secure by treaty with the Iroquois. As that fact became generally known, it pointed up the weakness of the confederation government. One Connecticut leader wondered, "What is to defend us from the ambition and rapacity of New York, when she has spread over that vast territory, which she claims and holds?"

Land Ordinances and the Northwest Territory

The congress ignored western New York and turned instead to the Ohio Valley to make good on the promise of western expansion. Congressman Thomas Jefferson, charged with drafting a policy, proposed dividing the territory north of the Ohio River and east of the Mississippi—the Northwest Territory—into nine new states with evenly spaced east-west boundaries and townships ten miles square. He even advocated giving, not selling, the land to settlers, because future property taxes on the improved land would be payment enough. Jefferson's aim was to encourage rapid and democratic settlement and to discourage land speculation. Jefferson projected representative governments in the new states; they would not become colonies of the older states. Finally, Jefferson's draft prohibited slavery in the nine new states.

The congress adopted parts of Jefferson's plan in the Ordinance of 1784: the rectangular grid, the nine states, and the guarantee of self-government and eventual statehood. What the congress found too radical was the proposal to give away the land; it badly needed immediate revenue. The slavery prohibition also failed, by a vote of seven to six states.

A year later, the congress revised the legislation with procedures for mapping and selling the land. The Ordinance of 1785 called for three to five states, divided into townships six miles square, further divided into thirty-six sections of 640 acres, each section enough for four family farms (Map 8.2). Reduced to easily mappable squares, the land would be sold at public auction for a minimum of one dollar an acre, with highly

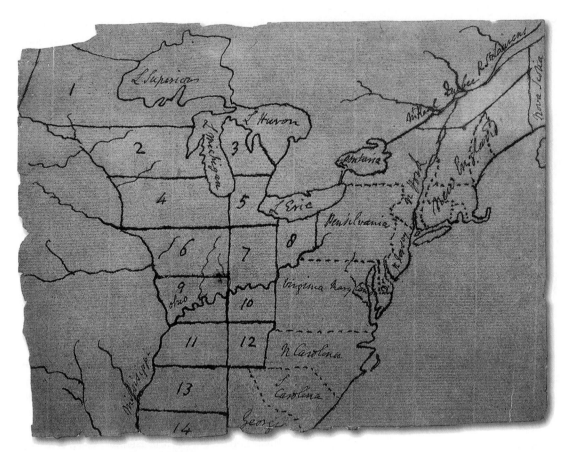

VISUAL ACTIVITY

Jefferson's Map of the Northwest Territory

Thomas Jefferson proposed nine states in his initial plan for the Northwest Territory in 1784. Straight lines and right angles held a strong appeal for him. But such regularity ignored inconvenient geographic features such as rivers and even more inconvenient political facts such as Indian territorial claims. William L. Clements Library, University of Michigan.

READING THE IMAGE: What does this map indicate about Jefferson's vision of the Northwest Territory?

CONNECTIONS: What were the problems with Jefferson's design for the division of the territory? Why did the congress alter it in the land ordinances of 1784, 1785, and 1787?

desirable land bid up for more. Two further restrictions applied: The minimum purchase was 640 acres, and payment had to be in hard money or in certificates of debt from Revolutionary days. This effectively meant that the land's first owners would be prosperous speculators. The grid of invariant squares further enhanced speculation, allowing buyers and sellers to operate without ever setting foot on the acreage. The commodification of land had been taken to a new level.

Speculators who held the land for resale avoided direct contact with the most serious obstacle to settlement: the dozens of Indian tribes that claimed the land as their own. The treaty signed at Fort Stanwix in 1784 was followed in 1785 by the Treaty of Fort McIntosh, which

similarly coerced partial cessions of land from the Delaware, Wyandot, Chippewa, and Ottawa tribes. Finally, in 1786, a united Indian meeting near Detroit issued an ultimatum: No cession would be valid without the unanimous consent of the tribes. For two more decades, violent Indian wars in Ohio and Indiana would continue to impede white settlement (as discussed in "Ohio Indians in the Northwest" in chapter 9).

A third land act, called the **Northwest Ordinance** of 1787, set forth a three-stage process by which settled territories would advance to statehood. First, the congress would appoint officials for a sparsely populated territory who would adopt a legal code and appoint local magistrates to administer justice. When the male population of voting age and landowning status

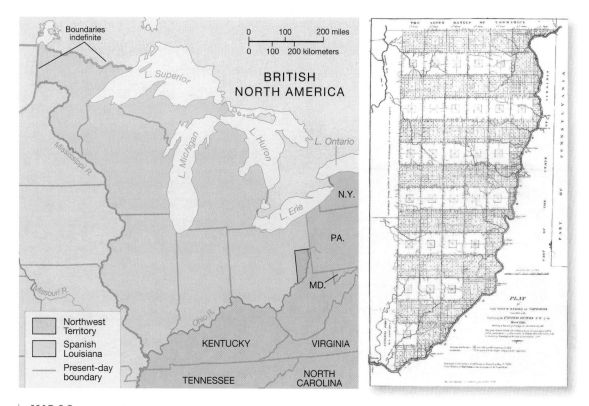

MAP 8.2

The Northwest Territory and Ordinance of 1785

Surveyors ventured into the eastern edge of the Northwest Territory in the 1780s and produced this first map (right) showing neat 6-mile square townships, each subdivided into one-mile squares containing sixteen 40-acre farms. Jefferson got his straight lines and right angles after all; compare this map to his on page 210. Plat Map © TNGenNet Inc. 2002.

(fifty acres) reached 5,000, the territory could elect its own legislature and send a nonvoting delegate to the congress. When the population of voting citizens reached 60,000, the territory could write a state constitution and apply for full admission to the Union. At all three territorial stages, the inhabitants were subject to taxation to support the Union, in the same manner as were the original states.

The Northwest Ordinance of 1787 was perhaps the most important legislation passed by the confederation government. It ensured that the new United States, so recently released from colonial dependency, would not itself become a colonial power—at least not with respect to white citizens. The mechanism it established allowed for the orderly expansion of the United States across the continent in the next century.

Nonwhites were not forgotten or neglected in the 1787 ordinance. The brief document acknowledged the Indian presence and promised that "the utmost good faith shall always be observed towards the Indians; their lands and property shall never be taken from them without their consent; and, in their property, rights, and liberty, they shall never be invaded or disturbed, unless in just and lawful wars authorized by Congress." The 1787 ordinance further pledged that "laws founded in justice and humanity, shall from time to time be made for preventing wrongs being done to them." Such promises indicated noble intentions, but they were not generally honored in the decades to come.

Jefferson's original and remarkable suggestion to prohibit slavery in the Northwest Territory resurfaced in the 1787 ordinance, passing this time without any debate. Probably the addition of a fugitive slave provision in the act set southern congressmen at ease: Escaped slaves caught north of the Ohio River would be returned south. Also, abundant territory south of the Ohio remained available for the spread of slavery. The ordinance thus acknowledged and supported slavery even as it barred

A Newly Cleared Frontier Farm
It took lots of muscle and sweat to turn the densely wooded land of the Northwest Territory into farms. Men with axes and oxen chopped down trees and dragged the logs into piles, to be transformed into log cabins and split-rail fences. Note the smoke: When burned, wood provided the leading energy source for all heat and cooking. The Granger Collection, New York.

it from one region. Still, the prohibition of slavery in the Northwest Territory perpetuated the dynamic of gradual emancipation in the North. North-South sectionalism based on slavery was slowly taking shape.

The Requisition of 1785 and Shays's Rebellion, 1786–1787

Without an impost amendment and with public land sales projected but not yet realized, the confederation again requisitioned the states to contribute revenue. In 1785 the amount requested was $3 million, four times larger than the previous year's levy. Of this sum, 30 percent was needed for the government's operating costs, and another 30 percent was earmarked to pay debts owed to foreign lenders, who insisted on payment in gold or silver. The remaining 40 percent was to go to Americans who owned government bonds, the IOUs of the Revolutionary years. A significant slice of that 40 percent represented the interest (but not the principal) owed

to army officers for their recently issued "commutation certificates." This was a tax that, if collected, was going to hurt.

At this time, states were struggling under state tax levies. The legislatures of several states without major ports (and the import duties that ports generated) were already pressing higher tax bills onto their farmer citizens in order to retire state debts from the Revolution. New Jersey and Connecticut fit this profile, and both state legislatures voted to ignore the confederation's requisition. In New Hampshire, town meetings voted to refuse to pay, because they could not. In 1786, two hundred armed insurgents surrounded the New Hampshire capitol to protest the taxes but were driven off by an armed militia. The shocked assemblymen backed off from an earlier order to haul delinquent taxpayers into courts. Rhode Island, North Carolina, and Georgia responded to their constituents' protests by issuing abundant amounts of paper money and allowing taxes to be paid in greatly depreciated currency.

Nowhere were the tensions so extreme as in Massachusetts. For four years in a row, a fiscally conservative legislature, dominated by the coastal commercial centers, had passed tough tax laws to pay state creditors who required payment in hard money, not cheap paper. Then in March 1786, the legislature in Boston loaded the federal requisition onto the bill. In June, farmers in southeastern Massachusetts marched on a courthouse in an effort to close it down, and petitions of complaint about oppressive taxation poured in from the western two-thirds of the state. In July 1786, when the legislature adjourned, having yet again ignored their complaints, dissidents held a series of conventions and called for revisions to the state constitution to promote democracy, eliminate the elite upper house, and move the capital farther west in the state.

Still unheard in Boston, the dissidents targeted the county courts, the local symbol of state authority. In the fall of 1786, several thousand armed men shut down courthouses in six counties; sympathetic local militias did not intervene. The insurgents were not predominantly poor or debt-ridden farmers; they included veteran soldiers and officers in the Continental army as well as town leaders. One was a farmer and onetime army captain, Daniel Shays.

The governor of Massachusetts, James Bowdoin, once a protester against British taxes, now characterized the western dissidents as illegal rebels. He vilified Shays as the chief leader, and a Boston newspaper claimed that Shays planned to burn Boston to the ground and overthrow the government. Another former radical, Samuel Adams, took the extreme position that "the man who dares rebel against the laws of a republic ought to suffer death." Those aging revolutionaries were not prepared to believe that representatives in a state legislature could seem to be as oppressive as monarchs. The dissidents challenged the assumption that popularly elected governments would always be fair and just.

Members of the Continental Congress had much to worry about. In nearly every state, the requisition of 1785 spawned some combination of crowd protests, demands for inflationary paper money, and anger at state authorities and alleged money speculators. The Massachusetts insurgency was the worst episode, and it seemed to be spinning out of control. In October,

the congress attempted to triple the size of the federal army, but fewer than 100 men enlisted. So Governor Bowdoin raised a private army, gaining the services of some 3,000 men with pay provided by wealthy and fearful Boston merchants.

In January 1787, the insurgents learned of the private army marching west from Boston, and 1,500 of them moved swiftly to capture a federal armory in Springfield to obtain weapons. But a militia band loyal to the state government beat them to the weapons facility and met their attack with gunfire; 4 rebels were killed and another 20 wounded. The final and bloodless encounter came at Petersham, where Bowdoin's army surprised the rebels and took several hundred of them prisoner. In the end, 2 men were executed for rebellion; 16 more sentenced to hang were reprieved at the last moment on the gallows. Some 4,000 men gained leniency by confessing their misconduct and swearing an oath of allegiance to the state. A special Disqualification Act prohibited the penitent rebels from voting, holding public office, serving on juries, working as schoolmasters, or operating taverns for up to three years.

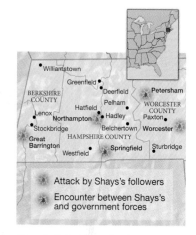

Shays's Rebellion, 1786–1787

Shays's Rebellion caused leaders throughout the country to worry about the confederation's ability to handle civil disorder. Inflammatory Massachusetts newspapers wrote about bloody mob rule spreading to other states. New York lawyer John Jay wrote to George Washington, "Our affairs seem to lead to some crisis, some revolution—something I cannot foresee or conjecture. I am uneasy and apprehensive; more so than during the war." Benjamin Franklin, in his eighties, shrewdly observed that in 1776 Americans had feared "an excess of power in the rulers" but now the problem was perhaps "a defect of obedience" in the subjects. Among such leaders, the sense of crisis in the confederation had greatly deepened.

REVIEW What were the most important factors in the failure of the Articles of Confederation?

Two Rebel Leaders
A Boston almanac of 1787 portrayed Daniel Shays (on the left) with another rebel leader, Job Shattuck, thought to be ringleaders in the rebellion against excessive taxation in Massachusetts. It is unlikely the artist ever saw either man. The cannon and drawn swords suggest the men are serious threats. This particular almanac series was pro-Constitution in 1788, so likely this picture is not meant to be sympathetic to the Shaysites. National Portrait Gallery, Smithsonian Institution/Art Resource, NY.

▶ The United States Constitution

Shays's Rebellion provoked an odd mixture of fear and hope that the government under the Articles of Confederation was losing its grip on power. A small circle of Virginians decided to try one last time to augment the powers granted to the government by the Articles. Their innocuous call for a meeting to discuss trade regulation led within a year to a total reworking of the national government, one with extensive powers and multiple branches based on differing constituencies.

From Annapolis to Philadelphia

The Virginians, led by James Madison, convinced the confederation congress to allow a September 1786 meeting of delegates at Annapolis, Maryland, to try again to revise the trade regulation pow-ers of the Articles. Only five states participated, and the delegates planned a second meeting for Philadelphia in May 1787. The congress reluctantly endorsed the Philadelphia meeting and limited its scope to "the sole and express purpose of revising the Articles of Confederation." But a few leaders, such as Alexander Hamilton of New York, had far more ambitious plans.

The fifty-five men who assembled at Philadelphia in May 1787 for the constitutional convention were generally those who had already concluded that there were serious weaknesses in the Articles of Confederation. Patrick Henry, author of the Virginia Resolves in 1765 and more recently state governor, refused to go to the convention, saying he "smelled a rat." Rhode Island declined to send delegates. Two men sent by New York's legislature to check the influence of fellow delegate Alexander Hamilton left in dismay in the middle of the convention, leaving Hamilton as the sole representative of the state.

The Pennsylvania Statehouse
The constitutional convention met in the Assembly Room of the Pennsylvania statehouse in the summer of 1787. Despite the heat, the delegates nailed the windows shut to foil eavesdroppers. The building is now called Independence Hall in honor of the signing of the Declaration of Independence there in 1776; this room has been meticulously restored.
© Tetra Images/Corbis.

This gathering of white men included no artisans, day laborers, or ordinary farmers. Two-thirds of the delegates were lawyers. Half had been officers in the Continental army. The majority had served in the confederation congress and knew its strengths and weaknesses. Seven men had been governors of their states and knew firsthand the frustrations of thwarted executive power. A few elder statesmen attended, such as Benjamin Franklin and George Washington, but on the whole the delegates were young, like Madison and Hamilton.

The Virginia and New Jersey Plans

The convention worked in secrecy, which enabled the men to freely explore alternatives without fear that their honest opinions would come back to haunt them. The Virginia delegation first laid out a fifteen-point plan that repudiated the principle of a confederation of states. Largely the work of Madison, the **Virginia Plan** set out a three-branch government composed of a two-chamber legislature, a powerful executive, and

a judiciary. It practically eliminated the voices of the smaller states by pegging representation in both houses of the congress to population. The theory was that government operated directly on people, not on states. Among the breathtaking powers assigned to the congress were the rights to veto state legislation and to coerce states militarily to obey national laws. To prevent the congress from having absolute power, the executive and judiciary could jointly veto its actions.

In mid-June, delegates from New Jersey, Connecticut, Delaware, and New Hampshire—all small states—unveiled an alternative proposal. The **New Jersey Plan**, as it was called, maintained the existing single-house congress of the Articles of Confederation in which each state had one vote. Acknowledging the need for an executive, it created a plural presidency to be shared by three men elected by the congress from among its membership. Where it sharply departed from the existing government was in the sweeping powers it gave to the new congress: the right to tax, regulate trade, and use force on unruly state governments. In favoring national power over states' rights, it aligned itself with the Virginia Plan. But the New Jersey Plan retained the confederation principle that the national government was to be an assembly of states, not of people.

For two weeks, delegates debated the two plans, focusing on the key issue of representation. The small-state delegates conceded that one house in a two-house legislature could be apportioned by population, but they would never agree that both houses could be. Madison was equally vehement about bypassing representation by state, which he viewed as the fundamental flaw in the Articles.

The debate seemed deadlocked, and for a while the convention was "on the verge of dissolution, scarce held together by the strength of a hair," according to one delegate. Only in mid-July did the so-called Great Compromise break the stalemate and produce the basic structural features of the emerging **United States Constitution**. Proponents of the competing plans agreed on a bicameral legislature. Representation in the lower house, the House of Representatives, would be apportioned by population, and representation in the upper house, the Senate, would come from all the states equally, with each state represented by two independently voting senators.

Representation by population turned out to be an ambiguous concept once it was subjected to rigorous discussion. Who counted? Were slaves, for example, people or property? As people, they would add weight to the southern delegations in the House of Representatives, but as property they would add to the tax burdens of those states. What emerged was the compromise known as the **three-fifths clause**: All free persons plus "three-fifths of all other Persons" constituted the numerical base for the apportionment of representatives.

Using "all other Persons" as a substitute for "slaves" indicates the discomfort delegates felt in acknowledging in the Constitution the existence of slavery. The words *slave* and *slavery* appear nowhere in the document, but slavery figured in two places besides the three-fifths clause. Government power over trade regulation naturally included the slave trade, which the Constitution euphemistically described as "the Migration or Importation of such Persons as any of the States now shall think proper to admit." Another provision contrived to guarantee the return of fugitive slaves using awkward, lawyer-like prose: "No person, held to Service or Labour in one State, under the Laws thereof, escaping into another, shall, in Consequence of any Law

or Regulation therein, be discharged from such Service or Labour but shall be delivered up on Claim of the party to whom such Service or Labour may be due." Although slavery was nowhere named, nonetheless it was recognized, protected, and thereby perpetuated by the U.S. Constitution.

Democracy versus Republicanism

The delegates in Philadelphia made a distinction between democracy and republicanism new to the American political vocabulary. Pure democracy was now taken to be a dangerous thing. As a Massachusetts delegate put it, "The evils we experience flow from the excess of democracy." The delegates still favored republican institutions, but they created a government that gave direct voice to the people only in the House and that granted a check on that voice to the Senate, a body of men elected not by direct popular vote but by the state legislatures. Senators served for six years, with no limit on reelection; they were protected from the whims of democratic majorities, and their long terms fostered experience and maturity in office.

Similarly, the presidency evolved into a powerful office out of the reach of direct democracy. The delegates devised an electoral college whose only function was to elect the president and vice president. Each state's legislature would choose the electors, whose number was the sum of representatives and senators for the state, an interesting blending of the two principles of representation. The president thus would owe his office not to the Congress, the states, or the people, but to a temporary assemblage of distinguished citizens who could vote their own judgment on the candidates. His term of office was four years, but he could be reelected without limitation.

The framers had developed a far more complex form of federal government than that provided by the Articles of Confederation. To curb the excesses of democracy, they devised a government with limits and checks on all three of its branches. They set forth a powerful president who could veto legislation passed in Congress, but they gave Congress the power to override presidential vetoes. They set up a national judiciary to settle disputes between states and citizens of different states. They separated the branches of government not only by functions and by reciprocal checks but also by deliberately basing the election of each branch on different universes of voters—voting citizens (the House), state legislators (the Senate), and the electoral college (the presidency).

The convention carefully listed the powers of the president and of Congress. The president could initiate policy, propose legislation, and veto acts of Congress; he could command the military and direct foreign policy; and he could appoint the entire judiciary, subject to Senate approval. Congress held the purse strings: the power to levy taxes, to regulate trade, and to coin money and control the currency. States were expressly forbidden to issue paper money. Two more powers of Congress—to "provide for the common defence and general Welfare" of the country and "to make all laws which shall be necessary and proper" for carrying out its powers—provided elastic language that came closest to Madison's wish to grant sweeping powers to the new government.

While no one was entirely satisfied with every line of the Constitution, only three dissenters refused to sign the document. The Constitution specified a mechanism for ratification that avoided the dilemma faced earlier by the confederation government: Nine states, not all thirteen, had to ratify it, and special ratifying conventions elected only for that purpose, not state legislatures, would make the crucial decision.

> **REVIEW** Why did the Constitution proposed at the Philadelphia convention include multiple checks on the three branches of government?

▶ Ratification of the Constitution

Had a popular vote been taken on the Constitution in the fall of 1787, it probably would have been rejected. In the three most populous states—Virginia, Massachusetts, and New York—substantial majorities opposed a powerful new national government. North Carolina and Rhode Island refused to call ratifying conventions. Seven of the eight remaining states were easy victories for the Constitution, but securing the approval of the ninth proved difficult. Pro-Constitution forces, called Federalists, had to strategize very shrewdly to defeat anti-Constitution forces, called Antifederalists.

The Federalists

Proponents of the Constitution moved swiftly into action. They first secured agreement from an uneasy confederation congress, to defer a vote and instead send the Constitution to the states for their consideration. The pro-Constitution forces next called themselves **Federalists**, a word that implied endorsement of a confederated government. Their opponents thus became known as Antifederalists, a label that made them sound defensive and negative, lacking a program of their own.

To gain momentum, the Federalists targeted the states most likely to ratify quickly. Delaware ratified in early December, before the Antifederalists had even begun to campaign. Pennsylvania, New Jersey, and Georgia followed within a month (Map 8.3). Delaware and New Jersey were small states surrounded by more powerful neighbors; a government that would regulate trade and set taxes according to population was an attractive proposition. Georgia sought the protection that a stronger national government would afford against hostile Indians and Spanish Florida to the south. "If a weak State with the Indians on its back and the Spaniards on its flank does not see the necessity of a General Government there must I think be wickedness or insanity in the way," said Federalist George Washington.

Another three easy victories came in Connecticut, Maryland, and South Carolina. Again, merchants, lawyers, and urban artisans in general favored the new Constitution, as did large landowners and slaveholders. Antifederalists in these states tended to be rural, western, and noncommercial, men whose access to news was limited and whose participation in state government was tenuous.

Massachusetts was the first state to give the Federalists serious difficulty. The vote to select the ratification delegates decidedly favored the Antifederalists, whose strength lay in the western areas of the state, home to Shays's Rebellion. One rural delegate from Worcester County voiced widely shared suspicions: "These lawyers and men of learning and money men that talk so finely, and gloss over matters so smoothly, to make us poor illiterate people swallow down the pill, expect to get into Congress themselves; they expect to be the managers of the Constitution and get all the power and all the money into their own hands, and then they will swallow up all us little folks." But another western farmer said he knew "the worth of good government by

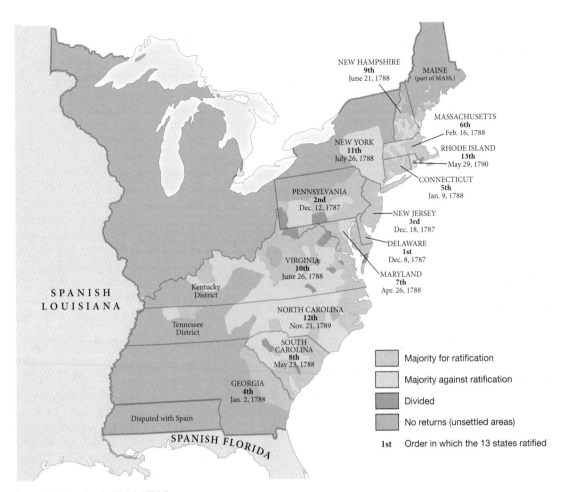

MAP ACTIVITY

Map 8.3   Ratification of the Constitution, 1788–1790

Populated areas cast votes for delegates to state ratification conventions. This map shows Antifederalist strength generally concentrated in backcountry, noncoastal, and non-urban areas, but with significant exceptions (for example, Rhode Island).

READING THE MAP: Where was Federalist strength concentrated? How did the distribution of Federalist and Antifederalist sentiment affect the order of state ratifications of the Constitution?

CONNECTIONS: What objections did Antifederalists have to the new U.S. Constitution? How might their locations have affected their view of the Federalist argument?

the want of it," a clear reference to the chaos of the Shaysite rebellion. He urged his fellow farmers to work with the elite leaders; "they are all embarked on the same cause with us, and we must swim or sink together. . . . We shall never have another opportunity." By such arguments and by a vigorous Federalist newspaper campaign, the Antifederalists' initial lead was slowly eroded. In the end, the Federalists won in Massachusetts by a slim margin and only with promises that amendments to the Constitution would be taken up in the first Congress.

By May 1788, eight states had ratified; only one more was needed. North Carolina and Rhode Island were hopeless for the Federalist cause, and New Hampshire seemed nearly as bleak. More worrisome was the failure to win over the largest and most economically critical states, Virginia and New York.

The Antifederalists

The **Antifederalists** were a composite group, united mainly in their desire to block the Constitution. Although much of their strength came from backcountry areas long suspicious of eastern elites, many Antifederalist leaders came from the same social background as Federalist leaders; economic class alone did not differentiate them. The Antifederalists also drew strength in states that were already on sure economic footing, such as New York which could afford to remain independent. Probably the biggest appeal of the Antifederalists' position lay in the long-nurtured fear that distant power might infringe on people's liberties.

But by the time eight states had ratified the Constitution, the Antifederalists faced a difficult task. First, they were no longer defending the status quo now that the momentum lay with the Federalists. Second, it was difficult to defend the confederation government with its admitted flaws. Even so, they remained genuinely fearful that the new government would be too distant from the people and could thus become corrupt or tyrannical. "The difficulty, if not impracticability, of exercising the equal and equitable powers of government by a single legislature over an extent of territory that reaches from the Mississippi to the western lakes, and from them to the Atlantic ocean, is an insuperable objection to the adoption of the new system," wrote Mercy Otis Warren, an Antifederalist woman writing under the name "A Columbia Patriot."

The new government was indeed distant. In the proposed House of Representatives, the only directly democratic element of the Constitution, one member represented some 30,000 people. How could that member really know or communicate with his whole constituency, Antifederalists worried? One Antifederalist essayist contrasted the proposed model with the personal character of state-level representation: "The members of our state legislature are annually elected—they are subject to instructions—they are chosen within small circles—they are sent but a small distance from their respective homes. Their conduct is constantly known to their constituents. They frequently see, and are seen, by the men whose servants they are." They also worried that representatives would always be elites and thus "ignorant of the sentiments of the middling and much more of the lower class of citizens, strangers to their ability, unacquainted with their wants, difficulties, and distress," as one Maryland man worried.

The Federalists generally agreed that the elite would be favored for national elections. Indeed, Federalists wanted power to reside with intelligent, virtuous leaders like themselves. They did not envision a government constituted of every class of people. "Fools and knaves have voice enough in government already," joked one Federalist, without being guaranteed representation in

VISUAL ACTIVITY

Mercy Otis Warren
Sister and wife of prominent Massachusetts revolutionaries, Mercy Otis Warren was well positioned to know about revolutionary politics. Abigail and John Adams were close friends until she broke with them in 1788 over her support for Antifederalism. At age thirty-five, in 1763, she sat for Boston artist John Singleton Copley wearing a shimmering blue silk gown ornamented with expensive lace. Museum of Fine Arts, Boston, Massachusetts/Bequest of Winslow Warren/The Bridgeman Art Library.
READING THE IMAGE: How does the artist convey grace and ease as features of feminine beauty? Copley painted two other women in 1763—two from Salem and Mrs. Warren from Barnstable, Massachusetts—each wearing the same blue dress. What might that suggest about Copley's studio practices, about fashion, or about the purpose of family portraits?
CONNECTIONS: What role could upper-class women play in the debate over the Constitution?

Was the New United States a Christian Country?

Rebecca Samuel, a Jewish resident of Virginia, conveyed her excitement about the new U.S. Constitution when she wrote her German parents in 1791 that finally "Jew and Gentile are as one" in the realm of politics and citizenship. Other voices were distinctly less approving. An Antifederalist pamphlet warned that the pope could become president; another feared that "a Turk, a Jew, a Roman Catholic, and what is worse than all, a Universalist, may be President."

The document that produced such wildly different reactions was indeed remarkable for the conspicuous absence of religion. The Constitution did not invoke Christianity as a state religion. It made no reference to an almighty being, and it specifically promised, in Article 6, section 3, that "no religious test shall ever be required as a qualification to any office or public trust under the United States."

Many Christian leaders were stunned at the Constitution's near silence on religion, a turnabout from most state constitutions. A New Yorker warned that "should the Citizens of America be as irreligious as her Constitution, we will have reason to tremble, lest the Governor of the universe . . . crush us to atoms." A delegate to North Carolina's ratifying convention predicted that the Constitution was "an invitation for Jews and pagans of every kind to come among us." A concerned Presbyterian minister asked Alexander Hamilton why religion was not in the Constitution. Hamilton reportedly quipped, "Indeed, Doctor, we forgot it."

Measured against the practices of state governments, Hamilton's observation is hardly credible. The men who wrote the state constitutions actively debated qualifications for voting and officeholding. Along with factors like property ownership, race, gender, and age, many also argued for religious qualifications.

Most leaders of the 1780s took for granted that Christianity was the one true faith and the essential foundation of morality. All but two state constitutions assumed the primacy of Protestantism, and one-third of them collected public taxes to support Christian churches. Every state but one required officeholders to take a Christian oath. For example, members of Pennsylvania's legislature swore to "acknowledge the Scripture of the Old and New Testament to be given by divine inspiration."

Governors proclaimed fast days and public thanksgivings in the name of the Holy Trinity. Chaplains led legislatures in Christian prayer. Jurors and witnesses swore Christian oaths. New England states passed Sabbath laws prohibiting all work or travel on Sunday. Blasphemy laws punished people who cursed the Christian God or Jesus.

Although close to half the state constitutions did include freedom of religious conscience as an explicit right, this right promised nothing about political equality. How then did the U.S. Constitution come to be such a break from the immediate past? Had the Constitution's writers really just forgotten about religion?

Not James Madison of Virginia. Madison arrived at the constitutional convention fresh from a hard-fought battle in Virginia to establish religious liberty free from all state interference. Opponents sponsored a bill to support Christian ministers with tax money; Madison instead secured passage in 1786 of the Virginia Statute for Religious Freedom, a document drafted several years earlier by Thomas Jefferson. The statute guaranteed freedom of conscience and prohibited any distinctions in "civil capacities" based on religion. In Jefferson's distinctive formulation, the statute asserted "that our civil rights have no dependence on our religious opinions any more than our opinions in physics or geometry." There could be no religious tests for officeholding thereafter in Virginia and no state funding of ministers.

The Virginia Statute expressed Madison's ideal, but on practical grounds he preferred that the U.S.

proportion to their total population. Alexander Hamilton claimed that mechanics and laborers preferred to have their social betters represent them. Antifederalists disagreed: "In reality, there will be no part of the people represented, but the rich. . . . It will literally be a government in the hands of the few to oppress and plunder the many." (See "Historical Question," above.)

Antifederalists fretted over many specific features of the Constitution, such as the prohibition on state-issued paper money or the federal power to control the time and place of elections. The most widespread objection was the Constitution's glaring omission of any guarantees of individual liberties in a bill of rights like those contained in many state constitutions.

In the end, a small state—New Hampshire—provided the decisive ninth vote for ratification on June 21, 1788, following an intensive and successful lobbying effort by Federalists.

Touro Synagogue
This 1759 synagogue in Newport, Rhode Island, is the oldest Jewish house of worship still standing in the United States. President Washington visited "the Hebrew Congregation" there in 1790 and wrote: "It is now no more that toleration is spoken of, as if it was by the indulgence of one class of people, that another enjoyed the exercise of their inherent natural rights." Touro Synagogue/photo John T. Hopf.

Constitution say little about religion since state laws reflected a variety of positions. When Antifederalists demanded a bill of rights, Madison drew up a list for the first Congress to consider. Two on his list dealt with religion, but only one was approved: "Congress shall make no law respecting an establishment of religion, or prohibiting the free exercise thereof." In a stroke, Madison placed religious worship and the privileging of any one church beyond Congress's power. His second proposal failed to gain traction: "No State shall violate the equal rights of conscience." Evidently, the states wanted to keep their Christian-only rules that violated dissenters' consciences and kept them out of office.

Gradually, states deleted restrictive laws, but as late as 1840 Jews still could not hold public office in four states. Well into the twentieth century, Sunday laws in some states forced business closings on the Christian Sabbath, creating economic hardship for those whose religion prohibited work on Saturday. The guarantee of freedom of conscience in religion was implanted in various founding documents in the 1770s and 1780s, but it took many years to fulfill Jefferson's and Madison's larger vision of what true religious liberty means: the freedom for religious belief to be independent of civil status.

Questions for Consideration

1. Why do you think so many state constitutions allowed only Protestants to hold political office?

2. What point was Jefferson making when he compared opinions about religion to opinions about physics or geometry as relevant factors for officeholding?

Connect to the Big Idea

C Is the Constitution's silence about religious qualifications for officeholding in any way parallel to its lack of specific property qualifications for voting or officeholding?

The Big Holdouts: Virginia and New York

Four states still remained outside the new union, and a glance at a map demonstrated the necessity of pressing the Federalist case in the two largest, Virginia and New York (see Map 8.3). In Virginia, an influential Antifederalist group led by Patrick Henry and George Mason made the outcome uncertain. The Federalists finally but barely won ratification by proposing twenty specific amendments that the new government would promise to consider.

New York voters tilted toward the Antifederalists out of a sense that a state so large and powerful need not relinquish so much authority to the new federal government. But New York was also home to some of the most persuasive Federalists. Starting in October 1787, Alexander Hamilton collaborated with James Madison and

"Success to the Tobacco Plant"
As soon as nine states ratified the Constitution, the Federalists staged spectacular victory celebrations intended to demonstrate national unity behind the new government. Philadelphia's parade, on July 4, 1788, mobilized several thousand participants marching under occupational banners representing farmers, brewers, tobacconists, lawyers, and others. This banner was carried by the local sellers of tobacco products, who likely applauded a national government empowered to regulate commerce among the states. Friends of the Thomas Leiper House and the Library Company of Philadelphia

New York lawyer John Jay on a series of eighty-five essays on the political philosophy of the new Constitution. Published in New York newspapers and later republished as *The Federalist Papers*, the essays brilliantly set out the failures of the Articles of Confederation and offered an analysis of the complex nature of the Federalist position. In one of the most compelling essays, number 10, Madison challenged the Antifederalists' heartfelt conviction that republican government had to be small-scale. Madison argued that a large and diverse population was itself a guarantee of liberty. In a national government, no single faction could ever be large enough to subvert the freedom of other groups. "Extend the sphere, and you take in a greater variety of parties and interests; you make it less probable that a majority of the whole will have a common motive to invade the rights of other citizens," Madison asserted. He called it "a republican remedy for the diseases most incident to republican government."

At New York's ratifying convention, Antifederalists predominated, but impassioned debate and lobbying—plus the dramatic news of Virginia's ratification—finally tipped the balance to the Federalists. Even so, the Antifederalists' approval of the document was accompanied by a list of twenty-four individual rights and thirty-three structural changes they hoped to see in the Constitution. New York's ratification ensured the legitimacy of the new government, yet it took another year and a half for Antifederalists in North Carolina to come around. Fiercely independent Rhode Island held out until May 1790, and even then it ratified by only a two-vote margin.

In less than twelve months, the U.S. Constitution was both written and ratified. The Federalists had faced a formidable task, but by building momentum and promising consideration of a bill of rights, they did indeed carry the day.

> **REVIEW**   Why did Antifederalists oppose the Constitution?

▶ Conclusion: The "Republican Remedy"

Thus ended one of the most intellectually tumultuous and creative periods in American history.

The period began in 1775 with a confederation government that could barely be ratified because of its requirement of unanimity, but there was no reaching unanimity on the western lands, an impost, and the proper way to respond to unfair taxation in a republican state. The new Constitution offered a different approach to these problems by loosening the grip of impossible unanimity and by embracing the ideas of a heterogeneous public life and a carefully balanced government that together would prevent any one part of the public from tyrannizing another. The genius of James Madison to anticipate that diversity of opinion was not only an unavoidable reality but also a hidden strength of the new society beginning to take shape. This is what he meant in Federalist essay number 10 when he spoke of the "republican remedy" for the troubles most likely to befall a government in which the people are the source of authority.

Despite Madison's optimism, political differences remained keen and worrisome to many. The Federalists still hoped for a society in which leaders of exceptional wisdom would discern the best path for public policy. They looked backward to a society of hierarchy, rank, and benevolent rule by an aristocracy of talent, but they created a government with forward-looking checks and balances as a guard against corruption, which they figured would most likely emanate from the people. The Antifederalists also looked backward, but to an old order of small-scale direct democracy and local control, in which virtuous people kept a close eye on potentially corruptible rulers. The Antifederalists feared a national government led by distant, self-interested leaders who needed to be held in check. In the 1790s, these two conceptions of republicanism and of leadership would be tested in real life.

See the Selected Bibliography for this chapter in the Appendix.

8 Chapter Review

MAKE IT STICK

LearningCurve

Go online and use LearningCurve to see what you know. Then review the key terms and answer the questions.

KEY TERMS

Articles of Confederation (p. 197)
republicanism (p. 201)
gradual emancipation (p. 205)
Newburgh Conspiracy (p. 207)
Treaty of Fort Stanwix (p. 209)
Northwest Ordinance (p. 210)
Shays's Rebellion (p. 213)
Virginia Plan (p. 215)
New Jersey Plan (p. 215)
United States Constitution (p. 216)
three-fifths clause (p. 216)
Federalists (p. 217)
Antifederalists (p. 218)

REVIEW QUESTIONS

1. Why was the confederation government's authority so limited? (pp. 197–200)

2. What were the limits of citizenship, rights, and freedom within the various states? (pp. 201–207)

3. What were the most important factors in the failure of the Articles of Confederation? (pp. 207–213)

4. Why did the Constitution proposed at the Philadelphia convention include multiple checks on the three branches of government? (pp. 214–217)

5. Why did Antifederalists oppose the Constitution? (pp. 217–222)

MAKING CONNECTIONS

1. Leaders in the new nation held that voting should be restricted to men possessing independence of mind. What did they mean by that? Who did they mean to exclude from voting?

2. Twenty-first-century Americans see a profound tension between the Revolutionary ideals of liberty and equality and the persistence of American slavery. Did Americans in the late eighteenth century see a tension?

3. What proposals were offered to manage the sale and settlement of the Northwest Territory, the confederation's greatest financial asset? How did the final Ordinance of 1787 shape the nation's expansion?

LINKING TO THE PAST

1. Compare and contrast the complaints against taxation connected with the Stamp Act in 1765 and those resulting from the congressional requisition of 1785. What were the principal arguments in each case? In either case, was it simply a matter of people refusing to pay to support government functions? Why do you think anti–Stamp Act activists like Samuel Adams took a negative view of the 1786 tax protests? (See chapter 6.)

2. Thomas Paine's pamphlet *Common Sense*, which sharply criticized the monarchy, was widely circulated and hailed by rebellious colonists in 1776. In light of the colonists' negative view toward monarchical power leading up to the Revolutionary War, how do you explain the powerful presidency that the victorious Americans set up in 1787? (See chapter 7.)

9

The New Nation Takes Form

1789–1800

CONTENT LEARNING OBJECTIVES

After reading and studying this chapter, you should be able to:

- Identify the sources of stability and change in the 1790s.

- Explain Alexander Hamilton's three-part economic program, including the parts that were adopted and those that failed, and why the program was controversial.

- Understand how foreign and domestic conflict, including fighting in the Ohio Valley, the Haitian Revolution, and the wars between England and France, influenced the early Republic.

- Understand how the Federalist and Republican parties developed, and in what ways the 1796 election, the XYZ affair, and the Alien and Sedition Acts polarized the two.

WASHINGTON'S GIFT TO HIS WIFE
George Washington sat for several official portraits during his presidency but he commissioned this personal one himself, in 1789, as a gift for his wife. The miniature could be worn as a pendant or pin. Private Collection/Photo © Christie's Images/The Bridgeman Art Library

ALEXANDER HAMILTON, THE MAN WHO BRILLIANTLY UNIFIED the pro-Constitution Federalists of 1788, headed the Treasury Department in the new government and thereby became the most polarizing figure of the 1790s.

Hamilton grew up on a small West Indies island, the son of an unmarried mother who died when he was eleven. He developed a fierce ambition to overcome his disadvantages and make good. After serving an apprenticeship to a trader, the bright lad made his way to New York City where he soon gained entry to college. During the American Revolution, he wrote political articles for a newspaper that caught the eye of General George Washington, who was moved to select the nineteen-year-old to be his close aide. In the 1780s, Hamilton practiced law in New York and participated in the constitutional convention in Philadelphia. His shrewd political tactics greatly aided the ratification process.

A Cinderella story characterized Hamilton's private life too. Handsome and now well connected, he married a wealthy merchant's daughter. He had a magnetic charm that attracted both men and women; at social gatherings he excelled. Late-night parties, however, never interfered with Hamilton's prodigious capacity for work.

As secretary of the treasury, Hamilton took quick action to build the economy. "If a Government appears to be confident of its own powers, it is the surest way to inspire the same confidence in others," he remarked. He immediately tackled the country's unpaid Revolutionary War debt, producing a complex proposal to fund the debt and pump millions of dollars into the U.S. economy. He drew up a plan for a national banking system to manage the money supply. And he designed a system of government subsidies and tariff policies to promote the development of manufacturing interests.

Hamilton was both visionary and practical, a gifted man with remarkable political intuitions. Yet this magnetic man made enemies; the "founding fathers" of the 1770s and 1780s became competitors and even bitter rivals in the 1790s. Both political philosophy and personality clashes created friction.

Hamilton's charm no longer worked with James Madison, now a representative in Congress and an opponent of all of Hamilton's economic plans. His charm had never worked with John Adams, the new vice president, who privately called him "the bastard brat of a Scotch pedlar" motivated by "disappointed Ambition and unbridled malice and revenge." Years later, when asked why he had deserted Hamilton, Madison coolly replied, "Colonel Hamilton deserted me." Hamilton assumed that government was safest when in the hands of "the rich, the wise, and the good"—by which he meant America's commercial elite. By contrast, agrarian values ran deep with Jefferson and Madison, and they were suspicious of get-rich-quick speculators, financiers, and manufacturing development.

The personal and political antagonisms of this first generation of American leaders left their mark on the young country. Leaders generally agreed on Indian policy in the new republic—peace when possible, war when necessary—but on little else. No one was prepared for the intense and passionate polarization over economic and foreign policy. The disagreements were articulated around particular events and policies: taxation and the public debt, a new treaty with Britain, a rebellion in Haiti, and a near-war with France. At their heart, these disagreements sprang from opposing ideologies on the value of democracy, the nature of leadership, and the limits of federal power.

By 1800, the oppositional politics ripening between Hamiltonian and Jeffersonian politicians would begin to crystallize into political parties, the Federalists and the Republicans. To the citizens of that day, this was an unhappy development.

***Alexander Hamilton*, by John Trumbull**
Hamilton was confident, handsome, audacious, brilliant, and very hardworking. Ever slender, in marked contrast to the more corpulent leaders of his day, he posed for this portrait in 1792, at the age of thirty-seven and at the height of his power. Everett Collection Historical/Alamy

► The Search for Stability

After the struggles of the 1780s, the most urgent task in establishing the new government was to secure stability. Leaders sought ways to heal old divisions, and the first presidential election offered the means to do that in the person of George Washington, who enjoyed widespread veneration. People trusted him to exercise the untested and perhaps elastic powers of the presidency.

Congress had important work as well in initiating the new government. Congress quickly agreed on the Bill of Rights, which answered the concerns of many Antifederalists. Beyond politics, cultural change in the area of gender also enhanced political stability. The private virtue of women was mobilized to bolster the public virtue of male citizens and to enhance political stability. Republicanism was forcing a rethinking of women's relation to the state.

Washington Inaugurates the Government

George Washington was elected president in February 1789 by a unanimous vote of the electoral college. (John Adams got just half as many votes; he became vice president, but his pride was wounded.) Washington perfectly embodied the republican ideal of disinterested, public-spirited leadership. Indeed, he cultivated that image through astute ceremonies such as the dramatic surrender of his sword to the Continental Congress at the end of the war, symbolizing the subservience of military power to the law.

Once in office, Washington calculated his moves, knowing that every step set a precedent and that any misstep could be dangerous for the fragile government. Congress debated a title for Washington, ranging from "His Highness" to "His Majesty, the President"; Washington favored "His High Mightiness." But in the end, republican simplicity prevailed. The final title was simply "President of the United States of America," and the established form of address became "Mr. President," a subdued yet dignified title reserved for property-owning white males.

Washington's genius in establishing the presidency lay in his capacity for implanting his own reputation for integrity into the office itself. In the political language of the day, he was "virtuous," meaning that he took pains to

CHRONOLOGY

1789	• George Washington inaugurated first president. • French Revolution begins. • First Congress meets. • Fort Washington erected in western Ohio.
1790	• Congress approves Hamilton's debt plan. • Judith Sargent Murray publishes "On the Equality of the Sexes." • National capital moved to Philadelphia. • Indians in Ohio defeat General Josiah Harmar.
1791	• States ratify Bill of Rights. • Bank of the United States chartered. • Ohio Indians defeat General Arthur St. Clair. • Congress passes whiskey tax. • Haitian Revolution begins. • Hamilton issues *Report on Manufactures*.
1793	• Anglo-French Wars commence in Europe. • Washington issues Neutrality Proclamation. • Eli Whitney invents cotton gin.
1794	• Whiskey Rebellion. • Battle of Fallen Timbers.
1795	• Treaty of Greenville. • Jay Treaty.
1796	• John Adams elected president.
1797	• XYZ affair.
1798	• Quasi-War with France erupts. • Alien and Sedition Acts. • Virginia and Kentucky Resolutions.
1800	• Thomas Jefferson elected president.

Federal Hall, the site of George Washington's Inauguration, April 30, 1789
New York's old City Hall, built in 1700, got a classical makeover in 1788 when it became the seat of the new federal government. Notice the triangular center gable with its giant-sized seal of the United States. Washington took the oath of office on this balcony before a crowd of 10,000. Following a 21-gun salute, the president delivered a near-inaudible ten-minute inaugural address in the senate chamber. Library of Congress.

elevate the public good over private interest and projected honesty and honor over ambition. He remained aloof, resolute, and dignified, to the point of appearing wooden at times. He encouraged pomp and ceremony to create respect for the office, traveling with six horses to pull his coach, hosting formal balls, and surrounding himself with uniformed servants. He even held weekly "levees," as European monarchs did, hour-long audiences granted to distinguished visitors (including women), at which Washington appeared attired in black velvet, with a feathered hat and a polished sword. The president and his guests bowed, avoiding the egalitarian familiarity of a handshake. But he always managed, perhaps just barely, to avoid the extreme of royal splendor.

Washington chose talented and experienced men to preside over the newly created Departments of War, Treasury, and State. For the Department of War, Washington selected General Henry Knox, former secretary of war in the confederation government. For the

Treasury—an especially tough job in view of revenue conflicts during the confederation (see "Confederation and Taxation" in chapter 8)—the president appointed Alexander Hamilton, known for his general brilliance and financial astuteness. To lead the State Department, which handled foreign policy, Washington chose Thomas Jefferson, a master diplomat and the current minister to France. For attorney general, Washington picked Edmund Randolph, a Virginian who had attended the constitutional convention but who had turned Antifederalist during ratification. For chief justice of the Supreme Court, Washington designated John Jay, a New York lawyer who had helped to write *The Federalist Papers*.

Soon Washington began to hold regular meetings with these men, thereby establishing the precedent of a presidential cabinet. (Vice President John Adams was not included; his only official duty, to preside over the Senate, he found "a punishment." To his wife he complained, "My country has in its wisdom contrived for me the most insignificant office.") No one anticipated that two decades of party turbulence would emerge from the brilliant but explosive mix of Washington's first cabinet.

The Bill of Rights

An important piece of business for the First Congress, meeting in 1789, was the passage of the **Bill of Rights**. Seven states had ratified the Constitution with the strong expectation that their concerns about individual liberties and limitations to federal power would be addressed through the amendment process. The Federalists of 1787 had thought an enumeration of rights unnecessary, but in 1789 Congressman James Madison understood that healing the divisions of the 1780s was of prime importance: "It will be a desirable thing to extinguish from the bosom of every member of the community, any apprehensions that there are those among his countrymen who wish to deprive them of the liberty for which they valiantly fought and honorably bled."

Drawing on existing state constitutions with bills of rights, Madison enumerated guarantees of freedom of speech, press, and religion; the right to petition and assemble; and the right to be free from unwarranted searches and seizures. One amendment asserted the right to keep and bear arms in support of a "well-regulated militia," to which Madison added, "but no person religiously scrupulous of bearing arms, shall be compelled to render military service in person." That provision for what a later century would call "conscientious objector" status failed to gain acceptance in Congress.

In September 1789, Congress approved a set of twelve amendments and sent them to the states for approval; by 1791, ten were eventually ratified. The First through Eighth dealt with individual liberties, and the Ninth and Tenth concerned the boundary between federal and state authority.

Still, not everyone was entirely satisfied. State ratifying conventions had submitted some eighty proposed amendments. Congress never considered proposals to change structural features of the new government, and Madison had no intention of reopening debates about the length of the president's term or the power to levy excise taxes. He also had no thought to use the Bill of Rights to address the status of enslaved people. But others capitalized on the First Amendment's right to petition to force the First Congress into a bitter debate over slavery (see "Historical Question," page 230).

Significantly, no one complained about one striking omission in the Bill of Rights: the right to vote. Only much later was voting seen as a fundamental liberty requiring protection by constitutional amendment—indeed, by four amendments. The Constitution deliberately left the definition of eligible voters to the states because of the existing wide variation in local voting practices. Most of these practices were based on property qualifications, but some touched on religion and, in one unusual case (New Jersey), on sex and race (see "Who Are 'the People'?" in chapter 8).

The Republican Wife and Mother

The exclusion of women from political activity did not mean they had no civic role or responsibility. A flood of periodical articles in the 1790s by both male and female writers reevaluated courtship, marriage, and motherhood in light of republican ideals. Tyrannical power in the ruler, whether king or husband, was declared a thing of the past. Affection, not duty, bound wives to their husbands and citizens to their government. In republican marriages, the writers claimed, women had the capacity to reform the morals and manners of men. One male author promised women that "the solidity and stability of the liberties of your country rest with you; since Liberty is never sure, 'till Virtue reigns triumphant. . . . While you thus keep our country virtuous, you maintain its independence."

Until the 1790s, public virtue was strictly a masculine quality. But another sort of virtue enlarged in importance: sexual chastity, a private asset prized as a feminine quality. Essayists of the 1790s explicitly advised young women to use sexual virtue to increase public virtue in men. "Love and courtship . . . invest a lady with more authority than in any other situation that falls to the lot of human beings," one male essayist proclaimed.

Republican ideals also cast motherhood in a new light. Throughout the 1790s, advocates for female education, still a controversial proposition, argued that education would produce better mothers, who in turn would produce better citizens, a concept historians call republican motherhood. Benjamin Rush, a Pennsylvania physician and educator, called for female education because "our ladies should be qualified . . . in instructing their sons in the principles of liberty and government." A series of essays by Judith Sargent Murray of Massachusetts favored

How Did America's First Congress Address the Question of Slavery?

In its opening months, the First Congress had an ambitious agenda. It established executive departments, the judiciary, and a federal postal system. It crafted the Bill of Rights, debated Alexander Hamilton's *Report on Public Credit*, and ratified its first Indian treaty. Tackling slavery was nowhere on its agenda. Congressmen assumed that key North-South compromises embedded in the Constitution had resolved the issue. But they were wrong: An angry debate over slavery burst forth in early 1790.

In mid-February, citizens of Pennsylvania and New York petitioned Congress to "exercise justice and mercy" and to end the "trafficking in the persons of fellow-men"— that is, the slave trade. The petitioners were Quakers, members of a religion with a long-standing moral objection to slavery. The pragmatic James Madison urged the representatives to refer the petitions to a congressional committee, thus keeping them out of public view. Representatives from South Carolina and Georgia instead urged immedi-

ate dismissal, citing the Constitution's ban on interference with the slave trade before 1808. Reaching no agreement, the Congress postponed discussion for a day.

But the next day brought another petition, not coincidentally. Drawn up by a largely Quaker group called the Pennsylvania Abolition Society, it asked Congress "to discourage every species of traffic in the persons of our fellow-men" and to "countenance the restoration of liberty" to slaves. The petition quoted the Constitution to prove the government's duty to "promote the general welfare, and secure the blessings of liberty" for all. That Benjamin Franklin's signature topped the list of petitioners gave it significant political clout.

This second petition was not just about the Atlantic slave trade, which was indeed protected for twenty years by the Constitution. It called for Congress to legislate on the domestic buying and selling of slaves, about which the Constitution was silent. Further, restoring liberty to slaves

required an emancipation law, again something not barred by the Constitution. No method was specified "for removing this inconsistency from the character of the American people," but the petitioners expressed confidence in a merciful Congress.

The petitions touched off an explosive debate in the House. Several northern representatives tried to use them to reopen the contentious issue; representatives from the deep South were adamantly opposed. A rare moment of contemptuous humor surfaced when a South Carolina member asserted that during ratification, "We took each other, with our mutual bad habits and respective evils, for better, for worse; the Northern States adopted us with our slaves, and we adopted them with their Quakers." No other levity was to be heard. Southerners cited biblical justifications for slavery, argued that slavery civilized slaves, predicted economic collapse if slavery ended, and called the petitioners fanatics. Madison finally got his way: The petitions were referred to a committee, amid mounting concern that newspaper coverage of the debate would create rebelliousness among slaves.

A month later, that committee's report defined a middle road in clarifying the powers of Congress over slavery. As expected, the report affirmed that Congress could not end the slave trade before 1808, but it also concluded that Congress could neither force emancipation nor deny it. And while the

education that would remake women into self-confident, rational beings. Her first essay, published in 1790, was boldly titled "On the Equality of the Sexes." In a subsequent essay on education, she reassured readers that educated women would retain their "characteristic trait" of sweetness. Murray thus reassured readers that education would not undermine women's compliant natures.

Although women's obligations as wives and mothers were now infused with political meaning, traditional gender relations remained unaltered. The analogy between marriage and civil society worked precisely because of the self-subordination inherent in the term *virtue*. Men should put the public good first, before selfish desires, just as women must put their husbands and families first, before themselves. Women

"WORK & BE HAPPY": The Pennsylvania Abolition Society, circa 1800

Philadelphia Quakers founded the Pennsylvania Abolition Society in 1775. Quickly they attracted 2,000 members to their program of "improving the Condition of the African Race," which included schools and jobs. A white Quaker man assists a slave to step out of his chains and shackles, while the implements of agricultural work with their promise of cultivated fields beyond await this newly freed worker. Seal of the Pennsylvania Society for Promoting Abolition of Slavery [E 441. A58 vol. 15 no. 1 p. 53], Historical Society of Pennsylvania.

report held that Congress had no authority to regulate slave treatment, it urged southern legislatures to pass humanitarian laws regulating the provision of food and housing and the protection of slave women and families. Southern representatives strongly objected to this third pronouncement, touching off yet another bitter public debate in Congress.

In the end, a shorter report was hammered out in debate as the formal reply to the petitioners, in which the key provision read: "The Congress have no authority to interfere in the emancipation of slaves, or in the treatment of them within any of the States; it remaining with the several States alone to provide any regulation therein, which humanity and true policy may require." The final vote on this amended report was a squeaker, with 29 ayes to 25 nays.

The Quaker groups conceded and ceased filing petitions, but a discouraged Benjamin Franklin made one last attempt to shape public opinion by writing a satirical essay for a Philadelphia newspaper. In it, the elder statesman ridiculed the proslavery speeches by transposing their exact arguments into a bogus document by a purported North African Muslim leader explaining why his country's fifty thousand Christian slaves were better off enslaved than free. It was vintage Franklin—funny, smart, and cutting. It was also Franklin's final public pronouncement; he died suddenly three weeks later, at the age of eighty-four. The congressional report launched against his 1790 petition stood for more than four decades as the silencing mechanism against any attempt at the federal level to disrupt slavery.

Questions for Consideration

1. Why did Congress answer the Quaker petitioners? Did it have to?

2. What was the result of the Quakers' efforts to abolish slavery? Do you think they were astute political strategists?

3. What was the South Carolina representative implying when he ironically referred to southern slaves and northern Quakers as "mutual bad habits and respective evils"? Do you think he was talking about slavery as an institution or slaves as people?

Connect to the Big Idea

C What powers did Congress have over the institution of slavery, according to the Constitution?

might gain literacy and knowledge, but only in the service of improved domestic duty. In Federalist America, wives and citizens alike should feel affection for and trust in their rulers; neither should ever rebel.

REVIEW How did political leaders in the 1790s attempt to overcome the divisions of the 1780s?

▶ Hamilton's Economic Policies

Compared to the severe financial instability of the 1780s, the 1790s brimmed with opportunity, as seen in improved trade, transportation, and banking. In 1790, the federal government moved from New York City to Philadelphia, a more

Republican Womanhood: Judith Sargent Murray
The young woman in this 1772 portrait became known in the 1790s as America's foremost spokeswoman for woman's equality. Judith Sargent Murray published essays under the pen name "Constantia." She argued that women had "natural powers" of mind fully the equal of men's. George Washington and John Adams each bought a copy of her collected essays published in 1798. John Singleton Copley, Portrait of Mrs. John Stevens (Judith Sargent, later Mrs. John Murray). Daniel J. Terra Art Acquisition Endowment Fund 2000.6. Terra Foundation for American Art, Chicago/Art Resource, NY.

central location with a substantial mercantile class. There, Alexander Hamilton, secretary of the treasury, embarked on multiple plans to solidify the government's economic base. But controversy ensued. His ambitious plans to fund the national debt, set up a national bank, promote manufacturing through trade laws, and raise revenue via a tax on whiskey mobilized severe opposition.

Agriculture, Transportation, and Banking

Dramatic increases in international grain prices, caused by underproduction in war-stricken Europe, motivated American farmers to boost agricultural production for the export trade. From the Connecticut River valley to the Chesapeake, farmers planted more wheat, generating new jobs for millers, coopers, dockworkers, and ship builders.

Cotton production also boomed, spurred by market demand from

Major Roads in the 1790s

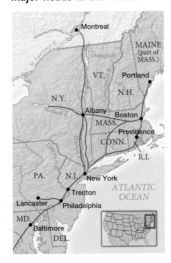

British textile manufacturers and a mechanical invention. Limited amounts of smooth-seed cotton had long been grown in the coastal areas of the South, but this variety of cotton did not prosper in the drier inland regions. Greenseed cotton grew well inland, but its rough seeds stuck to the cotton fibers and were labor-intensive to remove. In 1793, Yale graduate Eli Whitney devised a machine called a gin that easily separated out the seeds; cotton production soared, giving a boost to transatlantic trade with Britain, whose factories eagerly processed the raw cotton into cloth.

A surge of road building further stimulated the economy. Before 1790, one road connected Maine to Georgia, but with the establishment of the U.S. Post Office in 1792, road mileage increased sixfold. Private companies also built toll roads, such as the Lancaster Turnpike west of Philadelphia, the Boston-to-Albany turnpike, and a third road from Virginia to Tennessee. By 1800, a

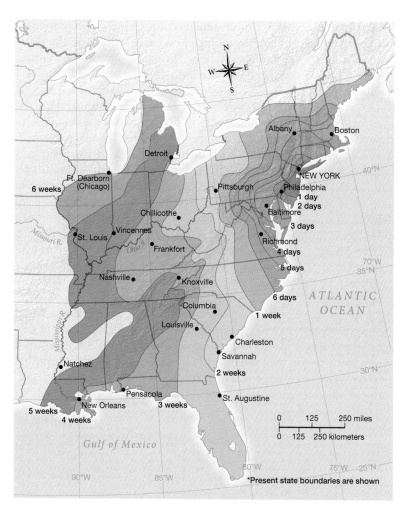

MAP ACTIVITY

Map 9.1   Travel Times From New York City in 1800

Notice that travel out of New York extends over a much greater distance in the first week than in subsequent weeks. River corridors in the West and East speeded up travel—but only going downriver. Also notice that travel by sea (along the coast) was much faster than land travel.

READING THE MAP: Compare this map to the map "Major Roads in the 1790s" (page 232) and to Map 9.2 (page 239). What physical and cultural factors account for the slower travel times west of Pittsburgh? **CONNECTIONS:** Why did Americans in the 1790s become so interested in traveling long distances? How did travel times affect the U.S. economy?

---

dense network of dirt, gravel, and plank roadways connected towns in southern New England and the Middle Atlantic states, spurring the establishment of commercial stage companies. A trip from New York to Boston took four days; from New York to Philadelphia, less than two (Map 9.1). In 1790, Boston had only three stagecoach companies; by 1800, there were twenty-four.

A third development signaling economic resurgence was the growth of commercial banking. During the 1790s, the number of banks nationwide multiplied tenfold, from three to twenty-nine in 1800. Banks drew in money chiefly through the sale of stock. They then made loans in the form of banknotes, paper currency backed by the gold and silver from stock sales. By issuing two or three times as much money in banknotes as they held in hard money, they were creating new money for the economy.

The U.S. population expanded along with economic development, propelled by large average family size and better than adequate food and land resources. As measured by the first two federal censuses in 1790 and 1800, the population grew from 3.9 million to 5.3 million, an increase of 35 percent.

The Public Debt and Taxes

The upturn in the economy, plus the new taxation powers of the government, suggested that the government might soon repay its wartime debt, amounting to more than $52 million owed to foreign and domestic creditors. But Hamilton had a different plan. He issued a *Report on Public Credit* in January 1790, recommending that the debt be funded—but not repaid immediately—at full value. This meant that old certificates of debt would be rolled over into new bonds, which would earn interest until they were retired several years later. There would still be a public debt, but it would be secure, giving its holders a direct financial stake in the new government. The bonds would circulate, injecting millions of dollars of new money into the economy. "A national debt if not excessive will be to us a national blessing; it will be a powerful cement of our union," Hamilton wrote to a financier. Hamilton's goal was to make the new country creditworthy, not debt-free.

Funding the debt in full was controversial because speculators had already bought up debt certificates cheaply, and Hamilton's report touched off further speculation. Hamilton compounded controversy with his proposal to add to the federal debt another $25 million that some state governments still owed to individuals. During the war, states had obtained supplies by issuing IOUs to farmers, merchants, and moneylenders. Some states, such as Virginia and New York, had paid off these debts entirely. Others, such as Massachusetts, had partially paid them off through heavy taxation of the people. About half the states had made little headway. Hamilton called for the federal government to assume these state debts and combine them with the federal debt, in effect consolidating federal power over the states.

Congressman James Madison strenuously objected to putting windfall profits in the pockets of speculators. He instead proposed a complex scheme to pay both the original holders of the federal debt and the speculators, each at fair fractions of the face value. He also strongly objected to assumption of all the states' debts. A large debt was dangerous, Madison warned, especially because it would lead to high taxation. Secretary of State Jefferson was also fearful of Hamilton's proposals: "No man is more ardently intent to see the public debt soon and sacredly paid off than I am. This exactly marks the difference between Colonel Hamilton's views and mine, that I would wish the debt paid tomorrow; he wishes it never to be paid, but always to be a thing where with to corrupt and manage the legislature."

A solution to this impasse arrived when Jefferson invited Hamilton and Madison to dinner. Over good food and wine, Hamilton secured the reluctant Madison's promise to restrain his opposition. In return, Hamilton pledged to back efforts to locate the nation's new capital city in

VISUAL ACTIVITY

1790 Census Page

This page summarizes the tally of the first federal census, data that determined representation in Congress and proportional taxation of the states. Notice the five classifications: free white males sixteen or older, the same under sixteen, free white females, "all other free persons," and slaves. Separating white males at sixteen provided a rough measure of military strength. U.S. Census Bureau.

READING THE IMAGE: Which northern states still had slaves? Which state had the largest population? Which had the largest white population?

CONNECTIONS: Why did the census separate males from females? Free from enslaved? Who might "all other free persons" include? Since women, children, and "all other free persons" counted for purposes of apportionment, could it be said that those groups were represented in the new government?

The Return for SOUTH CAROLINA having been made since the foregoing Schedule was originally printed, the whole Enumeration is here given complete, except for the N. Western Territory, of which no Return has yet been published.

DISTICTS	Free white Males of 16 years and upwards, including heads of families.	Free white Males under sixteen years.	Free white Females, including heads of families.	All other free persons.	Slaves.	Total.
Vermont	22435	22328	40505	255	16	85539
N. Hampshire	36086	34851	70160	630	158	141885
Maine	24384	24748	46870	538	NONE	96540
Massachusetts	95453	87289	190582	5463	NONE	378787
Rhode Island	16019	15799	32652	3407	948	68825
Connecticut	60523	54403	117448	2808	2764	237946
New York	83700	78122	152320	4654	21324	340120
New Jersey	45251	41416	83287	2762	11423	184139
Pennsylvania	110788	106948	206363	6537	3737	434373
Delaware	11783	12143	22384	3899	8887	59094
Maryland	55915	51339	101395	8043	103036	319728
Virginia	110936	116135	215046	12866	292627	747610
Kentucky	15154	17057	28922	114	12430	73677
N. Carolina	69988	77506	140710	4975	100572	393751
S. Carolina	35576	37722	66880	1801	107094	249073
Georgia	13103	14044	25739	398	29264	82548

Total number of Inhabitants of the United States exclusive of S. Western and N. Territory.	Free white Males of 21 years and upwards.	Free Males under 21 years of age.	Free white Females.	All other free persons.	Slaves.	Total.
	807094	791850	1541263	59150	694280	3893635
S. W. territory	6271	10277	15365	361	3417	35691
N. Ditto	—	—	—	—	—	—

the South, along the Potomac River, an outcome that was sure to please Virginians. In early July 1790, Congress voted for the Potomac site, and in late July Congress passed the debt package, assumption and all.

The First Bank of the United States and the *Report on Manufactures*

The second and third major elements of Hamilton's economic plan were his proposal to create a national Bank of the United States and his program to encourage domestic manufacturing. Arguing that banks were the "nurseries of national wealth," Hamilton modeled his bank plan on European central banks that used their government's money to invigorate the economy. According to Hamilton's plan, the central bank was to be capitalized at $10 million, a sum larger than all the hard money in the entire nation. The federal government would hold 20 percent of the bank's stock, making the bank in effect the government's fiscal agent, holding its revenues derived from import duties, land sales, and various other taxes. The other 80 percent of the bank's capital would come from private investors, who could buy stock in the bank with either hard money (silver or gold) or the recently funded and thus sound federal securities. Because of its size and the privilege of being the only national bank, the central bank would help stabilize the economy by exerting prudent control over credit, interest rates, and the value of the currency.

Concerned that a few rich bankers might have undue influence over the economy, Madison tried but failed to stop the plan in Congress. Jefferson advised President Washington that the Constitution did not permit Congress to charter banks. Hamilton countered that Congress had explicit powers to regulate commerce and a broad mandate "to make all laws which shall be necessary and proper for carrying into execution the foregoing powers." Washington sided with Hamilton and signed the Bank of the United States into law in February 1791, giving it a twenty-year charter.

When the bank's privately held stock went on sale in Philadelphia, Boston, and New York City in July, it sold out in a few hours, touching off a lively period of speculative trading by hundreds of urban merchants and artisans. A discouraged Madison reported that in New York "the Coffee House is an eternal buzz with the gamblers." Wide swings in the stock's price pained Jefferson. "The spirit of gaming, once it

has seized a subject, is incurable. The tailor who has made thousands in one day, tho' he has lost them the next, can never again be content with the slow and moderate earnings of his needle."

The third component of Hamilton's plan was issued in December 1791 in the *Report on Manufactures*, a proposal to encourage the production of American-made goods. Domestic manufacturing was in its infancy, and Hamilton aimed to mobilize the new powers of the federal government to grant subsidies to manufacturers and to impose moderate tariffs on those same products from overseas. Hamilton's plan targeted manufacturing of iron goods, arms and ammunition, coal, textiles, wood products, and glass. Among the blessings of manufacturing, he counted the new employment opportunities that would open to children and unmarried young women, who he assumed were underutilized in agricultural societies. The *Report on Manufactures*, however, was never approved by Congress, and indeed never even voted on. Many confirmed agriculturalists in Congress feared that manufacturing was a curse rather than a blessing. Madison and Jefferson in particular were alarmed by stretching the "general welfare" clause of the Constitution to include public subsidies to private businesses.

The Whiskey Rebellion

Hamilton's plan to restore public credit required new taxation to pay the interest on the large national debt. In deference to the merchant class, Hamilton did not propose a general increase in import duties, nor did he propose land taxes, which would have fallen hardest on the nation's wealthiest landowners. Instead, he convinced Congress in 1791 to pass a 25 percent excise tax on whiskey, to be paid by farmers bringing grain to the distillery and then passed on to whiskey consumers in higher prices. Members of Congress from eastern states favored the tax—especially New Englanders, where the favorite drink was rum. A New Hampshire representative observed that the country would be "drinking down the national debt," an idea he evidently found acceptable. More seriously, Virginia representative James Madison approved, in the hope that the tax might promote "sobriety and thereby prevent disease and untimely deaths."

Not surprisingly, the new excise tax proved unpopular. In 1791, farmers in Kentucky and the western parts of Pennsylvania, Virginia, Maryland, and the Carolinas forcefully conveyed their resentment to Congress. One farmer complained that he had already paid half his grain to the local distillery for distilling his rye, and now the distiller was taking the new whiskey tax out of the farmer's remaining half. "If this is not an oppressive tax, I am at a loss to describe what is so," the farmer wrote. Congress responded with modest modifications to the tax in 1792, but even so, discontent—along with tax evasion—was rampant. In some places, crowds threatened to tar and feather tax collectors. Four counties in Pennsylvania established committees of correspondence and held rallies. Hamilton admitted to Congress that the revenue was far less than anticipated. But rather than abandon the law, he tightened up the prosecution of tax evaders.

In western Pennsylvania, Hamilton had one ally, a stubborn tax collector named John Neville who refused to quit even after a group of spirited farmers burned him in effigy. In May 1794, Neville filed charges against seventy-five farmers and distillers for tax evasion. His action touched off the **Whiskey Rebellion**. In July, he and a federal marshal were ambushed in Allegheny County by a forty-man crowd. Neville's house was then burned down by a crowd of five hundred. At the end of July, seven thousand Pennsylvania farmers planned a march—or perhaps an attack, some thought—on Pittsburgh to protest the tax.

In response, President Washington nationalized the Pennsylvania militia and set out, with Hamilton at his side, at the head of thirteen thousand soldiers. A worried Philadelphia newspaper criticized the show of force: "Shall torrents of blood be spilled to support an odious excise system?" But in the end, no blood was spilled. By the time the army arrived in late September, the demonstrators had dispersed. No battles were fought, and no shots were exchanged. Twenty men were rounded up and charged with high treason, but only two were convicted, and Washington soon pardoned both.

Had the federal government overreacted? Thomas Jefferson thought so; he saw the event as a replay of Shays's Rebellion of 1786, when tax protesters had been met with military force (see "The Requisition of 1785 and Shays's Rebellion 1786–1787" in chapter 8). The rebel farmers agreed; they felt entitled to protest oppressive taxation. Hamilton and Washington, however, thought that laws passed by a republican government must be obeyed. To them, the Whiskey Rebellion presented an opportunity for the new federal government to flex its muscles and stand up to civil disorder.

REVIEW   Why were Hamilton's economic policies controversial?

VISUAL ACTIVITY

An Exciseman, 1792

This crude cartoon targets the hated figure of the whiskey tax collector, shown making off with two barrels of the drink. An evil imp hooks him by the nose to deliver him to the gallows where is he roasted over a flaming barrel of whiskey. © Philadelphia History Museum at the Atwater Kent/The Bridgeman Art Library.

READING THE IMAGE: The words above the two small figures on the right read, "Let us tar and feather the rascal." Are they equipped to carry out that threat? What punishment does the tax collector experience in addition to being hanged, according to the picture on the left?

CONNECTIONS: Why might ordinary citizens have targeted the tax collector? Where else could citizens go to complain about excessive federal taxation?

▶ Conflict on America's Borders and Beyond

While the whiskey rebels challenged federal leadership from within the country, disorder threatened the United States from external sources as well. From 1789 onward, serious trouble brewed in four directions. To the southwest, the loosely confederated Creek Indians pushed back against the westward-moving white southern population, giving George Washington an opportunity to test diplomacy. To the northwest, a powerful confederation of Indian tribes in the Ohio Country fiercely resisted white encroachment, resulting in a brutal war. At the same time, conflicts between the major European powers forced Americans to take sides and nearly pulled the country into another war. And to the south, a Caribbean slave rebellion raised fears that racial war would be imported to the United States. Despite these grave prospects, Washington won reelection to the presidency unanimously in the fall of 1792.

Creeks in the Southwest

An urgent task of the new government was to take charge of Indian affairs while avoiding the costs of warfare. Some twenty thousand Indians affiliated with the Creeks occupied lands extending from Georgia into what is now Mississippi, and border skirmishes with land-hungry Georgians were becoming a frequent occurrence. Washington and his secretary of war, Henry Knox, singled out one Creek chief, Alexander McGillivray, and sent a delegation to Georgia for preliminary treaty negotiations.

McGillivray had a mixed-race history that prepared him to be a major cultural broker. His French-Creek mother conferred a legitimate claim to Creek leadership, while his Scottish fur-trading father provided exposure to literacy and numeracy. Fluent in English and near fluent in Spanish, McGillivray spoke several Creek languages and had even studied Greek and Latin. In the 1770s, he worked for the British distributing gifts to various southern tribes; in the 1780s, he gained renown for brokering negotiations with the Spanish in Florida.

The chief reluctantly met with Knox's delegates and spurned the substantial concessions the American negotiators offered, chief among them a guarantee of the Creeks' extensive tribal lands. McGillivray sent the negotiators away, enjoying, as he wrote to a Spanish trader, the

Alexander McGillivray, 1790
Artist John Trumbull approached the Creek delegation in New York City for treaty negotiations and asked them to sit for individual portraits. They "possessed a dignity of manner, form, countenance and expression, worthy of Roman Senators," Trumbull recalled, but all declined. So the artist made five drawings "by stealth." McGillivray here wears an American military coat, a present from President Washington. The New York Public Library/Art Resource, NY.

spectacle of the self-styled "masters of the new world" having "to bend and supplicate for peace at the feet of a people whom shortly before they despised."

A year later, Secretary Knox reopened diplomatic relations. To coax McGillivray to the treaty table, Knox invited him to New York City to meet with the president. McGillivray arrived in a triumphal procession of various lesser Creek chiefs and was accorded the honors of a head of state.

The negotiations stretched out for a month, resulting in the 1790 Treaty of New York that looked much like Knox's original plan: Creek tribal lands were guaranteed, with a promise of boundary protection by federal troops against land-seeking settlers. The Creeks were assured of annual payments in money and trade goods, including "domestic animals and implements of husbandry"—words that hinted at a future time when the Creeks would become more agricultural and thus less in need of expansive hunting grounds.

The Creeks promised to accept the United States alone as its trading partner, shutting out Spain.

Actually, both sides had made promises they could not keep. McGillivray figured that the Creeks' interests were best served by maintaining creative tension between the American and Spanish authorities, and by 1792, he had signed an agreement with the Spanish governor of New Orleans, in which each side offered mutual pledges to protect against encroachments by Georgia settlers. By the time Alexander McGillivray died in 1793, his purported leadership of the Creeks was in serious question, and the Treaty of New York joined the list of treaties never implemented. Its promise of federal protection of Creek boundaries was unrealistic from the start, and its pledge of full respect for Creek sovereignty also was only a promise on paper.

At the very start of the new government, in dealing with the Creeks, Washington and Knox tried to find a different way to approach Indian affairs, one rooted more in British than in American experience. But in the end, the demographic imperative of explosive white population growth and westward-moving, land-seeking settlers, together with the economic imperative of land speculation, meant that confrontation with the native population was nearly inevitable. As Washington wrote in 1796, "I believe scarcely any thing short of a Chinese Wall, or line of Troops will restrain Land Jobbers, and the encroachment of Settlers, upon Indian Territory."

Ohio Indians in the Northwest

Tribes of the Ohio Valley were even less willing to negotiate with the new federal government. Left vulnerable by the 1784 Treaty of Fort Stanwix (see "The Treaty of Fort Stanwix" in chapter 8), in which Iroquois tribes in New York had relinquished Ohio lands to the Americans, the Shawnee, Delaware, Miami, and other groups local to Ohio stood their ground. To confuse matters further, British troops still occupied half a dozen forts in the northwest, protecting an ongoing fur trade between British traders and Indians and thereby sustaining Indians' claims to that land.

Under the terms of the Northwest Ordinance (see "Land Ordinances and the Northwest Territory" in chapter 8), the federal government started to survey and map eastern Ohio, and settlers were eager to buy. So Washington sent units of the U.S. Army into Ohio's western half, to subdue the various tribes. Fort Washington, built on the Ohio River in 1789 at the site of

present-day Cincinnati, became the command post for three major invasions of Indian country (Map 9.2). The first occurred in the fall of 1790, when General Josiah Harmar marched with 1,400 men into Ohio's northwest region, burning Indian villages. His inexperienced troops were ambushed by Miami and Shawnee Indians led by their chiefs, Little Turtle and Blue Jacket. Harmar lost one-eighth of his soldiers and retreated.

Harmar's defeat spurred enhanced efforts to clear Ohio for permanent American settlement. General Arthur St. Clair, the military governor of the Northwest Territory, had pursued peaceful tactics in the 1780s, signing treaties with Indians for land in eastern Ohio—dubious treaties, as it happened, since the Indian negotiators were not authorized to yield land. In the wake of Harmar's bungled operation, St. Clair geared up for military action, and in the fall of 1791 he and two thousand men (accompanied by two hundred women camp followers) traveled north from Fort Washington along Harmar's route, erecting two more fortified structures—Fort Jefferson and Fort Hamilton—deep in Indian country. Despite that show of military might, a surprise attack by Indians at the headwaters of the Wabash River left 55 percent of the Americans dead or wounded; only three of the women escaped alive. "The savages seemed not to fear anything we could do," wrote an officer afterward. "The ground was literally covered with the dead." The Indians captured valuable weaponry and scalped and dismembered the dying on the field of battle. With more than nine hundred lives lost, this was the most stunning American loss in the history of the U.S. Indian wars.

Washington doubled the U.S. military presence in Ohio and appointed a new commander, General Anthony Wayne of Pennsylvania, nicknamed "Mad Anthony" for his headstrong, hard-drinking style of leadership. About the Ohio natives, Wayne wrote, "I have always been of the opinion that we never should have a permanent peace with those Indians until they were made to experience our superiority." Throughout 1794, Wayne's army engaged in skirmishes with various tribes. Chief Little Turtle of the Miami tribe advised negotiation; in his view, Wayne's large army looked overpowering. But Blue Jacket of the Shawnees counseled continued warfare, and his view prevailed.

The decisive action came in August 1794 at the battle of Fallen Timbers, near the Maumee River, where a recent tornado had felled many trees. The confederated Indians—mainly Ottawas, Potawatomis, Shawnees, and Delawares numbering around eight hundred—ambushed the

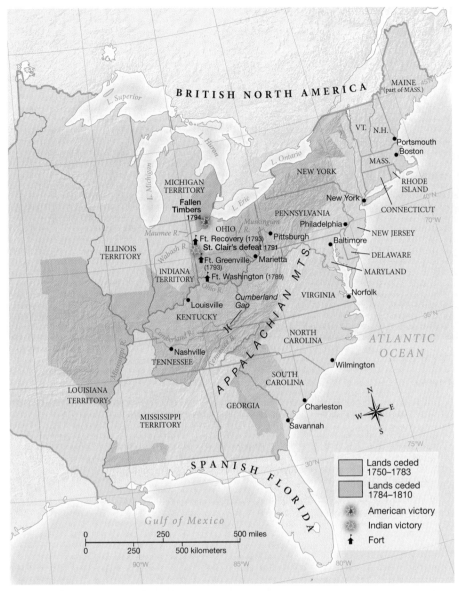

Map legend:
- Lands ceded 1750–1783
- Lands ceded 1784–1810
- American victory
- Indian victory
- Fort

Americans but were underarmed, and Wayne's troops made effective use of their guns and bayonets. The Indians withdrew and sought refuge at nearby Fort Miami, still held by the British, but their former allies locked the gate and refused protection. The surviving Indians fled to the woods, their ranks decimated.

Fallen Timbers was a major defeat for the Indians. The Americans had destroyed cornfields and villages on the march north, and with winter approaching, the Indians' confidence was sapped. They reentered negotiations in a much less powerful bargaining position. In 1795, about a thousand Indians representing nearly a dozen tribes met with Wayne and other American emissaries to work out the **Treaty of Greenville**. The Americans offered treaty goods (calico shirts, axes, knives, blankets, kettles, mirrors, ribbons, thimbles, and abundant wine and liquor casks) worth $25,000 and promised additional shipments every year. The government's idea was to create a dependency on American goods to keep the Indians friendly. In exchange, the Indians ceded most of Ohio to the Americans; only the northwest part of the territory was reserved solely for the Indians.

The treaty brought temporary peace to the region, but it did not restore a peaceful life to the Indians. The annual allowance from the United States too often came in the form of liquor. "More of us have died since the Treaty of Greenville than we lost by the years of war before, and it is all owing to the introduction of liquor among

VISUAL ACTIVITY

Treaty of Greenville, 1795

This contemporary painting purports to depict the signing of the Treaty of Greenville. An American officer kneels and writes—not a likely posture for drafting a treaty. One Indian gestures emphatically as if to dictate terms, but in fact the treaty was completely favorable to the United States. Although Indians from a dozen Ohio tribes gathered at the signing ceremony, this picture shows very few Indians. © Chicago History Museum, USA/The Bridgeman Art Library.

READING THE IMAGE: How likely is it that the artist actually witnessed the signing of the treaty? Are there clues in the painting that offer evidence?

CONNECTIONS: How did the Jay Treaty of 1795 (page 242) influence the Indians' willingness to capitulate to an unfavorable treaty with the U.S. government?

us," said Chief Little Turtle in 1800. "This liquor that they introduce into our country is more to be feared than the gun and tomahawk."

France and Britain

While Indian battles engaged the American military in the west, another war overseas to the east was also closely watched. In 1789, monarchy came under attack in France, bringing on a revolution whose democratic ideals inspired Americans in many states to celebrate the victory of the French people. Dozens of pro-French political clubs, called Democratic or Republican Societies, sprang up around the country. Even fashions expressed symbolic solidarity, causing some American women to don sashes and cockades made with ribbons of the French Revolution's

red, white, and blue colors. Pro-French headgear for committed women included an elaborate turban, leading one horrified Federalist newspaper editor to chastise the "fiery frenchified dames" thronging Philadelphia's streets. In Charleston, South Carolina, a pro-French pageant in 1793 united two women as partners, one representing France and the other America. The women repudiated their husbands "on account of ill treatment" and "conceived the design of living together in the strictest union and friendship." Most likely, this ceremony was not the country's first civil union but instead a richly metaphorical piece of street theater in which the spurned husbands represented the French and British monarchs. In addition to these symbolic actions, the growing exchange of political and intellectual ideas across the Atlantic helped plant

Revolutionary Solidarity
In the early 1790s, Americans enthused by the French Revolution might accessorize with a tricolor cockade—a distinctive bow made from red, white, and blue ribbons. Parisian revolutionary fashions (as shown in this French picture) were copied and worn in American cities. Such clothing made an easily grasped statement about political partisanship. Bibliothèque Nationale de France.

the seeds of a woman's rights movement in America (see "Beyond America's Borders," page 242).

Anti–French Revolution sentiments also ran deep. Vice President John Adams, who lived in France in the 1780s, trembled to think of radicals in France or America. "Too many Frenchmen, after the example of too many Americans, pant for the equality of persons and property," Adams said. "The impracticability of this, God Almighty has decreed, and the advocates for liberty, who attempt it, will surely suffer for it."

Support for the French Revolution remained a matter of personal conviction until 1793, when Britain and France went to war and divided loyalties now framed critical foreign policy debates. Pro-French Americans remembered France's critical help during the American Revolution and wanted to offer aid now. But those shaken by the report of the guillotining of thousands of French people—including the monarch—as well as those with strong commercial ties to Britain sought ways to stay neutral.

In May 1793, President Washington issued the Neutrality Proclamation, which contained friendly assurances to both sides, in an effort to stay out of European wars. Yet American ships continued to trade between the French West Indies and France. In early 1794, the British expressed their displeasure by capturing more than three hundred of these vessels near the West Indies. Clearly, the president thought, something had to be done to assert American power.

Washington tapped John Jay, the chief justice of the Supreme Court and a man of strong pro-British sentiments, to negotiate commercial relations in the British West Indies and secure compensation for the seized American ships. Jay was also directed to address southerners' demands for reimbursement for the slaves evacuated by

France, Britain, and Woman's Rights in the 1790s

During the 1770s and 1780s, no one in America wondered publicly about rights for women. Boycotts by the Daughters of Liberty before the Revolution did not challenge gender hierarchy, nor did New Jersey's handful of women voters (see "Who Are 'the People'?" in chapter 8). It took radical ideas from France and Britain to spark new ideas challenging women's subordinate status in American society.

In France between 1789 and 1793, the revolution against monarchy enlarged ideas about citizenship and led some women to call themselves citoyennes, female citizens. Women's political clubs, such as the Society of Republican Revolutionary Women in Paris, sent petitions and gave speeches to the National Assembly, demanding education, voting rights, and a curbing of patriarchal powers of men over women. In 1791, Frenchwoman Olympe de Gouges rewrote the male revolutionaries' document *The Declaration of the Rights of Man into The Rights of Woman*, a manifesto asserting that "all women are born free and remain equal to men in rights." Another prominent woman, Anne Josèphe Théroigne de Méricourt, maintained a political salon (intellectual gathering), marched around Paris in masculine riding attire, and

addressed crowds engaged in violent street actions. Her vision went beyond political rights to the social customs that dictated women's subordination: "It is time for women to break out of the shameful incompetence in which men's ignorance, pride, and injustice have so long held us captive."

Although the male National Assembly never approved voting rights for French women in that era, it did reform French civil and family law in the early 1790s. Marriage was removed from the control of the church, divorce was legalized, and the age of majority for women was lowered. A far-reaching change in inheritance law required division of a patriarch's estate among all his children, regardless of age, sex, and even legitimacy. By contrast, most American states adopted traditional English family law virtually unchanged.

French feminism traveled across the Channel to Britain and inspired the talented Mary Wollstonecraft. Born into a respectable but downwardly mobile family, Wollstonecraft took work as a governess before establishing herself as a writer in London. There she met the radical Thomas Paine and the philosopher William Godwin, along with other leading

artists and intellectuals. In 1792, she published *A Vindication of the Rights of Woman*, offering a contrast to Paine's 1791 book *The Rights of Man*. Paine wrote about property and politics as fundamental rights and never considered women; Wollstonecraft argued that women also had inherent rights. She spoke forcefully about the intellectual equality of the sexes that would become evident once women could get an equal education. She championed female economic independence and, most radically, suggested that traditional marriage at its worst was legalized prostitution.

Wollstonecraft's book created an immediate sensation in America. Excerpts appeared in periodicals, bookstores stocked the London edition, and by 1795 there were three American reprints. Some women readers were cautious. A sixty-year-old Philadelphian, Elizabeth Drinker, reflected in her diary that Wollstonecraft "speaks my mind" on some issues but not others; "I am not for quite so much independence." A youthful Priscilla Mason delivered a commencement address at her academy, inspired by Wollstonecraft to condemn "the high and mighty lords" (men) who denied women education and professional opportunities. "Happily, a

---

the British during the war as well as western settlers' demands to end the British occupation of frontier forts and their continuing involvement in the northwest fur trade.

Jay returned from his diplomatic mission with a treaty that no one could love. First, the **Jay Treaty** completely failed to address the captured cargoes or the lost property in slaves. Second, it granted the British a lenient eighteen months

to withdraw from the frontier forts. (Despite that leniency, this provision projecting the end of British presence in the Northwest disheartened the Indians negotiating the Treaty of Greenville in Ohio and loomed as a significant factor in their decision to make peace.) Finally, the treaty called for repayment with interest of the debts that some American planters still owed to British firms dating from the Revolutionary War.

FRONTISPIECE.

Publish'd at Philad? *Decr 1st 1792.*

Woman's Rights in the *Lady's Magazine*, 1792
A Philadelphia periodical published this engraving to accompany excerpts from Mary Wollstonecraft's *A Vindication of the Rights of Woman*. The kneeling woman in eighteenth-century garb holds out a paper entitled "Rights of Woman" to Lady Liberty, imploring her to embrace this new concept. Notice the objects arranged below Lady Liberty. What do they suggest about the picture's interpretation of the "rights of woman"? Library of Congress.

The interest in the rights of woman faded fast, however. The unhappy fate of de Gouges, guillotined in France in 1794, was soon followed by news of Wollstonecraft's death in childbirth in 1797. Soon thereafter, William Godwin, father of her infant daughter, published details of her unconventional personal life: love affairs, two children conceived out of wedlock, and two suicide attempts. "Her licentious practice renders her memory odious to every friend of virtue," declared a prominent American minister in 1801, shutting down nearly all possibility for continued public admiration of Wollstonecraft and her ideas about women.

America in a Global Context

1. Contrast the radical ideas of Mary Wollstonecraft with the more moderate concept of "republican motherhood," which summarizes American women's contributions to civil society and family life.

2. Why might Wollstonecraft's unconventional personal life have cast doubt on the value of her ideas about the rights of woman?

Connect to the Big Idea

C How did the struggle for woman's rights reflect the struggle to define the new American nation?

more liberal way of thinking begins to prevail," Mason predicted.

Male readers' responses were also varied. Aaron Burr, a senator from New York, called Wollstonecraft's book "a work of genius." A Fourth of July speaker in New Jersey in 1793 proclaimed that "the Rights of Woman are no longer strange sounds to an American ear" and called for revisions in state law codes. Critics of Wollstonecraft were not in short supply. A New York orator on that same July Fourth rejected Wollstonecraft with the claim that woman's rights really meant a woman's duty "to submit to the control of that government she has voluntarily chosen"—namely, the government of a husband.

In exchange for such generous terms, Jay secured limited trading rights in the West Indies and agreement that some issues—boundary disputes with Canada and the damage and loss claims of shipowners—would be decided later by arbitration commissions.

When newspapers published the terms of the treaty, powerful opposition quickly emerged. Citizens' petitions, newspaper editorials, and public gatherings mobilized public opinion from North to South to a degree not seen before in the early Republic. The debate raised the question of whether citizens could presume to instruct elected officials, or whether they had to accept the judgment of those officials and await the next election to register their displeasure. The negative reactions got ugly. In Massachusetts, disrespectful graffiti ("Damn John Jay!") appeared on walls, and effigies of Jay along with copies of the treaty were ceremoniously burned in noisy street demonstrations. When the Senate passed the treaty in mid-1795 by a vote of 20 to 10, a bare minimum of the two-thirds majority required, and the president signed it, the anti-Treaty opposition among many ordinary citizens refused to evaporate.

The controversy continued well into 1796. Opponents of the Jay Treaty in the House of Representatives called for hearings on the matter, demanding that the president disclose secret diplomatic documents. Washington refused. The House lacked constitutional authority to vote on treaties, but it did have primary power over all spending bills. Anti–Jay Treaty congressmen hoped to hamstring the hated agreement by defunding its key provisions. In the end, the final vote on appropriations for the treaty passed, but only by a 3-vote margin.

The year-long struggle over the Jay Treaty revealed an emerging and as yet uncharted role in politics for public opinion, voiced by an aroused citizenry and frequently managed and shaped by newspaper editors and local political clubs. It also brought to the fore a bitter division among elected politicians that emerged along the same lines as the Hamilton-Jefferson split on economic policy.

The Haitian Revolution

In addition to the Indian troubles and the European war across the Atlantic, another bloody conflict to the south polarized and even terrorized many Americans in the 1790s. The French colony of Saint Domingue, in the western third of the large Caribbean island of Hispaniola, became engulfed in revolution starting in 1791. Bloody war raged for more than a decade, resulting in 1804 in the birth of the Republic of Haiti, the first and only independent black state to arise out of a successful slave revolution.

The **Haitian Revolution** was a complex event involving many participants, including the diverse local population and, eventually, three European countries. Some 30,000 whites dominated the island in 1790, running sugar and coffee plantations with close to

half a million blacks, two-thirds of them of African birth. The white French colonists were not the only plantation owners, however. About 28,000 free mixed-race people (*gens de couleur*) owned one-third of the island's plantations and nearly a quarter of the slave labor force. Despite their economic status, these mixed-race planters were barred from political power, but they aspired to it.

The French Revolution of 1789 was the immediate catalyst for rebellion in this already tense society. First, white colonists challenged the white royalist government in an effort to link Saint Domingue with the new revolutionary government in France. Next, the mixed-race planters rebelled in 1791, demanding equal civil rights with the whites. No sooner was this revolt viciously suppressed than another part of the island's population rose up; thousands of slaves armed with machetes and torches wreaked devastation. In 1793, the civil war escalated to include French, Spanish, and British troops fighting the inhabitants and also one another. Led by former slave Toussaint L'Ouverture, slaves and free blacks in alliance with Spain occupied the northern regions of the island, leaving a thousand plantations in ruins and tens of thousands of people dead. Thousands of white and mixed-race planters, along with some of their slaves, fled to Spanish Louisiana and southern cities in the United States.

White Americans followed the revolution in horror through newspapers and refugees' accounts. A few sympathized with the impulse for liberty, but many more feared that violent black insurrection might spread to the United States. Many black American slaves also followed the revolution, for the news of the success of a first-ever massive revolution by slaves traveled quickly in this oral culture.

The Haitian Revolution provoked naked fear of a race war in white southerners. Jefferson, agonizing over the contagion of liberty in 1797, wrote another Virginia slaveholder that "if something is not done, and soon done, we shall be the murderers of our own children . . . ; the revolutionary storm, now sweeping the globe, will be upon us, and happy if we make timely provision to give it an easy passage over our land. From the present state of things in Europe and America, the day which brings our combus-

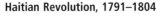

Haitian Revolution, 1791–1804

CUBA
(Sp.)

HISPANIOLA   ATLANTIC
              OCEAN
Le Cap • • Fort Dauphin
SAINT
DOMINGUE   SANTO
(France)   DOMINGO
              (Spain)
Port-au-Prince

Caribbean Sea

Beginning of slave revolt, 1791

Border of Saint Domingue/
Santo Domingo, 1790

Border of Haiti/
Santo Domingo, 1820

Toussaint L'Ouverture
This French engraving made around 1800 depicts the Haitian leader in full military dress and feathered hat commandingly issuing a document to French officers. Library of Congress.

▶ Federalists and Republicans

By the mid-1790s, polarization over Hamilton's economic program, the French Revolution, Haiti, and most crucially the Jay Treaty had led to two distinct and consistent rival political groups: **Federalists** and **Republicans**. Federalist leaders supported Britain in foreign policy and commercial interests at home, while Republicans rooted for liberty in France and worried about monarchical Federalists at home. The labels did not yet describe full-fledged political parties; such division was still thought to be a sign of failure of the experiment in government. Yet newspapers increasingly backed one group or the other; party lines were being drawn. Washington's decision not to seek a third term led to serious partisan electioneering in the presidential and congressional elections of 1796. Federalist John Adams won the presidency, but party strife accelerated over failed diplomacy in France, bringing the country to the brink of war. Pro-war and antiwar antagonism created a major crisis over political free speech, militarism, and fears of sedition and treason.

tion must be near at hand; and only a single spark is wanting to make that day to-morrow."

Jefferson's cataclysmic fears were not shared by New Englanders. Timothy Pickering of Massachusetts, in Washington's cabinet since 1795, chastised the inconsistent Jefferson for supporting French revolutionaries while condemning black Haitians fighting for freedom just because they had "a skin not colored like our own." Not that Pickering supported either type of violent revolutionary—he did not. But he and his political allies, soon to be called the Federalists, were far more willing to contemplate trade and diplomatic relations with the emerging black republic of Haiti.

REVIEW   Why did the United States feel vulnerable to international threats in the 1790s?

The Election of 1796

Washington struggled to appear to be above party politics, and in his farewell address he stressed the need to maintain a "unity of government" reflecting a unified body politic. He also urged the country to "steer clear of permanent alliances with any portion of the foreign world." The leading contenders for his position, John Adams of Massachusetts and Thomas Jefferson of Virginia, in theory agreed with him, but around them raged a party contest split along pro-British versus pro-French lines.

Adams and Jefferson were not adept politicians in the modern sense, skilled in the arts of persuasion and intrigue. Bruised by his conflicts with Hamilton, Jefferson had resigned as secretary of state in 1793 and retreated to Monticello, his home in Virginia. Adams's job as vice presi-

John and Abigail Adams
The artist Gilbert Stuart painted these portraits in 1800; Adams was sixty-five and his wife was fifty-six. A friend once listed Adams's shortcomings as a politician: "He can't dance, drink, game, flatter, promise, dress, swear with gentlemen, and small talk and flirt with the ladies." But luckily, Adams had a secret weapon to keep him resilient: Abigail, his wife, a woman of astute intellect and wisdom. National Gallery of Art, Washington, D.C.

dent kept him closer to the political action, but his personality often put people off. He was temperamental, thin-skinned, and quick to take offense.

The leading Federalists informally caucused and chose Adams as their candidate, with Thomas Pinckney of South Carolina to run with him. The Republicans in Congress settled on Aaron Burr of New York to pair with Jefferson. The Constitution did not anticipate parties and tickets. Instead, each electoral college voter could cast two votes for any two candidates, but on only one ballot. The top vote-getter became president, and the next-highest assumed the vice presidency. (This procedural flaw was corrected by the Twelfth Amendment, adopted in 1804.) With only one ballot, careful maneuvering was required to make sure that the chief rivals for the presidency did not land in the top two spots.

A failed effort by Alexander Hamilton to influence the outcome of the election landed the country in just such a position. Hamilton did not trust Adams; he preferred Pinckney, and he tried to influence southern electors to throw their support to the South Carolinian. But his plan backfired: Adams was elected president with 71 electoral votes; Jefferson came in second with 68 and thus became vice president. Pinckney got 59 votes, while Burr trailed with 30.

Adams's inaugural speech pledged neutrality in foreign affairs and respect for the French people, which made Republicans hopeful. To please Federalists, Adams retained three cabinet members from Washington's administration—the secretaries of state, treasury, and war. But the three were Hamilton loyalists, passing off Hamilton's judgments and advice as their own to the unwitting Adams. Vice President Jefferson extended a conciliatory hand to Adams, but the Hamiltonian cabinet ruined the honeymoon. Jefferson's advice was spurned, and he withdrew from active counsel of the president.

The XYZ Affair

From the start, Adams's presidency was in crisis. France retaliated for the British-friendly Jay Treaty by abandoning its 1778 alliance with the United States. French privateers—armed private vessels—started detaining American ships carrying British goods; by March 1797, more than three hundred American vessels had been seized. To avenge these insults, Federalists started murmuring openly about war with France. Adams preferred negotiations and dispatched a three-man commission to France in the fall of 1797. But at the same time, he asked Congress to approve expenditures on increased naval defense.

When the three American commissioners arrived in Paris, French officials would not receive them. Finally, the French minister of foreign affairs, Talleyrand, sent three French agents—unnamed and later known to the American public as X, Y, and Z—to the American commissioners with the information that $250,000 might grease the wheels of diplomacy and that a $12 million loan to the French government would be the price of a peace treaty. Incensed, the commissioners brought news of the bribery attempt to the president.

Americans reacted to the **XYZ affair** with shock and anger. Even staunch pro-French Republicans began to reevaluate their allegiance. The Federalist-dominated Congress appropriated money for an army of ten thousand soldiers and repealed all prior treaties with France. In 1798, twenty naval warships launched the United States into its first undeclared war, called the Quasi-War by historians to underscore its uncertain legal status. The main scene of action was the Caribbean, where more than one hundred French ships were captured.

There was no home-front unity in this time of undeclared war; antagonism only intensified between Federalists and Republicans. Because the chance of a land invasion by France seemed remote, some Republicans began to fear that the Federalists wanted that enlarged army to threaten domestic dissenters. Adams's cabinet strenuously backed the army build-up, making the president increasingly mistrustful of their advice. He was beginning to suspect that his cabinet was more loyal to Hamilton than to himself.

Party antagonism in the realm of public opinion spiraled out of control. Republican newspapers heaped abuse on Adams. One denounced him as "a person without patriotism, without philosophy, and a mock monarch." Pro-French mobs roamed the streets of Philadelphia, the capital, and Adams, fearing for his personal safety, stocked weapons in his presidential quarters. Federalists, too, went on the offensive. In Newburyport, Massachusetts, they lit a huge bonfire and burned issues of the state's Republican newspapers. Officers in a New York militia unit drank a menacing toast on July 4, 1798: "One and but one party in the United States." A Federalist editor ominously declared that "he who is not for us is against us."

The Alien and Sedition Acts

With tempers so dangerously high and fears that political dissent was akin to treason, Federalist leaders moved to muffle the opposition. In mid-1798, Congress passed the Sedition Act, which not only made conspiracy and revolt illegal but also criminalized any speech or words that defamed the president or Congress. One Federalist warned of the threat that existed "to overturn and ruin the government by publishing the most shameless falsehoods against the representatives of the people." In all, twenty-

five men, almost all Republican newspaper editors, were charged with sedition; twelve were convicted. (See "Documenting the American Promise," page 248.)

Congress also passed two Alien Acts. The first extended the waiting period for an alien to achieve citizenship from five to fourteen years and required all aliens to register with the federal government. The second empowered the president in time of war to deport or imprison without trial any foreigner suspected of being a danger to the United States. The clear intent of these laws was to harass French immigrants already in the United States and to discourage others from coming.

Republicans strongly opposed the **Alien and Sedition Acts** on the grounds that the acts conflicted with the Bill of Rights, but they did not have the votes to revoke the acts in Congress, nor could the federal judiciary, dominated by Federalist judges, be counted on to challenge them. Jefferson and Madison turned to the state legislatures, the only other competing political arena, to press their opposition. Each man anonymously drafted a set of resolutions condemning the acts and convinced the legislatures of Virginia and Kentucky to present them to the federal government in late fall 1798. The **Virginia and Kentucky Resolutions** tested the novel argument that state legislatures have the right to judge and even nullify the constitutionality of federal laws, bold claims that held risk that one or both men could be accused of sedition. The resolutions in fact made little dent in the Alien and Sedition Acts, but the idea of a state's right to nullify federal law did not disappear. It would resurface several times in decades to come, most notably in a major tariff dispute in 1832 and in the sectional arguments that led to the Civil War.

Amid all the war hysteria and sedition fears in 1798, President Adams regained his balance. He was uncharacteristically restrained in pursuing opponents under the Sedition Act, and he finally refused to declare war on France, as extreme Federalists wished. No doubt he was beginning to realize how much he had been the dupe of Hamilton. He also shrewdly realized that France was not eager for war and that a peaceful settlement might be close at hand. In January 1799, a peace initiative from France arrived in the form of a letter assuring Adams that diplomatic channels were open again and that new peace commissioners would be welcomed in France.

Adams accepted this overture and appointed new negotiators. By late 1799, the Quasi-War

The Crisis of 1798: Sedition

Republican newspaper editors criticized President John Adams with such venomous insults that civil war appeared possible. Federalists in Congress thus criminalized seditious words as a means to preserve the country. Republicans just redoubled their opposition.

DOCUMENT 1
Abigail Adams Complains of Sedition, 1798

A beleaguered Abigail Adams called repeatedly in letters to her sister for a sedition law to silence Benjamin Bache, editor of the Philadelphia Aurora.

(April 26): . . . Yet dairingly do the vile incendaries keep up in Baches paper the most wicked and base, voilent & calumniating abuse. . . . But nothing will have an Effect until Congress passes a Sedition Bill. . . . (April 28): . . . We are now wonderfully popular except with Bache & Co who in his paper calls the President old, querilous, Bald, blind, cripled, Toothless Adams. (May 10): . . . This Bache is cursing & abusing daily. If that fellow . . . is not surpressd, we shall come to a civil war. (May 26): . . . I wish the Laws of our Country were competant to punish the stirer up of sedition, the writer and Printer of base and unfounded calumny. . . . (June 19): . . . In any other Country Bache & all his papers would have been seazd and ought to be here, but congress are dilly dallying about passing a Bill enabling the President to seize suspisious persons, and their papers.

Source: *New Letters of Abigail Adams, 1788–1801*, edited by Stewart Mitchell, pp. 165, 167, 172, 179, 193. Copyright © 1974 by The American Antiquarian Society. Reprinted by permission of Houghton Mifflin Company. All rights reserved.

DOCUMENT 2
The Sedition Act of 1798

On July 14, Congress made sedition with malicious intent a federal crime.

SECTION 1. . . . if any persons shall unlawfully combine or conspire together, with intent to oppose any measure or measures of the government of the United States . . . , or to intimidate or prevent any person holding . . . office in or under the government of the United States, from undertaking, performing or executing his trust or duty, and if any person or persons, with intent as aforesaid, shall counsel, advise or attempt to procure any insurrection, riot, unlawful assembly. . . , he or they shall be deemed guilty of a high misdemeanor, and on conviction . . . shall be punished by a fine not exceeding five thousand dollars, and by imprisonment during a term not less than six months nor exceeding five years. . . .

SEC. 2. . . . If any person shall write, print, utter or publish . . . , any false, scandalous and malicious writing or writings against the government of the United States, or either house of the Congress of the United States, or the President of the United States, with intent to defame the said government . . . or to bring them . . . into contempt or disrepute; or to excite against them . . . the hatred of the good people of the United States . . . , then such person, being thereof convicted . . . shall be punished by a fine not exceeding two thousand dollars, and by imprisonment not exceeding two years.

Source: Excerpted text from congressional bill, July 14, 1798.

DOCUMENT 3
Matthew Lyon Criticizes John Adams, 1798

Matthew Lyon, congressman from Vermont, criticized Adams and was charged with sedition. Handed a four-month sentence and a fine of $1,000, Lyon ran for reelection from his cell—and won.

. . . Whenever I shall, on the part of the Executive, see every consideration of the public welfare swallowed up with France had subsided, and in 1800 the negotiations resulted in a treaty declaring "a true and sincere friendship" between the United States and France. But Federalists were not pleased; Adams lost the support of a significant part of his own party and sealed his fate as the first one-term president of the United States.

in a continual grasp for power, in an unbounded thirst for ridiculous pomp, foolish adulation, or selfish avarice; when I shall behold men of real merit daily turned out of office for no other cause but independence of sentiment; when I shall see men of firmness, merit, years, abilities, and experience, discarded on their application for office, for fear they possess that independence; . . . when I shall see the sacred name of religion employed as a State engine to make mankind hate and persecute one another, I shall not be their humble advocate.

Source: Matthew Lyon, Letter in *Spooner's Vermont Journal*, July 31, 1798. Quoted in *Matthew Lyon: New Man of the Democratic Revolution, 1749–1822* by Aleine Austin, pp. 108–9. Copyright © 1981 Aleine Austin. Reprinted with permission of Pennsylvania State University Press.

Source: Matthew Lyon, Essay in *Spooner's Vermont Journal*, July 31, 1798, pp. 1–2.

DOCUMENT 4
The Virginia Resolution, December 24, 1798

James Madison drafted the Virginia Resolution and had a trusted ally present it to the Virginia legislature, dominated by Republicans. (Jefferson did the same for Kentucky.) The document denounces the Alien and Sedition Acts and declares that states have the right to "interpose" to stop unconstitutional actions by the federal government.

RESOLVED . . . That this assembly most solemnly declares a warm attachment to the Union of the States, to maintain which it pledges all its powers; and that for this end, it is their duty to watch over and oppose every infraction of those principles which constitute the only basis of that Union, because a faithful observance of them, can alone secure its existence and the public happiness.

That this Assembly doth explicitly and peremptorily declare, that it views the powers of the federal government, as resulting from the compact, to which the states are parties; as limited by the plain sense and intention of the instrument constituting the compact; . . . and that in case of a deliberate, palpable, and dangerous exercise of other powers, not granted by the said compact, the states who are parties thereto, have the right, and are in duty bound, to interpose for arresting the progress of

the evil, and for maintaining within their respective limits, the authorities, rights and liberties appertaining to them. . . .

That the General Assembly doth particularly protest against the palpable and alarming infractions of the Constitution, in the two late cases of the "Alien and Sedition Acts" . . . ; the first of which exercises a power no where delegated to the federal government . . . ; and the other . . . exercises in like manner, a power not delegated by the constitution, but on the contrary, expressly and positively forbidden by one of the amendments thereto; a power, which more than any other, ought to produce universal alarm, because it is levelled against that right of freely examining public characters and measures, and of free communication among the people thereon, which has ever been justly deemed, the only effectual guardian of every other right.

Source: Avalon Project, Yale Law School, 1996. http://www.yale.edu. © 1996–2007 The Avalon Project at Yale Law School. Reprinted with permission.

Questions for Analysis and Debate

1. Why did the Federalists believe that the Sedition Act was necessary? What exactly was the threat, according to Abigail Adams? What threat is implied by the wording of the act?

2. Does Matthew Lyon's criticism of President Adams rise to the level of threat that the Federalists feared? How do you explain Lyon's guilty verdict? His reelection to Congress?

3. What might Madison have meant by "interpose" as the desired action by states? What could states actually do?

Connect to the Big Idea

⊙ What political or personal issues created the deep polarization between Federalists and Republicans that led to the Alien and Sedition Acts?

The election of 1800 was openly organized along party lines. The self-designated national leaders of each group met to handpick their candidates for president and vice president.

Adams's chief opponent was Thomas Jefferson. When the election was finally over, President Jefferson mounted the inaugural platform to announce, "We are all republicans, we are all

VISUAL ACTIVITY

Cartoon of the Lyon-Griswold Fight in Congress

Political tensions ran high in 1798. On the floor of Congress, Federalist Roger Griswold called Republican Matthew Lyon a coward. Lyon responded with some well-aimed spit, the first departure from the gentleman's code of honor. Griswold raised his cane to strike Lyon, whereupon Lyon grabbed fire tongs to defend himself. Madison later commented that the two should have dueled, the honorable way to avenge insults. Library of Congress.

READING THE IMAGE: Can you tell which figure is Lyon and which is Griswold? How? How do the other members of Congress react to the brawl, in this satirical cartoon? Are their reactions realistic?

CONNECTIONS: What, if anything, did this fight in Congress have to do with the rise of the Federalist and Republican political parties?

federalists," an appealing rhetoric of harmony appropriate to an inaugural address. But his formulation perpetuated a denial of the validity of party politics, a denial that ran deep in the founding generation of political leaders.

> REVIEW   How did war between Britain and France intensify the political divisions in the United States?

▶ Conclusion: Parties Nonetheless

American political leaders began operating the new government in 1789 with great hopes of unifying the country and overcoming selfish factionalism. The enormous trust in President Washington was the central foundation for those hopes, and Washington did not disappoint, becoming a model Mr. President with a blend of integrity and authority. Stability was further aided by easy passage of the Bill of Rights (to appease Antifederalists) and by attention to cultivating a virtuous citizenry of upright men supported and rewarded by republican womanhood. Yet the hopes of the honeymoon period soon turned to worries and then fears as major political disagreements flared up.

At the core of the conflict was a group of talented men—Hamilton, Madison, Jefferson, and Adams—so recently allies but now opponents. They diverged over Hamilton's economic program, over relations with the British and the Jay Treaty, over the French and Haitian revolutions, and over preparedness for war abroad and free speech at home. Hamilton was perhaps the driving force in these conflicts, but the antagonism was not about mere personality. Parties were taking shape not around individuals, but around principles, such as ideas about what constituted enlightened leadership, how powerful the federal government should be, who was the best ally in Europe, and when oppositional political speech turned into treason.

In his inaugural address of 1800, Jefferson offered his conciliatory assurance that Americans were at the same time "all republicans" and "all federalists," suggesting that both groups shared two basic ideas—the value of republican government, in which power derived from the people, and the value of the unique federal system of shared governance structured by the Constitution. But by 1800, Federalist and Republican defined competing philosophies of government. To at least some of his listeners, Jefferson's assertion of harmony across budding party lines could only have seemed bizarre. For the next two decades, these two groups would battle each other, each fearing that the success of the other might bring about the demise of the country.

See the Selected Bibliography for this chapter in the Appendix.

9 Chapter Review

 LearningCurve
Go online and use LearningCurve to see what you know. Then review the key terms and answer the questions.

KEY TERMS

Bill of Rights (p. 229)
Report on Public Credit (p. 233)
Report on Manufactures (p. 235)
Whiskey Rebellion (p. 236)
Treaty of Greenville (p. 239)
Jay Treaty (p. 242)
Haitian Revolution (p. 244)
Federalists (p. 245)
Republicans (p. 245)
XYZ affair (p. 247)
Alien and Sedition Acts (p. 247)
Virginia and Kentucky Resolutions (p. 247)

REVIEW QUESTIONS

1. How did political leaders in the 1790s attempt to overcome the divisions of the 1780s? (pp. 227–231)

2. Why were Hamilton's economic policies controversial? (pp. 231–236)

3. Why did the United States feel vulnerable to international threats in the 1790s? (pp. 237–245)

4. How did war between Britain and France intensify the political divisions in the United States? (pp. 245–250)

MAKING CONNECTIONS

1. Why did the Federalist alliance of the late 1780s fracture in the 1790s? Why was this development troubling to the nation? In your answer, cite specific ideological and political developments that hindered cooperation.

2. What provoked the Whiskey Rebellion? How did the government respond? In your answer, discuss the foundations and precedents of the conflict, as well as the significance of the government's response.

3. Americans held that virtue was pivotal to the success of their new nation. What did they mean by *virtue*? How did they hope to ensure that their citizens and their leaders possessed virtue?

4. The domestic politics of the new nation were profoundly influenced by conflicts beyond the nation's borders. Discuss how conflicts abroad contributed to domestic political developments in the 1790s.

LINKING TO THE PAST

1. Americans fought against the French in the Seven Years' War but welcomed them as allies during the Revolutionary War. Did either or both of those earlier experiences with France have any bearing on the sharp division in the 1790s between pro-French and anti-French political leaders in the United States? (See chapters 6 and 7.)

2. Shays's Rebellion appeared to some in 1786 to underscore the need for a stronger national government. Compare the Whiskey Rebellion to Shays's Rebellion. How were they similar and how were they different? Did the Constitution of 1787 make a difference in the authorities' response to rebellion? (See chapter 8.)

10 Republicans in Power

1800–1824

PATRIOTIC PITCHER, 1800
In this everyday pitcher, a militia officer poses near a cannon encircled by a toast: "Success to America Whose Militia Is Better Than Standing Armies." However, the nation's military preparedness was, in fact, woefully poor in 1800. Kahn Fine Antiques/photo courtesy of Antiques and Fine Arts.

CONTENT LEARNING OBJECTIVES

After reading and studying this chapter, you should be able to:

- Explain Thomas Jefferson's vision for the United States. Understand how the election of 1800 might be considered a "revolution." Identify the challenges and opportunities that Thomas Jefferson faced once in office.

- Explore the challenges and opportunities that James Madison faced once in office.

- Understand why the United States declared war on Britain in 1812 and identify the major turning points of the war.

- Recognize how the status of white women changed in the early Republic.

- Define the Missouri Compromise and its implications for the future direction of the country.

THE NAME TECUMSEH TRANSLATES AS "SHOOTING STAR," A FITTING name for the Shawnee chief who reached meteoric heights of fame among Indians during Thomas Jefferson's presidency. From Canada to Georgia, Tecumseh was by all accounts a charismatic leader. Graceful, eloquent, compelling, astute: Tecumseh was all these and more, a gifted natural commander, equal parts politician and warrior.

The Ohio Country, where Tecumseh was born in 1768, was home to some dozen Indian tribes. During the Revolutionary War, the region became a battleground, and Tecumseh lost his father and two brothers to American fighters. The Revolution's end in 1783 brought no peace to Indian country. The youthful Tecumseh fought at the battle of Fallen Timbers, a major Indian defeat, and stood by as eight treaties ceded much of Ohio to the Americans between 1795 and 1805.

Some resigned Indians looked for ways to accommodate, taking up farming, trade, and intermarriage with white settlers. Others spent their treaty payments on alcohol. Tecumseh's younger brother Tenskwatawa led an embittered life of idleness and drink. But Tecumseh rejected accommodation and instead campaigned for a return to ancient ways. Donning traditional animal-skin clothing, he traveled around the Great Lakes region persuading tribes to join his pan-Indian confederacy. The territorial governor of Indiana, William Henry Harrison, admired and feared Tecumseh, calling him "one of those uncommon geniuses which spring up occasionally to produce revolutions."

Even Tecumseh's dissolute brother was born anew. After a near-death experience in 1805, Tenskwatawa revived and recounted a startling vision of meeting the Master of Life. Renaming himself the Prophet, he urged his many Indian followers to regard whites as children of the Evil Spirit, destined to be destroyed.

President Thomas Jefferson worried about an organized Indian confederacy and its potential for a renewed alliance with the British in Canada. Those worries became a reality during Jefferson's second term in office (1805–1809). Although his first term (1801–1805) brought notable successes, such as the Louisiana Purchase and the Lewis and Clark expedition, his second term was consumed by the threat of war with either Britain or France, in a replay of the late-1790s tensions. When war came in 1812, the enemy was Britain, bolstered by a reenergized Indian-British alliance manifested in battles along the Canadian-U.S. border. Among the causes of the war were insults over international shipping rights and the capture of U.S. vessels, along with unresolved tensions with Indians in the Northwest and Southwest.

In the end, the War of 1812 settled little between the United States and Britain, but it was tragically conclusive for the Indians. Eight hundred warriors led by Tecumseh helped defend Canada against U.S. attacks, but the British did not reciprocate when the Indians were under threat. Tecumseh died on a Canadian battlefield in the fall of 1813. No Indian leader with his star power would emerge again east of the Mississippi.

Tecumseh's briefly unified Indian confederacy had no counterpart in the young Republic's confederation of states, where widespread unity behind a single leader proved impossible to achieve. Republicans did battle with Federalists during the Jefferson and Madison administrations, but then Federalists doomed their party by opposing the War of 1812. The next two presidents, James Monroe and John Quincy Adams, congratulated themselves on the Federalists' demise and Republican unity, but in fact divisions within their own party were extensive. Wives of politicians increasingly inserted themselves into this dissonant mix, managing their husbands' politicking and enabling them to appear above the fray and maintain the fiction of a nonpartisan state. That it was a fiction became sharply apparent in the most serious political crisis of this period, the Missouri Compromise of 1820.

Tecumseh

This 1848 engraving was adapted from an earlier drawing of Tecumseh made in a live sitting by a French fur trader in 1808. The engraver has given Tecumseh a British army officer's uniform, showing that he fought on the British side in the War of 1812. Notice the head covering and the medallion around Tecumseh's neck, marking his Indian identity. Library of Congress.

▶ Jefferson's Presidency

The first presidential election of the new century was an all-out partisan battle. A panicky Federalist newspaper in Connecticut predicted that a victory by Thomas Jefferson would produce a bloody civil war and usher in an immoral reign of "murder, robbery, rape, adultery and incest." Apocalyptic fears gripped parts of the South, where a frightful slave uprising seemed a possible consequence of Jefferson's victory. But nothing nearly so dramatic occurred. Jefferson later called his election the "revolution of 1800," referring to his repudiation of Federalist practices and his cutbacks in military spending and taxes. While he cherished a republican simplicity in governance, he inevitably encountered events that required decisive and sometimes expensive government action, including military action overseas to protect American shipping.

Turbulent Times: Election and Rebellion

The election of 1800 (Map 10.1) was historic for procedural reasons: It was the first election to be decided by the House of Representatives. Probably by mistake, Republican voters in the

MAP 10.1
The Election of 1800

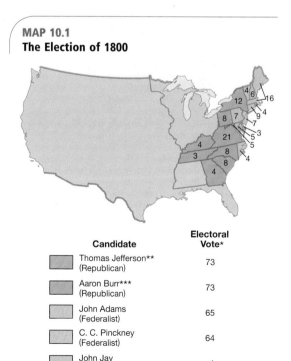

Candidate	Electoral Vote*
Thomas Jefferson** (Republican)	73
Aaron Burr*** (Republican)	73
John Adams (Federalist)	65
C. C. Pinckney (Federalist)	64
John Jay (Federalist)	1

*Before 1824, most presidential electors were chosen by state legislatures rather than by popular vote.
**Chosen president by House of Representatives.
***Chosen vice president by House of Representatives.

CHRONOLOGY

1800	• Thomas Jefferson and Aaron Burr tie in electoral college. • Gabriel's rebellion reported.
1801	• House of Representatives elects Jefferson president. • Barbary War with Tripoli begins.
1803	• *Marbury v. Madison.* • United States warned not to ship war goods to Britain or France. • Louisiana Purchase.
1804	• United States defeats Tripoli. • Jefferson meets with Osage Indians.
1804–1806	• Lewis and Clark expedition.
1807	• *Chesapeake* incident. • Embargo Act. • United States establishes trade with Comanche Indians.
1808	• James Madison elected president.
1809	• Treaty of Fort Wayne. • Non-Intercourse Act.
1811	• Battle of Tippecanoe.
1812	• United States declares war on Great Britain.
1813	• Tecumseh dies at battle of the Thames.
1814	• British attack Washington City. • Treaty of Ghent. • Hartford Convention.
1815	• Battle of New Orleans.
1816	• James Monroe elected president.
1819	• Adams-Onís Treaty.
1820	• Missouri Compromise.
1823	• Monroe Doctrine asserted.
1825	• John Quincy Adams elected president by House of Representatives.

How Could a Vice President Get Away with Murder?

On July 11, 1804, Vice President Aaron Burr shot Alexander Hamilton, the architect of the Federalist Party, in a duel on the cliffs of Weehawken, New Jersey, across the Hudson River from New York City. The pistol blast tore through a rib, demolished Hamilton's liver, and splintered his spine. Hamilton died the next day in agonizing pain.

How was it that a sitting vice president and a prominent political leader could put themselves at such risk? Two eminent attorneys, skilled in the legal negotiations meant to substitute for violent resolution of disputes, fired .54-caliber weapons at ten paces. Did anyone try to stop them?

Burr challenged Hamilton in late June after learning about a months'-old newspaper report that Hamilton "looked upon Mr. Burr to be a dangerous man, and one who ought not be trusted with the reins of government." Burr knew of Hamilton's low opinion of him, but now his private disparagement had made its way into print. Burr felt sure that Hamilton's remark cost him election to the governorship of New York.

Quite possibly, he was right. Suspecting that Jefferson would dump him from the federal ticket in the 1804 election, Burr decided to run for New York's highest office. He needed the support of New York's Federalist leadership, and he appeared to have it—until Hamilton's remark was circulated.

So on June 18, Burr challenged Hamilton to a duel if he did not disavow his comment. For three weeks, the men exchanged letters clarifying the nature of the insult that had aggrieved Burr. Hamilton the lawyer evasively quibbled over words, but at heart, he could not deny the insult nor spurn the challenge without injury to his own reputation. Both Burr

Pistols from the Burr-Hamilton Duel
These dueling pistols belonged to Hamilton's brother-in-law, who had once fought a non-injury duel with Aaron Burr. Hamilton's son Philip had borrowed them for his own fatal duel in 1799. During a cleaning in 1884, a hidden hair trigger came to light, allowing for a more rapid firing with one-twentieth the force of pull on the trigger. Hamilton gained no advantage from it.
Courtesy JPMorgan Chase History Program.

electoral college gave Jefferson and his running mate Senator Aaron Burr of New York an equal number of votes, an outcome possible because of the single balloting to choose both president and vice president. (To fix this problem, the Twelfth Amendment to the Constitution, adopted in 1804, provided for distinct ballots for the two offices.) That meant that the House had to choose between those two men, leaving the Federalist candidate, John Adams, out of the race. The vain and ambitious Burr declined to concede, so the sitting Federalist-dominated House of Representatives, in its waning days in early 1801, got to choose the president.

Some Federalists preferred Burr, believing that his character flaws made him susceptible to Federalist pressure. But the influential Alexander Hamilton, though no friend of Jefferson, recognized that the high-strung Burr would be more dangerous in the presidency. Jefferson was a "contemptible hypocrite" in Hamilton's opinion, but at least he was not corrupt. (In 1804, Burr shot and killed Hamilton in a formal but illegal duel. See "Historical Question," above.) Thirty-six ballots and six days later, Jefferson got the votes and Hamilton were locked in a highly ritualized procedure meant to uphold a gentleman's code of honor.

Each man had a trusted "second," in accord with the code of dueling, to deliver the letters and to assist at the duel. Only a handful of close friends knew of the challenge, and no one tried to stop it. Hamilton did not tell his wife. He wrote her a tender farewell letter, to be opened in the event of his death. He knew full well the pain dueling brought to loved ones, for three years earlier his nineteen-year-old son Philip had been killed in a duel, fought over heated words exchanged at a New York theater. Even when Hamilton's wife was called to his deathbed, she was first told he had a sudden illness. Women were excluded from the masculine world of dueling.

News of Hamilton's death spread quickly throughout the nation. New York shut down for the funeral, and the city council declared a six-week mourning period. Burr fled to Philadelphia, fearing retribution by crowds of mourners.

Northern newspapers expressed indignation over the illegal duel; not so in the South, where dueling was accepted as an extralegal remedy for insult. Many northern states had recently criminalized dueling, treating a challenge as a misdemeanor and a dueling death as a homicide. Even after death, the loser of an illegal duel could endure a range of penalties—being buried without a coffin, having a stake driven through the body, being strung up in public until the body rotted, or being donated to medical students for dissection. Hamilton's body was spared dishonor. But two ministers in succession refused to administer last rites to him because he was a duelist; one finally relented.

A coroner's jury in New York soon indicted Burr on misdemeanor charges for issuing a challenge, and a grand jury in New Jersey indicted him for murder. By that time, Burr was a fugitive from justice hiding out in South Carolina.

But not for long. Amazingly, he returned to Washington, D.C., in November 1804 to resume presiding over sessions of the Senate, a role he continued to perform until his term ended in March 1805. Federalists snubbed him, but eleven Republican senators petitioned New Jersey to drop its indictment on the grounds that "civilized nations" do not treat dueling deaths as "common murders." New Jersey did not pursue the murder charge. Burr freely visited New Jersey and New York for three more decades, paying no penalty for killing Hamilton.

Few would doubt that Burr was a scoundrel, albeit a brilliant one. A few years later, he was indicted for treason for a plot to break off part of the United States and start his own country in the Southwest.

(He dodged that bullet, too.) Hamilton certainly thought Burr a scoundrel, and when that opinion reached print, Burr had cause to defend his honor under the etiquette of dueling. The accuracy of Hamilton's charge was of no account.

Dueling redressed questions of honor, not questions of fact. Dueling held sway in the South for several more decades, but in the North the custom became extremely rare by the 1820s, discouraged by the tragedy of Hamilton's death and by the rise of a legalistic society that now preferred evidence, interrogation, and monetary judgments to avenge injury.

Questions for Consideration

1. Why did men who made their living by the legal system go outside the law and turn to the centuries-old ritual of the duel?

2. Why did Hamilton conceal from his wife that he was negotiating a challenge for a duel?

3. Was Hamilton's death a criminal act?

4. How could Burr remain vice president?

Connect to the Big Idea

⊙ What effect did Hamilton's death have on the viability and power of the Federalist Party?

---

he needed to win the presidency. This election demonstrated a remarkable feature of the new government: No matter how hard fought the campaign, the leadership of the nation could shift from one group to its rivals in a peaceful transfer of power.

As the country struggled over its white leadership crisis, a twenty-four-year-old blacksmith named Gabriel, the slave of Thomas Prossor, plotted rebellion in Virginia. Inspired by the Haitian Revolution (see "The Haitian Revolution" in chapter 9), Gabriel was said to be organizing a thousand slaves to march on the state capital of Richmond and take the governor, James Monroe, hostage. On the appointed day, however, a few nervous slaves went to the authorities with news of Gabriel's rebellion, and within days scores of implicated conspirators were jailed and brought to trial.

One of the jailed rebels compared himself to the most venerated icon of the early Republic: "I have nothing more to offer than what General Washington would have had to offer, had he been taken by the British and put to trial by them." Such talk invoking the specter of a black George Washington worried white Virginians, and in the fall of 1800 twenty-seven black men were hanged for allegedly contemplating rebellion. Finally, Jefferson advised Governor Monroe to halt the hangings. "The world at large will forever condemn us if we indulge a principle of revenge," Jefferson wrote.

The Jeffersonian Vision of Republican Simplicity

Once elected, Thomas Jefferson turned his attention to establishing his administration in clear contrast to the Federalists. For his inauguration, the first in the newly established District of Columbia, he dressed in everyday clothing to strike a tone of republican simplicity, and he walked to the Capitol for the modest swearing-in ceremony. As president, he scaled back Federalist building plans for Washington and cut the government budget.

Martha Washington and Abigail Adams had received the wives of government officials at weekly teas, thereby cementing social relations in the governing class. But Jefferson, a longtime widower, disdained female gatherings and avoided the women of Washington City. He abandoned George Washington's practice of holding weekly formal receptions. He preferred small dinner parties with carefully chosen politicos, either all Republicans or all Federalists (and all male). At these intimate dinners, the president exercised influence and strengthened informal relationships that would help him govern.

Jefferson was no Antifederalist; he had supported the Constitution in 1788. But events of the 1790s had caused him to worry about the stretching of powers in the executive branch. Jefferson had watched with distrust as Hamiltonian policies refinanced the public debt, established a national bank, and secured commercial ties with Britain (see "The Public Debt and Taxes" in chapter 9). These policies seemed to Jefferson to promote the interests of greedy speculators and profiteers at the expense of the rest of the country. In Jefferson's vision, the source of true liberty in America was the independent farmer, someone who owned and worked his land both for himself and for the market.

Jefferson set out to dismantle Federalist innovations. He reduced the size of the army by a third, preferring a militia-based defense, and he cut back the navy to six ships. With the consent of Congress, he abolished all federal taxes based on population or whiskey. Government revenue would now derive solely from customs duties and the sale of western land. This strategy benefited the South, where three-fifths of the slaves counted for representation but not for taxation now. By the end of his first term, Jefferson had deeply reduced Hamilton's cherished national debt.

A limited federal government, according to Jefferson, maintained a postal system, federal courts, and coastal lighthouses; it collected customs duties and conducted the census. The president had one private secretary, a young man named Meriwether Lewis, and Jefferson paid him out of his own pocket. The Department of State employed 8 people: Secretary James Madison, 6 clerks, and a messenger. The Treasury Department was by far the largest

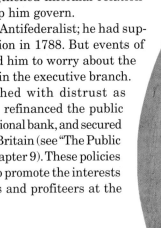

***Thomas Jefferson,* by John Trumbull, 1788 (detail)**
This portrait captures Jefferson when he lived in Paris as a diplomat with his daughters and slave Sally Hemings. In 1802, a scandal erupted when a journalist charged that Jefferson had fathered children by Hemings. DNA evidence and historical evidence of Jefferson's whereabouts at the start of Hemings's pregnancies make a powerful case that he did father some and perhaps all of her children. Image copyright © The Metropolitan Museum of Art. Bequest of Cornelia Cruger, 1923 (24.19.1). Image source: Art Resource, NY.

unit, with 73 revenue commissioners, auditors, and clerks, plus 2 watchmen. The entire payroll of the executive branch amounted to a mere 130 people in 1801.

However, 217 government workers lay beyond Jefferson's command, all judicial and military appointments made by John Adams as his very last-minute act in office. Jefferson refused to honor those "midnight judges" whose hires had not yet been fully processed. One disappointed job seeker, William Marbury, sued the new secretary of state, James Madison, for failure to make good on the appointment. This action gave rise to a landmark Supreme Court case, *Marbury v. Madison*, decided in 1803. The Court ruled that although Marbury's commission was valid and the new president should have delivered it, the Court could not compel him to do so. What made the case significant was little noted at the time: The Court found that the grounds of Marbury's suit, resting in the Judiciary Act of 1789, were in conflict with the Constitution. For the first time, the Court disallowed a federal law on the grounds that it was unconstitutional.

Dangers Overseas: The Barbary Wars

Jefferson's desire to keep government and the military small met a severe test in the western Mediterranean Sea, where U.S. trading interests ran afoul of several states on the northern coast of Africa. For well over a century, Morocco, Algiers, Tunis, and Tripoli, called the Barbary States by Americans, controlled all Mediterranean shipping traffic by demanding large annual payments (called "tribute") for safe passage. Countries electing not to pay found their ships and crews at risk for seizure. After several years in the 1790s when some hundred American crew members were taken captive and held in slavery, the United States agreed to pay $50,000 a year in tribute.

In May 1801, when the monarch of Tripoli failed to secure a large increase in his tribute, he declared war on the United States. Jefferson considered such payments extortion, and he sent four warships to the Mediterranean to protect U.S. shipping. From 1801 to 1803, U.S. frigates engaged in skirmishes with north African privateers.

Then, in late 1803, the USS *Philadelphia* ran aground near Tripoli's harbor and was captured along with its 300-man crew. In response, in early 1804 a U.S. naval ship commanded by Lieutenant Stephen Decatur sailed into the harbor after dark guided by an Arabic-speaking pilot to fool harbor sentries. Decatur's crew set the *Philadelphia* on fire, rendering it useless to the Tripoli monarch. Later that year, a small force of U.S. ships attacked the harbor and damaged or destroyed nineteen Tripolitan ships and bombarded the city, winning high praise and respect from European governments. Yet the sailors from the *Philadelphia* remained in captivity.

In 1805, William Eaton, an American officer stationed in Tunis, requested a thousand Marines to invade Tripoli, but Secretary of State James Madison rejected the plan. On his own, Eaton

SAVING THE LIFE OF COMMODORE DECATUR.

Stephen Decatur, Celebrated Hero of the Tripolitan War, 1804
Stephen Decatur, just twenty-five, won soaring praise from the American public for his daring nighttime raid into Tripoli's harbor to burn the USS *Philadelphia*. Decatur's fame grew when, six months later, he led ten men into combat against some fifty Tripolitan sailors. An 1850s artist re-created the dramatic moment when a wounded American took a saber blow for Decatur, who forthwith shot his attacker. © Look and Learn/The Bridgeman Art Library.

assembled a force of four hundred men (mostly Greek and Egyptian mercenaries plus eight Marines) and marched them over five hundred miles of desert for a surprise attack on Tripoli's second-largest city. Amazingly, he succeeded. The monarch of Tripoli yielded, released the prisoners taken from the *Philadelphia*, and negotiated a treaty in 1805 with the United States.

Periodic attacks by Algiers and Tunis continued to plague American ships during Jefferson's second term of office and into his successor's. This Second Barbary War ended in 1815 when the hero of 1804, Stephen Decatur, now a captain, arrived on the northern coast of Africa with a fleet of twenty-seven ships. By show of force, he engineered three treaties that put an end to the tribute system and provided reparations for damages to U.S. ships. Decatur was widely hailed for restoring honor to the United States.

REVIEW How did Jefferson's views of the role of the federal government differ from those of his predecessors?

▶ Opportunities and Challenges in the West

In 1803, an unanticipated opportunity presented itself when France offered to sell its territory west of the Mississippi River to the United States. President Jefferson set aside his usually cautious exercise of federal power and quickly took up the offer. He soon launched four expeditions into the prairie and mountains to explore this huge acquisition of land. The powerful Osage of the Arkansas River valley responded to overtures for an alliance and were soon lavishly welcomed by Jefferson in Washington City, but the even more powerful Comanche of the southern Great Plains stood their ground against all invaders. Meanwhile, the expedition by Lewis and Clark, the longest and northernmost trek of the four launched by Jefferson, mapped U.S. terrain all the way to the Pacific Ocean, giving a boost to expansionist aspirations.

The Louisiana Purchase

In 1763, at the end of the Seven Years' War, a large area west of the United States shifted from France to Spain, but Spain never effectively controlled it (see "The War and Its Consequences" in chapter 6). Centered on the Great Plains, it was home to Indian tribes, most notably the powerful and expansionist Comanche nation.

New Orleans was Spain's principal stronghold, a city of French origins and population, strategically sited on the Mississippi River near its outlet to the Gulf of Mexico. Spain profited modestly from trade taxes it imposed on the small flow of agricultural products shipped down the river from American farms in the western parts of Kentucky and Tennessee.

Spanish officials in New Orleans and St. Louis (another city of French origins) worried that their sparse population could not withstand an anticipated westward movement of Americans. At first they hoped for a Spanish-Indian alliance to halt the expected demographic wave, but defending many hundreds of miles along the Mississippi River against Americans on the move was a daunting prospect. Thus, in 1800 Spain struck a secret deal to return this trans-Mississippi territory to France, in the hopes that a French Louisiana would provide a buffer zone between Spain's more valuable holdings in northern Mexico and the land-hungry Americans. The French emperor Napoleon accepted the transfer and agreed to Spain's condition that France could not sell Louisiana to anyone without Spain's permission.

From the U.S. perspective, Spain had proved a weak western neighbor, but France was another story. Jefferson was so alarmed by the rumored transfer that he instructed Robert R. Livingston, America's minister in France, to try to buy New Orleans. When Livingston hinted that the United States might seize it if buying was not an option, the French negotiator asked him to name his price for the entire Louisiana Territory from the Gulf of Mexico north to Canada. Livingston shrewdly stalled and within days accepted the bargain price of $15 million (Map 10.2).

On the verge of war with Britain, France needed both money and friendly neutrality from the United States, and it got both from the quick sale of the Louisiana Territory. In addition, the recent and costly loss of Haiti as a colony made a French presence in New Orleans less feasible as well. But in selling Louisiana to the United States, France had broken its agreement with Spain, which protested that the sale was illegal.

Moreover, there was no clarity on the western border of this land transfer. Spain claimed that the border was about one hundred miles west of the Mississippi River, while in Jefferson's eyes it was some eight hundred miles farther west, defined by the crest of the Rocky Mountains. When Livingston pressured the French negotiator to clarify his country's understanding of the boundary, the negotiator replied, "I can give you no direction. You have made a noble bargain for yourself, and I suppose you will make the most of it."

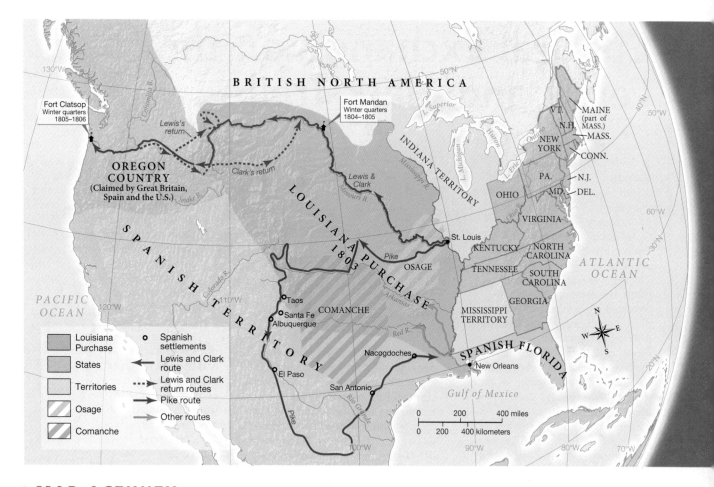

MAP ACTIVITY

Map 10.2   Jefferson's Expeditions in the West, 1804–1806

The Louisiana Purchase of 1803 brought the United States a large territory without clear boundaries. Jefferson sent off four scientific expeditions to take stock of the land's possibilities and to assess the degree of potential antagonism from Indian and Spanish inhabitants.

READING THE MAP: How did the size of the newly acquired territory compare to the land area of the existing American states and territories? What natural features of the land might have suggested boundaries for the Louisiana Purchase? Did those natural features coincide with actual patterns of human habitation already in place?

CONNECTIONS: What political events in Europe created the opportunity for the Jefferson administration to purchase Louisiana? How did the acquisition of Louisiana affect Spain's hold on North America?

Jefferson gained congressional approval for the **Louisiana Purchase**, but without the votes of Federalist New England, which feared that such a large acquisition of land would be detrimental to Federalist Party strength. In late 1803, the American army took formal control of the Louisiana Territory, and the United States nearly doubled in size—at least on paper.

The Lewis and Clark Expedition

Jefferson quickly launched four government-financed expeditions up the river valleys of the new territory to establish relationships with Indian tribes and to determine Spanish influence and presence. The first set out in 1804 to explore the upper reaches of the Missouri River. Jefferson appointed twenty-eight-year-old Meriwether Lewis, his secretary, to head the expedition and instructed him to investigate Indian cultures, to collect plant and animal specimens, and to chart the geography of the West. (See "Visualizing History," page 262.) Congress wanted the expedition to scout locations for military posts, negotiate fur trade agreements, and identify river routes to the West (see Map 10.2).

Cultural Exchange on the Lewis and Clark Trail

Lewis and Clark carried many gifts for the Indians they anticipated meeting as they traveled up the Missouri River toward the Rocky Mountains. Intended to signal goodwill and respect, some of the gifts held other subtle meanings as well.

Upon encountering new tribes, the explorers presented high-ranking Indian leaders with silver medals bearing the likeness of President Jefferson, in two-, three-, or four-inch sizes. Imagine the Indian recipients' reactions. What specific message might the image of the president convey? The explorers traveled with ornamental trinkets ("ear bobs," silk handkerchiefs, ivory combs, ribbons) as well as practical goods (brass buttons, needles and

Thomas Jefferson's Peace Medal, 1801

thread, blankets, calico shirts) that demonstrated American manufacturing and handcraft. They carried a few small mirrors and magnifying glasses but on one occasion found that making fire with the latter engendered suspicion, not goodwill. Blue glass beads—portable and inexpensive—

were a sought-after gift, leading Clark to observe that beads "may be justly compared to gold and Silver among civilized nations."

Jefferson pointedly urged Lewis to take small hand-cranked corn mills, to acculturate the native women to American household technology. Indian women, with full charge of corn agriculture and its preparation as food, used mortars and pestles to pulverize dried kernels. Each time Lewis and Clark presented tribal chiefs

Blue Trade Beads

For his co-leader, Lewis chose Kentuckian William Clark, a veteran of the 1790s Indian wars. With a crew of forty-five, including expert rivermen, gunsmiths, hunters, interpreters, a cook, and Clark's slave named York, the explorers left St. Louis in the spring of 1804, working their way northwest up the Missouri River. They camped for the winter at a Mandan village in what is now central North Dakota. The Mandan Indians were familiar with British and French traders from Canada, but the black man York created a sensation. Reportedly, the Indians rubbed moistened fingers over the man's skin to see whether the color was painted on.

The following spring, the explorers headed west, accompanied by a sixteen-year-old Shoshoni woman named Sacajawea. Kidnapped by Mandans at about age ten, she had been sold to a French trapper as a slave/wife. Hers was not a unique story among Indian women; such women knew several languages, making them valuable translators and mediators. Further, Sacajawea and her new baby allowed the American expedition to appear peaceful to suspicious tribes.

As Lewis wrote in his journal, "No woman ever accompanies a war party of Indians in this quarter."

The **Lewis and Clark expedition** reached the Pacific Ocean at the mouth of the Columbia River in November 1805. When the two leaders returned home the following year, they were greeted as national heroes. They had established favorable relations with dozens of Indian tribes; they had collected invaluable information on the peoples, soils, plants, animals, and geography of the West; and they had inspired a nation of restless explorers and solitary imitators.

Osage and Comanche Indians

The three additional expeditions set forth between 1804 and 1806 to probe the contested southwestern border of the Louisiana Purchase. The first exploring party left from Natchez, Mississippi, and ascended the Red River to the Ouachita River, ending at a hot springs in present-day Arkansas. Two years later, the second group followed the Red River west into eastern with a corn mill and demonstrated its use, the recipients seemed to be "highly pleased." Yet a year later, a fur trader visiting the Mandans wrote, "I saw the remains of an excellent large corn mill, which the foolish fellows had demolished to barb their arrows."

The explorers received gifts as well. The most impressive was the necklace shown here, made of 35 four-inch grizzly bear claws. The explorers encountered a number of Indian men wearing bear claw "collars" (Lewis's term for it). For many tribes, bears were sacred animals, and their claws embodied spiritual power. Grizzlies are large (up to nine hundred pounds) and aggressive, so acquiring so many claws from multiple bears without the use of firearms took extraordinary courage. Such an ornament clearly signaled that the wearer of it was a man of courage and power.

Corn Mill Grinder

SOURCES: Jefferson's medal: Brooklyn Museum of Art, New York, USA/The Bridgeman Art Library; trade beads: Ralph Thompson Collection of the Lewis & Clark Fort Mandan Foundation, Washburn, ND; corn mill: The Colonial Williamsburg Foundation. Gift of Mr. Allan Jobson; bear claw necklace: © President and Fellows of Harvard College, Peabody Museum of Archaeology and Ethnology. Harvard University, PM#41-54-10/99700 (digital file 60740049).

Grizzly Bear Claw Necklace

Questions for Analysis

1. On what basis do you think the explorers chose to distribute the three sizes of the medals bearing Jefferson's likeness?

2. Did the explorers perhaps fail in their mission by giving the mill for grinding corn to male leaders instead of to women? Or could this repurposing of the food grinder be read as a rejection by the women themselves of Americans' gendered practices?

3. Why might Indians bestow the rare grizzly-claw necklace on the explorers? Did it honor their manly courage? Or promote a spiritual brotherhood? Or might it have been intended to discourage further shootings of the sacred bears?

Connect to the Big Idea

C Why was the territory of the Louisiana Purchase important to President Jefferson, and why did he send Lewis and Clark to explore it?

Texas, and the third embarked from St. Louis and traveled west, deep into the Rockies. This third group, led by Zebulon Pike, had gone too far, in the view of the Spaniards: Pike and his men were arrested, taken to northern Mexico, and soon released.

Of the scores of Indian tribes in this lower Great Plains region, two enjoyed reputations for territorial dominance. The Osage ruled the land between the Missouri and the lower Arkansas rivers, while the trading and raiding grounds of the Comanche stretched from the upper Arkansas River to the Rockies and south into Texas, a vast area called Comanchería. Both were formidable tribes that proved equal to the Spaniards. The Osage accomplished this through careful diplomacy and periodic shows of strength, the Comanche by expert horsemanship, a brisk trade in guns and captives, and a readiness to employ deadly force.

In 1804, Jefferson invited Osage tribal leaders to Washington City and greeted them with ceremonies and gifts. He positioned the Osage as equals of the Americans: "The great spirit

has given you strength & has given us strength, not that we might hurt one another, but to do each other all the good in our power." Jefferson wanted a trade agreement that would introduce new agricultural tools to the Osage: hoes and ploughs for the men; spinning wheels and looms for the women. These gendered tools signified a departure from the native gender system in which women tended crops while men hunted game. With an agricultural civilization, men would give up the hunt and thus need far less land to sustain their communities. Jefferson expressed his hope that "commerce is the great engine by which we are to coerce them, & not war."

In exchange, the Osage asked for protection against Indian refugees displaced by American settlers east of the Mississippi. Jefferson's Osage alliance soon proved to be quite expensive, driven up by the costs of providing defense, brokering treaties, and giving gifts all around. In 1806, a second ceremonial visit to Washington and other eastern cities by a dozen Osage leaders cost the federal government $10,000.

Comanche Feats of Horsemanship, 1834

Pennsylvania artist George Catlin toured the Great Plains and captured Comanche equestrian warfare in training. "Every young man," Catlin wrote, learned "to drop his body upon the side of his horse at the instant he is passing, effectually screened from his enemies' weapons. . . . [H]e will hang whilst his horse is at fullest speed, carrying with him his bow and his shield, and also his long lance . . . which he will wield upon his enemy as he passes." Smithsonian American Art Museum, Washington, DC/Art Resource, NY.

READING THE IMAGE: Is there a riderless horse in this picture? Is this unusual expert riding skill an offensive or defensive posture?

CONNECTIONS: How did the Comanches' formidable presence in the Great Plains affect American westward settlement?

These promising peace initiatives were short-lived. By 1808, intertribal warfare was on the rise, and the governor of the Louisiana Territory declared that the U.S. government no longer had an obligation to protect the Osage. Jefferson's presidency was waning, and soon the practice of whittling away Indian lands through coercive treaties, so familiar to men like Tecumseh, reasserted itself. Four treaties between 1808 and 1839 years shrank the Osage lands, and by the 1860s they were relocated to present-day Oklahoma.

By contrast, the Comanche resisted attempts to dominate them. European maps marking Spanish ownership of vast North American lands simply did not correspond to the reality on the ground, and for decades after the Louisiana Purchase of 1803, nothing much changed. In 1807, a newly appointed U.S. Indian agent invited Comanche leaders to Natchitoches in Louisiana where he proclaimed an improbable solidarity with the Comanche: "It is now so long since our Ancestors came from beyond the great Water that we have no remembrance of it. We ourselves are Natives of the Same land that you are, in other words white Indians, we therefore Should feel & live together like brothers & Good Neighbours." Trade relations flourished, with American traders allowed to enter Comanchería to attend local market fairs, selling weapons, cloth, and household metal goods in exchange for horses, bison, and furs. No matter what the map of the United States looked like, on the ground Comanchería remained under the control of the Comanches and thus off-limits to settlement by white Americans until the late nineteenth century (see Map 10.2).

REVIEW   What was the significance of the Louisiana Purchase for the United States?

► Jefferson, the Madisons, and the War of 1812

Jefferson easily retained the presidency in the election of 1804, trouncing Federalist Charles Cotesworth Pinckney of South Carolina. A looming problem was the threat of war with both France and Britain that led Jefferson to try a novel tactic, an embargo. His successor, James Madison, continued with a modified embargo, but his much narrower margin of victory over

Pinckney in the election of 1808 indicated growing dissatisfaction with the Jefferson-Madison handling of foreign policy.

Madison broke with Jefferson on one very domestic matter: He allowed his gregarious wife, Dolley Madison, to participate in serious politics. Under James Madison's leadership, the country declared war in 1812 on Britain and on Tecumseh's Indian confederacy. The two-year war cost the young nation its White House and its Capitol, but victory was proclaimed at the end nonetheless.

Impressment and Embargo

In 1803, France and Britain went to war, and both repeatedly warned the United States not to ship arms to the other. Britain acted on these threats in 1806, stopping U.S. ships to inspect cargoes for military aid to France and seizing suspected deserters from the British navy, along with many Americans. Ultimately, 2,500 U.S. sailors were "impressed" (taken by force) by the British, who needed them for their war with France. In retaliation against the **impressments** of American sailors, Jefferson convinced Congress to pass a nonimportation law banning particular British-made goods.

Jefferson found one event particularly provoking. In June 1807, the American ship *Chesapeake*, harboring some British deserters, was ordered to stop by the British frigate *Leopard*. When the *Chesapeake* refused, the *Leopard* opened fire, killing three Americans—right at the mouth of the Chesapeake Bay, well within U.S. territory. In response, Congress passed the **Embargo Act of 1807**, prohibiting U.S. ships from traveling to all foreign ports, a measure that brought a swift halt to all overseas trade carried in American vessels. Though a drastic measure, the embargo was meant to forestall war by forcing concessions from the British through economic pressure.

The Embargo Act of 1807 was a disaster. From 1790 to 1807, U.S. exports had increased fivefold, but the embargo brought commerce to a standstill. In New England, the heart of the shipping industry, unemployment rose. Grain plummeted in value, river traffic halted, tobacco rotted in the South, and cotton

went unpicked. Protest petitions flooded Washington. The federal government suffered too, for import duties were a significant source of revenue. The Federalist Party, in danger of fading away after its weak showing in the election of 1804, began to revive.

Secretary of State James Madison was chosen by Republican caucuses—informal political groups that orchestrated the selection of candidates. The Federalist caucuses again chose Pinckney. Madison won, but Pinckney secured 47 electoral votes, nearly half of Madison's total. Support for the Federalists remained centered in New England, where the shipping industry suffered heavy losses in the embargo. The Republicans still held the balance of power nationwide.

Dolley Madison and Social Politics

Although women could not vote and supposedly left politics to men, the female relatives of Washington politicians took on several overtly political functions that greased the wheels of the affairs of state. They networked through dinners, balls, receptions, and the intricate custom of "calling," in which men and women paid brief visits at each other's homes. Webs of friendship and influence in turn facilitated female political lobbying. It was not uncommon for women in this social set to write letters of recommendation for men seeking government work.

Dolley Madison developed elaborate social networks during Jefferson's presidency that were of great benefit during her husband's administration. Called by some the "presidentress," Mrs. Madison struck a balance between queenliness and republican openness. She dressed the part in resplendent clothes, and she opened three elegant rooms in the executive mansion for a weekly open-house party called "Mrs. Madison's crush" or "squeeze." In contrast to George and Martha Washington's stiff, brief receptions, the Madisons' parties went on for hours, with scores or even hundreds of guests milling about, talking, and eating. Members of Congress, cabinet officers, distinguished guests, envoys from foreign countries, and their wives attended with regularity. Mrs. Madison's weekly squeeze was

The Chesapeake Incident, June 22, 1807

VISUAL ACTIVITY

Dolley Madison, by Rembrandt Peale

The "presidentress" of the Madison administration sat for this portrait in 1817 when she was close to fifty and just exiting from the White House. She wears a fashionable satin empire waist dress featuring a low-cut bodice and flowing gown that dropped from the high waistline straight to the ground. Mrs. Madison was noted for her unusual turbans and her unfailing good cheer, as her impish smile conveys. ©Bettmann/Corbis.

READING THE IMAGE: Does the scarf around her shoulders appear to have a functional value for this outfit? Is there any function associated with the collar around her neck?

CONNECTIONS: What kind of role were female relatives of politicians expected to play in the early Republic?

an essential event for gaining political access, trading information, and establishing informal channels that would smooth the governing process.

In 1810–1811, the Madisons' house acquired its present name, the White House. The many guests experienced simultaneously the splendor of the executive mansion and the atmosphere of republicanism that made it accessible to so many. Dolley Madison, ever an enormous political asset to her rather shy husband, understood well the symbolic function of the White House to enhance the power and legitimacy of the presidency.

Tecumseh and Tippecanoe

While the Madisons cemented alliances at home, difficulties with Britain and France overseas and with Indians in the old Northwest continued to increase. The Shawnee chief Tecumseh (see pages 253–54) actively solidified

Indian Lands Ceded in the Northwest Territory before 1810

his confederacy, while the more northern tribes renewed their ties with supportive British agents in Canada, a potential source of food and weapons. If the United States went to war with Britain, serious repercussions on the frontier would clearly follow.

Shifting demographics put the Indians under pressure. The 1810 census counted some 230,000 Americans in Ohio, while another 40,000 inhabited the territories of Indiana, Illinois, and Michigan. The Indian population of the same area was much smaller, probably about 70,000.

Up to 1805, Indiana's territorial governor, William Henry Harrison, had negotiated a series of treaties in a divide-and-conquer strategy aimed at extracting Indian lands for paltry payments. But with the rise to power of Tecumseh and his brother Tenskwatawa, the Prophet, Harrison's strategy faltered. A fundamental part of Tecumseh's message was the assertion that all Indian lands were held in common by all the tribes. "No tribe has the right to sell [these lands], even to each other, much less to strangers . . . ," Tecumseh said. "Sell a country! Why not sell the air, the great sea, as well as the earth? Didn't the Great Spirit make them all for the use of his children?" In 1809, while Tecumseh was away on a recruiting trip, Harrison assembled the leaders of the Potawatomi, Miami, and Delaware tribes to negotiate the Treaty of Fort Wayne. After promising (falsely) that this was the last cession of land the United States would seek, Harrison secured three million acres at about two cents per acre.

Battle of Tippecanoe, 1811

When he returned, Tecumseh was furious with both Harrison and the tribal leaders. Leaving his brother in charge at Prophetstown on the Tippecanoe River, the Shawnee chief left to seek alliances with tribes in the South. In November 1811, Harrison decided to attack Prophetstown with a thousand men. The two-hour battle resulted in the deaths of sixty-two Americans and forty Indians before the Prophet's forces fled. The Americans won the **battle of Tippecanoe**, but Tecumseh was now more ready than ever to make war on the United States.

The War of 1812

The Indian conflicts in the old Northwest soon merged into the wider conflict with Britain, now known as the War of 1812. Between 1809 and 1812, Madison teetered between declaring either Britain or France American's primary enemy, as attacks by both countries on U.S. ships continued. In 1809, Congress replaced Jefferson's embargo with the Non-Intercourse Act, which prohibited trade only with Britain and France and their colonies, thus opening up other trade routes to alleviate the economic distress of American shippers, farmers, and planters. By 1811, the country was seriously divided and on the verge of war.

The new Congress seated in March 1811 contained several dozen young Republicans from the West and South who would come to be known as the **War Hawks**. Led by thirty-four-year-old Henry Clay from Kentucky and twenty-nine-year-old John C. Calhoun from South Carolina, they welcomed a war with Britain both to justify attacks on the Indians and to bring an end to impressment. Many were also expansionists, looking to occupy Florida and threaten Canada. Clay was elected Speaker of the House, an extraordinary honor for a newcomer, and Calhoun won a seat on the Foreign Relations Committee. The War Hawks approved major defense expenditures, and the army soon quadrupled in size.

In June 1812, Congress declared war on Great Britain in a vote divided along sectional lines: New England and some Middle Atlantic states opposed the war, fearing its effect on commerce, while the South and West strongly favored it. Ironically, Britain had just announced that it would stop the search and seizure of American ships, but the war momentum would not be slowed. The Foreign Relations Committee issued an elaborate justification titled *Report on the Causes and Reasons for War*, written mainly by Calhoun and containing extravagant language about Britain's "lust for power," "unbounded tyranny," and "mad ambition." These were fighting words in a war that was in large measure about insult and honor.

The War Hawks proposed an invasion of Canada, confidently predicting victory in four weeks. Instead, the war lasted two and a half years, and Canada never fell. The northern invasion turned out to be a series of blunders that revealed America's grave unpreparedness for war against the unexpectedly powerful British and Indian forces (Map 10.3). By the fall of 1812, the outlook was grim.

Worse, the New England states were slow to raise troops, and some New England merchants carried on illegal trade with Britain. The fall presidential election pitted Madison against DeWitt Clinton of New York, nominally a Republican but able to attract the Federalist vote. Clinton picked up electoral votes from all of New England, with the exception of Vermont, and from New York, New Jersey, and part of Maryland. Madison won in the electoral college, 128 to 89, but his margin of victory was considerably smaller than in 1808.

In late 1812 and early 1813, the tide began to turn in the Americans' favor. First came some victories at sea. Then the Americans attacked York (now Toronto) and burned it in April 1813.

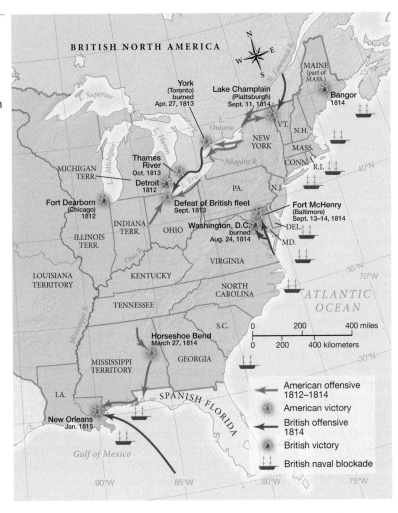

MAP 10.3

The War of 1812

During the War of 1812, battles were fought along the Canadian border and in the Chesapeake region. The most important American victory came in New Orleans two weeks after a peace agreement had been signed in England.

A few months later, Commodore Oliver Hazard Perry defeated the British fleet at the western end of Lake Erie. Emboldened, General Harrison drove an army into Canada from Detroit and in October 1813 defeated the British and Indians at the battle of the Thames, where Tecumseh was killed.

Creek Indians in the South who had allied with Tecumseh's confederacy were also plunged into war. Some 10,000 living in the Mississippi Territory put up a spirited fight against U.S. forces for ten months. But the **Creek War** ended suddenly in March 1814 when a general named Andrew Jackson led 2,500 Tennessee militiamen in a bloody attack called the Battle of Horseshoe Bend. More than 550 Indians were killed, and several hundred more died trying to escape across a river. Later that year, General Jackson extracted from the defeated tribe a treaty relinquishing thousands of square miles of their land to the United States.

Washington City Burns: The British Offensive

In August 1814, British ships sailed into the Chesapeake Bay, landing 5,000 troops and throwing the capital into a panic. Families evacuated, banks hid their money, and government clerks carted away boxes of important papers. Dolley Madison, with dinner for guests cooking over the fire, fled with her husband's papers, while servants rescued a portrait of George Washington. As the cook related, "When the British did arrive, they ate up the very dinner, and drank the wines, &c., that I had prepared for the President's party." Then the British torched the White House, the Capitol, a newspaper office, and a well-stocked arsenal. Instead of trying to hold the city, the British headed north and attacked Baltimore, but a fierce defense by the Maryland militia thwarted that effort.

In another powerful offensive that same month, British troops marched from Canada into

The Burning of Washington City
This engraving celebrates Britain's attack on Washington, D.C., in 1814. Disciplined troops control the street in front of the burning White House; the dome of the blazing Capitol is on the right. Some soldiers sought trophies of war that night. Below is James Madison's medicine chest, plundered by a British soldier. In 1939, his descendant returned the souvenir to President Franklin D. Roosevelt. Engraving: Anne S. K. Brown Military Collection, Brown University Library; medicine chest: FDR Library.

New York State, but a series of mistakes cost them a naval skirmish at Plattsburgh on Lake Champlain, and they retreated to Canada. Five months later, another large British army landed in lower Louisiana and, in early January 1815, encountered General Andrew Jackson and his militia just outside New Orleans. Jackson's forces carried the day. The British suffered between 2,000 and 3,000 casualties, the Americans fewer than 80. Jackson instantly became known as the hero of the **battle of New Orleans**. No one in the United States knew that negotiators in Europe had signed a peace agreement two weeks earlier.

The Treaty of Ghent, signed in December 1814, settled few of the surface issues that had led to war. Neither country could claim victory, and no land changed hands. Instead, the treaty reflected a mutual agreement to give up certain goals. The Americans dropped their plea for an end to impressments, which in any case subsided as soon as Britain and France ended their war in 1815. They also gave up any claim to Canada. The British agreed to stop all aid to the Indians. Nothing was said about shipping rights. The most concrete result was a plan for a future commission to determine the exact boundary between the United States and Canada.

Antiwar Federalists in New England could not gloat over the war's ambiguous conclusion because of an ill-timed and seemingly unpatriotic move on their part. The region's leaders had convened a secret meeting in Hartford, Connecticut, in December 1814 to discuss a series of proposals aimed at reducing the South's power and breaking Virginia's lock on the presidency. They proposed abolishing the Constitution's three-fifths

clause as a basis of representation; requiring a two-thirds vote instead of a simple majority for imposing embargoes, admitting states, or declaring war; limiting the president to one term; and prohibiting the election of successive presidents from the same state. They even discussed secession from the Union but rejected that path. Coming just as peace was achieved, however, the **Hartford Convention** looked very unpatriotic. The Federalist Party never recovered, and within a few years it was reduced to a shadow of its former self, even in New England.

No one really won the War of 1812; however, Americans celebrated as though they had, with parades and fireworks. The war gave rise to a new spirit of nationalism. The paranoia over British tyranny evident in the 1812 declaration of war was laid to rest, replaced by pride in a more equal relationship with the old mother country. Indeed, in 1817 the two countries signed the Rush-Bagot disarmament treaty (named after its two negotiators), which limited each country to a total of four naval vessels, each with just a single cannon, to patrol the vast watery border between them. It was the most successful disarmament treaty for a century to come.

The biggest winners in the War of 1812 were the young men, once called War Hawks, who took up the banner of the Republican Party and carried it in new, expansive directions. These young politicians favored trade, western expansion, internal improvements, and the energetic development of new economic markets. The biggest losers of the war were the Indians. Tecumseh was dead, his brother the Prophet was discredited, the prospects of an Indian confederacy were dashed, the Creeks' large homeland was seized, and the British protectors were gone.

REVIEW   Why did Congress declare war on Great Britain in 1812?

▶ Women's Status in the Early Republic

Dolley Madison's pioneering role as "presidentress" showed that elite women could assume an active presence in civic affairs. But, as with the 1790s cultural compromise that endorsed female education to make women into better wives and mothers (see "The Republican Wife and Mother" in chapter 9), Mrs. Madison and her female circle practiced politics to further their husbands' careers. There was little talk of the "rights of woman." Indeed, from 1800 to 1825, key institutions central to the shaping of women's lives—the legal system, marriage, and religion—proved fairly resistant to change. Nonetheless, the trend toward increased commitment to female education that began in the 1780s and 1790s continued in the first decades of the nineteenth century.

Women and the Law

In English common law, wives had no independent legal or political personhood. The legal doctrine of *feme covert* (covered woman) held that a wife's civic life was completely subsumed by her husband's. A wife was obligated to obey her husband; her property was his, her domestic and sexual services were his, and even their children were legally his. Women had no right to keep their wages, to make contracts, or to sue or be sued. American state legislatures generally passed up the opportunity to rewrite the laws of domestic relations even though they redrafted other British laws in light of republican principles. Lawyers never paused to defend, much less to challenge, the assumption that unequal power relations lay at the heart of marriage.

The one aspect of family law that changed in the early Republic was divorce. Before the Revolution, only New England jurisdictions recognized a limited right to divorce; by 1820, every state except South Carolina did so. However, divorce was uncommon and in many states could be obtained only by petition to the state's legislature, a daunting obstacle for many ordinary people. A mutual wish to terminate a marriage was never sufficient grounds for a legal divorce. A New York judge affirmed that "it would be aiming a deadly blow at public morals to decree a dissolution of the marriage contract merely because the parties requested it. Divorces should never be allowed, except for the protection of the innocent party, and for the punishment of the guilty." States upheld the institution of marriage both to protect persons they thought of as naturally dependent (women and children) and to regulate the use and inheritance of property. (Unofficial self-divorce, desertion, and bigamy were remedies that ordinary people sometimes chose to get around the law, but all were socially unacceptable.) Legal enforcement of marriage as an unequal relationship played a major role in maintaining gender inequality in the nineteenth century.

Single adult women could own and convey property, make contracts, initiate lawsuits, and pay taxes. They could not vote (except in New Jersey before 1807), serve on juries, or practice law, so their civil status was limited. Single women's economic status was often limited as well, by custom as much as by law. Job prospects were few and low-paying. Unless they had inherited adequate property or could live with married siblings, single adult women in the early Republic very often were poor.

None of the legal institutions that structured white gender relations applied to black slaves. As property themselves, under the jurisdiction of slave owners, they could not freely consent to any contractual obligations, including marriage. The protective features of state-sponsored unions were thus denied to black men and women in slavery. But this also meant that slave unions did not establish unequal power relations between partners backed by the force of law, as did marriages among the free.

Women and Church Governance

In most Protestant denominations around 1800, white women made up the majority of congregants. Yet church leadership of most denominations

The Universal Friend.

VISUAL ACTIVITY

**Women and the Church:
Jemima Wilkinson**

In this engraving, Jemima Wilkinson, "the Publick Universal Friend," wears a clerical collar and body-obscuring robe, much as a male minister would wear, in keeping with the claim that the former Jemima was now a person without gender. Wilkinson's hair is swept back from the forehead and curled at the neck in the style of men's powdered wigs of the 1790s. From *History of Yates County* by Stafford C. Cleveland, 1873.

READING THE IMAGE: Was Wilkinson merely masculinized by dress and deportment, or did the "Universal Friend" truly transcend gender?

CONNECTIONS: Why was it so difficult for women to attain religious authority in the early Republic? What allowed a few to rise above social limitations?

rested in men's hands. There were some exceptions, however. In Baptist congregations in New England, women served along with men on church governance committees, deciding on the admission of new members, voting on hiring ministers, and even debating doctrinal points. Quakers, too, had a history of recognizing women's spiritual talents. Some were accorded the status of minister, capable of leading and speaking in Quaker meetings.

Between 1790 and 1820, a small and highly unusual set of women actively engaged in open preaching. Most were from Freewill Baptist groups centered in New England and upstate New York. Others came from small Methodist sects, and yet others rejected any formal religious affiliation. Probably fewer than a hundred such women existed, but several dozen traveled beyond their local communities, creating converts and controversy. They spoke from the heart, without prepared speeches, often exhibiting trances and claiming to exhort (counsel or warn) rather than to preach.

The best-known exhorting woman was Jemima Wilkinson, who called herself "the Publick Universal Friend." After a near-death experience from a high fever, Wilkinson proclaimed her body no longer female or male but the incarnation of the "Spirit of Light." She dressed in men's clothes, wore her hair in a masculine style, shunned gender-specific pronouns, and preached openly in Rhode Island and Philadelphia. In the early nineteenth century, Wilkinson established a town called New Jerusalem in western New York with some 250 followers. Her fame was sustained by periodic newspaper articles that fed public curiosity about her lifelong cross dressing and her unfeminine forcefulness.

The decades from 1790 to the 1820s marked a period of unusual confusion, ferment, and creativity in American religion. New denominations blossomed, new styles of religiosity gripped adherents, and an extensive periodical press devoted to religion popularized all manner of theological and institutional innovations. In such a climate, the age-old tradition of gender subordination came into question here and there among the most radically democratic of the churches. But the presumption of male authority over women was deeply entrenched in American culture. Even denominations that had allowed women to participate in church governance began to pull back, and most churches reinstated patterns of hierarchy along gender lines.

Female Education

First in the North and then in the South, states and localities began investing in public schools to foster an educated citizenry deemed essential

One Woman's Quest to Provide Higher Education for Women

Talented young men seeking the mental enrichment and career boost of higher education saw their opportunities expand rapidly in the early Republic. By 1830, six dozen colleges offered them training in science, history, religion, literature, and philosophy. Not a single one admitted females.

With the spread of district schools and female academies, however, the number of girls trained for advanced study was on the rise. The winning rationale for female education—that mothers molded the character of rising generations—worked well to justify basic schooling. But a highly intellectual woman, negatively termed a "bluestocking," was thought to put her very femininity at risk. Some critics sounded a more practical note: "When girls become scholars, who is to make the puddings and pies?"

The academic aspirations of Emma Hart—born in Connecticut in 1787 as the sixteenth in a farm family of seventeen children—were encouraged by her father, who read Shakespeare at night to his large brood. After attending the local district school and an academy for girls,

Emma taught at the district school before moving to Vermont to head the Middlebury Female Academy, founded in 1800. There, she taught sixty adolescents in an underheated building.

Emma ran the academy for two years until she married a Middlebury physician and banker named John Willard in 1809. Marriage for white women usually ended outside employment, so Emma's life now focused on child care and domestic duties. Yet she found time to read books in her husband's well-stocked library, including political philosophy, medical treatises, physiology texts, and Euclid's geometry.

Four years into their marriage, John Willard suffered severe financial losses, leading Emma Willard to open an advanced girls' school in her home. She patterned her courses on those at nearby Middlebury College for men, and her rigorous curriculum soon drew students from all over the Northeast. One satisfied father with political connections persuaded the Willards to relocate to his home state of New York with the promise to help them secure state funding for a school.

Emma drew up a formal proposal in 1819, arguing that advanced female education would both enhance motherhood and supply excellent teachers needed for a projected state-supported school system. Though her proposal was endorsed by Governor DeWitt Clinton, John Adams, and Thomas Jefferson, the New York assembly failed to fund Willard's school. Local citizens in Troy supplied Willard with a building, however, and in 1821 the Troy Female Seminary opened with students coming from many states. Coursework included "masculine" subjects such as Latin, Greek, mathematics, and science in addition to modern languages and literature. Willard taught geometry and trigonometry herself and hired other teachers for classes in astronomy, botany, geology, chemistry, and zoology. She soon forged a cooperative alliance with the neighboring Rensselaer Polytechnic Institute. Just like Harvard and Princeton, her seminary required a course in moral philosophy, taught by Willard herself to the senior class using the same texts employed at the male colleges.

in a republic. Young girls attended district schools along with boys, and by 1830, girls had made rapid gains, in many places approaching male literacy rates. Basic literacy and numeracy formed the curriculum taught to white children aged roughly six to eleven. (Far fewer schools addressed the needs of free black children, whether male or female.)

More advanced female education came from a growing number of private academies. Judith Sargent Murray, the Massachusetts author who had called for equality of the sexes around 1790 (see "The Republican Wife and Mother" in chapter 9), predicted in 1800 that "a new era in female history" would emerge because "female academies are everywhere establishing." Some dozen were founded in the 1790s, and by 1830 that number had grown to nearly two hundred. Students of ages 12 to 16 came from elite families as well as those of middling families with intellectual aspirations, such as ministers' daughters.

The three-year curriculum included both ornamental arts and solid academics. The former strengthened female gentility: drawing, needlework, music, and French conversation. The academic subjects included English grammar, literature, history, the natural sciences, geography, and elocution (the art of effective public speaking). The most ambitious female academies equaled the training offered at male colleges

Willard invited the public to weeklong examinations, where students solved algebra problems and geometry proofs on chalkboards and gave twenty-minute discourses on history and philosophy. Educated men were particularly encouraged to question the students, to put to rest any "lurking suspicion, that the learning which a female possesses must be superficial." One minister was astonished, and pleased, to see "Euclid discussed by female lips." By emphasizing geometry, Willard vindicated her claim that women could equal men in logic. But she took pains to make sure her students preserved "feminine delicacy" and avoided "the least indelicacy of language or behavior, such as too much exposure of the person."

More than the rigorous curriculum inspired these young women. Willard was an exemplary role model, beloved by many of her students for her dedication and confidence. One student recalled that her "great distinction seemed to me to be a supreme confidence in herself and, as a consequence, a stubborn faith in the capacity of her own sex." Willard graciously gave much of the credit to her unusually supportive husband: "He entered into the full spirit of my views, with a disinterested zeal for the sex whom, as he had come to believe, his own had unjustly neglected."

The Troy Female Seminary flourished; it still exists today as the

Emma Willard School. From 1821 to 1871, more than 12,000 girls attended; it was larger than most men's colleges. Ministers' daughters received a discount on tuition, and many girls were allowed to defer payment until they were wage-earning teachers. Nearly 5,000 graduates in the first fifty years became teachers, and some 150 directed their own schools scattered across the nation. When the marquis de Lafayette, aging hero of the American Revolution, visited Willard's school in 1824, he pronounced it a "Female University." Willard took pleasure in his recognition of her success.

Portrait of Emma Willard
Emma Willard, founder of the famed and rigorous Troy Female Seminary, was an exemplary role model to her students. Elizabeth Cady, a student in the 1830s and later an important figure in the woman's rights movement, recalled that Willard had a "profound self respect (a rare quality in a woman) which gave her a dignity truly regal." Her confidence shines through in this portrait. The Granger Collection, New York.

Questions for Consideration

1. How did Emma Willard's own life demonstrate the importance of female education for a family's financial security?

2. Compare the occupation of Emma Willard with that of Dolley Madison. In what ways were these women similar? How did they differ?

Connect to the Big Idea

C What difference might it make for large numbers of females to attain literacy over the course of the first decades of the early Republic?

such as Harvard, Yale, Dartmouth, and Princeton, with classes in Latin, rhetoric, theology, moral philosophy, algebra, geometry, and even chemistry and physics.

Two of the best-known female academies were the Troy Female Seminary in New York, founded by Emma Willard in 1821, and the Hartford Seminary in Connecticut, founded by Catharine Beecher in 1822. (See "Seeking the American Promise," above.) Unlike theological seminaries that trained men for the clergy, Troy and Hartford prepared their female students to teach, on the grounds that women made better teachers than did men. Author Harriet Beecher Stowe, educated at her sister's school and then

a teacher there, agreed: "If men have more knowledge they have less talent at communicating it. Nor have they the patience, the long-suffering, and gentleness necessary to superintend the formation of character."

The most immediate value of advanced female education lay in the self-cultivation and confidence it provided. Following the model of male colleges, female graduation exercises showcased speeches and recitations performed in front of a mixed-sex audience of family, friends, and local notables. Elocution, a common subject offering in the academies, taught the young women the art of persuasion along with correct pronunciation and the skill of fluent speaking. Academies also took care to promote a pleasing female modesty. Female pedantry or intellectual immodesty triggered the stereotype of the "bluestocking," a British term of hostility for a too-learned woman doomed to fail in the marriage market.

By the mid-1820s, the total annual enrollment at the female academies equaled enrollment at the near six dozen male colleges in the United States. Both groups accounted for only about 1 percent of their age cohorts in the country at large, indicating that advanced education was clearly limited to a privileged few. Among the male students, this group disproportionately filled the future rosters of ministers, lawyers, judges, and political leaders. Most female graduates in time married and raised families, but first many of them became teachers at academies and district schools. A large number also became minor authors, contributing essays and poetry to newspapers, editing periodicals, and publishing novels. The new attention to the training of female minds laid the foundation for major changes in the gender system as girl students of the 1810s matured into adult women of the 1830s.

> **REVIEW**   How did the civil status of American women and men differ in the early Republic?

► Monroe and Adams

Virginians continued their hold on the presidency with the election of James Monroe in 1816 and again in 1820, when Monroe garnered all but one electoral vote. The collapse of the Federalist Party ushered in an apparent period of one-party rule, but politics remained highly partisan. At the state level, increasing political engagement sparked a drive for universal white male suffrage. At the national level, ill feelings were stirred by a sectional crisis in 1820 over the admission of Missouri to the Union, and foreign policy questions involving European claims to Latin American animated sharp disagreements as well. Four candidates vied for the presidency in 1824 in an election decided by the House of Representatives. One-party rule was far from harmonious.

From Property to Democracy

Up to 1820, presidential elections occurred in the electoral college, at a remove from ordinary voters. The excitement generated by state elections, however, created an insistent pressure for greater democratization of presidential elections.

In the 1780s, twelve of the original thirteen states enacted property qualifications based on the time-honored theory that only male

VISUAL ACTIVITY

"We Owe Allegiance to No Crown"
John Woodside, a Philadelphia sign painter, made his living creating advertisements for hotels and taverns, and he specialized in patriotic banners carried in parades. At some point in his long career from 1815 to 1850, he created this scene of a youthful sailor receiving a laurel wreath, the ancient Greek symbol of victory, by a breezy Miss Liberty (identified by the liberty cap on a stick). Picture Research Consultants & Archives.
READING THE IMAGE: What might the chain at the sailor's feet indicate? What do you think the slogan on the banner means? What do you see in the picture that would help date it? (Hint: Examine the flag. And for the truly curious, consider the history of men's facial hair styles.)
CONNECTIONS: How and why does the painting reference the War of 1812? Regardless of the painting's date, what message do you think Woodside is trying to convey here?

Painting on a patriotic motif by John A. Woodside of Philadelphia, in the early 1800s.

freeholders—landowners, as distinct from tenants or servants—had sufficient independence of mind to be entrusted with the vote. Of course, not everyone accepted that restricted idea of the people's role in government (see "Equality and Slavery" in chapter 8). In the 1790s, Vermont became the first state to enfranchise all adult males, and four other states soon broadened suffrage considerably by allowing all male taxpayers to vote. As new states joined the union, most opted for suffrage for all free white men, which added pressure for eastern states to consider broadening their suffrage laws. Between 1800 and 1830, greater democratization became a contentious issue.

Not everyone favored expanded suffrage; propertied elites tended to defend the status quo. But others managed to get legislatures to call new constitutional conventions in which questions of suffrage, balloting procedures, apportionment, and representation were debated. By 1820, half a dozen states passed suffrage reform, some choosing universal manhood suffrage while others tied the vote to tax status or militia service. In the remainder of the states, the defenders of landed property qualifications managed to delay expanded suffrage for two more decades. But it was increasingly hard to persuade the disfranchised that landowners alone had a stake in government. Proponents of the status quo began to argue instead that the "industry and good habits" necessary to achieve a propertied status in life were what gave landowners the right character to vote. Opponents fired back blistering attacks. One delegate to New York's constitutional convention said, "More integrity and more patriotism are generally found in the labouring class of the community than in the higher orders." Owning land was no more predictive of wisdom and good character than it was of a person's height or strength, said another observer.

Both sides of the debate generally agreed that character mattered, and many ideas for ensuring an electorate of proper wisdom came up for discussion. The exclusion of paupers and felons convicted of "infamous crimes" found favor in legislation in many states. Requiring literacy tests and raising the voting age to a figure in the thirties were debated but ultimately discarded. The exclusion of women required no discussion in the constitutional conventions, so firm was the legal power of *feme covert* mandating the subjugation of married women to their husbands. But in one exceptional moment, at the Virginia constitutional convention in 1829, a delegate wondered aloud why unmarried women older than twenty-one could not vote; he was quickly silenced with the argument that all women lacked the "free agency and intelligence" necessary for wise voting.

Free black men's enfranchisement was another story, generating much discussion at all the conventions. Under existing freehold qualifications, a small number of propertied black men could vote; universal or taxpayer suffrage would inevitably enfranchise many more. Many delegates at the various state conventions spoke against that extension, claiming that blacks as a race lacked prudence, independence, and knowledge. With the exception of New York, which retained the existing property qualification for black voters as it removed it for whites, the general pattern was one of expanded suffrage for whites and a total eclipse of suffrage for blacks.

The Missouri Compromise

The politics of race produced the most divisive issue during Monroe's term. In February 1819, Missouri—so recently the territory of the powerful Osage Indians—applied for statehood. Since 1815, four other states had joined the Union (Indiana, Mississippi, Illinois, and Alabama) following the blueprint laid out by the Northwest Ordinance of 1787. But Missouri posed a problem. Although much of its area was on the same latitude as the free state of Illinois, its territorial population included ten thousand slaves brought there by southern planters.

That anomaly—a mostly northern state with the profile of a southern population—led a New York congressman, James Tallmadge Jr., to propose two amendments to the statehood bill. The first stipulated that slaves born in Missouri after statehood would be free at age twenty-five, and the second declared that no new slaves could be imported into the state. Tallmadge's model was New York's gradual emancipation law of 1799 (see "Equality and Slavery" in chapter 8). It did not strip slave owners of their current property, and it allowed them full use of the labor of newborn slaves well into their prime productive years. Still, southern congressmen objected because in the long run the amendments would make Missouri a free state, presumably no longer allied with southern economic and political interests. Just as southern economic power rested on slave labor, southern political power drew extra strength from the slave population because of the three-fifths rule. In 1820, the South owed seventeen of its seats in the House of Representatives to its slave population.

Tallmadge's amendments passed in the House by a close and sharply sectional vote of North against South. The ferocious debate led a Georgia representative to observe that the question had started "a fire which all the waters of the ocean could not extinguish. It can be extinguished only in blood." The Senate, with an even number of slave and free states, voted down the amendments, and Missouri statehood was postponed until the next congressional term.

In 1820, a compromise emerged. Maine, once part of Massachusetts, applied for statehood as a free state, balancing against Missouri as a slave state. The Senate further agreed that the southern boundary of Missouri—latitude 36°30′—extended west, would become the permanent line dividing slave from free states, guaranteeing the North a large area where slavery was banned (Map 10.4). The House also approved the **Missouri Compromise**, thanks to expert deal brokering by Kentucky's Henry Clay. The whole package passed because seventeen northern congressmen decided that minimizing sectional conflict was the best course and voted with the South.

President Monroe and former president Jefferson at first worried that the Missouri crisis would reinvigorate the Federalist Party as the party of the North. But even ex-Federalists agreed that the split between free and slave states was too dangerous a fault line to be permitted to become a shaper of national politics. When new parties did develop in the 1830s, they took pains to bridge geography, each party developing a presence in both North and South. Monroe and Jefferson also worried about the future of slavery. Both understood slavery to be deeply problematic, but, as Jefferson said, "we have the wolf by the ears, and we can neither hold him, nor safely let him go. Justice is in one scale, and self-preservation in the other."

The Monroe Doctrine

New foreign policy challenges arose even as Congress struggled with the slavery issue. In

MAP ACTIVITY

Map 10.4 The Missouri Compromise, 1820

After a difficult battle in Congress, Missouri entered the Union in 1821 as part of a package of compromises. Maine was admitted as a free state to balance slavery in Missouri, and a line drawn at latitude 36°30′ put most of the rest of the Louisiana Territory off-limits to slavery in the future.

READING THE MAP: How many free and how many slave states were there prior to the Missouri Compromise? What did the admission of Missouri as a slave state threaten to do?
CONNECTIONS: Who precipitated the crisis over Missouri, what did he propose, and where did the idea come from? Who proposed the Missouri Compromise, and who benefited from it?

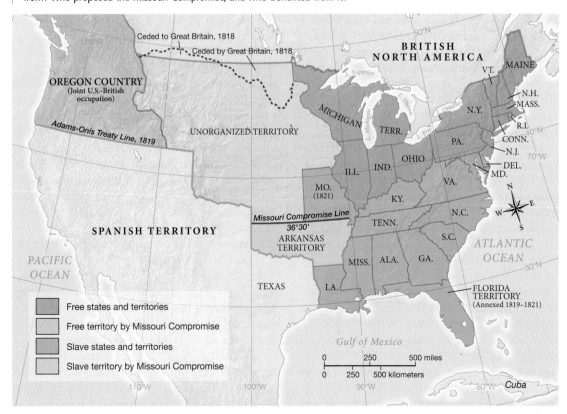

1816, U.S. troops led by General Andrew Jackson invaded Spanish Florida in search of Seminole Indians harboring escaped slaves. Once there, Jackson declared himself the commander of northern Florida, demonstrating his power in 1818 by executing two British men who he claimed were dangerous enemies. In asserting rule over the territory, and surely in executing the two British subjects on Spanish land, Jackson had gone too far. Privately, President Monroe was distressed and pondered court-martialing Jackson, prevented only by Jackson's immense popularity as the hero of the battle of New Orleans. Instead, John Quincy Adams, the secretary of state, negotiated with Spain the Adams-Onís Treaty, which delivered Florida to the United States in 1819 and finally settled the disputed borders of the Louisiana Purchase. In exchange, the Americans agreed to abandon any claim to Texas or Cuba. Southerners viewed this as a large concession, having eyed both places as potential acquisitions for future slave states.

Spain at that moment was preoccupied with its colonies in South America. One after another, Chile, Colombia, Peru, and finally Mexico declared themselves independent in the early 1820s. To discourage Spain and other European countries from reconquering these colonies, Monroe in 1823 formulated a declaration of principles on South America, known in later years as the Monroe Doctrine. The president warned that "the American Continents, by the free and independent condition which they have assumed and maintain, are henceforth not to be considered as subjects for future colonization by any European power." Any attempt to interfere in the Western Hemisphere would be regarded as "the manifestation of an unfriendly disposition towards the United States." In exchange for noninterference by Europeans, Monroe pledged that the United States would stay out of European struggles.

The Election of 1824

Monroe's nonpartisan administration was the last of its kind, a throwback to eighteenth-century ideals, as was Monroe, with his powdered wig and knee breeches. Monroe's cabinet contained men of sharply different philosophies, all calling themselves Republicans. Secretary of State John Quincy Adams represented the urban Northeast; South Carolinian John C. Calhoun spoke for the planter aristocracy as secretary of war; and William H. Crawford of Georgia, secretary of the treasury, was a proponent of Jeffersonian states' rights and limited federal power. Even before the end of Monroe's first term, these men and others began to maneuver for the election of 1824.

Crucially helping them to maneuver were their wives, who accomplished some of the work of modern campaign managers by courting men—and women—of influence. Louisa Catherine Adams had a weekly party for guests numbering in the hundreds. The somber Adams lacked charm—"I am a man of reserved, cold, austere, and forbidding manners," he once wrote—but his abundantly

Election Sewing or Trinket Boxes from 1824
Women could express support for a presidential candidate by purchasing a sewing box emblazoned with his face. The box to the left bears John Quincy Adams's picture; the box top (not visible here) has a velvet pincushion printed with the slogan "Be Firm for Adams." The competing box on the right features Andrew Jackson's likeness under glass on top of the cover. © David J. & Janice L. Frent Collection/CORBIS.

charming (and hardworking) wife made up for that. She attended to the etiquette of social calls, sometimes making two dozen in a morning, and counted sixty-eight members of Congress as her regular guests. This was smart politics, in case the House of Representatives wound up deciding the 1824 election—which it did.

John Quincy Adams (and Louisa Catherine) were ambitious for the presidency, but so were others. Candidate Henry Clay, Speaker of the House and negotiator of the Treaty of Ghent with Britain in 1814, promoted a new "American System," a package of protective tariffs to encourage manufacturing and federal expenditures for internal improvements such as roads and canals. Treasurer William Crawford was a favorite of Republicans from Virginia and New York, even after he suffered an incapacitating stroke in mid-1824. Calhoun was another serious contender, having served in Congress and in several cabinets. A southern planter, he attracted northern support for his backing of internal improvements and protective tariffs.

The final candidate was an outsider and a latecomer: General Andrew Jackson of Tennessee. Jackson had far less national political experience than the others, but he enjoyed great celebrity from his military career. In 1824, on the anniversary of the battle of New Orleans, the Adamses threw a spectacular ball in his honor, hoping that some of Jackson's charisma would rub off on Adams, who was not yet thinking of Jackson as a rival for office. Not long after, Jackson's supporters put his name forward for the presidency, and voters in the West and South reacted with enthusiasm, Adams was dismayed, and Calhoun dropped out of the race and shifted his attention to winning the vice presidency.

Along with democratizing the vote, eighteen states (out of the full twenty-four) had put the power to choose members of the electoral college directly in the hands of voters, making the 1824 election the first one to have a popular vote tally for the presidency. Jackson proved by far to be the most popular candidate, winning 153,544 votes. Adams was second with 108,740, Clay won 47,136 votes, and the debilitated Crawford garnered 46,618. This was not a large turnout, probably amounting to just over a quarter of adult white males. Nevertheless, the election of 1824 marked a new departure in choosing presidents. Partisanship energized the electorate; apathy and a low voter turnout would not recur until the twentieth century.

In the electoral college, Jackson received 99 votes, Adams 84, Crawford 41, and Clay 37

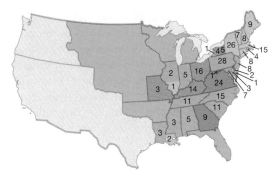

Candidate*	Electoral Vote	Popular Vote	Percent of Popular Vote
John Q. Adams	84	108,740	30.5
Andrew Jackson	99	153,544	43.1
Henry Clay	37	47,136	13.2
W. H. Crawford	41	46,618	13.1

*No distinct political parties

Note: Because no candidate garnered a majority in the electoral college, the election was decided in the House of Representatives. Although Clay was eliminated from the running, as Speaker of the House he influenced the final decision in favor of Adams.

MAP 10.5
The Election of 1824

(Map 10.5). Jackson lacked a majority, so the House of Representatives stepped in for the second time in U.S. history. Each congressional delegation had one vote; according to the Constitution's Twelfth Amendment, passed in 1804, only the top three candidates joined the runoff. Thus Henry Clay was out of the race and in a position to bestow his support on another candidate.

Jackson's supporters later characterized the election of 1824 as the "corrupt bargain." Clay backed Adams, and Adams won by one vote in the House in February 1825. Clay's support made sense on several levels. Despite strong mutual dislike, he and Adams agreed on issues such as federal support to build roads and canals. More-over, Clay was uneasy with Jackson's volatile temperament and unstated political views and with Crawford's diminished capacity. What made Clay's decision look "corrupt" was that immediately after the election, Adams offered to appoint Clay secretary of state—and Clay accepted.

In fact, there probably was no concrete bargain; Adams's subsequent cabinet appointments demonstrated his lack of political astuteness. But Andrew Jackson felt that the election had been stolen from him, and he wrote bitterly that "the Judas of the West [Clay] has closed the contract and will receive the thirty pieces of silver."

The Adams Administration

John Quincy Adams, like his father, was a one-term president. His career had been built on diplomacy, not electoral politics, and despite his wife's deftness in the art of political influence, his own political horse sense was not well developed. With his cabinet choices, he welcomed his opposition into his inner circle. He asked Crawford to stay on in the Treasury. He retained an openly pro-Jackson postmaster general even though that position controlled thousands of nationwide patronage appointments. He even asked Jackson to become secretary of war. With Calhoun as vice president (elected without opposition by the electoral college) and Clay at the State Department, the whole argumentative crew would have been thrust into the executive branch. Crawford and Jackson had the good sense to decline the appointments.

Adams had lofty ideas for federal action during his presidency, and the plan he put before Congress was sweeping. Adams called for federally built roads, canals, and harbors. He proposed a national university in Washington as well as government-sponsored scientific research. He wanted to build observatories to advance astronomical knowledge and to promote precision in timekeeping, and he backed a decimal-based system of weights and measures. In all these endeavors, Adams believed he was continuing the legacy of Jefferson and Madison, using the powers of government to advance knowledge. But his opponents feared he was too Hamiltonian, using federal power inappropriately to advance commercial interests.

Whether he was more truly Federalist or Republican was a moot point. Lacking the give-and-take political skills required to gain congressional support, Adams was unable to implement much of his program. He scorned the idea of courting voters to gain support and using the patronage system to enhance his power. He often made appointments (to posts such as customs collectors) to placate enemies rather than to reward friends. A story of a toast offered to the president may well have been mythical, but it came to summarize Adams's precarious hold on leadership. A dignitary raised a glass and said, "May he strike confusion to his foes," to which another voice scornfully chimed in, "as he has already done to his friends."

REVIEW Why did partisan conflict increase during the administrations of Monroe and Adams?

▶ Conclusion: Republican Simplicity Becomes Complex

The Jeffersonian Republicans at first tried to undo much of what the Federalists had created in the 1790s, but their promise of a simpler government gave way to the complexities of domestic and foreign issues. The Louisiana Purchase and the Barbary Wars required powerful government responses, and the challenges posed by Britain on the seas finally drew American into declaring war on the onetime mother country. The War of 1812, joined by restive Indian nations fighting with the British, was longer and more costly than anticipated, and it ended inconclusively.

The war elevated to national prominence General Andrew Jackson, whose popularity with voters in the 1824 election surprised traditional politicians and threw the one-party rule of Republicans into a tailspin. John Quincy Adams had barely assumed office in 1825 before the election campaign of 1828 was off and running. Reformed suffrage laws ensured that appeals to the mass of white male voters would be the hallmark of all nineteenth-century elections after 1824. In such a system, Adams and men like him were at a great disadvantage.

Ordinary American women, whether white or free black, had no place in government. Male legislatures maintained women's *feme covert* status, keeping wives dependent on husbands. A few women found a pathway to greater personal autonomy through religion, while many others benefited from expanded female schooling in schools and academies. These substantial gains in education would blossom into a major transformation of gender in the 1830s and 1840s.

Two other developments would prove momentous in later decades. The bitter debate over slavery that surrounded the Missouri Compromise accentuated the serious divisions between northern and southern states—divisions that would only widen in the decades to come. And Jefferson's long embargo and Madison's wartime trade stoppage gave a big boost to American manufacturing by removing competition with British factories. When peace returned in 1815, the years of independent development burst forth into a period of sustained economic growth that continued nearly unabated into the mid-nineteenth century.

See the Selected Bibliography for this chapter in the Appendix.

10 Chapter Review

MAKE IT STICK

LearningCurve
Go online and use LearningCurve to see what you know. Then review the key terms and answer the questions.

KEY TERMS

Marbury v. Madison (p. 259)
Louisiana Purchase (p. 261)
Lewis and Clark expedition (p. 262)
impressment (p. 265)
Embargo Act of 1807 (p. 265)
battle of Tippecanoe (p. 267)
War Hawks (p. 267)
Creek War (p. 268)
battle of New Orleans (p. 269)
Hartford Convention (p. 269)
feme covert (p. 270)
Missouri Compromise (p. 276)

REVIEW QUESTIONS

1. How did Jefferson's views of the role of the federal government differ from those of his predecessors? (pp. 255–260)

2. What was the significance of the Louisiana Purchase for the United States? (pp. 260–264)

3. Why did Congress declare war on Great Britain in 1812? (pp. 264–270)

4. How did the civil status of American women and men differ in the early Republic? (pp. 270–274)

5. Why did partisan conflict increase during the administrations of Monroe and Adams? (pp. 274–279)

MAKING CONNECTIONS

1. When Jefferson assumed the presidency following the election of 1800, he expected to transform the national government. Describe President Jefferson's republican vision and his successes and failures in implementing it. Did subsequent Republican presidents advance the same objectives?

2. How did the United States strengthen its control of territory in North America in the early nineteenth century via diplomatic, military, and political means?

3. Although the United States denied its female citizens equality in public life, some women were able to exert considerable influence. How did they do so?

LINKING TO THE PAST

1. Compare the British-Indian alliance in the Revolutionary War with the British-Indian alliance in the War of 1812. Were there any reasons for men like Tecumseh to think that the alliance might work out better the second time? (See chapter 7.)

2. How do you think the Federalist supporters of the Constitution in 1787–1788 felt about the steady decline in states' property qualifications for male voters that occurred between 1800 and 1824? Did the democratization of voting necessarily undermine the Constitution's restrictions on direct democracy in the federal government? (See chapter 8.)

11 The Expanding Republic

1815–1840

CONTENT LEARNING OBJECTIVES

After reading and studying this chapter, you should be able to:

- Identify several contributing factors to the "market revolution."
- Describe political changes that led to the second party system.
- Identify the Democrats', the Whigs', and Andrew Jackson's political agendas.
- Explain both sides of the controversy over the Indian Removal Act of 1829.
- Explain the Second Great Awakening, and identify the major social reform movements it fueled.
- Identify the issues and challenges that faced Martin Van Buren.
- Explain how slavery emerged as a campaign issue in 1836 and how the Panic of 1837 affected the country and Van Buren's administration.

HOUSEHOLD CLOCK
A revolution in household timekeeping devices accompanied the speedup of commerce and transportation in the early republic. By the mid 1820s, inexpensive, mass-manufactured clocks became commonplace, indicating the increased importance of punctuality. Willard House and Clock Museum.

IN 1837, AUDIENCES THROUGHOUT MASSACHUSETTS WITNESSED THE astonishing spectacle of two sisters from a wealthy southern family delivering impassioned speeches about the evils of slavery. Women lecturers were rare in the 1830s, but Sarah and Angelina Grimké were on a mission, channeling a higher power to authorize their outspokenness. Angelina explained that "whilst in the act of speaking I am favored to forget little 'I' entirely & to feel altogether hid behind the great cause I am pleading." In their seventy-nine speaking engagements that year, forty thousand women—and men—came to hear them.

Not much in their family background predicted the sisters' radical break with tradition. They grew up in elite surroundings in Charleston, South Carolina, where their father was chief justice of the state supreme court, yet they somehow managed to develop independent minds and a hatred of slavery. In the 1820s, both sisters moved to Philadelphia and joined the Quakers' Society of Friends.

The abolitionist movement was in its infancy in the 1830s, centered around Boston's William Lloyd Garrison, editor of the *Liberator*, who demanded an immediate end to slavery. In 1835, Angelina Grimké wrote to Garrison, describing herself as a white southern exile from slavery, and Garrison published her letter. Her rare voice of personal testimony caused a stir and propelled her into her new public career.

The sisters' 1837 extended tour of Massachusetts led to a doubling of membership in northern antislavery societies. Newspapers and religious leaders fiercely debated the Grimkés' boldness in presuming to lecture men, and the sisters defended their stand: "Whatever is morally right for a man to do is morally right for a woman to do," Angelina wrote. "I recognize no rights but human rights." Sarah produced a set of essays titled *Letters on the Equality of the Sexes* (1838), the first American treatise asserting women's equality with men.

The Grimké sisters' innovative radicalism was part of a vibrant, contested public life that came alive in the United States of the 1830s. This decade—often summed up as the Age of Jackson, in honor of the larger-than-life president—was a time of rapid economic, political, and social change. Andrew Jackson's bold self-confidence mirrored the new confidence of American society in the years after 1815. An entrepreneurial spirit gripped the country, producing a market revolution of unprecedented scale. Old social hierarchies eroded; ordinary men dreamed of moving high up the ladder of success. Stunning advances in transportation and economic productivity fueled such dreams and propelled thousands to travel west or to cities. Urban growth and technological change fostered the diffusion of a distinctive and lively public culture, spread mainly through the increased circulation of newspapers and also by thousands of public lecturers, like the Grimké sisters, allowing popular opinions to coalesce and intensify.

Expanded communication transformed politics dramatically. Sharp disagreements over the best way to promote individual liberty, economic opportunity, and national prosperity in the new economy defined key differences between presidential parties emerging in the early 1830s, attracting large numbers of white male voters into their ranks. Religion became democratized as well. A nationwide evangelical revival brought its adherents the certainty that salvation was now available to all.

Yet there were downsides. Steamboats blew up, banks and businesses periodically collapsed, alcoholism rates soared, Indians were killed or relocated farther west, and slavery continued to expand. The brash confidence that turned some people into rugged, self-promoting individuals inspired others to think about the human costs of rapid economic expansion and thus about reforming society in dramatic ways. The common denominator was a faith that people and societies could shape their own destinies.

Grimké Sisters

Sarah and Angelina Grimké sat for these portraits around 1840, at ages 48 and 35. Day caps were typical indoor wear for most older women and for Quaker women of all ages. Caps kept hair neat and in place. As important, they signaled modesty, in contrast to fancily coiffed or loose hair, which sent a different signal. Library of Congress.

▶ The Market Revolution

The return of peace in 1815 unleashed powerful forces that revolutionized the organization of the economy. Spectacular changes in transportation facilitated the movement of commodities, information, and people, while textile mills and other factories created many new jobs, especially for young unmarried women. Innovations in banking, legal practices, and tariff policies promoted swift economic growth.

This was not yet an industrial revolution, as was beginning in Britain, but rather a market revolution fueled by traditional sources—water, wood, beasts of burden, and human muscle. What was new was the accelerated pace of economic activity and the scale of the distribution of goods. The nature and scale of production and consumption changed Americans' economic behavior, attitudes, and expectations. The new economy also carried great risk, which periodically resulted in economic crashes.

Improvements in Transportation

Before 1815, transportation in the United States was slow and expensive; it cost as much to ship a crate over thirty miles of domestic roads as it did to send it across the Atlantic Ocean. A stagecoach trip from Boston to New York took four days. But between 1815 and 1840, networks of roads, canals, steamboats, and finally railroads dramatically raised the speed and lowered the cost of travel (Map 11.1).

Improved transportation moved goods into wider markets. It moved passengers, too, allowing young people as well as adults to take up new employment in cities or factory towns. Transportation also facilitated the flow of political information via the U.S. mail with its bargain postal rates for newspapers, periodicals, and books. Enhanced public transport was expensive and produced uneven economic benefits, so presidents from Jefferson to Monroe were reluctant to fund it with federal dollars. Instead, private investors pooled resources and chartered transport companies, receiving significant subsidies and monopoly rights from state governments. Turnpike and roadway mileage increased dramatically after 1815, reducing shipping costs. Stagecoach companies proliferated, and travel time on main routes was cut in half.

CHRONOLOGY

1807	• Robert Fulton sets off steamboat craze.
1816	• Second Bank of the United States chartered.
1817	• American Colonization Society founded.
1819	• Economic panic.
1825	• Erie Canal completed in New York.
1826	• American Temperance Society founded.
1828	• Tariff of Abominations. • Andrew Jackson elected president.
1829	• David Walker's *Appeal . . . to the Coloured Citizens of the World*. • Baltimore and Ohio Railroad begun.
1830	• Indian Removal Act.
1830–1831	• Charles Grandison Finney preaches in Rochester, New York.
1831	• William Lloyd Garrison starts *Liberator*.
1832	• Massacre of Sauk and Fox Indians. • *Worcester v. Georgia*. • Jackson vetoes charter renewal of Bank of the United States. • New England Anti-Slavery Society founded.
1833	• South Carolina nullifies federal tariffs. • New York and Philadelphia antislavery societies founded. • New York Female Moral Reform Society founded.
1834	• Female mill workers strike in Lowell, Massachusetts, and again in 1836.
1836	• Martin Van Buren elected president. • American Temperance Union founded.
1837	• Economic panic.
1838	• Cherokee Trail of Tears.
1839	• Economic panic.
1840	• William Henry Harrison elected president.

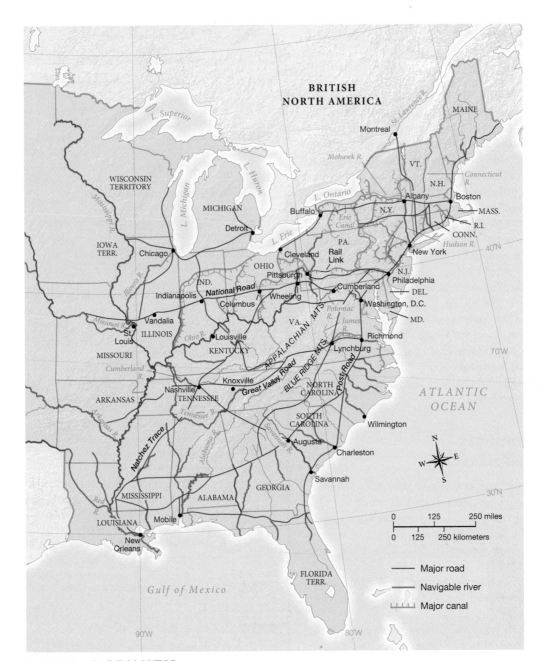

MAP ACTIVITY

Map 11.1 Routes of Transportation in 1840

Transportation advances cut travel times significantly. On the Erie Canal, goods and people could move from New York City to Buffalo in four days, a two-week trip by road. Steamboats cut travel time from New York to New Orleans from four weeks by road to less than two weeks by river.

READING THE MAP: In what parts of the country were canals built most extensively? Were most of them within a single state's borders, or did they encourage interstate travel and shipping?

CONNECTIONS: What impact did the Erie Canal have on the development of New York City? How did improvements in transportation affect urbanization in other parts of the country?

Water travel was similarly transformed. In 1807, Robert Fulton's steam-propelled boat, the *Clermont*, churned up the Hudson River from New York City to Albany, touching off a steam-boat craze on eastern rivers and the Great Lakes. By the early 1830s, more than seven hundred steamboats were in operation on the Ohio and Mississippi rivers.

The Erie Canal at Lockport
The Erie Canal, completed in 1825, was impressive not only for its length of 350 miles but also for its elevation, requiring the construction of eighty-three locks. The biggest engineering challenge came at Lockport, twenty miles northeast of Buffalo, where the canal traversed a steep slate escarpment. Work crews—mostly immigrant Irishmen—used gunpowder and grueling physical labor to blast the deep artificial gorge shown here. Department of Rare Books and Special Collections, Rush Rhees Library, University of Rochester.

Steamboats were not benign advances, however. The urgency to cut travel time led to overstoked furnaces, sudden boiler explosions, and terrible mass fatalities. An investigation of an accident near Cincinnati in 1838, in which 150 passengers were killed, charged: "Such disasters have their foundation in the present mammoth evil of our country, an inordinate love of gain. We are not satisfied with getting rich, but we must get rich in a day. We are not satisfied with traveling at a speed of ten miles an hour, but we must fly." By the mid 1830s, nearly three thousand Americans had been killed in steamboat accidents, leading to the first federal attempt to regulate safety on vessels used for interstate commerce. Environment costs were also large: Steamboats had to load fuel—"wood up"—every twenty miles or so, resulting in mass deforestation. By the 1830s, the banks of many main rivers were denuded of trees, and forests miles back from the rivers fell to the ax. The smoke from wood-burning steamboats created America's first significant air pollution.

Canals were another major innovation of the transportation revolution. Canal boats powered by mules moved slowly—less than five miles per hour—but the low-friction water enabled one mule to pull a fifty-ton barge. Several states commenced major government-sponsored canal enterprises, the most impressive being the **Erie Canal**, finished in 1825, covering 350 miles between Albany and Buffalo and linking the port of New York City with the entire Great Lakes region. Wheat and flour moved east, household goods and tools moved west, and passengers went in both directions. By the 1830s, the cost of shipping by canal fell to less than one-tenth of the cost of overland transport, and New York City quickly blossomed into the premier commercial city in the United States.

In the 1830s, private railroad companies heavily subsidized by state legislatures began to give canals competition. The nation's first railroad, the Baltimore and Ohio, laid thirteen miles of track in 1829, and by 1840, three thousand more miles of track materialized nationwide. Rail lines in the 1830s were generally short, on the order of twenty to one hundred miles. They did not yet provide an efficient distribution system for goods, but passengers flocked to experience the marvelous speeds of fifteen to twenty miles per hour. Railroads and other advances in transportation served to unify the country culturally and economically.

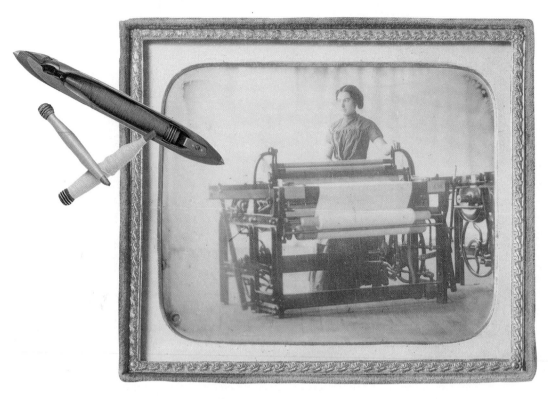

Mill Worker Tending a Power Loom, 1850
This young woman's main task was the frequent restocking of the wooden shuttle with spindles of thread (shown here), which traveled mechanically over and under the threads mounted on the loom. The worker also had to be alert for sudden breaks of thread, which required a fast shutdown of the loom and a quick repair. Mill worker: American Textile History Museum, Lowell, MA; Shuttle with spindles: Picture Research Consultants & Archives.

Factories, Workingwomen, and Wage Labor

Transportation advances accelerated manufacturing after 1815, creating an ever-expanding market for goods. The two leading industries, textiles and shoes, altered methods of production and labor relations. Textile production was greatly spurred by the development of water-driven machinery built near fast-coursing rivers. Shoe manufacturing, still using the power and skill of human hands, involved only a reorganization of production. Both industries pulled young women into wage-earning labor for the first time.

The earliest American textile factory was built in the 1790s by an English immigrant in Pawtucket, Rhode Island. By 1815, nearly 170 spinning mills stood along New England rivers. While British manufacturers hired entire families for mill work, American factory owners innovated by hiring young women, assumed to be cheap to hire because of their limited employment options and their short-term prospects, since most left to get married.

In 1821, a group of Boston entrepreneurs founded the town of Lowell on the Merrimack River, centralizing all aspects of cloth production: combing, shrinking, spinning, weaving, and dyeing. By 1836, the eight **Lowell mills** employed more than five thousand young women, who lived in carefully managed company-owned boarding-houses. Corporation rules at the Lowell mills required church attendance and prohibited drinking and unsupervised courtship; dorms were locked at 10 p.m. A typical mill worker earned $2 to $3 for a seventy-hour

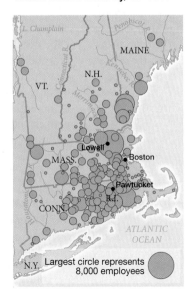

Cotton Textile Industry, ca. 1840

Largest circle represents 8,000 employees

week, more than a seamstress or domestic servant could earn but less than a young man's wages.

Despite the long hours, young women embraced factory work as a means to earn spending money and build savings before marriage; several banks in town held the nest eggs of thousands of workers. Also welcome was the unprecedented, though still limited, personal freedom of living in an all-female social space, away from parents and domestic tasks. In the evening, the women could engage in self-improvement activities, such as attending public lectures. In 1837, 1,500 mill girls crowded Lowell's city hall to hear the Grimké sisters speak about the evils of slavery.

In the mid-1830s, worldwide growth and competition in the cotton market impelled mill owners to speed up work and decrease wages. The workers protested, emboldened by their communal living arrangement and by their relative independence as temporary employees. In 1834 and again in 1836, hundreds of women at Lowell went out on strike (see "Documenting the American Promise," page 288). Such strikes spread; in 1834, mill workers in Dover, New Hampshire, denounced their owners for trying to turn them into "slaves." Their assertiveness surprised many, but ultimately the ease of replacing them undermined their bargaining power, and owners in the 1840s began to shift to immigrant families as their primary labor source.

The shoe manufacturing industry centered in eastern New England reorganized production and hired women, including wives, as shoebinders. Male shoemakers still cut the leather and made the soles in shops, but female shoebinders working from home now stitched the upper parts of the shoes. Working from home meant that wives could contribute to family income—unusual for most wives in that period—and still perform their domestic chores.

In the economically turbulent 1830s, shoebinder wages fell. Unlike mill workers, female shoebinders worked in isolation, a serious hindrance to organized protest. In Lynn, Massachusetts, a major shoemaking center, women used female church networks to organize resistance, communicating via religious newspapers. The Lynn shoebinders who demanded higher wages in 1834 built on a collective sense of themselves as women. "Equal rights should be extended to all—to the weaker sex as well as the stronger," they proclaimed.

In the end, the Lynn shoebinders' protests failed to achieve wage increases. At-home workers all over New England continued to accept low wages, and even in Lynn many women shied away from organized protest, preferring to situate their work in the context of family duty (helping their husbands to finish the shoes) instead of market relations.

Bankers and Lawyers

Entrepreneurs like the Lowell factory owners relied on innovations in the banking system to finance their ventures. Between 1814 and 1816, the number of state-chartered banks in the United States more than doubled from fewer than 90 to 208. By 1830, there were 330, and by 1840 hundreds more. Banks stimulated the economy by making loans to merchants and manufacturers and by enlarging the money supply. Borrowers were issued loans in the form of banknotes—certificates unique to each bank—that were used as money for all transactions. Neither federal nor state governments issued paper money, so banknotes issued by hundreds of individual banks became the country's currency. Constant uncertainty about the true worth of a banknote injected extra risk into the economy. Additionally, the sheer variety of notes in circulation created ideal conditions for counterfeiters to get into the action.

Bankers exercised great power over the economy, deciding who would get loans and what the discount rates would be. The most powerful bankers sat on the board of directors for the **second Bank of the United States**, headquartered in Philadelphia and featuring eighteen branches throughout the country. The twenty-year charter of the first Bank of the United States had expired in 1811, and the second Bank of the United States opened for business in 1816 under another twenty-year charter. The rechartering of this bank would become a major issue in the 1832 presidential campaign.

Lawyer-politicians too exercised economic power, by refashioning commercial law to enhance the prospects of private investment. In 1811, states started to rewrite their laws of incorporation (allowing the chartering of businesses by states), and the number of corporations expanded rapidly, from about twenty in 1800 to eighteen hundred by 1817. Incorporation protected individual investors from being held liable for corporate debts. State lawmakers also wrote laws of eminent domain, empowering states to buy land for roads and canals even from unwilling sellers. In such ways, entrepreneurial lawyers created the legal foundation for an economy that favored ambitious individuals interested in maximizing their own wealth.

Not everyone applauded these developments. Andrew Jackson, himself a skillful lawyer turned

Mill Girls Stand Up to Factory Owners, 1834

Lowell's first large "turn out" by mill girls came in February 1834, when factory owners announced a 15 percent wage cut. Newspaper accounts played up the spectacle of young women, thought to be docile, taking to the streets in protest. After four days, the strike fizzled when the inexperienced workers realized that the owners could easily replace them. But lessons were learned, and a later Lowell "turn out," in 1836, was sustained for several months.

DOCUMENT 1
The Lowell Journal Reports the Strike, February 18, 1834

A town newspaper favorable to the factory owners characterized the work stoppage as a delusional farce led by a small number of "wicked girls."

The Factory Girls.—It has become known, from rumor, that a considerable number of the girls employed in the mills of this town turned out on Friday last, to prevent a reduction in wages. . . . It was proposed, some time since, to make a very small reduction in the wages of all of the hands on the first of March, and notices to that effect were posted in the mills. . . .

Upon this, several wicked and malicious girls . . . undertook to get up a *turn out*, with a view to threaten the agents with an entire stoppage of the works, in order to exact the higher rates of wages. . . . On Friday and Saturday from 800 to 1000 girls revolted under the most laughable delusions, that mischief could invent. The first day, processions were formed of about 700 girls, who listened to sundry stimulative exhortations, . . . and marched through the streets, ankle-deep in mud. . . . Saturday became a day of repentance to many; and they would gladly have returned to their business, but for a pledge, cunningly devised, that each who did so, should forfeit five dollars to the rebels. The Sabbath afforded opportunity for a little more cool reflection, and on Monday morning, a large concourse attended by a parcel of idle men and boys, heard another speech. . . . The result of the whole matter is, that a few of the ring-leaders are refused entrance into the mills, and most of the disaffected, having learned the truth, and becoming sensible of the wicked misrepresentations of which they had nearly been the victims, are returning to their work, ready to take a diminished price, and continue to labor at wages which will give them from one and a half, to two and a half dollars per week, more than their board.—This, to be sure, is not so much as they have had in past times, nor so much as we hope they will soon have again, but it is more than they can get in any other occupation in New England.

Source: *The Lowell Journal*, February 18, 1834, as reprinted in the *New-York Spectator*, March 6, 1834. Gale Database, "Nineteenth-century U.S. Newspapers."

DOCUMENT 2
Anonymous Mill Girls, "Union Is Power"

A position paper, quickly drafted, framed the strikers' goals in terms of "rights" and appealed to the patriotic spirit of the American Revolution to justify their actions.

Our present object is to have union and exertion, and we remain in possession of our own unquestionable rights.

politician, spoke for a large and mistrustful segment of the population when he warned about the potential abuses of power "which the moneyed interest derives from a paper currency which they are able to control [and] from the multitude of corporations with exclusive privileges which they have succeeded in obtaining in the different states." Jacksonians believed that ending government-granted privileges was the way to maximize individual liberty and economic opportunity.

Booms and Busts

One aspect of the economy that the lawyer-politicians could not control was the threat of financial collapse. The boom years from 1815 to

We circulate this paper, wishing to obtain the names of all who imbibe the spirit of our patriotic ancestors, who preferred privation to bondage, and parted with all that renders life desirable—and even life itself—to procure independence for their children. The oppressing hand of avarice would enslave us; and to gain their object, they very gravely tell us of the pressure of the times; this we are already sensible of, and deplore it. If any are in want of assistance, the Ladies will be compassionate, and assist them; but we prefer to have the disposing of our charities in our own hands; and as we are free, we would remain in possession of what kind Providence has bestowed upon us, and remain daughters of freemen still.

All who patronize this effort, we wish to have discontinue their labors until terms of reconciliation are made.

Resolved, That we will not go back into the mills to work unless our wages are continued to us as they have been.

Resolved, That none of us will go back unless they receive us all as one.

Source: Printed in *The Man*, February 22, 1834. Published in New York City by G. H. Evans. American Periodicals Series Online.

DOCUMENT 3
A Strike Leader Speaks Out, Mid-March, 1834

A month later, one of the leaders explained that the strike was caused not only by reduced wages but also by anger at the insolence of wealthy factory owners. Her remarks were published in The Man, *a New York paper friendly to workingmen's issues.*

The Lowell Girls have been censured in no measured terms by the Federal press of the east, for the "turn out.". . . One of the girls has turned round on her accusers, and while she does not outstep the modesty of her sex, her spirit would do credit to any parentage in these or other days. Hear the yankee girl:

"We do not estimate our *Liberty* by dollars and cents; consequently it was not the reduction of *wages* alone which caused the excitement, but that *haughty,*

overbearing disposition—that *purse proud insolence,* which was becoming more and more apparent—that spirit of tyranny so manifest at present among the *avaricious* and wealthy manufacturers of this and the old country.

"I have only to add, that if the proprietors and agents are not satisfied with alluring us from our homes—from the peaceful abodes of our childhood, under the false promises of a great reward, and then casting us upon the world, . . . merely because we would not be slaves—. . . let them bring down upon us the whole influence of the *rich* and *noble*, the *proud* and the *mighty*, all piled upon the *United States Bank*—steep us in poverty to the very dregs, but we beseech them not to asperse our characters, or *stigmatize* us as *disorderly* persons. Grant us this favor, and give us the privilege of breathing the air of freedom in its *purity*, and we will be content."

Source: *The Man*, March 20, 1834. Published in New York City by G. H. Evans. American Periodicals Series Online.

Questions for Analysis and Debate

1. Does the *Lowell Journal* adequately explain how a few "ringleaders" could motivate more than eight hundred female workers to engage in street protests?

2. Why do the strikers invoke Revolutionary-era ideals of independence and liberty and the phrase "daughters of freemen"? Do these young women feel subordinate and deferential to the factory owners? Were they in fact subordinates?

3. How did the *Lowell Journal* excuse the wage reduction? What did the strike leader mean by "purse proud insolence"? What are the class dimensions of this episode?

Connect to the Big Idea

C How was the "turn out" of female workers at Lowell an unintended consequence of the "Market Revolution"?

1818 exhibited a volatility that resulted in the first sharp, large-scale economic downturn in U.S. history. Americans called this downturn a "panic," and the pattern was repeated in the 1830s. Some blamed the panic of 1819 on the second Bank of the United States for failing to control an economic bubble and then contracting the money supply, sending tremors throughout the economy. The crunch was made worse by a financial crisis in Europe in the spring of 1819. Overseas, prices for American cotton, tobacco, and wheat plummeted by more than 50 percent. Thus, when the banks began to call in their outstanding loans, American debtors involved in the commodities trade could not come up with the money. Business and personal bankruptcies skyrocketed. The intricate

Second Bank of the United States, Philadelphia
Along with the growth of state banks came a second federal Bank of the United States, chartered by Congress in 1816. It was headquartered in Philadelphia in this imposing Greek Revival building, constructed between 1818 and 1824. The architecture conveyed solidity, security, and timeless permanence. Despite appearances, the bank lost its charter during Andrew Jackson's presidency and ceased to exist. Library Company of Philadelphia / The Bridgeman Art Library.

web of credit and debt relationships meant that almost everyone with even a toehold in the new commercial economy was affected by the panic. Thousands of Americans lost their savings and property, and unemployment estimates suggest that half a million people lost their jobs.

Recovery took several years. Unemployment declined, but bitterness lingered, ready to be stirred up by politicians in the decades to come. The dangers of a system dependent on extensive credit were now clear. In one folksy formulation that circulated around 1820, a farmer compared credit to "a man pissing in his breeches on a cold day to keep his arse warm—very comfortable at first but I dare say . . . you know how it feels afterwards."

By the mid-1820s, the economy was back on track, driven by increases in productivity, consumer demand for goods, and international trade. Despite the panic of 1819, credit financing continued to fuel the system. A network of credit and debt relations grew dense by the 1830s in a system that encouraged speculation and risk

taking. A pervasive optimism about continued growth supported the elaborate system, but a single business failure could produce many innocent victims. Well after the panic of 1819, an undercurrent of anxiety about rapid economic change continued to shape the political views of many Americans.

REVIEW   Why did the United States experience a market revolution after 1815?

▶ The Spread of Democracy

Just as the market revolution held out the promise, if not the reality, of economic opportunity for all who worked, the political transformation of the 1830s held out the promise of political opportunity for hundreds of thousands of new voters. During Andrew Jackson's presidency (1829–1837), the second American party system took shape, defined by Jackson's charismatic personality expressed in his efforts to dominate Congress. Not until 1836, however, would the parties have distinct names and consistent programs transcending the particular personalities running for office. Over those years, more men could and did vote, responding to new methods of arousing voter interest.

Popular Politics and Partisan Identity

The election of 1828, pitting Andrew Jackson against John Quincy Adams, was the first presidential contest in which the popular vote determined the outcome. In twenty-two out of twenty-four states, voters—not state legislatures—designated the number of electors committed to a particular candidate. More than a million voters participated, three times the number in 1824 and nearly half the free male population, reflecting the high stakes that voters perceived in the Adams-Jackson rematch. Throughout the 1830s, voter turnout continued to rise and reached 70 percent in some localities, partly because of the disappearance of property qualifications in all but three states and partly because of heightened political interest.

The 1828 election inaugurated new campaign styles. State-level candidates routinely gave speeches at rallies, picnics, and banquets. Adams and Jackson still declined such appearances as undignified, but Henry Clay of Kentucky, campaigning for Adams, earned the nickname "the Barbecue Orator." Campaign rhetoric became more informal and even blunt. The Jackson camp established many Hickory Clubs, trading on Jackson's popular nickname, "Old Hickory," from a common Tennessee tree suggesting resilience and toughness.

Partisan newspapers in ever-larger numbers defined issues and publicized political personalities as never before. Improved printing technology and rising literacy rates fueled a great expansion of newspapers of all kinds (Table 11.1). Party leaders dispensed subsidies and other favors to secure the support of papers, even in remote towns and villages. Political news stories traveled swiftly in the mail, gaining coverage by reprintings in sympathetic newspapers. Presidential campaigns were now coordinated in a national arena.

Politicians at first identified themselves as Jackson or Adams men, honoring the fiction of Republican Party unity. By 1832, however, the

TABLE 11.1	THE GROWTH OF NEWSPAPERS, 1820–1840			
	1820	1830	1835	1840
U.S. population (in millions)	9.6	12.8	15.0	17.1
Number of newspapers published	500	800	1,200	1,400
Daily newspapers	42	65	—	138

terminology had evolved to National Republicans, who favored federal action to promote commercial development, and Democratic Republicans, who promised to be responsive to the will of the majority. Between 1834 and 1836, National Republicans came to be called **Whigs**, while Jackson's party became simply the **Democrats**.

The Election of 1828 and the Character Issue

The campaign of 1828 was the first national election dominated by scandal and character questions. Claims about morality, honor, and discipline became central because voters used them to comprehend the kind of public official each man would make. Jackson and Adams presented two radically different styles of manhood.

John Quincy Adams was vilified by his opponents as an elitist, a bookish academic, and even a monarchist. They attacked his "corrupt bargain" of 1824—the alleged election deal between Adams and Henry Clay (see "The Election of 1824" in chapter 10). Adams's supporters countered by playing on Jackson's fatherless childhood to portray him as the bastard son of a prostitute. Worse, the cloudy circumstances around his marriage to Rachel Donelson Robards in 1791 gave rise to the story that Jackson was a seducer and an adulterer, having married a woman whose divorce from her first husband was not entirely legal. Pro-Adams newspapers howled that Jackson was sinful and impulsive, while portraying Adams as pious, learned, and virtuous.

Editors in favor of Adams played up Jackson's violent temper, as evidenced by his participation in many duels, brawls, and canings. Jackson's supporters used the same stories to project Old Hickory as a tough frontier hero who knew how to command obedience. As for learning, Jackson's rough frontier education gave him a "natural sense," wrote a Boston editor, that "can never be acquired by reading books—it can only be acquired, in perfection, by reading men."

Jackson won a sweeping victory, with 56 percent of the popular vote and 178 electoral votes to Adams's 83 (Map 11.2). Old Hickory took most

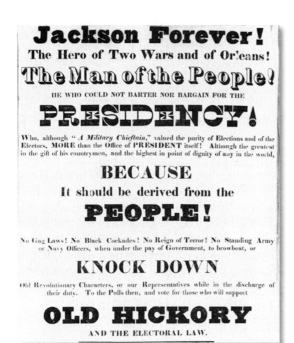

Campaign Poster from 1828
This poster praises Andrew Jackson as a war hero and "man of the people" and reminds readers that Jackson, who won the popular vote in 1824, did not stoop to "bargain for the presidency," as John Quincy Adams presumably had in his dealings with Henry Clay (see "The Election of 1824" in chapter 10). © Collection of the New-York Historical Society, USA/The Bridgeman Art Library.

Candidate	Electoral Vote	Popular Vote	Percent of Popular Vote
Andrew Jackson (Democratic Republican)	178	647,286	56
John Q. Adams (National Republican)	83	508,064	44

MAP 11.2
The Election of 1828

of the South and West and carried Pennsylvania and New York as well; Adams carried the remainder of the East. Jackson's vice president was John C. Calhoun, who had just served as vice president under Adams but had broken with Adams's policies.

After 1828, national politicians no longer deplored the existence of political parties. They were coming to see that parties mobilized and delivered voters, sharpened candidates' differences, and created party loyalty that surpassed loyalty to individual candidates and elections. Adams and Jackson clearly symbolized the competing ideas of the emerging parties: a moralistic, top-down party (the Whigs) ready to make major decisions to promote economic growth competing against a contentious, energetic party (the Democrats) ready to embrace liberty-loving individualism.

Jackson's Democratic Agenda

Before the inauguration in March 1829, Rachel Jackson died. Certain that the ugly campaign had hastened his wife's death, the president went into deep mourning, his depression worsened by constant pain from a bullet still lodged in his

chest from an 1806 duel and by mercury poisoning from the medicines he took. Aged sixty-two, Jackson carried only 140 pounds on his six-foot-one frame. His adversaries doubted that he would make it to a second term. His supporters, however, went wild at his March 1829 inauguration. Thousands cheered his ten-minute inaugural address, the shortest in history. An open reception at the White House turned into a near riot as well-wishers jammed the premises, used windows as doors, stood on furniture for a better view of the great man, and broke thousands of dollars' worth of china and glasses. During his presidency, Jackson continued to offer unprecedented hospitality to the public. The courteous Jackson, committed to his image as president of the "common man," held audiences with unannounced visitors throughout his two terms.

Past presidents had tried to lessen party conflict by including men of different factions in their cabinets, but Jackson would have only loyalists, a political tactic followed by most later presidents. For secretary of state, the key job, he tapped New Yorker Martin Van Buren, one of the shrewdest politicians of the day. Throughout the federal government, from postal clerks to ambassadors, Jackson replaced competent civil servants with party loyalists. Jackson's appointment practices were termed a "spoils system" by his opponents, after a Democratic politician coined the affirmative slogan "to the victor belong the spoils."

Jackson's agenda quickly emerged. Fearing that intervention in the economy inevitably favored some groups at the expense of others, Jackson favored a Jeffersonian limited federal government. He therefore opposed federal support of transportation and grants of monopolies and charters that benefited wealthy investors. Like Jefferson, he anticipated the rapid settlement of the country's interior, where land sales would spread economic democracy to settlers. Thus, establishing a federal policy to remove the Indians from this area had high priority. Jackson was freer than previous presidents with the use of the presidential veto power over Congress. In 1830, he vetoed a highway project in Maysville, Kentucky, Henry Clay's home state. The Maysville Road veto articulated Jackson's principled stand that citizens' tax dollars could be spent only on projects of a "general, not local" character. In all, Jackson used the veto twelve times; all previous presidents combined had exercised that right a total of nine times.

REVIEW Why did Andrew Jackson defeat John Quincy Adams so dramatically in the 1828 election?

Jackson Defines the Democratic Party

In his two terms as president, Andrew Jackson worked to implement his vision of a politics of opportunity for all white men. To open land for white settlement, he favored the relocation of all eastern Indian tribes. He dramatically confronted John C. Calhoun and South Carolina when that state tried to nullify the tariff of 1828. Disapproving of all government-granted privilege, Jackson challenged and defeated the Bank of the United States. In all this, he greatly enhanced the power of the presidency.

Indian Policy and the Trail of Tears

Probably nothing defined Jackson's presidency more than his efforts to solve what he saw as the Indian problem. Thousands of Indians lived in the South and the old Northwest, and many remained in New England and New York. In his first message to Congress in 1829, Jackson, famed for his battles with the Creek and Seminole tribes in the 1810s, declared that removing the Indians to territory west of the Mississippi was the only way to save them. White civilization destroyed Indian resources and thus doomed the Indians,

VISUAL ACTIVITY

Andrew Jackson as "The Great Father"
In 1828, a new process of commercial lithography brought political cartooning to new prominence. Out of some sixty satirical cartoons lampooning Jackson, only one featured his controversial Indian policy. This cropped cartoon lacks the cartoonist's caption, important for understanding the artist's intent. Still, the visual humor of Jackson cradling Indians packs an immediate punch. William L. Clements Library, University of Michigan.
READING THE IMAGE: Examine the body language conveyed in the various characters' poses. Are the Indians depicted as children or as powerless, miniature adults? What is going on in the picture on the wall, and how does it relate to Jackson's Indian removal policy?
CONNECTIONS: Did the Jackson administration protect the Indians? How might Jackson have convinced himself that he was protecting the Indians from certain doom?

he claimed: "That this fate surely awaits them if they remain within the limits of the states does not admit of a doubt. Humanity and national honor demand that every effort should be made to avert so great a calamity." Jackson never publicly wavered from this seemingly noble theme, returning to it in his next seven annual messages.

Prior administrations had experimented with different Indian policies. Starting in 1819, Congress funded missionary associations eager to "civilize" native peoples by converting them to Christianity and to whites' agricultural practices. The federal government had also pursued aggressive treaty making with many tribes, dealing with the Indians as foreign nations (see "Creeks in the Southwest" in chapter 9 and "Osage and Comanche Indians" in chapter 10). In contrast, Jackson saw Indians as subjects of the United States (neither foreigners nor citizens) who needed to be relocated to assure their survival. Congress agreed and passed the **Indian Removal Act of 1830**. About 100 million acres of eastern land would be vacated for eventual white settlement under this act authorizing ethnic expulsion (Map 11.3).

The Indian Removal Act generated widespread controversy. Newspapers, public lecturers, and local clubs debated the expulsion law, and public opinion, especially in the North, was heated.

MAP ACTIVITY

Map 11.3   Indian Removal and the Trail of Tears

The federal government under President Andrew Jackson pursued a vigorous policy of Indian removal in the 1830s, forcibly moving tribes west to land known as Indian Territory (present-day Oklahoma). In 1838, as many as a quarter of the Cherokee Indians died on the route known as the Trail of Tears.

READING THE MAP: From which states were most of the Native Americans removed? Through which states did the Trail of Tears go?

CONNECTIONS: Before Jackson's presidency, how did the federal government view Native Americans, and what policy initiatives were undertaken by the government and private groups? How did Jackson change the government's policy toward Native Americans?

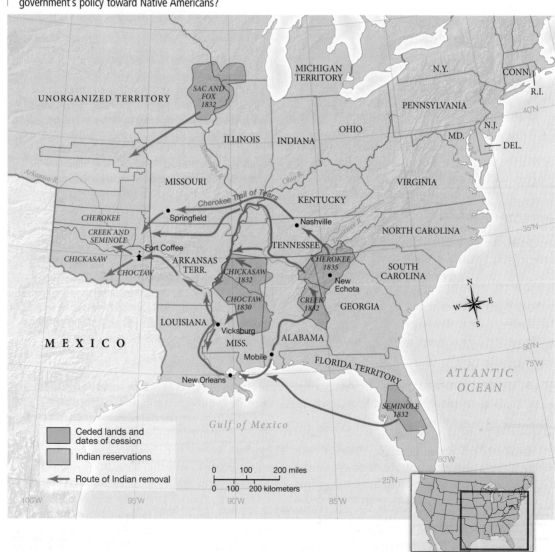

"One would think that the guilt of African slavery was enough for the nation to bear, without the additional crime of injustice to the aborigines," one writer declared in 1829. In an unprecedented move, thousands of northern white women signed antiremoval petitions. Between 1830 and 1832, women's petitions rolled into Washington, arguing that sovereign peoples on the road to Christianity were entitled to stay on their land. Jackson ignored the petitions.

For many northern tribes, diminished by years of war, removal was already under way. But not all went quietly. In 1832 in western Illinois, Black Hawk, a leader of the Sauk and Fox Indians who had fought in alliance with Tecumseh in the War of 1812 (see "The War of 1812" in chapter 10), resisted removal. Volunteer militias attacked and chased the Indians into southern Wisconsin, where, after several skirmishes and a deadly battle (later called the Black Hawk War), Black Hawk was captured and some four hundred of his people were massacred.

The large southern tribes—the Creek, Chickasaw, Choctaw, Seminole, and Cherokee—proved even more resistant to removal. Georgia Cherokees had already taken several assimilationist steps. They had adopted written laws, including, in 1827, a constitution modeled on the U.S. Constitution. Two hundred of the wealthiest Cherokee men had intermarried with whites, adopting white styles of housing, dress, and cotton agriculture, including the ownership of slaves. They developed a written alphabet and published a newspaper and Christian prayer books in their language. These features helped make their cause attractive to the northern white women who petitioned the government on their behalf. Yet most of the seventeen thousand Cherokees maintained cultural continuity with past traditions.

In 1831, when Georgia announced its plans to seize all Cherokee property, the tribal leadership took their case to the U.S. Supreme Court. In *Worcester v. Georgia* (1832), the Court upheld the territorial sovereignty of the Cherokee people, recognizing their existence as "a distinct community, occupying its own territory, in which the laws of Georgia can have no force." An angry President Jackson ignored the Court and pressed the Cherokee tribe to move west: "If they now refuse to accept the liberal terms offered, they can only be liable for whatever evils and difficulties may arise. I feel conscious of having done my duty to my red children."

The Cherokee tribe remained in Georgia for two more years without significant violence.

Cherokee Deer Hide Coat
Durable, supple, and nearly airtight, tanned deer hides made excellent clothing material. This knee-length coat, decorated with red buttons and fringe, dates from the first quarter of the nineteenth century and was still in the possession of Cherokees in Oklahoma in the 1930s. It very likely traveled to Oklahoma with its owner on the Trail of Tears in 1838. National Museum of the American Indian, Smithsonian Institution (catalogue number 02/0353). Photo by David Heald.

Then, in 1835, a small, unauthorized faction of the acculturated leaders signed a treaty selling all the tribal lands to the state, which rapidly resold the land to whites. Chief John Ross, backed by several thousand Cherokees, petitioned the U.S. Congress to ignore the bogus treaty to no avail. Most Cherokees refused to move, so in May 1838, the deadline for voluntary removal, federal troops arrived to remove them. Under armed guard, the Cherokees embarked on a 1,200-mile journey west that came to be called the **Trail of Tears**. Nearly a quarter of the Cherokees died en route from the hardship. Survivors joined the fifteen thousand Creek, twelve thousand Choctaw, five thousand Chickasaw, and several thousand Seminole Indians also forcibly relocated to Indian Territory (which became the state of Oklahoma in 1907).

In his farewell address to the nation in 1837, Jackson professed his belief in the humanitarian benefits of Indian removal: "This unhappy race . . . are now placed in a situation where we may well hope that they will share in the blessings of civilization and be saved from the degradation and destruction to which they were rapidly hastening while they remained in the states." Perhaps Jackson genuinely believed that removal was necessary, but for the forcibly removed tribes, the costs of relocation were high.

The Tariff of Abominations and Nullification

Just as Indian removal in Georgia had pitted a state against a federal power, in the form of a Supreme Court ruling, a second explosive issue also pitted a state against federal regulation. This was the issue of federal tariff policy, strongly opposed by South Carolina.

Federal tariffs as high as 33 percent on imports such as textiles and iron goods had been passed in 1816 and again in 1824 in an effort to shelter new American manufacturers from foreign competition. Some southern congressmen opposed the steep tariffs, fearing they would reduce overseas shipping and thereby hurt cotton exports. In 1828, Congress passed a revised tariff that came to be known as the Tariff of Abominations. A bundle of conflicting duties, some as high as 50 percent, the legislation contained provisions that pleased and angered every economic and sectional interest.

South Carolina in particular suffered from the Tariff of Abominations. Worldwide prices for cotton had declined in the late 1820s, and the falloff in shipping caused by the high tariffs further hurt the South. In 1828, a group of South Carolina politicians headed by John C. Calhoun advanced a doctrine called **nullification**. They argued that when Congress overstepped its powers, states had the right to nullify Congress's acts. As precedents, they pointed to the Virginia and Kentucky Resolutions of 1798, intended to invalidate the Alien and Sedition Acts (see "The Alien and Sedition Acts" in chapter 9). Congress had erred in using tariff policy to benefit specific industries, they claimed; tariffs should be used only to raise revenue.

On assuming the presidency in 1829, Jackson ignored the South Carolina statement of nullification and shut out Calhoun, his new vice president, from influence or power. Tariff revisions in early 1832 brought little relief to the South. Sensing futility, Calhoun resigned the vice presidency and became a senator to better serve his state. Finally, strained to their limit, South Carolina leaders took the radical step of declaring federal tariffs null and void in their state as of February 1, 1833. The constitutional crisis was out in the open.

In response, Jackson sent armed ships to Charleston harbor and threatened to invade the state. He pushed through Congress the Force Bill, defining South Carolina's stance as treason and authorizing military action to collect federal tariffs. At the same time, Congress moved quickly to pass a revised tariff that was more acceptable to the South, reducing tariffs to their 1816 level.

On March 1, 1833, Congress passed both the new tariff and the Force Bill. South Carolina withdrew its nullification of the old tariff—and then nullified the Force Bill. It was a symbolic gesture since Jackson's show of muscle was no longer necessary.

Yet the question of federal power versus states' rights was far from settled. The implied threat behind nullification was secession, a position articulated in 1832 by some South Carolinians whose concerns went beyond tariff policy. In the 1830s, the political moratorium on discussions of slavery agreed on at the time of the Missouri Compromise (see "The Missouri Compromise" in chapter 10) was coming unglued, and new northern voices opposed to slavery gained increasing attention. If and when a northern-dominated federal government decided to end slavery, the South Carolinians thought, the South should nullify such laws or else remove itself from the Union.

The Bank War and Economic Boom

Along with the tariff and nullification, President Jackson fought another political battle, over the Bank of the United States. With twenty-nine branches, the bank handled the federal government's deposits, extended credit and loans, and issued banknotes—by 1830, the most stable currency in the country. Jackson, however, thought the bank concentrated undue economic power in the hands of a few.

National Republican (Whig) senators Daniel Webster and Henry Clay decided to force the issue. They convinced the bank to apply for charter renewal in 1832, well before the fall election, even though the existing charter ran until 1836. They fully expected that Congress's renewal would force Jackson to follow through on his rhetoric with a veto, that the unpopular veto would cause Jackson to lose the election, and that the bank would survive on an override vote by a new Congress swept into power on the anti-Jackson tide.

At first, the plan seemed to work. The bank applied for rechartering, Congress voted to renew, and Jackson, angry over being manipulated, issued his veto. But it was a brilliantly written veto, positioning Jackson as the champion of the democratic masses. "Many of our rich men have not been content with equal protection and equal benefits, but have besought us to make them richer by act of Congress," Jackson wrote.

Clay and his supporters found Jackson's economic ideas and his rhetoric of class antagonism so absurd that they distributed thousands of copies of the bank veto as campaign material

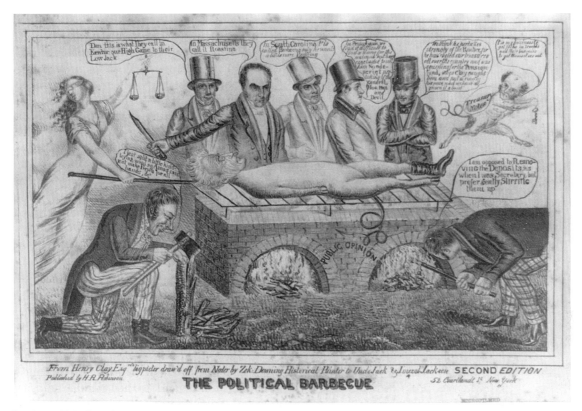

The Political Barbecue, 1834
Political cartooning became a high art in the 1830s. Here, Pig Jackson roasts on a barbecue grill, fed by the fires of "public opinion" kindled by his decision to take down the Bank of the United States. Political opponents happy to see him get cooked include Henry Clay, Daniel Webster, and Nicholas Biddle, president of the bank. The cartoon is a fantasy: Public opinion generally backed Jackson. Library of Congress.

for their own party. A confident Henry Clay headed his party's ticket for the presidency. But the plan backfired. Jackson's framing of the bank controversy in the language of class conflict resonated with many Americans. Jackson won the election easily, gaining 55 percent of the popular vote and 219 electoral votes to Clay's 49. Jackson's party still controlled Congress, so no override was possible. The second Bank of the United States would cease to exist after 1836.

Jackson wanted to destroy the bank sooner. Calling it a "monster," he ordered the sizable federal deposits to be removed from its vaults and redeposited into Democratic-inclined state banks. In retaliation, the Bank of the United States raised interest rates and called in loans. This action caused a brief decline in the economy in 1833 and actually enhanced Jackson's claim that the bank was too powerful for the good of the country.

Unleashed and unregulated, the economy went into high gear in 1834. Just at this moment, an excess of silver from Mexican mines made its way into American banks, giving bankers license to print ever more banknotes. From 1834 to 1837,

inflation soared; prices of basic goods rose more than 50 percent. States quickly chartered hundreds of new private banks, each issuing its own banknotes. Entrepreneurs borrowed and invested money, and the webs of credit and debt relationships that were the hallmark of the American economy grew denser yet. The market in western land sales also heated up. In 1834, about 4.5 million acres of the public domain had been sold, the highest annual volume since 1818. By 1836, the total reached an astonishing 20 million acres (Figure 11.1).

In one respect, the economy attained an admirable goal: The national debt disappeared, and from 1835 to 1837, for the only time in American history, the government had a monetary surplus. But much of that surplus consisted of questionable bank currencies—"bloated, diseased" currencies, in Jackson's vivid terminology. While the boom was on, however, few stopped to worry about the consequences if and when the bubble burst.

REVIEW   What were the most significant policies of Andrew Jackson's presidency?

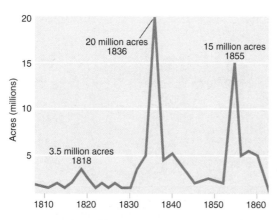

FIGURE 11.1 Western Land Sales, 1810–1860
Land sales peaked in the 1810s, 1830s, and 1850s as Americans rushed to speculate in western land sold by the federal government. The surges in 1818 and 1836 demonstrate the volatile, speculative economy that suddenly collapsed in the panics of 1819 and 1837.

▶ Cultural Shifts, Religion, and Reform

The growing economy, booming by the mid-1830s, transformed social and cultural life. For many families, especially in the commercialized Northeast, standards of living rose, consumption patterns changed, and the nature and location of work were altered. All this had a direct impact on the duties of men and women and on the training of youths for the economy of the future.

Along with economic change came an unprecedented revival of evangelical religion known as the Second Great Awakening. Among the most serious adherents of evangelical Protestantism were men and women of the new merchant classes, whose self-discipline in pursuing market ambitions meshed well with the message of self-discipline in pursuit of spiritual perfection. Not content with individual perfection, many of these people sought to perfect society as well, by defining excessive alcohol consumption, nonmarital sex, and slavery as three major evils of modern life in need of correction. Three social movements championing temperance, moral reform, and abolition gained strength from evangelistic Christianity.

The Family and Separate Spheres

The centerpiece of new ideas about gender relations was the notion that husbands found their status and authority in the new world of work, leaving wives to tend the hearth and home. Sermons, advice books, periodicals, and novels reinforced the idea that men and women inhabited separate spheres and had separate duties. "To woman it belongs . . . to elevate the intellectual character of her household [and] to kindle the fires of mental activity in childhood," wrote Mrs. A. J. Graves in a popular book titled *Advice to American Women*. For men, by contrast, "the absorbing passion for gain, and the pressing demands of business, engross their whole attention." In particular, the home, now said to be the exclusive domain of women, was sentimentalized as the source of intimacy, love, and safety, a refuge from the cruel and competitive world of market relations.

Some new aspects of society gave substance to this formulation of separate spheres. Men's work was undergoing profound change after 1815 and increasingly brought cash to the household, especially in the manufacturing and urban Northeast. Farmers and tradesmen sold products in a market, and bankers, bookkeepers, shoemakers, and canal diggers earned regular salaries or wages. Furthermore, many men now worked away from the home, at an office or a store.

A woman's domestic role was more complicated than the cultural prescriptions indicated. Although the vast majority of married white women did not hold paying jobs, their homes required time-consuming labor. But the advice books treated housework as a loving familial duty, thus rendering it invisible in an economy that evaluated work by how much cash it generated. In reality, many wives contributed to family income by taking in boarders or sewing for pay. Wives in the poorest classes, including most free black wives, did not have the luxury of husbands earning adequate wages; for them, work as servants or laundresses helped augment family income.

Idealized notions about the feminine home and the masculine workplace gained acceptance in the 1830s because of the cultural ascendancy of the commercialized Northeast, with its domination of book and periodical publishing. Men seeking manhood through work and pay could embrace competition and acquisitiveness, while women established femininity through dutiful service to home and family. This particular formulation of gender difference helped smooth the path for the first generation of Americans experiencing the market revolution, and both men and women of the middle classes benefited. Men were set free to pursue wealth, and women gained moral authority within the home. Beyond white families of the middle and upper classes, however, these new gender ideals had limited applicability. And new

VISUAL ACTIVITY

The Caverly Family at Home, 1836
Itinerant amateur artists journeyed the back roads of antebellum America, painting individuals and families in standard repetitive poses. This picture of a New Hampshire family lists the names and ages at the bottom: Azariah, 44, George, 3, Sarah Jane, 7 months, and Eliza, 24. Gift of Stephen C. Clark. Fenimore Art Museum, Cooperstown, New York. Photograph by Richard Walker.
READING THE IMAGE: What do you make of little George's outfit? Are there clues within the picture that this is a male child? How are gender differences established in this image? What might the large age difference between husband and wife suggest?
CONNECTIONS: How did the heightened attention to gender differences correlate with the changing economy and politics of Jacksonian America?

voices like those of the Grimké sisters challenged whether "virtue" and "duty" had separate masculine and feminine manifestations. Despite their apparent authority in printed material of the period, these gender ideals were never all-pervasive.

The Education and Training of Youths

The market economy required expanded opportunities for training youths of both sexes. By the 1830s, in both the North and the South, state-supported public school systems were the norm, designed to produce pupils of both sexes able, by age twelve to fourteen, to read, write, and participate in marketplace calculations. Literacy rates for white females climbed dramatically, rivaling the rates for white males for the first time. The fact that taxpayers paid for children's education created an incentive to seek an inexpensive teach-

ing force. By the 1830s, school districts replaced male teachers with young females, for, as a Massachusetts report on education put it, "females can be educated cheaper, quicker, and better, and will teach cheaper after they are qualified."

Advanced education continued to expand in the 1830s, with an additional two dozen colleges for men and several more female seminaries offering education on a par with the male colleges. Still, only a very small percentage of young people attended institutions of higher learning. The vast majority of male youths left public school at age fourteen to apprentice in specific trades or to embark on business careers by seeking entry-level clerkships, abundant in the growing urban centers. Young women headed for mill towns or cities in unprecedented numbers, seeking work in the expanding service sector as seamstresses and domestic servants. Changes in patterns of youth employment meant that

Women Graduates of Oberlin College, Class of 1855
Oberlin College, founded by abolitionists in the 1830s, admitted men and women of both races. In the early years, black students were all male, and women students were all white. By 1855 black women had integrated the Ladies' Department. Each student wears a dark dress with a detachable lace collar. Note the uniform hairstyles, parted down the middle, with well-oiled locks lustrously coiled over the ears. Oberlin College Archives.

large numbers of youngsters escaped the watchful eyes of their parents, a cause of great concern for moralists of the era. Advice books published by the hundreds instructed youths in the virtues of hard work and delayed gratification.

The Second Great Awakening

A newly invigorated version of Protestantism gained momentum in the 1820s and 1830s as the economy reshaped gender and age relations. The earliest manifestations of this fervent piety, which historians call the **Second Great Awakening**, appeared in 1801 in Kentucky, when a crowd of ten thousand people camped out on a hillside at Cane Ridge for a revival meeting that lasted several weeks. By the 1810s and 1820s, "camp meetings" had spread to the Atlantic seaboard states, accelerating and intensifying the emotional impact of the revival.

The gatherings attracted women and men hungry for a more immediate access to spiritual peace, one not requiring years of soul-searching. One eyewitness reported that "some of the people were singing, others praying, some crying for mercy. . . . At one time I saw at least five hundred swept down in a moment as if a battery of a thousand guns had been opened upon them, and then immediately followed shrieks and shouts that rent the very heavens."

From 1800 to 1820, church membership doubled in the United States, much of it among the evangelical groups. Methodists, Baptists, and Presbyterians formed the core of the new movement, which attracted women more than men; wives and mothers typically recruited husbands and sons to join them.

A central leader of the Second Great Awakening was a lawyer turned minister named Charles Grandison Finney. Finney lived in western New York, where the completion of the Erie Canal in 1825 fundamentally altered the social and economic landscape overnight. Growth and prosperity came with other, less admirable side effects, such as prostitution, drinking, and gaming. Finney saw New York canal towns as especially ripe for evangelical awakening. In Rochester, he sustained a six-month revival through the winter of 1830–31, generating thousands of converts.

Finney's message, directed primarily at the business classes, argued for a public-spirited outreach to the less-than-perfect to foster their salvation. Evangelicals promoted Sunday schools to bring piety to children; they battled to honor the Sabbath by ending mail delivery, stopping public transport, and closing shops on Sundays. Many women formed missionary societies that distributed millions of Bibles and religious tracts. Through such avenues, evangelical religion offered women expanded spheres of influence. Finney adopted the tactics of Jacksonian-era politicians—publicity, argumentation, rallies, and speeches—to sell his cause. His object, he said, was to get Americans to "vote in the Lord Jesus Christ as the governor of the Universe."

The Temperance Movement and the Campaign for Moral Reform

The evangelical fervor animated vigorous campaigns to eliminate alcohol abuse and eradicate sexual sin. Millions of Americans took the temperance pledge to abstain from strong drink, and thousands became involved in efforts to end prostitution.

Alcohol consumption had risen steadily in the decades up to 1830. All classes imbibed. A lively saloon culture fostered masculine camaraderie along with extensive alcohol consumption among laborers, while in elite homes the after-dinner whiskey or sherry was commonplace. Colleges before 1820 routinely served students a pint of ale with meals, and the military included rum in the daily ration.

Organized opposition to drinking first surfaced in the 1810s among health and religious reformers. In 1826, Lyman Beecher, a Connecticut minister of an "awakened" church, founded the **American Temperance Society**, which warned that drinking led to poverty, idleness, crime, and family violence. Temperance lecturers spread the word, and middle-class drinking began a steep decline. One powerful tool of persuasion was the temperance pledge, which many business owners began to require of employees.

In 1836, leaders of the temperance movement regrouped into a new society, the American Temperance Union, which demanded total abstinence from its adherents. The intensified war against alcohol moved beyond individual moral suasion into the realm of politics as reformers sought to deny taverns liquor licenses. By 1845, temperance advocates had put an impressive dent in alcohol consumption, which diminished to one-quarter of the per capita consumption of 1830.

More controversial than temperance was a social movement called "moral reform," which first aimed at public morals in general but quickly narrowed to a campaign to eradicate sexual sin. In 1833, a group of Finneyite women started the **New York Female Moral Reform Society**. Its members insisted that uncontrolled male sexual expression, manifested in seduction and prostitution, posed a serious threat to society in general and to women in particular. Within five years, more than four thousand auxiliary groups of women had sprung up, mostly in New England, New York, Pennsylvania, and Ohio.

In its analysis of the causes of licentiousness and its conviction that women had a duty to speak out about unspeakable things, the Moral Reform Society pushed the limits of what even the men in the evangelical movement could tolerate. Yet these women did not regard themselves as radicals. They were simply pursuing the logic of a gender system that defined home protection and morality as women's special sphere and a religious conviction that called for the eradication of sin.

VISUAL ACTIVITY

"Signing the Pledge" in the 1840s
This lithograph celebrates a hard-won moment in the life of a hard-luck family. A temperance worker convinces the father to sign an oath to abstain from alcohol, while his wife exhibits prayerful gratitude. The temperance pledge was a major tool used by anti-alcohol advocates to curb drinking: Could it have really worked? Consider the power of religious oaths in a society infused with religious belief. The Granger Collection, New York.
READING THE IMAGE: How does the artist let us know this is a picture about temperance? Can you find five clues to this family's social and economic standing?
CONNECTIONS: What groups or people were most concerned to define alcohol consumption as a major problem needing fixing? Why?

Organizing against Slavery

More radical still was the movement in the 1830s to abolish the sin of slavery. The abolitionist movement had its roots in Great Britain in the late 1700s. (See "Beyond America's Borders," page 302.) Previously, the American Colonization Society, founded in 1817 by Maryland and Virginia planters, promoted gradual individual emancipation of slaves followed by colonization in Africa. By the early 1820s, several thousand ex-slaves had been transported to Liberia on the West African coast. But not surprisingly, newly freed men and women often were not eager to emigrate; their African roots were three or more generations in the past. Colonization was too gradual (and expensive) to have much impact on American slavery.

Around 1830, northern challenges to slavery intensified, beginning in free black communities. In 1829, a Boston printer named David Walker

Transatlantic Abolition

Abolitionism blossomed in the United States in the 1830s, but its roots stretched back to the 1780s in Britain and America. Developments in both countries led to a transatlantic antislavery movement with shared ideas, strategies, activists, songs, and, eventually, victories.

An important source of antislavery sentiment derived from the Quaker religion, with its deep convictions regarding human equality. But moral sentiment alone does not make a political movement. English Quakers, customarily an apolitical group, awoke to sudden antislavery zeal in 1783, triggered in part by the loss of the imperial war for America and the debate it spurred about citizenship and slavery. The end of the war also brought a delegation of Philadelphia Quakers to meet with the London group, and an immediate result was the first petition requesting that Parliament abolish the slave trade.

The English Quakers, now joined by a scattering of evangelical Anglicans and Methodists, formed the Society for Effecting the Abolition of the Slave Trade in 1787 and in just five years became a force to be reckoned with. They amassed thousands of signatures on petitions to Parliament. They organized a boycott of slave-produced sugar from the British West Indies that involved 300,000 Britons. (Women, the traditional cooks of English families, were essential to the effort.) In 1789, the society scored a publicity coup by publishing two chilling illustrations of slave ships stacked with human cargo. These images, reprinted by the thousands, created a sensation. The society mobilized the resulting groundswell of antislavery sentiment to pressure Parliament once again. A sympathetic member of that body, the Methodist William Wilberforce, brought the anti–slave trade issue to a debate and vote in 1791; it lost.

Meanwhile, Pennsylvania Quakers in 1784 launched their own Society for Promoting the Abolition of Slavery, which worked to end slavery in that state and petitioned the confederation congress—unsuccessfully—to end American participation in the international slave trade. When the First Congress met in 1790, this antislavery society delivered two petitions in quick succession, one to ban the slave trade and a second to ban slavery itself (see chapter 9, "Historical Question," page 230). In rejecting both petitions, Congress pointed to the U.S. Constitution's clause that prohibited federal regulation of the trade before 1808.

The antislavery movement also took root in France, with the founding of the Société des Amis des Noirs (Society of the Friends of Blacks) in 1788. Inspired by Quaker groups in London and Philadelphia, the Société sent petitions to the French National Assembly. All three antislavery groups, in close communication, agreed that ending the slave trade was the critical first step in abolishing slavery. That goal was achieved once the revolution of *liberté and égalité* came to France; a 1794 decree of the National Assembly freed all French colonial slaves and termed them citizens.

Success came more slowly in Britain and America. In 1807, Parliament finally made it illegal for British ships to transport Africans into slavery. A year later, the United States also banned the international slave trade. The rapid natural increase of the African American population made passage of this law relatively easy. Older slave states along the coast supported the ban because it actually increased the value of their native-born slaves who were sold and transported west in the domestic slave trade.

British antislavery forces took a new tack in the 1820s, when women became active and pushed beyond the ban on trade. Quaker widow Elizabeth Heyrick authored *Immediate Not Gradual Abolition* in 1824, prompting the formation of scores of all-women societies. American women abolitionists soon published *An Appeal . . . to the Coloured Citizens of the World*, which condemned racism, invoked the egalitarian language of the Declaration of Independence, and hinted at racial violence if whites did not change their prejudiced ways. In 1830, at the inaugural National Negro Convention meeting in Philadelphia, forty blacks from nine states discussed the racism of American society and proposed emigration to Canada. In 1832 and 1833, a twenty-eight-year-old black woman named Maria Stewart delivered public lectures on slavery and racial prejudice to black audiences in Boston. Her lectures gained wider circulation when they were published in a national publication called the *Liberator*.

The *Liberator*, founded in 1831 in Boston, took antislavery agitation to new heights. Its founder and editor, William Lloyd Garrison, advocated immediate abolition: "On this subject, I do not wish to think, or speak, or write, with moderation. No! No! Tell a man whose house is on fire to give a moderate alarm; tell him to moderately rescue his wife from the hands of the ravisher; tell the mother to gradually extricate her followed suit. Abolitionists again bombarded Parliament with a massive petition campaign, and 30 percent of the 1.3 million signatures submitted in 1833 were women's. That year, Parliament finally passed the Abolition of Slavery Act, which freed all slave children under age six and gradually phased out slavery for everyone older during a four-year apprenticeship. The act also provided financial compensation for owners (£20 million), a key proviso made possible by the relatively small number of slave owners in the British slaveholding colonies.

The success of the British movement generated even greater transatlantic communication. In 1840, British and American abolitionists came together in full force at the World Anti-Slavery Convention in London. Most of the 409 delegates were from Britain and the West Indies, although 53 Americans and half a dozen French delegates also attended. Ten days of meetings produced speeches and reports on the worldwide practice of slavery, along with debates over various economic and religious strategies to end it. A key plan was to publicize throughout America the British movement's success in achieving emancipation. The delegates closed their meeting fully energized by their international congress, called to propose international solutions to an international problem.

Description of a Slave Ship

This powerful and often-reprinted image combines a precise technical rendering of a British ship (normally evoking pride in Britons) with the horrors of a crowded mass of dark human flesh. Newberry Library, Chicago, Illinois, USA/The Bridgeman Art Library.

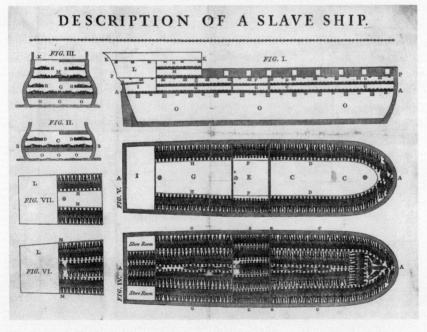

DESCRIPTION OF A SLAVE SHIP.

America in a Global Context

1. What were some of the tactics that British abolitionists used to advance their cause?

2. What factors help explain why the emancipation of slaves came earliest in France, and then four decades later in Britain and seven decades later in the United States?

Connect to the Big Idea

C What parts of American abolitionism owed their origins and inspiration to European models? Do you think there were aspects of American abolitionism that would have emerged even without any European models? Why or why not?

babe from the fire into which it has fallen—but urge me not to use moderation in a cause like the present." In 1832, Garrison's supporters started the New England Anti-Slavery Society.

Similar groups were organized in Philadelphia and New York in 1833. Soon a dozen antislavery newspapers and scores of antislavery lecturers were spreading the word and inspiring the formation of new local societies, which numbered thirteen hundred by 1837. Confined entirely to the North, their membership totaled a quarter of a million men and women.

Many white northerners, even those who opposed slavery, were not prepared to embrace the abolitionist call for emancipation. From 1834 to 1838, there were more than a hundred eruptions of serious mob violence against abolitionists and free blacks. On one occasion, antislavery headquarters in Philadelphia and a black church and orphanage were burned to the ground. In another incident, Illinois abolitionist editor Elijah Lovejoy was killed by a rioting crowd attempting to destroy his printing press. When the Grimké sisters lectured in 1837 (see pages 281–82), some

Controversy over Abolitionism

Mob violence erupted in northern cities with regularity when abolitionist speakers came to town. This 1837 poster from Poughkeepsie, New York, exemplifies the extremely inflammatory language that kindled riots. Antislavery societies raised money to support these lecture tours, one way being the weekly pledge. This contribution box is inscribed with biblical passages and the symbolic yet disturbing image of the slave in chains. Poster: Library of Congress; box: Boston Public Library/Rare Books Department—Courtesy of the Trustees.

OUTRAGE.

Fellow Citizens,

AN

ABOLITIONIST,

of the most revolting character is among you, exciting the feelings of the North against the South. A seditious Lecture is to be delivered

THIS EVENING,

at 7 o'clock, at the Presbyterian Church in Cannon-street. You are requested to attend and unite in putting down and silencing by peaceable means this tool of evil and fanaticism. Let the rights of the States guaranteed by the Constitution be protected.

Feb. 27, 1837. *The Union forever!*

authorities tried to intimidate them and deny them meeting space. The following year, rocks shattered windows when Angelina Grimké gave a speech at a female antislavery convention in Philadelphia. After the women vacated the building, a mob burned the building to the ground.

Despite these dangers, large numbers of northern women played a prominent role in abolition. They formed women's auxiliaries and held fairs to sell handmade crafts to support male lecturers in the field. They circulated antislavery petitions, presented to the U.S. Congress with tens of thousands of signatures. At first women's petitions were framed as respectful memorials to Congress about the evils of slavery, but soon they demanded political action to end slavery in the District of Columbia, under Congress's jurisdiction. By such fervent tactics, antislavery women asserted their claim to be heard on political issues independently of their husbands and fathers.

Garrison particularly welcomed women's activity, despite the potential for danger. The 1837 Massachusetts speaking tour of the Grimké sisters brought out respectful audiences of thousands but also drew intimidation from some quarters. The state leaders of the Congregational Church in Massachusetts banned the sisters from speaking in their churches. While a modest woman deserved deference and protection, church leaders said, immodest women presumptuously instructing men in public forfeited feminine privileges. "When she assumes the place and tone of man as a public reformer, our care and protection of her seem unnecessary; we put ourselves in self-defence against her . . . her character becomes unnatural."

By the late 1830s, the cause of abolition divided the nation as no other issue did. Even among abolitionists, significant divisions emerged. The Grimké sisters, radicalized by the public reaction to their speaking tour, began to write and speak about woman's rights. Angelina Grimké compared the silencing of women to the silencing of slaves: "The denial of our duty to act, is a bold denial of our right to act; and if *we* have no right to act, then may we well be termed 'the white slaves of the North'—for, like our brethren in bonds, we must seal our lips in silence and despair." The Grimkés were opposed by moderate abolitionists who were unwilling to mix the new and controversial issue of woman's rights with their first cause, the rights of blacks.

The many men and women active in reform movements in the 1830s found their initial inspiration in evangelical Protestantism's dual message: Salvation was open to all, and society needed to be perfected. Their activist mentality squared well with the interventionist tendencies of the Whig Party forming in opposition to Andrew Jackson's Democrats.

REVIEW How did evangelical Protestantism contribute to the social reform movements of the 1830s?

▶ Van Buren's One-Term Presidency

By the mid-1830s, a vibrant and tumultuous political culture occupied center stage in American life. Andrew Jackson, too ill to stand for a third term, made way for Martin Van Buren, who faced tough opposition from an array of opposing Whigs and even from slave-owning Jacksonians. Van Buren was a skilled politician, but soon after his inauguration the country faced economic collapse. A shattering panic in 1837, followed by another in 1839, brought the country its worst economic depression yet.

The Politics of Slavery

Sophisticated party organization was the specialty of Martin Van Buren, nicknamed "the Little Magician" for his consummate political skills. First a senator and then governor, the New Yorker became Jackson's secretary of state and then his running mate in 1832, replacing John C. Calhoun. His eight years in the volatile Jackson administration required the full measure of his political deftness as he sought repeatedly to save Jackson from both his enemies and his own obstinacy.

Jackson clearly favored Van Buren for the nomination in 1836, but starting in 1832, the major political parties had developed nominating conventions to choose their candidates. In 1835, Van Buren got the convention nod unanimously, to the dismay of his archrival, Calhoun, who then worked to discredit Van Buren among southern proslavery Democrats. Van Buren spent months assuring them that he was a "northern man with southern principles." This was a credible line since his Dutch family hailed from the Hudson River counties where New York slavery had once flourished, and his own family had owned slaves as late as the 1810s, permitted under New York's gradual emancipation law.

Calhoun was able to stir up trouble for Van Buren because southerners were becoming increasingly alarmed by the rise of northern antislavery sentiment. When, in late 1835, abolitionists prepared to circulate in the South a million pamphlets condemning slavery, a mailbag of their literature was hijacked at the post office in Charleston, South Carolina, and ceremoniously burned along with effigies of leading abolitionists. President Jackson condemned the theft but issued approval for individual postmasters to exercise their own judgment about whether to allow incendiary materials to reach their destination. Abolitionists saw this as censorship of the mail.

The petitioning tactics of abolitionists escalated sectional tensions. When hundreds of antislavery petitions inundated Congress, proslavery congressmen responded by passing a "gag rule" in 1836. The gag rule prohibited entering the documents into the public record on the grounds that what the abolitionists prayed for was unconstitutional and, further, an assault on the rights of white southerners, as one South Carolina representative put it. Abolitionists like the Grimké sisters considered the gag rule to be an abridgment of free speech. They also argued that, tabled or not, the petitions were effective. "The South already turns pale at the number sent," Angelina Grimké said in a speech exhorting more petitions to be circulated.

Van Buren shrewdly seized on both mail censorship and the gag rule to express his prosouthern sympathies. Abolitionists were "fanatics," he repeatedly claimed, possibly under the influence of "foreign agents" (British abolitionists). He dismissed the issue of abolition in the District of Columbia as "inexpedient" and promised that if he was elected president, he would not allow any interference in southern "domestic institutions."

Elections and Panics

Although the elections of 1824, 1828, and 1832 clearly bore the stamp of Jackson's personality, by 1836 the party apparatus was sufficiently developed to give Van Buren, a backroom politician, a shot at the presidency. Local and state committees existed throughout the country, and more than four hundred newspapers were Democratic partisans.

The Whigs had also built state-level organizations and newspaper loyalty. They had no top contender with nationwide support, so three regional candidates opposed Van Buren. Senator Daniel Webster of Massachusetts could deliver New England, home to reformers, merchants, and manufacturers; Senator Hugh Lawson White of Tennessee attracted proslavery voters still suspicious of the northern Magician; and the aging General William Henry Harrison, now residing in Ohio and remembered for his Indian war heroics in 1811, pulled in the western anti-Indian vote. Not one of the three candidates had the ability to win the presidency, but together they came close to denying Van Buren a majority vote. Van Burenites called the three-Whig strategy a deliberate plot to derail the election and move it to the House of Representatives.

In the end, Van Buren won with 170 electoral votes, while the other three received a total of 113. But Van Buren's victories came from narrow majorities, far below those Jackson had commanded. Although Van Buren had pulled together a national Democratic Party with wins in both the North and the South, he had done it at the cost of committing northern Democrats to the proslavery agenda. And running three candidates had maximized the Whigs' success by drawing Whigs into office at the state level.

Going Ahead or *Gone to Smash*: An Entrepreneur Struggles in the 1830s

The spectacular boom of the 1830s gave life to the dream of get-rich-quick entrepreneurship, promising a level of comfort and even affluence previously unimagined. A new slang term, *go-aheadism*, captured the enthusiasm of the day. But this cocky confidence also had a downside, identified by a New York diarist who lamented that *go-aheadism* had made Americans "the most careless, reckless, headlong people on the face of the earth." Soon enough, a rich vocabulary also defined business failure: *gone to smash, fizzled, wiped out, busted, up a tree*, and *GTT*—for "gone to Texas," a location outside the United States (until 1845) and therefore out of reach of U.S. law.

Benjamin Rathbun epitomized both *go-aheadism* and *gone to smash* failure in the turbulent 1830s. A shy man who was never seen to smile, he shrewdly identified Buffalo, New York, as the perfect location for his first business venture, a fancy hotel. Buffalo, a boomtown, linked the Erie Canal with the Great Lakes, where scores of steamboats departed daily for Ohio and Michigan. The town's population doubled from 1830 to 1835, and doubled again, to eighteen thousand inhabitants, by 1840. Fueling this boom were brokerage houses that lined Buffalo's streets, lending money at high interest rates to borrowers speculating in real estate and business.

The success of the Eagle Hotel enabled Rathbun to become Buffalo's biggest self-made man. In eight years, he built a vast empire of real estate, building construction, banks, stores, and transportation. More than two thousand employees—more than a third of all adult males in Buffalo—were on his payroll. This empire required business acumen, astute management, and a steady influx of borrowed banknotes issued by New York City creditors. Rathbun's trusted younger brother, Lyman, headed financial operations, while Rathbun kept his eye on the big picture: designing the grand architecture of Buffalo (ninety-nine buildings) and cornering the land on the American side of Niagara Falls for profitable resale. Some people believed that Rathbun owned the falls themselves.

Collapse came suddenly in 1836. Rathbun learned that his creditors in New York City had lost faith in him and were selling his IOUs to brokers at a steep discount, a process known as "note shaving." To cover the much higher interest rates charged by the new note holders, the Rathbuns negotiated more loans, supposedly backed by a dozen cosigners from the Buffalo business community guaranteeing payment if the brothers failed. When Rathbun applied for a $500,000 loan in an attempt to consolidate his debt, the dozen endorsements were revealed to be forgeries. Benjamin Rathbun was convicted of fraud and sentenced to five years' hard labor in state prison; brother Lyman disappeared with trunks full of money— "GTT," many people said.

Rathbun's spectacular failure plunged Buffalo into a severe depression eight months in advance of the panic of 1837. Although deliberate fraud brought him down, his *wipeout* highlighted the inherent difficulties in an economy of note shaving and discounting, where loans of millions of dollars were granted on the basis of a few signatures. Historians calculate that something like one-fifth of all businessmen in the 1830s *fizzled* or went *up a tree*.

Massive failures in the five years after 1837 led to two striking innovations in business law and loan practices. First, the federal government passed the U.S. Bankruptcy Act of 1841, a controversial and short-term law that enabled failed debtors to wipe debts away legally, paying creditors a fraction of what was owed. Debtors gained release from crushing debt but had to endure the humiliation of having notices of their bankruptcies printed in the newspapers.

Second, the credit rating industry was born in 1841 when a failed businessman opened the

When Van Buren took office in March 1837, the financial markets were already quaking; by April, the country was plunged into crisis. The causes of the **panic of 1837** were multiple and far-ranging. Bad harvests in Europe and a large trade imbalance between Britain and the United States caused the Bank of England to start calling in loans to American merchants. Failures in various crop markets and a 30 percent downturn in international cotton prices fed the growing disaster. Cotton merchants in the South could no longer meet their obligations to New York

The Eagle Hotel, Buffalo, 1825
Benjamin Rathbun (shown here scowling) bought this three-story building in 1825, doubled it in size, and turned it into the finest hotel west of New York City. The Eagle became the meeting place for all civic and professional groups in early Buffalo. The marquis de Lafayette, French hero of the American Revolution, stayed at the Eagle in 1825 on his U.S. tour. Hotel: Courtesy of the Buffalo History Museum, used by permission. Rathbun: Courtesy of the Buffalo History Museum, used by permission.

Mercantile Agency in New York City. For a $50 subscription fee, lenders could tap into large books containing confidential information gathered by hundreds of agents around the country who assessed the credit-worthiness of local businessmen. Church (and saloon) attendance, family stability, and punctuality were often factors in grading business-men's reputations for prudence and reliability.

Had it been in existence in 1836, the Mercantile Agency might have unmasked Rathbun's fraud through semiannual checks on his reputation. The Bankruptcy Act no doubt helped the many debt-saddled Buffalo

men who had been caught out by Rathbun's failure. His liquidated estate paid out first to the thousands of workers on his payroll, second to the lawyers, and third to preferred creditors, leaving hundreds of thousands of dollars of debt unpaid.

When Rathbun left prison in 1843, he rejoined his wife, now running a lowly boardinghouse in Buffalo. Soon the Rathbuns moved to New York City, where the one-time proprietor of Buffalo's Eagle Hotel returned to his first occupation. With financial help from cousins, he leased a building for the first in a series of increasingly seedy hotels that he ran until his death.

Questions for Consideration

1. What factors led to the Rathbuns' downfall?

2. How did the new credit rating agency, established in reaction to the panic of 1837, intend to prevent economic crises?

Connect to the Big Idea

⊙ What were the causes of the panic of 1837? Did Jackson's war against the Bank of the United States have any connection to the panic?

creditors, whose firms began to fail—ninety-eight of them in March and April 1837 alone. Frightened citizens thronged the banks to try to get their money out, and businesses rushed to liquefy their remaining assets to pay off debts. Prices of stocks, bonds, and real estate fell 30 to 40 percent. The

familiar events of the panic of 1819 unfolded again, with terrifying rapidity, and the credit market tumbled like a house of cards. Newspapers describing the economic free fall generally used the language of emotional states—excitement, anxiety, terror, panic. Such words focused on human reactions to the crisis rather than on the structural features of the economy that had interacted to amplify the downturn. The vocabulary for understanding the wider economy was still quite limited, making it hard to track the bigger picture of the workings of capitalism. (See "Seeking the American Promise," page 306.)

Instead, many observers looked to politics, religion, and character flaws to explain the crisis. Some Whig leaders were certain that Jackson's antibank and hard-money policies were responsible for the ruin. New Yorker Philip Hone, a wealthy Whig, called the Jackson administration "the most disastrous in the annals of the country" for its "wicked interference" in banking and monetary matters. Others framed the devastation as retribution for the frenzy of speculation that had gripped

the nation. A religious periodical in Boston hoped that Americans would now moderate their greed: "We were getting to think that there was no end to the wealth, and could be no check to the progress of our country; that economy was not needed, that prudence was weakness." In this view, the panic was a wakeup call, a blessing in disguise. Others identified the competitive, profit-maximizing capitalist system as the cause and looked to Britain and France for new socialist ideas calling for the common ownership of the means of production. American socialists, though few in number, were vocal and imaginative, and in the early 1840s several thousand developed utopian alternative communities (as discussed in chapter 12).

The panic of 1837 subsided by 1838, but in 1839 another run on the banks and ripples of

VISUAL ACTIVITY

The Panic of 1837

A sad family with an unemployed father confronts the fallout of the panic of 1837. The wife and children complain of hunger, the house is stripped nearly bare, and rent collectors loom in the doorway. The only support system for the unemployed in 1837 was the local almshouse, where families were split up and living conditions were harsh. Library of Congress.

READING THE IMAGE: What does the clothing worn by family members suggest about their customary economic standing? Can you guess why the artist put sketches of Andrew Jackson and Martin Van Buren on the wall?

CONNECTIONS: What caused the panic of 1837, and why were its consequences suffered by so many people?

SPECIE CLAWS.

business failures deflated the economy, creating a second panic. President Van Buren called a special session of Congress to consider creating an independent treasury system to perform some of the functions of the defunct Bank of the United States. Such a system, funded by government deposits, would deal only in hard money and would exert a powerful moderating influence on inflation and the credit market. But Van Buren encountered strong resistance in Congress, even among Democrats. The treasury system finally won approval in 1840, but by then Van Buren's chances of winning a second term in office were virtually nil.

In 1840, the Whigs settled on William Henry Harrison to oppose Van Buren. The campaign drew on voter involvement as no other presidential campaign ever had. The Whigs borrowed tricks from the Democrats: Harrison was touted as a common man born in a log cabin (in reality, he was born on a Virginia plantation), and campaign parades featured toy log cabins held aloft. His Indian-fighting days, now thirty years behind him, were played up to give him a Jacksonian aura. Whigs staged festive rallies around the country, drumming up mass appeal with candlelight parades and song shows, and women participated in rallies as never before. Some 78 percent of eligible voters cast ballots—the highest percentage ever in American history.

Harrison took 53 percent of the popular vote and won a resounding 234 electoral college votes to Van Buren's 60. A Democratic editor lamented, "We have taught them how to conquer us!"

> **REVIEW**   How did slavery figure as a campaign issue in the election of 1836?

▶ Conclusion: The Age of Jackson or the Era of Reform?

Harrison's election closed a decade that had brought the common man and democracy to the forefront of American politics. Economic transformations loom large in explaining the fast-paced changes of the 1830s. Transportation advances put goods and people in circulation, augmenting urban growth and helping to create a national culture, and water-powered manufacturing began to change the face of wage labor. Trade and banking mushroomed, and western land once occupied by Indians was auctioned off in a landslide of sales. Two

periods of economic downturn—including the panic of 1819 and the panics of 1837 and 1839—offered sobering lessons about speculative fever.

Andrew Jackson symbolized this age of opportunity for many. His fame as an aggressive general, Indian fighter, champion of the common man, and defender of slavery attracted growing numbers of voters to the emergent Democratic Party, which championed personal liberty, free competition, and egalitarian opportunity for all white men.

Jackson's constituency was challenged by a small but vocal segment of the population troubled by serious moral problems that Jacksonians preferred to ignore. Inspired by the Second Great Awakening, reformers targeted personal vices (illicit sex and intemperance) and social problems (prostitution, poverty, and slavery) and joined forces with evangelicals and wealthy lawyers and merchants (North and South) who appreciated a national bank and protective tariffs. The Whig Party was the party of activist moralism and state-sponsored entrepreneurship. Whig voters were, of course, male, but thousands of reform-minded women broke new ground by signing political petitions on the issues of Indian removal and slavery. A few exceptional women, like Sarah and Angelina Grimké, captured the national limelight by offering powerful testimony against slavery and in the process pioneering new pathways for women to contribute a moral voice to politics.

National politics in the 1830s were more divisive than at any time since the 1790s. The new party system of Democrats and Whigs reached far deeper into the electorate than had the Federalists and Republicans. Stagecoaches and steamboats carried newspapers from the cities to the backwoods, politicizing voters and creating party loyalty. Politics acquired immediacy and excitement, causing nearly four out of five white men to cast ballots in 1840.

High rates of voter participation would continue into the 1840s and 1850s. Unprecedented urban growth, westward expansion, and early industrialism marked those decades, sustaining the Democrat-Whig split in the electorate. But critiques of slavery, concerns for free labor, and an emerging protest against women's second-class citizenship complicated the political scene of the 1840s, leading to third-party political movements. One of these third parties, called the Republican Party, would achieve dominance in 1860 with the election of an Illinois lawyer, Abraham Lincoln, to the presidency.

See the Selected Bibliography for this chapter in the Appendix.

11 Chapter Review

MAKE IT STICK

LearningCurve
Go online and use LearningCurve to see what you know. Then review the key terms and answer the questions.

KEY TERMS

Erie Canal (p. 285)
Lowell mills (p. 286)
second Bank of the United States (p. 287)
Whigs (p. 291)
Democrats (p. 291)
Indian Removal Act of 1830 (p. 294)
Trail of Tears (p. 295)
nullification (p. 296)
Second Great Awakening (p. 300)
American Temperance Society (p. 301)
New York Female Moral Reform Society (p. 301)
panic of 1837 (p. 306)

REVIEW QUESTIONS

1. Why did the United States experience a market revolution after 1815? (pp. 283–290)

2. Why did Andrew Jackson defeat John Quincy Adams so dramatically in the 1828 election? (pp. 291–293)

3. What were the most significant policies of Andrew Jackson's presidency? (pp. 293–297)

4. How did evangelical Protestantism contribute to the social reform movements of the 1830s? (pp. 298–304)

5. How did slavery figure as a campaign issue in the election of 1836? (pp. 305–307)

MAKING CONNECTIONS

1. How did the market revolution that began in the 1810s affect Americans' work and domestic lives? Consider how gender contributed to these developments.

2. Discuss how Jackson benefited from, and contributed to, the vibrant political culture of the 1830s. Cite specific national developments.

3. Describe Andrew Jackson's response to the "Indian problem" during his presidency. How did his policies revise or continue earlier federal policies?

4. Discuss the objectives and strategies of two reform movements of the 1830s and how they relate to larger political and economic trends.

LINKING TO THE PAST

1. How were the economic circumstances and social anxieties that gave rise to the Second Great Awakening similar to, and different from, those that encouraged the First Great Awakening? (See chapter 5.)

2. Compare the development of political parties in the 1790s (Federalists and Republicans) with the second development of parties in the 1830s (Whigs and Democrats). Were the parties of the 1830s in any way the descendants of the two of the 1790s? Or were they completely different? (See chapter 9.)

12 The New West and the Free North

1840–1860

CONTENT LEARNING OBJECTIVES

After reading and studying this chapter, you should be able to:

- Identify the fundamental changes that transformed the American economy from 1840 to 1860.

- Compare and contrast the promises and realities of free labor, including how free-labor proponents explained economic inequality in America.

- Explain how the American nation expanded its boundaries and define the concept of "manifest destiny."

- Describe the issues that surrounded the debate on the annexation of Texas and Oregon, how the United States provoked war with Mexico and the consequences of the war.

- Describe the "evangelical temperament," and the reforms evangelical Protestants proposed, and explain how the women's rights movement evolved from other reform movements.

GOLD NUGGET
Gold! Nuggets like this one scooped from a California river drove easterners crazy with excitement. Only a few of the quarter of a million men who joined the gold rush got rich. Wolffy/Alamy

EARLY IN NOVEMBER 1842, ABRAHAM LINCOLN AND HIS NEW WIFE, Mary, moved into their first home in Springfield, Illinois, a small rented room on the second floor of the Globe Tavern, the nicest place that Abraham had ever lived and the worst place that Mary had ever inhabited. She grew up in Lexington, Kentucky, attended by slaves in the elegant home of her father, a prosperous merchant and banker. In March 1861, the Lincolns moved into the presidential mansion in Washington, D.C.

Abraham Lincoln climbed from the Globe Tavern to the White House by work, ambition, and immense talent—traits he had honed since boyhood. Lincoln and many others celebrated his rise from humble origins as an example of the opportunities in the free-labor economy of the North and West. They attributed his spectacular ascent to his individual qualities and tended to ignore the help he received from Mary and many others.

Born in a Kentucky log cabin in 1809, Lincoln grew up on small, struggling farms as his family migrated west. His father, Thomas Lincoln, who had been born in Virginia, never learned to read and, as his son recalled, "never did more in the way of writing than to bunglingly sign his own name." Lincoln's mother, Nancy, could neither read nor write. In 1816, Thomas Lincoln moved his young family from Kentucky to the Indiana wilderness where Abraham learned the arts of agriculture, but "there was absolutely nothing to excite ambition for education," Lincoln recollected. In contrast, Mary Todd received ten years of schooling in Lexington's best private academies for young women.

In 1830, Thomas Lincoln decided to move farther west and headed to central Illinois. The next spring, when Thomas moved yet again, Abraham set out on his own, a "friendless, uneducated, penniless boy," as he described himself.

By dogged striving, Abraham Lincoln gained an education and the respect of his Illinois neighbors, although a steady income eluded him for years. The newlyweds received help from Mary's father, including eighty acres of land and a yearly allowance of about $1,100 for six years that helped them move out of their room above the Globe Tavern and into their own home. Abraham eventually built a thriving law practice in Springfield, Illinois, and served in the state legislature and in Congress. Mary helped him in many ways, rearing their sons, tending their household, and integrating him into her wealthy and influential extended family in Illinois and Kentucky. Mary also shared Abraham's keen interest in politics and ambition for power. With Mary's support, Abraham became the first president born west of the Appalachian Mountains.

Like Lincoln, millions of Americans believed they could make something of themselves, whatever their origins, so long as they were willing to work. Individuals who were lazy, undisciplined, or foolish had only themselves to blame if they failed, advocates of free labor ideology declared. Work was a prerequisite for success, not a guarantee. This emphasis on work highlighted the individual efforts of men and tended to slight the many crucial contributions of women and family members to the successes of men like Lincoln. In addition, the rewards of work were skewed toward white men and away from women and free African Americans, as antislavery and women's rights reformers pointed out. Nonetheless, the promise of such rewards spurred efforts that shaped the contours of America, plowing new fields and building railroads that pushed the boundaries of the nation ever westward to the Pacific Ocean. The nation's economic, political, and geographic expansion raised anew the question of whether slavery should also move west, the question that Lincoln and other Americans confronted repeatedly following the Mexican-American War, yet another outgrowth of the nation's ceaseless westward movement.

► Economic and Industrial Evolution

During the 1840s and 1850s, Americans experienced a profound economic transformation. Since 1800, the total output of the U.S. economy had multiplied twelvefold. Four fundamental changes in American society fueled this remarkable economic growth. First, millions of Americans moved from farms to towns and cities, Abraham Lincoln among them. Second, factory workers (primarily in towns and cities) increased to about 20 percent of the labor force by 1860. Third, a shift from water power to steam as a source of energy raised productivity, especially in factories and transportation. Railroads in particular harnessed steam power, speeding transport and cutting costs. Fourth, agricultural productivity nearly doubled during Lincoln's lifetime, spurring the nation's economic growth more than any other factor.

Historians often refer to this cascade of changes as an industrial revolution. However, these changes did not cause an abrupt discontinuity in America's economy or society, which remained overwhelmingly agricultural. Old methods of production continued alongside the new. The changes in the American economy during the 1840s and 1850s might better be termed "industrial evolution."

Agriculture and Land Policy

The foundation of the United States' economic growth lay in agriculture. A French traveler in the United States noted that Americans had "a general feeling of hatred against trees." Although the traveler exaggerated, trees limited agricultural productivity because farmers had to spend much time and energy clearing trees to make fields suitable for cultivation. As farmers pushed westward in a quest for cheap land, they encountered the Midwest's comparatively treeless prairie, where they could spend less time clearing land and more time with a plow and hoe. Rich prairie soils yielded bumper crops, enticing farmers to migrate to the Midwest by the tens of thousands between 1830 and 1860. The populations of Indiana, Illinois, Michigan, Wisconsin, and Iowa exploded tenfold between 1830 and 1860, ten times faster than the growth of the nation as a whole.

Labor-saving improvements in farm implements also boosted agricultural productivity. Inventors tinkered to craft stronger, more

CHRONOLOGY

1830	• *The Book of Mormon* published.
1836	• Battle of the Alamo. • Texas declares independence from Mexico.
1837	• Steel plow patented.
1840s	• Practical mechanical reapers created. • Fourierist communities founded.
1841	• First wagon trains head west on Oregon Trail. • Vice President John Tyler becomes president when William Henry Harrison dies.
1844	• James K. Polk elected president. • Samuel F. B. Morse demonstrates telegraph.
1845	• Term *manifest destiny* coined. • Texas enters Union as slave state. • Potato blight spurs Irish immigration.
1846	• Bear Flag Revolt. • Congress declares war on Mexico. • United States and Great Britain divide Oregon Country.
1847	• Mormons settle in Utah.
1848	• Treaty of Guadalupe Hidalgo. • Oneida community organized. • Seneca Falls convention.
1849	• California gold rush begins.
1850	• Utah Territory annexed. • Railroads granted six square miles of land for every mile of track.
1851	• Fort Laramie conference marks the beginning of Indian concentration.
1855	• Massachusetts integrates public schools.
1857	• Mormon War.
1861	• California connected to nation by telegraph.

efficient plows. In 1837, John Deere made a strong, smooth steel plow that sliced through prairie soil so cleanly that farmers called it the "singing plow." Deere's company produced more than ten thousand plows a year by the late 1850s. Human and animal muscles provided the energy for plowing, but Deere's plows permitted farmers to break more ground and plant more crops.

Improvements in wheat harvesting also increased farmers' productivity. In 1850, most farmers harvested wheat by hand, cutting two or three acres a day. In the 1840s, Cyrus McCormick and others experimented with designs for **mechanical reapers**, and by the 1850s a McCormick reaper that cost between $100 and $150 allowed a farmer to harvest twelve acres a day. Improved reapers and plows,

usually powered by horses or oxen, allowed farmers to cultivate more land, doubling the corn and wheat harvests between 1840 and 1860.

Federal land policy made possible the leap in agricultural productivity. Up to 1860, the United States continued to be land-rich and labor-poor. Territorial acquisitions made the nation a great deal richer in land, adding more than a billion acres with the Louisiana Purchase (see "The Louisiana Purchase" in chapter 10) and vast territories following the Mexican-American War. The federal government made most of this land available for purchase to attract settlers and to generate revenue. Millions of ordinary farmers bought federal land for just $1.25 an acre, or $50 for a forty-acre farm that could support a family. Millions of other farmers squatted on unclaimed federal land, and

VISUAL ACTIVITY

Mechanical Reaper Advertisement

This advertisement for the mechanical reaper manufactured by the Lagonda Agricultural Works in Ohio illustrates the labor saved—and the labor still required—to harvest wheat. The revolving reel pulled the stalks of wheat toward a cutter and piled the cut grain on a platform. One man pushed the cut wheat onto the ground where another man bound into sheaves. Library of Congress.

READING THE IMAGE: What kinds of labor are represented by the two men standing on each side of the oval picture of the reaper? What kinds of labor were saved by the mechanical reaper and what kinds were required?

CONNECTIONS: How did reapers and other improvements increase agricultural productivity?

carved out farms. By making land available on relatively easy terms, federal land policy boosted the increase in agricultural productivity that fueled the nation's impressive economic growth.

Manufacturing and Mechanization

Changes in manufacturing arose from the nation's land-rich, labor-poor economy. In Europe's land-poor, labor-rich economies, meager opportunities in agriculture supplied plenty of factory workers and kept wages low. In the United States, western expansion and government land policies buoyed agriculture, keeping millions of people on the farm—80 percent of the nation's 31 million people lived in rural areas in 1860—and thereby limiting the supply of workers for manufacturing and elevating wages. Because of this relative shortage of workers, American manufacturers searched constantly for ways to save labor.

Mechanization allowed manufacturers to produce more with less labor. In general, factory workers produced twice as much (per unit of labor) as agricultural workers. The practice of manufacturing and then assembling interchangeable parts spread from gun making to other industries and became known as the **American system**. Standardized parts produced by machine allowed manufacturers to employ unskilled workers, who were much cheaper than highly trained craftsmen. A visitor to a Springfield, Massachusetts, gun factory noted in 1842, for example, that standardized parts made the trained gunsmith's "skill of the eye and hand, [previously] acquired by practice alone . . . no longer indispensable." Factories remained small, however. Even in heavily mechanized industries, factories seldom employed more than twenty or thirty workers.

Manufacturing and agriculture meshed into a dynamic national economy. New England led the nation in manufacturing, shipping goods such as guns, clocks, plows, and axes west and south, while southern and western states sent commodities such as wheat, pork, whiskey, tobacco, and cotton north and east. Between 1840 and 1860, coal production in Pennsylvania, Ohio, and elsewhere multiplied eightfold, cutting prices in half and powering innumerable coal-fired steam engines. Even so, by 1860 coal accounted for less than a fifth of the nation's energy consumption, and, even in manufacturing, muscles provided thirty times more energy than steam did.

American manufacturers specialized in producing for the gigantic domestic market rather than for export. British goods dominated the international market and usually were cheaper and better than American-made products. U.S. manufacturers supported tariffs to minimize British competition, but their best protection from British competitors was to please their American customers, most of them farmers. The burgeoning national economy was accelerated by the growth of railroads, which linked farmers and factories in new ways.

Railroads: Breaking the Bonds of Nature

Railroads captured Americans' imagination because they seemed to break the bonds of nature. (See "Visualizing History," page 316.) When canals and rivers froze in winter or became impassable during summer droughts, trains steamed ahead, averaging more than twenty miles an hour during the 1850s. Above all, railroads gave cities not blessed with canals or navigable rivers a way to compete for rural trade.

In 1850, trains steamed along 9,000 miles of track, almost two-thirds of it in New England and the Middle Atlantic states. By 1860, several railroads spanned the Mississippi River, connecting frontier farmers to the nation's 30,000 miles of track, approximately as much as in all of the rest of the world combined (Map 12.1). In 1857, for example, France had just 3,700 miles of track, while England and Wales had 6,400 miles. The massive expansion of American railroads helped catapult the nation to the world's second greatest industrial power, after Great Britain.

The Telegraph

Samuel F. B. Morse received a patent for the telegraph in 1840. With a series of taps on a telegraph key like this, operators sent short and long pulses of electricity that translated into letters and numbers. Stimulated by the railroad industry by 1861, telegraph wires webbed the nation. Cheap, efficient, and fast communication changed American businesses, newspapers, government, and everyday life. Division of Work & Industry, National Museum of American History, Smithsonian Institution

The Path of Progress

Westward the Star of Empire Takes its Way—Near Council Bluffs, Iowa

In addition to speeding transportation, railroads propelled the growth of other industries, such as iron and communications. Iron production grew five times faster than the population during the decades up to 1860, in part to meet railroads' demand. Railroads also stimulated the fledgling telegraph industry. In 1844, Samuel F. B. Morse demonstrated the potential of his telegraph by transmitting an electronic message between Washington, D.C., and Baltimore. By 1861, more than fifty thousand miles of telegraph wire stretched across the continent to the Pacific Ocean, often alongside railroad tracks, accelerating communications of all sorts.

In contrast to the government ownership of railroads common in other industrial nations, private corporations built and owned almost all American railroads. But the railroads received massive government aid, especially federal land grants. Up to 1850, the federal government had granted a total of seven million acres of federal land to various turnpike, highway, and canal projects. In 1850, Congress approved a precedent-setting grant to railroads of six square miles of federal land for each mile of track laid. By 1860, Congress had granted railroads more than twenty million acres of federal land, thereby underwriting construction costs and promoting the expansion of the rail network, the settlement of federal land, and the integration of the domestic market.

The railroad boom of the 1850s signaled the growing industrial might of the American economy. Like other industries, railroads succeeded because they served both farms and cities. But transportation was not revolutionized overnight. Most Americans in 1860 were still far more familiar with horses than with locomotives. Even

This painting depicts a mid-nineteenth-century landscape of agricultural and industrial progress. Created by Andrew Melrose to celebrate the recently built railroad connecting Chicago and Council Bluffs, Iowa, almost four hundred miles to the west, the painting contrasts the irregularity of nature with the new principles of order imposed on the natural landscape by human beings.

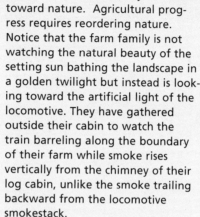

Detail of Farmhouse

The natural order is illustrated by the forest on the right side of the painting, by the rock-studded vegetation on either side of the rail bed, and by the deer scampering across the tracks.

The locomotive barreling down the tracks is barely visible behind its blazing headlight, which illuminates the way forward and startles the deer accustomed to shadowed hiding places in the forest. The immense power of the locomotive contrasts with the skittish, vulnerable deer. suggesting the unstoppable momentum of industrial progress.

The left side of the painting shows a frontier farm cultivated by

a family standing in the shadow of the log cabin. The principles of agricultural order represented by the farm are somewhat different from those of the industrial order represented by the railroad and the natural order represented by the forest. The stumps littering the fields suggest the farm family's attitudes toward nature. Agricultural progress requires reordering nature. Notice that the farm family is not watching the natural beauty of the setting sun bathing the landscape in a golden twilight but instead is looking toward the artificial light of the locomotive. They have gathered outside their cabin to watch the train barreling along the boundary of their farm while smoke rises vertically from the chimney of their log cabin, unlike the smoke trailing backward from the locomotive smokestack.

Overall, the painting depicts the benefits and costs of progress for the farm family, the forest, the deer, the railroad, and American society in general

SOURCE: Autry National Center, Los Angeles; 92.147.1

Detail of Deer Crossing Tracks

Questions for Analysis

1. How do the principles of order represented by the locomotive and railroad tracks contrast with the natural order?

2. How does the agricultural order compare with the industrial and natural order in the painting?

3. How does the painting portray the costs and benefits of progress?

Connect to the Big Idea

C How did Americans alter the physical landscape of the nation in the early nineteenth century?

by 1875, trains carried only about a third of the mail; most of the rest still went by horseback or stagecoach.

The economy of the 1840s and 1850s linked an expanding, westward-moving population in farms and cities with muscles, animals, machines, steam, and railroads. Abraham Lincoln planted corn and split fence rails as a young man before he moved to Springfield, Illinois, and became a successful attorney who defended, among others, railroad corporations. His mobility—westward, from farm to city, from manual to mental labor, and upward—illustrated the direction of economic change and the opportunities that beckoned enterprising individuals.

REVIEW Why did the United States become a leading industrial power in the nineteenth century?

▶ Free Labor: Promise and Reality

The nation's impressive economic performance did not reward all Americans equally. Native-born white men tended to do better than immigrants. With few exceptions, women were excluded from opportunities open to men. Tens of thousands of women worked as seamstresses, laundresses, domestic servants, factory hands, and teachers but had little opportunity to aspire to higher-paying jobs. In the North and West, slavery was slowly eliminated in the half century after the American Revolution, but most free African Americans were relegated to dead-end jobs as laborers and servants. Discrimination against immigrants, women, and free blacks did not trouble most white men. With certain notable

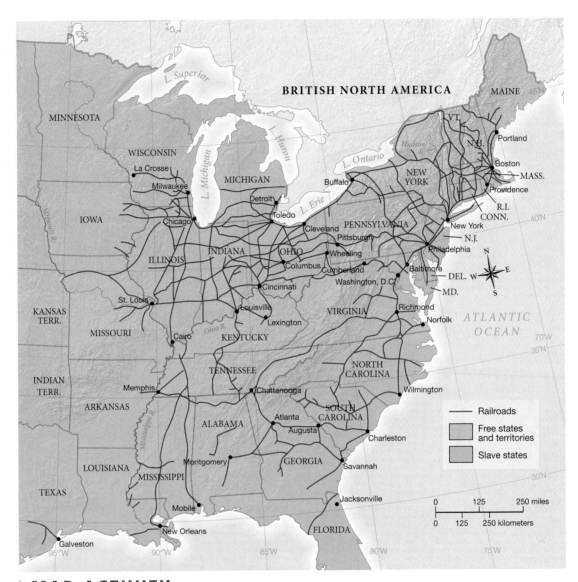

MAP ACTIVITY

Map 12.1   Railroads In 1860
Railroads were a crucial component of the revolutions in transportation and communications that transformed nineteenth-century America. The railroad system reflected the differences in the economies of the North and South.

READING THE MAP: In which sections of the country was most of the railroad track laid by the middle of the nineteenth century? What cities served as the busiest railroad hubs?

CONNECTIONS: How did the expansion of railroad networks affect the American economy? Why was the U.S. government willing to grant more than twenty million acres of public land to the private corporations that ran the railroads?

exceptions, they considered it proper and just, the outcome of the free labor system that rewarded hard work and, ideally, education.

The Free-Labor Ideal

During the 1840s and 1850s, leaders throughout the North and West emphasized a set of ideas that seemed to explain why the changes under way in their society benefited some people more than others. They referred again and again to the advantages of what they termed *free labor*. (The word *free* referred to laborers who were not slaves. It did not mean laborers who worked for nothing.) By the 1850s, free-labor ideas described a social and economic ideal that accounted for both the successes and the shortcomings of the economy and society taking shape in the North and West.

Spokesmen for the free-labor ideal celebrated hard work, self-reliance, and independence. They proclaimed that the door to success was open not just to those who inherited wealth or status but also to self-made men such as Abraham Lincoln. Free labor, Lincoln argued, was "the just and generous, and prosperous system, which opens the way for all—gives hope to all, and energy, and progress, and improvement of condition to all." Free labor permitted farmers and artisans to enjoy the products of their own labor, and it also benefited wageworkers. "The prudent, penniless beginner in the world," Lincoln asserted, "Labors for wages awhile, saves a surplus with which to buy tools or land, for himself; then labors on his own account another while, and at length hires another new beginner to help him." Wage labor, Lincoln claimed, was the first rung on the ladder toward self-employment and eventually hiring others.

The free-labor ideal affirmed an egalitarian vision of human potential. Lincoln and other spokesmen stressed the importance of universal education to permit "heads and hands [to] cooperate as friends." Throughout the North and West, communities supported public schools to make the rudiments of learning available to young children. In rural areas, where the labor of children was more difficult to spare, schools typically enrolled no more than half the school-age children. Textbooks and teachers—most of whom were young women—drummed into students the lessons of the free-labor system: self-reliance, discipline, and, above all else, hard work. "Remember that all the ignorance, degradation, and misery in the world is the result of indolence and vice," one textbook intoned. Both in and outside school, free-labor ideology emphasized labor as much as freedom.

Economic Inequality

The free-labor ideal made sense to many Americans, especially in the North and West, because it seemed to describe their own experiences. Lincoln frequently referred to his humble beginnings as a hired laborer and implicitly invited his listeners to consider how far he had come. In 1860, his assets of $17,000 easily placed him in the wealthiest 5 percent of the population. A few men became much richer. Most Americans, however, measured success in more modest terms. The average wealth of adult white men in the North in 1860 barely topped $2,000. Nearly half of American men had no wealth at all; about 60 percent owned no land. Because property possessed by married women

was normally considered to belong to their husbands, women typically had less wealth than men. Free African Americans had still less; 90 percent of them were propertyless. (See "Beyond America's Borders," page 320.)

Free-labor spokesmen considered these economic inequalities a natural outgrowth of freedom—the inevitable result of some individuals being both luckier and more able and willing to work. These inequalities also demonstrate the gap between the promise and the performance of the free-labor ideal. Economic growth permitted many men to move from being landless squatters to landowning farmers and from being hired laborers to independent, self-employed producers. But many more Americans remained behind, landless and working for wages. Even those who realized their aspirations often had a precarious hold on their independence. Bad debts, market volatility, crop failure, sickness, or death could quickly eliminate a family's gains.

Seeking out new opportunities in pursuit of free-labor ideals created restless social and geographic mobility. While fortunate people such as Abraham Lincoln rose far beyond their

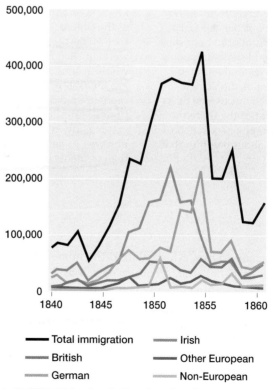

FIGURE 12.1 Antebellum Immigration, 1840–1860
Immigration shot up in the mid-1840s. Between 1848 and 1860, nearly 3.5 million immigrants entered the United States.

Global Prosperity in the 1850s

By the 1850s, the U.S. economy had achieved a remarkable economic transformation. In 1801, when president-elect Thomas Jefferson rode horseback the 180 miles from his home in Monticello, Virginia, to Washington, D.C., he and his horse had to swim across several rivers that lacked bridges or ferries. In 1861, when president-elect Abraham Lincoln traveled more than 1,000 miles to Washington from his home in Springfield, Illinois, he did not need to get wet swimming across rivers. He rode the entire way on railroads. The changes that made Lincoln's journey possible created an American economy that produced more goods and services per capita than that of any other country in the world, except one—Great Britain.

In the 1850s, some countries in the world produced more total goods and services than the United States. But since they had much larger populations than the United States, they produced much less per capita. For example, China produced huge quantities of goods and services, roughly four times more than the United States did. But since the Chinese population was about twenty times greater than that of the United States, the per capita production of China was only about one-fifth that of the United States.

In other words, if all the goods and services in China and the United States in 1850 had been shared equally by the people who lived in each country, each person in China would have had only one-fifth as much as each person in the United States. Of course, all goods and services were never shared equally in either country (or in any other country for that matter). Rich people had more than poor people; landowners had more than laborers; slave owners had more than slaves; and so on. Still, per capita production can serve as an imperfect but revealing indicator of the general prosperity of a country's economy.

Like China, African countries were about one-fifth as prosperous as the United States. India, Japan, Mexico, and Brazil had somewhat more prosperous economies, with per capita production about one-third that of the United States. European countries such as Russia, Spain, and Italy were about half as prosperous as the United States. Overall, more than 90 percent of the people in the world in 1850 lived in countries whose economies produced half or less (much less, for most people) per capita than did the economy of the United States. In other words, the vast majority of the global population was, in general, much poorer than residents of the United States.

The American economy surpassed even the two largest countries of western continental Europe, France and Germany. Both countries, like the United States, had started to industrialize, making them far more prosperous than most of the world. But they lagged behind the United States in per capita production. Germany's per capita production was about 80 percent of that of the United States; France's was about 90 percent.

Great Britain, the most prosperous country in the world in 1850, surpassed the per capita production of the United States by 30 percent. With a population of 21 million, slightly fewer than the 23 million residents of the United States, Britain produced a whopping 45 percent of the world's manufactured goods.

Many factors contributed to Britain's economic leadership, but three were especially important. First, most people in Britain had moved to towns and cities by 1850. Rural folks made up only 22 percent of Britain's population, compared to 85 percent of the U.S. population. Many urban dwellers worked in industries that, in general, were more productive than agriculture, boosting British output. Second, wages were relatively high in Britain, giving manufacturers a big incentive to replace costly labor with machinery. Although machinery

social origins, others shared the misfortune of a merchant who, an observer noted, "has been on the sinking list all his life." In search of better prospects, roughly two-thirds of the rural population moved every decade, and population turnover in cities was even greater.

Immigrants and the Free-Labor Ladder

The risks and uncertainties of free labor did not deter millions of immigrants from entering the United States during the 1840s and 1850s. Almost 4.5 million immigrants arrived between 1840 and 1860, six times more than had come during the previous two decades (Figure 12.1).

Nearly three-fourths of the immigrants who arrived in the United States between 1840 and 1860 came from either Germany or Ireland. The majority of the 1.4 million Germans who entered during these years were skilled tradesmen and their families. Roughly a quarter were farmers, many of whom settled in Texas. German Americans were often Protestants and usually occupied the middle stratum of independent producers than in the rest of the world. Low coal prices gave manufacturers a cheap energy source, making it less costly for them to adopt innovative industrial techniques that boosted production—such as steam power. In 1850, coal consumption in Britain was ten times greater than in France and seven times greater than in Germany and the United States. Britain's unique combination of cheap energy, high wages, and a large urban population helped make it the most productive and prosperous country in the world in 1850.

America in a Global Context

1. In 1850, how did U.S. prosperity compare to that in the rest of the world?

2. Why did Britain have the world's leading economy in 1850?

3. To what extent is per capita production a misleading measure of prosperity? Can you think of better measures?

4. What questions does the pattern of global prosperity and poverty in 1850 raise about immigration to the United States?

Connect to the Big Idea

⊙ How did the comparative economic prosperity of the United States influence the experiences and ideas of Americans during the 1850s?

Poverty and Prosperity

The prosperous couple entering the door brings blankets and parcels probably containing food to this poverty-stricken family living in a barren attic. The charity provided by the benevolent couple offered a small measure of temporary relief, but it did not promise a long-term solution to the poor family's plight. The clothing and bodily postures in the painting highlight the contrast between poverty and prosperity in the mid-nineteenth century. The Granger Collection, New York.

required capital outlays to set up and maintain, it was far more efficient and tireless than wageworkers.

Manufacturers in both Britain and the United States had similar incentives to industrialize, but British producers did so first and with far greater effectiveness than did those in the United States, in large measure because Britain had a cheap and nearly inexhaustible source of energy—coal, the third crucial factor in Britain's economic leadership. Britain had a unique endowment of coal resources that could be mined relatively inexpensively, making coal prices much lower

celebrated by free-labor spokesmen; relatively few worked as wage laborers or domestic servants.

Irish immigrants, in contrast, entered at the bottom of the free-labor ladder and struggled to climb up. Nearly 1.7 million Irish immigrants arrived between 1840 and 1860, nearly all of them desperately poor and often weakened by hunger and disease. Potato blight caused a catastrophic famine in Ireland in 1845 and returned repeatedly in subsequent years. Many Irish people crowded into ships and set out for America, where they congregated in northeastern cities. As one immigrant group declared, "All we

want is to get out of Ireland; we must be better anywhere than here."

Roughly three out of four Irish immigrants worked as laborers or domestic servants. Irish men dug canals, loaded ships, laid railroad track, and did odd jobs while Irish women worked in the homes of others—cooking, washing, ironing, minding children, and cleaning house. Almost all Irish immigrants were Catholic, which set them apart from the overwhelmingly Protestant native-born residents. Many natives regarded the Irish as hard-drinking, unruly, half-civilized folk. Job

VISUAL ACTIVITY

A German Immigrant in New York

This 1855 painting depicts a German immigrant in New York City asking directions from an African American man cutting firewood. Like many other German immigrants, the man shown here appears relatively well off. Unlike most Irish immigrants, who arrived without family members, the German immigrant is accompanied by his daughter and son. North Carolina Museum of Art, Raleigh, purchased with funds from the State of North Carolina (52.9.2)

READING THE IMAGE: How does the clothing of the German immigrant compare to that of the black man cutting wood and the white laborer on the right? What racial attitudes are illustrated by the painting?

CONNECTIONS: How did mid-nineteenth century immigrants compare to native-born Americans?

announcements commonly stated, "No Irish need apply." One immigrant recalled that Irish laborers were thought of as "nothing . . . more than dogs . . . despised and kicked about." Despite such prejudices, native residents hired Irish immigrants because they accepted low pay and worked hard.

In America's labor-poor economy, Irish laborers could earn more in one day than in several weeks in Ireland. In America, one immigrant explained in 1853, there was "plenty of work and plenty of wages plenty to eat and no land lords thats enough what more does a man want." But many immigrants also craved respect and decent working conditions.

Amidst the opportunities for some immigrants and native-born laborers, the free-labor system often did not live up to the optimistic vision outlined by Abraham Lincoln. Many wage laborers could not realistically aspire to become independent, self-sufficient property holders, despite the claims of free-labor proponents.

REVIEW   How did the free-labor ideal account for economic inequality?

▶ The Westward Movement

Beginning in the 1840s, the nation's swelling population, booming economy, and boundless confidence propelled a new era of rapid westward migration. Until then, the overwhelming majority of Americans lived east of the Mississippi River. Under the banner of manifest destiny, Americans encountered Native Americans, who inhabited the plains, deserts, and rugged coasts of the west; the British, who claimed the Oregon Country; and the Mexicans, whose flag flew over the vast expanse of the Southwest. Nevertheless, by 1850 the United States stretched to the Pacific and included the Utah Territory with its Mormon settlement.

Frontier settlers took the land and then, with the exception of the Mormons, lobbied their government to acquire the territory they had settled. The human cost of aggressive expansionism was high. The young Mexican nation lost a war and half of its territory. Two centuries of Indian wars, which ended east of the Mississippi during the 1830s, continued for an-other half century in the West.

Manifest Destiny

Most Americans believed that the superiority of their institutions and white culture bestowed on them a God-given right to spread across the continent. They imagined the West as a howling wilderness, empty and undeveloped. If they recognized Indians and Mexicans at all, they dismissed them as primitives who would have to be redeemed, shoved aside, or exterminated. The West provided young men especially an arena in which to "show their manhood." Most Americans believed that the West needed the civilizing power of the hammer and the plow, the ballot box and the pulpit, which had transformed the East.

In 1845, a New York political journal edited by John L. O'Sullivan coined the term *manifest destiny* to justify white settlers taking the land they coveted. O'Sullivan called on Americans to resist any effort to thwart "the fulfillment of our manifest destiny to overspread the continent allotted by Providence for the free development of our yearly multiplying millions . . . [and] for the development of the great experiment of liberty and federative self-government entrusted to us." Almost overnight, the magic phrase *manifest destiny* swept the nation, providing an ideological shield for conquering the West.

As important as national pride and racial arrogance were to manifest destiny, economic gain made up its core. Land hunger drew hundreds of thousands of Americans westward. Some politicians, moreover, had become convinced that national prosperity depended on capturing the rich trade of the Far East. To trade with Asia, the United States needed the Pacific coast ports that stretched from San Diego to Puget Sound. The United States and Asia must "talk together, and trade together," Missouri senator Thomas Hart Benton declared. "Commerce is a great civilizer." In the 1840s, American economic expansion came wrapped in the rhetoric of uplift and civilization.

Oregon and the Overland Trail

American expansionists and the British competed for the Oregon Country—a vast region bounded on the west by the Pacific Ocean, on the east by the Rocky Mountains, on the south by the forty-second parallel, and on the north by Russian Alaska. In 1818, the United States and Great Britain decided on "joint occupation" that would leave Oregon "free and open" to settlement by both countries. By the 1820s, a handful of American fur traders and "mountain men" roamed the region.

In the late 1830s, settlers began to trickle along the **Oregon Trail**, following a path blazed by the mountain men (Map 12.2). The first wagon trains headed west in 1841, and by 1843 about 1,000 emigrants a year set out from Independence, Missouri. By 1869, when the first transcontinental railroad was completed, approximately 350,000 migrants had traveled west in wagon trains.

Emigrants encountered the Plains Indians, a quarter of a million Native Americans scattered over the area between the Mississippi River and the Rocky Mountains. Some were farmers who lived peaceful, sedentary lives, but a

***Kee-O-Kuk, the Watchful Fox, Chief of the Tribe*, by George Catlin, 1835** In the 1830s, artist George Catlin, convinced that Indian cultures would soon disappear, traveled the West painting Native Americans in their own environments. Keokuk, chief of the Sauk and Fox, struggled with the warrior Black Hawk (see "Indian Policy and the Trail of Tears" in chapter 11) about how to deal with whites. Black Hawk fought American expansion; Keokuk believed that war was fruitless. Smithsonian American Art Museum, Washington, DC/Art Resource, NY.

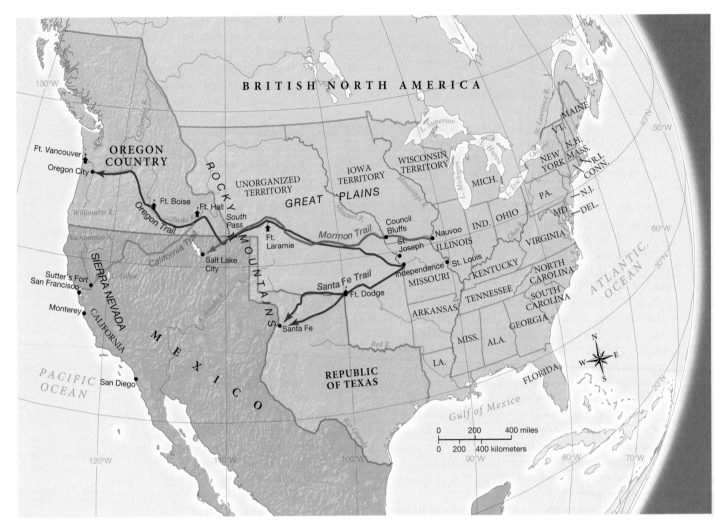

MAP 12.2

Major Trails West

In the 1830s, wagon trains began snaking their way to the Southwest and the Pacific coast. Deep ruts, some of which can still be seen today, soon marked the most popular routes.

majority—the Sioux, Cheyenne, Shoshoni, and Arapaho of the central plains and the Kiowa, Wichita, and Comanche of the southern plains— were horse-mounted, nomadic, nonagricultural peoples whose warriors symbolized the "savage Indian" in the minds of whites.

Horses, which had been brought to North America by Spaniards in the sixteenth century, permitted the Plains tribes to become highly mobile hunters of buffalo. They came to depend on buffalo for nearly everything—food, clothing, shelter, and fuel. Competition for buffalo led to war between the tribes. Young men were introduced to warfare early, learning to ride ponies at breakneck speed while firing off arrows and, later, rifles with astounding accuracy. "A Comanche on his feet is out of his element," observed western artist George Catlin, "but the moment he lays his hands upon his

horse, his *face* even becomes handsome, and he gracefully flies away like a different being."

The Plains Indians struck fear in the hearts of whites on the wagon trains. But Native Americans had far more to fear from whites. Indians killed fewer than four hundred emigrants on the trail between 1840 and 1860, while whites brought alcohol and deadly epidemics. Moreover, white hunters slaughtered buffalo for the international hide market and sometimes just for sport.

The government constructed a chain of forts along the Oregon Trail (see Map 12.2) and adopted a new Indian policy: "concentration." In 1851, government negotiators at the Fort Laramie conference persuaded the Plains Indians to sign agreements that cleared a wide corridor for wagon trains by restricting Native Americans to specific areas that whites promised they would never violate. This policy of concentration became the seedbed for the subsequent policy of reservations. But whites would not keep out of Indian territory, and Indians would not easily give up their traditional ways of life. Struggle for control of the West meant warfare for decades to come.

Still, Indians threatened emigrants less than life on the trail did. Emigrants could count on at least six months of grueling travel. With nearly two thousand miles to go and traveling no more than fifteen miles a day, the pioneers endured parching heat, drought, treacherous rivers, disease, physical and emotional exhaustion, and, if the snows closed the mountain passes before they got through, freezing and starvation. It was

Plains Indians and Trails West in the 1840s and 1850s

said that a person could walk from Missouri to the Pacific stepping only on the graves of those who had died heading west.

Men usually found Oregon "one of the greatest countries in the world." From "the Cascade mountains to the Pacific, the whole country can be cultivated," exclaimed one eager settler. When women reached Oregon, they found that neighbors were scarce and things were in a "primitive state." One young wife arrived with only her husband, one stew pot, and three knives. Work seemed unending. "I am a very old woman," declared twenty-nine-year-old Sarah Everett. "My face is thin sunken and wrinkled, my hands bony withered and hard." Another settler observed, "A woman that

VISUAL ACTIVITY

Pioneer Family on the Trail West

In 1860, W. G. Chamberlain photographed these unidentified travelers momentarily at rest by the upper Arkansas River in Colorado. We do not know their fates, but we can only hope that they fared better than many of the families that braved the trip. Denver Public Library, Western History Collection/The Bridgeman Art Library.

READING THE IMAGE: Based on this photograph, what were some of the difficulties faced by pioneers traveling west?

CONNECTIONS: How did wagon trains change the western United States?

can not endure almost as much as a horse has no business here." Yet despite the ordeal of the trail and the difficulties of starting from scratch, emigrants kept coming.

The Mormon Exodus

Not every wagon train heading west was bound for the Pacific Slope. One remarkable group of religious emigrants halted near the Great Salt Lake in what was then Mexican territory. After years of persecution in the East, the **Mormons** fled west to find religious freedom and communal security.

In the 1820s, an upstate New York farm boy named Joseph Smith Jr. said that he was visited by an angel who led him to golden tablets buried near his home. With the aid of magic stones, he translated the mysterious language on the tablets to produce *The Book of Mormon*, which he published in 1830. It told the story of an ancient Hebrew civilization in the New World and predicted the appearance of an American prophet who would reestablish Jesus Christ's undefiled kingdom in America. Converts, attracted to the promise of a pure faith in the midst of antebellum America's social turmoil and rampant materialism, flocked to the new Church of Jesus Christ of Latter-Day Saints (the Mormons).

Neighbors branded Mormons heretics and drove Smith and his followers from New York to Ohio, then to Missouri, and finally in 1839 to Nauvoo, Illinois, where they built a prosperous community. But after Smith sanctioned "plural marriage" (polygamy), non-Mormons arrested Smith and his brother. On June 27, 1844, a mob stormed the jail and shot both men dead.

The embattled church turned to an extraordinary new leader, Brigham Young, who oversaw a great exodus. In 1846, traveling in 3,700 wagons, 12,000 Mormons made their way to Iowa and then, the following year, to their new home beside the Great Salt Lake. Young described the region as a barren waste, "the paradise of the lizard, the cricket and the rattlesnake." Within ten years, however, the Mormons developed an irrigation system that made the desert bloom. Under Young's stern leadership, the Mormons built a thriving community using cooperative labor, not the individualistic and competitive enterprise common among most emigrants.

In 1850, the Mormon kingdom was annexed to the United States as Utah Territory. Shortly afterward, Brigham Young announced that many Mormons practiced polygamy. Although only one Mormon man in five had more than one wife (Young had twenty-three), Young's statement forced the U.S. government to establish its authority in Utah. In 1857, 2,500 U.S. troops invaded Salt Lake City in what was known as the Mormon War. The bloodless occupation illustrated that most Americans viewed the Mormons as a threat to American morality and institutions.

VISUAL ACTIVITY

Mormon Family
The rest of America found the Mormon practice of polygamy deeply offensive. In 1890, the Mormons officially abandoned plural marriages, but in this photograph from Salt Lake City in the 1850s, a husband, his three wives, and their five children sit for a family portrait. The Church of Jesus Christ of Latter-Day Saints.
READING THE IMAGE: How would you describe the family's attitude about their unusual family constellation—at ease and proud or uneasy and embarrassed?
CONNECTIONS: Why would most Americans find the Mormon practice of plural marriages so disturbing?

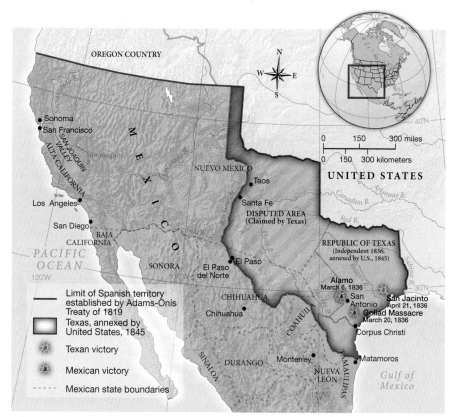

MAP 12.3

Texas and Mexico in the 1830s
As Americans spilled into lightly populated and loosely governed northern Mexico, Texas and then other Mexican provinces became contested territory.

The Mexican Borderlands

In the Mexican Southwest, westward-moving Anglo-American pioneers confronted northern-moving Spanish-speaking frontiersmen. On this frontier as elsewhere, national cultures, interests, and aspirations collided. Mexico won its independence from Spain in 1821 (Map 12.3), but the young nation was plagued by civil wars, economic crises, quarrels with the Roman Catholic Church, and devastating raids by the Comanche, Apache, and Kiowa. Mexico found it increasingly difficult to defend its sparsely populated northern provinces, especially when faced with a neighbor convinced of its superiority and bent on territorial acquisition.

The American assault began quietly. In the 1820s, Anglo-American traders drifted into Santa Fe, a remote outpost in the northern province of New Mexico. The traders made the long trek southwest along the Santa Fe Trail (see Map 12.2) with wagons crammed with inexpensive American manufactured goods and returned home with Mexican silver, furs, and mules.

The Mexican province of Texas attracted a flood of Americans who had settlement, not long-distance trade, on their minds (see Map 12.3). Wanting to populate and develop its northern territory, the Mexican government granted the American Stephen F. Austin a huge tract of land along the Brazos River. In the 1820s, Austin offered land at only ten cents an acre, and thousands of Americans poured across the border. Most were Southerners who brought cotton and slaves with them.

By the 1830s, the settlers had established a thriving plantation economy in Texas. Americans numbered 35,000, while the *Tejano* (Spanish-speaking) population was less than 8,000. Few Anglo-American settlers were Roman Catholic, spoke Spanish, or cared about assimilating into Mexican culture. Afraid of losing Texas to the new arrivals, the Mexican government in 1830 banned further immigration to Texas from the United States and outlawed the introduction of additional slaves. The Anglo-Americans made it clear that they wanted to be rid of the "despotism of the sword and the priesthood" and to govern themselves.

When the Texan settlers rebelled, General Antonio López de Santa Anna ordered the Mexican army northward. In February 1836, the army arrived at the outskirts of San Antonio. Commanded by Colonel William B. Travis from Alabama, the rebels included the Tennessee frontiersman Davy Crockett and the Louisiana adventurer James Bowie, as well as a handful of Tejanos. They took refuge in a former Franciscan mission

***Fandango,* by Theodore Gentilz, 1844**
A small and resourceful Tejano community managed to develop a ranching economy in the harsh frontier conditions of Texas. The largest Hispanic population concentrated in San Antonio, where settlers reproduced as best they could the cultural traditions they carried with them. Here, well-dressed men and women perform a Spanish dance called the fandango. Daughters of the Republic of Texas Library at the Alamo.

known as the Alamo. Santa Anna sent wave after wave of his 2,000-man army crashing against the walls until the attackers finally broke through and killed all 187 rebels. A few weeks later, outside the small town of Goliad, Mexican forces captured and executed almost 400 Texans as "pirates and outlaws." In April 1836, at San Jacinto, General Sam Houston's army adopted the massacre of Goliad as a battle cry and crushed Santa Anna's troops in a surprise attack. The Texans had succeeded in establishing the **Lone Star Republic**, and the following year the United States recognized the independence of Texas from Mexico.

Earlier, in 1824, in an effort to increase Mexican migration to the province of California, the

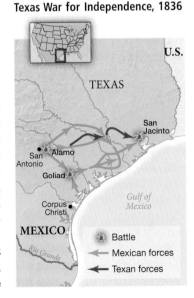

Texas War for Independence, 1836

Mexican government granted *ranchos*—huge estates devoted to cattle raising—to new settlers. *Rancheros* ruled over near-feudal empires worked by Indians whose condition sometimes approached that of slaves. In 1834, *rancheros* persuaded the Mexican government to confiscate the Franciscan missions and make their vast lands available to new settlement, a development that accelerated the decline of the California Indians. Devastated by disease, the Indians, who had numbered approximately 300,000 when the Spanish arrived in 1769, had declined to half that number by 1846.

Despite the efforts of the Mexican government, California in 1840 had a population of only 7,000 Mexican settlers.

Non-Mexican settlers numbered only 380, but among them were Americans who championed manifest destiny. They sought to convince American emigrants who were traveling the Oregon Trail to head southwest on the California Trail (see Map 12.2). As a New York newspaper observed in 1845, "Let the tide of emigration flow toward California and the American population will soon be sufficiently numerous to play the Texas game." Few Americans in California wanted a war, but many dreamed of living again under the U.S. flag.

In 1846, American settlers in the Sacramento Valley took matters into their own hands. Prodded by John C. Frémont, a former army captain and explorer who had arrived with a party of sixty buckskin-clad frontiersmen spoiling for a fight, the Californians raised an independence movement known as the Bear Flag Revolt. By then, James K. Polk, a champion of aggressive expansion, sat in the White House.

> **REVIEW** Why did westward migration expand dramatically in the mid-nineteenth century?

Expansion and the Mexican-American War

Although emigrants acted as the advance guard of American empire, there was nothing automatic about the U.S. annexation of territory in the West. Acquiring territory required political action. In the 1840s, the politics of expansion became entangled with sectionalism and the slavery question. Texas, Oregon, and the Mexican borderlands also thrust the United States into dangerous diplomatic crises with Great Britain and Mexico.

Aggravation between Mexico and the United States escalated to open antagonism in 1845 when the United States annexed Texas. Absorbing territory still claimed by Mexico set the stage for war. But it was President James K. Polk's insistence on having Mexico's other northern provinces that made war certain. The war was not as easy as Polk anticipated, but it ended in American victory and the acquisition of a new American West. The discovery of gold in one of the nation's new territories, California, prompted a massive wave of emigration that nearly destroyed Native American and *Californio* societies.

The Politics of Expansion

Texans had sought admission to the Union almost since winning their independence from Mexico in 1836. Constant border warfare between Mexico and the Republic of Texas in the decade following the revolution underscored the precarious nature of independence. But any suggestion of adding another slave state to the Union outraged most Northerners, who applauded westward expansion but imagined the expansion of liberty, not slavery.

John Tyler, who became president in April 1841 when William Henry Harrison died one month after taking office, understood that Texas was a dangerous issue. Adding to the danger, Great Britain began sniffing around Texas, apparently contemplating adding the young republic to its growing empire. In 1844, Tyler, an ardent expansionist, decided to risk annexing the Lone Star Republic. However, howls of protest erupted across the North. Future Massachusetts senator Charles Sumner deplored the "insidious" plan to annex Texas and carve from it "great slaveholding states." The Senate soundly rejected the annexation treaty.

During the election of 1844, the Whig nominee for president, Henry Clay, in an effort to woo northern voters, came out against annexation of Texas. "Annexation and war with Mexico are identical," he declared. When news of Clay's statement reached Andrew Jackson at his plantation in Tennessee, he chuckled, "Clay [is] a dead political Duck." In Jackson's shrewd judgment, no man who opposed annexation could be elected president.

The Democratic nominee, Tennessean James K. Polk, vigorously backed annexation. To make annexation palatable to Northerners, the Democrats cleverly yoked the annexation of Texas to the annexation of Oregon, thus tapping the desire for expansion in the free states of the North as well as in the slave states of the South. The Democratic platform called for the "reannexation of Texas" and the "reoccupation of Oregon." The statement that the United States was merely reasserting existing rights was poor history but good politics.

When Clay finally recognized the popularity of expansion, he waffled, hinting that he might accept the annexation of Texas after all. His retreat succeeded only in alienating antislavery opinion in the North. James G. Birney, the candidate of the fledgling Liberty Party, denounced Clay as "rotten as a stagnant fish pond" and picked up the votes of thousands of disillusioned

Polk and Dallas Banner, 1844
In 1844, Democratic presidential nominee James K. Polk and vice presidential nominee George M. Dallas campaigned under this banner. The extra star spilling over into the red and white stripes symbolizes Polk's vigorous support for annexing the huge slave republic of Texas, which had declared its independence from Mexico eight years earlier.
© David J. & Janice L. Frent Collection/CORBIS

Clay supporters. In the November election, Polk won a narrow victory.

In his inaugural address on March 4, 1845, Polk underscored his faith in America's manifest destiny. "This heaven-favored land," he proclaimed, enjoyed the "most admirable and wisest system of well-regulated self-government . . . ever devised by human minds." He asked, "Who shall assign limits to the achievements of free minds and free hands under the protection of this glorious Union?"

The nation did not have to wait for Polk's inauguration to see results from his victory. One month after the election, President Tyler announced that the triumph of the Democratic Party provided a mandate for the annexation of Texas "promptly and immediately." In February 1845, after a fierce debate between antislavery and proslavery forces, Congress approved a joint resolution offering the Republic of Texas admission to the United States. Texas entered as the fifteenth slave state.

While Tyler delivered Texas, Polk had promised Oregon, too. Westerners particularly demanded that the new president make good on the Democratic pledge "Fifty-four forty or Fight"—that is, all of Oregon, right up to Alaska (54° 40′ was the southern latitude of Russian Alaska). But Polk was close to war with Mexico

and could not afford a war with Britain over U.S. claims in Canada. He renewed an old offer to divide Oregon along the forty-ninth parallel. Westerners cried betrayal, but when Britain accepted the compromise, the nation gained an enormous territory peacefully. When the Senate approved the treaty in June 1846, the United States and Mexico were already at war.

The Mexican-American War, 1846–1848

From the day he entered the White House, Polk craved Mexico's remaining northern provinces: California and New Mexico, land that today makes up California, Nevada, Utah, most of New Mexico and Arizona, and parts of Wyoming and Colorado. Since the 1830s, Indians had attacked Mexican ranches and towns, killing thousands, and the Polk administration invoked Mexico's inability to control its northern provinces to denigrate its claims to them. Polk hoped to buy the territory, but when the Mexicans refused to sell, he concluded that military force would be needed to realize the United States' manifest destiny.

Polk ordered General Zachary Taylor to march his 4,000-man army 150 miles south from its position on the Nueces River, the southern

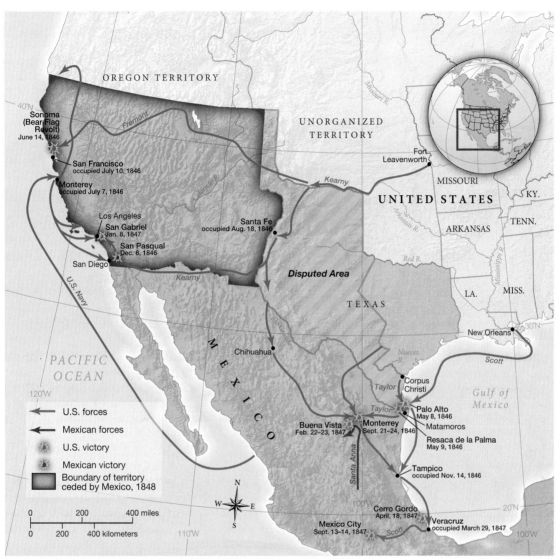

Map 12.4 The Mexican-American War, 1846–1848
American and Mexican soldiers skirmished across much of northern Mexico, but the major battles took place between the Rio Grande and Mexico City.

boundary of Texas according to the Mexicans, to the banks of the Rio Grande, the boundary claimed by Texans (Map 12.4). Lieutenant George G. Meade, who would later command troops at Gettysburg, admitted, "I hope for a war and a speedy battle." Viewing the American advance as aggression, Mexican cavalry on April 25, 1846, attacked a party of American soldiers, killing or wounding 16 and capturing the rest.

On May 11, the president told Congress, "Mexico has passed the boundary of the United States, has invaded our territory, and shed American blood upon American soil." Thus "war exists, and, notwithstanding all our efforts to avoid it, exists by the act of Mexico herself." Congress passed a declaration of war and began raising an army. The U.S. Army was pitifully

small, only 8,600 soldiers. Faced with the nation's first foreign war, against a Mexican army that numbered more than 30,000, Polk called for volunteers. More than 30,000 Tennesseans competed for the state's 3,000 allotted positions. Eventually, more than 112,000 white Americans (40 percent were immigrants; blacks were banned) joined the army to fight in Mexico.

Despite the flood of volunteers, the war divided the nation. Northern Whigs in particular condemned the war. The Massachusetts legislature claimed that the war was being fought for the "triple object of extending slavery, of strengthening the slave power, and of obtaining control of the free states." On January 12, 1848, a gangly freshman Whig representative from Illinois rose in the House of

***Batalla del Sacramento,* by Julio Michaud y Thomas**
Most images of the Mexican-American War were created by artists from the United States, but Mexicans also recorded the war. In this hand-colored lithograph, Mexican artist Julio Michaud y Thomas depicts the February 1847 battle in which 1,100 American troops engaged 3,000 Mexicans on the banks of the Sacramento River near Chihuahua.
Yale Collection of Western Americana, Beinecke Rare Book and Manuscript Library.

Representatives. He likened the president's views to the "half-insane mumbling of a fever dream" and proclaimed Polk a "bewildered, confounded, and miserably perplexed man." Before Abraham Lincoln sat down, he had questioned Polk's intelligence, honesty, and sanity. The president ignored the upstart representative, but antislavery, antiwar Whigs kept up the attack throughout the conflict.

President Polk expected a short war in which U.S. armies would occupy Mexico's northern provinces and defeat the Mexican army in a decisive battle or two, after which Mexico would sue for peace and the United States would keep the territory its armies occupied.

At first, Polk's strategy seemed to work. In May 1846, Zachary Taylor's troops drove south from the Rio Grande and routed the Mexican army, first at Palo Alto, then at Resaca de la Palma (see Map 12.4). "Old Rough and Ready," as Taylor was affectionately known among his troops, became an instant war hero. Polk rewarded Taylor for his victories by making him commander of the Mexican campaign.

A second prong of the campaign centered on Colonel Stephen Watts Kearny, who led a 1,700-man army from Missouri into New Mexico. Without firing a shot, U.S. forces took Santa Fe in August 1846. Kearny then marched to San Diego, where he encountered a major Mexican rebellion against American rule. In January 1847, after several clashes and severe losses, U.S. forces occupied Los Angeles. California and New Mexico were in American hands.

By then, Taylor had driven deep into the interior of Mexico. In September 1846, after house-to-house fighting, he had taken the city of Monterrey. Taylor then pushed his 5,000 troops southwest, where the Mexican hero of the Alamo, General Antonio López de Santa Anna, was concentrating an army of 21,000. On February 23, 1847, Santa Anna's troops attacked Taylor at Buena Vista. The Americans won the day but suffered heavy casualties. The Mexicans suffered even greater losses (some 3,400 dead, wounded, and missing, compared with 650 Americans). During the night, Santa Anna withdrew his battered army.

The series of uninterrupted victories in northern Mexico fed the American troops' sense of invincibility. "No American force has ever thought of being defeated by any amount of Mexican troops," one soldier declared. The Americans worried about other hazards, however. "I can assure you that fighting is the least dangerous & arduous part of a soldier's life," one young man declared. Letters home told of torturous marches across arid wastes alive with tarantulas, scorpions, and rattlesnakes. Others recounted dysentery, malaria, smallpox, cholera, and yellow fever. Of the 13,000 American soldiers who died (some 50,000 Mexicans perished), fewer than 2,000 fell to Mexican bullets and shells. Disease killed most of the others. Medicine was so primitive that, as one Tennessee man observed, "nearly all who take sick die."

Victory in Mexico

Despite heavy losses on the battlefield, Mexico refused to trade land for peace. One American soldier captured the Mexican mood: "They cannot submit to be deprived of California after the loss of Texas, and nothing but the conquest of their Capital will force them to such a humiliation." President Polk had arrived at the same conclusion. While Taylor occupied the north, Polk ordered General Winfield Scott to land an army on the Gulf coast of Mexico and march 250 miles inland to Mexico City. The plan entailed enormous risk because Scott would have to cut himself off from supplies and lead his men deep into enemy country against a much larger army.

An amphibious landing on March 9, 1847, near Veracruz put some 10,000 American troops ashore. After furious shelling, Veracruz surrendered. In April 1847, Scott's forces moved westward, following the path blazed more than three centuries earlier by Hernán Cortés to "the halls of Montezuma" (see "The Conquest of Mexico" in chapter 2).

After the defeat at Buena Vista, Santa Anna had returned to Mexico City, where he rallied

MAP ACTIVITY

Map 12.5   Territorial Expansion by 1860
Less than a century after its founding, the United States spread from the Atlantic seaboard to the Pacific coast. War, purchase, and diplomacy had gained a continent.

READING THE MAP: List the countries from which the United States acquired land. Which nation lost the most land because of U.S. expansion?

CONNECTIONS: Who coined the phrase *manifest destiny*? When? What does it mean? What areas targeted for expansion were the subjects of debate during the presidential campaign of 1844?

The Gold Rush

The discovery of gold in California stimulated imaginations around the world. But getting to gold country was not easy. Americans in the East could sail 18,000 miles around the tip of South America; or sail to the Atlantic side of the Isthmus of Panama, slog through the jungle to the Pacific, and wait for a ship to San Francisco; or walk overland across the continent. Nothing got easier when they arrived in California. The West presented emigrants with unprecedented challenges and only occasionally fulfillment.

DOCUMENT 1
James Marshall, Account of His Discovery of Gold, 1891

While building a sawmill on the American River for Swiss rancher John Sutter, James Marshall found gold on January 24, 1848. Marshall gave several accounts of his discovery, but this is probably his first. Marshall never benefited from his discovery and died bitter and penniless.

One morning in January—it was a clear, cold morning; I shall never forget that morning—as I was taking my usual walk along the race after shutting off the water, my eye was caught with the glimpse of something shining in the bottom of the ditch. There was about a foot of water running then. I reached my hand down and picked it up; it made my heart thump, for I was certain it was gold. The piece was about half the size and of the shape of a pea. Then I saw another piece. . . .

When I returned to our cabin for breakfast I showed the two pieces to my men. They were all a good deal excited, and had they not thought that the gold only existed in small quantities they would have abandoned everything and left me to finish my job alone. However, to satisfy them, I told them that as soon as we had the mill finished we would devote a week or two to gold hunting and see what we could make out of it.

. . . [W]e thought it our best policy to keep it as quiet as possible till we should have finished our mill. But there was a great number of disbanded Mormon soldiers in and about the fort, and when they came to hear of it, why it just spread like a wildfire, and soon the whole country was in a bustle. . . .

Source: James W. Marshall, "Marshall's Own Account of the Gold Discovery," *Century Illustrated Magazine*, no. 4 (Feb. 1891): 537–39.

DOCUMENT 2
Sarah Royce, Memoir of the Journey to California in 1849, 1932

In 1849, Sarah Royce, with her husband and two-year-old daughter, left New York for California. Her memoir of their journey westward by covered wagon recounts the family's encounters with Indians, cholera, thirst, and hunger. Thirty years later she wrote her memories, and in 1932 her son published them. Here she describes traveling through a desert southwest of Salt Lake City.

There was no moon yet, but by starlight we had for some time seen, only too plainly, the dead bodies of cattle lying here and there on both sides of the road. As we advanced they increased in numbers, and presently we saw two or three wagons. At first we thought we had

his ragged troops and marched them east to set a trap for Scott in the mountain pass at Cerro Gordo. Knifing through Mexican lines, the Americans almost captured Santa Anna, who fled the field on foot. So complete was the victory that Scott gloated to Taylor, "Mexico no longer has an army." But Santa Anna, ever resilient, again rallied the Mexican army. Some 30,000 troops took up defensive positions on the outskirts of Mexico City and began melting down church bells to cast new cannons.

In August 1847, Scott began his assault on the Mexican capital. The fighting proved the most brutal of the war. Santa Anna backed his army into the city, fighting each step of the way. At the battle of Churubusco, the Mexicans took 4,000 casualties in a single day and the Americans more than 1,000. At the castle of overtaken a company but, coming close, no sign of life appeared. . . . Everything indicated a complete break down, and a hasty flight. Some animals were lying nearly in front of a wagon, apparently just as they had dropped down, while loose yokes and chains indicated that part of the teams had been driven on, laden probably with some necessaries of life; for the contents of the wagons were scattered in confusion, the most essential articles alone evidently having been thought worth carrying. . . . It was not a very encouraging scene but our four oxen still kept their feet; we would drive on a little farther, out of this scene of ruin, bait them, rest ourselves, and go on. We did so, but soon found that what we supposed an exceptional misfortune must have been the common fate of many companies; for at still shortening intervals, scenes of ruin similar to that just described kept recurring till we seemed to be but the last, little, feeble struggling band at the rear of a routed Army.

Source: Sarah Royce, *A Frontier Lady* (New Haven, CT: Yale University Press, 1932), 51–53.

DOCUMENT 3
Daniel B. Woods, Life of a California Miner, 1849

Daniel B. Woods, a Philadelphia schoolteacher, reached the diggings in California in 1849. He soon discovered that mining was very hard work, and he suspected that he would never get rich. He poured his frustration and disillusionment into his diary and after sixteen months quit gold country.

July 9th [1849]. To-day we have made $20 each. One of the conclusions at which we are rapidly arriving is that the "chances of our making a fortune in the old mines are about the same as those in favor of our drawing a prize in a lottery." No kind of work is so uncertain.

July 10th. We made three dollars each to-day. This life of severe hardship and exposure has affected my health. Our diet consists of hard bread, flour, which we eat half-cooked, and salt pork, with occasionally a salmon which we purchase of the Indians. Vegetables are not to be procured. Our feet are wet all day, while a hot sun shines down upon our heads, and the very air parches the skin like the hot air of an oven. Our drinking water comes down to us thoroughly impregnated with the mineral substances washed through a thousand cradles above us.

After our days of labor, exhausted and faint, we *retire*— if this word may be applied to the simple act of lying down in our clothes—robbing our feet of their boots to make a pillow of them, and wrapping blankets about us, on a bed of pine boughs, or on the ground, beneath the clear, bright stars of night. . . .

Aug. 23d. After all our preparations and hopes, our toil early and late, toil of the most laborious kind, digging down in the channel of the river till the water was up to our knees, giving ourselves barely time to eat, we have made but $4 each. We sat down on the rocks, and looked at the small ridge of gold in the pan, and at each other. One fell to swearing, another to laughing.

Source: Daniel B. Woods, *Sixteen Months at the Gold Diggings* (New York: Harper & Brothers, 1851), 57–63.

Questions for Analysis and Debate

1. What was James Marshall's primary concern after he discovered gold?

2. What was Sarah Royce's initial understanding of her nighttime encounter?

3. What were the chief sources of Daniel Woods's frustration and disillusionment?

Connect to the Big Idea

C How did the realities of Gold Rush California fit with the promises of manifest destiny?

Chapultepec, American troops scaled the walls and fought the Mexican defenders hand to hand. After Chapultepec, Mexico City officials persuaded Santa Anna to evacuate the city to save it from destruction, and on September 14, 1847, Scott rode in triumphantly.

On February 2, 1848, American and Mexican officials signed the **Treaty of Guadalupe Hidalgo** in Mexico City. Mexico agreed to give up all claims to Texas north of the Rio Grande and to cede the provinces of New Mexico and California—more than 500,000 square miles—to the United States (see Map 12.4). The United States agreed to pay Mexico $15 million and to assume $3.25 million in claims that American citizens had against Mexico. Some Americans clamored for all of Mexico, but the treaty gave the president

Miners, Auburn Ravine, California, 1852
The three white miners on the left of the photograph were separated from the four Chinese miners on the right by more than a sluice box. Whites welcomed Chinese into gold country as hired laborers, not as independent miners like themselves. Getty Images.

all he wanted. In March 1848, the Senate ratified the treaty. Polk had his Rio Grande border, his Pacific ports, and all the land that lay between.

The American triumph had enormous consequences. Less than three-quarters of a century after its founding, the United States had achieved its self-proclaimed manifest destiny to stretch from the Atlantic to the Pacific (Map 12.5). It would enter the industrial age with vast new natural resources and a two-ocean economy, while Mexico faced a sharply diminished economic future.

Golden California

Another consequence of the Mexican defeat was that California gold poured into American, not Mexican, pockets. In January 1848, James Marshall discovered gold in the American River in the foothills of the Sierra Nevada. His discovery set off the **California gold rush**, one of the wildest mining stampedes in the world's history. Between 1849 and 1852, more than

250,000 "forty-niners," as the would-be miners were known, descended on the Golden State. In less than two years, Marshall's discovery transformed California from foreign territory to statehood.

Gold fever quickly spread around the world. A stream of men of various races and nationalities poured into California. Only a few struck it rich, and life in the goldfields was nasty, brutish, and often short. The prospectors faced cholera and scurvy, exorbitant prices for food (eggs cost a dollar apiece), deadly encounters with claim jumpers, and endless backbreaking labor. (See "Documenting the American Promise," page 334.)

By 1853, San Francisco had grown into a raw, booming city of 50,000 that depended as much on gold as did the mining camps inland. Enterprising individuals learned that there was money to be made tending to the needs of miners. Hotels, saloons, restaurants, laundries, brothels, and stores of all kinds exchanged goods and services for miners' gold dust and nuggets. Violent crime was an everyday occurrence. In 1851, the Committee of Vigilance determined to bring order to the city. Members pledged that "no thief, burglar, incendiary or assassin shall escape punishment, either by the quibbles of the law, the insecurity of prisons, the carelessness or corruption of the police, or a laxity of those who pretended to administer justice." Lynchings proved the committee meant business.

Establishing civic order was made more difficult by California's diversity and Anglo bigotry. The Chinese attracted special scrutiny. By 1851, 25,000 Chinese lived in California, and their religion, language, dress, queues (long pigtails), eating habits, and use of opium convinced many Anglos that they were not fit citizens of the Golden State. In 1850, the California legislature passed the Foreign Miners' Tax Law, which levied high taxes on non-Americans to drive them from the goldfields, except as hired laborers working on claims owned by Americans. The Chinese were segregated residentially and occupationally, and along with blacks and Indians, denied public education and the right to testify in court.

Opponents demanded a halt to Chinese immigration, but Chinese leaders in San Francisco fought back. Admitting deep cultural differences, they insisted that "in the important matters we are good men. We honor our parents; we take care of our children; we are industrious and peaceable; we trade much; we are trusted for small and large sums; we pay our debts; and are honest, and of course must tell the truth." Their protestations offered little protection, however, and racial violence grew.

Anglo-American prospectors asserted their dominance over other groups, especially Native Americans and the Californios, Spanish and Mexican settlers who had lived in California for decades. Despite the U.S. government's pledge to protect Mexican and Spanish land titles, Americans took the land of the rancheros and through discriminatory legislation pushed Hispanic professionals, merchants, and artisans into the ranks of unskilled labor. Mariano Vallejo, a leading Californio, said of the forty-niners, "The good ones were few and the wicked many."

For Indians, the gold rush was catastrophic. Numbering about 150,000 in 1848, the Indian population of California fell to 25,000 by 1854. Starvation, disease, and a declining birthrate took a heavy toll. Indians also fell victim to wholesale murder. The nineteenth-century historian Hubert Howe Bancroft described white behavior toward Indians during the gold rush as "one of the last human hunts of civilization, and the basest and most brutal of them all."

The forty-niners created dazzling wealth: In 1852, 81 million ounces of gold, nearly half of the world's production, came from California. However, most miners eventually took up farming, opened small businesses, or worked for wages for the corporations that took over the mining industry. Other Americans traded furs, hides, and lumber and engaged in whaling and the China trade in tea, silk, and porcelain. Still, as one Californian observed, the state was separated "by thousands of miles of plains, deserts, and almost impossible mountains" from the rest of the Union. Some dreamers imagined a railroad that would someday connect the Golden State with the thriving agriculture and industry of the East. Others imagined a country transformed not by transportation but by progressive individual and institutional reform.

REVIEW Why did the United States go to war with Mexico?

► Reforming Self and Society

While manifest destiny, the Mexican-American War, and the California gold rush transformed the nation's boundaries, many Americans sought personal and social reform. The emphasis on self-discipline and individual effort at the core of the free-labor ideal led Americans to believe that insufficient self-control caused the major social problems of the era. Evangelical Protestants struggled to control individuals' propensity to sin. Temperance advocates exhorted drinkers to control their taste for alcohol. Only about one-third of Americans belonged to a church in 1850, but the influence of evangelical religion reached far beyond church members.

The evangelical temperament—a conviction of righteousness coupled with energy, self-discipline, and faith that the world could be improved—animated most reformers. However, a few activists pointed out that certain fundamental injustices lay beyond the reach of individual self-control. Transcendentalists and utopians believed that perfection required rejecting the competitive, individualistic values of mainstream society. Woman's rights activists and abolitionists sought to reverse the subordination of women and to eliminate the enslavement of blacks by changing laws, social institutions, attitudes, and customs. These reformers confronted the daunting challenge of repudiating widespread beliefs in male supremacy and white supremacy and somehow challenging the entrenched institutions that reinforced those views: the family and slavery.

The Pursuit of Perfection: Transcendentalists and Utopians

A group of New England writers who came to be known as transcendentalists believed that individuals should conform neither to the dictates of the materialistic world nor to the dogma of formal religion. Instead, people should look within themselves for truth and guidance. The leading transcendentalist, Ralph Waldo Emerson—an essayist, poet, and lecturer—proclaimed that the power of the solitary individual was nearly limitless. The novelist Herman Melville ridiculed the inward gaze and confident egoism of transcendentalism as "oracular gibberish" and "self-conceit" that represented less an alternative to mainstream values than an extreme form of the rampant individualism of the age.

Unlike transcendentalists who sought to turn inward, a few reformers tried to change the world by organizing utopian communities as alternatives to prevailing social arrangements. Although these communities never attracted more than a few thousand people, the activities of their members demonstrated dissatisfaction with the larger society and efforts to realize their visions of perfection.

Some communities set out to become models of perfection whose success would point the way toward a better life for everyone. During the 1840s, more than two dozen communities organized themselves around the ideas of Charles Fourier. Members of Fourierist phalanxes, as these communities were called, believed that individualism and competition were evils that denied the basic truth that "men . . . are brothers and not competitors." Phalanxes aspired to replace competition with harmonious cooperation based on communal ownership of property. But Fourierist communities failed to realize their lofty goals, and few survived more than two or three years.

The **Oneida community** went beyond the Fourierist notion of communalism. John Humphrey Noyes, the charismatic leader of Oneida, believed that American society's commitment to private property made people greedy and selfish. Noyes claimed that the root of private property lay in marriage, in men's conviction that their wives were their exclusive property. Drawing from a substantial inheritance, Noyes organized the Oneida community in New York in 1848 to abolish marital property rights by permitting sexual intercourse between any consenting man and woman in the community. Noyes also required all members to relinquish their economic property to the community. Most of their neighbors considered Oneidans adulterers and blasphemers. Yet the practices that set Oneida apart from its mainstream neighbors strengthened the community, and it survived long after the Civil War.

Woman's Rights Activists

Women participated in the many reform activities that grew out of evangelical churches. Women church members outnumbered men two to one and worked to put their religious ideas into practice by joining peace, temperance, antislavery, and other societies. Involvement in reform organizations gave a few women activists practical experience in such political arts as speaking in public, running a meeting, drafting resolutions, and circulating petitions. The abolitionist Lydia Maria Child pointed out in 1841 that "those who urged women to become missionaries and form tract societies . . . have changed the household utensil to a living energetic being and they have no spell to turn it into a broom again."

In 1848, about three hundred reformers led by Elizabeth Cady Stanton and Lucretia Mott gathered at Seneca Falls, New York, for the first national woman's rights convention in the United States. As Stanton recalled, "The general discontent I felt with women's portion as wife, mother, housekeeper, physician, and spiritual guide, [and] the wearied anxious look of the majority of women impressed me with a strong feeling that some active measure should be taken to right the wrongs of society in general, and of women in particular." The **Seneca Falls Declaration of Sentiments** set an ambitious agenda to demand civil liberties for women and to right the wrongs of society. The declaration proclaimed that "the history of mankind is a history of repeated injuries and usurpations on

BLOOMERISM—AN AMERICAN CUSTOM.

Bloomers and Woman's Emancipation
This 1851 British cartoon lampoons bloomers, the trouser-like garment worn beneath shortened skirts by two cigar-smoking American women. Bloomers were invented in the United States as an alternative to the uncomfortable, confining, and awkward dresses worn by the "respectable" women on the right. In the 1850s, Elizabeth Cady Stanton and other woman's rights activists wore bloomers and urged all American women to do likewise. The New York Public Library/Art Resource, NY.

the part of man toward woman, having in direct object the establishment of an absolute tyranny over her." In the style of the Declaration of Independence (see appendix I, page A-1), the Seneca Falls declaration demanded that women "have immediate admission to all the rights and privileges which belong to them as citizens of the United States," particularly the "inalienable right to the elective franchise."

Nearly two dozen other woman's rights conventions assembled before 1860, repeatedly calling for suffrage and an end to discrimination against women. But women had difficulty receiving a respectful hearing, much less achieving legislative action. Even so, the Seneca Falls declaration served as a pathbreaking manifesto of dissent against male supremacy and of support for woman suffrage, and it inspired many women to challenge the barriers that limited their opportunities.

Stanton and other activists sought fair pay and expanded employment opportunities for women by appealing to free-labor ideology. Woman's rights advocate Paula Wright Davis urged Americans to stop discriminating against able and enterprising women: "Let [women] . . . open a Store, . . . learn any of the lighter mechanical Trades, . . . study for a Profession, . . . be called to the lecture-room, [and] . . . the Temperance rostrum . . . [and] let her be appointed [to serve in the Post Office]." Some women pioneered in these and many other occupations during the 1840s and 1850s. Woman's rights activists also

succeeded in protecting married women's rights to their own wages and property in New York in 1860. But discrimination against women persisted, as most men believed that free-labor ideology required no compromise of male supremacy.

Abolitionists and the American Ideal

During the 1840s and 1850s, abolitionists continued to struggle to draw the nation's attention to the plight of slaves and the need for emancipation. Former slaves Frederick Douglass, Henry Bibb, and Sojourner Truth lectured to reform audiences throughout the North about the cruelties of slavery. Abolitionists published newspapers, held conventions, and petitioned Congress, but they never attracted a mass following among white Americans. Many white Northerners became convinced that slavery was wrong, but they still believed that blacks were inferior. Many other white Northerners shared the common view of white Southerners that slavery was necessary and even desirable. The westward extension of the nation during the 1840s offered abolitionists an opportunity to link their unpopular ideal to a goal that many white Northerners found much more attractive—limiting the geographic expansion of slavery, an issue that moved to the center of national politics during the 1850s (see "The Wilmot Proviso and the Expansion of Slavery" in chapter 14).

Abolitionist Meeting

This rare daguerreotype portrays an abolitionist meeting in New York in 1850. Frederick Douglass, who had escaped from slavery in Maryland, is seated on the platform next to the woman at the table. One of the nation's most eloquent abolitionists, Douglass also supported equal rights for women. The man behind Douglass is Gerrit Smith, a wealthy and militant abolitionist whose funds supported many reform activities. Digital image courtesy of the Getty's Open Content Program.

Black leaders rose to prominence in the abolitionist movement during the 1840s and 1850s. African Americans had actively opposed slavery for decades, but a new generation of leaders came to the forefront in these years. Frederick Douglass, Henry Highland Garnet, William Wells Brown, Martin R. Delany, and others became impatient with white abolitionists' appeals to the conscience of the white majority. In 1843, Garnet urged slaves to choose "Liberty or Death" and rise in insurrection against their masters, an idea that alienated almost all white people and had little influence among slaves. To express their own uncompromising ideas, black abolitionists founded their own newspapers and held their own antislavery conventions, although they still cooperated with sympathetic whites.

The commitment of black abolitionists to battling slavery grew out of their own experiences with white supremacy. The 250,000 free African Americans in the North and West constituted less than 2 percent of the total population in 1860. They confronted the humiliations of racial discrimination in nearly every arena of daily life. Only Maine, Massachusetts, New Hampshire, and Vermont permitted black men to vote; New York imposed a special property-holding requirement on black—but not white—voters, effectively excluding most black men from the franchise. The pervasive racial discrimination both handicapped and energized black abolitionists. Some cooperated with the efforts of the **American Colonization Society** to send freed slaves and other black Americans to Liberia in West Africa. Others sought to move to Canada, Haiti, or elsewhere. As one African American from Michigan wrote, "it is impracticable, not to say impossible, for the whites and blacks to live together, and upon terms of social and civil equality, under the same government." Most black American leaders refused to embrace emigration and worked against racial prejudice in their own communities, organizing campaigns against segregation, particularly in transportation and education. Their most notable success came in 1855 when Massachusetts integrated its public schools. Elsewhere, white supremacy continued unabated.

Outside the public spotlight, free African Americans in the North and West contributed to the antislavery cause by quietly aiding fugitive slaves. Harriet Tubman escaped from slavery in Maryland in 1849 and repeatedly risked her freedom and her life to return to the South to escort slaves to freedom. When the opportunity arose, free blacks in the North provided fugitive slaves with food, a safe place to rest, and a helping hand. An outgrowth of the antislavery sentiment and opposition to white supremacy that unified nearly all African Americans in the North, this **underground railroad** ran mainly through black neighborhoods, black churches, and black homes.

REVIEW Why were women especially prominent in many nineteenth-century reform efforts?

▶ Conclusion: Free Labor, Free Men

During the 1840s and 1850s, a cluster of interrelated developments—population growth, steam power, railroads, and the growing mechanization of agriculture and manufacturing—meant greater economic productivity, a burst of output from farms and factories, and prosperity for many. Diplomacy with Great Britain and war with Mexico handed the United States 1.2 million square miles and more than 1,000 miles of Pacific coastline. One prize of manifest destiny, California, almost immediately rewarded its new owners with tons of gold. Most Americans believed that the new territory and vast riches were appropriate rewards for the nation's stunning economic progress and superior institutions.

To Northerners, industrial evolution confirmed the choice they had made to eliminate slavery and promote free labor as the key to independence, equality, and prosperity. Like Abraham Lincoln, millions of Americans could point to their personal experiences as evidence of the practical truth of the free-labor ideal. But millions of others knew that in the free-labor system, poverty and wealth continued to rub shoulders. Free-labor enthusiasts denied that the problems were inherent in the country's social and economic systems. Instead, they argued, most social ills—including poverty and dependency—sprang from individual deficiencies. Consequently, many reformers focused on personal self-control and discipline, on avoiding sin and alcohol. Other reformers focused on woman's rights and the abolition of slavery. They challenged widespread conceptions of male supremacy and black inferiority, but neither group managed to overcome the prevailing free-labor ideology based on individualism, racial prejudice, and notions of male superiority.

By midcentury, half of the nation had prohibited slavery, and half permitted it. The North and the South were animated by different economic interests, cultural values, and political aims. Each celebrated its regional identity and increasingly disparaged that of the other. Not even the victory over Mexico could bridge the deepening divide between North and South.

See the Selected Bibliography for this chapter in the Appendix.

12 Chapter Review

LearningCurve
Go online and use LearningCurve to see what you know. Then review the key terms and answer the questions.

KEY TERMS

mechanical reapers (p. 314)
American system (p. 315)
manifest destiny (p. 323)
Oregon Trail (p. 323)
Mormons (p. 326)
Lone Star Republic (p. 328)
Treaty of Guadalupe Hidalgo (p. 335)
California gold rush (p. 336)
Oneida community (p. 338)
Seneca Falls Declaration of Sentiments (p. 338)
American Colonization Society (p. 340)
underground railroad (p. 340)

REVIEW QUESTIONS

1. Why did the United States become a leading industrial power in the nineteenth century? (pp. 313–317)

2. How did the free-labor ideal account for economic inequality? (pp. 317–321)

3. Why did westward migration expand dramatically in the mid-nineteenth century? (pp. 322–329)

4. Why did the United States go to war with Mexico? (pp. 329–337)

5. Why were women especially prominent in many nineteenth-century reform efforts? (pp. 337–340)

MAKING CONNECTIONS

1. Discuss migration to two different regions. What drew the migrants, and how did the U.S. government contribute to their efforts?

2. How did the ideology of manifest destiny contribute to mid-nineteenth-century expansion? Discuss its implications for individual migrants and the nation.

3. How did the Mexican-American War affect national political and economic developments in subsequent decades?

4. How did nineteenth-century reform movements draw on the free-labor ideal to pursue specific reforms?

LINKING TO THE PAST

1. In what ways were the North's economy, society, and political structure during the 1840s and 1850s shaped by the American Revolution and the Constitution? (See chapters 7 and 8.)

2. The nation's mighty push westward in the 1840s and 1850s extended a history of expansion that was as old as the nation itself. How was expansion to the West between 1840 and 1860 similar to and different from expansion between 1800 and 1820? (See chapter 10.)

13 The Slave South
1820–1860

CONTENT LEARNING OBJECTIVES

After reading and studying this chapter, you should be able to:

- Identify the ways slavery, a plantation-based economy, and biracialism distinguished the antebellum South from the North.

- Explain how a plantation was physically organized, and describe the roles of the plantation master and mistress. Define the ideology of paternalism and its role on the plantation.

- Describe the lives led by slaves in the Old South and the elements that contributed to a semi-autonomous slave culture.

- Explain why free blacks posed an ideological dilemma for white Southerners and why their freedom was precarious.

- Identify the "plain folk" of the Old South.

- Explain how the South became both increasingly democratized during the second quarter of the nineteenth century and planters managed to retain their power.

GOURD FIDDLE
Found in Maryland, this slave-made gourd fiddle is an example of the musical instruments that African Americans crafted and played throughout the South. Music provided slaves with a relief from the rigors of slavery. Smithsonian Institution Collections, National Museum of American History, Behring Center.

NAT TURNER WAS BORN A SLAVE IN SOUTHAMPTON COUNTY, VIRGINIA, in October 1800. His parents noticed special marks on his body, which they said were signs that he was "intended for some great purpose." His master said that he learned to read without being taught. As an adolescent, he adopted an austere lifestyle of Christian devotion and fasting. In his twenties, he received visits from the "Spirit," the same spirit, he believed, that had spoken to the ancient prophets. In time, Nat Turner began to interpret these things to mean that God had appointed him an instrument of divine vengeance for the sin of slaveholding.

On the morning of August 22, 1831, he set out with six friends—Hark, Henry, Sam, Nelson, Will, and Jack—to punish slave owners. Turner struck the first blow, an ax to the head of his master, Joseph Travis. The rebels killed all of the white men, women, and children they encountered. By noon, they had visited eleven farms and slaughtered fifty-seven whites. Along the way, they had added fifty or sixty men to their army. Word spread quickly, and soon the militia and hundreds of local whites gathered. They quickly captured or killed all of the rebels except Turner, who hid out for about ten weeks before being captured in nearby woods. Within a week, he was tried, convicted, and executed. By then, forty-five slaves had stood trial, twenty had been convicted and hanged, and another ten had been banished from Virginia. Frenzied whites had killed

Horrid Massacre in Virginia
No contemporary images of Nat Turner are known to exist. This woodcut simply imagines the rebellion as a nightmare in which black brutes took the lives of innocent whites. Although there was never another rebellion as large as Turner's, images of black violence continued to haunt white imaginations. Library of Congress.

another hundred or more blacks—insurgents and innocent bystanders—in their counterattack against the rebellion.

White Virginians blamed the rebellion on outside agitators. In 1829, David Walker, a freeborn black man living in Boston, had published his *Appeal . . . to the Coloured Citizens of the World*, an invitation to slaves to rise up in bloody revolution, and copies had fallen into the hands of Virginia slaves. Moreover, on January 1, 1831, the Massachusetts abolitionist William Lloyd Garrison had published the first issue of the *Liberator*, his fiery newspaper (see "Organizing against Slavery" in chapter 11).

In the months following the insurrection, the Virginia legislature reaffirmed the state's determination to preserve slavery by passing laws that strengthened the institution and further restricted free blacks. A professor at the College of William and Mary, Thomas R. Dew, published a vigorous defense of slavery that became the bible of Southerners' proslavery arguments. More than ever, the nation was divided along the Mason-Dixon line, the surveyors' mark that in colonial times had established the boundary between Maryland and Pennsylvania but half a century later divided the free North and the slave South.

Black slavery increasingly molded the South into a distinctive region. In the decades after 1820, Southerners, like Northerners, raced westward; but unlike Northerners who spread small farms, manufacturing, and free labor, Southerners spread slavery, cotton, and plantations. Geographic expansion meant that slavery became more vigorous and more profitable than ever, embraced more people, and increased the South's political power. Antebellum Southerners sometimes found themselves at odds with one another—not only slaves and free people but also women and men; Indians, Africans, and Europeans; and aristocrats and common folk. Nevertheless, beneath this diversity, a distinctively southern society and culture were forming. The South became a slave society, and most white Southerners were proud of it.

▶ The Growing Distinctiveness of the South

From the earliest settlements, inhabitants of the southern colonies had shared a great deal with northern colonists. Most whites in both sections were British and Protestant, spoke a common language, and celebrated their victorious revolution against British rule. The creation of the new nation under the Constitution in 1789 forged political ties that bound all Americans. The beginnings of a national economy fostered economic interdependence and communication across regional boundaries. White Americans everywhere praised the prosperous young nation, and they looked forward to its seemingly boundless future.

Despite these national similarities, Southerners and Northerners grew increasingly different. The French political observer Alexis de Tocqueville believed he knew why. "I could easily prove," he asserted in 1831, "that almost all the differences which may be noticed between the character of the Americans in the Southern and Northern states have originated in slavery." And a quarter of a century later, neither Northerners nor Southerners liked developments on the other side of the Mason-Dixon line. "On the subject of slavery," the *Charleston Mercury* declared, "the North and South . . . are not only two Peoples, but they are rival, hostile Peoples." Even more than the cotton-based agriculture that dominated the region, slavery made the South different, and it was the differences between the North and South, not the similarities, that increasingly shaped antebellum American history.

Cotton Kingdom, Slave Empire

In the first half of the nineteenth century, millions of Americans migrated west. In the South, the stampede began after the Creek War of 1813–1814, which divested the Creek Indians of 24 million acres and initiated the government campaign to remove Indian people living east of the Mississippi River to the West. Hard-driving slaveholders seeking virgin acreage for new plantations, ambitious farmers looking for patches of cheap land for small farms, striving herders and drovers pushing their hogs and cattle toward fresh pastures—everyone felt the pull of western land.

CHRONOLOGY

1808	• External slave trade outlawed.
1810s–1850s	• Suffrage extended throughout South to all adult white males.
1820s–1830s	• Southern legislatures enact slave codes. • Southern legislatures restrict free blacks. • Southern intellectuals fashion systematic defense of slavery.
1822	• Denmark Vesey executed.
1829	• *Appeal . . . to the Coloured Citizens of the World* published.
1830	• Southern slaves number approximately two million.
1831	• Nat Turner's rebellion. • First issue of the *Liberator* published.
1836	• Arkansas admitted to Union as slave state.
1840	• Cotton accounts for more than 60 percent of nation's exports.
1845	• Texas and Florida admitted to Union as slave states.
1860	• Southern slaves number nearly four million, one-third of South's population.

But more than anything it was cotton that propelled Southerners westward. South of the **Mason-Dixon line**, climate and geography were ideally suited for the cultivation of cotton. By the 1830s, cotton fields stretched from the Atlantic seaboard to central Texas. Heavy migration led to statehood for Arkansas in 1836 and for Texas and Florida in 1845. Cotton production soared to nearly 5 million bales in 1860, when the South produced three-fourths of the world's supply. The South—especially that tier of states from South Carolina west to Texas called the Lower South—had become the **cotton kingdom** (Map 13.1).

The cotton kingdom was also a slave empire. The South's cotton boom rested on the backs of

MAP ACTIVITY

Map 13.1   Cotton Kingdom, Slave Empire: 1820 and 1860

As the production of cotton soared, the slave population increased dramatically. Slaves continued to toil in tobacco and rice fields, but in Alabama, Mississippi, and Texas, they increasingly worked on cotton plantations.

READING THE MAP: Where was slavery most prevalent in 1820? In 1860? How did the spread of slavery compare with the spread of cotton?

CONNECTIONS: How much of the world's cotton was produced in the American South in 1860? How did the number of slaves in the American South compare with that in the rest of the world? What does this suggest about the South's cotton kingdom?

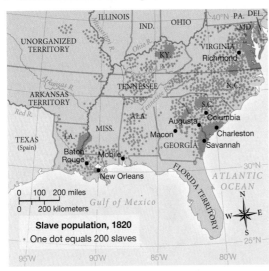

Slave population, 1820
· One dot equals 200 slaves

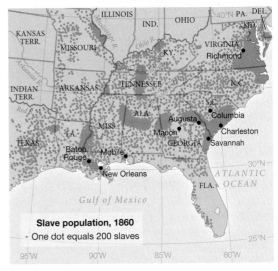

Slave population, 1860
· One dot equals 200 slaves

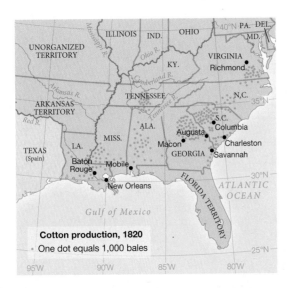

Cotton production, 1820
· One dot equals 1,000 bales

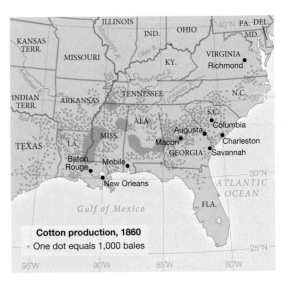

Cotton production, 1860
· One dot equals 1,000 bales

slaves. As cotton agriculture expanded westward, whites shipped more than a million enslaved men, women, and children from the Atlantic coast across the continent in what has been called the "Second Middle Passage," a massive deportation that dwarfed the transatlantic slave trade to North America. (See "Visualizing History," page 348.) Victims of this brutal domestic slave trade marched hundreds of miles southwest to the Lower South, where they literally cut new plantations from the forests. Cotton, slaves, and plantations moved west together.

The slave population grew enormously. Southern slaves numbered fewer than 700,000 in 1790, about 2 million in 1830, and almost 4 million by 1860. By 1860, the South contained more slaves than all the other slave societies in the New World combined. The extraordinary

The Upper and Lower South

growth was not the result of the importation of slaves, which the federal government outlawed in 1808. Instead, the slave population grew through natural reproduction; by midcentury, most U.S. slaves were native-born Southerners.

The South in Black and White

By 1860, one in every three Southerners was black (approximately 4 million blacks to 8 million whites). In the Lower South states of Mississippi and South Carolina, blacks constituted the majority (Figure 13.1). The contrast with the North was striking: In 1860, only one Northerner in seventy-six was black (about 250,000 blacks to 19 million whites).

The presence of large numbers of African Americans had profound consequences for the South. Southern culture—language, food, music,

FIGURE 13.1   Black and White Populations in the South, 1860
Blacks represented a much larger fraction of the population in the South than in the North, but considerable variation existed from state to state. Only one Missourian in ten, for example, was black, while Mississippi and South Carolina had black majorities. States in the Upper South were "whiter" than states in the Lower South, despite the Upper South's greater number of free blacks.

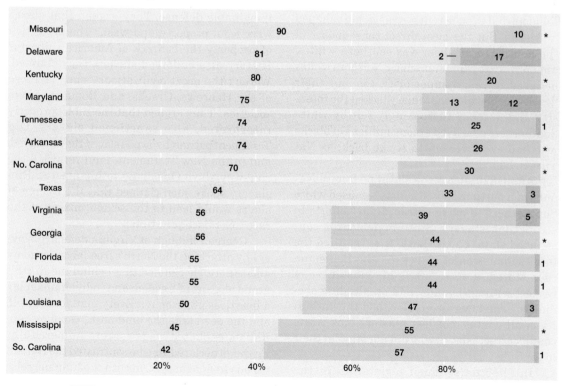

The Auction Block

"American Slave Market," 1852

religion, and even accents—was in part shaped by blacks. But the most direct consequence of the South's biracialism was southern whites' commitment to white supremacy. Northern whites believed in racial superiority, too, but their dedication to white supremacy lacked the intensity and urgency increasingly felt by white Southerners who lived among millions of blacks who had every reason to strike back, as Nat Turner had.

After 1820, attacks on slavery—from slaves and from northern abolitionists—caused white Southerners to make extraordinary efforts to strengthen slavery. State legislatures constructed **slave codes** (laws) that required the total submission of slaves. As the Louisiana code stated, a slave "owes his master . . . a respect without bounds, and an absolute obedience." The laws also underlined the authority of all whites, not just masters. Any white could "correct" slaves who did not stay "in their place."

Intellectuals joined legislators in the campaign to strengthen slavery. The South's academics, writers, and clergy employed every

imaginable defense. They argued that slaves were legal property, and wasn't the protection of property the bedrock of American liberty? History also endorsed slavery, they claimed. Weren't the great civilizations—such as those of the Hebrews, Greeks, and Romans—slave societies? They argued that the Bible, properly interpreted, also sanctioned slavery. Old Testament patriarchs owned slaves, they observed, and in the New Testament, Paul returned the runaway slave Onesimus to his master. Pro-slavery spokesmen claimed that the freeing of slaves would lead to the sexual mixing of the races, or **miscegenation**.

George Fitzhugh of Virginia defended slavery by attacking the North's free-labor economy and society. He claimed that behind the North's grand slogans of freedom and individualism lay a heartless philosophy: "Every man for himself, and the devil take the hindmost." Gouging capitalists exploited wageworkers unmercifully, Fitzhugh declared, and he contrasted the North's vicious free-labor system with the humane relations that he said prevailed between masters and slaves because slaves were valuable capital

The slave trade was a familiar sight throughout the South. African Americans were bought and sold at public auction, as depicted here, and at private sales. Between 1820 and 1860, some one million slaves entered the interstate slave trade that supplied labor to the booming Cotton South. Perhaps twice as many slaves were sold locally. In the "American Slave Market," the artist captures the buyers, traders, and slaves at the precise moment of sale. In this painting, the buyers—the well-dressed gentlemen in top hats—who gather around the auctioneer show no regret or embarrassment, only anticipation. One hopeful purchaser wears a more casual hat, perhaps indicating that he is a poorer man who was seeking to purchase his first slave.

The artist also depicts the slave traders, or "Negro speculators" as contemporaries called them. The auctioneer stands in the center with what appears to be a bill of sale. The other traders wear more casual clothes, indicating that they are not of the same social class as the buyers. One trader holds a long switch in case the slaves get out of line. Long

before the auction began, the traders would have been busy preparing their merchandise for market. They fattened slaves, plucked grey hairs, and provided slaves with clean clothes to convince buyers that their slaves were young, healthy, and had years of work left in them.

Every slave dreaded the appearance of a slave trader at the gate of the plantation. Falling into the hands of a trader meant separation from family, probably for life, and a new existence under an unknown master. The men, women, and children huddled on the ground are clearly anxious about their fates. Whether any of these women are the mothers of the children portrayed here is unclear. In any case, traders often sold children separately and by the pound. The male slave standing in the middle of the group wears what appears to be a kind of skirt, which may suggest his African origins and perhaps his intransigence.

The contrast between the eager white gentlemen and the miserable slaves could not be starker. But the artist complicates the simple composition of white and black by adding a black

man to the group of potential buyers and a black woman who is probably a slave, walking by with a basket on her head, observing the cruel drama.

source: © Chicago History Museum, USA/The Bridgeman Art Library

Questions for Analysis

1. What is the slave with arm raised seeming to say?

2. Why do the prospective buyers not show any guilt or embarrassment about participating in this sale of human beings?

3. Are all of the prospective buyers white? Is the artist correct that a black man can purchase a slave in the South?

4. What do you suppose the woman with the basket on her head is thinking?

Connect to the Big Idea

C Why were slave sales crucial to the smooth function of the slave economy?

---

that masters sought to protect. John C. Calhoun, an influential southern politician, declared that in the states where slavery had been abolished, "the condition of the African, instead of being improved, has become worse," while in the slave states, the Africans "have improved greatly in every respect."

But at the heart of the defense of slavery lay the claim of black inferiority. Black enslavement was both necessary and proper, slavery's defenders argued, because Africans were lesser beings. Rather than exploitative, slavery was a mass civilizing effort that lifted lowly blacks from African barbarism and savagery, taught them disciplined work, and converted them to soul-saving Christianity. According to Virginian Thomas R. Dew, most slaves were grateful. He declared that "the slaves of a good master are his warmest, most constant, and most devoted friends." (See "Documenting the American Promise," page 352.)

African slavery encouraged southern whites to unify around race rather than to divide by class. The grubbiest, most tobacco-stained white man could proudly proclaim his superiority to

all blacks and his equality with the most refined southern planter. Georgia attorney Thomas R. R. Cobb observed that every white Southerner "feels that he belongs to an elevated class. It matters not that he is no slaveholder; he is not of the inferior race; he is a freeborn citizen." Consequently, the "poorest meets the richest as an equal; sits at his table with him; salutes him as a neighbor; meets him in every public assembly, and stands on the same social platform." In the South, Cobb boasted, "there is no war of classes." By providing every white Southerner membership in the ruling race, slavery helped whites bridge differences in wealth, education, and culture.

The Plantation Economy

As important as slavery was in unifying white Southerners, only about a quarter of the white population lived in slaveholding families. Most slaveholders owned fewer than five slaves. Only about 12 percent of slaveholders owned twenty or more, the number of slaves that historians consider necessary to distinguish a **planter**

THE FRUITS OF AMALGAMATION.

VISUAL ACTIVITY

The Fruits of Amalgamation
In this lithograph from 1839, Edward W. Clay of Philadelphia attacked abolitionists by imagining the miscegenation (also known as "amalgamation") that would come from emancipation. He drew a beautiful white woman, her two black children, and her dark-skinned, ridiculously overdressed husband, resting his feet in his wife's lap. American Antiquarian Society, Worcester, Massachusetts / The Bridgeman Art Library.
READING THE IMAGE: What are the races of the servant and the couple at the door, and what do you think the artist is saying?
CONNECTIONS: In the opinion of abolitionists, who was responsible for miscegenation and why?

from a farmer. Despite their small numbers, planters dominated the southern economy. In 1860, 52 percent of the South's slaves lived and worked on **plantations**. Plantation slaves produced more than 75 percent of the South's export crops, the backbone of the region's economy. While slavery was dying elsewhere in the New World (only Brazil and Cuba still defended slavery at midcentury), slave plantations increasingly dominated southern agriculture.

The South's major cash crops—tobacco, sugar, rice, and cotton—grew on plantations (Map 13.2). Tobacco, the original plantation crop in North America, had shifted westward in the

nineteenth century from the Chesapeake to Tennessee and Kentucky. Large-scale sugar production began in 1795, when Étienne de Boré built a modern sugar mill in what is today New Orleans, and sugar plantations were confined almost entirely to Louisiana. Commercial rice production began in the seventeenth century, and like sugar, rice was confined to a small geographic area, a narrow strip of coast stretching from the Carolinas into Georgia.

But by the nineteenth century, cotton reigned as king of the South's plantation crops. Cotton became commercially significant in the 1790s after the invention of a new cotton gin by Eli

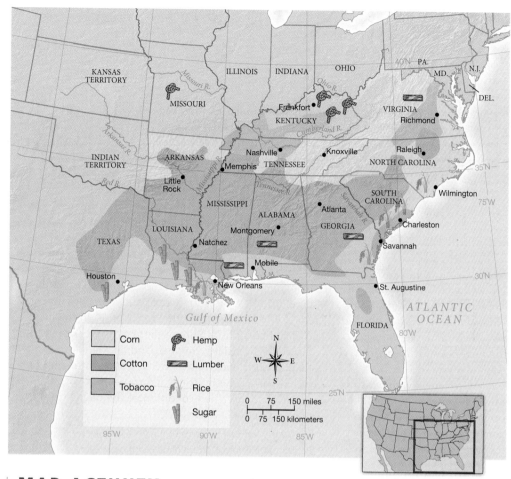

MAP ACTIVITY

Map 13.2   The Agricultural Economy of the South, 1860
Cotton dominated the South's agricultural economy, but the region grew a variety of crops and was largely self-sufficient in foodstuffs.

READING THE MAP: In what type of geographic areas were rice and sugar grown? After cotton, what crop commanded the greatest agricultural area in the South? In which region of the South was this crop predominantly found?

CONNECTIONS: What role did the South play in the U.S. economy in 1860? How did the economy of the South differ from that of the North?

Whitney (see "Agriculture, Transportation, and Banking" in chapter 9). Cotton was relatively easy to grow and took little capital to get started—just enough for land, seed, and simple tools. Thus, small farmers as well as planters grew cotton. But planters, whose extensive fields were worked by gangs of slaves, produced three-quarters of the South's cotton, and cotton made planters rich.

Plantation slavery also enriched the nation. By 1840, cotton accounted for more than 60 percent of American exports. Most of the cotton was shipped to Great Britain, the world's largest manufacturer of cotton textiles. Much of the profit

from the sale of cotton overseas returned to planters, but some went to northern middlemen who bought, sold, insured, warehoused, and shipped cotton to the mills in Great Britain. As one New York merchant observed, "Cotton has enriched all through whose hands it has passed." As middlemen invested their profits in the booming northern economy, industrial development received a burst of much-needed capital. Furthermore, southern plantations benefited northern industry by providing an important market for textiles, agricultural tools, and other manufactured goods.

The economies of the North and South steadily diverged. While the North developed a mixed

Defending Slavery

White Southerners who defended slavery were rationalizing their economic interests and racial privileges, of course, but they also believed what they said about slavery being just, necessary, and godly. Whatever their specific arguments, they agreed with the *Charleston Mercury* that without slavery, the South would become a "most magnificent jungle."

DOCUMENT 1
John C. Calhoun, Speech before the U.S. Senate, 1837

When abolitionists began to denounce slavery as sinful and odious, John C. Calhoun, the South's leading proslavery politician, rose to defend the institution as "a positive good." Calhoun devoted part of his speech to the argument that enslavement benefited the slaves themselves.

Be it good or bad, it [slavery] has grown up with our society and institutions, and is so interwoven with them, that to destroy it would be to destroy us as a people. But let me not be understood as admitting, even by implication, that the existing relations between the two races in the slaveholding States is an evil: far otherwise; I hold it to be a good. . . . I appeal to facts. Never before has the black race of Central Africa, from the dawn of history to the present day, attained a condition so civilized and so improved, not only physically, but morally and intellectually. It came to us in a low, degraded, and savage condition, and in the course of a few generations, it has grown up under the fostering care of our institutions, reviled they have been, to its present comparatively civilized condition. This, with the rapid increase of numbers, is conclusive proof of the general happiness of the race, in spite of all the exaggerated tales to the contrary. . . .

I hold that in the present state of civilization, where two races of different origin, and distinguished by color, and other physical differences, as well as intellectual, are brought together, the relation now existing in the slave-holding States between the two, is, instead of an evil, a good—a positive good. . . .

I may say with truth, that in few countries so much is left to the share of the laborer, and so little exacted from him, or where there is more kind attention paid to him in sickness or infirmities of age. Compare his condition with the tenants of the poor houses in the more civilized portions of Europe—look at the sick, and the old and infirm slave, on one hand, in the midst of his family and friends, under the kind superintending care of his master and mistress, and compare it with the forlorn and wretched condition of the pauper in the poor house.

Source: John C. Calhoun, "Speech on the Reception of Abolition Petitions, Delivered in the Senate, February 6th, 1837," in *Speeches of John C. Calhoun, Delivered in the House of Representatives and in the Senate of the United States*, edited by Richard K. Cralle (Appleton, 1853), 625–33.

DOCUMENT 2
William Harper, *Memoir on Slavery*, 1837

William Harper—judge, politician, and academic—defended slavery by denouncing abolitionists, particularly the "atrocious philosophy" of "natural equality and inalienable rights" that they used to support their attacks on slavery.

All men are born free and equal. Is it not palpably nearer the truth to say that no man was ever born free, and that

economy—agriculture, commerce, and manufacturing—the South remained overwhelmingly agricultural. Year after year, planters funneled the profits they earned from land and slaves back into more land and more slaves. With its capital flowing into agriculture, the South did not develop many factories. By 1860, only 10 percent of the nation's industrial workers lived in the South. Some cotton mills sprang up, but the region that produced 100 percent of the nation's cotton manufactured less than 7 percent of its cotton textiles.

no two men were ever born equal? . . . Wealth and poverty, fame or obscurity, strength or weakness, knowledge or ignorance, ease or labor, power or subjection, mark the endless diversity in the condition of men. . . .

It is the order of nature and of God, that the being of superior faculties and knowledge, and therefore of superior power, should control and dispose of those who are inferior. It is as much in the order of nature, that men should enslave each other, as that other animals should prey upon each other.

Moralists have denounced the injustice and cruelty which have been practiced towards our aboriginal Indians, by which they have been driven from their native seats and exterminated.

. . . No doubt, much fraud and injustice has been practiced in the circumstances and manner of their removal. Yet who has contended that civilized man had no moral right to possess himself of the country? That he was bound to leave this wide and fertile continent, which is capable of sustaining uncounted myriads of a civilized race, to a few roving and ignorant barbarians? Yet if any thing is certain, it is certain that there were no means by which he could possess the country, without exterminating or enslaving them. Slave and civilized man cannot live together, and the savage can only be tamed by being enslaved or by having slaves.

Source: William Harper, *Memoir of Slavery* (J. S. Burges, 1838).

DOCUMENT 3
Thornton Stringfellow, "The Bible Argument: or, Slavery in the Light of Divine Revelation," 1856

Reverend Thornton Stringfellow, a Baptist minister from Virginia, defended human bondage based on his reading of the Bible. He makes a case that Jesus himself approved of the relationship between master and slave.

Jesus Christ recognized this institution [slavery] as one that was lawful among men, and regulated its relative duties. . . . I affirm then, first, (and no man denies,) that Jesus Christ has not abolished slavery by a prohibitory

command: and second, I affirm, he has introduced no new moral principle which can work its destruction, under the gospel dispensation; and that the principle relied on for this purpose, is a fundamental principle of the Mosaic law, under which slavery was instituted by Jehovah himself. . . .

To the church at Colosse . . . Paul in his letter to them, recognizes the three relations of wives and husbands, parents and children, servants and masters, as relations existing among the members . . . and to the servants and masters he thus writes: "Servants obey in all things your masters, according to the flesh: not with eye service, as men pleasers, but in singleness of heart, fearing God: and whatsoever you do, do it heartily, as to the Lord and not unto men; knowing that of the Lord ye shall receive the reward of the inheritance, for ye serve the Lord Christ. . . . Masters give unto your servants that which is just and equal, knowing that you also have a master in heaven."

Source: *Slavery Defended: The Views of the Old South* by Eric L. McKitrick, editor. Published by Prentice-Hall, 1963. Reprinted with permission. *Cotton Is King and Pro-Slavery Arguments* by Thornton Stringfellow (Pritchard, Abbott & Loomis, 1860), 459–546.

Questions for Analysis and Debate

1. According to John C. Calhoun, what were slavery's chief benefits for blacks? How did his proslavery convictions shape his argument?

2. Why do you suppose William Harper interjected Americans' treatment of Indians into his defense of slavery?

3. According to Thornton Stringfellow, the Bible instructs both masters and slaves about their duties. What are their respective obligations?

Connect to the Big Idea

C What were the underlying motives behind the defense of slavery?

Without significant economic diversification, the South developed fewer cities than the North and West. In 1860, it was the least urban region in the country. Whereas nearly 37 percent of New England's population lived in cities, less than 12 percent of Southerners were urban dwellers. Because the South had so few cities and industrial jobs, it attracted small numbers of European immigrants. Seeking economic opportunity, not competition with slaves (whose labor would keep wages low), immigrants steered northward. In 1860,

13 percent of all Americans were born abroad. But in nine of the fifteen slave states, only 2 percent or less of the population was foreign-born.

Northerners claimed that slavery was a backward labor system, and compared with Northerners, Southerners invested less of their capital in industry, transportation, and public education. But few Southerners perceived economic weakness in their region. Indeed, planters' pockets were never fuller than in the 1850s, thanks to the South's near monopoly on cotton, the hottest commodity in the international marketplace. Planters' decisions to reinvest in cotton ensured the momentum of the plantation economy and the political and social relationships rooted in it.

> **REVIEW**   Why did the nineteenth-century southern economy remain primarily agricultural?

▶ Masters and Mistresses in the Big House

Nowhere was the contrast between northern and southern life more vivid than on the plantations of the South. A plantation typically included a "big house," where the plantation owner and his family lived, and a slave quarter. Near the big house were the kitchen, storehouse, smokehouse (for curing and preserving meat), and hen coop. More distant were the barns, toolsheds, artisans' workshops, and overseer's house. Large plantations sometimes had an infirmary and a chapel for slaves. Depending on the crop, there was also a tobacco shed, a rice mill, a sugar refinery, or a cotton gin house. Lavish or plain, plantations everywhere had an underlying similarity (Figure 13.2).

The plantation was the home of masters, mistresses, and slaves. A hierarchy of rigid roles and duties governed their relationships. Presiding was the master, who by law ruled his wife, children, and slaves as dependents under his dominion and protection.

Paternalism and Male Honor

Whereas smaller planters supervised the labor of their slaves themselves, larger planters hired overseers who went to the fields with the slaves, leaving the planters free to concentrate on marketing, finance, and the general affairs of the plantation. Planters also found time to escape to town to discuss cotton prices, to the courthouse and legislature to debate politics, and to the woods to hunt and fish.

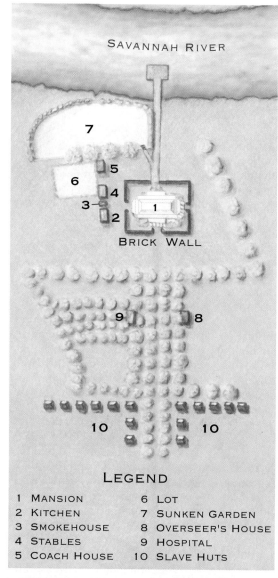

SAVANNAH RIVER

BRICK WALL

LEGEND

1	MANSION	6	LOT
2	KITCHEN	7	SUNKEN GARDEN
3	SMOKEHOUSE	8	OVERSEER'S HOUSE
4	STABLES	9	HOSPITAL
5	COACH HOUSE	10	SLAVE HUTS

FIGURE 13.2   A Southern Plantation
Slavery determined how masters laid out their plantations and where they situated their "big houses" and
slave quarters. This model of the Hermitage, the mansion
built in 1830 for Henry McAlpin, a Georgia rice planter,
shows the overseer's house poised halfway between the
owner's mansion and the slave huts. Adapted from *Back of
the Big House: The Architecture of Plantation Slavery* by John Michael
Vlach. Copyright © 1993 by the University of North Carolina Press.
Reprinted with permission of the University of North Carolina Press.
Original illustration property of the Historic American Buildings Survey, a
division of the National Park Service.

Increasingly, planters characterized their
mastery in terms of what they called "Christian
guardianship" and what historians have called
paternalism. The concept of paternalism denied
that the form of slavery practiced in the South
was brutal and exploitative. Instead, paternalism

claimed that plantations benefited all. In exchange for the slaves' work and obedience,
masters provided basic care and necessary guidance for a childlike, dependent people. In 1814,
Thomas Jefferson captured the essence of the
advancing ideal: "We should endeavor, with
those whom fortune has thrown on our hands,
to feed & clothe them well, protect them from
ill usage, require such reasonable labor only as
is performed voluntarily by freemen, and be led
by no repugnancies to abdicate them, and our
duties to them." A South Carolina rice planter
insisted, "I manage them as my children."

Paternalism was part propaganda and part
self-delusion. But it was also economically
shrewd. Masters increasingly recognized slaves
as valuable assets, particularly after the nation
closed its external slave trade in 1808 and the
cotton boom stimulated the demand for slaves.
The expansion of the slave labor force could
come only from natural reproduction. As one
slave owner declared in 1849, "It behooves
those who own them to make them last as long
as possible."

One consequence of paternalism and economic self-interest was a small improvement
in slaves' welfare. Diet improved, although
nineteenth-century slaves still ate mainly fatty
pork and cornmeal. Housing improved, although
the cabins still had cracks large enough, slaves
said, for cats to slip through. Clothing improved,
although slaves seldom received much more
than two crude outfits a year and perhaps a
pair of cheap shoes. Workdays remained sunup
to sundown, but planters often offered a rest
period in the heat of the day. Most planters
ceased the colonial practice of punishing slaves
by branding and mutilation.

Paternalism should not be mistaken for "Ol'
Massa's" kindness and goodwill. It encouraged
better treatment because it made economic
sense to provide at least minimal care for
valuable slaves. Nor did paternalism require
that planters put aside their whips. They could
whip and still claim that they were only fulfilling their responsibilities as guardians of
their naturally lazy and at times insubordinate
black dependents. State laws gave masters
nearly "uncontrolled authority over the body"
of the slave, according to one North Carolina
judge, and whipping remained planters' basic
form of coercion. (See "Historical Question,"
page 356.)

Paternalism never won universal acceptance
among planters, but by the nineteenth century
it had become a kind of communal standard.

How Often Were Slaves Whipped?

There is little doubt that the whipping of slaves was widespread and acceptable in the South. We know from white sources that whipping was the prescribed method of physical punishment on most antebellum plantations. Masters' instructions to overseers authorized whippings and often established the number of strokes an overseer could administer. Some planters allowed fifteen lashes, some fifty, and some one hundred. But slave owners' instructions, as revealing as they are, tell us more about the severity of beating than about their frequency.

Remembrances of former slaves confirm that whipping was widespread and frequent. In the 1930s, a government program gathered testimony from more than 2,300 elderly African Americans about their experiences as slaves. Their accounts offer grisly evidence of the cruelty of slavery. "You say how did our Master treat his slaves?" asked one woman. "Scandalous, they treated them just like dogs." She was herself whipped "till the blood dripped to the ground." Bert Strong never personally felt the sting of the lash, but he recalled hearing slaves on other farms "hollering when they get beat." He said, "They beat them till it a pity." Beatings occurred often, but how often?

The diary of Bennet H. Barrow, the master of Highland plantation in West Feliciana Parish, Louisiana, provides a rare picture of a master's punishment of his slaves. For a twenty-three-month period in 1840–1841, Barrow meticulously recorded every one of the 160 whippings he administered or ordered, which amounted to one whipping every four and a half days. Barrow's records establish that 60 of the 77 slaves who worked in his fields were whipped in this period, with 80 percent of the males and 70 percent of the females being whipped at least once. Most of the 17 field slaves who escaped being beaten were children and pregnant women.

In most instances, Barrow recorded not only the fact of a whipping but also his reasons for administering it. All sorts of "rascality" made Barrow reach for his whip. The provocations included family quarrels in the slave quarter, impudence, running away, and failure to keep curfew. But nearly 80 percent of the reasons were related to poor work. Barrow gave beatings for picking "very trashy cotton," for "not picking as well as he can," and for failing to pick the prescribed weight of cotton. One slave claimed to have lost his eyesight and for months refused to work,

until Barrow "gave him 25 cuts yesterday morning & ordered him to work Blind or not." Some planters used whips that raised welts, caused blisters, and bruised. Others resorted to rawhide and cowhide whips that broke the skin, caused scarring, and sometimes permanently maimed. Occasionally, slaves were beaten to death.

Whipping was not Barrow's only means of inflicting pain. His diary mentions confining slaves to a plantation jail, putting them in chains, shooting them, breaking a "sword cane" over one slave's head, having slaves mauled by dogs, placing them in stocks, "staking down" slaves for hours, holding their heads under water, and a variety of punishments intended to ridicule and to shame, including making men wear women's clothing and do "women's work," such as the laundry. Still, Barrow's preferred instrument of punishment was the whip.

On the Barrow plantation, as on many others, whipping was public. Victims were often tied to a stake in the quarter, and the other slaves were made to watch. In a real sense, the entire slave population on the plantation experienced a whipping every four and a half days, and all were familiar with its terror and agony.

Was whipping effective? Did it produce a hardworking, efficient, and conscientious labor force? Not according to Barrow's own record. No evidence indicates that whipping changed the slaves' behavior. What Barrow considered bad work continued. Unabated whipping is

With its notion that slavery imposed on masters a burden and a duty, paternalism provided slaveholders with a means of rationalizing their rule. But it also provided some slaves with leverage in controlling the conditions of their lives. Slaves learned to manipulate the slaveholder's need to see himself as a good master. To avoid a reputation as a cruel tyrant, planters sometimes negotiated with slaves, rather than just

resorting to the whip. Masters sometimes granted slaves small garden plots in which they could work for themselves after working all day in the fields, or they gave slaves a few days off and a dance when they had gathered the last of the cotton.

Virginia statesman Edmund Randolph argued that slavery created in white southern men a "quick and acute sense of personal liberty" and itself evidence of the failure of punishment to achieve the master's will. Slaves knew the rules, yet they continued to act "badly." And they continued to suffer.

Did Barrow whip as often as other planters whipped? We simply do not know. Still, the Barrow evidence allows us to speculate profitably on the frequency of whipping by large planters. We do know that Barrow did not consider himself a cruel man. He bitterly denounced his neighbor as "the most cruel Master i ever knew of" for castrating three of his slaves. Like most whites, he believed that the lash was essential to get the work done, and he used it no more than he believed absolutely necessary. Still, Barrow's whip fell on someone's back every few days.

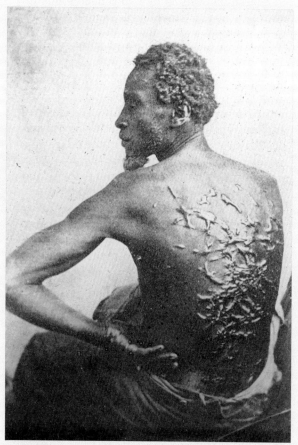

Gordon

This photograph of Gordon, a runaway slave from Baton Rouge, Louisiana, was taken on April 2, 1863. Frederick W. Mercer, an assistant surgeon with the Forty-seventh Massachusetts Regiment, examined four hundred other runaways and found many "to be as badly lacerated." Publication of Gordon's photograph in the popular *Harper's Weekly* made him a symbol of slavery's terrible brutality.

© Massachusetts Historical Society, Boston, MA / The Bridgeman Art Library.

Questions for Consideration

1. How could slaveholders, who increasingly saw themselves as "Christian guardians" to their slaves, have justified whipping them?

2. Why do you suppose masters relied on whipping as the preferred form of punishment?

3. Why do you suppose Barrow gave the overwhelming majority of whippings because of poor work?

Connect to the Big Idea

Ⓒ How did paternalism affect the quality of slaves' living and working conditions?

---

a "disdain for every abridgement of personal independence." Indeed, prickly individualism and aggressive independence became crucial features of the southern concept of honor. Social standing, political advancement, and even self-esteem rested on an honorable reputation. Defending honor became a male passion. Andrew Jackson's mother reportedly told her son, "Never tell a lie, nor take what is not your own, nor sue anybody for slander or assault and battery. *Always settle them cases yourself.*"

Among planters, such advice sometimes led to dueling, a ritual that had arrived from Europe in the eighteenth century. It died out in the North, but in the South, even after legislatures banned it, gentlemen continued to defend their honor with pistols at ten paces. Duels were fought by Andrew Jackson, whose wife one foolish man slandered, as well as by two college students who happened at dinner to reach simultaneously for the last piece of trout.

Southerners also expected an honorable gentleman to be a proper patriarch. Nowhere in America was masculine power more accentuated. Planters allowed no opposition from any of their dependents, black or white. The master's absolute dominion sometimes led to miscegenation. Laws prohibited interracial sex, but as long as slavery gave white men extraordinary power, slave women were forced to submit to the sexual demands of the men who owned them.

In time, as the children of one elite family married the children of another, ties of blood and kinship, as well as ideology and economic interest, linked planters to one another. Aware of what they shared as slaveholders, planters worked together to defend their common interests. The values of the big house—slavery, honor, male domination—washed over the boundaries of plantations and flooded all of southern life.

The Southern Lady and Feminine Virtues

Like their northern counterparts, southern ladies were expected to possess the feminine virtues of piety, purity, chastity, and obedience within the context of marriage, motherhood, and domesticity. Countless toasts praised the southern lady as the perfect complement to her husband, the commanding patriarch. She was physically weak, "formed only for the less laborious occupations," and thus dependent on male protection. To gain this protection, she exhibited modesty and delicacy, possessed beauty and grace, and cultivated refinement and charm. The lady, southern men said proudly, was an "ornament."

Chivalry—the South's romantic ideal of male-female relationships—glorified the lady while it subordinated her. Chivalry's underlying assumptions about the weakness of women and the protective authority of men resembled the paternalistic defense of slavery. Just as the slaveholder's mastery was written into law, so too were the paramount rights of husbands. Married women lost almost all their property rights to their husbands. Women throughout the nation found divorce difficult, but southern women found it almost impossible.

Daughters of planters confronted chivalry's demands at an early age. At their private boarding schools, they learned to be southern ladies, reading literature, learning languages, and studying the appropriate drawing-room arts. Elite women began courting young and married early. Kate Carney exaggerated only slightly

VISUAL ACTIVITY

Black Woman Holding White Child, ca. 1855

Most of the white children who grew up in the Big House had slave nurses, or nannies. The fact that this nannie is included in the portrait of the child indicates her importance in the white household. Library of Congress.

READING THE IMAGE: If she was important, however, why is her face hidden behind the child?

CONNECTIONS: As a female house servant, what other obligations might this nannie have had in the Big House?

Varina Howell Davis, 1849
Elite plantation women often had expensive lockets like this, in which their portraits were painted in miniature on ivory. In 1845, eighteen-year-old Varina Howell married Jefferson Davis, a man twice her age and the future president of the Confederate States of America. National Portrait Gallery, Smithsonian Institution/Art Resource, NY.

when she despaired in her diary: "Today, I am seventeen, getting quite old, and am not married." Yet marriage meant turning their fates over to their husbands and making enormous efforts to live up to their region's lofty expectations. Caroline Merrick of Louisiana told a friend in 1859, "We owe it to our husbands, children, and friends to represent as nearly as possible the ideal which they hold so dear."

Proslavery advocates claimed that slavery freed white women from drudgery. Surrounded "by her domestics," declared Thomas R. Dew, "she ceases to be a mere beast of burden" and "becomes the cheering and animating center of the family circle." In reality, however, having servants required the plantation mistress to work long hours. She managed the big house, directly supervising sometimes more than a dozen slaves. One slaveholder remembered that his boyhood home had "two cooks, two washer-women, one dining room servant, two seamstresses, one house girl, one house boy, one carriage driver, one hostler [stableman], one gardener, [and] one errand boy." And, he added, "they were all under the supervision of my mother." But unlike her husband, the mistress had no overseer. All house servants answered directly to her. She assigned them tasks each morning, directed their work throughout the day, and punished them when she found fault.

Whereas masters used their status as slaveholders as a springboard into public affairs, mistresses' lives were circumscribed by the plantation. Masters left when they pleased, but mistresses had heavy responsibilities, and

besides they needed chaperones to travel. When they could, they went to church, but women spent most days at home, where they often became lonely. In 1853, Mary Kendall wrote how much she enjoyed her sister's letter: "For about three weeks I did not have the pleasure of seeing one white female face, there being no white family except our own upon the plantation."

As members of slaveholding families, mistresses lived privileged lives. But they also had grounds for discontent. No feature of plantation life generated more anguish among mistresses than miscegenation. Mary Boykin Chesnut of Camden, South Carolina, confided in her diary, "Ours is a monstrous system, a wrong and iniquity. Like the patriarchs of old, our men live all in one house with their wives and their concubines; and the mulattos one sees in every family partly resemble the white children. Any lady is ready to tell you who is the father of all the mulatto children in everybody's household but her own. Those, she seems to think drop from the clouds."

But most planters' wives, including Chesnut, accepted slavery. After all, the privileged life of a mistress rested on slave labor as much as a master's did. Mistresses enjoyed the rewards of their class and race. But these rewards came at a price. Still, the heaviest burdens of slavery fell not on those who lived in the big house, but on those who toiled to support them.

REVIEW Why did the ideology of paternalism gain currency among planters in the nineteenth century?

▶ Slaves in the Quarter

On most plantations, only a few hundred yards separated the big house and the slave quarter. But the distance was great enough to provide slaves with some privacy. Out of eyesight and earshot of the big house, slaves drew together and built lives of their own. They created families, worshipped God, and developed an African American community and culture. Individually and collectively, slaves found ways to resist their bondage.

Despite the rise of plantations, almost half of the South's slaves lived and worked elsewhere. Most labored on small farms, where they wielded a hoe alongside another slave or two and perhaps their master. But by 1860, almost half a million slaves (one in eight) did not work in agriculture at all. Some lived in towns and cities, where they worked as domestics, day laborers, bakers, barbers, tailors, and more. Other slaves, far from urban centers, toiled as fishermen, lumbermen, railroad workers, and deckhands on riverboats. Slaves could also be found in most of the South's factories. Nevertheless, a majority of slaves (52 percent) counted plantations as their workplaces and homes.

Work

Whites enslaved blacks for their labor, and all slaves who were capable of productive labor worked. Former slave Carrie Hudson recalled that children who were "knee high to a duck" were sent to the fields to carry water to thirsty workers or to protect ripening crops from hungry birds. Others helped in the slave nursery, caring for children even younger than themselves, or in the big house, where they swept floors or shooed flies in the dining room. When slave boys and girls reached the age of eleven or twelve, masters sent most of them to the fields. After a lifetime of labor, old women left the fields to care for the small children and spin yarn, and old men moved on to mind livestock and clean stables.

The overwhelming majority of plantation slaves worked as field hands. Planters sometimes assigned men and women to separate gangs, the women working at lighter tasks and the men doing the heavy work of clearing and breaking the land. But women also did heavy work. "I had to work hard," Nancy Boudry remembered, and "plow and go and split wood just like a man." The backbreaking labor and the monotonous routines caused one ex-slave to observe that the "history of one day is the history of every day."

A few slaves (about one in ten) became house servants. Nearly all of those (nine out of ten) were women. They cooked, cleaned, babysat, washed clothes, and did the dozens of other tasks the master and mistress required. House servants were constantly on call, with no time that was entirely their own. Since no servant could please constantly, most bore the brunt of white frustration and rage. Ex-slave Jacob Branch of Texas remembered, "My poor mama! Every washday old Missy give her a beating."

Even rarer than house servants were skilled artisans. In the cotton South, no more than one slave in twenty (almost all men) worked in a skilled trade. Most were blacksmiths and carpenters, but slaves also worked as masons, mechanics, millers, ginsmiths, and shoemakers. Skilled slave fathers took pride in teaching their crafts to their sons. "My pappy was one of the black smiths and worked in the shop," John Mathews remembered. "I had to help my pappy in the shop when I was a child and I learnt how

Isaac Jefferson
In this 1845 daguerreotype, seventy-year-old Isaac Jefferson proudly poses in the apron he wore while practicing his crafts as a tinsmith and nail maker. Isaac, his wife, and their two children were slaves of Thomas Jefferson. Isaac worked at Jefferson's home, Monticello, until 1820, when he moved to Petersburg, Virginia. Special Collections Department, University of Virginia Library.

to beat out the iron and make wagon tires, and make plows."

Rarest of all slave occupations was that of slave driver. Probably no more than one male slave in a hundred worked in this capacity. These men were well named, for their primary task was driving other slaves to work harder in the fields. In some drivers' hands, the whip never rested. Ex-slave Jane Johnson of South Carolina called her driver the "meanest man, white or black, I ever see." But other drivers showed all the restraint they could. "Ole Gabe didn't like that whippin' business," West Turner of Virginia remembered. "When Marsa was there, he would lay it on 'cause he had to. But when old Marsa wasn't lookin', he never would beat them slaves."

Normally, slaves worked from what they called "can to can't," from "can see" in the morning to "can't see" at night. Even with a break at noon for a meal and rest, it made for a long day. For slaves, Lewis Young recalled, "work, work, work, 'twas all they do."

Family and Religion

From dawn to dusk, slaves worked for the master, but at night and all day Sunday and usually Saturday afternoon, slaves were left largely to themselves. Bone tired perhaps, they nonetheless used the time to develop what mattered most to them. Over the generations, they created a community and a culture of their own that sustained them.

Though severely battered, the black family survived slavery. Young men and women in the quarter fell in love, married, and set up housekeeping in cabins of their own. But no laws recognized slave marriage, and therefore no master was legally obligated to honor the bond. While plantation records show that some slave marriages were long-lasting, the massive deportation associated with the Second Middle Passage destroyed hundreds of thousands of slave families.

In 1858, a slave named Abream Scriven wrote to his wife, who lived on a neighboring plantation in South Carolina. "My dear wife," he began, "I take the pleasure of writing you . . . with much regret to inform you I am Sold to man by the name of Peterson, a Treader and Stays in New Orleans." Before he left for Louisiana, Scriven asked his wife to "give my love to my father and mother and tell them good Bye for me. And if we do not meet in this world I hope to meet in heaven. . . . My dear wife for you and my children my pen cannot express the griffe I feel to be parted from you all." He closed with

"Family Outside Cabin, 1862"
On a plantation just outside Beaufort, South Carolina, this poor, proud, but unnamed family includes at least four generations. Because of slavery's assault of the family life of slaves, very few blacks could gather as many generations. Library of Congress.

words no master would have permitted in a slave's marriage vows: "I remain your truly husband until Death." The letter makes clear Scriven's love for and commitment to his family; it also demonstrates slavery's massive assault on family life in the quarter.

Masters sometimes permitted slave families to work on their own, "overwork," as it was called. In the evenings and on Sundays, they tilled gardens, raised pigs and fowl, and chopped wood, selling the products in the market for a little pocket change. "Den each fam'ly have some chickens and sell dem and de eggs and maybe go huntin' and sell de hides and git some money," a former Alabama slave remembered. "Den us buy what am Sunday clothes with dat money, sech as hats and pants and shoes and dresses." Slave children remembered the extraordinary efforts their parents made to sustain their families, and they held them in high esteem.

Religion also provided slaves with a refuge and a reason for living. In the nineteenth century, evangelical Baptists and Methodists had great success in converting slaves from their African beliefs. Planters promoted Christianity in the quarter because they believed that the slaves' salvation was part of the obligation of paternalism; they also hoped that religion would make slaves more obedient. South Carolina slaveholder Charles Colcock Jones, the leading missionary to the slaves, instructed them "to count their Masters 'worthy of all honour,' as those whom God has placed over them in this world." But slaves laughed up their sleeves at such messages. "That old white preacher just was telling us slaves to be good to our masters," one ex-slave said with a chuckle. "We ain't cared a bit about that stuff he was telling us 'cause we wanted to sing, pray, and serve God in our own way."

Meeting in their cabins or secretly in the woods, slaves created an African American Christianity that served their needs, not the masters'. Laws prohibited teaching slaves to read, but a few could read enough to struggle with the Bible. They interpreted the Christian message themselves. Rather than obedience, their faith emphasized justice. Slaves believed that God kept score and that the accounts of this world would be settled in the next. "God is punishing some of them old suckers and their children right now for the way they use to treat us poor colored folks," one ex-slave declared. But the slaves' faith also spoke to their experiences in this world. In the Old Testament, they discovered Moses, who delivered his people from slavery, and in the New Testament, they found Jesus,

who offered salvation to all. Jesus' message of equality provided a potent antidote to the planters' claim that blacks were an inferior people whom God condemned to slavery.

Christianity did not entirely drive out traditional African beliefs. Even slaves who were Christians sometimes continued to believe that conjurers, witches, and spirits possessed the power to injure and protect. Moreover, slaves' Christian music, preaching, and rituals reflected the influence of Africa, as did many of their secular activities, such as wood carving, quilt making, dancing, and storytelling. But by the mid-nineteenth century, black Christianity had assumed a central place in slaves' quest for freedom. In the words of one spiritual, "O my Lord delivered Daniel / O why not deliver me too?"

Resistance and Rebellion

Slaves did not suffer slavery passively. They were, as whites said, "troublesome property." Slaves understood that accommodation to what they could not change was the price of survival, but in a hundred ways they protested their bondage. Theoretically, the master was all-powerful and the slave powerless. But sustained by their families, religion, and community, slaves engaged in day-to-day resistance against their enslavers.

The spectrum of slave resistance ranged from mild to extreme. Telling a pointed story by the fireside in a slave cabin was probably the mildest form of protest. But when the weak got the better of the strong, as they did in tales of Br'er Rabbit and Br'er Fox (*Br'er* is a contraction of *Brother*), listeners could enjoy the thrill of a vicarious victory over their masters. Protest in the fields was riskier and included putting rocks in their cotton bags before having them weighed, feigning illness, and pretending to be so thickheaded that they could not understand the simplest instruction. Slaves broke so many hoes that owners outfitted the tools with oversized handles. Slaves so mistreated the work animals that masters switched from horses to mules, which could absorb more abuse. Although slaves worked hard in the master's fields, they also sabotaged his interests.

Running away was a common form of protest, but except along the borders with northern states and with Mexico, escape to freedom was almost impossible. Most runaways could hope only to escape for a few days. They sought temporary respite from hard labor or avoided punishment, and their "lying out," as it was known, usually ended when the runaway, worn-out and ragged,

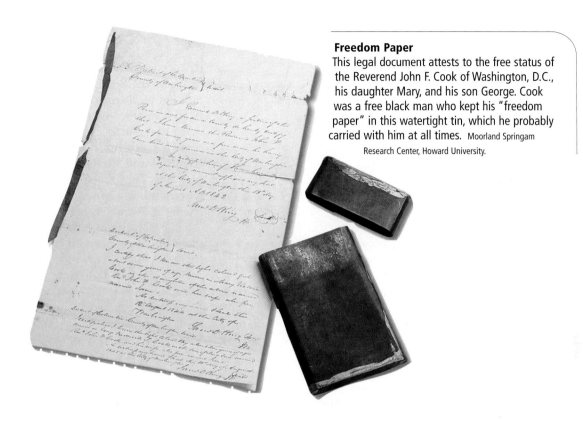

Freedom Paper

This legal document attests to the free status of the Reverend John F. Cook of Washington, D.C., his daughter Mary, and his son George. Cook was a free black man who kept his "freedom paper" in this watertight tin, which he probably carried with him at all times. Moorland Springam Research Center, Howard University.

gave up or was finally chased down by slave-hunting dogs.

Although resistance was common, outright rebellion—a violent assault on slavery by large numbers of slaves—was very rare. Conditions gave rebels almost no chance of success. By 1860, whites in the South outnumbered blacks two to one and were heavily armed. Moreover, communication between plantations was difficult, and the South provided little protective wilderness into which rebels could retreat and defend themselves. Rebellion, as Nat Turner's experience showed (see pages 343–44), was virtual suicide.

Despite steady resistance and occasional rebellion, slaves did not have the power to end their bondage. Slavery thwarted their hopes and aspirations. It broke some and crippled others. But slavery's destructive power had to contend with the resiliency of the human spirit. Slaves fought back physically, culturally, and spiritually. Not only did they survive bondage, but they also created in the quarter a vibrant African American culture that buoyed them up during long hours in the fields and brought them joy and hope in the few hours they had to themselves.

REVIEW   What types of resistance did slaves participate in, and why did slave resistance rarely take the form of rebellion?

▶ The Plain Folk

Most whites in the South did not own slaves, not even one. In 1860, more than six million of the South's eight million whites lived in slaveless households. Some slaveless whites lived in cities and worked as artisans, mechanics, and traders. Others lived in the country and worked as storekeepers, parsons, and schoolteachers. But most "plain folk" were small farmers. Perhaps three out of four were **yeomen**, small farmers who owned their own land. As in the North, farm ownership provided a family with an economic foundation, social respectability, and political standing. Unlike their northern counterparts, however, southern yeomen lived in a region whose economy and society were increasingly dominated by unfree labor.

The Cotton Belt

In an important sense, the South had more than one white yeomanry. The huge southern landscape provided space enough for two yeoman societies, separated roughly along geographic lines. Yeomen throughout the

South had much in common, but the life of a small farm family in the cotton belt—the flatlands that spread from South Carolina to Texas—differed from the life of a family in the upcountry—the area of hills and mountains. And some rural slaveless whites were not yeomen; they owned no land at all and were sometimes desperately poor.

Upcountry of the South

Plantation-Belt Yeomen

Plantation-belt yeomen lived within the orbit of the planter class. Small farms outnumbered plantations in the **plantation belt**, but they were dwarfed in importance. Small farmers grew mainly food crops, particularly corn, but they also produced a few 400-pound bales of cotton each year. Large planters measured their crop in hundreds of bales. Small farmers' cotton tied them to planters. Unable to afford cotton gins or baling presses of their own, they relied on slave owners to gin and bale their cotton. With no link to merchants in the port cities, plantation-belt yeomen also turned to better-connected planters to ship and sell their cotton.

A network of relationships placed small farmers and planters together. Planters hired out surplus slaves to ambitious yeomen who wanted to expand cotton production. They sometimes chose overseers from among the sons of local farm families. Plantation mistresses occasionally nursed ailing neighbors. Family ties could span class lines, making planter and yeoman kin as well as neighbors. Yeomen helped police slaves by riding in slave patrols, which nightly scoured country roads to make certain that no slaves were moving about without permission. On Sundays, plantation dwellers and plain folk came together in church to worship.

Plantation-belt yeomen may have envied, and at times even resented, wealthy slaveholders, but small farmers learned to accommodate. Planters made accommodation easier by going out of their way to behave as good neighbors and avoid direct exploitation of slaveless whites in their community. As a consequence, rather than raging at the oppression of the planter regime, the typical plantation-belt yeoman sought entry into it. He dreamed of adding acreage to his farm, buying a few slaves of his own, and retiring from exhausting field work.

Upcountry Yeomen

By contrast, the hills and mountains of the South resisted the spread of slavery and plantations. In the western parts of Virginia, North Carolina, and South Carolina; in northern Georgia and Alabama; and in eastern Tennessee and Kentucky, the higher elevation, colder climate, rugged terrain, and poor transportation made it difficult for commercial agriculture to make headway. As a result, planters and slaves were scarce. Geographically isolated, the up-country was a yeoman stronghold.

All members of the **upcountry** farm family worked their tasks depending on their sex and age. Husbands labored in the fields, and with their sons they cleared, plowed, planted, and cultivated primarily food crops—corn, wheat, beans, sweet potatoes, and perhaps some fruit. Women and their daughters labored in and about the cabin. One upcountry farmer remembered that his mother "worked in the house cooking, spinning, weaving [and doing] patchwork." Women also tended the vegetable garden, kept a cow and some chickens, preserved food, cleaned their homes, fed their families, and cared for their children. Male and female tasks were equally crucial to the farm's success, but as in other white southern households, the male patriarch ruled the domestic sphere.

The typical upcountry yeoman also grew a little cotton or tobacco, but food production was more important than cash crops. Not much currency changed hands in the upcountry. Barter was common. A yeoman might trade his small cotton or tobacco crop to a country store owner for a little salt, bullets, needles, and nails, or swap extra sweet potatoes for a plow from a blacksmith or for leather from a tanner. Networks of exchange and mutual assistance tied individual homesteads to the larger community. Farm families joined together in logrolling, house and barn raising, and cornhusking.

Even the hills had some plantations and slaves, but the few upcountry folks who owned slaves usually had only two or three. As a result, slaveholders had much less social and economic power, and yeomen had more. But the upcountry did not oppose slavery. As long as plain folk there were free to lead their own lives, they defended slavery and white supremacy just as staunchly as other white Southerners.

Poor Whites

The majority of slaveless white Southerners were hardworking, landholding small farmers, but Northerners held a different image of this group. They believed that slavery had condemned most whites to poverty and backwardness. One antislavery advocate charged that the South harbored three classes: "the slaves on whom devolves all the regular industry, the slaveholders who reap all the fruits, and an idle and lawless rabble who live dispersed over vast plains little removed from absolute barbarism." Critics called this third class a variety of derogatory names: hillbillies, crackers, rednecks, and poor white trash. According to critics, poor whites were not just whites who were poor. They were also supposedly ignorant, diseased, and degenerate.

Contrary to northern opinion, only about one in four nonslaveholding rural white men was landless and very poor. Some worked as tenants, renting land and struggling to make a go of it. Others survived by herding pigs and cattle. And still others worked for meager wages, ditching, mining, logging, and laying track for railroads.

Some poor white men earned reputations for mayhem and violence. One visitor claimed that a "bowie-knife was a universal, and a pistol a not at all unusual companion." Edward Isham, an illiterate roustabout, spent about as much time fighting as he did working. When he was not engaged in ear-biting, eye-gouging free-for-alls, he gambled, drank, stole, had run-ins with the law, and in 1860 murdered a respected slaveholder, for which he was hanged.

Unlike Isham, most poor white men did not engage in ferocious behavior but worked hard and dreamed of becoming yeomen. The Lipscomb family illustrates the possibility of upward mobility. In 1845, Smith and Sally Lipscomb and their children abandoned their worn-out land in South Carolina for Benton County, Alabama. "Benton is a mountainous country but ther is a heep of good levil land to tend in it," Smith wrote back to his brother. Alabama, Smith said, "will be better for the rising generation if not for ourselves but I think it will be the best for us all that live any length of time."

Because they had no money to buy land, they squatted on seven unoccupied acres. With the help of neighbors, they built a 22-by-24-foot cabin, a detached kitchen, and two stables. In the first year, Smith and his sons produced several bales of cotton and enough food for the table. The women worked just as hard in the cabin, and Sally contributed to the family's income by selling homemade shirts and socks. In time, the Lipscombs bought land and joined the Baptist church, completing their transformation to respectable yeomen.

Many poor whites succeeded in climbing the economic ladder, but in the 1850s upward mobility slowed. The cotton boom of that decade caused planters to expand their operations, driving the price of land beyond the reach of poor families. Whether they gained their own land or not, however, poor whites shared common cultural traits with yeoman farmers.

The Culture of the Plain Folk

The lives of most plain folk revolved around farms, family, a handful of neighbors, the local church, and perhaps a country store. Work occupied most hours, but plain folk still found time for pleasure. "Dancing they are all fond of," a visitor to North Carolina discovered, "especially when they can get a fiddle, or bagpipe." But the most popular pastimes of men and boys were fishing and hunting. A traveler in Mississippi recalled that his host sent "two of his sons, little fellows that looked almost too small to shoulder a gun," for food. "One went off towards the river and the other struck into the forest, and in a few hours we were feasting on delicious venison, trout and turtle."

Plain folk did not have much "book learning." Private academies charged fees that yeomen could not afford, and public schools were scarce. "Education is not extended to the masses here as at the North," observed a northern visitor in the 1850s. Although most people managed to pick up the "three R's," approximately one southern white man in five was illiterate in 1860, and the rate for white women was even higher. "People here prefer talking to reading," a Virginian remarked. Telling stories, reciting ballads, and singing hymns were important activities in yeoman culture.

Plain folk spent more hours in revival tents than in classrooms. Preachers spoke day and night to save souls. Baptists and Methodists adopted revivalism most readily and by midcentury had become the South's largest religious groups. By emphasizing free choice and individual worth, the plain folk's religion was hopeful and affirming. Hymns and spirituals provided guides to right and wrong—praising humility and steadfastness, condemning drunkenness and profanity. Above all, hymns spoke of the eventual release from worldly sorrows and the assurance of eternal salvation.

REVIEW   Why did the lives of plantation-belt yeomen and upcountry yeomen diverge?

Camp Meeting, Mid-Nineteenth Century

Camp meetings, or revivals, were a key feature of southern evangelical Christianity. Many preachers were itinerants who spoke wherever they could draw a crowd. Here an earnest clergyman preaches his message in an open field to an audience that includes both the reverent and the not-so-reverent. Private Collection/Picture Research Consultants & Archives.

READING THE IMAGE: What does the dress of the people in the audience say about their class position?

CONNECTIONS: Why were camp meetings so important to southern Methodists and Baptists?

▶ Black and Free: On the Middle Ground

All white Southerners—slaveholders and slaveless alike—considered themselves superior to all blacks. But not every black Southerner was a slave. In 1860, some 260,000 (approximately 6 percent) of the region's 4.1 million African Americans were free. What is surprising is not that their numbers were small but that they existed at all. According to proslavery thinking, blacks were supposed to be slaves; only whites were supposed to be free. Blacks who were free stood out, and whites made them targets of oppression. But a few found success despite the restrictions placed on them by white Southerners.

Precarious Freedom

The population of **free blacks** swelled after the Revolutionary War, when the natural rights philosophy of the Declaration of Independence, the egalitarian message of evangelical Protestantism, and a depression in the tobacco economy of the Upper South, led to a brief flurry of emancipation—the act of freeing from slavery. The soaring numbers of free blacks worried white Southerners, who, because of the cotton boom, wanted more slaves, not more blacks who were free.

In the 1820s and 1830s, state legislatures stemmed the growth of the free black population and shrank the liberty of those blacks who had gained their freedom. New laws denied masters the right to free their slaves. Other laws subjected free blacks to special taxes, prohibited them from interstate travel, denied them the right to have schools and to participate in politics, and required them to carry "freedom papers" to prove they were not slaves. Increasingly, whites subjected free blacks to the same laws as slaves. Free blacks could not testify under oath in a court of law or serve on juries. Free blacks were forbidden to strike whites, even to defend themselves. "Free negroes belong to a degraded caste of society," a South Carolina judge said in 1848. "They are in no respect on a perfect equality with the white man . . . . They ought, by law, to be compelled to demean themselves as inferiors."

Laws confined most free African Americans to poverty and dependence. Typically, free blacks were rural, uneducated, unskilled agricultural laborers and domestic servants who had to scramble to survive. Opportunities of any kind—for work, education, or community—were slim. Planters believed that free blacks set a bad example for slaves, subverting the racial subordination that was the essence of slavery.

Whites feared that free blacks might lead slaves in rebellion. In 1822, whites in Charleston accused Denmark Vesey, a free black carpenter, of conspiring with plantation slaves to slaughter Charleston's white inhabitants. The authorities rounded up scores of suspects, who, prodded by torture and the threat of death, implicated others in a "plot to riot in blood, outrage, and rapine." Although the city fathers never found any weapons and Vesey and most of the accused steadfastly denied the charges of conspiracy, officials hanged thirty-five black men, including Vesey, and banished another thirty-seven blacks from the state.

Achievement Despite Restrictions

Despite increasingly harsh laws and stepped-up persecution, free African Americans made the most of the advantages their status offered. Unlike slaves, free blacks could legally marry and pass on their heritage of freedom to their children. Freedom also meant that they could choose occupations and own property. For most, however, these economic rights proved only theoretical, for a majority of the South's free blacks remained propertyless.

Still, some free blacks escaped the poverty and degradation whites thrust on them. Particularly in the South's cities, a free black elite emerged. Consisting of light-skinned African Americans, this group worked at skilled trades, as tailors, carpenters, mechanics, and the like. Their customers were prominent whites—planters, merchants, and judges—who appreciated their able, respectful service. Urban whites enforced many of the restrictive laws only sporadically, allowing free blacks room to maneuver. They operated schools for their children and traveled in and out of their states, despite laws forbidding both activities. They worshipped with whites (in separate seating) and lived scattered about in white neighborhoods, not in ghettos. And some owned slaves. Of the 3,200 black slaveholders (barely 1 percent of the free black population), most owned only a few family members whom they could not legally free. Others owned slaves in large numbers and exploited them for labor.

One such free black slave owner was William Ellison of South Carolina. Born a slave in 1790, Ellison bought his freedom in 1816 and set up business as a cotton gin maker, a trade he had learned as a slave. His business grew with the cotton boom, and by 1835 he was prosperous enough to purchase the home of a former governor of the state. By the time of his death in 1861, he had become a cotton planter, with sixty-three slaves and an 800-acre plantation.

Most free blacks neither became slaveholders nor sought to raise a slave rebellion, as whites accused Denmark Vesey of doing. Rather, most free blacks simply tried to preserve their freedom, which was under increasing attack. Unlike blacks in the North whose freedom was secure, free blacks in the South clung to a precarious freedom by seeking to impress whites with their reliability, economic contributions, and good behavior.

REVIEW Why did many state legislatures pass laws restricting free blacks' rights in the 1820s and 1830s?

▶ The Politics of Slavery

By the mid-nineteenth century, all southern white men—planters and plain folk—and no southern black men, even those who were free, could vote. But even after the South's politics became democratic for white males, political power remained unevenly distributed. The non-slaveholding white majority wielded less political power than their numbers indicated. The slaveholding white minority wielded more. With a well-developed sense of class interest, slaveholders engaged in party politics, campaigns, and officeholding, and as a result they received significant benefits from state governments. Nonslaveholding whites were concerned mainly with preserving their liberties and keeping their taxes low. They asked government for little of an economic nature, and they received little.

Slaveholders sometimes worried about non-slaveholders' loyalty to slavery, but most whites accepted the planters' argument that the existing social order served *all* Southerners' interests. Slavery rewarded every white man—no matter how poor—with membership in the South's white ruling race. It also provided the means by which nonslaveholders might someday advance into the ranks of the planters. White men in the South argued furiously about many things, but they agreed that they should take land from Indians, promote agriculture, uphold white supremacy and masculine privilege, and defend slavery from its enemies.

The Democratization of the Political Arena

In the first half of the nineteenth century, Southerners eliminated the wealth and property requirements that had once restricted political participation. By the 1850s, every state had extended the right to vote to all adult white males. Most southern states also removed the property requirements for holding state offices. To be sure, undemocratic features lingered. Plantation districts still wielded disproportionate power in several state legislatures. Nevertheless, southern politics took place within an increasingly democratic political structure, as it did elsewhere in the nation.

White male suffrage ushered in an era of vigorous electoral competition in the South. Eager voters rushed to the polls to exercise their new rights. Candidates crisscrossed their electoral districts, treating citizens to barbecues and bands, rum and races, as well as stirring oratory.

In the South, it seemed, "everybody talked politics everywhere," even the "illiterate and shoeless."

As politics became aggressively democratic, it also grew fiercely partisan. From the 1830s to the 1850s, Whigs and Democrats battled for the electorate's favor. Both parties presented themselves as the plain white folk's best friend. All candidates declared their allegiance to republican equality and pledged themselves to defend the people's liberty. And each party sought to portray the other as a collection of rich, snobbish, selfish men who had antidemocratic designs up their silk sleeves.

Planter Power

Whether Whig or Democrat, southern officeholders were likely to be slave owners. The power that slaveholders exerted over slaves did not translate directly into political authority over whites, however. In the nineteenth century, political power could only be won at the ballot box, and almost everywhere nonslaveholders were in the majority. Yet year after year, proud and noisily egalitarian common men elected wealthy slaveholders.

By 1860, the percentage of slave owners in state legislatures ranged from 41 percent in Missouri to nearly 86 percent in North Carolina (Table 13.1). Legislators not only tended to own slaves; they also often owned large numbers. The percentage of planters (individuals with twenty or more slaves) in southern legislatures in 1860 ranged from 5.3 percent in Missouri to 55.4 percent in South Carolina. Even in North Carolina, where only 3 percent of the state's white families belonged to the planter class, more than 36 percent of state legislators were planters. Clearly, plain folk did not throw the planters out of office.

Upper-class dominance of southern politics reflected the elite's success in persuading the yeoman majority that what was good for slaveholders was also good for plain folk. In reality, the South had, on the whole, done well by common white men. Most had farms of their own. They participated as equals in a democratic political system. They enjoyed an elevated social status, above all blacks and in theory equal to all other whites. They commanded patriarchal authority over their households. And as long as slavery existed, they could dream of joining the planter class. Slaveless white men found much to celebrate in the slave South.

Most slaveholders took pains to win the plain folk's trust and to nurture their respect. One nonslaveholder told his wealthy neighbor that he had a bright political future because he never thought himself "too good to sit down & talk to a poor man." Mary Boykin Chesnut complained about the fawning attention her husband, U.S. senator from South Carolina, showed to poor men, including one who had "mud sticking up through his toes." But smart candidates found ways to convince wary plain folk of their democratic convictions and egalitarian sentiments, whether they were genuine or not. Walter L. Steele, who ran for a seat in the North Carolina legislature in 1846, detested campaigning for votes, but he learned, he said, to speak with a "candied tongue."

Georgia politics illustrate how well planters protected their interests in state legislatures. In 1850, about half of the state's revenues came from taxes on slaves, the principal form of planter wealth. However, the tax rate on slaves was trifling, only about one-fifth the rate on land. Moreover, planters benefited from public spending far more than other groups did. Financing railroads—which carried cotton to market—was the largest state expenditure. The legislature also established low tax rates on land, the principal form of yeomen wealth, which meant that the typical yeoman's annual tax bill was small. Still, relative to their

TABLE 13.1	PERCENT OF SLAVEHOLDERS AND PLANTERS IN SOUTHERN LEGISLATURES, 1860	
Legislature	Slaveholders	Planters*
North Carolina	85.8%	36.6%
South Carolina	81.7	55.4
Alabama	76.3	40.8
Mississippi	73.4	49.5
Georgia	71.6	29.0
Virginia	67.3	24.2
Tennessee	66.0	14.0
Louisiana	63.8	23.5
Kentucky	60.6	8.4
Florida	55.4	20.0
Texas	54.1	18.1
Maryland	53.4	19.3
Arkansas	42.0	13.0
Missouri	41.2	5.3

*Planters: Owned 20 or more slaves.

SOURCE: Adapted from Ralph A. Wooster, *The People in Power: Courthouse and Statehouse in the Lower South, 1850–1860*, page 40. Copyright © 1975 by Ralph A. Wooster. Courtesy of the University of Tennessee Press.

wealth, large slaveholders paid less than did other whites. Relative to their numbers, they got more. Slaveholding legislators protected planters' interests and gave the impression of protecting the small farmers' interests as well.

In addition to politics, slaveholders defended slavery in other ways. In the 1830s, Southerners decided that slavery was too important to debate. "So interwoven is [slavery] with our interest, our manners, our climate and our very being," one man declared in 1833, "that no change can ever possibly be effected without a civil commotion from which the heart of a patriot must turn with horror." Powerful whites dismissed slavery's critics from college faculties, drove them from pulpits, and hounded them from political life. Sometimes antislavery Southerners fell victim to vigilantes and mob violence. One could defend slavery; one could even delicately suggest mild reforms. But no Southerner could any longer safely call slavery evil or advocate its destruction.

In the South, therefore, the rise of the common man occurred alongside the continuing, even growing, power of the planter class. Rather than pitting slaveholders against nonslaveholders, elections remained an effective means of binding the region's whites together. Elections affirmed the sovereignty of white men, whether planter or plain folk, and the subordination of African Americans. Those twin themes played well among white women as well. Though unable to vote, white women supported equality for whites and slavery for blacks. In the antebellum South, the politics of slavery helped knit together all of white society.

REVIEW   How did planters retain political power in a democratic system?

▶ Conclusion: A Slave Society

By the early nineteenth century, northern states had either abolished slavery or put it on the road to extinction, while southern states were building the largest slave society in the New World. Regional differences increased over time, not merely because the South became more and more dominated by slavery, but also because developments in the North rapidly propelled it in a very different direction.

By 1860, one-third of the South's population was enslaved. Bondage saddled blacks with enormous physical and spiritual burdens: hard labor, harsh treatment, broken families, and, most important, the denial of freedom itself. Although degraded and exploited, they were not defeated. Out of African memories and New World realities, blacks created a life-affirming African American culture that sustained and strengthened them. Their families, religion, and community provided defenses against white racism and power. Defined as property, they refused to be reduced to things. Perceived as inferior beings, they rejected the notion that they were natural slaves.

The South was not merely a society with slaves; it had become a slave society. Slavery shaped the region's economy, culture, social structure, and politics. Whites south of the Mason-Dixon line believed that racial slavery was necessary and just. By making all blacks a pariah class, all whites gained a measure of equality and harmony.

Many features of southern life helped to confine class tensions among whites: the wide availability of land, rapid economic mobility, the democratic nature of political life, the patriarchal power among all white men, and, most of all, slavery and white supremacy. All stress along class lines did not disappear, however, and anxious slaveholders continued to worry that yeomen would defect from the proslavery consensus. But during the 1850s, white Southerners' near universal acceptance of slavery would increasingly unite them in political opposition to their northern neighbors.

See the Selected Bibliography for this chapter in the Appendix.

13 | Chapter Review

MAKE IT STICK

 **LearningCurve**

Go online and use LearningCurve to see what you know. Then review the key terms and answer the questions.

KEY TERMS

Mason-Dixon line (p. 346)
cotton kingdom (p. 346)
slave codes (p. 348)
miscegenation (p. 348)
planter (p. 349)
plantation (p. 350)
paternalism (p. 355)
chivalry (p. 358)
yeomen (p. 363)
plantation belt (p. 364)
upcountry (p. 364)
free black (p. 366)

REVIEW QUESTIONS

1. Why did the nineteenth-century southern economy remain primarily agricultural? (pp. 345–354)

2. Why did the ideology of paternalism gain currency among planters in the nineteenth century? (pp. 354–359)

3. What types of resistance did slaves participate in, and why did slave resistance rarely take the form of rebellion? (pp. 360–363)

4. Why did the lives of plantation-belt yeomen and upcountry yeomen diverge? (pp. 363–365)

5. Why did many state legislatures pass laws restricting free blacks' rights in the 1820s and 1830s? (pp. 366–367)

6. How did planters retain political power in a democratic system? (pp. 367–369)

MAKING CONNECTIONS

1. How did cotton's profitability shape the region's antebellum development?

2. How did southern white legislators and intellectuals attempt to strengthen the institution of slavery in the 1820s? What prompted them to do this?

3. Discuss the variety of ways in which slaves attempted to resist slavery. What were the short- and long-term effects of their efforts?

4. Despite vigorous political competition in the South, by 1860 legislative power was largely concentrated in the hands of a regional minority—slaveholders. Why were slaveholders politically dominant?

LINKING TO THE PAST

1. Compare and contrast Northerners' defense of free labor and white Southerners' defense of slave labor. (See chapter 12.)

2. How did President Andrew Jackson's Indian removal policies pave the way for the South's cotton empire? (See chapter 11.)

14 The House Divided
1846–1861

After reading and studying this chapter, you should be able to:

- Explain why the question of extending slavery to federal territories was the focus of constitutional debate from 1846 to 1860. Define the Wilmot Proviso, including who supported and opposed it, and why.

- Relate how the debate over the expansion of slavery affected the election of 1848. Explain what led to the Compromise of 1850.

- Determine what destroyed the second American party system in the 1850s, and how the electorate realigned.

- Describe how Kansas was settled and organized, and how it got the name "Bleeding Kansas." Explain the *Dred Scott* decision and how it shaped the perceptions of the North.

- Explain the political rise of Abraham Lincoln.

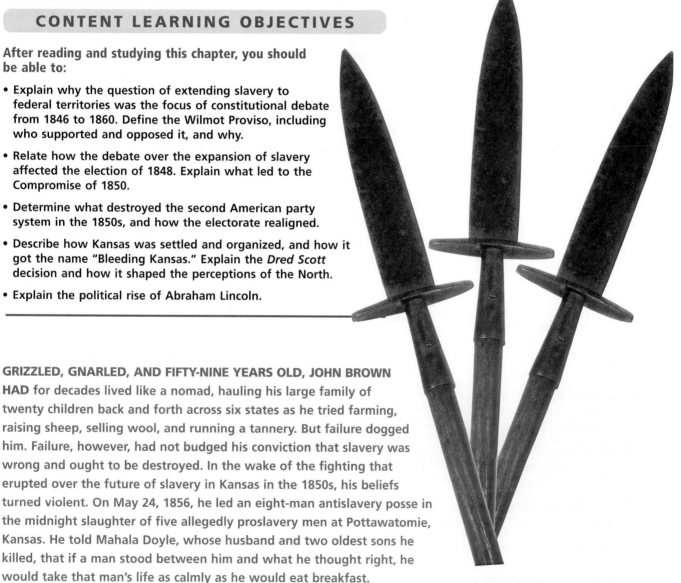

GRIZZLED, GNARLED, AND FIFTY-NINE YEARS OLD, JOHN BROWN HAD for decades lived like a nomad, hauling his large family of twenty children back and forth across six states as he tried farming, raising sheep, selling wool, and running a tannery. But failure dogged him. Failure, however, had not budged his conviction that slavery was wrong and ought to be destroyed. In the wake of the fighting that erupted over the future of slavery in Kansas in the 1850s, his beliefs turned violent. On May 24, 1856, he led an eight-man antislavery posse in the midnight slaughter of five allegedly proslavery men at Pottawatomie, Kansas. He told Mahala Doyle, whose husband and two oldest sons he killed, that if a man stood between him and what he thought right, he would take that man's life as calmly as he would eat breakfast.

After the killings, Brown slipped out of Kansas and reemerged in the East, where for thirty months he begged money to support his vague plan for military operations against slavery. On the night of October 16, 1859, Brown took his war against slavery into the South. With only twenty-one men, including five African Americans, he invaded Harpers Ferry, Virginia. His band seized the town's armory and rifle works, but the invaders were immediately surrounded. When Brown refused to surrender, federal troops under Colonel Robert E. Lee charged with bayonets. Although a few of

JOHN BROWN'S PIKES
In 1859 John Brown brought his abolitionist war to Harpers Ferry, Virginia. He carried with him 950 pikes, which he expected to put into the hands of rebelling slaves. © Chicago History Museum, USA/The Bridgeman Art Library.

Brown's raiders escaped, federal forces killed ten of his men (including two of his sons) and captured seven, among them Brown.

Months before the raid, Brown had claimed, "When I strike, the bees will begin to swarm." Brown said he would arm slaves and they would then fight a war of liberation. Brown, however, neglected to inform the slaves when he had arrived in Harpers Ferry, and the few who knew of his arrival wanted nothing to do with his enterprise. "It was not a slave insurrection," Abraham Lincoln observed. "It was an attempt by white men to get up a revolt among slaves, in which the slaves refused to participate. In fact, it was so absurd that the slaves, with all their ignorance, saw plainly enough it could not succeed."

White Southerners viewed Brown's raid as proof that Northerners actively sought to incite slaves in bloody rebellion. Sectional tension was as old as the Constitution, but hostility had escalated with the outbreak of war with Mexico in May 1846 (see "The Mexican American War, 1846–1848" in chapter 12). Only three months after the war began, national expansion and the slavery issue intersected when Representative David Wilmot introduced a bill to prohibit slavery in any territory that might be acquired as a result of the war. After that, the problem of slavery in the territories became the principal wedge that divided the nation.

"Mexico is to us the forbidden fruit," South Carolina senator John C. Calhoun declared at the war's outset. "The penalty of eating it [is] to subject our institutions to political death." For a decade and a half, the slavery issue intertwined with the fate of former Mexican land, poisoning the national political debate. Slavery proved powerful enough to transform party politics into sectional politics. Rather than Whigs and Democrats confronting one another across party lines, Northerners and Southerners eyed one another hostilely across the Mason-Dixon line. As the nation lurched from crisis to crisis, southern disaffection and alienation mounted, and support for compromise eroded. The era began with a crisis of union and ended with the Union in even graver peril. As Abraham Lincoln predicted in 1858, "A house divided against itself cannot stand."

John Brown

In this 1859 photograph, John Brown appears respectable, but contemporaries debated his mental state and moral character, and the debate still rages. Critics argue that he was a bloody terrorist, a religious fanatic who believed that he was touched by God for a great purpose. Admirers see a selfless hero, a shrewd political observer who recognized that only violence would end slavery in America. Library of Congress.

► The Bitter Fruits of War

Victory in the Mexican-American War brought vast new territories in the West into the United States. The gold rush of 1849 transformed the sleepy frontier of California into a booming economy (see "Golden California" in chapter 12). The 1850s witnessed new "rushes," for gold in Colorado and silver in Nevada's Comstock Lode. The phenomenal economic growth of the West demanded the attention of the federal government, but it quickly became clear that Northerners and Southerners had very different visions of the West, particularly the place of slavery in its future. From 1846, when it first appeared that the war with Mexico might mean new territory for the United States, politicians battled over whether to ban slavery from former Mexican land or permit it to expand to the Pacific. In 1850 Congress patched together a plan that Americans hoped would last. This plan for expansion envisioned stability only for the Anglo Americans, however. Native Americans in the West would soon see their traditional way of life disrupted. (See "Visualizing History," page 374.)

The Wilmot Proviso and the Expansion of Slavery

Most Americans agreed that the Constitution left the issue of slavery to the individual states to decide. Northern states had done away with slavery, while southern states had retained it. But what about slavery in the nation's territories? The Constitution states that "Congress shall have power to . . . make all needful rules and regulations respecting the territory . . . belonging to the United States." The debate about slavery, then, turned toward Congress.

The spark for the national debate appeared in August 1846 when a Democratic representative from Pennsylvania, David Wilmot, proposed that Congress bar slavery from all lands acquired in the war with Mexico. The Mexicans had abolished slavery in their country, and Wilmot declared, "God forbid that we should be the means of planting this institution upon it."

Regardless of party affiliation, Northerners lined up behind the **Wilmot Proviso**. Many supported free soil, by which they meant territory in which slavery would be prohibited, because they wanted to preserve the West for **free labor**, for hardworking, self-reliant free men, not for

CHRONOLOGY

1820	• Missouri Compromise.
1846	• Wilmot Proviso introduced.
1847	• Wilmot Proviso defeated in Senate. • "Popular sovereignty" compromise offered.
1848	• Free-Soil Party founded. • Zachary Taylor elected president.
1849	• California gold rush.
1850	• Taylor dies; Vice President Millard Fillmore becomes president. • Compromise of 1850 becomes law.
1852	• *Uncle Tom's Cabin* published. • Franklin Pierce elected president.
1853	• Gadsden Purchase.
1854	• American (Know-Nothing) Party emerges. • Kansas-Nebraska Act. • Republican Party founded.
1856	• "Bleeding Kansas." • "Sack of Lawrence." • Pottawatomie massacre. • James Buchanan elected president.
1857	• *Dred Scott* decision. • Congress rejects Lecompton constitution. • Panic of 1857.
1858	• Lincoln-Douglas debates; Douglas wins Senate seat.
1859	• John Brown raids Harpers Ferry.
1860	• Abraham Lincoln elected president. • South Carolina secedes from Union.
1861	• Six other Lower South states secede. • Confederate States of America formed.

Games among the Sioux

Neither proslavery Southerners nor antislavery Northerners were much concerned about the Native Americans who inhabited the western lands they coveted. But Seth Eastman (1808–1875), who graduated from the U.S. Military Academy at West Point in 1829 and began a long career in the U.S. Army, recorded sympathetically the lives he encountered. While stationed at Fort Snelling in present-day Minnesota, he began observing the local Indians and learning their languages. (He also married Wakanin ajin win, the fifteen-year-old daughter of a Dakota chief, whom he left behind when he was transferred.) He began to paint scenes of the everyday lives of Indians—marriage customs, the gathering of wild rice, and games. Because he was a military officer, he spent more time in the field than any other artist. And because his duties were often light, he was prolific, producing hundreds of carefully done paintings.

In *Ball Playing among the Sioux Indians*, Eastman captures Sioux playing an early version of lacrosse. Eastman's second wife, Virginia-born Mary Henderson Eastman, who was also a student of Indian cultures, said that the object of the game was "to get the ball (a piece of baked clay covered with deer skin) beyond a certain line." She added, "This is rough play, limbs are often broken and lives lost." Eastman captures the speed and the danger of the game. Some men have their sticks raised; others have been knocked to the ground. Yet it is clearly a game, not warfare (although rough games like this certainly helped prepare young men for war). Most of the sticks are on the ground, going for the ball. Spectators—men and women—enjoy the action from a nearby hillside. Eastman sets the game in the majestic West—green grass, open fields, craggy mountains, and a glorious cloud-filled sky. It adds up to a painting that is both beautiful and painstakingly accurate.

As an artist, Eastman was a realist, painting Indian life as he saw it lived. He was a meticulous craftsman, owing perhaps to his training in topographical drawing (map

---

slaveholders and slaves. But support also came from those who were simply anti-South. New slave territories would eventually mean new slave states. Wilmot himself said his proposal would blunt *"the power* of slaveholders" in the national government.

Additional support for free soil came from Northerners who were hostile to blacks and wanted to reserve new land for whites. Wilmot himself blatantly encouraged racist support when he declared, "I would preserve for free white labor a fair country, a rich inheritance, where the sons of toil, of my own race and own color, can live without the disgrace which association with negro slavery brings upon free labor." It is no wonder that some called the Wilmot Proviso the "White Man's Proviso."

The thought that slavery might be excluded in the territories outraged white Southerners. Like Northerners, they regarded the West as a ladder for economic and social opportunity. They also believed that

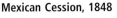

Mexican Cession, 1848

the exclusion of slavery was a slap in the face to southern veterans of the Mexican-American War. "When the war-worn soldier returns home," one Alabaman asked, "is he to be told that he cannot carry his property to the country won by his blood?" In addition, southern leaders also sought to maintain political parity with the North to protect the South's interests, especially slavery. The need seemed especially urgent in the 1840s, when the North's population and wealth were booming. James Henry Hammond of South Carolina predicted that ten new states would be carved from the acquired Mexican land. If free soil won, the North would "ride over us roughshod" in Congress, he claimed. "Our only safety is in *equality* of power."

Foes of slavery's expansion and foes of slavery's exclusion squared off in the nation's capital. Because Northerners had a majority in the House, they easily passed the Wilmot Proviso. In the Senate, however, where slave states outnumbered free

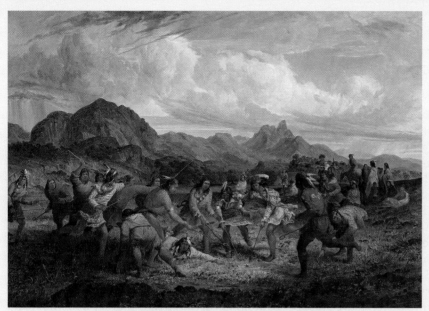

Ball Playing Among the Sioux Indians (1851)

as he could the customs of the Chippewa, Winnebago, and Sioux that he had come to know.

SOURCE: Corcoran Gallery of Art, Washington D.C., USA/ The Bridgeman Art Library.

Questions for Analysis

1. How would easterners viewing this painting have known that it was a scene from the West?

2. Does the artist present a hostile or a benevolent landscape?

3. What is the artist suggesting by placing spectators on the hill?

Connect to the Big Idea

C Would *Ball Playing among the Sioux Indians* have challenged or confirmed most Americans' view of Native Americans, and why?

making) at West Point. Unlike artists who sought to thrill stay-at-home whites with glimpses of savage ways or to move them to admiration through romanticized portraits, Eastman sought to record as closely

states fifteen to fourteen, Southerners defeated it in 1847. Senator John C. Calhoun of South Carolina denied that Congress had the constitutional authority to exclude slavery from the nation's territories. He argued that because the territories were the "joint and common property" of all the states, Congress could not bar citizens of one state from migrating with their property (including slaves) to the territories. Whereas Wilmot demanded that Congress slam shut the door to slavery, Calhoun called on Congress to hold the door wide open.

Senator Lewis Cass of Michigan offered a compromise through the doctrine of **popular sovereignty**, by which the people who settled the territories would decide for themselves slavery's fate. This solution, Cass argued, sat squarely in the American tradition of democracy and local self-government. Popular sovereignty's most attractive feature was its ambiguity about the precise moment when settlers could determine slavery's fate. Northern advocates believed that the decision on slavery could be made as soon as the first territorial legislature assembled. With free-soil majorities likely because of the North's greater population, they would shut the door to slavery immediately. Southern supporters believed that popular sovereignty guaranteed

that slavery would be unrestricted throughout the entire territorial period. Only when settlers in a territory drew up a constitution and applied for statehood could they decide the issue of slavery. By then, slavery would have sunk deep roots. As long as the matter of timing remained vague, popular sovereignty gave hope to both sides.

When Congress ended its session in 1848, no plan had won a majority in both houses. Northerners who demanded no new slave territory anywhere, ever, and Southerners who demanded entry for their slave property into all territories, or else, staked out their extreme positions. Unresolved in Congress, the territorial question naturally became an issue in the presidential election of 1848.

The Election of 1848

When President Polk, worn-out and ailing, chose not to seek reelection, the Democratic convention nominated Lewis Cass of Michigan, the man most closely associated with popular sovereignty. The Whigs nominated a Mexican-American War hero, General Zachary Taylor, a man who had never voted and who had no known political opinions. The Whigs declined to adopt a party platform, betting that the combination of a military hero and total silence on the slavery issue would unite their divided party. Taylor, who owned more than one hundred slaves on plantations in Mississippi and Louisiana, was hailed by Georgia politician Robert Toombs as a "Southern man, a slaveholder, a cotton planter."

Antislavery Whigs balked. Senator Charles Sumner called for a major political realignment, "one grand Northern party of Freedom." In the summer of 1848, antislavery Whigs and antislavery Democrats founded the Free-Soil Party, nominating a Democrat, Martin Van Buren, for president and a Whig, Charles Francis Adams, for vice president. The platform boldly proclaimed, "Free soil, free speech, free labor, and free men."

The November election dashed the hopes of the Free-Soilers. They did not carry a single state. Taylor won the all-important electoral vote 163 to 127, carrying eight of the fifteen slave states and seven of the fifteen free states (Map 14.1). (Wisconsin had entered the Union earlier in 1848 as the fifteenth free state.) Northern voters were not yet ready for Sumner's "one grand Northern party of Freedom," but the struggle over slavery in the territories had shaken the major parties badly.

Debate and Compromise

Zachary Taylor was very much a mystery when he entered the White House in March 1849. Almost immediately, the slaveholding president

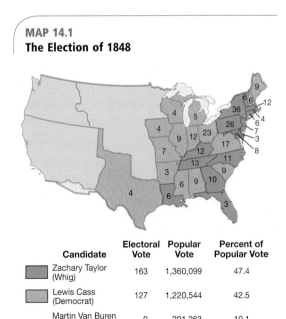

MAP 14.1
The Election of 1848

Candidate	Electoral Vote	Popular Vote	Percent of Popular Vote
Zachary Taylor (Whig)	163	1,360,099	47.4
Lewis Cass (Democrat)	127	1,220,544	42.5
Martin Van Buren (Free-Soil)	0	291,263	10.1

shocked the nation by championing a free-soil solution to the Mexican cession. Believing that he could avoid further sectional strife if California and New Mexico skipped the territorial stage, Taylor encouraged the settlers to apply for admission to the Union as states. Predominantly antislavery, the settlers began writing free-state constitutions. "For the first time," Mississippian Jefferson Davis lamented, "we are about permanently to destroy the balance of power between the sections."

Congress convened in December 1849, beginning one of the most contentious and most significant sessions in its history. President Taylor urged Congress to admit California as a free state immediately and to admit New Mexico, which lagged behind a few months, as soon as it applied. Southerners exploded. A North Carolinian declared that Southerners who would "consent to be thus degraded and enslaved, ought to be whipped through their fields by their own negroes."

Into this rancorous scene stepped Senator Henry Clay of Kentucky, the architect of Union-saving compromises in the Missouri and nullification crises (see chapters 10 and 11). Clay offered a series of resolutions meant to answer and balance "all questions in controversy between the free and slave states, growing out of the subject of slavery." Admit California as a free state, he proposed, but organize the rest of the Southwest without restrictions on slavery. Require Texas to abandon its claim to parts of New Mexico, but compensate it by assuming its preannexation debt. Abolish the domestic slave trade in Washington, D.C., but confirm slavery itself in the nation's capital. Affirm Congress's lack of authority to interfere with the interstate slave trade, and enact a more effective fugitive slave law.

Both antislavery advocates and "fire-eaters" (as radical Southerners who urged secession from the Union were called) savaged Clay's plan. Senator Salmon P. Chase of Ohio ridiculed it as "sentiment for the North, substance for the South." Senator Henry S. Foote of Mississippi denounced it as more offensive to the South than the speeches of abolitionists William Lloyd Garrison, Wendell Phillips, and Frederick Douglass combined. The most ominous response came from Calhoun, who argued that the fragile political unity of North and South depended on continued equal representation in the Senate, which Clay's plan for a free California destroyed. "As things now stand," he said in February 1850, the South "cannot with safety remain in the Union."

VISUAL ACTIVITY

Henry Clay Offering His California Compromise to the Senate on 5 February 1850
Artist Peter F. Rothermel captures the high intensity of the seventy-three-year-old Kentuckian's last significant political act. Citizens who packed the galleries of the U.S. Senate had come to hear the renowned orator explain that his package of compromises required mutual concessions from both North and South but no sacrifice of "great principle" from either. Friends called his performance the "crowning grace to his public life." The Granger Collection, New York.

READING THE IMAGE: What about the painting suggests either that the artist admired Clay and his effort for compromise or found his effort silly and wrongheaded?
CONNECTIONS: How did Northerners and Southerners respond to Clay's claim that his compromise required no sacrifice of "great principle"?

Massachusetts Senator Daniel Webster then addressed the Senate. Like Clay, Webster defended compromise. He told Northerners that the South had legitimate complaints, but he told Southerners that secession from the Union would mean civil war. He argued that the Wilmot Proviso's ban on slavery in the territories was reckless and unnecessary because the harsh climate effectively prohibited the expansion of cotton and slaves into the new American Southwest. Why, then, "taunt" Southerners with the proviso? "I would not take pains uselessly

to reaffirm an ordinance of nature, nor to reenact the will of God," Webster declared.

Free-soil forces recoiled from what they saw as Webster's desertion. Senator William H. Seward of New York responded that Webster's and Clay's compromise with slavery was "radically wrong and essentially vicious." He rejected Calhoun's argument that Congress lacked the constitutional authority to exclude slavery from the territories. In any case, Seward said, there was a "higher law than the Constitution"—the law of God—to ensure freedom in all the public domain. Claiming that God was a Free-Soiler did nothing to cool the superheated political atmosphere.

In May 1850, the Senate considered a bill that joined Clay's resolutions into a single comprehensive package. Clay bet that a majority of Congress wanted compromise and that the members would vote for the package, even though it contained provisions they disliked. But the strategy backfired. Free-Soilers and proslavery Southerners voted down the comprehensive plan.

Fortunately for those who favored a settlement, Senator Stephen A. Douglas, a rising Democratic star from Illinois, broke the bill into its parts and skillfully ushered each through Congress. The agreement Douglas won in September 1850 was very much the one Clay had proposed in January. California entered the Union as a free state. New Mexico and Utah became territories where slavery would be decided by popular sovereignty. Texas accepted its boundary with New Mexico and received $10 million from the federal government. Congress ended the slave trade in the District of Columbia but enacted a more stringent fugitive slave law. In September, Millard Fillmore, who had become president when Zachary Taylor died in July, signed into law each bill, collectively known as the **Compromise of 1850** (Map 14.2).

The nation breathed a sigh of relief, for the Compromise preserved the Union and peace for the moment. But as some understood, the Compromise of 1850 was not a true compromise at all. Douglas's parliamentary skill, not a spirit of conciliation, was responsible for the legislative success. The Compromise scarcely touched the deep conflict over slavery. Free-Soiler Salmon Chase observed, "The question of slavery in the territories has been avoided. It has not been settled."

REVIEW How might the Compromise of 1850 have eased sectional tensions?

MAP 14.2
The Compromise of 1850
The patched-together sectional agreement was both clumsy and unstable. Few Americans—in either North or South—supported all five parts of the Compromise.

Legend:
- Free state or territory
- Slave state
- Opened to slavery by principle of popular sovereignty
- • Slave trade ended

▶ The Sectional Balance Undone

The Compromise of 1850 began to come apart almost immediately. Surprisingly, the thread that unraveled it was not slavery in the territories, the crux of the disagreement, but runaway slaves in New England, a part of the settlement that had previously received little attention. The implementation of the Fugitive Slave Act brought the horrors of slavery into the North. Moreover, millions of Northerners who never saw a runaway slave confronted slavery through Harriet Beecher Stowe's *Uncle Tom's Cabin*, a novel that vividly depicts the brutality of the South's "peculiar institution." Congress did its part to undo the Compromise as well. Four years after Congress stitched the sectional compromise together, it ripped the threads out. With the Kansas-Nebraska Act in 1854, it again posed the question of slavery in the territories, the deadliest of all sectional issues.

The Fugitive Slave Act

The issue of runaway slaves was as old as the Constitution, which contained a provision for the return of any "person held to service or labor in one state" who escaped to another. In 1793, a federal law gave muscle to the provision by authorizing slave owners to enter other states to recapture their slave property. Proclaiming the 1793 law a license to kidnap free blacks, northern states in the 1830s began passing "personal liberty laws" that provided fugitives with some protection.

Some northern communities also formed vigilance committees to help runaways. Each year, a few hundred slaves escaped into free states and found friendly northern "conductors" who put them aboard the underground railroad, which was not a railroad at all but a series of secret "stations" (hideouts) on the way to Canada. Harriet Tubman, an escaped slave from Maryland, returned more than a dozen times and guided more than three hundred slaves to freedom in this way.

Fugitive Ellen Craft in Disguise
In 1848, William and Ellen Craft, a slave couple from Macon, Georgia, executed a daring escape. Light-skinned, Ellen disguised herself as a sickly southern gentleman who was traveling to Philadelphia for medical treatment. She carried her arm in a sling to explain why she couldn't sign travel documents. William acted as her personal servant as they anxiously made their way by train to Savannah, then on to Philadelphia by boat and train. The Crafts told their daring story throughout the North until the Fugitive Slave Law of 1850 drove them to Britain, where adoring crowds greeted them as celebrities. *Documenting the American South*, The University of North Carolina at Chapel Hill Library.

Furious about northern interference, Southerners in 1850 insisted on the stricter fugitive slave law that was part of the Compromise. According to the **Fugitive Slave Act**, to seize an alleged slave, a slaveholder simply had to appear before a commissioner and swear that the runaway was his. The commissioner earned $10 for every individual returned to slavery but only $5 for those set free. Most galling to Northerners, the law stipulated that all citizens were expected to assist officials in apprehending runaways. That required Northerners to become slave catchers.

In Boston in February 1851, an angry crowd overpowered federal marshals and snatched a runaway named Shadrach from a courtroom, put him on the underground railroad, and whisked him off to Canada. Three years later, when another Boston crowd rushed the courthouse in a failed attempt to rescue runaway Anthony Burns, a guard was shot dead. To white Southerners, it seemed that fanatics of the "higher law" creed had whipped Northerners into a frenzy of massive resistance.

Actually, the overwhelming majority of fugitives claimed by slaveholders were re-enslaved peacefully. But brutal enforcement of the unpopular law had a radicalizing effect in the North, particularly in New England. Textile owner Amos A. Lawrence said that "we went to bed one night old fashioned, conservative, Compromise Union Whigs & waked up stark mad abolitionists." He exaggerated, but to Southerners, Northerners had betrayed the Compromise and the Constitution. "The continued existence of the United States as one nation," warned the *Southern Literary Messenger*, "depends upon the full and faithful execution of the Fugitive Slave Bill."

Uncle Tom's Cabin

The spectacle of shackled African Americans being herded south seared the conscience of every Northerner who witnessed such a scene. But even more Northerners were turned against slavery by a novel. Harriet Beecher Stowe, a white Northerner who had never set foot on a plantation, made the South's slaves into flesh-and-blood human beings almost more real than life.

A member of a famous clan of preachers, teachers, and reformers, Stowe despised the slave catchers and wrote to expose the sin of slavery. Published as a book in 1852, *Uncle Tom's Cabin, or Life among the Lowly*, became a blockbuster hit, selling 300,000 copies in its first year and more than 2 million copies within ten years. Stowe's characters leaped from the page. Here was the gentle slave Uncle Tom, a Christian saint who forgave those who beat him to death; the courageous slave Eliza, who fled with her child across the frozen Ohio River; and the fiendish overseer Simon Legree, whose Louisiana plantation was a nightmare of torture and death.

Stowe aimed her most powerful blows at slavery's destructive impact on the family. Her character Eliza succeeds in keeping her son from being sold away, but other mothers are not so fortunate. When told that her infant has been sold, Lucy drowns herself. Driven half mad by the sale of a son and daughter, Cassy decides "never again [to] let a child live to grow up!" She gives her third child an opiate and watches as "he slept to death." Northerners shed tears and sang praises to *Uncle Tom's Cabin*.

What Northerners accepted as truth, Southerners denounced as slander. The Virginian George F. Holmes proclaimed Stowe a member of the "Woman's Rights" and "Higher Law"

Uncle Tom's Cabin Poster

After Congress passed the Fugitive Slave Act in 1850, Harriet Beecher Stowe's outraged sister-in-law told her, "Now Hattie, if I could use a pen as you can, I would write something that will make this whole nation feel what an accursed thing slavery is." This poster advertising the novel Stowe wrote calls it "The Greatest Book of the Age." The novel fueled the growing antislavery crusade. The Granger Collection, New York.

Filibusters: The Underside of Manifest Destiny

Each year, the citizens of Caborca, a small town in the northern state of Sonora, Mexico, celebrate the defeat there in 1857 of an American army. The invaders did not wear the uniform of the U.S. Army, but instead marched as the private "Arizona Colonization Company" under the command of Henry A. Crabb, a Mississippian who had followed the gold rush to California. When the governor of Sonora faced an insurrection, he invited Crabb to help him repress his enemies in exchange for mineral rights and land.

Crabb marched his band of sixty-eight heavily armed ex-miners south from Los Angeles, but by the time the Americans arrived, the governor had put down the insurgency, and the Mexicans turned on the American invaders. Every American except one died either in battle or at the hands of Mexican firing squads. Crabb's head was preserved in alcohol and placed on display as a symbol of victory.

Henry Crabb was one of thousands of American adventurers, known as "*filibusters*" (from the Spanish *filibustero*, meaning "free-booter" or "pirate"), who in the mid-nineteenth century joined private armies that invaded foreign

Filibustering in Nicaragua
In this image of a pitched battle in Nicaragua in 1856, Costa Ricans on foot fight American filibusters on horseback. Costa Rican soldiers and their Central American allies defeated William Walker's *filibusteros* in 1857. The Pierce administration had already extended diplomatic recognition to Walker's regime, and white Southerners had cheered Walker's attempt to "introduce civilization" in Nicaragua and to develop its resources "with slave labor." *London Illustrated Times*, May 24, 1856.

countries throughout the Western Hemisphere. Although these expeditions violated the U.S. Neutrality Act of 1818, private American armies attacked Canada, Mexico, Ecuador, Honduras, Cuba, and Nicaragua and planned invasions of places as far away as the Hawaiian

schools and dismissed the novel as a work of "intense fanaticism." The New Orleans *Crescent* called Stowe "part quack and part cutthroat," a fake physician who came with arsenic in one hand and a pistol in the other to treat diseases she had "never witnessed." Although it is impossible to measure precisely the impact of a novel on public opinion, *Uncle Tom's Cabin* clearly helped to crystallize northern sentiment against slavery and to confirm white Southerners' suspicion that they no longer received any sympathy in the free states.

Other writers—ex-slaves who knew life in slave cabins firsthand—also produced stinging indictments of slavery. Solomon Northup's compelling *Twelve Years a Slave* (1853) sold 27,000 copies in two years, and the powerful *Narrative of the Life of Frederick Douglass, as Told by Himself* (1845) eventually sold more than 30,000 copies. But no work touched the North's conscience as did the novel by a free white woman. A decade after its publication, when Stowe visited Abraham Lincoln at the White House, he reportedly said, "So you are kingdom. The federal government usually cracked down on filibusters, fearing that private invasions would jeopardize legitimate diplomatic efforts to promote trade and acquire territory.

Men joined filibustering expeditions for reasons that ranged from personal gain to validating manhood. Many saw themselves as carrying on the work of manifest destiny, extending America's reach beyond Texas, California, and Oregon, the prizes of the 1830s and 1840s. In addition, during the 1840s and 1850s, when Northerners insisted on containing slavery's spread to the North and West, Southerners became filibusters to expand slavery south beyond the U.S. border. A leading proslavery ideologue, George Fitzhugh, defended filibustering through historical comparison: "They who condemn the modern filibuster . . . must also condemn the discoverers and settlers of America, of the East Indies of Holland, and of the Indian and Pacific Oceans."

One of the most vigorous filibusters to appeal to southern interests was Narciso López, a Venezuelan-born Cuban who dedicated himself to the liberation of Cuba from Spanish rule. López claimed that Spain was planning to free Cuba's slaves, and he told Southerners that "self-preservation" demanded that they seize the island. In 1851, after gaining the support of Governor John Quitman of Mississippi, López and his army invaded Cuba. The Spaniards crushed the invasion,

killing 200 filibusters, shipping 160 prisoners to Spain, executing 50 invaders by firing squad, and publicly garroting López. John Quitman gathered another army of several thousand, but federal authorities intervened and ended the threat to Cuba.

The most successful of all filibusters was William Walker of Tennessee, a restless adventurer who longed for an empire of his own south of the border. In May 1855, Walker and an army of fifty-six men sailed from San Francisco to the west coast of Nicaragua. Two thousand reinforcements and a civil war in Nicaragua gave Walker his victory. He had himself proclaimed president, legalized slavery, and called on Southerners to come raise cotton, sugar, and coffee in "a magnificent country." Walker's regime survived only until 1857, when a coalition of Central American countries sent Walker packing. Walker doggedly launched four other attacks on Nicaragua, but in 1860 Honduran forces captured and shot him.

Filibustering had lost steam by the time of the U.S. Civil War, but the Confederacy paid a diplomatic price for its association with filibustering. The Guatemalan minister Antonio José de Irisarri declared that there was "no foreign Nation which can have less cause for sympathy with the enemies of the American Union, than the Republics of Central America, because from the Southern States were set on foot those filibustering expeditions." No Central

American nation recognized Confederate independence.

The peoples of Central America and the Caribbean, like the inhabitants of Sonora, still harbor bitter memories of filibusters' private wars of imperialism and honor those who fought off American advances. In 1951, on the centennial of López's invasion, Cubans erected a monument at the very spot where his ill-fated army came ashore. Costa Ricans celebrate Juan Santamaria as their national martyr for his courage in battling William Walker. Memories of the invasions by nineteenth-century filibusters set the stage for anti-American sentiment in Latin America that lingers to this day.

America in a Global Context

1. How did supporters of filibustering justify the practice?

2. What was the relationship between filibustering and sectional politics in the United States in the 1840s and 1850s?

3. Why would an expansionist-minded U.S. government frown on filibustering?

Connect to the Big Idea

⊙ How did filibustering reflect the growing divide between the interests of free and slave states?

the little woman who wrote the book that made this great war."

The Kansas-Nebraska Act

As the 1852 election approached, the Democrats and Whigs sought to close the sectional rifts that had opened within their parties. For their presidential nominee, the Democrats turned to Franklin Pierce of New Hampshire. Pierce's well-known sympathy with southern views on public issues caused his northern critics to

include him among the "doughfaces," northern men malleable enough to champion southern causes. The Whigs chose another Mexican-American War hero, General Winfield Scott of Virginia. But the Whigs' northern and southern factions were hopelessly divided, and the Democrat Pierce carried twenty-seven states to Scott's four and won the electoral college vote 254 to 42 (see Map 14.4, page 384). The Free-Soil Party lost almost half of the voters who had turned to it in the tumultuous political atmosphere of 1848.

Eager to leave the sectional controversy behind, the new president turned swiftly to foreign expansion. Manifest destiny remained robust. (See "Beyond America's Borders," page 380.) Pierce's major objective was Cuba, which was owned by Spain and in which slavery flourished, but when antislavery Northerners blocked Cuba's acquisition to keep more slave territory from entering the Union, Pierce turned to Mexico.

Gadsden Purchase, 1853

In 1853, diplomat James Gadsden negotiated a $10 million purchase of some 30,000 square miles of land in present-day Arizona and New Mexico. The Gadsden Purchase furthered the dream of a transcontinental railroad to California and Pierce's desire for a southern route through Mexican territory. Talk of a railroad ignited rivalries in cities from New Orleans to Chicago as they maneuvered to become the eastern terminus. Inevitably in the 1850s, the contest for a transcontinental railroad became a sectional struggle over slavery.

Illinois's Democratic senator Stephen A. Douglas badly wanted the transcontinental railroad for Chicago. Any railroad that ran west from Chicago would pass through a region that Congress in 1830 had designated a "permanent" Indian reserve (see "Indian Policy and the Trail of Tears" in chapter 11). Douglas proposed giving this vast area between the Missouri River and the Rocky Mountains an Indian name, Nebraska, and then throwing the Indians out. Once the region achieved territorial status, whites could survey and sell the land, establish a civil government, and build a railroad.

Nebraska lay within the Louisiana Purchase and, according to the Missouri Compromise of 1820, was closed to slavery (see "The Missouri Compromise" in chapter 10). Douglas needed southern votes to pass his Nebraska legislation, but Southerners had no incentive to create another free territory or to help a northern city win the transcontinental railroad. Southerners, however, agreed to help if Congress organized Nebraska according to popular sovereignty. That meant giving slavery a chance in Nebraska Territory and reopening the dangerous issue of slavery expansion.

In January 1854, Douglas introduced his bill to organize Nebraska Territory, leaving to the settlers themselves the decision about slavery. At southern insistence, and even though he knew it would "raise a hell of a storm," Douglas added an explicit repeal of the Missouri Compromise. Free-Soilers branded Douglas's plan "a gross violation of a sacred pledge" and an "atrocious plot" to transform free land into a "dreary region of despotism, inhabited by masters and slaves."

Undaunted, Douglas skillfully shepherded the explosive bill through Congress in May 1854. Nine-tenths of the southern members (Whigs and Democrats) and half of the northern Democrats cast votes in favor of the bill. Like Douglas, most northern supporters believed that popular sovereignty would make Nebraska free territory. The **Kansas-Nebraska Act** divided the huge territory in two: Nebraska and Kansas (Map 14.3). With this act, the government pushed the Plains Indians farther west, making way for farmers and railroads.

Free state or territory

Slave state or territory

Voters to decide on allowing slavery, Compromise of 1850

Voters to decide on allowing slavery, Kansas-Nebraska Act, 1854

MAP ACTIVITY

Map 14.3   The Kansas-Nebraska Act, 1854
Americans hardly thought twice about dispossessing the Indians of land guaranteed them by treaty, but many worried about the outcome of repealing the Missouri Compromise and opening up the region to slavery.

READING THE MAP: How many slave states and how many free states does the map show? Estimate the percentage of new territory likely to be settled by slaveholders.

CONNECTIONS: Who would be more likely to support changes in government legislation to discontinue the Missouri Compromise—slaveholders or free-soil advocates? Why?

REVIEW   Why did the Compromise of 1850 fail to achieve sectional peace?

▶ Realignment of the Party System

Since the early 1830s, Whigs and Democrats had organized and channeled political conflict in the nation. This party system dampened sectionalism and strengthened the Union. To achieve national political power, the Whigs and Democrats had to retain their strength in both the North and South. Strong northern and southern wings required that each party compromise and find positions acceptable to both sections.

The Kansas-Nebraska controversy shattered this stabilizing political system. In place of two national parties with bisectional strength, the mid-1850s witnessed the development of one party heavily dominated by one section and another party entirely limited to the other section. Rather than "national" parties, the country had what one critic disdainfully called "geographic" parties, a development that thwarted political compromise between the sections.

The Old Parties: Whigs and Democrats

As early as the Mexican-American War, members of the Whig Party had clashed over the future of slavery in annexed Mexican lands. By 1852, the Whig Party could please its proslavery southern wing or its antislavery northern wing but not both. The Whigs' miserable showing in the election of 1852 made it clear that they were no longer a strong national party. By 1856, after more than two decades of contesting the Democrats, they were hardly a party at all (Map 14.4).

The collapse of the Whig Party left the Democrats as the country's only national party. Popular sovereignty provided a doctrine that many Democrats could support. Even so, popular sovereignty very nearly undid the party. When Stephen Douglas applied the doctrine to the part of the Louisiana Purchase where slavery had been barred, he divided northern Democrats and destroyed the dominance of the Democratic Party in the free states. After 1854, the Democrats were a southern-dominated party. Still, gains in the South more than balanced Democratic losses in the North, and during the 1850s Democrats elected two presidents and won majorities in Congress in almost every election.

The breakup of the Whigs and the disaffection of many northern Democrats set millions of Americans politically adrift. As they searched for new political harbors, Americans found that the death of the old party system created a multitude of fresh political alternatives.

The New Parties: Know-Nothings and Republicans

Dozens of new political organizations vied for voters' attention. Out of the confusion, two emerged as true contenders. One grew out of the slavery controversy, a coalition of indignant antislavery Northerners. The other arose from an entirely different split in American society, between native Protestants and Roman Catholic immigrants.

The wave of immigrants that arrived in America from 1845 to 1855 produced a nasty backlash among Protestant Americans, who feared that the Republic was about to drown in a sea of Roman Catholics from Ireland and Germany (see Figure 12.1, page 322). Nativists (individuals who were anti-immigrant) began to organize, first into secret fraternal societies and then in 1854 into a political party. Recruits swore never to vote for either foreign-born or Roman Catholic candidates and not to reveal

VISUAL ACTIVITY

Know-Nothing Cartoon

This cartoon underscores the Know-Nothing contention that hard-drinking Irish and German immigrants were stealing elections and polluting American democracy. In addition to the Irishman's whiskey and the German's beer, the artist completes the negative stereotypes by giving the Irishman his shillelagh (club) and the German his pipe. The Granger Collection, New York.

READING THE IMAGE: What is taking place behind the Irishman and German, and how does it spell danger for the Republic?

CONNECTIONS: In what parts of the nation would you suppose the Know-Nothing message had its greatest appeal?

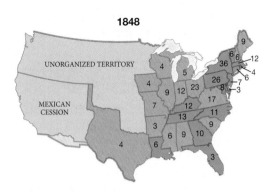

1848

Candidate	Electoral Vote	Popular Vote	Percent of Popular Vote
Zachary Taylor (Whig)	163	1,360,099	47.4
Lewis Cass (Democrat)	127	1,220,544	42.5
Martin Van Buren (Free-Soil)	0	291,263	10.1

1852

Candidate	Electoral Vote	Popular Vote	Percent of Popular Vote
Franklin Pierce (Democrat)	254	1,601,274	50.9
Winfield Scott (Whig)	42	1,386,580	44.1
John P. Hale (Free-Soil)	5	155,825	5.0

1856

Candidate	Electoral Vote	Popular Vote	Percent of Popular Vote
James Buchanan (Democrat)	174	1,838,169	45.3
John C. Frémont (Republican)	114	1,341,264	33.1
Millard Fillmore (American)	8	874,534	21.6

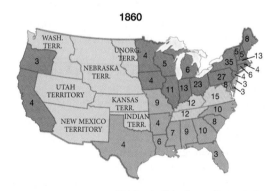

1860

Candidate	Electoral Vote	Popular Vote	Percent of Popular Vote
Abraham Lincoln (Republican)	180	1,866,452	39.9
John C. Breckinridge (Southern Democrat)	72	847,953	18.1
Stephen A. Douglas (Northern Democrat)	12	1,375,157	29.4
John Bell (Constitutional Union)	39	590,631	12.6

MAP ACTIVITY

Map 14.4 Political Realignment, 1848–1860

In 1848, slavery and sectionalism began taking their toll on the country's party system. The Whig Party was an early casualty. By 1860, national parties—those that contended for votes in both North and South—had been replaced by regional parties.

READING THE MAP: Which states did the Democrats pick up in 1852 compared to 1848? Which of these states did the Democrats lose in 1856? Compare the general geographic location of the states won by the Republicans in 1856 versus those won in 1860.

CONNECTIONS: In the 1860 election, which party benefited the most from the western and midwestern states added to the Union since 1848? Why do you think these states chose to back this party?

any information about the organization. When questioned, they said, "I know nothing." Officially, they were the American Party, but most Americans called them Know-Nothings.

The Know-Nothings enjoyed dazzling success in 1854 and 1855. They captured state legislatures throughout the nation and claimed dozens of seats in Congress. Democrats and Whigs described the Know-Nothing's phenomenal record as a "tornado," a "hurricane," and "a freak of political insanity." But by 1855, an observer might reasonably have concluded that the Know-Nothings had emerged as the successor to the Whigs.

The Know-Nothings were not the only new party making noise, however. One of the new antislavery organizations provoked by the Kansas-Nebraska Act called itself the **Republican Party.** The Republicans attempted to unite all those who opposed the extension of slavery into any territory of the United States.

The Republican creed tapped into the basic beliefs and values of Northerners. Slavery, Republicans believed, degraded the dignity of white labor by associating work with blacks and servility. As evidence, they pointed to the South, where, one Republican claimed, nonslaveholding whites "retire to the outskirts of civilization, where they live a semi-savage life, sinking deeper and more hopelessly into barbarism with every succeeding generation." Republicans warned that the insatiable slaveholders of the South, whom antislavery Northerners called the "Slave Power," were conspiring through their control of the Democratic Party to expand slavery, subvert liberty, and undermine the Constitution.

Only by restricting slavery to the South, Republicans believed, could free labor flourish elsewhere. In the North, one Republican declared in 1854, "every man holds his fortune in his own right arm; and his position in society, in life, is to be tested by his own individual character." Without slavery, western territories would provide vast economic opportunity for free men. Powerful images of liberty and opportunity attracted a wide range of Northerners to the Republican cause.

Women as well as men rushed to the new Republican Party. Indeed, three women helped found the party in Ripon, Wisconsin, in 1854. Although they could not vote and suffered from other legal handicaps, women nevertheless participated in partisan politics by writing campaign literature, marching in parades, giving speeches, and lobbying voters. Women's antislavery fervor attracted them to the Republican Party, and participation in party politics in turn nurtured the woman's rights movement. Susan B. Anthony, who attended Republican meetings throughout the 1850s, found that her political activity made her disfranchisement all the more galling. She and other women in the North worked on behalf of antislavery and woman suffrage and the right of married women to control their own property. (See "Seeking the American Promise," page 386.)

The Election of 1856

The election of 1856 revealed that the Republicans had become the Democrats' main challenger, and slavery in the territories, not immigration,

The Realignment of Political Parties

Whig Party

1848	Whig Party divides into two factions over slavery; Whigs adopt no platform and nominate war hero Zachary Taylor, who is elected president.
1852	Whigs nominate war hero General Winfield Scott for president; deep divisions in party result in humiliating loss.
1856	Shattered by sectionalism, Whig Party fields no presidential candidate.

Democratic Party

1848	President Polk declines to run again; Democratic Party nominates Lewis Cass, the man most closely associated with popular sovereignty, but avoids firm platform position on expansion of slavery.
1852	To bridge rift in party, Democrats nominate northern war veteran with southern views, Franklin Pierce, for president; he wins with 50.9 percent of popular vote.
1856	Democrat James Buchanan elected president on ambiguous platform; his prosouthern actions in office alienate northern branch of party.
1860	Democrats split into northern Democrats and southern Democrats; each group fields its own presidential candidate.

Free-Soil Party

1848	Breakaway antislavery Democrats and antislavery Whigs found Free-Soil Party; presidential candidate Martin Van Buren takes 10.1 percent of popular vote, mainly from Whigs.
1852	Support for Free-Soil Party ebbs in wake of Compromise of 1850; Free-Soil presidential candidate John P. Hale wins only 5 percent of popular vote.

American (Know-Nothing) Party

1851	Anti-immigrant American (Know-Nothing) Party formed.
1854–1855	American Party succeeds in state elections and attracts votes from northern and southern Whigs in congressional elections.
1856	Know-Nothing presidential candidate Millard Fillmore wins only Maryland; party subsequently disbands.

Republican Party

1854	Republican Party formed to oppose expansion of slavery in territories; attracts northern Whigs, northern Democrats, and Free-Soilers.
1856	Republican presidential candidate John C. Frémont wins all but five northern states, establishing Republicans as main challenger to Democrats.
1860	Republican Abraham Lincoln wins all northern states except New Jersey and is elected president in four-way race against divided Democrats and southern Constitutional Union Party.

"A Purse of Her Own": Petitioning for the Right to Own Property

In the early Republic, as today, having money and deciding how to spend it was a fundamental aspect of independent adulthood. Yet antebellum married women were denied this privilege, because of the laws of *coverture*, which placed wives under the full legal control of their husbands (see "Women and The Law" in chapter 10). By law, husbands made all the financial decisions in a household. Even money that a wife earned or brought into a marriage from gifts or inheritance was not hers to control as long as she remained married. Ernestine Potowsky Rose of New York City thought that was wrong, and she became the first woman in the United States to take action to change the law.

Born in Poland in 1810, Ernestine Potowsky was the daughter of a rabbi, which meant that her destiny was fixed: an arranged marriage, many children, and a life strictly governed by religious law. Ernestine rejected this fate and left home for London. There, at age nineteen, she married William Rose, a like-minded socialist intellectual. The couple later emigrated to the United States and settled in New York City, where William, a jeweler, started a business.

Ernestine soon learned of a bill presented in 1837 in the New York assembly proposing that married women, "equally with males and unmarried females, possess the rights of *life*, *liberty*, and PROPERTY, and are equally entitled to be protected in all three." But opponents feared that it would undermine a central pillar of marriage: the assumption that husband and wife shared identical interests. Predictably, the bill failed to pass.

The devastating panics of 1837 and 1839 (see "Elections and Panics" in chapter 11), and the resulting bankruptcies, soon changed some traditionalists' minds about wives and property. Men in several state legislatures crafted laws that shielded a wife's inherited property from creditors collecting debts from her husband. Mississippi led the way in 1839, and by 1848 eighteen states had modified property laws in the name of family protection.

In New York, as support for such a law grew, Ernestine Rose mobilized a new constituency of women around the argument that married women should be able to own and control property. She circulated petitions and spoke from public platforms, often joined by Elizabeth Cady Stanton, a young wife from western New York. In April 1848, three months before the Seneca Falls woman's rights convention (see "Women's Rights Activists" in chapter 12), the New York assembly finally awarded married women sole authority over property they brought to a marriage.

Rose welcomed the new law but recognized its key shortcoming: It made no provision for wages earned by a married woman. Nor did it alter inheritance laws that limited a widow's share of her husband's estate. Speaking at every national woman's rights convention from 1850 to 1860, Rose argued for women's economic independence. In 1853, she itemized the limited belongings allowed to a widow if her husband died without a will: "As to the personal property, after all debts and liabilities are discharged, the widow receives one-half of it; and, in addition, the law allows her, her own wearing apparel, her own ornaments, proper to her station, one bed, with appurtenances for the same, a stove, the Bible, family pictures, and all the school-books; also all spinning wheels and weaving looms, one table, six chairs, ten cups and saucers, one tea-pot, one sugar dish, and six spoons." While her audience laughed appreciatively, Rose questioned whether the spoons would be teaspoons, "since a widow might live on tea only." Spinning wheels, long gone in 1853, needed no elaboration from her to make the law sound pathetically out-of-date.

Of particular concern to Rose was the plight of poor wives. She and Susan B. Anthony encountered women trapped in marriages with husbands who failed to support their dependents. Anthony, herself a lifelong single woman, recalled that "as I passed from town to town I was made to feel the great evil of women's utter dependence on man. . . .

was the election's principal issue. When the Know-Nothings insisted on a platform that endorsed the Kansas-Nebraska Act, most of the Northerners walked out, and the party came apart. The few Know-Nothings who remained nominated ex-president Millard Fillmore.

The Republican platform focused mostly on "making every territory free." When they labeled slavery a "relic of barbarism," they signaled that they had written off the South. For president, they nominated the soldier and California adventurer John C. Frémont. Frémont lacked political credentials, but his wife, Jessie Frémont, the daughter of Senator Thomas Hart Benton of Missouri, knew the political map well. Though careful to maintain a proper public image, the

Ernestine Rose
Ernestine Rose, in her mid-forties when this photograph was taken, managed to hold a smile for the several minutes required to capture her image on a photographic plate. Getty Images.

ciaries of this law were women whose husbands were incompetent to support them or who had deserted them. These husbands now had no right to their wives' hard-gained earnings.

The revised New York law made other important changes to coverture. A wife could now sue (or be sued), make legal contracts of her own, and serve as joint guardian of her children, "with equal powers, rights and duties in regard to them." These changes, adopted in many states after 1860, began the long (and still ongoing) process of elevating women to equality with men.

Questions for Consideration

1. What do the laws of coverture reveal about how married women were viewed in antebellum America?

2. Why did a woman need "a purse of her own"?

3. Why did men eventually agree to grant married women property rights?

Connect to the Big Idea

C What about women's condition drew women in the North to the antislavery campaign?

Woman must have a purse of her own."

Rose's efforts paid off. In 1860, New York amended its law to include a wife's wages as her own, but only if she earned the money outside the household. Money earned selling eggs or caring for boarders still went directly into the husband's pocket. Perhaps the most significant benefi-

vivacious young mother and antislavery zealot helped attract voters and draw women into politics.

The Democrats, successful in 1852 in bridging sectional differences by nominating a northern man with southern principles, chose another "doughface," James Buchanan of Pennsylvania. They portrayed the Republicans as extremists ("Black Republican Abolitionists") whose support for the Wilmot Proviso risked pushing the South out of the Union.

The Democratic strategy carried the day for Buchanan, who won 174 electoral votes against Frémont's 114 and Fillmore's 8 (see Map 14.4, page 384). But the big news was that the Republicans, campaigning under the banner

"Free soil, Free men, Frémont," carried all but five of the states north of the Mason-Dixon line. Sectionalism had fashioned a new party system, one that spelled danger for the Democrats and the nation. Indeed, war had already broken out between proslavery and antislavery forces in the distant Kansas Territory.

REVIEW   Why did the Whig Party disintegrate in the 1850s?

▶ Freedom under Siege

Events in Kansas Territory in the mid-1850s underscored the Republicans' contention that the slaveholding South presented a profound threat to "free soil, free labor, and free men." Kansas reeled with violence that Republicans argued was southern in origin. Republicans also pointed to the brutal beating by a Southerner of a respected northern senator on the floor of Congress. Even the Supreme Court, in the Republicans' view, reflected the South's drive toward minority rule and tyranny. Then, in 1858, the issues dividing North and South received an extraordinary hearing in a senatorial contest in Illinois, when the nation's foremost Democrat debated a resourceful Republican.

"Bleeding Kansas"

Three days after the House of Representatives approved the Kansas-Nebraska Act in 1854, Senator William H. Seward of New York boldly challenged the South. "Come on then, Gentlemen

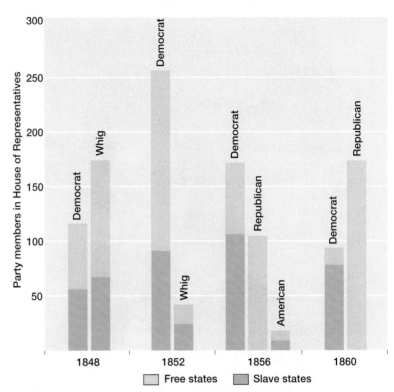

FIGURE 14.1   Changing Political Landscape, 1848–1860
The polarization of American politics between free states and slave states occurred in little more than a decade.

of the Slave States," he cried, "since there is no escaping your challenge, I accept it in behalf of the cause of freedom. We will engage in competition for the virgin soil of Kansas, and God give the victory to the side which is stronger in numbers as it is in right." Because of Stephen Douglas, popular sovereignty would determine whether Kansas became slave or free. Free-state and slave-state settlers each sought a majority at the ballot box, claimed God's blessing, and kept their rifles ready.

Emigrant aid societies sprang up to promote settlement from free states or slave states. Missourians, already bordered on the east by the free state of Illinois and on the north by the free state of Iowa, especially thought it important to secure Kansas for slavery. Thousands of rough frontiersmen, egged on by Missouri senator David Rice Atchison, invaded Kansas. "There are eleven hundred coming over from Platte County to vote," Atchison reported, "and if that ain't enough we can send five thousand—enough to kill every God-damned abolitionist in the Territory." Not surprisingly, proslavery candidates swept the territorial elections in November 1854. When Kansas's first territorial legislature met, it enacted a raft of proslavery laws, including a statute prohibiting antislavery men from holding office or serving on juries. Ever-pliant President Pierce endorsed the work of the fraudulently elected legislature. Free-soil Kansans did not.

"Bleeding Kansas," 1850s

They elected their own legislature, which promptly banned both slaves and free blacks from the territory. Organized into two rival governments and armed to the teeth, Kansans verged on civil war.

Fighting broke out on the morning of May 21, 1856, when several hundred proslavery men raided the town of Lawrence, the center of free-state settlement. Only one man died, but the "Sack of Lawrence," as free-soil forces called it, inflamed northern opinion. Elsewhere in Kansas, news of events in Lawrence provoked John Brown, a free-soil settler, to announce that "it was better that a score of bad men should die than that one man who came here to make Kansas a Free State should be driven out" and to lead the posse that massacred five allegedly proslavery settlers along Pottawatomie Creek (see page 371). After that, guerrilla war engulfed the territory.

Just as "Bleeding Kansas" gave the fledgling Republican Party fresh ammunition for its battle against the Slave Power, so too did an event that occurred in the national capital. In May 1856, Senator Charles Sumner of Massachusetts delivered a speech titled "The Crime against Kansas," which included a scalding personal attack on South Carolina senator Andrew P. Butler. Sumner described Butler as a "Don Quixote" who had taken as his mistress "the harlot, slavery."

Armed Settlers Near Lawrence, Kansas

Armed with rifles, knives, swords, and pistols, these tough antislavery men gathered for a photograph near the free-soil town of Lawrence in 1856. Equally well-armed proslavery men attacked and briefly occupied Lawrence that same year.
Kansas State Historical Society.

Preston Brooks, a young South Carolina member of the House and a kinsman of Butler's, felt compelled to defend the honor of his aged relative. On May 22, Brooks entered the Senate, where he found Sumner working at his desk. He beat Sumner over the head with his cane until Sumner lay bleeding and unconscious on the floor. Brooks resigned his seat in the House, only to be promptly reelected. In the North, the southern hero became an arch-villain. Like "Bleeding Kansas," "Bleeding Sumner" provided the Republican Party with a potent symbol of the South's "twisted and violent civilization."

The *Dred Scott* Decision

Political debate over slavery in the territories became so heated in part because the Constitution lacked precision on the issue. In 1857, in the case of *Dred Scott v. Sandford*, the Supreme Court announced its understanding of the meaning of the Constitution regarding slavery in the territories. The Court's decision demonstrated that it enjoyed no special immunity from the sectional and partisan passions that were convulsing the land.

In 1833, an army doctor bought the slave Dred Scott in St. Louis, Missouri, and took him as his personal servant to Fort Armstrong, Illinois, and then to Fort Snelling in Wisconsin Territory. Back in St. Louis in 1846, Scott, with the help of white friends, sued to prove

that he and his family were legally entitled to their freedom. Scott argued that living in Illinois, a free state, and Wisconsin, a free territory, had made his family free and that they remained free even after returning to Missouri, a slave state.

In 1857, Chief Justice Roger B. Taney, who hated Republicans and detested racial equality, wrote the Court's *Dred Scott* decision. First, the Court ruled that Scott could not legally claim violation of his constitutional rights because he was not a citizen of the United States. When the Constitution was written, Taney said, blacks "were regarded as beings of an inferior order . . . so far inferior, that they had no rights which the white man was bound to respect." Second, the laws of Dred Scott's home state, Missouri, determined his status, and thus his travels in free areas did not make him free. Third, Congress's power to make "all needful rules and regulations" for the territories did not include the right to prohibit slavery. The Court explicitly declared the Missouri Compromise unconstitutional, even though it had already been voided by the Kansas-Nebraska Act.

The Taney Court's extreme proslavery decision outraged Republicans. By denying the federal government the right to exclude slavery in the territories, it cut the legs out from under the

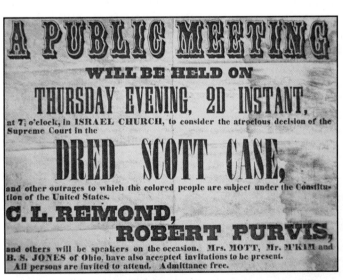

Dred Scott
This portrait of Dred Scott was painted in 1857, the year of the Supreme Court's decision. African Americans in the North were particularly alarmed by the Court's ruling. Although the Court rejected Scott's suit, he gained his freedom in May 1857 when a white man purchased and freed Scott and his family. Portrait: © Collection of the New-York Historical Society, USA/The Bridgeman Art Library. Poster: Private Collection/Peter Newark American Pictures/The Bridgeman Art Library.

Republican Party. Moreover, as the *New York Tribune* lamented, the decision cleared the way for "all our Territories . . . to be ripened into Slave States." Particularly frightening to African Americans in the North was the Court's declaration that free blacks were not citizens and had no rights.

The Republican rebuttal to the *Dred Scott* ruling relied heavily on the dissenting opinion of Justice Benjamin R. Curtis. Scott *was* a citizen of the United States, Curtis argued. At the time of the writing of the Constitution, free black men could vote in five states and participated in the ratification process. Scott *was* free. Because slavery was prohibited in Wisconsin, the "involuntary servitude of a slave, coming into the Territory with his master, should cease to exist." The Missouri Compromise *was* constitutional. The Founders had meant exactly what they said: Congress had the power to make "*all* needful rules and regulations" for the territories, including barring slavery.

Unswayed by Curtis's dissent, the Court in a seven-to-two decision, validated an extreme statement of the South's territorial rights. John C. Calhoun's claim that Congress had no authority to exclude slavery became the law of the land. White Southerners cheered. One gloated that the *Dred Scott* decision was the "funeral sermon of Black Republicanism . . . crushing and annihilating the anti-slavery platform." Ironically, the *Dred Scott* decision actually strengthened the young Republican Party. Indeed, that "outrageous decision," one Republican argued, was "the best thing that could have happened," for it provided powerful evidence of the Republicans' claim that a hostile "Slave Power" conspired against northern liberties.

Prairie Republican: Abraham Lincoln

By reigniting the sectional flames, the *Dred Scott* case provided Republican politicians with fresh challenges and fresh opportunities. Abraham Lincoln had long since put behind him his hardscrabble log-cabin beginnings in Kentucky and Indiana. Now living in Springfield, Illinois, he earned good money as a lawyer, but politics was his life. "His ambition was a little engine that knew no rest," observed his law partner William Herndon. Lincoln had served as a Whig in the Illinois state legislature and in the House of Representatives, but he had not held public office since 1849.

Convinced that slavery was a "monstrous injustice," a "great moral wrong," and an "unqualified evil to the negro, the white man, and the State," Lincoln condemned the Kansas-Nebraska Act of 1854 for giving slavery a new life and in 1856 joined the Republican Party. He accepted that the Constitution permitted slavery in those states where it existed, but he believed that Congress could contain its spread. Penned in, plantation slavery would wither, Lincoln believed, and in time Southerners would end slavery themselves.

Lincoln held what were, for his times, moderate racial views. Although he denounced slavery and defended black humanity, he also viewed black equality as impractical and unachievable. "Negroes have natural rights . . . as other men have," he said, "although they cannot enjoy them here." Insurmountable white prejudice made it impossible to extend full citizenship to blacks in America, he believed. In Lincoln's mind, social stability and black progress required that slavery end and that blacks leave the country.

Lincoln envisioned the western territories as "places for poor people to go to, and better their conditions." But slavery's expansion threatened free men's basic right to succeed. The Kansas-Nebraska Act and the *Dred Scott* decision persuaded him that slaveholders were engaged in a dangerous conspiracy to nationalize slavery. The next step, Lincoln warned, would be "another Supreme Court decision, declaring that the Constitution of the United States does not permit a State to exclude slavery from its limits." Unless the citizens of Illinois woke up, he warned, the Supreme Court would make "Illinois a slave State."

In Lincoln's view, the nation could not "endure, permanently half slave and half free." Either opponents of slavery would arrest its spread and place it on the "course of ultimate extinction," or its advocates would see that it became legal in "*all* the States, *old* as well as *new*—*North* as well as *South*." Lincoln's convictions that slavery was wrong and that Congress must stop its spread formed the core of the Republican ideology. In 1858, Republicans in Illinois chose him to challenge the nation's premier Democrat, who was seeking reelection to the U.S. Senate.

The Lincoln-Douglas Debates

When Stephen Douglas learned that the Republican Abraham Lincoln would be his opponent for the Senate, he observed: "He is the strong man of the party—full of wit, facts, dates —and the best stump speaker, with his droll ways and dry jokes, in the West. He is as honest as he is shrewd, and if I beat him my victory will be hardly won."

Not only did Douglas have to contend with a formidable foe, but the previous year, the nation's economy had experienced a sharp downturn. Prices had plummeted, thousands of businesses had failed, and many were unemployed. As a Democrat, Douglas had to go before the voters as a member of the party whose policies stood accused of causing the panic of 1857.

Douglas's response to another crisis in 1857, however, helped shore up his standing in Illinois. Proslavery forces in Kansas met in the town of Lecompton, drafted a proslavery constitution, and applied for statehood. Everyone knew that free-soilers outnumbered proslavery settlers, but President Buchanan instructed Congress to admit Kansas as the sixteenth slave state. Senator Douglas broke with the Democratic administration and denounced the Lecompton constitution; Congress killed the Lecompton bill. (When Kansans reconsidered the Lecompton constitution in an honest election, they rejected it six to one. Kansas entered the Union in 1861 as a free state.) By denouncing the fraudulent proslavery constitution, Douglas declared his independence from the South and, he hoped, made himself acceptable at home.

A relative unknown and a decided underdog in the Illinois election, Lincoln challenged Douglas to debate him face-to-face. The two met in seven communities for what would become a legendary series of debates. To the thousands who stood straining to see and hear, they must have seemed an odd pair. Douglas was five feet four inches tall, broad, and stocky; Lincoln was six feet four, angular, and lean. Douglas was in perpetual motion, darting across the platform, shouting, and jabbing the air; Lincoln stood still and spoke deliberately. Douglas wore the latest fashion and dazzled audiences with his flashy vests. Lincoln wore good suits but managed to look rumpled anyway.

The two men debated the crucial issues of the age—slavery and freedom. Lincoln badgered Douglas with the question of whether he favored the spread of slavery. He tried to force Douglas into the damaging admission that the Supreme Court had repudiated Douglas's own territorial solution, popular sovereignty. At Freeport, Illinois, Douglas admitted that settlers could not now pass legislation barring slavery, but he argued that they could ban slavery just as effectively by not passing protective laws,

Abraham Lincoln (1858)
This photograph was taken in Pittsfield, Illinois, two weeks before the final Lincoln-Douglas debate. It portrays Lincoln as an intense and focused campaigner, a man intent on forcing Douglas to debate the central issue— the morality of slavery. Library of Congress.

such as those found in slave states. Southerners condemned Douglas's "Freeport Doctrine" and charged him with trying to steal the victory they had gained with the *Dred Scott* decision. Lincoln chastised his opponent for his "don't care" attitude about slavery, for "blowing out the moral lights around us."

Douglas worked the racial issue. He called Lincoln an abolitionist and an egalitarian enamored of "our colored brethren." Put on the defensive, Lincoln reaffirmed his faith in white rule: "I will say, then, that I am not, nor ever have been, in favor of bringing about in any way the social and political equality of the white and black race." But unlike Douglas, who told racist jokes, Lincoln was no negrophobe. He tried to steer the debate back to what he considered the true issue: the morality and future of slavery. "Slavery is wrong," Lincoln repeated, because "a man has the right to the fruits of his own labor."

As Douglas predicted, the election was hard-fought and closely contested. Until the adoption of the Seventeenth Amendment in 1911, citizens voted for state legislators, who in turn selected U.S. senators. Since Democrats won a slight majority in the Illinois legislature, the members returned Douglas to the Senate. But the **Lincoln-Douglas debates** thrust Lincoln, the prairie Republican, into the national spotlight.

> **REVIEW** Why did the *Dred Scott* decision strengthen northern suspicions of a "Slave Power" conspiracy?

▶ The Union Collapses

From the Republican perspective, the Kansas-Nebraska Act, the Brooks-Sumner affair, the *Dred Scott* decision, and the Lecompton constitution amounted to irrefutable evidence of the South's aggressive promotion of slavery. White Southerners, of course, saw things differently. They were the ones who were under siege, they declared. They believed that Northerners were itching to use their numerical advantage to attack slavery, and not just in the territories. Republicans had made it clear that they were unwilling to accept the *Dred Scott* ruling as the last word on the issue of slavery expansion. And John Brown's attempt to incite a slave insurrection in Virginia in 1859 proved to Southerners that Northerners would do anything to end slavery.

Talk of leaving the Union had been heard for years, but until the final crisis, Southerners had used secession as a ploy to gain concessions within the Union, not to destroy it. Then the 1850s delivered powerful blows to Southerners' confidence that they could remain in the Union and protect slavery. When the Republican Party won the White House in 1860, many Southerners concluded that they would have to leave.

The Aftermath of John Brown's Raid

For his attack on Harpers Ferry, John Brown stood trial for treason, murder, and incitement of slave insurrection. "To hang a fanatic is to make a martyr of him and fledge another brood of the same sort," cautioned one newspaper, but on December 2, 1859, Virginia executed Brown. In life, he was a ne'er-do-well, but, as the poet Stephen Vincent Benét observed, "he knew how to die." Brown told his wife that he was "determined to make the utmost possible out of a defeat." He told the court: "If it is deemed necessary that

I should forfeit my life for the furtherance of the ends of justice, and mingle my blood further with the blood of . . . millions in this slave country whose rights are disregarded by wicked, cruel, and unjust enactments, I say, let it be done."

After Brown's execution, Americans across the land contemplated the meaning of his life and death. Some Northerners celebrated his "splendid martyrdom." Ralph Waldo Emerson likened Brown to Christ when he declared that Brown made "the gallows as glorious as the cross." Most Northerners did not advocate bloody rebellion, however. Like Lincoln, they concluded that Brown's noble antislavery ideals could not "excuse violence, bloodshed, and treason."

Still, when northern churches marked John Brown's hanging with tolling bells, hymns, and prayer vigils, white Southerners contemplated what they had in common with people who "regard John Brown as a martyr and a Christian hero, rather than a murderer and robber." Georgia senator Robert Toombs announced solemnly that Southerners must "never permit this Federal government to pass into the traitorous hands of the black Republican party."

Republican Victory in 1860

When the Democrats converged on Charleston for their convention in April 1860, fire-eating Southerners denounced Stephen Douglas and demanded a platform that included federal protection of slavery in the territories, a goal of extreme proslavery Southerners for years. "Ours are the institutions which are at stake; ours is the property that is to be destroyed; ours is the honor at stake," shouted the Alabaman William Lowndes Yancy. When the delegates approved a platform with popular sovereignty, representatives from the entire Lower South and Arkansas stomped out of the convention. The remaining Democrats adjourned to meet a few weeks later in Baltimore, where they nominated Douglas for president.

When bolting southern Democrats reconvened, they approved a platform with a federal slave code and nominated Vice President John C. Breckinridge of Kentucky. Southern moderates, however, refused to support Breckinridge. They formed the Constitutional Union Party to provide voters with a Unionist choice. Instead of adopting a platform and confronting the slavery question, the Constitutional Union Party merely approved a vague resolution pledging "to recognize no political principle other than *the Constitution . . . the Union . . . and the Enforcement*

VISUAL ACTIVITY

John Brown Going to His Hanging, by Horace Pippin, 1942
The grandparents of Horace Pippin, a Pennsylvania artist, were slaves. His grandmother witnessed the hanging of John Brown, and this painting recalls the scene she so often described to him. Pippin used a muted palette to establish the bleak setting, but he also managed to convey its striking intensity. Historically accurate, the painting depicts Brown tied and sitting erect on his coffin, passing resolutely before the silent, staring white men. The black woman in the lower right corner presumably is Pippin's grandmother. Romare Bearden, another African American artist, recalled the central place of John Brown in black memory: "Lincoln and John Brown were as much a part of the actuality of the Afro-American experience, as were the domino games and the hoe cakes for Sunday morning breakfast. I vividly recall the yearly commemorations for John Brown." Courtesy of the Pennsylvania Academy of Fine Arts, Philadelphia. www.pafa.org. John Lambert Fund.

READING THE IMAGE: What was the artist trying to convey about the tone of John Brown's execution? According to the painting, what were the feelings of those gathered to witness the event?

CONNECTIONS: How did Brown's trial and execution contribute to the growing split between North and South?

of the Laws." For president, they nominated former senator John Bell of Tennessee.

The Republicans smelled victory, but they needed to carry nearly all the free states to win. To make their party more appealing, they expanded their platform beyond antislavery. They hoped that free homesteads, a protective tariff, a transcontinental railroad, and a guarantee of immigrant political rights would provide an agenda broad enough to unify the North.

While reasserting their commitment to stop the spread of slavery, they also denounced John Brown's raid as "among the gravest of crimes" and confirmed the security of slavery in the South.

The foremost Republican, William H. Seward, had made enemies with his radical "higher law" doctrine, which claimed that there was a higher moral law than the Constitution, and with his "irrepressible conflict" speech, in which he

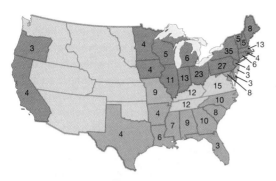

Candidate	Electoral Vote	Popular Vote	Percent of Popular Vote
Abraham Lincoln (Republican)	180	1,866,452	39.9
John C. Breckinridge (Southern Democrat)	72	847,953	18.1
Stephen A. Douglas (Northern Democrat)	12	1,375,157	29.4
John Bell (Constitutional Union)	39	590,631	12.6

MAP 14.5
The Election of 1860

declared that North and South were fated to collide. Lincoln, however, since bursting onto the national scene in 1858 had demonstrated his clear purpose, good judgment, and solid Republican credentials. That, and his residence in Illinois, a crucial state, made him attractive to the party. On the third ballot, the delegates chose Lincoln. Defeated by Douglas in a state contest less than two years earlier, Lincoln now stood ready to take him on for the presidency.

The election of 1860 was like none other in American politics. It took place in the midst of the nation's severest crisis. Four major candidates crowded the presidential field. Rather than a four-cornered contest, however, the election broke into two contests, each with two candidates. In the North, Lincoln faced Douglas; in the South, Breckinridge confronted Bell. So outrageous did Southerners consider the Republican Party that they did not even permit Lincoln's name to appear on the ballot in ten of the fifteen slave states.

On November 6, 1860, Lincoln swept all of the eighteen free states except New Jersey, which split its electoral votes between him and Douglas. Although Lincoln received only 39 percent of the popular vote, he won easily in the electoral college with 180 votes, 28 more than he needed for victory (Map 14.5). Lincoln did not win because his opposition was splintered. Even

if the votes of his three opponents had been combined, Lincoln still would have won. He won because his votes were concentrated in the free states, which contained a majority of electoral votes. Ominously, however, Breckinridge, running on a southern-rights platform, won the entire Lower South, plus Delaware, Maryland, and North Carolina.

Secession Winter

Anxious Southerners immediately began debating what to do. Although Breckinridge had carried the South, a vote for "southern rights" was not necessarily a vote for secession. Besides, slightly more than half of the Southerners who had voted had cast ballots for Douglas and Bell, two stout defenders of the Union. "The people of the South have too much sense to attempt the ruin of the government," Lincoln predicted.

Southern Unionists tried to calm the fears that Lincoln's election triggered. Former congressman Alexander Stephens of Georgia asked what Lincoln had done to justify something as extreme as secession. Had he not promised to respect slavery where it existed? In Stephens's judgment, secession might lead to war, which would loosen the hinges of southern society and possibly even open the door to slave insurrection. "Revolutions are much easier started than controlled," he warned. "I consider slavery much more secure in the Union than out of it."

Secessionists emphasized the dangers of delay. "Mr. Lincoln and his party assert that this doctrine of equality applies to the negro," former Georgia governor Howell Cobb declared, "and necessarily there can exist no such thing as property in our equals." Lincoln's election without a single electoral vote from the South meant that Southerners were powerless to defend themselves within the Union, Cobb argued. Why wait, he asked, for abolitionists to attack? As for war, there would be none. The Union was a voluntary compact, and Lincoln would not coerce patriotism. If Northerners did resist with force, secessionists argued, one southern woodsman could whip five of Lincoln's greasy mechanics.

For all their differences, southern whites agreed that they had to defend slavery. John Smith Preston of South Carolina spoke for the overwhelming majority when he declared, "The South cannot exist without slavery." They disagreed about whether the mere presence of a Republican in the White House made it necessary to exercise what they considered a legitimate right to secede.

The debate about what to do was briefest in South Carolina, which seceded from the Union on December 20, 1860. By February 1861, the six other Lower South states followed in South Carolina's footsteps. In general, slaveholders spearheaded secession, while nonslaveholders in the Piedmont and mountain counties, where slaves were relatively few, displayed the greatest attachment to the Union. In February, representatives from South Carolina, Georgia, Florida, Alabama, Mississippi, Louisiana, and Texas met in Montgomery, Alabama, where they created the **Confederate States of America**. Mississippi senator Jefferson

Secession of the Lower South, December 1860–February 1861

Davis became president, and Alexander Stephens of Georgia, who had spoken so eloquently about the dangers of revolution, became vice president. In March 1861, Stephens declared that the Confederacy's "cornerstone" was "the great truth that the negro is not equal to the white man; that slavery, subordination to the superior race, is his natural and moral condition."

Lincoln's election had split the Union. Now secession split the South. Seven slave states seceded during the winter, but the eight slave states of the Upper South rejected secession, at least for the moment. The Upper South had a smaller stake in slavery. Barely half as many white families in the Upper South held slaves (21 percent) as in the Lower South (37 percent). Slaves represented twice as large a percentage of the population in the Lower South (48 percent) as in the Upper South (23 percent). Consequently, whites in the Upper South had fewer fears that Republican ascendancy meant economic catastrophe, social chaos, and racial war. Lincoln would need to do more than just be elected to provoke them into secession.

The nation had to wait until March 4, 1861, when Lincoln took office, to see what he would do. (Presidents-elect waited four months to take office until 1933, when the Twentieth Amendment to the Constitution shifted the inauguration to January 20.) He chose to stay in Springfield after his election and to say nothing. "Lame-duck" president James Buchanan sat in Washington and did nothing. Congress's efforts at cobbling together a peace-saving compromise came to nothing.

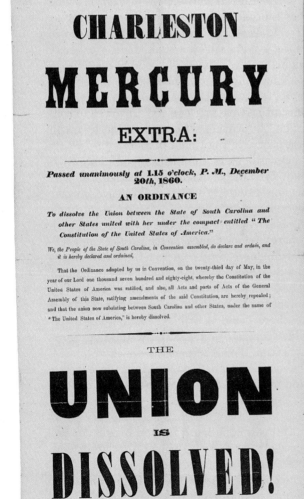

CHARLESTON MERCURY

EXTRA:

Passed unanimously at 1.15 o'clock, P. M., December 20th, 1860.

AN ORDINANCE

To dissolve the Union between the State of South Carolina and other States united with her under the compact entitled "The Constitution of the United States of America."

We, the People of the State of South Carolina, in Convention assembled, do declare and ordain, and it is hereby declared and ordained,

That the Ordinance adopted by us in Convention, on the twenty-third day of May, in the year of our Lord one thousand seven hundred and eighty-eight, whereby the Constitution of the United States of America was ratified, and also, all Acts and parts of Acts of the General Assembly of this State, ratifying amendments of the said Constitution, are hereby repealed; and that the union now subsisting between South Carolina and other States, under the name of "The United States of America," is hereby dissolved.

THE

UNION IS DISSOLVED!

The Union Is Dissolved
On December 20, 1860, the *Charleston Mercury* put out this special edition of the paper to celebrate South Carolina's secession from the Union. Six weeks earlier, on hearing the news that Lincoln had won the presidency, the Mercury had predicted as much, announcing, "The revolution of 1860 has been initiated." Gilder Lehrman Collection, New York, USA/The Bridgeman Art Library.

Lincoln began his inaugural address with reassurances to the South. He had "no lawful right" to interfere with slavery where it existed, he declared again, adding for emphasis that he had "no inclination to do so." Conciliatory about slavery, Lincoln proved inflexible about the Union. The Union, he declared, was "perpetual." Secession was "anarchy" and "legally void." The Constitution required him to execute the law "in all the States."

The decision for war or peace rested in the South's hands, Lincoln said. "You can have no conflict, without being yourselves the aggressors. *You* have no oath registered in Heaven to destroy the government, while I shall have the most solemn one to 'preserve, protect, and defend' it."

REVIEW   Why were the states of the Lower and Upper South divided on the question of secession during the winter of 1860–61?

▶ Conclusion: Slavery, Free Labor, and the Failure of Political Compromise

As their economies, societies, and cultures diverged in the nineteenth century, Northerners and Southerners expressed different concepts of the American promise and the place of slavery within it. Their differences crystallized into political form in 1846 when David Wilmot proposed banning slavery in any territory won in the Mexican-American War. "As if by magic," a Boston newspaper observed, "it brought to a head the great question that is about to divide the American people." Discovery of gold and other precious metals in the West added urgency to the controversy over slavery in the territories. Congress attempted to address the issue with the Compromise of 1850, but the Fugitive Slave Act and the publication of *Uncle Tom's Cabin* hardened northern sentiments against slavery and confirmed southern suspicions of northern ill will. The bloody violence that erupted in Kansas in 1856 and the incendiary *Dred Scott* decision in 1857 further eroded hope for a solution to this momentous question.

During the extended crisis of the Union that stretched from 1846 to 1861, the slavery question intertwined with national politics. The traditional Whig and Democratic parties struggled to hold together as new parties, most notably the Republican Party, emerged. Politicians fixed their attention on the expansion of slavery, but from the beginning Americans recognized that the controversy had less to do with slavery in the territories than with the future of slavery in the nation.

For more than seventy years, statesmen had found compromises that accepted slavery and preserved the Union. But as each section grew increasingly committed to its labor system, Americans discovered that accommodation had limits. In 1859, John Brown's militant antislavery pushed white Southerners to the edge. In 1860, Lincoln's election convinced whites in the Lower South that slavery and the society they had built on it were at risk in the Union, and they seceded. But it remained to be seen whether disunion would mean war.

See the Selected Bibliography for this chapter in the Appendix.

14 Chapter Review

MAKE IT STICK

LearningCurve
Go online and use LearningCurve to see what you know. Then review the key terms and answer the questions.

KEY TERMS

Wilmot Proviso (p. 373)
free labor (p. 373)
popular sovereignty (p. 375)
Compromise of 1850 (p. 377)
Uncle Tom's Cabin (p. 378)
Fugitive Slave Act (p. 379)
Kansas-Nebraska Act (p. 382)
Republican Party (p. 385)
"Bleeding Kansas" (p. 389)
Dred Scott decision (p. 390)
Lincoln-Douglas debates (p. 393)
Confederate States of America (p. 396)

REVIEW QUESTIONS

1. How might the Compromise of 1850 have eased sectional tensions? (pp. 376–377)

2. Why did the Compromise of 1850 fail to achieve sectional peace? (pp. 378–382)

3. Why did the Whig Party disintegrate in the 1850s? (pp. 383–387)

4. Why did the *Dred Scott* decision strengthen northern suspicions of a "Slave Power" conspiracy? (pp. 390–392)

5. Why were the states of the Lower and Upper South divided on the question of secession during the winter of 1860–61? (pp. 395–397)

MAKING CONNECTIONS

1. Compromise between slave and free states collapsed with secession. Why did compromise fail at this moment?

2. In the 1850s, many Americans supported popular sovereignty as the best solution to the explosive question of slavery in the western territories. Why was this solution so popular, and why did it ultimately prove inadequate?

3. In the 1840s and 1850s, the United States witnessed the realignment of its long-standing two-party system. Why did the old system fall apart, what emerged to take its place, and how did this process contribute to the coming of the Civil War?

4. Abraham Lincoln believed that he had staked out a moderate position on the question of slavery. Why, then, did some southern states determine that his election necessitated the radical act of secession?

LINKING TO THE PAST

1. How did social and economic developments in the South during the first half of the nineteenth century influence the decisions that southern politicians made in the 1840s and 1850s? (See chapter 13.)

2. How did the policies of the Republican Party reflect the free-labor ideals of the North? (See chapter 12.)

15 The Crucible of War

1861–1865

After reading and studying this chapter, you should be able to:

• Describe what each side was fighting for, and why they each believed they would win.

• Compare the Union's military results in the East and West in 1861 and 1862, and explain the significance of the Union blockade.

• Explain how the Civil War was transformed into a war to end slavery.

• Examine how the war affected Union and Confederate societies and economies, and how African Americans and women took part in the war effort.

• Describe how General Grant accomplished his plan for Union victory from 1863 to 1865 and why the Confederacy collapsed.

UNION PARADE DRUM
Drums signaled soldiers to report for breakfast, roll call, and guard duty, but the most important use of drums was on the battlefield where they communicated orders from commanding officers to their troops. Photo courtesy Allan Katz Americana, Woodbridge, CT.

ON THE NIGHT OF SEPTEMBER 21, 1862, IN WILMINGTON, North Carolina, twenty-four-year-old William Gould and seven other runaway slaves crowded into a small boat on the Cape Fear River. They rowed hard throughout the night, reaching the Atlantic Ocean by dawn. They made for the Union navy patrolling offshore. At 10:30 that morning, the USS *Cambridge* took the men aboard. Astonishingly, on that same day President Abraham Lincoln revealed his intention to issue a proclamation of emancipation freeing the slaves in the Confederate states. Although Gould was not legally free, the U.S. Navy needed sailors and cared little about the formal status of runaway slaves. Within days, all eight runaways became sailors in the U.S. Navy.

William Gould could read and write, and he began keeping a diary. In some ways, Gould's naval experience looked like that of a white sailor. He found duty on a ship in the blockading squadron both boring and exhilarating, as days of tedious work were occasionally interrupted by a moment of "daring exploit."

But Gould's Civil War experience was shaped by his race. Like most black men in the Union military, he saw service as an opportunity to fight slavery. Gould linked union and freedom, "the holiest of all causes." Gould witnessed a number of ugly racial incidents, however. When a black regiment came aboard, "they were treated verry rough by the crew," he said. The white sailors "refused to let them eat off the mess pans and called them all kinds of names[;] . . . in all they was treated shamefully."

Still, Gould was proud of his service in the navy and monitored the progress of racial equality during the war. In March 1865, he celebrated the "passage of an amendment of the Con[sti]tution prohibiting slavery througho[ut] the United States." And a month later, he thrilled to the "Glad Tidings that the Stars and Stripe[s] had been planted over the Capital of the D—nd Confederacy by the invincible Grant." He added, we must not forget the "Mayrters to the cau[se] of Right and Equality."

Early in the war, black abolitionist Frederick Douglass challenged the friends of freedom to *be up and doing;—now is your time*." But for the first eighteen months of the war, federal soldiers officially fought only to uphold the Constitution and preserve the nation. Only with the Emancipation Proclamation in 1863 did the northern war effort take on a dual purpose: to save the Union and to free the slaves.

As the world's first modern war, the Civil War transformed America. It mobilized the entire populations of North and South, harnessed the productive capacities of both economies, and produced battles that fielded 200,000 soldiers and created casualties in the tens of thousands. The carnage lasted four years and cost the nation between 620,000 and 750,000 lives. The war helped mold the modern American nation-state, and the federal government emerged with new power and responsibility over national life. It tore families apart and pushed women into new work and roles. But because the war ended slavery, it had truly revolutionary meaning.

Recalling the Civil War years, Frederick Douglass said, "It is something to couple one's name with great occasions." It *was* something— for William Gould and millions of other Americans. Whether they fought for the Confederacy or the Union, whether they labored behind the lines to supply Yankee or rebel soldiers, whether they prayed for the safe return of Northerners or Southerners, all Americans endured the crucible of war. But the war affected no group more than the nearly 4 million African Americans who saw its beginning as slaves and emerged as free people.

The Crew of the USS *Hunchback*

African Americans served as sailors in the federal military long before they were permitted to become soldiers. They initially served only as coal heavers, cooks, and stewards, but within a year some black sailors joined their ships' gun crews. The *Hunchback* was one of the Union's innovative ironclad ships. National Archives.

▶ "And the War Came"

Abraham Lincoln faced the worst crisis in the history of the nation: disunion. He revealed his strategy to save the Union in his inaugural address on March 4, 1861. He was firm yet conciliatory. First, he denied the right of secession and sought to stop its spread by avoiding any act that would push the skittish Upper South (North Carolina, Virginia, Maryland, Delaware, Kentucky, Tennessee, Missouri, and Arkansas) out of the Union. Second, he sought to reassure the seceding Lower South (South Carolina, Georgia, Florida, Alabama, Mississippi, Louisiana, and Texas) that the Republicans would not abolish slavery. Lincoln believed that Unionists there would assert themselves and overturn the secession decision. Always, Lincoln denied the right of secession and upheld the Union.

His counterpart, Jefferson Davis, fully intended to establish the Confederate States of America as an independent republic. To achieve permanence, Davis had to sustain the secession fever that had carried the Lower South out of the Union. Even if the Lower South held firm, however, the Confederacy would remain weak without additional states. Davis watched for opportunities to add new stars to the Confederate flag.

Neither man sought war; both wanted to achieve their objectives peacefully. As Lincoln later observed, "Both parties deprecated war, but one of them would *make* war rather than let the nation survive, and the other would *accept* war rather than let it perish. And the war came."

Attack on Fort Sumter

Major Robert Anderson and some eighty U.S. soldiers occupied Fort Sumter, which was perched on a tiny island at the entrance to Charleston harbor in South Carolina. The fort with its American flag became a hated symbol of the nation that Southerners had abandoned, and they wanted federal troops out. Sumter was also a symbol to Northerners, a beacon affirming federal authority in the seceded states.

Lincoln decided to hold the fort, but Anderson and his men were running dangerously short of food. In early April 1861, Lincoln authorized a peaceful expedition to bring supplies, but not military reinforcements, to the fort. The president understood that in seeking to relieve the fort he risked war, but his plan honored his inaugural promises to defend federal property and to

CHRONOLOGY

1861
- Attack on Fort Sumter.
- Four Upper South states join Confederacy.
- First battle of Bull Run (Manassas).
- First Confiscation Act.

1862
- Grant captures Fort Henry and Fort Donelson.
- Battle of Glorieta Pass.
- Battle of Pea Ridge.
- Battle of Shiloh.
- Confederate Congress authorizes draft.
- Homestead Act.
- Virginia peninsula campaign.
- Second Confiscation Act.
- Militia Act.
- Battle of Antietam.

1863
- Emancipation Proclamation.
- National Banking Act.
- Congress authorizes draft.
- Fall of Vicksburg to Union forces.
- Lee defeated at battle of Gettysburg.
- New York City draft riots.

1864
- Grant appointed Union general in chief.
- Wilderness campaign.
- Fall of Atlanta.
- Lincoln reelected.
- Fall of Savannah.

1865
- Fall of Petersburg and Richmond.
- Lee surrenders to Grant.
- Lincoln assassinated; Vice President Andrew Johnson becomes president.

Fort Sumter
The Confederate bombardment that began the Civil War on April 12, 1861, lobbed more than 4,000 rounds at Fort Sumter. Shrapnel from thirty-three hours of cannon fire shredded this flag. When Union major Robert Anderson surrendered on April 13, he and his men marched out of the fort under this tattered banner. When Anderson returned in April 1865, he raised this very flag.
Photograph: Minnesota Historical Society; flag: United Daughters of the Confederacy.

the rebellion, several times that number rushed to defend the flag. Democrats responded as fervently as Republicans. Stephen A. Douglas, the recently defeated Democratic candidate for president, pledged his support and noted, "There can be no neutrals in this war, *only patriots—or traitors.*" But the people of the Upper South found themselves torn.

The Upper South Chooses Sides

The Upper South faced a horrendous choice: either to fight against the Lower South or to fight against the Union. Many who only months earlier had rejected secession now embraced the Confederacy. To vote against southern independence was one thing, to fight fellow Southerners quite another. Thousands felt betrayed, believing that Lincoln had promised to achieve a peaceful reunion by waiting patiently for Unionists to retake power in the seceding states. It was a "politician's war," one man declared, but he conceded that "this is no time now to discuss the causes, but it is the duty of all who regard Southern institutions of value to side with the South, make common cause with the Confederate States and sink or swim with them."

Virginia, Arkansas, Tennessee, and North Carolina joined the Confederacy (Map 15.1). But in the border states of Delaware, Maryland, Kentucky, and Missouri, Unionism triumphed. Only in Delaware, where slaves accounted for less than 2 percent of the population, was the victory easy. In Maryland, Unionism needed a helping hand. Lincoln suspended the writ of habeas corpus, essentially setting aside constitutional guarantees that protect citizens from arbitrary arrest and detention, and he ordered U.S. troops into Baltimore. Maryland's legislature rejected secession.

The struggle turned violent in the West. In Missouri, Unionists won a narrow victory, but southern-sympathizing guerrilla bands roamed the state for the duration of the war, terrorizing civilians and soldiers alike. In Kentucky, Unionists also narrowly defeated secession, but the prosouthern minority claimed otherwise. Throughout the border states, secession divided families. Seven of Kentuckian Henry Clay's grandsons fought: four for the Confederacy and three for the Union.

Lincoln understood that the border states—particularly Kentucky—contained indispensable resources, population, and wealth and also controlled major rivers and railroads. "I think to lose Kentucky is nearly the same as to lose

avoid using military force unless first attacked. Masterfully, Lincoln had shifted the fateful decision of war or peace to Jefferson Davis.

On April 9, Davis and his cabinet met to consider the situation in Charleston harbor. Davis argued for military action, but his secretary of state, Robert Toombs of Georgia, replied: "Mr. President, at this time it is suicide, murder, and will lose us every friend at the North. You will wantonly strike a hornet's nest which extends from mountain to ocean, and legions now quiet will swarm out and sting us to death." But Davis ordered Confederate troops in Charleston to take the fort before the relief expedition arrived. Thirty-three hours of bombardment on April 12 and 13 reduced the fort to rubble. On April 14, Major Anderson offered his surrender and lowered the U.S. flag. The Confederates had Fort Sumter, but they also had war.

On April 15, when Lincoln called for 75,000 militiamen to serve for ninety days to put down

MAP 15.1

Secession, 1860–1861
After Lincoln's election, the fifteen slave states debated what to do. Seven states quickly left the Union, four left after the firing on Fort Sumter, and four remained loyal to the Union.

Legend:
- Seceded before fall of Fort Sumter
- Seceded after fall of Fort Sumter
- Slave state loyal to Union
- Free state
- Territory
- 1 Order of secession

the whole game," Lincoln said. "Kentucky gone, we can not hold Missouri, nor, as I think, Maryland. These all against us, . . . we would as well consent to separation at once."

In the end, only eleven of the fifteen slave states joined the Confederate States of America. Moreover, the four seceding Upper South states contained significant numbers of people who felt little affection for the Confederacy. Dissatisfaction was so rife in the western counties of Virginia that in 1863 citizens there voted to create the separate state of West Virginia, loyal to the Union. Still, the acquisition of four new states greatly strengthened the Confederacy's drive for national independence.

REVIEW Why did the attack on Fort Sumter force the Upper South to choose sides?

▶ The Combatants

Only slaveholders had a direct economic stake in preserving slavery, but most whites in the Confederacy defended the institution, the way of life built on it, and the Confederate nation. The degraded and subjugated status of blacks elevated the status of the poorest whites. "It is enough that one simply belongs to the superior and ruling race, to secure consideration and respect." Moreover, Yankee "aggression" was no longer a mere threat; it was real and at the South's door.

For Northerners, the South's failure to accept the democratic election of a president and its firing on the nation's flag challenged the rule of law, the authority of the Constitution, and the ability of the people to govern themselves. As an Indiana soldier told his wife, a "good government is the best thing on earth. Property is nothing without it, because it is not protected; a family is nothing without it, because they cannot be educated." Only a Union victory, Lincoln declared, would secure America's promise "to elevate the condition of man."

Northerners and Southerners rallied behind their separate flags, fully convinced that they were in the right and that God was on their side. Yankees took heart from their superior power, but the rebels believed they had advantages that nullified every northern strength. Both sides mobilized swiftly in 1861, and each devised what it believed would be a winning military and diplomatic strategy.

How They Expected to Win

The balance sheet of northern and southern resources reveals enormous advantages for the Union (Figure 15.1). The twenty-three states remaining in the Union had a population of 22.3 million; the eleven Confederate states had a population of only 9.1 million, of whom 3.67 million (40 percent) were slaves. The North's economic advantages were even more overwhelming. Yet Southerners expected to win—for some good reasons—and they came very close to doing so.

FIGURE 15.1   Resources of the Union and the Confederacy
The Union's enormous statistical advantages failed to convince Confederates that their cause was doomed.

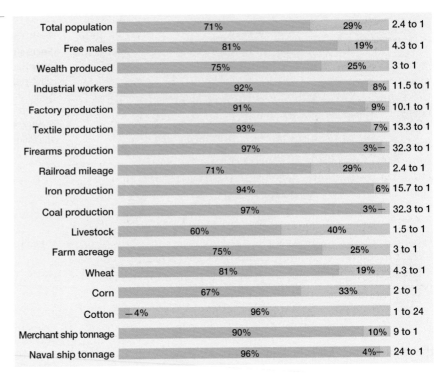

	Union	Confederacy	Ratio
Total population	71%	29%	2.4 to 1
Free males	81%	19%	4.3 to 1
Wealth produced	75%	25%	3 to 1
Industrial workers	92%	8%	11.5 to 1
Factory production	91%	9%	10.1 to 1
Textile production	93%	7%	13.3 to 1
Firearms production	97%	3%—	32.3 to 1
Railroad mileage	71%	29%	2.4 to 1
Iron production	94%	6%	15.7 to 1
Coal production	97%	3%—	32.3 to 1
Livestock	60%	40%	1.5 to 1
Farm acreage	75%	25%	3 to 1
Wheat	81%	19%	4.3 to 1
Corn	67%	33%	2 to 1
Cotton	—4%	96%	1 to 24
Merchant ship tonnage	90%	10%	9 to 1
Naval ship tonnage	96%	4%—	24 to 1

Southerners knew they bucked the military odds, but hadn't the liberty-loving colonists in 1776 also done so? "Britain could not conquer three million," a Louisianan proclaimed, and "the world cannot conquer the South." How could anyone doubt the outcome of a contest between lean, hard, country-born rebel warriors defending family, property, and liberty, and soft, flabby, citified Yankee mechanics waging an unconstitutional war?

The South's confidence also rested on its belief that northern prosperity depended on the South's cotton. Without cotton, New England textile mills would stand idle. Without planters purchasing northern manufactured goods, northern factories would drown in their own unsold surpluses. And without the foreign exchange earned by the overseas sales of cotton, the financial structure of the entire Yankee nation would collapse. A Virginian spoke for most Confederates when he declared that in the South's ability to "withhold the benefits of our trade, we hold a power over the North more powerful than a powerful army in the field."

Cotton would also make Europe a powerful ally of the Confederacy, Southerners reasoned. Of the 900 million pounds of cotton Britain imported annually, more than 700 million pounds came from the American South. If the supply was interrupted, sheer economic need would make Britain (and perhaps France) a Confederate ally. And because the British navy ruled the seas, the North would find Britain a formidable foe.

The Confederacy devised a military strategy to exploit its advantages and minimize its limitations. It recognized that a Union victory required the North to defeat and subjugate the South, but a Confederate victory required only that the South stay at home, blunt invasions, avoid battles that risked annihilating its army, and outlast the North's will to fight. When an opportunity presented itself, the South would strike the invaders. Like the American colonists, the South could win independence by not losing the war.

The Lincoln administration countered with an aggressive strategy designed to take advantage of its superior resources. Lincoln declared a naval blockade of the Confederacy to deny it the ability to sell cotton abroad, giving the South far fewer dollars to pay for war goods. Lincoln also ordered the Union army into Virginia, at the same time planning a march through the Mississippi valley that would cut the Confederacy in two.

Most Americans thought of war in terms of their most recent experience, the Mexican-American War in the 1840s. In Mexico, fighting had taken relatively small numbers of lives and had inflicted only light damage on the countryside. They could not imagine the four ghastly years of bloodletting that lay ahead.

Lincoln and Davis Mobilize

Mobilization required effective political leadership, and at first glance the South appeared to have the advantage. Jefferson Davis brought to the Confederate presidency a distinguished political career, including experience in the U.S. Senate. He was also a West Point graduate, a combat veteran and authentic hero of the Mexican-American War, and a former secretary of war. Dignified and ramrod straight, with "a jaw sawed in steel," Davis appeared to be everything a nation could want in a wartime leader.

By contrast, Abraham Lincoln brought to the White House one lackluster term in the House of Representatives and almost no administrative experience. His sole brush with anything military was as a captain in the militia in the Black Hawk War, a brief struggle in Illinois in 1832 in which whites expelled the last Indians from the state. The lanky, disheveled Illinois lawyer-politician looked anything but military or presidential in his bearing.

Davis, however, proved to be less than he appeared. Although he worked hard, he had no gift for military strategy yet intervened often in military affairs. He was an even less able political leader. Quarrelsome and proud, he had an acid tongue that made enemies the Confederacy could ill afford. In his defense, the Confederacy's intimidating problems might have defeated an even more talented leader.

With Lincoln the North got far more than met the eye. He proved himself a master politician and a superb leader. When forming his cabinet, Lincoln appointed the ablest men, no matter that they were often his chief rivals and critics. He appointed Salmon P. Chase secretary of the treasury, knowing that Chase had presidential ambitions. As secretary of state, he chose his chief opponent for the Republican nomination in 1860, William H. Seward. Despite his civilian background, Lincoln displayed an innate understanding of military strategy. No one was more crucial in mapping the Union war plan.

Lincoln and Davis began gathering their armies. Confederates had to build almost everything from scratch, and Northerners had to channel their superior numbers and industrial resources to war. On the eve of the war, the federal army numbered only 16,000 men. One-third of the officers followed the example of the Virginian Robert E. Lee, resigning their commissions and heading south. The U.S. Navy was in better shape. Forty-two ships were in service, and a large merchant marine would in time provide more ships and sailors for the Union cause. Possessing a much weaker navy, the South pinned its hopes on its armies.

The Confederacy made prodigious efforts to build factories to supply its armies with tents, blankets, shoes, and uniforms, but even when factories produced what soldiers needed, southern railroads often could not deliver the goods. And each year, more railroads were captured, destroyed, or left in disrepair. Food production proved less of a problem, but food sometimes rotted before it reached the soldiers. The one bright spot was the Confederacy's Ordnance Bureau, headed by Josiah Gorgas. In April 1864, Gorgas proudly observed: "Where three years ago we were not making a gun, a pistol nor a sabre, no shot nor shell . . . we now make all these in quantities to meet the demands of our large armies."

Recruiting and supplying huge armies required enormous new revenues. At first, the Union and the Confederacy sold war bonds, which essentially were loans from patriotic citizens. In addition, both sides turned to taxes. Eventually, both began printing paper money. Inflation soared, but the Confederacy suffered more because it financed a greater part of its wartime costs through the printing press. Prices in the Union rose by about 80 percent during the war, while inflation in the Confederacy topped 9,000 percent.

Within months of the bombardment of Fort Sumter, both sides found men to fight and ways to supply them. But the underlying strength of the northern economy gave the Union the decided advantage. With their military and industrial muscles beginning to ripple, Northerners became itchy for action that would smash the rebellion.

The Minié Ball
None of the Union army's weaponry proved more vital than a French innovation by Captain Claude Minié. In 1848, Minié created an inch-long bullet that was rammed down a rifle barrel and would spin as it left the muzzle. The spin gave the bullet greater distance and accuracy than bullets fired from smoothbore weapons. Bullets caused more than 90 percent of battle wounds. Picture Research Consultants & Archives.

Horace Greeley's *New York Tribune* began to chant: "Forward to Richmond! Forward to Richmond!"

> **REVIEW** Why did the South believe it could win the war despite numerical disadvantages?

▶ Battling It Out, 1861–1862

During the first year and a half of the war, armies fought major campaigns in both the East and West. While the eastern campaign was more dramatic, Lincoln had trouble finding a capable general, and the fighting ended in a stalemate. Battles in the West proved more decisive. Union general Ulysses S. Grant won important victories in Kentucky and Tennessee. As Yankee and rebel armies pounded each other on land, the navies fought on the seas and on the rivers of the South. In Europe, Confederate and U.S. diplomats competed for advantage in the corridors of power. All the while, casualty lists on both sides reached appalling lengths.

Stalemate in the Eastern Theater

In the summer of 1861, Lincoln ordered the 35,000 Union troops assembling outside Washington to attack the 20,000 Confederates defending Manassas, a railroad junction in Virginia about thirty miles southwest of Washington. On July 21, the army forded Bull Run, a branch of the Potomac River, and engaged the southern forces (Map 15.2). But fast-moving southern reinforcements blunted the Union attack and then counterattacked. What began as an orderly Union retreat turned into a panicky stampede.

By Civil War standards, the casualties (wounded and dead) at the **battle of Bull Run** (or **Manassas**, as Southerners called the battle) were light, about 2,000 Confederates and 1,600 Federals. The significance of the battle lay in the lessons North-

Peninsula Campaign, 1862

erners and Southerners drew from it. For Southerners, it confirmed the superiority of rebel fighting men and the inevitability of Confederate nationhood. Manassas was "*one of the decisive battles of the world*," a Georgian proclaimed. It "*has* secured our independence." On the other hand, defeat sobered Northerners. It was a major setback, admitted the *New York Tribune*, but "let us go to work, then, with a will." Within four days of the disaster, the president authorized the enlistment of 1 million men for three years.

Lincoln also found a new general, the young George B. McClellan, whom he appointed commander of the newly named Army of the Potomac. Having graduated from West Point second in his class, the thirty-four-year-old McClellan believed that he was a great soldier and that Lincoln was a dunce, the "original Gorilla." A superb administrator and organizer, McClellan energetically whipped his dispirited soldiers into shape, but for all his energy, McClellan lacked decisiveness. Lincoln wanted a general who would advance, take risks, and fight, but McClellan went into winter quarters. "If General McClellan does not want to use the army I would like to *borrow* it," Lincoln declared in frustration.

Finally, in May 1862, McClellan launched his long-awaited offensive. He transported his highly polished army, now 130,000 strong, to the mouth of the James River and began slowly moving up the Yorktown peninsula toward Richmond. When he was within six miles of the Confederate capital, General Joseph Johnston hit him like a hammer. In the assault, Johnston was wounded and was replaced by Robert E. Lee, who would become the South's most celebrated general. Lee named his command the Army of Northern Virginia.

The contrast between Lee and McClellan could hardly have been greater. McClellan brimmed with conceit; Lee was courteous and reserved. On the battlefield, McClellan grew timid and irresolute, and Lee became audaciously, even recklessly, aggressive. And Lee had at his side in the peninsula campaign military men of real talent: Thomas J. Jackson, nicknamed "Stonewall" for holding the line at Manassas, and

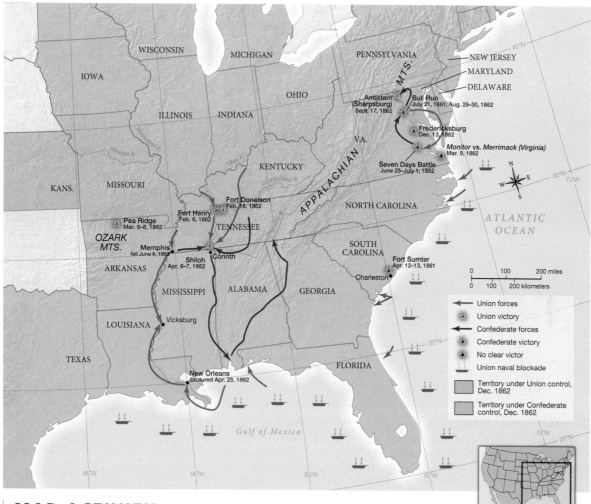

MAP ACTIVITY

Map 15.2   The Civil War, 1861–1862

While most eyes were focused on the eastern theater, especially the ninety-mile stretch of land between Washington, D.C., and the Confederate capital of Richmond, Virginia, Union troops were winning strategic victories in the West.

READING THE MAP: In which states did the Confederacy and the Union each win the most battles during this period? Which side used or followed water routes most for troop movements and attacks?

CONNECTIONS: Which major cities in the South and West fell to Union troops in 1862? Which strategic area did those Confederate losses place in Union hands? How did this outcome affect the later movement of troops and supplies?

James E. B. ("Jeb") Stuart, a dashing twenty-nine-year-old cavalry commander who rode circles around Yankee troops.

Lee's assault initiated the Seven Days Battle (June 25–July 1) and began McClellan's march back down the peninsula. By the time McClellan reached safety, 30,000 men from both sides had died or been wounded. Although Southerners suffered twice the casualties of Northerners, Lee had saved Richmond. Lincoln fired McClellan and replaced him with General John Pope.

In August, north of Richmond, at the second battle of Bull Run, Lee's smaller army battered Pope's forces and sent them scurrying back to Washington. Lincoln ordered Pope to Minnesota to pacify the Indians and restored McClellan to command. Lincoln had not changed his mind about McClellan's capacity as a warrior, but he had concluded, "There is no man in the Army who can lick these troops of ours into shape half as well as he. . . . If he can't fight himself, he excels in making others ready to fight."

The Dead of Antietam
In October 1862, photographer Mathew Brady opened an exhibition that presented the battle of Antietam as the soldiers saw it. A *New York Times* reporter observed, "Mr. Brady has done something to bring to us the terrible reality and earnestness of the war. If he has not brought bodies and laid them in our door-yards and along [our] streets, he had done something very like it." Library of Congress.

Believing that he had the enemy on the run, Lee pushed his army across the Potomac and invaded Maryland. A victory on northern soil would dislodge Maryland from the Union, Lee reasoned, and might even cause Lincoln to sue for peace. On September 17, 1862, McClellan's forces engaged Lee's army at Antietam Creek (see Map 15.2). With "solid shot . . . cracking skulls like eggshells," according to one observer, the armies went after each other. At Miller's Cornfield, the firing was so intense that "every stalk of corn in the . . . field was cut as closely as could have been done with a knife." By nightfall, 6,000 men lay dead or dying on the battlefield, and 17,000 more had been wounded. The **battle of Antietam** would be the bloodiest day of the war and sent the battered Army of Northern Virginia limping back home. McClellan claimed to have saved the North, but Lincoln again removed him from command of the Army of the Potomac and appointed General Ambrose Burnside.

Though bloodied, Lee found an opportunity in December to punish the enemy at Fredericksburg, Virginia, where Burnside's 122,000 Union troops faced 78,500 Confederates dug in behind a stone wall on the heights above the Rappahannock River. Half a mile of open ground separated the armies. "A chicken could not live on that field when we open on it," a Confederate artillery officer predicted. Yet Burnside ordered a frontal assault. When the shooting ceased, the Federals counted nearly 13,000 casualties, the Confederates fewer than 5,000. The battle of Fredericksburg was one of the Union's worst defeats. As 1862 ended, the North seemed no nearer to ending the rebellion than it had been when the war began. Rather than checkmate, military struggle in the East had reached stalemate.

Union Victories in the Western Theater

While most eyes focused on events in the East, the decisive early encounters of the war were taking place between the Appalachian Mountains and the Ozarks (see Map 15.2). Confederates

VISUAL ACTIVITY

Battle of Fredericksburg, 1862

This painting by Private John Richards (1831–1889) of the New York Volunteers captures the behind-the-lines Union activity at the battle of Fredericksburg. Long rows of fresh troops await orders to march up the hill to join the fighting underway in the distance. Barely visible, the cavalry charges off into one of the Union's greatest failures. These foot soldiers will follow the cavalry soon. Private Collection/Peter Newark Military Pictures/The Bridgeman Art Library.

READING THE IMAGE: What does the artist portray in the lower left of the painting? What are the lines of wagons hauling?

CONNECTIONS: At Fredericksburg, General Ambrose Burnside joined the list of failed Union generals. What other Union defeats can be attributed, at least in part, to failed Union leadership?

wanted Missouri and Kentucky, states they claimed but did not control. Federals wanted to split Arkansas, Louisiana, and Texas from the Confederacy by taking control of the Mississippi River and to occupy Tennessee, one of the Confederacy's main producers of food, mules, and iron—all vital resources.

Before Union forces could march on Tennessee, they needed to secure Missouri to the west. Union troops swept across Missouri to the border of Arkansas, where in March 1862 they encountered a 16,000-man Confederate army, which included three regiments of Indians from the so-called Five Civilized Tribes—the Choctaw, Chickasaw, Creek, Seminole, and Cherokee. The Union victory at the battle of Pea Ridge left Missouri free of Confederate troops, but guerrilla bands led by the notorious William Clarke Quantrill and "Bloody Bill" Anderson burned, tortured, scalped, and murdered Union civilians and soldiers until the final year of the war.

Even farther west, Confederate armies sought to fulfill Jefferson Davis's vision of a slaveholding empire stretching all the way to the Pacific. Both sides recognized the immense value of the gold and silver mines of California,

VISUAL ACTIVITY

Native American Recruits

Both the Union and the Confederacy enrolled Indian soldiers. Here, a Union recruiter swears in two recruits. Cherokee chief John Ross, who signed with the Confederacy, likened his difficult choice to that of a man in a flood who sees a log floating by. "By refusing [the log] he is a doomed man. By seizing hold of it he has a chance for his life." Wisconsin Historical Society, WHS-1909.

READING THE IMAGE: What does the clothing of these Indians suggest may have been their motive for joining?

CONNECTIONS: As the Union's search for more soldiers expanded, who else was caught in the Northerner's net?

Battle of Glorieta Pass, 1862

Nevada, and Colorado. And both sides bolstered their armies in the Southwest with Mexican Americans. A quick strike by Texas troops took Santa Fe, New Mexico, in the winter of 1861–62. Then in March 1862, a band of Colorado miners ambushed and crushed southern forces at Glorieta Pass, outside Santa Fe, effectively ending dreams of a Confederate empire beyond Texas.

The principal western battles took place in Tennessee, where General Ulysses S. Grant emerged as the key northern commander. Grant, a West Point graduate who served in Mexico, was a thirty-nine-year-old dry-goods clerk in Galena, Illinois, when the war began. Gentle at home, he became pugnacious on the battle-field. "The art of war is simple," he said. "Find out where your enemy is, get at him as soon as you can and strike him as hard as you can, and keep moving on." Grant's philosophy of war as attrition would take a huge toll in human life, but it played to the North's superiority in manpower. Later, to critics who wanted the president to sack Grant because of his drinking, Lincoln would say, "*I can't spare this man. He fights.*"

In February 1862, operating in tandem with U.S. Navy gunboats, Grant captured Fort Henry on the Tennessee River and Fort Donelson on the Cumberland (see Map 15.2). Defeat forced the Confederates to withdraw from all of Kentucky and most of Tennessee, but Grant followed.

On April 6, General Albert Sidney Johnston's army surprised Grant at Shiloh Church in Tennessee. Union troops were badly mauled the first day, but Grant remained cool and brought up reinforcements throughout the night. The next morning, the Union army counterattacked, driving the Confederates before it. The **battle of Shiloh** was terribly costly to both sides; there were 20,000 casualties, among them General Johnston. Grant later said that after Shiloh he "gave up all idea of saving the Union except by complete conquest."

Although no one knew it at the time, Shiloh ruined the Confederacy's bid to control the theater of operations in the West. The Yankees quickly captured the strategic town of Corinth, Mississippi; the river city of Memphis; and the South's largest city, New Orleans. By the end of 1862, the far West and most—but not all—of the Mississippi valley lay in Union hands. At the same time, the outcome of the struggle in another theater of war was also becoming clearer.

The Atlantic Theater

When the war began, the U.S. Navy's blockade fleet consisted of about three dozen ships to patrol more than 3,500 miles of southern coastline, and rebel merchant ships were able to slip in and out of southern ports nearly at will. Taking on cargoes in the Caribbean, sleek Confederate blockade runners brought in vital supplies—guns and medicine. But with the U.S. Navy commissioning a new blockader almost weekly, the naval fleet eventually numbered 150 ships on duty, and the Union navy dramatically improved its score.

Unable to build a conventional navy equal to the expanding U.S. fleet, the Confederates experimented with a radical new maritime design: the ironclad warship. At Norfolk, Virginia, the wooden hull of the *Merrimack* was layered with two-inch-thick armor plate. Rechristened *Virginia*, the ship steamed out in March 1862 and sank two wooden federal ships (see Map 15.2). When the *Virginia* returned to finish off the federal blockaders the next morning, it was challenged by the *Monitor*, a federal ironclad of even more radical design, topped with a revolving turret holding two eleven-inch guns. On March 9, the two ships hurled shells at each other for two hours, but the battle ended in a draw.

The Confederacy never found a way to break the **Union blockade** despite exploring many naval innovations, including a new underwater vessel—the submarine. By 1865, the blockaders were intercepting about half of the southern ships attempting to break through. The Union navy, a southern naval officer observed, "shut the Confederacy out from the world, deprived it of supplies, weakened its military and naval

Major Battles of the Civil War, 1861–1862

April 12–13, 1861	Attack on Fort Sumter
July 21, 1861	First battle of Bull Run (Manassas)
February 6, 1862	Battle of Fort Henry
February 16, 1862	Battle of Fort Donelson
March 6–8, 1862	Battle of Pea Ridge
March 9, 1862	Battle of the *Merrimack* (the *Virginia*) and the *Monitor*
March 26, 1862	Battle of Glorieta Pass
April 6–7, 1862	Battle of Shiloh
May–July 1862	McClellan's peninsula campaign
June 6, 1862	Fall of Memphis
June 25–July 1, 1862	Seven Days Battle
August 29–30, 1862	Second battle of Bull Run (Manassas)
September 17, 1862	Battle of Antietam
December 13, 1862	Battle of Fredericksburg

strength." The Confederacy was sealed off, with devastating results.

International Diplomacy

What the Confederates could not achieve on the seas, they sought to achieve through international diplomacy. They based their hope for European intervention on King Cotton. In theory, cotton-starved European nations would have no choice but to break the Union blockade and recognize the Confederacy. Southern hopes were not unreasonable, for at the height of the "cotton famine" in 1862, when 2 million British workers were unemployed, Britain tilted toward recognition. Along with several other European nations, Britain granted the Confederacy "belligerent" status, which enabled it to buy goods and build ships in European ports. But no country challenged the Union blockade or recognized the Confederate States of America as a nation, a bold act that probably would have drawn that country into war.

King Cotton diplomacy failed for several reasons. A bumper cotton crop in 1860 meant that the warehouses of British textile manufacturers bulged with surplus cotton throughout 1861. In 1862, when a cotton shortage did occur, European manufacturers found new sources in India, Egypt, and elsewhere (Figure 15.2).

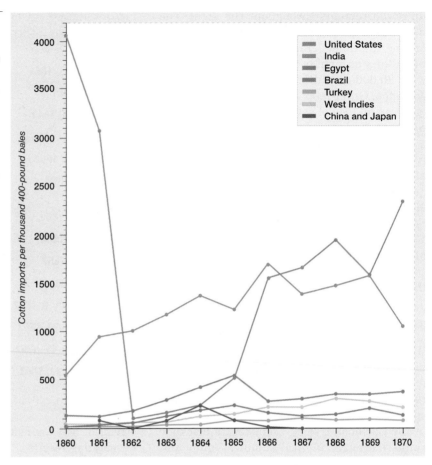

FIGURE 15.2 **Global Comparison: European Cotton Imports, 1860–1870**
In 1860, the South enjoyed a near monopoly in supplying cotton to Europe's textile mills, but the Civil War almost entirely halted its exports. Figures for Europe's importation of cotton for 1861 to 1865 reveal one of the reasons the Confederacy's King Cotton diplomacy failed: Europeans found other sources of cotton. Which countries were most important in filling the void? When the war ended in 1865, cotton production resumed in the South, and exports to Europe again soared. Did the South regain its near monopoly? How would you characterize the United States' competitive position five years after the war?

In addition, the development of a brisk trade between the Union and Britain—British war material for American grain and flour—helped offset the decline in textiles and encouraged Britain to remain neutral.

Europe's temptation to intervene disappeared for good in 1862. Union military successes in the West made Britain and France think twice about linking their fates to the struggling Confederacy. Moreover, in September 1862, Lincoln announced a new policy that made an alliance with the Confederacy an alliance with slavery—a commitment the French and British, who had outlawed slavery in their empires and looked forward to its eradication worldwide, were not willing to make. After 1862, the South's cause was linked irrevocably with slavery and reaction, and the Union's cause was linked with freedom and democracy. The Union, not the Confederacy, had won the diplomatic stakes.

REVIEW Why did the Confederacy's bid for international support fail?

▶ Union *and* Freedom

For a year and a half, Lincoln insisted that the North fought strictly to save the Union and not to abolish slavery. Nevertheless, the war for union became a war for African American freedom. Each month the conflict dragged on, it became clearer that the Confederate war machine depended heavily on slavery. Rebel armies used slaves to build fortifications, haul material, tend horses, and perform camp chores. On the southern home front, slaves labored in ironworks and shipyards, and they grew the food that fed both soldiers and civilians. As Frederick Douglass put it, slavery was the "stomach of this rebellion." Slavery undergirded the Confederacy as certainly as it had the Old South. In the field among Union military commanders, in the halls of Congress, and in the White House, the truth gradually came into focus: To defeat the Confederacy, the North would have to destroy slavery. "I am a slow walker," Lincoln said, "but I never walk back." Lincoln's Emancipation Proclamation began the work, and soon African Americans flooded into the Union army, where they fought against the Confederacy and for black freedom.

From Slaves to Contraband

Lincoln detested human bondage, but as president he felt compelled to act prudently in the interests of the Union. He doubted his right under the Constitution to tamper with the "domestic institutions" of any state, even states in rebellion. An astute politician, Lincoln worked within the tight limits of public opinion. The issue of black freedom was particularly explosive in the loyal border states, where slaveholders threatened to jump into the arms of the Confederacy at even the hint of emancipation.

Black freedom also raised alarms in the free states. The Democratic Party gave notice that adding emancipation to the goal of union would make the war strictly a Republican affair. Moreover, many white Northerners were not about to risk their lives to satisfy what they considered abolitionist "fanaticism." "We Won't Fight to Free the Nigger," one popular banner read. They feared that emancipation would propel "two or three million semi-savages" northward, where they would crowd into white neighborhoods, compete for white jobs, and mix with white "sons and daughters." Thus, emancipation threatened to dislodge the loyal slave states from the Union, alienate the Democratic Party, deplete the armies, and perhaps even spark race warfare.

Yet proponents of emancipation pressed Lincoln as relentlessly as did the anti-emancipation forces. Abolitionists argued that by seceding, Southerners had forfeited their right to the protection of the Constitution and that Lincoln could—as the price of their treason—legally confiscate their property in slaves. When Lincoln refused, abolitionists scalded him. Frederick Douglass labeled him "the miserable tool of traitors and rebels."

The Republican-dominated Congress declined to leave slavery policy entirely in President Lincoln's hands. In August 1861, Congress approved the Confiscation Act, which allowed the seizure of any slave employed directly by the Confederate military. It also fulfilled the free-soil dream of prohibiting slavery in the territories and abolished slavery in Washington, D.C. Democrats and border-state representatives voted against even these mild measures.

Slaves, not politicians, became the most insistent force for emancipation. By escaping their masters by the tens of thousands and running away to Union lines, they forced slavery on the North's wartime agenda. Runaways made Northerners answer a crucial question: Were the runaways now free, or were they still slaves who, according to the fugitive slave law, had to be returned to their masters? At first, Yankee military officers sent the fugitives back. But Union armies needed laborers, and at Fort Monroe, Virginia, General Benjamin F. Butler called runaways **contraband of war**, meaning "confiscated property," and put them to work. Congress made Butler's practice national policy in March 1862 when it forbade returning fugitive slaves to their masters. Slaves were still not legally free, but there was a tilt toward emancipation.

Human Contraband
These refugees from slavery crossed the Rappahannock River in Virginia in August 1862 to seek sanctuary with a federal army. Most slaves fled with little more than the clothes on their backs, but not all escaped slavery empty-handed. The oxen, horse, wagon, and goods seen here could have been purchased during slavery, "borrowed" from the former master, or gathered during flight.
Library of Congress.

Lincoln's policy of noninterference with slavery gradually crumbled. To calm Northerners' racial fears, Lincoln offered colonization, the deportation of African Americans from the United States to Haiti, Panama, or elsewhere. In the summer of 1862, he told a delegation of black visitors that racial prejudice among whites made it impossible for blacks to achieve equality in the United States. One African American responded, "This is our country as much as it is yours, and we will not leave it." Congress voted a small amount of money to underwrite colonization, but practical limitations and stiff black opposition sank the scheme.

While Lincoln was developing his own antislavery initiatives, he snuffed out actions that he believed would jeopardize northern unity. He was particularly alert to Union commanders who tried to dictate slavery policy from the field. In August 1861, when John C. Frémont, former Republican presidential nominee and now commander of federal troops in Missouri, freed the slaves belonging to Missouri rebels, Lincoln forced the general to revoke his edict. The following May, when General David Hunter freed the slaves in Georgia, South Carolina, and Florida, Lincoln countermanded his order. Events moved so rapidly, however, that Lincoln found it impossible to control federal policy on slavery.

From Contraband to Free People

On August 22, 1862, Lincoln replied to an angry abolitionist who demanded that he attack slavery. "My paramount objective in this struggle *is* to save the Union," Lincoln said, "and is *not* either to save or destroy slavery. If I could save the Union without freeing *any* slave I would do it, and if I could save it by freeing *all* the slaves I would do it; and if I could save it by freeing some and leaving others alone I would also do that." At first glance, Lincoln seemed to restate his old position that union was the North's sole objective. Instead, Lincoln announced that slavery was no longer untouchable and that he would emancipate every slave if doing so would preserve the Union.

By the summer of 1862, events were tumbling rapidly toward emancipation. On July 17, Congress adopted the second Confiscation Act. The first had confiscated slaves employed by the Confederate military; the second declared all slaves of rebel masters "forever free of their servitude." In theory, this breathtaking measure freed most Confederate slaves, for slaveholders formed the backbone of the rebellion. Congress had traveled far since the war began.

Lincoln had too. By July, 1862, the president had come to believe that emancipation was "a military necessity, absolutely essential to the preservation of the Union." The lengthening casualty lists had finally brought him around. In September, he announced his preliminary **Emancipation Proclamation** that promised to free *all* the slaves in the seceding states on January 1, 1863. The limitations of the proclamation—it exempted the loyal border states and the Union-occupied areas of the Confederacy—caused some to ridicule the act. The *Times* (London) observed cynically, "Where he has no power Mr. Lincoln will set the negroes free, where he retains power he will consider them as slaves." But Lincoln had no power to free slaves in loyal states, and invading Union armies would liberate slaves in the Confederacy as they advanced.

By presenting emancipation as a "military necessity," Lincoln hoped to disarm his conservative critics. Emancipation would deprive the Confederacy of valuable slave laborers, shorten the war, and thus save lives. Democrats, however, fumed that the "shrieking and howling abolitionist faction" had captured the White House and made it "a nigger war." Democrats gained thirty-four congressional seats in the November 1862 elections. House Democrats quickly proposed a resolution branding emancipation "a high crime against the Constitution." The Republicans, who maintained narrow majorities in both houses of Congress, barely beat it back.

As promised, on New Year's Day 1863, Lincoln issued the final Emancipation Proclamation. In addition to freeing the slaves in the rebel states, the Emancipation Proclamation also committed the federal government to the fullest use of African Americans to defeat the Confederate enemy.

The War of Black Liberation

Even before Lincoln proclaimed emancipation a Union war aim, African Americans in the North had volunteered to fight. Military service, one black volunteer declared, would mean "the elevation of a downtrodden and despised race." But the War Department, doubtful of blacks' abilities and fearful of white reaction to serving side by side with them, refused to make black men soldiers. Instead, the army employed black men as manual laborers; black women sometimes found employment as laundresses and cooks. The navy, however,

Black Dock Workers, Virginia
Hundreds of thousands of able-bodied free blacks and runaways cleared forests, built roads, erected bridges, constructed fortifications, and transported supplies for the U.S. Army. Their labor became indispensable to the war effort, and as one Northerner remembered, "The truth was we never could get enough of them." These men unloaded Union ships at an unnamed Virginia dock. National Archives.

accepted blacks from the outset, including runaway slaves such as William Gould (see pages 399–400).

As Union casualty lists lengthened, Northerners gradually and reluctantly turned to African Americans to fill the army's blue uniforms. With the Militia Act of July 1862, Congress authorized enrolling blacks in "any military or naval service for which they may be found competent." After the Emancipation Proclamation, whites—like it or not—were fighting and dying for black freedom, and few insisted that blacks remain out of harm's way behind the lines. Indeed, whites insisted that blacks share the danger, especially after March 1863, when Congress resorted to the draft to fill the Union army.

The military was far from color-blind. The Union army established segregated black regiments, paid black soldiers $10 per month rather than the $13 it paid whites, refused blacks the opportunity to become commissioned officers, punished blacks as if they were slaves, and assigned blacks to labor battalions rather than to combat units. Still, when the war ended, 179,000 African American men had served in the Union army. An astounding 71 percent of black men ages eighteen to forty-five in the free states wore Union blue, a participation rate substantially higher than that of white men.

In time, whites allowed blacks to put down their shovels and to shoulder rifles. At the battles of Port Hudson and Milliken's Bend on the Mississippi River and at Fort Wagner in Charleston harbor, black courage under fire finally dispelled notions that African Americans could not fight. More than 38,000 black soldiers died in the Civil War, a mortality rate that was higher than that of white troops. Blacks played a crucial role in the triumph of the Union and the destruction of slavery in the South. (See "Seeking the American Promise," page 416.)

From the beginning, African Americans viewed the Civil War as a revolutionary struggle to overthrow slavery and to gain equality for their entire race. "Once let the black man get

The Right to Fight: Black Soldiers in the Civil War

"**A** war undertaken and brazenly carried on for the perpetual enslavement of colored men, calls logically and loudly for colored men to help suppress it," black leader Frederick Douglass declared at the beginning of the war. But it was only in 1863 that the lengthening casualty lists finally convinced the Lincoln administration to begin aggressively recruiting black soldiers.

In February 1863, James Henry Gooding, a twenty-six-year-old seaman from New Bedford, enlisted in the 54th Massachusetts Colored Regiment. Like most black soldiers, Gooding viewed military service as an opportunity to strike blows against slavery and white prejudice. The destruction of slavery, he believed, "depends on the free black men of the North" because "those who are in bonds must have some one to open the door; when the slave sees the white soldier approach, he dares not trust him and why? Because he has heard that *some* have treated him worse than their owners in rebellion. But if the slave sees a black soldier, he knows he has got a friend." Fighting for the Union also offered a chance to attack white racism. In military service lay "the germs of the elevation of a downtrodden and

despised race," Gooding believed, the chance for African Americans "to make themselves a people."

Fighting, Gooding said, offered blacks a chance to destroy the "foul aspersion that they were not men." According to the white commander of the 59th U.S. Colored Infantry, when an ex-slave put on a uniform of army blue, the change was dramatic: "Yesterday a filthy, repulsive 'nigger,' to-day a neatly-attired man; yesterday a slave, to-day a freeman; yesterday a civilian, to-day a soldier." Others noticed the same transformation: "Put a United States uniform on his back and the *chattel* is a man." Black veterans agreed. "This was the biggest thing that ever happened in my life," one ex-soldier remembered. "I felt like a man with a uniform and a gun in my hand." Another said, "I felt freedom in my bones."

Black courage under fire ended skepticism about the capabilities of African American troops. As one white officer observed after a battle, "They seemed like men who were fighting to vindicate their manhood and they did it well." The truth is, another remarked, "they have fought their way into the respect of all the army." After the 54th served coura-

geously in South Carolina, Gooding reported: "It is not for us to blow our horn; but when a regiment of white men gave us three cheers as we were passing them, it shows that we did our duty as men should."

Yet discrimination within the Union army continued. When the government refused to pay blacks the same as whites, the 54th refused to accept unequal pay. Gooding wrote to President Lincoln himself to explain his regiment's decision: "Now the main question is, Are we Soldiers, or are we Labourers? . . . Now your Excellency, we have done a Soldier's Duty. Why Can't we have a Soldier's pay?" The 54th's principled stance helped reverse the government's position, and in June 1864 Congress equalized the pay of black and white soldiers.

As Union troops advanced deeper into the Confederacy, former slaves greeted black soldiers as heroes. In March 1865, the white officer of a black regiment in North Carolina reported that black soldiers "stepped like lords & conquerors. The frantic demonstrations of the negro population will never die out of my memory. Their cheers & heartfelt 'God bress ye's' & cries of 'De chains is broke; De chains is broke' mingled sublimely

upon his person the brass letters, U.S.; let him get an eagle on his button, and a musket on his shoulder and bullets in his pocket," Frederick Douglass predicted, "and there is no power on earth which can deny that he has earned the right of citizenship." When black men became soldiers, they and their families gained new confidence and self-esteem. Military service taught them new skills and introduced them to political struggle as they battled for their rights within

the army. Wartime experiences stood them in good stead when the war of liberation was over and the battle for equality began. But first there was a rebellion to put down. Victory depended as much on what happened behind the lines as on the battlefields.

REVIEW   How did the war for union become a war for black freedom?

with the lusty shout of our brave sol-diery." Hardened and disciplined by their military service, black soldiers drew tremendous strength from their participation in the Union effort. Despite their second-class status, they found army life a great counter-weight to the degradation and dependency of slavery.

Eager to shoulder the rights, privileges, and responsibilities of freedom, black veterans often took the lead in the hard struggle for equality after the war. Blacks in the Union army that occupied the South after 1865 assumed a special obliga-tion to protect former slaves. "The fact is," one black chaplain said, "when colored soldiers are about they [whites] are afraid to kick col-ored women and abuse colored peo-ple on the Streets, as they usually do." Black veterans believed that their military service entitled African Americans not only to freedom but also to civil and political rights. Sergeant Henry Maxwell announced: "We want two more boxes besides the cartridge box—the ballot and the jury box." Black men had demon-strated what they could do if permit-ted to become soldiers; they now demanded the chance to perform as citizens.

James Henry Gooding did not have a chance to participate in the postwar struggle for equal rights. Wounded and captured at the battle of Olustee in Florida, he was sent to the infamous Confederate prison Andersonville, where he died on July 19, 1864.

Company E, 4th U.S. Colored Infantry, Fort Lincoln, Virginia
The Lincoln administration was slow to accept black soldiers into the Union army, but eventually the valor of black troops eroded white skepticism. The white commander of a unit made up of former slaves celebrated their courage after their first skirmish: "No officer in this regiment now doubts that the key to the successful prosecution of this war lies in the unlimited employment of black troops." Library of Congress.

Questions for Consideration

1. Why did the Union resist enrolling black troops?

2. Why was the right to fight so im-portant to black men?

3. How did military service affect black men?

Connect to the Big Idea

○ In what ways do you think military service by black men would have been important to the entire black community?

▶ The South at War

By seceding, Southerners brought on themselves a firestorm of unimaginable fury. Monstrous losses on the battlefield nearly bled the Confederacy to death. Southerners on the home front also suffered, even at the hands of their own government. Efforts by the Davis admin-istration in Richmond to centralize power in order to fight the war convinced some men and women that the Confederacy had betrayed them. They charged Richmond with tyranny when it impressed goods and slaves and drafted men into the army. War also meant severe economic deprivation. Shortages and inflation hurt every-one, some more than others. By 1863, unequal suffering meant that planters and yeomen who had stood together began to drift apart. Most disturbing of all, slaves became open participants in the destruction of slavery and the Confederacy.

VISUAL ACTIVITY

John Wallace Comer, C.S.A., with his servant, Burrell
Many slaveholders took personal servants with them to war. These slaves cooked, washed, and cleaned for their owners. Owners sometimes dressed their servants in uniforms, as Comer did, which led some observers to conclude erroneously that slaves were members of the Confederate military. Alabama Department of Archives and History, Montgomery, Alabama.

READING THE IMAGE: How would you describe the expressions on the men's faces? Similar? Different?

CONNECTIONS: What are the possible ramifications of slaveholders bringing "body servants" to war? How were nonslaveholding soldiers, who did their own chores, likely to have responded?

Revolution from Above

As a Confederate general observed, Southerners were engaged in a total war "in which the whole population and the whole production . . . are to be put on a war footing, where every institution is to be made auxiliary to war." Jefferson Davis faced the task of building an army and navy from almost nothing, supplying them from factories that were scarce and anemic, and paying for it all from a treasury that did not exist. Finding eager soldiers proved easiest. Hundreds of officers defected from the U.S. Army, and hundreds of thousands of eager young rebels volunteered to follow them.

The Confederacy's economy and finances proved tougher problems. Because of the Union blockade, the government had no choice but to build an industrial sector itself. Government-owned clothing and shoe factories, mines, arsenals, and powder works sprang up. The government also harnessed private companies, such as the huge Tredegar Iron Works in Richmond, to the war effort. Paying for the war became the most difficult task. A flood of paper money caused debilitating inflation. By Christmas 1864, a Confederate soldier's monthly pay no longer bought a pair of socks. The Confederacy

manufactured much more than most people imagined possible, but it never produced all that the South needed.

Richmond's war-making effort brought unprecedented government intrusion into the private lives of Confederate citizens. In April 1862, the Confederate Congress passed the first conscription (draft) law in American history. All able-bodied white males between the ages of eighteen and thirty-five (later seventeen and fifty) were liable to serve in the rebel army. The government adopted a policy of impressment, which allowed officials to confiscate food, horses, wagons, and whatever else they wanted from private citizens and to pay for them at below-market rates. After March 1863, the Confederacy legally impressed slaves, employing them as military laborers.

Richmond's centralizing efforts ran head on into the South's traditional values of states' rights and unfettered individualism. Southerners lashed out at what Georgia governor Joseph E. Brown denounced as the "dangerous usurpation by Congress of the reserved right of the States." Richmond and the states struggled for control of money, supplies, and soldiers, with damaging consequences for the war effort.

Hardship Below

Hardships on the home front fell most heavily on the poor. The draft stripped yeoman farms of men, leaving the women and children to grow what they ate. Government agents took 10 percent of harvests as a "tax-in-kind" on agriculture. Like inflation, shortages afflicted the entire population, but the rich lost luxuries while the poor lost necessities. In the spring of 1863, bread riots broke out in a dozen cities and villages across the South. In Richmond, a mob of nearly a thousand hungry women broke into shops and took what they needed.

"Men cannot be expected to fight for the Government that permits their wives & children to starve," one Southerner observed. Although a few wealthy individuals shared their bounty and the Confederate and state governments made efforts at social welfare, every attempt fell short. In late 1864, one desperate farmwife told her husband, "I have always been proud of you, and since your connection with the Confederate army, I have been prouder of you than ever before. I would not have you do anything wrong for the world, but before God, Edward, unless you come home, we must die." When the war ended, one-third of the soldiers had already gone home. A Mississippi deserter explained, "We are poor men and are willing to defend our country but our families [come] first." (See "Documenting the American Promise," page 420.)

Yeomen perceived a profound inequality of sacrifice. They called it "a rich man's war and a poor man's fight." The draft law permitted a man who had money to hire a substitute to take his place. Moreover, the "twenty-Negro law" exempted one white man on every plantation with twenty or more slaves. The government intended this law to provide protection for white women and to see that slaves tended the crops, but yeomen perceived it as rich men evading military service. A Mississippian complained that stay-at-home planters sent their slaves into the fields to grow cotton while in plain view "poor soldiers' wives are plowing with *their own* hands to make a subsistence for themselves and children—while their husbands are suffering, bleeding and dying for their country." In fact, most slaveholders went off to war, but the extreme suffering of common folk and the relative immunity of planters increased class friction.

The Richmond government hoped that the crucible of war would mold a region into a nation. Officials actively promoted Confederate nation-alism to "excite in our citizens an ardent and enduring attachment to our Government and its institutions." Clergymen assured their congregations that God had blessed slavery and the new nation. Jefferson Davis claimed that the Confederacy was part of a divine plan and asked citizens to observe national days of fasting and prayer. But these efforts failed to win over thousands of die-hard Unionists, and animosity between yeomen and planters increased. The war also threatened to rip the southern social fabric along its racial seam.

The Disintegration of Slavery

The legal destruction of slavery was the product of presidential proclamation, congressional legislation, and eventually constitutional amendment, but the practical destruction of slavery was the product of war, what Lincoln called war's "friction and abrasion." Slaves took advantage of the upheaval to reach for freedom. Some half a million of the South's 4 million slaves ran away to Union military lines. More than 100,000 runaways took up arms as federal soldiers and sailors and attacked slavery directly. Other men and women stayed in the slave quarter, where they staked their claim to more freedom.

War disrupted slavery in a dozen ways. Almost immediately, it called the master away, leaving the mistress to assume responsibility for the plantation. But mistresses could not maintain traditional standards of slave discipline in wartime, and the balance of power shifted. Slaves got to the fields late, worked indifferently, and quit early. Some slaveholders responded violently; most saw no alternative but to strike bargains—offering gifts or part of the crop—to keep slaves at home and at work. An Alabaman complained that she "begged . . . what little is done." Slaveholders had believed that they "knew" their slaves, but they learned that they did not. When the war began, a North Carolina woman praised her slaves as "diligent and respectful." When it ended, she said, "As to the idea of a *faithful servant, it is all a fiction*." Whites' greatest fear—retaliatory violence—rarely occurred, but slaves gradually undermined white mastery and expanded control over their own lives.

REVIEW   How did wartime hardship in the South contribute to class friction?

Home and Country

Christian Marion Epperly and his wife, Mary Epperly, lived in the Blue Ridge Mountains of Virginia. Although neither was an ardent secessionist, Marion entered the Confederate army as a private early in 1862. He hated army life and longed for his wife and children. Mary was equally heartsick without Marion. Despite their limited schooling, the couple's letters reveal how plain folks wrestled with the tangled issues of loyalty and obligation.

DOCUMENT 1
Letter from Chickahominy Creek, Virginia, May 16, 1862

During the peninsula campaign in Virginia, as Union general George B. McClellan was approaching the Confederate capital of Richmond, Marion wrote to Mary from near the action.

I think the people will be bound to suffer for something to eat[;] the grain is all destroid and nearly all the fenses is burnt up from yorktown to Richmond: it looks distressing just to travel along the road: the wheat up waist hi some of it and horses and cattle has eat the most of it to the ground and I think the yankees will make a finish of the ballans [balance] that is left but the[y] cant doo much more damage than our army did[;] our own men killed all the cattle and hogs & sheep that the farmers had[,] even took ther chickens[;] every thing is totally destroid in this part of the State. . . .

I hope and pray this awful war will soon come to a close some way or another[,] any way to get pease in the world wonst more[;] it seems to me I had drather be at home and live on bred and water than to have this war hanging over us but I pray god pease will soon be made[.] I dont think the war can last long.

DOCUMENT 2
Letter from Camp near Bells Bridge, Tennessee, August 15, 1863

By the summer of 1863, Marion's regiment had moved to Tennessee, where he notices increasing war weariness, desertions, and disillusionment with the Confederacy.

You don't know how glad I would be if I was just thar with you this morning to see the sun rise over the hills in Virginia again[,] for every thing seames so sad and desolate here this morning; it seames like the absens of dear friends and the present condition of things has brought deep refletion and sadnes upon every heart, and [men] are growing weary and getting out of heart and leaving the Army everry day. I cant tell wheather it will be for the better or wheather it will make things wors: but I hope it is a way god has provided to bring this war and time of sorrow to an end and to give us pease in our land again: Thoug I believe the south first started on a just course but our own wickedness and disobedians has brought us to what we are and I firmly believe wee will be bound to give up to subjugation[.] I don't think the south will stand much longer, and I am sorrow to say it for wee will be a ruined people while time ma [may] last, but wee ought to submit to any thing to have this awwful war ended.

▶ The North at War

Although little fighting took place on northern soil, almost every family had a son, husband, father, or brother in uniform. Moreover, total war blurred the distinction between home front and battlefield. As in the South, men marched off to fight, but preserving the country was also women's work. For civilians as well as soldiers, for women as well as men, war was transforming.

The need to build and fuel the Union war machine strengthened the federal government and boosted the economy. The Union sent nearly 2 million men into the military and still increased production in almost every area. But because the rewards and burdens of patriotism were distributed unevenly, the North experienced sharp, even violent, divisions. Workers confronted employers, whites confronted blacks, and Democrats confronted Republicans. Still,

DOCUMENT 3
Letter from Floyd County, Virginia, August 16, 1863

Mary longs for peace and argues that desertion will end the war.

Oh how much beter satisfied would I be if you was just hear with me this beatiful Sabath morning. I feel as if my troubles on earth would all be over if you was just at home to stay wonst more[,] but god sent it upon us and we will have to bear with it the best we can but I do pray that he may soon end this destressing time some way[.] I would be willing for it to end most any way just so it would end[.] Dear Marion I think if the head men dont soon end this war that the soldiers will for they are runing way from down east by hundreds[;] they was five hundard went through hear last weak and well armed and they say they wont go back any more and I dont blame them for it[.] I wish they would all runaway and these head men would be oblige to fight it out but as long as they can stay at home and speculate off of the poor soulders they dont care how long the war lasts[.] Serious Smith wrote a leter the 9 of this month and he wrote that they had to pay 15 dolars for a bushel of taters . . . how can the poor soulders make out and only get a leven [eleven] dolars a month[?]

DOCUMENT 4
Letter from Outskirts of Dalton, Georgia, March 25, 1864

As his regiment is backing toward Atlanta, trying to fend off Sherman, Marion considers what has gone wrong with the Confederacy.

I dont think it will last much longer if the souldiers doo what they say they will doo[;] they are all verry tired of this war and the way it is carried on[.] I think wee all have stud it about as long as we can unless our leading men dos a heap better than they ever have yet: if they wer God fearing men I would think wee would prosper but so long as they [seek] the Bottom of a Whiskey Barl and frolick around bad places just so long we will hafto fight and suffer. . . . we was all Born in a free land and I think wee ought to stil be free and not be bound down wors than slaves[;] we wonst had a union and was living happy and had all man can wish for[;] now we are cut off from that union and what are wee nothing but a ruend people as long as we shal live . . . dissatisfaction and wickedness all over the south[;] may God show us our errors and put us in the rite way and Bring us Back to our old union again.

Despite his doubts about the Confederacy and continued affection for the Union, Marion left the army without authorization only once, and after a few weeks at home in 1863, he returned to his regiment. Like many disillusioned soldiers, he fought in the rebel army to the very end.

Source: Christian M. Epperly Correspondence, Gilder Lehrman Collection, Pierpont Morgan Library, New York.

Questions for Analysis and Debate

1. How does Marion contrast life in the Union with life in the Confederacy?

2. In what ways does the Epperlys' perspective on the Confederacy reflect their social position as plain folk in Virginia society?

3. Marion makes clear why he had such affection for his home; he is much less clear about why he fought for the Confederacy. What might some of his reasons have been?

Connect to the Big Idea

Ⓒ How did class issues divide southern soldiers during the Civil War?

Northerners on the home front remained fervently attached to the Union.

The Government and the Economy

When the war began, the United States had no national banking system, no national currency, and no federal income tax. But the secession of eleven slave states cut the Democrats' strength in Congress in half and destroyed their capacity to resist Republican economic programs. The Legal Tender Act of February 1862 created a national currency, paper money that Northerners called "greenbacks." With the passage of the National Banking Act in February 1863, Congress established a system of national banks that by the 1870s had largely replaced the antebellum system of decentralized state banks. Congress also enacted a series of sweeping tax laws.

Union Army Horse Artillery, 1860–1865
Seen here in Virginia, a powerful battery of Union field artillery moved forward to assist infantry units. Each cannon required more than a dozen men and many horses to service it. Assignment to an artillery battery was dangerous for man and beast. Life expectancy for an artillery horse was less than eight months, and it is estimated that 1.5 million horses died in the war. ©CORBIS.

The Republicans' wartime legislation also aimed at integrating the West into the Union. In May 1862, Congress approved the Homestead Act, which offered 160 acres of public land to settlers who would live and labor on it. The Homestead Act bolstered western loyalty and in time resulted in more than a million new farms. The Pacific Railroad Act in July 1862 provided massive federal assistance for building a transcontinental railroad that ran from Omaha to San Francisco when completed in 1869. Congress further bound East and West by subsidizing the Pony Express mail service and a transcontinental telegraph.

Congress also created the Department of Agriculture and passed the Land-Grant College Act (also known as the Morrill Act after its sponsor, Representative Justin Morrill of Vermont), which set aside public land to support universities that emphasized "agriculture and mechanical arts." The Lincoln administration immeasurably strengthened the North's effort to win the war, but its initiatives also permanently changed the nation.

Women and Work at Home and at War

More than a million farm men were called to the military, and farm women added men's chores

to their own. "I met more women driving teams on the road and saw more at work in the fields than men," a visitor to Iowa reported in the fall of 1862. Rising production testified to their success in plowing, planting, and harvesting. Rapid mechanization assisted farm women in their new roles. Cyrus McCormick sold 165,000 of his reapers during the war years. The combination of high prices for farm products and increased production ensured that war and prosperity joined hands in the rural North.

In cities, women stepped into jobs vacated by men, particularly in manufacturing, and also into essentially new occupations such as government secretaries and clerks. The number of women working for wages rose 40 percent during the war. As more and more women entered the workforce, employers cut wages. In 1864, New York seamstresses working fourteen-hour days earned only $1.54 a week. Urban workers resorted increasingly to strikes to wrench decent salaries from their employers, but their protests rarely succeeded.

Most middle-class white women stayed home and contributed to the war effort in traditional ways. They sewed, wrapped bandages, and sold homemade goods at local fairs to raise money to aid the soldiers. Other women expressed their patriotism in an untraditional way. Defying prejudices about female delicacy, thousands of women on both sides volunteered to nurse the wounded. Many northern female volunteers worked through the U.S. Sanitary Commission, a huge civilian organization that bought and distributed clothing, food, and medicine, recruited doctors and nurses, and buried the dead.

Some volunteers went on to become paid military nurses. Dorothea Dix, well known for her efforts to reform insane asylums, was named superintendent of female nurses in April 1861. Eventually, some 3,000 nurses by 1863 served under her. Most nurses worked in hospitals behind the battle lines, but some, like Clara Barton, who later founded the American Red Cross, worked in battlefield units. Women who served in the war went on to lead the postwar movement to establish training schools for female nurses.

Politics and Dissent

At first, the bustle of economic and military mobilization seemed to silence politics, but bipartisan unity did not last. Within a year, Democrats

Women Doing Laundry for Federal Soldiers, ca. 1861
Some northern women were forced by their desperate financial circumstances to wash soldiers' dirty clothes to make a living. Army camps were difficult places for "respectable" women to work. One Union soldier discouraged his wife even from visiting, noting, "It is not a fit place for any woman, for there is all kinds of talk, songs and everything not good for them 2 hear." ©CORBIS.

were labeling the Republican administration a "reign of terror" and denouncing as unconstitutional Republican policies expanding federal power, subsidizing private business, and emancipating the slaves. In turn, Republicans were calling Democrats the party of "Dixie, Davis, and the Devil."

When the Republican-dominated Congress enacted the draft law in March 1863, Democrats had another grievance. The law required that all men between the ages of twenty and forty-five enroll and make themselves available for a lottery that would decide who went to war. It also allowed a draftee to hire a substitute or simply to pay a $300 fee and get out of his military obligation. As in the South, common folk could be heard chanting, "A rich man's war and a poor man's fight."

Linking the draft and emancipation, Democrats argued that Republicans employed an unconstitutional means (the draft) to achieve an unconstitutional end (emancipation). In the summer of 1863, antidraft, antiblack mobs went on rampages in northern cities. In July in New York City, Democratic Irish workingmen—crowded into filthy tenements, gouged by inflation, enraged by the draft, and dead set against fighting to free blacks—erupted in four days of rioting. The **New York City draft riots** killed at least 105 people, most of them black.

Lincoln called Democratic opposition to the war "the fire in the rear" and believed that it was even more threatening to national survival than were Confederate armies. The antiwar wing of the Democratic Party, the Peace Democrats—whom some called "Copperheads," after the poisonous snake—found their chief spokesman in Ohio congressman Clement Vallandigham. Vallandigham demanded: "Stop fighting. Make an armistice. . . . Withdraw your army from the seceding States."

In September 1862, in an effort to stifle opposition to the war, Lincoln placed under military arrest any person who discouraged enlistments, resisted the draft, or engaged in "disloyal" practices. Before the war ended, his administration imprisoned nearly 14,000 individuals, most in the border states. The administration's heavy-handed tactics suppressed free speech, but the campaign fell short of a reign of terror, for the majority of the prisoners were not northern Democratic opponents but Confederates, blockade runners, and citizens of foreign countries, and most of those arrested gained quick release. Still, the administration's net captured Vallandigham, who was arrested, convicted of treason, and banished.

> **REVIEW**   Why was the U.S. Congress able to pass such a bold legislative agenda during the war?

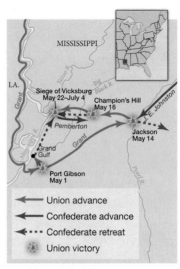

Vicksburg Campaign, 1863

► Grinding Out Victory, 1863–1865

In the early months of 1863, the Union's prospects looked bleak, and the Confederate cause stood at high tide. Then, in July 1863, the tide began to turn. The military man most responsible for this shift was Ulysses S. Grant. Elevated to supreme command in 1864, Grant knit together a powerful war machine that integrated a sophisticated command structure, modern technology, and complex logistics and supply systems. Grant's arithmetic was simple: Killing more of the enemy than he killed of you equaled "the complete over-throw of the rebellion."

The North ground out the victory battle by bloody battle. Still, Southerners were not deterred. The fighting escalated

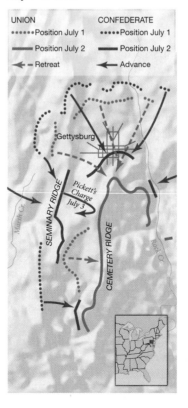

Battle of Gettysburg, July 1–3, 1863

in the last two years of the war. As national elections approached in the fall of 1864, Lincoln expected a war-weary North to reject him. Instead, northern voters declared their willingness to continue the war in the defense of the ideals of union and freedom. Lincoln lived to see victory, but only days after Lee surrendered, the president died from an assassin's bullet.

Vicksburg and Gettysburg

Vicksburg, Mississippi, situated on the eastern bank of the Mississippi River, stood between Union forces and complete control of the river. In May 1863, Union forces under Grant laid siege to the city in an effort to starve out the enemy. As the **siege of Vicksburg** dragged on, civilians ate mules and rats to survive. After six weeks, on July 4, 1863, nearly 30,000 rebels marched out of Vicksburg, stacked their arms, and surrendered unconditionally. A Yankee captain wrote home to his wife: "The backbone of the Rebellion is this day broken. The Confederacy is divided. . . . Vicksburg is ours. The Mississippi River is opened, and Gen. Grant is to be our next President."

On the same Fourth of July, word arrived that Union forces had crushed General Lee at Gettysburg, Pennsylvania (Map 15.3). Emboldened by his victory at Chancellorsville in May, Lee and his 75,000-man army had invaded Pennsylvania. On June 28, Union forces under General George G. Meade intercepted the Confederates at the small town of Gettysburg, where Union soldiers occupied the high ground. In three days of furious fighting, the Confederates failed to dislodge the Federals. The **battle of Gettysburg** cost Lee more than one-third of his army—28,000 casualties. "It's all my fault," he lamented. On the night of July 4, 1863, he marched his battered army back to Virginia.

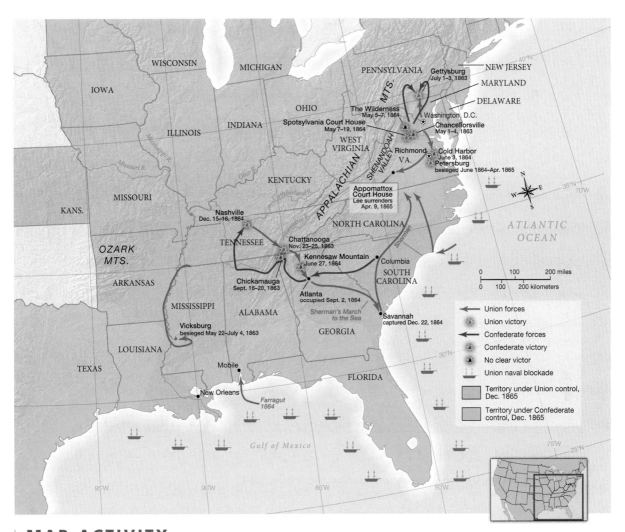

MAP ACTIVITY

Map 15.3   The Civil War, 1863–1865

Ulysses S. Grant's victory at Vicksburg divided the Confederacy at the Mississippi River. William Tecumseh Sherman's march from Chattanooga to Savannah divided it again. In northern Virginia, Robert E. Lee fought fiercely, but Grant's larger, better-supplied armies prevailed.

READING THE MAP: Describe the difference between Union and Confederate naval capacities. Were the battles shown on the map fought primarily in Union-controlled or in Confederate-controlled territory? (Look at the land areas on the map.)

CONNECTIONS: Did former slaves serve in the Civil War? If so, on which side(s), and what did they do?

The twin disasters at Vicksburg and Gettysburg proved to be the turning point of the war. The Confederacy could not replace the nearly 60,000 soldiers who were captured, wounded, or killed. It is hindsight, however, that permits us to see the pair of battles as decisive. At the time, the Confederacy still controlled the heartland of the South, and Lee still had a vicious sting. War-weariness threatened to erode the North's will to win before Union armies could destroy the Confederacy's ability to go on.

Grant Takes Command

In September 1863, Union general William Rosecrans placed his army in a dangerous situation in Chattanooga, Tennessee, where he had retreated after defeat at the battle of Chickamauga (see Map 15.3). Rebels surrounded the disorganized bluecoats and threatened to starve them into submission. Grant, now commander of Union forces between the Mississippi River and the Appalachians, arrived in nearby

VISUAL ACTIVITY

***The Dead Line*, by Robert Sneden, Andersonville Prison, 1864**
Union soldier Robert Sneden arrived at Andersonville in February 1864. Soon the sixteen-and-a-half acres were crammed with 33,000 Union prisoners. Sneden sketched this scene of a man being shot by a guard while trying to take part of a fence (the "dead line" that prisoners could not cross) for firewood. More than 13,000 prisoners perished at Andersonville. Virginia Historical Society, Richmond, Virginia, USA / The Bridgeman Art Library.
READING THE IMAGE: What does the painting suggest were among the hazards to the health of the prisoners at Andersonville?
CONNECTIONS: How might the state of the Confederate economy have affected conditions at Andersonville?

Chattanooga in October. Within weeks, he opened an effective supply line, broke the siege, and routed the Confederate army. The victory at Chattanooga on November 25 opened the door to Georgia. In March 1864, Lincoln asked Grant to come east to become the general in chief of all Union armies.

In Washington, General Grant implemented his grand strategy for a war of attrition. He ordered a series of simultaneous assaults from Virginia all the way to Louisiana. Two actions proved particularly significant. In one, General William Tecumseh Sherman, whom Grant appointed his successor to command the western armies, plunged southeast toward Atlanta. In the other, Grant, who took control of the Army

of the Potomac, went head-to-head with Lee in Virginia in May and June of 1864.

The fighting between Grant and Lee was particularly savage. At the battle of the Wilderness, where a dense tangle of forest often made it impossible to see more than ten paces, the armies pounded away at each other until approximately 18,000 Yankees and 11,000 rebels had fallen. At Spotsylvania Court House, frenzied men fought hand to hand for eighteen hours in the rain. One veteran remembered men "piled upon each other in some places four layers deep, exhibiting every ghastly phase of mutilation." (See "Historical Question," page 428.) Spotsylvania cost Grant another 18,000 casualties and Lee 10,000. Grant kept moving and attacked Lee again at Cold

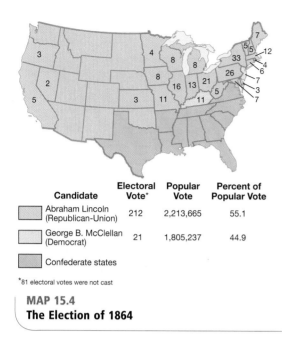

Candidate	Electoral Vote*	Popular Vote	Percent of Popular Vote
Abraham Lincoln (Republican-Union)	212	2,213,665	55.1
George B. McClellan (Democrat)	21	1,805,237	44.9
Confederate states			

*81 electoral votes were not cast

MAP 15.4
The Election of 1864

The Election of 1864

In the summer of 1864, with Sherman temporarily checked outside Atlanta and Grant bogged down in the siege of Petersburg, the Democratic Party smelled victory in the fall elections. Lincoln himself concluded, "It seems exceedingly probable that this administration will not be re-elected."

The Democrats were badly divided, however. Peace Democrats insisted on an armistice, while "war" Democrats supported the conflict but opposed Republican means of fighting it. The party tried to paper over the chasm by nominating a war candidate, General George McClellan, but adopting a peace platform that demanded that "immediate efforts be made for a cessation of hostilities." Republicans denounced the peace plank as a cut-and-run plan that "virtually proposed to surrender the country to the rebels in arms against us."

The capture of Atlanta in September turned the political tide in favor of the Republicans. Lincoln received 55 percent of the popular vote, but his electoral margin was a whopping 212 to McClellan's 21 (Map 15.4). Lincoln's party won a resounding victory, one that gave him a mandate to continue the war until slavery and the Confederacy were dead.

Harbor, where he suffered 13,000 additional casualties to Lee's 5,000.

Twice as many Union soldiers as rebel soldiers died in four weeks of fighting in Virginia, but because Lee had only half as many troops as Grant, his losses were equivalent to Grant's. Grant knew that the South could not replace the losses. Moreover, the campaign carried Grant to the outskirts of Petersburg, just south of Richmond, where he abandoned the costly tactic of the frontal assault and began a siege that immobilized both armies and dragged on for nine months.

Simultaneously, Sherman invaded Georgia. Skillful maneuvering, constant skirmishing, and one pitched battle, at Kennesaw Mountain, brought Sherman to Atlanta, which fell on September 2. Intending to "make Georgia howl," Sherman marched out of Atlanta on November 15 with 62,000 battle-hardened veterans, heading for Savannah, 285 miles away on the Atlantic coast. One veteran remembered, "[We] destroyed all we could not eat, stole their niggers, burned their cotton & gins, spilled their sorghum, burned & twisted their R. Roads and raised Hell generally." **Sherman's March to the Sea** aimed at destroying the will of white Southerners to continue the war. A few weeks earlier, General Philip H. Sheridan had carried out his own scorched-earth campaign in the Shenandoah Valley. When Sherman's troops entered an undefended Savannah in mid-December, the general telegraphed Lincoln that he had "a Christmas gift" for him. A month earlier, Union voters had bestowed on the president an even greater gift.

Major Battles of the Civil War, 1863–1865

May 1–4, 1863	Battle of Chancellorsville
July 1–3, 1863	Battle of Gettysburg
July 4, 1863	Fall of Vicksburg
September 16–20, 1863	Battle of Chickamauga
November 23–25, 1863	Battle of Chattanooga
May 5–7, 1864	Battle of the Wilderness
May 7–19, 1864	Battle of Spotsylvania Court House
June 3, 1864	Battle of Cold Harbor
June 27, 1864	Battle of Kennesaw Mountain
September 2, 1864	Fall of Atlanta
November–December 1864	Sheridan sacks Shenandoah Valley Sherman's "March to the Sea"
December 15–16, 1864	Battle of Nashville
December 22, 1864	Fall of Savannah
April 2–3, 1865	Fall of Petersburg and Richmond
April 9, 1865	Lee surrenders at Appomattox Court House

Why Did So Many Soldiers Die?

The American Civil War was the bloodiest conflict in American history (Figure 15.3). Precise numbers are hard to determine, but as many as 750,000 soldiers died. Why were the Civil War totals so horrendous?

This question is almost as old as the war itself, and in answering it historians have traditionally pointed to a variety of explanations: the scale and duration of the fighting; military strategy; battlefield technology; and the backward state of medicine. The sheer size of the armies—some battles involved more than 200,000 soldiers—ensured that battlefields would turn red with blood. Moreover, what most Americans expected to be a short war extended for four full years. In addition, armies fought with antiquated Napoleonic strategy. In the generals' eyes, the ideal soldier advanced with his comrades in a compact, close-order formation. But by the 1860s, military technology had made such frontal assaults deadly. Weapons with rifled barrels were replacing smoothbore muskets and cannons, and the new weapons' greater range and accuracy made sitting ducks of charging infantry units. As a result, battles took thousands of lives in a single day. On July 2, 1862, the morning after the battle at Malvern Hill in Virginia, a Union officer surveyed the scene: "Over 5,000 dead and wounded men were on the ground . . . enough were alive and moving to give to the field a singular crawling effect."

When the war began, Union and Confederate medical departments could not cope with skirmishes, much less large-scale battles. They had no ambulance corps to remove the wounded from the scene. They had no field hospitals. Wounded soldiers often lay on battlefields for hours, sometimes days. Only the shock of massive casualties compelled reform. Gradually, both North and South organized effective ambulance corps, built hospitals, and hired trained surgeons and nurses.

Soldiers did not always count speedy transportation to a hospital as a blessing, however. As one Union soldier said, "I had rather risk a battle than the Hospitals." Field doctors gained a reputation as butchers, but a wounded man's real enemy was medical ignorance. Physicians had almost no knowledge of the cause and transmission of disease or the benefits of antiseptics. Unaware of basic germ theory, surgeons spread infection almost every time they operated. They wore the same bloody smocks for days and washed their hands and their scalpels and saws in buckets of dirty water. Although surgeons used anesthesia (both ether and chloroform), soldiers often did not survive amputations, not because of the operations but because of the gangrene that inevitably followed. A Union doctor discovered in 1864 that bromine arrested gangrene, but the best that most amputees could hope for was maggots, which ate dead flesh on the stump and thus inhibited the spread of infection. The growing ranks of nurses, including Dorothea Dix and Clara Barton, improved wounded men's odds and alleviated their suffering. Still, during the Civil War, nearly one of every five wounded rebel soldiers died, and one of every six Yankees. A century later, in Vietnam, only one wounded American soldier in four hundred died.

Soldiers who avoided battlefield wounds and hospital infections still faced sickness. Deadly diseases such as dysentery and typhoid swept through crowded army camps, where latrines were often dangerously close to drinking-water supplies, and mosquitoes, flies, and body lice were more than nuisances. Pneumonia and malaria also cut down thousands. Quinine from South America proved an effective treatment for malaria, but by the end of the war the going price was $500 an ounce. Civilian relief agencies promoted hygiene in army camps and made some headway. Nevertheless, disease killed nearly twice as many soldiers as did combat. Many who died of disease were prisoners of war. Approximately 30,000 Northerners died in Confederate prisons, and approximately 26,000 Southerners died in Union prisons.

FIGURE 15.3 Civil War Deaths

The loss of life in the Civil War—as many as 750,000—was greater than the losses in all other American wars through the Vietnam War combined.

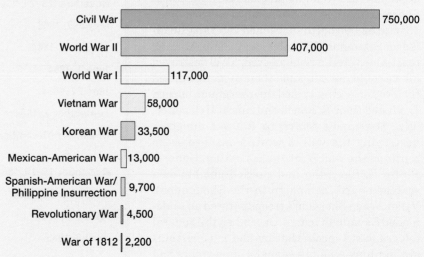

Civil War	750,000
World War II	407,000
World War I	117,000
Vietnam War	58,000
Korean War	33,500
Mexican-American War	13,000
Spanish-American War/ Philippine Insurrection	9,700
Revolutionary War	4,500
War of 1812	2,200

Wounded Men at Savage's Station

Misery did not end when the cannons ceased firing. Northern and southern surgeons performed approximately 60,000 amputations with simple instruments such as those included in this surgical kit. The wounded men shown here were but a fraction of those injured or killed during General George McClellan's peninsula campaign in 1862. Photo: Library of Congress; Surgical kit: © Chicago History Museum, USA/The Bridgeman Art Library.

Recently, historians have probed another explanation for the death toll, turning to soldiers' cultural attitudes and values to explain why they were willing to die in such great numbers. Some have explored how the nineteenth-century code of masculinity propelled valor on the battlefields, and how patriotism, for either the Union or the Confederacy, moved soldiers to risk everything. But scholars have focused most especially on how soldiers' religious beliefs about death made it easier for them to negotiate dying. The triumph of evangelical Protestantism in the early nineteenth century meant that Civil War soldiers faced death with calm resignation. They believed in a heaven that promised bodily resurrection and family reunion; the assurance of everlasting life, therefore, made it easier to face death. Culture, then, as well as the scope and length of the war, strategy, technology, and primitive medicine, helps explain the war's tremendous carnage.

Questions for Consideration

1. In what ways were Civil War strategists fighting the world's first "modern" war? In what ways were they still fighting a traditional-style war? How does this contrast account for the number of dead and wounded soldiers?

2. How did the high casualty rates lead to new opportunities for both women and blacks?

Connect to the Big Idea

Ⓒ Which economy—the Union's or the Confederacy's—was better able to cope with the loss of manpower to the military, and why?

The Confederacy Collapses

As 1865 dawned, military disaster littered the Confederate landscape. With the destruction of John B. Hood's army at Nashville in December 1864, the interior of the Confederacy lay in Yankee hands (see Map 15.3). Sherman's troops, resting momentarily in Savannah, eyed South Carolina hungrily. Farther north, Grant had Lee's army pinned down in Petersburg, a few miles from Richmond.

Some Confederates turned their backs on the rebellion. News from the battlefield made it difficult not to conclude that the Yankees had beaten them. When soldiers' wives begged their husbands to return home to keep their families from starving, the stream of deserters grew dramatically. Still, white Southerners had demonstrated a remarkable endurance for their cause. Half of the 900,000 Confederate soldiers had been killed or wounded, and ragged, hungry women and children had sacrificed throughout one of the bloodiest wars then known to history.

The end came with a rush. On February 1, 1865, Sherman's troops stormed out of Savannah into South Carolina, the "cradle of the Confederacy." In Virginia, Lee abandoned Petersburg on April 2, and Richmond fell on April 3. Grant pursued Lee until he surrendered on April 9, 1865, at Appomattox Court House, Virginia. Grant offered generous peace terms. He allowed Lee's men to return home and to keep their horses to help "put in a crop to carry themselves and their families through the next winter." With Lee gone, the remaining Confederate armies lost hope and gave up within two weeks. After four years, the war was over.

No one was more relieved than Lincoln, but his celebration was restrained. He told his cabinet that his postwar burdens would weigh almost as heavily as those of wartime. Seeking a distraction, Lincoln attended Ford's Theatre on the evening of Good Friday, April 14, 1865. John Wilkes Booth, an actor with southern sympathies, slipped into the president's box and shot Lincoln, who died the next morning. Vice President Andrew

Robert E. Lee and Friends, by Mathew Brady, 1865

One week after his surrender at Appomattox Court House, Robert E. Lee sat for this portrait by Mathew Brady, the country's foremost photographer. Lee is joined by his eldest son, Major General George Washington Custis Lee (left), and a longtime aide, Lieutenant Colonel Walter H. Taylor (right). Lee's sober, weary expression reflects four hard years of war and his final defeat. Already a matchless hero among white Southerners, Lee was well on his way toward saintly immortality. In 1868, one woman described Lee as "bathed in the white light which falls directly upon him from the smile of an approving and sustaining God." Library of Congress.

Johnson became president. The man who had led the nation through the war would not lead it during the postwar search for a just peace.

> REVIEW   Why were the siege of Vicksburg and the battle of Gettysburg crucial to the outcome of the war?

▶ Conclusion: The Second American Revolution

A transformed nation emerged from the crucible of war. Antebellum America was decentralized politically and loosely integrated economically. To bend the resources of the country to a Union victory, Congress enacted legislation that reshaped the nation's political and economic character. It created a transcontinental railroad and miles of telegraph lines to bind the West to the rest of the nation. The massive changes brought about by the war—the creation of a national government, a national economy, and a national spirit—led one historian to call the American Civil War the "Second American Revolution."

The Civil War also had a profound effect on individual lives. Millions of men put on blue or gray uniforms and fought and suffered for what they passionately believed was right. The war disrupted families, leaving women at home with additional responsibilities and giving others wartime work in factories, offices, and hospitals. It offered blacks new and more effective ways to resist slavery and agitate for equality.

The war devastated the South. Three-fourths of southern white men of military age served in the Confederate army, and half of them were wounded or killed or died of disease. The war destroyed two-fifths of the South's livestock, wrecked half of the farm machinery, and blackened dozens of cities and towns. The struggle also cost the North a heavy price in lives, but rather than devastating the land, the war set the countryside and cities humming with business activity. The radical shift in power from South to North signaled a new direction in American development: the long decline of agriculture and the rise of industrial capitalism.

Most revolutionary of all, the war ended slavery. Ironically, the South's war to preserve slavery destroyed it. Nearly 200,000 black men, including ex-slave William Gould, dedicated their wartime service to its eradication. Because slavery was both a labor and a racial system, the institution was entangled in almost every aspect of southern life. Slavery's uprooting inevitably meant fundamental change. But the full meaning of abolition remained unclear in 1865 and the status of ex-slaves would be the principal task of reconstruction.

See the Selected Bibliography for this chapter in the Appendix.

15 Chapter Review

MAKE IT STICK

LearningCurve
Go online and use LearningCurve to see what you know. Then review the key terms and answer the questions.

KEY TERMS

Fort Sumter (p. 401)
battle of Bull Run (Manassas) (p. 406)
battle of Antietam (p. 408)
battle of Shiloh (p. 411)
Union blockade (p. 411)
King Cotton diplomacy (p. 411)
contraband of war (p. 413)
Emancipation Proclamation (p. 414)
New York City draft riots (p. 423)
siege of Vicksburg (p. 424)
battle of Gettysburg (p. 424)
Sherman's March to the Sea (p. 427)

REVIEW QUESTIONS

1. Why did the attack on Fort Sumter force the Upper South to choose sides? (pp. 401–403)

2. Why did the South believe it could win the war despite numerical disadvantages? (pp. 403–405)

3. Why did the Confederacy's bid for international support fail? (pp. 411–412)

4. How did the war for union become a war for black freedom? (pp. 412–416)

5. How did wartime hardship in the South contribute to class friction? (pp. 417–419)

6. Why was the U.S. Congress able to pass such a bold legislative agenda during the war? (pp. 421–423)

7. Why were the siege of Vicksburg and the battle of Gettysburg crucial to the outcome of the war? (pp. 424–430)

MAKING CONNECTIONS

1. Despite loathing slavery, Lincoln embraced emancipation as a war objective late and with great caution. Why?

2. The Emancipation Proclamation did not accomplish the destruction of slavery on its own. How did a war over union bring about the end of slavery? In your answer, consider the direct actions of slaves and Union policymakers as well as indirect factors within the Confederacy.

3. In addition to restoring the Union and destroying slavery, what other significant changes did the war produce on the home front and in the nation's capital?

4. Brilliant military strategy alone did not determine the outcome of the war; victory also depended on generating revenue, material mobilization, diplomacy, and politics. In light of these considerations, explain why the Confederacy believed it would succeed and why it ultimately failed.

LINKING TO THE PAST

1. Why were white slaveholders surprised by the wartime behavior of slaves? (See chapter 13.)

2. In what ways did the Lincoln administration's wartime policies fulfill the prewar aspirations of Northerners? (See chapters 12 and 14.)

16 Reconstruction
1863–1877

CONTENT LEARNING OBJECTIVES

After reading and studying this chapter, you should be able to:

- Identify the challenges facing reconstruction efforts.

- Describe President Johnson's reconstruction plan and the ways in which it aligned and differed from Lincoln's.

- Recount the significance of the Fourteenth Amendment, and why President Johnson advised southern states to reject it. Explain the terms of radical reconstruction and how Johnson's interventions led some in Congress to seek his impeachment.

- Describe the provisions of the Fifteenth Amendment, and explain why some women's rights advocates were dissatisfied with it.

- Describe how congressional reconstruction altered life in the South. Explain why the North abandoned reconstruction, including the role of Grant's troubled presidency and the election of 1877 in this abandonment.

CARPETBAG
A carpetbag was a suitcase made from carpet. "Carpetbagger" was a derogatory name for rootless adventurers, which critics of Republican administrations in the South hurled at white Northerners who moved south during Reconstruction. © Elemental Studios/Alamy.

IN 1856, JOHN RAPIER, A FREE BLACK BARBER IN FLORENCE, ALABAMA, urged his four freeborn sons to flee the increasingly repressive and dangerous South. James T. Rapier chose Canada, where he went to live with his uncle in a largely black community and studied Greek and Latin in a log schoolhouse. In a letter to his father, he vowed, "I will endeavor to do my part in solving the problems [of African Americans] in my native land."

The Union victory in the Civil War gave James Rapier the opportunity to redeem his pledge. In 1865, after more than eight years of exile, the twenty-seven-year-old Rapier returned to Alabama, where he presided over the first political gathering of former slaves in the state. He soon discovered, however, that Alabama's whites found it agonizingly difficult to accept defeat and black freedom. They responded to the revolutionary changes under the banner "White Man—Right or Wrong—Still the White Man!"

During the elections of 1868, when Rapier and other Alabama blacks vigorously supported the Republican ticket, the recently organized Ku

Klux Klan went on a bloody rampage. A mob of 150 outraged whites scoured Rapier's neighborhood seeking four black politicians they claimed were trying to "Africanize Alabama." They caught and hanged three, but the "nigger carpetbagger from Canada" escaped. After briefly considering fleeing the state, Rapier decided to stay and fight.

In 1872, Rapier won election to the House of Representatives, where he joined six other black congressmen in Washington, D.C. Defeated for reelection in 1874 in a campaign marked by ballot-box stuffing, Rapier turned to cotton farming. But persistent black poverty and unrelenting racial violence convinced him that blacks could never achieve equality and prosperity in the South. He purchased land in Kansas and urged Alabama's blacks to escape with him. In 1883, however, before he could leave Alabama, Rapier died of tuberculosis at the age of forty-five.

Union general Carl Schurz had foreseen many of the troubles Rapier encountered in the postwar South. In 1865, Schurz concluded that the Civil War was "a revolution but half accomplished." Northern victory had freed the slaves, he observed, but it had not changed former slaveholders' minds about blacks' unfitness for freedom. Left to themselves, whites would "introduce some new system of forced labor, not perhaps exactly slavery in its old form but something similar to it." To defend their freedom, Schurz concluded, blacks would need federal protection, land of their own, and voting rights. Until whites "cut loose from the past, it will be a dangerous experiment to put Southern society upon its own legs."

As Schurz understood, the end of the war did not mean peace. Indeed, the nation entered one of its most turbulent eras—Reconstruction. Answers to the era's central questions—about the defeated South's status within the Union and the meaning of freedom for ex-slaves—came not only from Washington, D.C., where the federal government played an active role, but also from the state legislatures and county seats of the South, where blacks eagerly participated in politics. The Fourteenth and Fifteenth Amendments to the Constitution strengthened the claim of African Americans to equal rights. The struggle also took place on the South's farms and plantations, where former slaves sought to become free workers while former slaveholders clung to the Old South. A small band of white women joined in the struggle for racial equality, and soon their crusade broadened to include gender equality. Their attempts to secure voting rights for women were thwarted, however, just as were the effort of blacks and their allies to secure racial equality. In the contest to determine the consequences of Confederate defeat and emancipation, white Southerners prevailed.

James T. Rapier
In 1874, when Representative James T. Rapier spoke before Congress on behalf of a civil rights bill, he described the humiliation of being denied service at inns all along his route from Montgomery to Washington. Elsewhere in the world, he said, class and religion were invoked to defend discrimination. But in America, "our distinction is color." Alabama Department of Archives and History, Montgomery, Alabama.

▶ Wartime Reconstruction

Reconstruction did not wait for the end of war. As the odds of a northern victory increased, thinking about reunification quickened. Immediately, a question arose: Who had authority to devise a plan for reconstructing the Union? President Abraham Lincoln firmly believed that reconstruction was a matter of executive responsibility. Congress just as firmly asserted its jurisdiction. Fueling the argument were significant differences about the terms of reconstruction.

In their eagerness to formulate a plan for political reunification, neither Lincoln nor Congress gave much attention to the South's land and labor problems. But as the war rapidly eroded slavery and traditional plantation agriculture, Yankee military commanders in the Union-occupied areas of the Confederacy had no choice but to oversee the emergence of a new labor system. Freedmen's aspirations played little role in the plans that emerged.

"To Bind Up the Nation's Wounds"

As early as 1863, Lincoln began contemplating how "to bind up the nation's wounds" and achieve "a lasting peace." While deep compassion for the enemy guided his thinking about peace, his plan for reconstruction aimed primarily at shortening the war and ending slavery.

Lincoln's Proclamation of Amnesty and Reconstruction in December 1863 set out his terms. He offered a full pardon, restoring property (except slaves) and political rights, to most rebels willing to renounce secession and to accept emancipation. When 10 percent of a state's voting population had taken an oath of allegiance, the state could organize a new government and be readmitted into the Union. Lincoln's plan did not require ex-rebels to extend social or political rights to ex-slaves, nor did it anticipate a program of long-term federal assistance to freedmen. Clearly, the president looked forward to the rapid, forgiving restoration of the broken Union.

Lincoln's easy terms enraged abolitionists such as Wendell Phillips of Boston, who charged that the president "makes the negro's freedom a mere sham." He "is willing that the negro should be free but seeks nothing else for him."

CHRONOLOGY

1863	• Proclamation of Amnesty and Reconstruction.
1864	• Lincoln refuses to sign Wade-Davis bill.
1865	• Freedmen's Bureau established. • Lincoln assassinated; Andrew Johnson becomes president. • Black codes enacted. • Thirteenth Amendment becomes part of Constitution.
1866	• Congress approves Fourteenth Amendment. • Civil Rights Act. • American Equal Rights Association founded. • Ku Klux Klan founded.
1867	• Military Reconstruction Act. • Tenure of Office Act.
1868	• Impeachment trial of President Johnson. • Ulysses S. Grant elected president.
1869	• Congress approves Fifteenth Amendment.
1871	• Ku Klux Klan Act.
1872	• Liberal Party formed. • President Grant reelected.
1873	• Economic depression sets in. • *Slaughterhouse* cases. • Colfax massacre.
1874	• Democrats win majority in House of Representatives.
1875	• Civil Rights Act.
1876	• *United States v. Cruikshank.*
1877	• Rutherford B. Hayes becomes president; Reconstruction era ends.

Wartime Reconstruction

This cartoon from the presidential campaign of 1864 shows the "Rail Splitter" Abraham Lincoln leveraging the broken nation back together while his running mate, Andrew Johnson, who once was a tailor by trade, stitches the Confederate states securely back into the Union. Optimism that the task of reconstructing the nation after the war would be both quick and easy shines through the cartoon. The Granger Collection, New York.

Comparing Lincoln to the Union's most passive general, Phillips declared, "What McClellan was on the battlefield—'Do as little hurt as possible!'—Lincoln is in civil affairs—'Make as little change as possible!'" Phillips and other northern radicals called instead for a thorough overhaul of southern society. Their ideas proved to be too drastic for most Republicans during the war years, but Congress agreed that Lincoln's plan was inadequate.

In July 1864, Congress put forward a plan of its own. Congressman Henry Winter Davis of Maryland and Senator Benjamin Wade of Ohio jointly sponsored a bill that demanded that at least half of the voters in a conquered rebel state take the oath of allegiance before reconstruction could begin. The Wade-Davis bill also banned almost all ex-Confederates from participating in the drafting of new state constitutions. Finally, the bill guaranteed the equality of freedmen before the law. Congress's reconstruction would be neither as quick nor as forgiving as Lincoln's. When Lincoln refused to sign the bill and let it die, Wade and Davis charged the president with usurpation of power.

Undeterred, Lincoln continued to nurture the formation of loyal state governments under his own plan. Four states—Arkansas, Louisiana, Tennessee, and Virginia—fulfilled the president's requirements, but Congress refused to seat representatives from the "Lincoln states." Lincoln admitted that a government based of only 10 percent was not ideal, but he argued, "We shall sooner have the fowl by hatching the egg than by smashing it." Massachusetts's senator Charles Sumner responded, "The eggs of crocodiles can produce only crocodiles." In his last public address in April 1865, Lincoln defended his plan but for the first time expressed publicly his endorsement of suffrage for southern blacks, at least "the very intelligent, and . . . those who serve our cause as soldiers." The announcement demonstrated that Lincoln's thinking about reconstruction was still evolving. Four days later, he was dead.

Land and Labor

Of all the problems raised by the North's victory in the war, none proved more critical than the South's transition from slavery to free labor. As federal armies invaded and occupied the Confederacy, hundreds of thousands of slaves became free workers. In addition, Union armies controlled vast territories in the South where legal title to land had become unclear. The Confiscation Acts passed during the war punished "traitors" by taking away their property. The question of what to do with federally occupied land and how to organize labor on it engaged ex-slaves, ex-slaveholders, Union military commanders, and federal government officials long before the war ended.

In the Mississippi valley, occupying federal troops announced a new labor code. It required landholders to give up whipping, sign contracts with ex-slaves, pay wages, and provide food, housing, and medical care. The code required black laborers to enter into contracts, work diligently, and remain subordinate and obedient. Military leaders clearly had no intention of promoting a social or economic revolution. Instead, they sought to restore traditional plantation agriculture with wage labor. The effort resulted in a hybrid system that one contemporary called "compulsory free labor," something that satisfied no one.

Planters complained because the new system fell short of slavery. Blacks could not be "transformed by proclamation," a Louisiana sugar planter declared. Without the right to whip, he argued, the new labor system did not have a chance. Either Union soldiers must "*compel* the negroes to work," or the planters themselves must "be authorized and sustained in using force."

African Americans found the new regime too reminiscent of slavery to be called free labor. Its chief deficiency, they believed, was the failure to provide them with land of their own. Freedmen believed they had a moral right to land because they and their ancestors had worked it without compensation for centuries. "What's the use of being free if you don't own land enough to be buried in?" one man asked. Several wartime developments led freedmen to believe that the

VISUAL ACTIVITY

The Lord Is My Shepherd, 1863

Maine-born Eastman Johnson (1824–1906) did this painting only months after the Emancipation Proclamation. Its title comes from Psalm 23, which begins "The Lord is my shepherd; I shall not want." The painting captures a humble black man quietly reading his Bible and reminds us of one of the reasons freedmen struggled so hard for literacy. Smithsonian American Art Museum, Washington, DC/Art Resource, NY.

READING THE IMAGE: What is the artist saying about ex-slaves' capacity to live as free people?

CONNECTIONS: Why did southern whites in the Reconstruction era consider literacy for former slaves less a religious impulse than a dangerous political act?

federal government planned to undergird black freedom with landownership.

In January 1865, General William Tecumseh Sherman set aside part of the coast south of Charleston for black settlement. By June 1865, some 40,000 freedmen sat on 400,000 acres of "Sherman land." In addition, in March 1865, Congress passed a bill establishing the Bureau of Refugees, Freedmen, and Abandoned Lands. The **Freedmen's Bureau**, as it was called, distributed food and clothing to destitute Southerners and eased the transition of blacks from slaves to free persons. Congress also authorized the agency to divide abandoned and confiscated land into 40-acre plots, to rent them to freedmen, and eventually to sell them "with such title as the

The Meaning of Freedom

Although the Emancipation Proclamation itself did not free any slaves, it transformed the character of the war. Black people resolutely focused on the possibilities of freedom.

DOCUMENT 1
Letter from John Q. A. Dennis to Edwin M. Stanton, July 26, 1864

John Q. A. Dennis, formerly a slave in Maryland, wrote to ask Secretary of War Edwin M. Stanton for help in reuniting his family.

Boston. Dear Sir I am Glad that I have the Honour to Write you a few line I have been in troble for about four yars my Dear wife was taken from me Nov 19th 1859 and left me with three Children and I being a Slave At the time Could Not do Anny thing for the poor little Children for my master it was took me Carry me some forty mile from them So I Could Not do for them and the man that they live with half feed them and half Cloth them & beat them like dogs & when I was admitted to go to see them it use to brake my heart & Now I say again I am Glad to have the honour to write to you to see if you Can Do Anny thing for me or for my poor little Children I was keap in Slavy untell last Novr 1863. then the Good lord sent the Cornel borne [federal colonel William Birney?] Down their in Marland in worsester Co So as I have been recently freed I have but letle to live on but I am Striveing Dear Sir but what I went too know of you Sir is it possible for me to go & take my Children from those men that keep them in Savery if it is possible will you pleas give me a permit from your hand then I think they would let them go. . . . I want get the little Children out of Slavery. . . .

Source: *Freedom: A Documentary History of Emancipation, 1861–1867,* ser. 1, vol. 1, *The Destruction of Slavery,* 386, edited by Ira Berlin, Joseph P. Reidy, and Leslie S. Rowland. Copyright © 1985. Reprinted with the permission of Cambridge University Press.

DOCUMENT 2
Report from Reverend A. B. Randall, February 28, 1865

A. B. Randall, the white chaplain of a black regiment stationed in Little Rock, Arkansas, affirmed the importance of legal marriage to freed slaves and emphasized their conviction that emancipation was only the first step toward full freedom.

Weddings, just now, are very popular, and abundant among the Colored People. They have just learned, of the Special Order No. 15. of Gen Thomas [Adjutant General Lorenzo Thomas] by which, they may not only be lawfully married, but have their Marriage Certificates, Recorded; in a book furnished by the Government. . . . I have married, during the month, at this Post; Twenty five couples; mostly, those, who have families; & have been living together for years. . . . The Colord People here, generally consider, this war not only; their exodus, from bondage; but the road, to Responsibility; Competency; and an honorable Citizenship—God grant that their hopes and expectations may be fully realized.

Source: *Freedom: A Documentary History of Emancipation, 1861–1867,* ser. 2, vol. 1, *The Black Military Experience,* 712, edited by Ira Berlin, Joseph P. Reidy, and Leslie S. Rowland. Copyright © 1982. Reprinted with the permission of Cambridge University Press.

United States can convey." By June 1865, the Bureau had situated nearly 10,000 black families on a half million acres abandoned by fleeing planters. Other ex-slaves eagerly anticipated farms of their own.

Despite the flurry of activity, wartime reconstruction failed to produce agreement about whether the president or Congress had the authority to devise policy or what proper policy should be.

The African American Quest for Autonomy

Ex-slaves never had any doubt about what they wanted from freedom. They had only to contemplate what they had been denied as slaves. (See "Documenting the American Promise," above.) Slaves had to remain on their plantations; freedom allowed blacks to see what was on the other side

DOCUMENT 3
Petition "to the Union Convention of Tennessee Assembled in the Capitol at Nashville," January 9, 1865

In January 1865, black Tennesseans petitioned a convention of white Unionists debating the reorganization of state government.

We the undersigned petitioners, American citizens of African descent, natives and residents of Tennessee, and devoted friends of the great National cause, do most respectfully ask a patient hearing of your honorable body in regard to matters deeply affecting the future condition of our unfortunate and long suffering race. . . .

In the contest between the nation and slavery, our unfortunate people have sided, by instinct, with the former. . . . We will work, pray, live, and, if need be, die for the Union, as cheerfully as ever a white patriot died for his country. The color of our skin does not lessen in the least degree, our love either for God or for the land of our birth. . . .

We know the burdens of citizenship, and are ready to bear them. We know the duties of the good citizen, and are ready to perform them cheerfully, and would ask to be put in a position in which we can discharge them more effectually. . . .

This is a democracy—a government of the people. It should aim to make every man, without regard to the color of his skin, the amount of his wealth, or the character of his religious faith, feel personally interested in its welfare. Every man who lives under the Government should feel that it is his property, his treasure, the bulwark and defence of himself and his family. . . .

This is not a Democratic Government if a numerous, law-abiding, industrious, and useful class of citizens, born and bred on the soil, are to be treated as aliens and enemies, as an inferior degraded class, who must have no voice in the Government which they support, protect and defend, with all their heart, soul, mind, and body, both in peace and war. . . .

The possibility that the negro suffrage proposition may shock popular prejudice at first sight, is not a conclusive argument against its wisdom and policy. No proposition ever met with more furious or general opposition than the one to enlist colored soldiers in the United States army. The opponents of the measure exclaimed on all hands that the negro was a coward; that he would not fight; that one white man, with a whip in his hand could put to flight a regiment of them. . . . Yet the colored man has fought so well . . . .

The Government has asked the colored man to fight for its preservation and gladly has he done it. It can afford to trust him with a vote as safely as it trusted him with a bayonet.

Source: *Freedom: A Documentary History of Emancipation, 1861–1867*, ser. 2, vol. 1, *The Black Military Experience*, 811–16, edited by Ira Berlin, Joseph P. Reidy, and Leslie S. Rowland. Copyright © 1982. Reprinted with the permission of Cambridge University Press.

Questions for Analysis and Debate

1. How does John Q. A. Dennis interpret his responsibility as a father?

2. Why do you think ex-slaves wanted their marriages legalized?

3. Why, according to petitioners to the Union Convention of Tennessee, did blacks deserve voting rights?

Connect to the Big Idea

C How did ex-slaves embrace freedom following the Civil War?

---

of the hill. Slaves had to be at work in the fields by dawn; freedom permitted blacks to sleep through a sunrise. Freedmen also tested the etiquette of racial subordination. "Lizzie's maid passed me today when I was coming from church *without speaking to me*," huffed one plantation mistress.

To whites, emancipation looked like pure anarchy. Blacks, they said, had reverted to their natural condition: lazy, irresponsible, and wild.

Actually, former slaves were experimenting with freedom, but they could not long afford to roam the countryside, neglect work, and casually provoke whites. Soon, most were back at work in whites' kitchens and fields.

But they continued to dream of land and independence. "The way we can best take care of ourselves is to have land," one former slave declared in 1865, "and turn it and till it by our

VISUAL ACTIVITY

Harry Stephens and Family, 1866
The seven members of the Stephens family sit proudly for a photograph just after the Civil War ended. Many black families were not as fortunate as these Virginians. Separated by slavery or war, former slaves desperately sought news of missing family members through newspaper advertisements.
G. Gable, Summer Scene, 1866. Gilman Collection, Purchase, The Horace W. Goldsmith Foundation Gift, through Joyce and Robert Menschel, 2005 (2005.100.277) Image copyright © The Metropolitan Museum of Art. Image source: Art Resource, NY.

READING THE IMAGE: How does the Stephens family signal that they are free people, not slaves?

CONNECTIONS: How would white Southerners likely respond to the message delivered by this photograph?

own labor." Slavery had deliberately kept blacks illiterate, and freedmen emerged from bondage eager to learn to read and write. "I wishes the Childern all in School," one black veteran asserted. "It is beter for them then to be their Surveing a mistes [mistress]."

The restoration of broken families was another persistent black aspiration. Thousands of freedmen took to the roads in 1865 to look for kin who had been sold away or to free those who were being held illegally as slaves. A black soldier from Missouri wrote his daughters that he was coming for them. "I will have you if it cost me my life," he declared. "Your Miss Kitty said that I tried to steal you," he told them. "But I'll let her know that god never intended for a man to steal his own flesh and blood." And he swore that "if she meets me with ten thousand soldiers, she [will] meet her enemy."

Independent worship was another continuing aspiration. African Americans greeted freedom with a mass exodus from white churches, where they had been required to worship when slaves. Some joined the newly established southern branches of all-black northern churches, such as the African Methodist Episcopal Church. Others formed black versions of the major southern denominations, Baptists and Methodists.

REVIEW   To what extent did Lincoln's wartime plan for reconstruction reflect the concerns of newly freed slaves?

▶ Presidential Reconstruction

Abraham Lincoln died on April 15, 1865, just hours after John Wilkes Booth shot him at a Washington, D.C., theater. Chief Justice Salmon P. Chase immediately administered the oath of office to Vice President Andrew Johnson of Tennessee. Congress had adjourned in March and would not reconvene until December. Throughout the summer and fall, Johnson drew up and executed a plan of reconstruction without congressional advice.

Congress returned to the capital in December to find that, as far as the president and former Confederates were concerned, reconstruction was completed. Most Republicans, however, thought Johnson's plan made far too few demands of ex-rebels and made a mockery of the sacrifice of Union soldiers. They claimed that Johnson's leniency had acted as midwife to the rebirth of the Old South, that he had achieved political reunification at the cost of black freedom. Republicans in Congress then proceeded to dismantle Johnson's program and substitute a program of their own.

Johnson's Program of Reconciliation

Born in 1808 in Raleigh, North Carolina, Andrew Johnson was the son of illiterate parents. Self-educated and ambitious, Johnson moved to Tennessee, where he worked as a tailor, accumulated a fortune in land, acquired five slaves, and built a career in politics championing the South's common white people and assailing its "illegitimate, swaggering, bastard, scrub aristocracy." The only senator from a Confederate state to remain loyal to the Union, Johnson held the planter class responsible for secession. Less than two weeks before he became president, he announced what he would do to planters if he ever had the chance: "I would arrest them—I would try them—I would convict them and I would hang them."

A Democrat all his life, Johnson occupied the White House only because the Republican Party in 1864 had needed a vice presidential candidate who would appeal to loyal, Union-supporting Democrats. Johnson vigorously defended states' rights (but not secession) and opposed Republican efforts to expand the power of the federal government. A steadfast supporter of slavery, Johnson had owned slaves until 1862, when Tennessee rebels, angry at his Unionism, confiscated them. When he grudgingly accepted emancipation, it was more because he hated planters than sympathized with slaves. "Damn the negroes," he said. "I am fighting those traitorous aristocrats, their masters." The new president harbored unshakable racist convictions. Africans, Johnson said, were "inferior to the white man in point of intellect—better calculated in physical structure to undergo drudgery and hardship."

Like Lincoln, Johnson stressed the rapid restoration of civil government in the South. Like Lincoln, he promised to pardon most, but not all, ex-rebels. Johnson recognized the state governments created by Lincoln but set out his own requirements for restoring the other rebel states to the Union. All that the citizens of a state had to do was to renounce the right of secession, deny that the debts of the Confederacy were legal and binding, and ratify the Thirteenth Amendment abolishing slavery, which became part of the Constitution in December 1865.

Johnson also returned all confiscated and abandoned land to pardoned ex-Confederates, even if it was in the hands of freedmen. Reformers were shocked. Instead of punishing planters as he had promised, Johnson canceled the promising beginnings made by General Sherman and the Freedmen's Bureau to settle blacks on land of their own. As one freedman observed, "Things was hurt by Mr. Lincoln getting killed."

White Southern Resistance and Black Codes

In the summer of 1865, delegates across the South gathered to draw up the new state constitutions required by Johnson's plan of reconstruction. They refused to accept even the president's mild requirements. Refusing to renounce secession, the South Carolina and Georgia conventions merely "repudiated" their secession ordinances, preserving in principle their right to secede. South Carolina and Mississippi refused to disown their Confederate war debts. Mississippi rejected the Thirteenth Amendment, and Alabama rejected it in part. Despite this defiance, Johnson did nothing. White Southerners began to think that by standing up for themselves they could shape the terms of reconstruction.

New state governments across the South adopted a series of laws known as **black codes**, which made a travesty of black freedom. The codes sought to keep ex-slaves subordinate to whites by subjecting them to every sort of discrimination. Several states made it illegal for blacks to own a gun. Mississippi made insulting gestures and language by blacks a criminal offense. The codes barred blacks from jury duty. Not a single southern state granted any black the right to vote.

At the core of the black codes, however, lay the matter of labor. Legislators sought to hustle

The Black Codes
Titled *Selling a Freeman to Pay His Fine at Monticello, Florida*, this 1867 drawing from a northern magazine equates black codes with the reinstitution of slavery. The laws stopped short of reenslavement but sharply restricted blacks' freedom. In southern states, certain acts, such as breaking a labor contract, were made criminal offenses, the penalty for which could be involuntary plantation labor for a year. The Granger Collection, New York

freedmen back to the plantations. Whites were almost universally opposed to black landownership. Whitelaw Reid, a northern visitor to the South, found that the "man who should sell small tracts to them would be in actual personal danger." South Carolina attempted to limit blacks to either farmwork or domestic service by requiring them to pay annual taxes of $10 to $100 to work in any other occupation. Mississippi declared that blacks who did not possess written evidence of employment could be declared vagrants and be subject to involuntary plantation labor. Under so-called apprenticeship laws, courts bound thousands of black children— orphans and others whose parents they deemed

unable to support them—to work for planter "guardians."

Johnson refused to intervene. A staunch defender of states' rights, he believed that citizens of every state should be free to write their own constitutions and laws. Moreover, Johnson was as eager as other white Southerners to restore white supremacy. "White men alone must manage the South," he declared.

Johnson also recognized that his do-nothing response offered him political advantage. A conservative Tennessee Democrat at the head of a northern Republican Party, he had begun to look southward for political allies. Despite tough talk about punishing traitors, he personally pardoned fourteen thousand wealthy or high-ranking ex-Confederates. By pardoning powerful whites, by accepting governments even when they failed to satisfy his minimal demands, and by acquiescing in the black codes, he won useful southern friends.

In the fall elections of 1865, white Southerners dramatically expressed their mood. To represent them in Congress, they chose former Confederates. Of the eighty senators and representatives they sent to Washington, fifteen had served in the Confederate army, ten of them as generals. Another sixteen had served in civil and judicial posts in the Confederacy. Nine others had served in the Confederate Congress. One—Alexander Stephens—had been vice president of the Confederacy. As one Georgian remarked, "It looked as though Richmond had moved to Washington."

Expansion of Federal Authority and Black Rights

Southerners had blundered monumentally. They had assumed that what Andrew Johnson was willing to accept, Republicans would accept as well. But southern intransigence compelled even moderates to conclude that ex-rebels were a "generation of vipers," still untrustworthy and dangerous. The black codes became a symbol of southern intentions to "restore all of slavery but its name." "We tell the white men of Mississippi,"

the *Chicago Tribune* roared, "that the men of the North will convert the State of Mississippi into a frog pond before they will allow such laws to disgrace one foot of the soil in which the bones of our soldiers sleep and over which the flag of freedom waves."

The moderate majority of the Republican Party wanted only assurance that slavery and treason were dead. They did not champion black equality, the confiscation of plantations, or black voting, as did the radical minority within the party. But southern obstinacy had succeeded in forging unity (at least temporarily) among Republican factions. In December 1865, Republicans refused to seat the southern representatives elected in the fall elections. Rather than accept Johnson's claim that the "work of restoration" was done, Congress challenged his executive power.

Republican senator Lyman Trumbull declared that the president's policy meant that an ex-slave would "be tyrannized over, abused, and virtually reenslaved without some legislation by the nation for his protection." Early in 1866, the moderates produced two bills that strengthened the federal shield. The first, the Freedmen's Bureau bill, prolonged the life of the agency established by the previous Congress. Arguing that the Constitution never contemplated a "system for the support of indigent persons," President Andrew Johnson vetoed the bill. Congress failed by a narrow margin to override the president's veto.

The moderates designed their second measure, what would become the **Civil Rights Act of 1866**, to nullify the black codes by affirming African Americans' rights to "full and equal benefit of all laws and proceedings for the security of person and property as is enjoyed by white citizens." The act boldly required the end of racial discrimination in state laws and represented an extraordinary expansion of black rights and federal authority. The president argued that the civil rights bill amounted to "unconstitutional invasion of states' rights" and vetoed it. In essence, he denied that the federal government possessed the authority to protect the civil rights of African Americans.

In April 1866, an incensed Republican Party again pushed the civil rights bill through Congress and overrode the presidential veto. In July, it passed another Freedmen's Bureau bill and overrode Johnson's veto. For the first time in American history, Congress had overridden presidential vetoes of major legislation. As a worried South Carolinian observed, Johnson had succeeded in uniting the Republicans and probably touched off "a fight this fall such as has never been seen."

> **REVIEW**   When the southern states passed the black codes, how did the U.S. Congress respond?

Elizabeth Cady Stanton and Susan B. Anthony, 1870
Outspoken suffragists Elizabeth Cady Stanton (left) and Susan B. Anthony (right) were veteran reformers who advocated, among other things, better working conditions for labor, married women's property rights, liberalization of divorce laws, and women's admission into colleges and trade schools. Their passion for other causes led some conservatives to oppose women's political rights because they equated the suffragist cause with radicalism in general. ©Bettmann/ Corbis.

▶ Congressional Reconstruction

By the summer of 1866, President Andrew Johnson and Congress had dropped their gloves and stood toe-to-toe in a bare-knuckle contest unprecedented in American history. Johnson made it clear that he would not budge on either constitutional issues or policy. Moderate Republicans responded by amending the Constitution. But the obstinacy of Johnson and white Southerners pushed Republican moderates ever closer to the radicals and to acceptance of additional federal intervention in the South. To end presidential interference, Congress voted to impeach the president for the first time since the nation was formed. Soon after, Congress also debated whether to make voting rights color-blind, while women sought to make voting sex-blind as well.

The Fourteenth Amendment and Escalating Violence

In June 1866, Congress passed the **Fourteenth Amendment** to the Constitution, and two years later the states ratified it. The most important provisions of this complex amendment made all native-born or naturalized persons American citizens and prohibited states from abridging the "privileges and immunities" of citizens, depriving them of "life, liberty, or property without due process of law," and denying them "equal protection of the laws." By making blacks national citizens, the amendment provided a national guarantee of equality before the law. In essence, it protected blacks against violation by southern state governments.

The Fourteenth Amendment also dealt with voting rights. It gave Congress the right to reduce the congressional representation of states that withheld suffrage from some of its adult male population. In other words, white Southerners could either allow black men to vote or see their representation in Washington slashed. Whatever happened, Republicans stood to benefit from the Fourteenth Amendment. If southern whites granted voting rights to freedmen, Republicans would gain valuable black votes. If whites refused, the representatives of southern Democrats would plunge.

The Fourteenth Amendment's suffrage provisions ignored the small band of women who had emerged from the war demanding "the ballot for the two disenfranchised classes, negroes and women." Founding the American Equal Rights Association in 1866, Susan B. Anthony and Elizabeth Cady Stanton lobbied for "a government by the people, and the whole people; for the people and the whole people." They felt betrayed when their old antislavery allies refused to work for their goals. "It was the Negro's hour," Frederick Douglass explained. Senator Charles Sumner suggested that woman suffrage could be "the great question of the future."

The Fourteenth Amendment provided for punishment of any state that excluded voters on the basis of race but not on the basis of sex. The amendment also introduced the word *male* into the Constitution when it referred to a citizen's right to vote. Stanton predicted that "if that word 'male' be inserted, it will take us a century at least to get it out."

Tennessee approved the Fourteenth Amendment in July, and Congress promptly welcomed the state's representatives and senators back. Had President Johnson counseled other southern states to ratify this relatively mild amendment, they might have listened. Instead, Johnson advised Southerners to reject the Fourteenth Amendment and to rely on him to trounce the Republicans in the fall congressional elections.

Johnson had decided to make the Fourteenth Amendment the overriding issue of the 1866 elections and to gather its white opponents into a new conservative party, the National Union Party. The president's strategy suffered a setback when whites in several southern cities went on rampages against blacks. Mobs killed thirty-four blacks in New Orleans and forty-six blacks in Memphis. The slaughter shocked Northerners and renewed skepticism about Johnson's claim that southern whites could be trusted. "Who doubts that the Freedmen's Bureau ought to be abolished forthwith," a New Yorker observed sarcastically, "and the

Memphis Riots, May 1866
South Memphis, pictured in this lithograph from *Harper's Weekly*, was a shantytown where the families of black soldiers stationed at nearby Fort Pickering lived. The army commander refused to send troops to protect soldiers' families and property in early May 1866 when white mobs ran wild. The Granger Collection, New York City.

blacks remitted to the paternal care of their old masters, who 'understand the nigger, you know, a great deal better than the Yankees can.'"

The 1866 elections resulted in an overwhelming Republican victory. Johnson had bet that Northerners would not support federal protection of black rights and that a racist backlash would blast the Republican Party. But the war was still fresh in northern minds, and as one Republican explained, southern whites "with all their intelligence were traitors, the blacks with all their ignorance were loyal."

Reconstruction Military Districts

Radical Reconstruction and Military Rule

When Johnson continued to urge Southerners to reject the Fourteenth Amendment, every southern state except Tennessee voted it down. "The last one of the sinful ten," thundered Representative James A. Garfield of Ohio, "has flung back into our teeth the magnanimous offer of a generous nation." After the South rejected the moderates' program, the radicals seized the initiative.

Each act of defiance by southern whites had boosted the standing of the radicals within the Republican Party. Except for freedmen themselves, no one did more to make freedom the "mighty moral question of the age." Radicals such as Massachusetts senator Charles Sumner and Pennsylvania representative Thaddeus Stevens united in demanding civil and political equality. Southern states were "like clay in the hands of the potter," Stevens declared in January 1867, and he called on Congress to begin reconstruction all over again.

In March 1867, Congress overturned the Johnson state governments and initiated military rule of the South. The **Military Reconstruction Act** (and three subsequent acts) divided the ten unreconstructed Confederate states into five military districts. Congress placed a Union general in charge of each district and instructed him to "suppress insurrection, disorder, and violence" and to begin political reform. After the military had completed voter registration, which would include black men, voters in each state would elect delegates to conventions that would draw up new state constitutions. Each constitution would guarantee black suffrage.

When the voters of each state had approved the constitution and the state legislature had ratified the Fourteenth Amendment, the state could submit its work to Congress. If Congress approved, the state's senators and representatives could be seated, and political reunification would be accomplished.

Radicals proclaimed the provision for black suffrage "a prodigious triumph," for it extended far beyond the limited suffrage provisions of the Fourteenth Amendment. When combined with the disfranchisement of thousands of ex-rebels, it promised to cripple any neo-Confederate resurgence and guarantee Republican state governments in the South.

Despite its bold suffrage provision, the Military Reconstruction Act of 1867 disappointed those who also advocated the confiscation of southern plantations and their redistribution to ex-slaves. Thaddeus Stevens agreed with the freedman who said, "Give us our own land and we take care of ourselves, but without land, the old masters can hire us or starve us, as they please." But most Republicans believed they had provided blacks with what they needed: equal legal rights and the ballot. Besides, confiscation was too radical, even for some Radicals. Confiscating private property, declared the *New York Times*, "strikes at the root of all property rights in both sections. It concerns Massachusetts quite as much as Mississippi." If blacks were to get land, they would have to gain it themselves.

Declaring that he would rather sever his right arm than sign such a formula for "anarchy and chaos," Andrew Johnson vetoed the Military Reconstruction Act, but Congress overrode his veto. With the passage of the Reconstruction Acts of 1867, congressional reconstruction was virtually completed. Congress left whites owning most of the South's land but, in a departure that justified the term "radical reconstruction," had given black men the ballot.

Impeaching a President

Despite his defeats, Andrew Johnson had no intention of yielding control of reconstruction. In a dozen ways, he sabotaged Congress's will and encouraged southern whites to resist. He issued a flood of pardons, waged war against the Freedmen's Bureau, and replaced Union generals eager to enforce Congress's Reconstruction Acts with conservative officers eager to defeat them. Johnson claimed that he was merely defending the "violated Constitution." At bottom, however, the president subverted congressional reconstruction to protect southern whites from what he considered the horrors of "Negro domination."

Radicals argued that Johnson's abuse of constitutional powers and his failure to fulfill constitutional obligations to enforce the law were impeachable offenses. According to the Constitution, the House of Representatives can impeach and the Senate can try any federal official for "treason, bribery, or other high crimes and misdemeanors." But moderates interpreted the Constitution to mean violation of criminal statutes. As long as Johnson refrained from breaking the law, impeachment (the process of formal charges of wrongdoing against the president or other federal official) remained stalled.

Then in August 1867, Johnson suspended Secretary of War Edwin M. Stanton from office. As required by the Tenure of Office Act, which demanded the approval of the Senate for the removal of any government official who had been appointed with Senate approval, the president requested the Senate to consent to Stanton's dismissal. When the Senate balked, Johnson removed Stanton anyway. "Is the President crazy, or only drunk?" asked a dumbfounded Republican moderate. "I'm afraid his doings will make us all favor impeachment."

News of Johnson's open defiance of the law convinced every Republican in the House to vote for a resolution impeaching the president. Supreme Court chief justice Salmon Chase presided over the Senate trial, which lasted from March until May 1868. When the vote came, thirty-five senators voted guilty and nineteen not guilty. The impeachment forces fell one vote short of the two-thirds needed to convict.

After his trial, Johnson called a truce, and for the remaining ten months of his term, congressional reconstruction proceeded unhindered by presidential interference. Without interference from Johnson, Congress revisited the suffrage issue.

The Fifteenth Amendment and Women's Demands

In February 1869, Republicans passed the **Fifteenth Amendment** to the Constitution, which prohibited states from depriving any citizen of the right to vote because of "race, color, or previous condition of servitude." The Reconstruction Acts of 1867 already required black suffrage in the South; the Fifteenth Amendment extended black voting nationwide.

Some Republicans, however, found the final wording of the Fifteenth Amendment "lame and halting." Rather than absolutely guaranteeing the right to vote, the amendment merely prohibited exclusion on grounds of race. The distinction would prove to be significant. In time, white Southerners would devise tests of literacy and property and other apparently nonracial measures that would effectively disfranchise blacks yet not violate the Fifteenth Amendment. But an amendment that fully guaranteed the right to vote courted defeat outside the South. Rising antiforeign sentiment—against the Chinese in California and European immigrants in the Northeast—caused states to resist giving up total control of suffrage requirements. In March 1870, after three-fourths of the states had ratified it, the Fifteenth Amendment became part of the Constitution.

Woman suffrage advocates, however, were sorely disappointed with the Fifteenth Amendment's failure to extend voting rights to women. Elizabeth Cady Stanton and Susan B. Anthony condemned the Republicans' "negro first" strategy and pointed out that women remained "the only class of citizens wholly unrepresented in the government." Increasingly, activist women concluded that woman "must not put her trust in man." The Fifteenth Amendment severed the early feminist movement from its abolitionist roots. Over the next several decades, feminists established an independent suffrage crusade that drew millions of women into political life.

Republicans took enough satisfaction in the Fifteenth Amendment to conclude that black suffrage was the "last great point that remained to be settled of the issues of the war" and promptly scratched the "Negro question" from the agenda of national politics. Even that steadfast crusader for equality Wendell Phillips concluded that the black man now held "sufficient shield in his own hands. . . . Whatever he suffers will be largely now, and in future, his own fault." Northerners had no idea of the violent struggles that lay ahead.

REVIEW Why did Congress impeach President Andrew Johnson?

▶ The Struggle in the South

Northerners believed they had discharged their responsibilities with the Reconstruction Acts and the amendments to the Constitution, but Southerners knew that the battle had just begun. Black suffrage had destroyed traditional southern politics and established the foundation for the rise of the Republican Party. Gathering outsiders and outcasts, southern Republicans won elections, wrote new state constitutions, and formed new state governments.

Challenging the established class for political control was dangerous business. Equally dangerous were the confrontations that took place on southern farms and plantations, where blacks sought to give fuller meaning to their newly won legal and political equality. Ex-masters had their own ideas about the labor system that should replace slavery, and freedom remained contested territory. Southerners fought pitched battles with one another to determine the contours of their new world.

Freedmen, Yankees, and Yeomen

African Americans made up the majority of southern Republicans. After gaining voting rights in 1867, nearly all eligible black men registered to vote as Republicans, grateful to the party that had freed them and granted them the franchise. "It is the hardest thing in the world to keep a negro away from the polls," observed an Alabama white man. Southern blacks did not all have identical political priorities, but they united in their desire for education and equal treatment before the law.

Northern whites who made the South their home after the war were a second element of the South's Republican Party. Conservative white Southerners called them **carpetbaggers**, opportunists who stuffed all their belongings in a single carpet-sided suitcase and headed south to "fatten on our misfortunes." But most Northerners who moved south were young men who looked upon the South as they did the West—as a promising place to make a living. Northerners in the southern Republican Party supported programs that encouraged vigorous economic development along the lines of the northern free-labor model.

Southern whites made up the third element of the South's Republican Party. Approximately one out of four white Southerners voted Republican. The other three condemned the one who did as a traitor to his region and his race and called him a **scalawag**, a term for runty horses and low-down, good-for-nothing rascals. Yeoman farmers accounted for the majority of southern white Republicans. Some were Unionists who emerged from the war with bitter memories of Confederate persecution. Others were small farmers who wanted to end state governments' favoritism toward plantation owners. Yeomen supported initiatives for public schools and for expanding economic opportunity in the South.

The South's Republican Party, then, was made up of freedmen, Yankees, and yeomen—an improbable coalition. The mix of races, regions, and classes inevitably meant friction as each group maneuvered to define the party. But Reconstruction represented an extraordinary moment in American politics: Blacks and whites joined together in the Republican Party to pursue political change. Formally, of course, only men participated in politics—casting ballots and holding offices—but white and black women also played a part in the political struggle by joining in parades and rallies, attending stump speeches, and even campaigning.

Most whites in the South condemned southern Republicans as illegitimate and felt justified in doing whatever they could to stamp them out. Violence against blacks—the "white terror"—took brutal institutional form in 1866 with the formation in Tennessee of the **Ku Klux Klan**, a social club of Confederate veterans that quickly developed into a paramilitary organization supporting Democrats. The Klan went on a rampage of whipping, hanging, shooting, burning, and throat-cutting to defeat Republicans and restore white supremacy. (See "Historical Question," page 450.) Rapid demobilization of the Union army after the war left only twenty thousand troops to patrol the entire South. Without effective military protection, southern Republicans had to take care of themselves.

Republican Rule

In the fall of 1867, southern states held elections for delegates to state constitutional conventions, as required by the Reconstruction Acts. About 40 percent of the white electorate stayed home because they had been disfranchised or because they had decided to boycott politics. Republicans won three-fourths of the seats. About 15 percent of the Republican delegates to the conventions were Northerners who had moved south, 25 percent were African Americans, and 60 percent were white Southerners. As a British visitor observed, the delegate elections reflected "the mighty revolution that had taken place in America."

The reconstruction constitutions introduced two broad categories of changes in the South: those that reduced aristocratic privilege and increased democratic equality and those that expanded the state's responsibility for the general welfare. In the first category, the constitutions adopted universal male suffrage, abolished property qualifications for holding office, and made more offices elective and fewer appointed. In the second category, they enacted prison reform; made the state responsible for caring for orphans, the insane, and the deaf and mute; and exempted debtors' homes from seizure.

To Democrats, however, these progressive constitutions looked like wild revolution. Democrats were blind to the fact that no constitution confiscated and redistributed land, as virtually every former slave wished, or disfranchised ex-rebels wholesale, as most southern Unionists advocated. And they were convinced that the new constitutions initiated "Negro domination." In fact, although 80 percent of Republican voters were black men, only 6 percent of Southerners in Congress during Reconstruction were black (Figure 16.1). The sixteen black men in Congress included exceptional men, such as Representative James T. Rapier of Alabama (see pages 433–34). No state legislature experienced "Negro rule," despite black majorities in the populations of some states.

Southern voters ratified the new constitutions and swept Republicans into power. When the former Confederate states ratified the Fourteenth Amendment, Congress readmitted them. Southern Republicans then turned to a staggering array of problems. Wartime destruction littered the landscape. Making matters worse, racial harassment and reactionary violence dogged Southerners who sought reform. Democrats mocked Republican officeholders as ignorant field hands who had only "agricultural degrees" and "brick yard diplomas," but Republicans began a serious effort to rebuild and reform the region.

Activity focused on three areas—education, civil rights, and economic development. Every

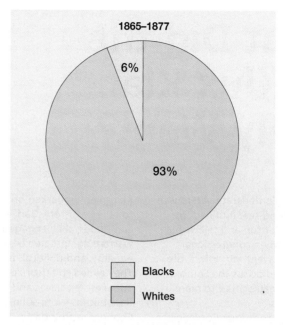

FIGURE 16.1 Southern Congressional Delegations, 1865–1877
The statistics contradict the myth of black domination of congressional representation during Reconstruction.

state inaugurated a system of public education. Before the Civil War, whites had deliberately kept slaves illiterate, and planter-dominated governments rarely spent tax money to educate the children of yeomen. By 1875, half of Mississippi's and South Carolina's eligible children were attending school. Although schools were underfunded, literacy rates rose sharply. Public schools were racially segregated, but education remained for many blacks a tangible, deeply satisfying benefit of freedom and Republican rule.

State legislatures also attacked racial discrimination and defended civil rights. Republicans especially resisted efforts to segregate blacks from whites in public transportation. Mississippi levied fines and jail terms for owners of railroads and steamboats that pushed blacks into "smoking cars" or to lower decks. But passing color-blind laws was one thing; enforcing them was another. A Mississippian complained: "Education amounts to nothing, good behavior counts for nothing, even money cannot buy for a colored man or woman decent treatment and the comforts that white people claim and can obtain." Despite the laws, segregation—later called Jim Crow—developed at white insistence. Determined to underscore the social inferiority

What Did the Ku Klux Klan Really Want?

In 1866, six Confederate veterans in Pulaski, Tennessee, founded the Ku Klux Klan for fun and fellowship. But by 1868, when congressional reconstruction went into effect, the Klan had spread across the South, and members had shifted to more serious matters.

According to former Confederate general and Georgia Democratic politician John B. Gordon, the Klan owed its popularity to the "instinct of self-preservation . . . the sense of insecurity and danger, particularly in those neighborhoods where the Negro population largely predominated." Everywhere whites looked, he said, they saw "great crime." Republican politicians marched ignorant freedmen to the polls, where they blighted honest government. Ex-slaves drove overseers from plantations and claimed the land for themselves. Black rapists made white women cower behind barred doors. It was necessary, Gordon declared, "in order to protect our families from outrage and preserve our own lives, to have something that we could regard as a brotherhood—a combination of the best men of the country, to act purely in self-defense."

Behind the Klan's high-minded and self-justifying rhetoric, however, lay another agenda. It was revealed in their actions, not their words.

Klansmen embarked on a campaign to reverse history. Garbed in robes and hoods, they engaged in guerrilla warfare against free labor, civil equality, and political democracy. They aimed to terrorize their enemies—ex-slaves and white Republicans—into submission. Changes in four particular areas of southern life proved flash points for Klan violence: racial etiquette, education, labor, and politics.

The Klan punished those blacks and whites who broke the Old South's racial code. The Klan considered "impudence" a punishable offense. Asked to define "impudence" before a congressional investigating committee, one white man responded: "Well, it is considered impudence for a negro not to be polite to a white man—not to pull off his hat and bow and scrape to a white man, as was done formerly." Klansmen whipped blacks for speaking disrespectfully, refusing to yield the sidewalk, and dressing well. Black women who "dress up and fix up like ladies" risked a midnight visit from the Klan. The Klan sought to restore racial subordination in every aspect of private and public life.

Klansmen also took aim at black education. White men found the sight of blacks in classrooms hard to stomach. Schools were easy targets,

and scores of them went up in flames. Teachers, male and female, were flogged, or worse. Klansmen drove northern-born teacher Alonzo B. Corliss from North Carolina for "teaching niggers and making them like white men." In Cross Plains, Alabama, the Klan hanged an Irish-born teacher along with four black men. Planters wanted ex-slaves back in the fields, not at desks. In 1869, an Alabama newspaper announced that the burning of a black school should be "a warning for them to stick hereafter to 'de shovel and de hoe,' and let their dirty-backed primers go."

Planters turned to the Klan as part of their effort to preserve plantation agriculture. An Alabama white admitted that in his area the Klan was "intended principally for the negroes who failed to work." Hooded bands "punished Negroes whose landlords had complained of them." Sharecroppers who disputed their share at "settling up time" risked a visit from the night riders. It was dangerous for freedmen to consider changing employers. "If we got out looking for some other place to go," an ex-slave from Texas remembered, "them KKK they would tend to Mister negro good and plenty."

Above all, the Klan terrorized Republicans. Klansmen became the military arm of the Democratic Party. They drove blacks from the polls on election day and assaulted Republican officeholders. Klansmen gave Andrew Flowers, a black politician in Chattanooga, a brutal beating and told him that they "did not intend any nigger to hold office in the United States." Jack Dupree, president of the Republican Club in Monroe County, Mississippi, a man known to "speak

of blacks, whites saw to it that separation by race became a feature of southern life long before the end of the Reconstruction era.

Republican governments also launched ambitious programs of economic development. They envisioned a South of diversified agriculture, roaring factories, and booming towns. State legislatures chartered scores of banks and industrial companies, appropriated funds to fix ruined levees and drain swamps, and went on a railroad-building binge. These efforts fell far short of solving the South's economic troubles, however.

Ku Klux Klan Rider in Tennessee about 1868
During Reconstruction, Klansmen wore robes of various designs and colors. Hooded horses added another element to the Klan's terror. The Klansman holds a flag that probably contained a motto that supported white supremacy. Courtesy of the Tennessee State Museum.

Klan murdered three scalawag members of the legislature and drove ten others from their homes. As one Georgia Republican commented after a Klan attack: "We don't call them [D]emocrats, we call them southern murderers."

It proved hard to arrest Klansmen and harder still to convict them. "If a white man kills a colored man in any of the counties of this State," observed a Florida sheriff, "you cannot convict him." Federal intervention—in the Ku Klux Klan Acts of 1870 and 1871—signaled an end to much of the Klan's power but not to counterrevolutionary violence in the South. Other groups continued the terror in the cause of white supremacy.

Questions for Consideration

1. What changes during Reconstruction particularly provoked the Klan? Why do you think these issues were so important to Klansmen?

2. Why did Klansmen believe that their actions were justified? Why do you think they hid their identities?

3. What southern traditions did the Klan seek to perpetuate?

Connect to the Big Idea

⊙ How did the Ku Klux Klan serve the counter-evolutionary goals of the South's Democratic Party?

his mind," had his throat cut and was disemboweled while his wife was forced to watch.

Political violence reached astounding levels. Arkansas experienced nearly three hundred political killings in the three months before the fall elections in 1868. Louisiana was even bloodier, suffering more than one thousand killings in the same year. In Georgia, the

Republican spending to stimulate economic growth also meant rising taxes and enormous debt that siphoned funds from schools and other programs.

The southern Republicans' record, then, was mixed. To their credit, the biracial party adopted an ambitious agenda to change the South. But money was scarce, the Democrats continued their harassment, and factionalism threatened the Republican Party from within. Moreover, corruption infected Republican governments. Nonetheless, the Republican Party

Students at a Freedmen's School in Virginia, ca. 1870s
"The people are hungry and thirsty after knowledge," a former slave observed immediately after the Civil War. African American leader Booker T. Washington remembered "a whole race trying to go to school." Students at this Virginia school stand in front of their log-cabin classroom reading books. For people long forbidden to learn to read and write, literacy symbolized freedom. Cook Collection, Valentine Richmond History Center, www.richmondhistorycenter.com.

made headway in its efforts to purge the South of aristocratic privilege and racist oppression. Republican governments had less success in overthrowing the long-established white oppression of black farm laborers in the rural South.

White Landlords, Black Sharecroppers

Ex-slaves who wished to escape slave labor and ex-masters who wanted to reinstitute old ways clashed repeatedly. Except for having to pay subsistence wages, planters had not been required to offer many concessions to emancipation. They continued to believe that African Americans would not work without coercion. A Tennessee man declared two years after the war ended that

blacks were "a trifling set of lazy devils who will never make a living without Masters." Whites moved quickly to restore as much of slavery as they could get away with.

Ex-slaves resisted every effort to turn back the clock. They argued that if any class could be described as "lazy," it was the planters, who, as one former slave noted, "lived in idleness all their lives on stolen labor." They believed that land of their own would anchor their economic independence and end planters' interference in their personal lives. They could then, for example, make their own decisions about whether women and children would labor in the fields. Indeed, within months after the war, perhaps one-third of black women abandoned field labor to work on chores in their own cabins just as poor white women did. Black women also

Black Woman in Cotton Fields, Thomasville, Georgia
Few images of everyday black women during the Reconstruction era survive. This 1895 photograph poignantly depicts the post–Civil War labor struggle, when white landlords wanted emancipated slaves to continue working in the fields. Freedom allowed some women to escape field labor, but not this Georgian. Her headdress protected her from the fierce heat, and her bare feet reveal the hardships of her life. Courtesy, Georgia Archives, Vanishing Georgia Collection tho096.

negotiated about work ex-mistresses wanted done in the big house. (See "Visualizing History," page 454.) Hundreds of thousands of black children enrolled in school. But without their own land, ex-slaves had little choice but to work on plantations.

Although forced to return to the planters' fields, they resisted efforts to restore slavelike conditions. Instead of working for wages, a South Carolinian observed, "the negroes all seem disposed to rent land," which increased their independence from whites. Out of this tug-of-war between white landlords and black laborers emerged a new system of southern agriculture.

Sharecropping was a compromise that offered something to both ex-masters and ex-slaves but satisfied neither. Under the new system, planters divided their cotton plantations into small farms that freedmen rented, paying with a share of each year's crop, usually half. Sharecropping gave blacks more freedom than the system of wages and labor gangs and released them from day-to-day supervision by whites. Black families abandoned the old slave quarters and built separate cabins for themselves on the patches of land they rented (Map 16.1). Still, most black families remained dependent on white landlords, who had the power to evict them at the end of each growing season. For planters, sharecropping offered a way to resume agricultural production, but it did not allow them to restore the old slave plantation.

Sharecropping introduced the country merchant into the agricultural equation. Land-lords supplied sharecroppers with land, mules, seeds, and tools, but blacks also needed credit to obtain essential food and clothing before they harvested their crops. Under an arrangement called a crop lien, a merchant would advance goods to a sharecropper in exchange for a *lien*, or legal claim, on the farmer's future crop. Some merchants charged exorbitant rates of interest, as much as 60 percent, on the goods they sold. At the end of the growing season, after the landlord had taken half of the farmer's crop for rent, the merchant took most of the rest. Sometimes, the farmer did not earn enough to repay the debt to the merchant, so he would have to borrow more from the merchant and begin the cycle again.

An experiment at first, sharecropping soon dominated the cotton South. Lien merchants forced tenants to plant cotton, which was easy to sell, instead of food crops. The result was excessive production of cotton and falling cotton prices, developments that cost thousands of small white farmers their land and pushed them into the great army of sharecroppers. The new sharecropping system of agriculture took shape just as the political power of Republicans in the South began to buckle under Democratic pressure.

REVIEW How did politics and economic concerns shape reconstruction in the South?

A Post-slavery Encounter

A Visit from the Old Mistress, 1876

Winslow Homer (1836–1910) is regarded by many as the nation's greatest nineteenth-century painter. He typically sketched and painted ordinary people in their everyday lives, and he was admired for his ability to convey drama and emotion on canvas. During the Civil War, Homer worked as an illustrator for *Harper's Weekly*, depicting scenes of the war for curious Northerners. In 1875, he traveled from his home in New York City to Virginia, where he observed firsthand the transformation of relationships between former slaves and their former owners. He composed *A Visit from the Old Mistress* from sketches he had made while traveling through Virginia.

In this painting, Homer captures the moment when a white woman arrives in the humble cabin of former slaves and encounters three black women, one of whom holds a toddler. Homer typically said little about his paintings, and there is much we don't know about the story being told in this work. Why has the old

mistress come? We can imagine that she has come to talk about work she wants done in the big house. If so, she would have come asking, not commanding, for the end of slavery meant that ex-slaves had control over their own labor and negotiated what they would be paid and the conditions under which they would work.

Notice the way Homer has arranged the subjects of his painting, with the former slaves on one side of the room and the former mistress on the other. What does the generous space between them suggest? How do the two sides compare? Look particularly at the women's clothing and their stance. What does the white woman's posture suggest? How are the three black women positioned, and what does this say about their attitude toward the old mistress? What do you detect in the facial expressions of the people in this image?

The end of slavery required wrenching readjustments in the lives of Southerners, black and white. Homer has captured a tense moment in that transition.

SOURCE: Smithsonian American Art Museum, Washington, DC/Art Resource, NY.

Questions for Analysis

1. How would you describe the conditions of these former slaves? Have they improved since emancipation?

2. White southerners often claimed that their slaves loved them. Do you see any signs of affection or loyalty in these black women for their former owner?

3. Do you think that this domestic scene reveals the artist's opinion about what he witnessed, or does *A Visit from the Old Mistress* try merely to capture truthfully a complex scene?

Connect to the Big Idea

C How might this painting have looked differently if it had been created before emancipation? (See chapters 13 and 15.)

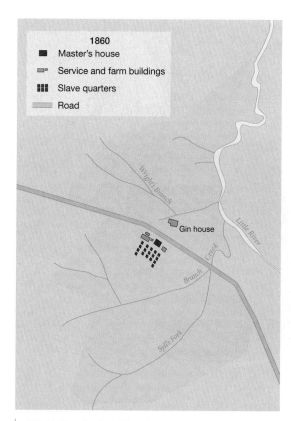

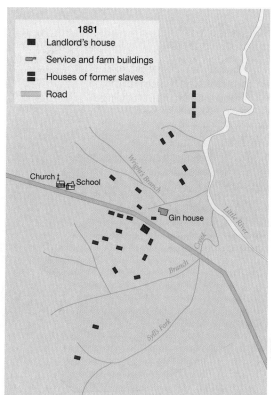

MAP ACTIVITY

Map 16.1 A Southern Plantation in 1860 and 1881
These maps of the Barrow plantation in Georgia illustrate some of the ways in which ex-slaves expressed their freedom. Freedmen and freedwomen deserted the clustered living quarters behind the master's house, scattered over the plantation, built family cabins, and farmed rented land. The former Barrow slaves also worked together to build a school and a church.

READING THE MAP: Compare the number and size of the slave quarters in 1860 with the homes of the former slaves in 1881. How do they differ? Which buildings were prominently located along the road in 1860, and which could be found along the road in 1881?

CONNECTIONS: How might the former master feel about the new configuration of buildings on the plantation in 1881? In what ways did the new system of sharecropping replicate the old system of plantation agriculture? In what ways was it different?

▶ Reconstruction Collapses

By 1870, after a decade of war and reconstruction, Northerners wanted to put "the southern problem" behind them. Practical business-minded men came to dominate the Republican Party, replacing the band of reformers and idealists who had been prominent in the 1860s. Civil war hero Ulysses S. Grant succeeded Andrew Johnson as president in 1869 and quickly be-came an issue himself, proving that brilliance on the battlefield does not necessarily translate into competence in the White House. As northern commitment to defend black

freedom eroded, southern commitment to white supremacy intensified. Without northern protection, southern Republicans were no match for the Democrats' economic coercion, political fraud, and bloody violence. One by one, Republican state governments fell in the South. The election of 1876 both confirmed and completed the collapse of reconstruction.

Grant's Troubled Presidency

In 1868, the Republican Party's presidential nomination went to Ulysses S. Grant, the North's favorite general. His Democratic opponent, Horatio Seymour of New York, ran on a platform

VISUAL ACTIVITY

Grant and Scandal

This anti-Grant cartoon by Thomas Nast, the nation's most celebrated political cartoonist, shows the president falling headfirst into the barrel of fraud and corruption that tainted his administration. During Grant's eight years in the White House, many members of his administration failed him. Sometimes duped, sometimes merely loyal, Grant stubbornly defended wrongdoers, even to the point of perjuring himself to keep an aide out of jail. Picture Research Consultants & Archives.

READING THE IMAGE: How does Thomas Nast portray President Grant's role in corruption? According to this cartoon, what caused the problems?

CONNECTIONS: How responsible was President Grant for the corruption that plagued his administration?

that blasted reconstruction as "a flagrant usurpation of power . . . unconstitutional, revolutionary, and void." The Republicans answered by "waving the bloody shirt"—that is, they reminded voters that the Democrats were "the party of rebellion." Despite a reign of terror in the South, costing hundreds of Republicans their lives, Grant gained a narrow 309,000-vote margin in the popular vote and a substantial victory (214 votes to 80) in the electoral college (Map 16.2).

Grant was not as good a president as he was a general. The talents he had demonstrated on the battlefield—decisiveness, clarity, and resolution—were less obvious in the White House. Grant sought both justice for blacks and sectional reconciliation. But he surrounded himself with fumbling kinfolk and old friends from his army days and made a string of dubious appointments that led to a series of damaging scandals. Charges of corruption tainted his vice president, Schuyler Colfax, and brought down two of his cabinet officers. Though never personally implicated in any scandal, Grant was aggravatingly naive and blind to the rot that filled his administration. Republican congressman James A. Garfield declared: "His imperturbability is amazing. I am in doubt whether to call it greatness or stupidity."

In 1872, anti-Grant Republicans bolted and launched the Liberal Party. To clean up the graft and corruption, Liberals proposed ending the spoils system, by which victorious parties rewarded

loyal workers with public office, and replacing it with a nonpartisan civil service commission that would oversee competitive examinations for appointment to office (as discussed in chapter 18). Liberals also demanded that the federal government remove its troops from the South and restore "home rule" (southern white control). Democrats liked the Liberals' southern policy and endorsed the Liberal presidential candidate, Horace Greeley,

MAP 16.2
The Election of 1868

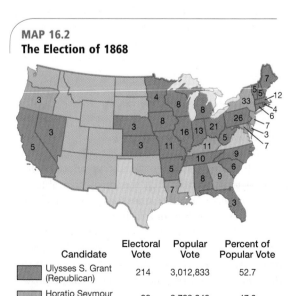

Candidate	Electoral Vote	Popular Vote	Percent of Popular Vote
Ulysses S. Grant (Republican)	214	3,012,833	52.7
Horatio Seymour (Democrat)	80	2,703,249	47.3
Nonvoting states (Reconstruction)			

the longtime editor of the *New York Tribune*. The nation, however, still felt enormous affection for the man who had saved the Union and reelected Grant with 56 percent of the popular vote.

Northern Resolve Withers

Although Grant genuinely wanted to see blacks' civil and political rights protected, he understood that most Northerners had grown weary of reconstruction and were increasingly willing to let southern whites manage their own affairs. Citizens wanted to shift their attention to other issues, especially after the nation slipped into a devastating economic depression in 1873. More than eighteen thousand businesses collapsed, leaving more than a million workers on the streets. Northern businessmen wanted to invest in the South but believed that recurrent federal intrusion was itself a major cause of instability in the region. Republican leaders began to question the wisdom of their party's alliance with the South's lower classes—its small farmers and sharecroppers. One member of Grant's administration proposed allying with the "thinking and influential native southerners . . . the intelligent, well-to-do, and controlling class."

Congress, too, wanted to leave reconstruction behind, but southern Republicans made that difficult. When the South's Republicans begged for federal protection from increasing Klan violence, Congress enacted three laws in 1870 and 1871 that were intended to break the back of white terrorism. The severest of the three, the Ku Klux Klan Act (1871), made interference with voting rights a felony. Federal marshals arrested thousands of Klansmen and came close to destroying the Klan, but they did not end all terrorism against blacks. Congress also passed the Civil Rights Act of 1875, which boldly outlawed racial discrimination in transportation, public accommodations, and juries. But federal authorities never enforced the law aggressively, and segregation remained the rule throughout the South.

By the early 1870s, the Republican Party had lost its leading champions of African American rights to death or defeat at the polls. Other Republicans concluded that the quest for black equality was mistaken or hopelessly naive. In May 1872, Congress restored the right of office holding to all but three hundred ex-rebels. Many Republicans had come to believe that traditional white leaders offered the best hope for honesty, order, and prosperity in the South.

Underlying the North's abandonment of reconstruction was unyielding racial prejudice.

Northerners had learned to accept black freedom during the war, but deep-seated prejudice prevented many from accepting black equality. Even the actions they took on behalf of blacks often served partisan political advantage. Northerners generally supported Indiana senator Thomas A. Hendricks's harsh declaration that "this is a white man's Government, made by the white man for the white man."

The U.S. Supreme Court also did its part to undermine reconstruction. The Court issued a series of decisions that significantly weakened the federal government's ability to protect black Southerners. In the *Slaughterhouse* cases (1873), the Court distinguished between national and state citizenship and ruled that the Fourteenth Amendment protected only those rights that stemmed from the federal government, such as voting in federal elections and interstate travel. Since the Court decided that most rights derived from the states, it sharply curtailed the federal government's authority to defend black citizens. Even more devastating, the *United States v. Cruikshank* ruling (1876) said that the reconstruction amendments gave Congress the power to legislate against discrimination only by states, not by individuals. The "suppression of ordinary crime," such as assault, remained a state responsibility. The Supreme Court did not declare reconstruction unconstitutional but eroded its legal foundation.

The mood of the North found political expression in the election of 1874, when for the first time in eighteen years the Democrats gained control of the House of Representatives. As one Republican observed, the people had grown tired of the "negro question, with all its complications, and the reconstruction of Southern States, with all its interminable embroilments." Reconstruction had come apart. Rather than defend reconstruction from its southern enemies, Northerners steadily backed away from the challenge. By the early 1870s, southern Republicans faced the forces of reaction largely on their own.

White Supremacy Triumphs

Reconstruction was a massive humiliation to most white Southerners. Republican rule meant intolerable insults: Black militiamen patrolled town streets, black laborers negotiated contracts with former masters, black maids stood up to former mistresses, black voters cast ballots, and black legislators such as James T. Rapier enacted laws. Whites fought back by extolling the "great Confederate cause," or Lost Cause. They celebrated their soldiers, "the noblest band of men who ever

"White Man's Country"
This silk ribbon from the 1868 presidential campaign between Republican Ulysses S. Grant and his Democratic opponent, New York governor Horatio Seymour, openly declares the Democrats' goal of white supremacy. During the campaign, Democratic vice presidential nominee Francis P. Blair Jr. promised that a Seymour victory would restore "white people" to power by declaring the reconstruction governments in the South "null and void." © David J. & Janice L. Frent Collection/CORBIS.

fought" and by making an idol of Robert E. Lee, the embodiment of the southern gentleman.

But the most important way white Southerners responded to reconstruction was their assault on Republican governments in the South. These Republican governments attracted more hatred than did any other political regimes in American history. The northern retreat from reconstruction permitted southern Democrats to set things right. Taking the name **Redeemers**, Democrats in the South promised to replace "bayonet rule" (a few federal troops continued to be stationed in the South) with "home rule." They promised that honest, thrifty Democrats would supplant corrupt tax-and-spend Republicans. Above all, Redeemers swore to save southern civilization from a descent into "African barbarism." As one man put it, "We must render this either a white man's government, or convert the land into a Negro man's cemetery."

Southern Democrats adopted a multipronged strategy to overthrow Republican governments. First, they sought to polarize the parties around race. They went about gathering all the South's white voters into the Democratic Party, leaving the Republicans to depend on blacks, who made up a minority of the population in almost every southern state. To dislodge whites from the Republican Party, Democrats fanned the flames of racism. A South Carolina Democrat crowed that his party appealed to the "proud

Caucasian race, whose sovereignty on earth God has proclaimed." Local newspapers published the names of whites who kept company with blacks, and neighbors ostracized offenders.

Democrats also exploited the severe economic plight of small white farmers by blaming it on Republican financial policy. Government spending soared during reconstruction, and small farmers saw their tax burden skyrocket. "This is tax time," a South Carolinian reported. "We are nearly all on our head about them. They are so high & so little money to pay with" that farmers were "selling every egg and chicken they can get." In 1871, Mississippi reported that one-seventh of the state's land—3.3 million acres—had been forfeited for nonpayment of taxes. The small farmers' economic distress had a racial dimension. Because few freedmen succeeded in acquiring land, they rarely paid taxes. In Georgia in 1874, blacks made up 45 percent of the population but paid only 2 percent of the taxes. From the perspective of a small white farmer, Republican rule meant that he was paying more taxes and paying them to aid blacks.

If racial pride, social isolation, and financial hardship proved insufficient to drive yeomen from the Republican Party, Democrats turned to terrorism. "Night riders" targeted white Republicans as well as blacks for murder and assassination. Whether white or black, a "dead Radical is very harmless," South Carolina Democratic leader Martin Gary told his followers.

But the primary victims of white violence were black Republicans. Violence escalated to an unprecedented ferocity on Easter Sunday in 1873 in tiny Colfax, Louisiana. The black majority in the area had made Colfax a Republican stronghold until 1872, when Democrats turned to intimidation and fraud to win the local election. Republicans refused to accept the result and occupied the courthouse in the middle of the town. After three weeks, 165 white men attacked. They overran the Republicans' defenses and set the courthouse on fire. When the blacks tried to surrender, the whites murdered them. At least 81 black men were slaughtered that day. Although the federal government indicted the attackers, the Supreme Court ruled that it did not have the right to prosecute. And since local whites would not prosecute neighbors who killed blacks, the defendants in the Colfax massacre went free.

Even before adopting the all-out white supremacist tactics of the 1870s, Democrats had taken control of the governments of Virginia, Tennessee, and North Carolina. The new campaign brought fresh gains. The Redeemers

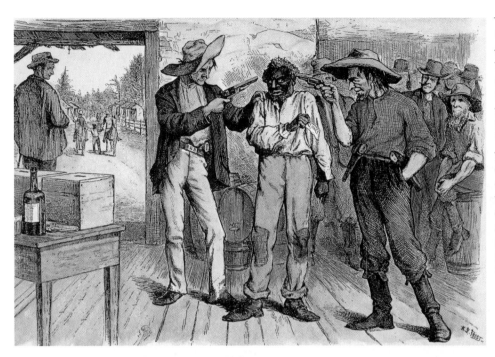

"Of Course He Wants to Vote the Democratic Ticket"
This Republican cartoon from the October 21, 1876, issue of *Harper's Weekly* comments sarcastically on the possibility of honest elections in the South. The caption reads: "You're free as air, ain't you? Say you are or I'll blow yer black head off." The cartoon demonstrates not only some Northerners' concern that violence would deliver the election to the Democrats but also the perception that white Southerners were crude, drunken, ignorant brutes. The Granger Collection, New York.

retook Georgia in 1871, Texas in 1873, and Arkansas and Alabama in 1874. As the state election approached in 1876, Governor Adelbert Ames appealed to Washington for federal troops to control the violence, only to hear from the attorney general that the "whole public are tired of these annual autumnal outbreaks in the South." Abandoned, Mississippi Republicans succumbed to the Democratic onslaught in the fall elections. By 1876, only three Republican state governments survived in the South (Map 16.3).

An Election and a Compromise

The year 1876 witnessed one of the most tumultuous elections in American history. The election took place in November, but not until March 2 of the following year did the nation know who would be inaugurated president on March 4. Sixteen years after Lincoln's election, Americans feared that a presidential election would again precipitate civil war.

The Democrats nominated New York's governor, Samuel J. Tilden, who immediately targeted the corruption of the Grant administration

and the "despotism" of Republican reconstruction. The Republicans put forward Rutherford B. Hayes, governor of Ohio. Privately, Hayes considered "bayonet rule" a mistake but concluded

---

MAP ACTIVITY

Map 16.3   The Reconstruction of the South
Myth has it that Republican rule of the former Confederacy was not only harsh but long. In most states, however, conservative southern whites stormed back into power in months or just a few years. By the election of 1876, Republican governments could be found in only three states, and they soon fell.

READING THE MAP: List in chronological order the readmission of the former Confederate states to the Union. Which states reestablished conservative governments most quickly?
CONNECTIONS: What did the former Confederate states need to do to be readmitted to the Union? How did reestablished conservative governments react to reconstruction?

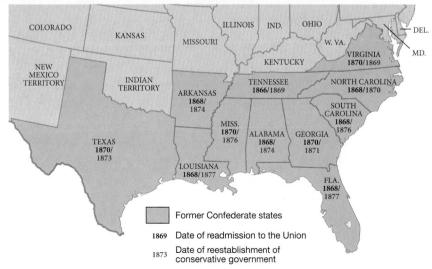

Former Confederate states

1869   Date of readmission to the Union

1873   Date of reestablishment of conservative government

that waving the bloody shirt remained the Republicans' best political strategy.

On election day, Tilden tallied 4,288,590 votes to Hayes's 4,036,000. But in the all-important electoral college, Tilden fell one vote short of the majority required for victory. The electoral votes of three states—South Carolina, Louisiana, and Florida, the only remaining Republican governments in the South—remained in doubt because both Republicans and Democrats in those states claimed victory. To win, Tilden needed only one of the nineteen contested votes. Hayes had to have all of them.

Congress had to decide who had actually won the elections in the three southern states and thus who would be president. The Constitution provided no guidance for this situation. Moreover, Democrats controlled the House, and Republicans controlled the Senate. Congress created a special electoral commission to arbitrate the disputed returns. All of the commissioners voted their party affiliation, giving every state to the Republican Hayes and putting him over the top in electoral votes (Map 16.4).

Some outraged Democrats vowed to resist Hayes's victory. Rumors flew of an impending coup and renewed civil war. But the impasse was broken when negotiations behind the scenes resulted in an informal understanding known as the **Compromise of 1877**. In exchange for a Democratic promise not to block Hayes's inauguration and to deal fairly with the freedmen,

Hayes vowed to refrain from using the army to uphold the remaining Republican regimes in the South and to provide the South with substantial federal subsidies for railroads.

Stubborn Tilden supporters bemoaned the "stolen election" and damned "His Fraudulency," Rutherford B. Hayes. Old-guard radicals such as William Lloyd Garrison denounced Hayes's bargain as a "policy of compromise, of credulity, of weakness, of subserviency, of surrender." But the nation as a whole celebrated, for the country had weathered a grave crisis. The last three Republican state governments in the South fell quickly once Hayes abandoned them and withdrew the U.S. Army. Reconstruction came to an end.

REVIEW Why did northern support for reconstruction collapse?

► Conclusion: "A Revolution but Half Accomplished"

In 1865, when General Carl Schurz visited the South, he discovered "a revolution but half accomplished." White Southerners resisted the passage from slavery to free labor, from white racial despotism to equal justice, and from white political monopoly to biracial democracy. The old elite wanted to get "things back as near to slavery as possible," Schurz reported, while African Americans such as James T. Rapier and some whites were eager to exploit the revolutionary implications of defeat and emancipation.

Although the northern-dominated Republican Congress refused to provide for blacks' economic welfare, it employed constitutional amendments to require ex-Confederates to accept legal equality and share political power with black men. Congress was not willing to extend such power to women, however. Conservative southern whites fought ferociously to recover their power and privilege. When Democrats regained control of politics, whites used both state power and private violence to wipe out many of the gains of Reconstruction, leading one observer to conclude that the North had won the war but the South had won the peace.

The Redeemer counterrevolution, however, did not mean a return to slavery. Northern victory in the Civil War ensured that ex-slaves no longer faced the auction block and could send

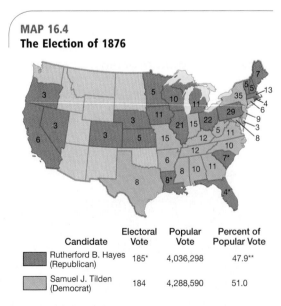

MAP 16.4
The Election of 1876

Candidate	Electoral Vote	Popular Vote	Percent of Popular Vote
Rutherford B. Hayes (Republican)	185*	4,036,298	47.9**
Samuel J. Tilden (Democrat)	184	4,288,590	51.0

*19 electoral votes were disputed.
**Percentages do not total 100 because some popular votes went to other parties.

their children to school, worship in their own churches, and work independently on their own rented farms. Sharecropping, with all its hardships, provided more autonomy and economic welfare than bondage had. It was limited freedom, to be sure, but it was not slavery.

The Civil War and emancipation set in motion the most profound upheaval in the nation's history. War destroyed the largest slave society in the New World and gave birth to a modern nation-state. The world of masters and slaves gave way to that of landlords and share-croppers. Washington increased its role in national affairs, and the victorious North set the nation's compass toward the expansion of industrial capitalism and the final conquest of the West.

Despite massive changes, however, the Civil War remained only a "half accomplished" revolution. By not fulfilling the promises the nation seemed to hold out to black Americans at war's end, Reconstruction represents a tragedy of enormous proportions. The failure to protect blacks and guarantee their rights had enduring consequences. It was the failure of the first reconstruction that made the modern civil rights movement necessary.

See the Selected Bibliography for this chapter in the Appendix.

16 Chapter Review

MAKE IT STICK

 LearningCurve

Go online and use LearningCurve to see what you know. Then review the key terms and answer the questions.

KEY TERMS

Freedmen's Bureau (p. 437)
black codes (p. 441)
Civil Rights Act of 1866 (p. 444)
Fourteenth Amendment (p. 444)
Military Reconstruction Act (p. 446)
Fifteenth Amendment (p. 447)
carpetbagger (p. 448)
scalawag (p. 448)
Ku Klux Klan (p. 448)
sharecropping (p. 451)
Redeemers (p. 458)
Compromise of 1877 (p. 460)

REVIEW QUESTIONS

1. To what extent did Lincoln's wartime plan for reconstruction reflect the concerns of newly freed slaves? (pp. 435–439)

2. When the southern states passed the black codes, how did the U.S. Congress respond? (pp. 441–444)

3. Why did Congress impeach President Andrew Johnson? (pp. 444–447)

4. How did politics and economic concerns shape reconstruction in the South? (pp. 448–455)

5. Why did northern support for reconstruction collapse? (pp. 456–461)

MAKING CONNECTIONS

1. Why and how did the federal government retreat from defending African Americans' civil rights in the 1870s?

2. Why was distributing plantation land to former slaves such a controversial policy? Why did Congress reject redistribution as a general policy?

3. After emancipation, how did ex-slaves exercise their new freedoms, and how did white Southerners attempt to limit them?

4. How did the identification of the Republican Party with Reconstruction policy affect the party's political fortunes in the 1870s?

LINKING TO THE PAST

1. In what ways did the attitudes and actions of President Johnson increase northern resolve to reconstruct the South and the South's resolve to resist reconstruction?

2. White women, abolitionists, and blacks all had hopes for a brighter future that were in some ways dashed during the turmoil of reconstruction. What specific goals of these groups slipped away? What political allies abandoned their causes, and why?

Appendix Directory

THE DECLARATION OF INDEPENDENCE

In Congress, July 4, 1776,

THE UNANIMOUS DECLARATION OF THE THIRTEEN UNITED STATES OF AMERICA

When in the course of human events, it becomes necessary for one people to dissolve the political bands which have connected them with another, and to assume, among the powers of the earth, the separate and equal station to which the laws of nature and of nature's God entitle them, a decent respect to the opinions of mankind requires that they should declare the causes which impel them to the separation.

We hold these truths to be self-evident, that all men are created equal; that they are endowed by their Creator with certain unalienable rights; that among these, are life, liberty, and the pursuit of happiness. That, to secure these rights, governments are instituted among men, deriving their just powers from the consent of the governed; that, whenever any form of government becomes destructive of these ends, it is the right of the people to alter or to abolish it, and to institute a new government, laying its foundation on such principles, and organizing its powers in such form, as to them shall seem most likely to effect their safety and happiness. Prudence, indeed, will dictate that governments long established, should not be changed for light and transient causes; and, accordingly, all experience hath shown, that mankind are more disposed to suffer, while evils are sufferable, than to right themselves by abolishing the forms to which they are accustomed. But, when a long train of abuses and usurpations, pursuing invariably the same object, evinces a design to reduce them under absolute despotism, it is their right, it is their duty, to throw off such government and to provide new guards for their future security. Such has been the patient sufferance of these colonies, and such is now the necessity which constrains them to alter their former systems of government. The history of the present King of Great Britain is a history of repeated injuries and usurpations, all having, in direct object, the establishment of an absolute tyranny over these States. To prove this, let facts be submitted to a candid world: He has refused his assent to laws the most wholesome and necessary for the public good.

He has forbidden his governors to pass laws of immediate and pressing importance, unless suspended in their operation till his assent should be obtained; and, when so suspended, he has utterly neglected to attend to them.

He has refused to pass other laws for the accommodation of large districts of people, unless those people would relinquish the right of representation in the legislature; a right inestimable to them, and formidable to tyrants only.

He has called together legislative bodies at places unusual, uncomfortable, and distant from the depository of their public records, for the sole purpose of fatiguing them into compliance with his measures.

He has dissolved representative houses repeatedly for opposing, with manly firmness, his invasions on the rights of the people.

He has refused, for a long time after such dissolutions, to cause others to be elected; whereby the legislative powers, incapable of annihilation, have returned to the people at large for their exercise; the state remaining in the mean-time exposed to all the danger of invasion from without, and convulsions within.

He has endeavoured to prevent the population of these States; for that purpose, obstructing the laws for naturalization of foreigners, refusing to pass others to encourage their migration hither, and raising the conditions of new appropriations of lands.

He has obstructed the administration of justice, by refusing his assent to laws for establishing judiciary powers.

He has made judges dependent on his will alone, for the tenure of their offices, and the amount and payment of their salaries.

He has erected a multitude of new offices, and sent hither swarms of officers to harass our people, and eat out their substance.

He has kept among us, in times of peace, standing armies, without the consent of our legislature.

He has affected to render the military independent of, and superior to, the civil power.

He has combined, with others, to subject us to a jurisdiction foreign to our Constitution, and unacknowledged by our laws; giving his assent to their acts of pretended legislation:

For quartering large bodies of armed troops among us:

For protecting them by a mock trial, from punishment, for any murders which they should commit on the inhabitants of these States:

For cutting off our trade with all parts of the world:

For imposing taxes on us without our consent:

For depriving us, in many cases, of the benefit of trial by jury:

For transporting us beyond seas to be tried for pretended offences:

For abolishing the free system of English laws in a neighboring province, establishing therein an arbitrary government, and enlarging its boundaries, so as to render it at once an example and fit instrument for introducing the same absolute rule into these colonies:

For taking away our charters, abolishing our most valuable laws, and altering, fundamentally, the powers of our governments:

For suspending our own legislatures, and declaring themselves invested with power to legislate for us in all cases whatsoever.

He has abdicated government here, by declaring us out of his protection, and waging war against us.

He has plundered our seas, ravaged our coasts, burnt our towns, and destroyed the lives of our people.

He is, at this time, transporting large armies of foreign mercenaries to complete the works of death, desolation, and tyranny, already begun, with circumstances of cruelty and perfidy scarcely paralleled in the most barbarous ages, and totally unworthy the head of a civilized nation.

He has constrained our fellow citizens, taken captive on the high seas, to bear arms against their country, to become the executioners of their friends, and brethren, or to fall themselves by their hands.

He has excited domestic insurrections amongst us, and has endeavored to bring on the inhabitants of our frontiers, the merciless Indian savages, whose known rule of warfare is an undistinguished destruction of all ages, sexes, and conditions.

In every stage of these oppressions, we have petitioned for redress; in the most humble terms; our repeated petitions have been answered only by repeated injury. A prince, whose character is thus marked by every act which may define a tyrant, is unfit to be the ruler of a free people.

Nor have we been wanting in attention to our British brethren. We have warned them, from time to time, of attempts made by their legislature to extend an unwarrantable jurisdiction over us. We have reminded them of the circumstances of our emigration and settlement here. We have appealed to their native justice and magnanimity, and we have conjured them, by the ties of our common kindred, to disavow these usurpations, which would inevitably interrupt our connections and correspondence. They, too, have been deaf to the voice of justice and consanguinity. We must, therefore, acquiesce in the necessity which denounces our separation, and hold them as we hold the rest of mankind, enemies in war, in peace, friends.

We, therefore, the representatives of the United States of America, in general Congress assembled, appealing to the Supreme Judge of the world for the rectitude of our intentions, do, in the name, and by authority of the good people of these colonies, solemnly publish and declare, that these united colonies are, and of right ought to be, free and independent states: that they are absolved from all allegiance to the British Crown, and that all political connection between them and the state of Great Britain is, and ought to be, totally dissolved; and that, as free and independent states, they have full power to levy war, conclude peace, contract alliances, establish commerce, and to do all other acts and things which independent states may of right do. And, for the support of this declaration, with a firm reliance on the protection of Divine Providence, we mutually pledge to each other our lives, our fortunes, and our sacred honor.

The foregoing Declaration was, by order of Congress, engrossed, and signed by the following members:

JOHN HANCOCK

New Hampshire
Josiah Bartlett
William Whipple
Matthew Thornton

Massachusetts Bay
Samuel Adams
John Adams
Robert Treat Paine
Elbridge Gerry

Rhode Island
Stephen Hopkins
William Ellery

Connecticut
Roger Sherman
Samuel Huntington
William Williams
Oliver Wolcott

New York
William Floyd
Phillip Livingston
Francis Lewis
Lewis Morris

New Jersey
Richard Stockton
John Witherspoon
Francis Hopkinson
John Hart
Abraham Clark

Pennsylvania
Robert Morris
Benjamin Rush
Benjamin Franklin
John Morton
George Clymer
James Smith

George Taylor
James Wilson
George Ross

Delaware
Caesar Rodney
George Read
Thomas M'Kean

Maryland
Samuel Chase
William Paca
Thomas Stone
Charles Carroll,
   of Carrollton

North Carolina
William Hooper
Joseph Hewes
John Penn

South Carolina
Edward Rutledge
Thomas Heyward, Jr.
Thomas Lynch, Jr.
Arthur Middleton

Virginia
George Wythe
Richard Henry Lee
Thomas Jefferson
Benjamin Harrison
Thomas Nelson, Jr.
Francis Lightfoot Lee
Carter Braxton

Georgia
Button Gwinnett
Lyman Hall
George Walton

Resolved, That copies of the Declaration be sent to the several assemblies, conventions, and committees, or councils of safety, and to the several commanding officers of the continental troops; that it be proclaimed in each of the United States, at the head of the army.

THE CONSTITUTION OF THE UNITED STATES*

Agreed to by Philadelphia Convention, September 17, 1787. Implemented March 4, 1789.

Preamble

We the people of the United States, in order to form a more perfect union, establish justice, insure domestic tranquility, provide for the common defense, promote the general welfare, and secure the blessings of liberty to ourselves and our posterity, do ordain and establish this Constitution for the United States of America.

Article I

Section 1 All legislative powers herein granted shall be vested in a Congress of the United States, which shall consist of a Senate and a House of Representatives.

Section 2 The House of Representatives shall be composed of members chosen every second year by the people of the several States, and the electors in each State shall have the qualifications requisite for electors of the most numerous branch of the State Legislature.

No person shall be a Representative who shall not have attained to the age of twenty-five years, and been seven years a citizen of the United States, and who shall not, when elected, be an inhabitant of that State in which he shall be chosen.

Representatives and direct taxes shall be apportioned among the several States which may be included within this Union, according to their respective numbers, *which shall be determined by adding to the whole number of free persons, including those bound to service for a term of years and excluding Indians not taxed, three-fifths of all other persons.* The actual enumeration shall be made within three years after the first meeting of the Congress of the United States, and within every subsequent term of ten years, in such manner as they shall by law direct. The number of Representatives shall not exceed one for every thirty thousand, but each State shall have at least one Representative; *and until such enumeration shall be made, the State of New Hampshire shall be entitled to choose three, Massachusetts eight, Rhode Island and Providence Plantations one, Connecticut five, New York six, New Jersey four, Pennsylvania eight, Delaware one, Maryland six, Virginia ten, North Carolina five, South Carolina five, and Georgia three.*

When vacancies happen in the representation from any State, the Executive authority thereof shall issue writs of election to fill such vacancies.

The House of Representatives shall choose their Speaker and other officers; and shall have the sole power of impeachment.

Section 3 The Senate of the United States shall be composed of two Senators from each State, *chosen by the legislature thereof,* for six years; and each Senator shall have one vote.

Immediately after they shall be assembled in consequence of the first election, they shall be divided as equally as may be into three classes. The seats of the Senators of the first class shall be vacated at the expiration of the second year, of the second class at the expiration of the fourth year, and of the third class at the expiration of the sixth year, so that one-third may be chosen every second year; *and if vacancies happen by resignation or otherwise, during the recess of the legislature of any State, the Executive thereof may make temporary appointments until the next meeting of the legislature, which shall then fill such vacancies.*

No person shall be a Senator who shall not have attained to the age of thirty years, and been nine years a citizen of the United States, and who shall not, when elected, be an inhabitant of that State for which he shall be chosen.

The Vice-President of the United States shall be President of the Senate, but shall have no vote, unless they be equally divided.

The Senate shall choose their other officers, and also a President pro tempore, in the absence of the Vice-President, or when he shall exercise the office of President of the United States.

The Senate shall have the sole power to try all impeachments. When sitting for that purpose, they shall be on oath or affirmation. When the President of the United States is tried, the Chief Justice shall preside: and no person shall be convicted without the concurrence of two-thirds of the members present.

Judgment in cases of impeachment shall not extend further than to removal from the office, and disqualification to hold and enjoy any office of honor, trust or profit under the United States: but the party convicted shall nevertheless be liable and subject to indictment, trial, judgment and punishment, according to law.

---

*Passages no longer in effect are in italic type.

Section 4 The times, places and manner of holding elections for Senators and Representatives shall be prescribed in each State by the legislature thereof; but the Congress may at any time by law make or alter such regulations, except as to the places of choosing Senators.

The Congress shall assemble at least once in every year, and such meeting *shall be on the first Monday in December, unless they shall by law appoint a different day.*

Section 5 Each house shall be the judge of the elections, returns and qualifications of its own members, and a majority of each shall constitute a quorum to do business; but a smaller number may adjourn from day to day, and may be authorized to compel the attendance of absent members, in such manner, and under such penalties, as each house may provide.

Each house may determine the rules of its proceedings, punish its members for disorderly behavior, and with the concurrence of two-thirds, expel a member.

Each house shall keep a journal of its proceedings, and from time to time publish the same, excepting such parts as may in their judgment require secrecy; and the yeas and nays of the members of either house on any question shall, at the desire of one-fifth of those present, be entered on the journal.

Neither house, during the session of Congress, shall, without the consent of the other, adjourn for more than three days, nor to any other place than that in which the two houses shall be sitting.

Section 6 The Senators and Representatives shall receive a compensation for their services, to be ascertained by law and paid out of the treasury of the United States. They shall in all cases except treason, felony and breach of the peace, be privileged from arrest during their attendance at the session of their respective houses, and in going to and returning from the same; and for any speech or debate in either house, they shall not be questioned in any other place.

No Senator or Representative shall, during the time for which he was elected, be appointed to any civil office under the authority of the United States, which shall have been created, or the emoluments whereof shall have been increased, during such time; and no person holding any office under the United States shall be a member of either house during his continuance in office.

Section 7 All bills for raising revenue shall originate in the House of Representatives; but the Senate may propose or concur with amendments as on other bills.

Every bill which shall have passed the House of Representatives and the Senate, shall, before it become a law, be presented to the President of the United States; if he approve he shall sign it, but if not he shall return it with objections to that house in which it shall have originated, who shall enter the objections at large on their journal, and proceed to reconsider it. If after such reconsideration two-thirds of that house shall agree to pass the bill, it shall be sent, together with the objections, to the other house, by which it shall likewise be reconsidered, and, if approved by two-thirds of that house, it shall become a law. But in all such cases the votes of both houses shall be determined by yeas and nays, and the names of the persons voting for and against the bill shall be entered on the journal of each house respectively. If any bill shall not be returned by the President within ten days (Sundays excepted) after it shall have been presented to him, the same shall be a law, in like manner as if he had signed it, unless the Congress by their adjournment prevent its return, in which case it shall not be a law.

Every order, resolution, or vote to which the concurrence of the Senate and House of Representatives may be necessary (except on a question of adjournment) shall be presented to the President of the United States; and before the same shall take effect, shall be approved by him, or being disapproved by him, shall be repassed by two-thirds of the Senate and House of Representatives, according to the rules and limitations prescribed in the case of a bill.

Section 8 The Congress shall have power

To lay and collect taxes, duties, imposts, and excises, to pay the debts and provide for the common defense and general welfare of the United States; but all duties, imposts and excises shall be uniform throughout the United States;

To borrow money on the credit of the United States;

To regulate commerce with foreign nations, and among the several States, and with the Indian tribes;

To establish an uniform rule of naturalization, and uniform laws on the subject of bankruptcies throughout the United States;

To coin money, regulate the value thereof, and of foreign coin, and fix the standard of weights and measures;

To provide for the punishment of counterfeiting the securities and current coin of the United States;

To establish post offices and post roads;

To promote the progress of science and useful arts by securing for limited times to authors and inventors the exclusive right to their respective writings and discoveries;

To constitute tribunals inferior to the Supreme Court;

To define and punish piracies and felonies committed on the high seas and offences against the law of nations;

To declare war, grant letters of marque and reprisal, and make rules concerning captures on land and water;

To raise and support armies, but no appropriation of money to that use shall be for a longer term than two years;

To provide and maintain a navy;

To make rules for the government and regulation of the land and naval forces;

To provide for calling forth the militia to execute the laws of the Union, suppress insurrections and repel invasions;

To provide for organizing, arming, and disciplining the militia, and for governing such part of them as may be employed in the service of the United States, reserving to the States respectively the appointment of the officers, and the authority of training the militia according to the discipline prescribed by Congress;

To exercise exclusive legislation in all cases whatsoever, over such district (not exceeding ten miles square) as may, by cession of particular States, and the acceptance of Congress, become the seat of the government of the United States, and to exercise like authority over all places purchased by the consent of the legislature of the State, in which the same shall be, for erection of forts, magazines, arsenals, dock-yards, and other needful buildings;—and

To make all laws which shall be necessary and proper for carrying into execution the foregoing powers, and all other powers vested by this Constitution in the government of the United States, or in any department or officer thereof.

Section 9 *The migration or importation of such persons as any of the States now existing shall think proper to admit shall not be prohibited by the Congress prior to the year one thousand eight hundred and eight; but a tax or duty may be imposed on such importation, not exceeding ten dollars for each person.*

The privilege of the writ of habeas corpus shall not be suspended, unless when in cases of rebellion or invasion the public safety may require it.

No bill of attainder or ex post facto law shall be passed.

No capitation, or other direct, tax shall be laid, unless in proportion to the census or enumeration herein before directed to be taken.

No tax or duty shall be laid on articles exported from any State.

No preference shall be given by any regulation of commerce or revenue to the ports of one State over those of another; nor shall vessels bound to, or from, one State be obliged to enter, clear, or pay duties in another.

No money shall be drawn from the treasury, but in consequence of appropriations made by law; and a regular statement and account of the receipts and expenditures of all public money shall be published from time to time.

No title of nobility shall be granted by the United States: and no person holding any office of profit or trust under them, shall, without the consent of the Congress, accept of any present, emolument, office, or title, of any kind whatever, from any king, prince, or foreign state.

Section 10 No State shall enter into any treaty, alliance, or confederation; grant letters of marque and reprisal; coin money; emit bills of credit; make anything but gold and silver coin a tender in payment of debts; pass any bill of attainder, ex post facto law, or law impairing the obligation of contracts, or grant any title of nobility.

No State shall, without the consent of Congress, lay any imposts or duties on imports or exports, except what may be absolutely necessary for executing its inspection laws: and the net produce of all duties and imposts, laid by any State on imports or exports, shall be for the use of the treasury of the United States; and all such laws shall be subject to the revision and control of the Congress.

No State shall, without the consent of Congress, lay any duty of tonnage, keep troops, or ships of war in time of peace, enter into any agreement or compact with another State, or with a foreign power, or engage in war, unless actually invaded, or in such imminent danger as will not admit of delay.

Article II

Section 1 The executive power shall be vested in a President of the United States of America. He shall hold his office during the term of four years, and, together with the Vice-President, chosen for the same term, be elected as follows:

Each State shall appoint, in such manner as the legislature thereof may direct, a number of electors, equal to the whole number of Senators and Representatives to which the State may be entitled in the Congress; but no Senator or Representative, or person holding an office of trust or profit under the United States, shall be appointed an elector.

The electors shall meet in their respective States, and vote by ballot for two persons, of whom one at least shall not be an inhabitant of the same State with themselves. And they shall make a list of all the persons voted for, and of the number of votes for each; which list they shall sign and certify, and transmit sealed to the seat of government of the United States, directed to the President of the Senate. The President of the Senate shall, in the presence of the Senate and House of Representatives, open all the certificates, and the votes shall then be counted. The person having the greatest number of votes shall be the President, if such number be a majority of the whole number of electors appointed; and if there be more than one who have such majority, and have an equal number of votes, then the House of Representatives shall immediately choose by ballot one of them for President; and if no person have a majority, then from the five highest on the list said house shall in like manner choose the President. But in choosing the President the votes shall be taken by States, the representation from each State having one vote; a quorum for this purpose shall consist of a member or members from two-thirds of the States, and a majority of all the States shall be necessary to a choice. In every case, after the choice of the President, the person having the greatest number of votes of the electors shall be the Vice-President. But if there should remain two or more who have equal votes, the Senate shall choose from them by ballot the Vice-President.

The Congress may determine the time of choosing the electors, and the day on which they shall give their votes; which day shall be the same throughout the United States.

No person except a natural-born citizen, *or a citizen of the United States at the time of the adoption of this Constitution*, shall be eligible to the office of President; neither shall any person be eligible to that office who shall not have attained to the age of thirty-five years, and been fourteen years a resident within the United States.

In cases of the removal of the President from office or of his death, resignation, or inability to discharge the powers and duties of the said office, the same shall devolve on the Vice-President, and the Congress may by law provide for the case of removal, death, resignation, or inability, both of the President and Vice-President, declaring what officer shall then act as President, and such officer shall act accordingly, until the disability be removed, or a President shall be elected.

The President shall, at stated times, receive for his services a compensation, which shall neither be increased nor diminished during the period for which he shall have been elected, and he shall not receive within that period any other emolument from the United States, or any of them.

Before he enter on the execution of his office, he shall take the following oath or affirmation:—"I do solemnly swear (or affirm) that I will faithfully execute the office of the President of the United States, and will to the best of my ability preserve, protect and defend the Constitution of the United States."

Section 2 The President shall be commander in chief of the army and navy of the United States, and of the militia of the several States, when called into the actual service of the United States; he may require the opinion, in writing, of the principal officer in each of the executive departments, upon any subject relating to the duties of their respective offices, and he shall have power to grant reprieves and pardons for offenses against the United States, except in cases of impeachment.

He shall have power, by and with the advice and consent of the Senate, to make treaties, provided two-thirds of the Senators present concur; and he shall nominate, and by and with the advice and consent of the Senate, shall appoint ambassadors, other public ministers and consuls, judges of the Supreme Court, and all other officers of the United States, whose appointments are not herein otherwise provided for, and which shall be established by law: but Congress may by law vest the appointment of such inferior officers, as they think proper, in the President alone, in the courts of law, or in the heads of departments.

The President shall have power to fill up all vacancies that may happen during the recess of the Senate, by granting commissions which shall expire at the end of their next session.

Section 3 He shall from time to time give to the Congress information of the state of the Union, and recommend to their consideration such measures as he shall judge necessary and expedient; he may, on extraordinary occasions, convene both houses, or either of them, and in case of disagreement between them, with respect to the time of adjournment, he may adjourn them to such time as he shall think proper; he shall receive ambassadors and other public ministers; he shall take care that the laws be faithfully executed, and shall commission all the officers of the United States.

Section 4 The President, Vice-President and all civil officers of the United States shall be removed from office on impeachment for, and on conviction of, treason, bribery, or other high crimes and misdemeanors.

Article III

Section 1 The judicial power of the United States shall be vested in one Supreme Court, and in such inferior courts as the Congress may from time to time ordain and establish. The judges, both of the Supreme and inferior courts, shall hold their offices during good behavior, and shall, at stated times, receive for their services a compensation which shall not be diminished during their continuance in office.

Section 2 The judicial power shall extend to all cases, in law and equity, arising under this Constitution, the laws of the United States, and treaties made, or which shall be made, under their authority;—to all cases affecting ambassadors, other public ministers and consuls;—to all cases of admiralty and maritime jurisdiction;—to controversies to which the United States shall be a party;—to controversies between two or more States;—*between a State and citizens of another State*;—between citizens of different States;— between citizens of the same State claiming lands under grants of different States, and between a State, or the citizens thereof, and foreign states, citizens or subjects.

In all cases affecting ambassadors, other public ministers and consuls, and those in which a State shall be party, the Supreme Court shall have original jurisdiction. In all the other cases before mentioned, the Supreme Court shall have appellate jurisdiction, both as to law and fact, with such exceptions, and under such regulations, as the Congress shall make.

The trial of all crimes, except in cases of impeachment, shall be by jury; and such trial shall be held in the State where said crimes shall have been committed; but when not committed within any State, the trial shall be at such place or places as the Congress may by Law have directed.

Section 3 Treason against the United States shall consist only in levying war against them, or in adhering to their enemies, giving them aid and comfort. No person shall be convicted of treason unless on the testimony of two witnesses to the same overt act, or on confession in open court.

The Congress shall have power to declare the punishment of treason, but no attainder of treason shall work corruption of blood, or forfeiture except during the life of the person attainted.

Article IV

Section 1 Full faith and credit shall be given in each State to the public acts, records, and judicial proceedings of every other State. And the Congress may by general laws prescribe the manner in which such acts, records, and proceedings shall be proved, and the effect thereof.

Section 2 The citizens of each State shall be entitled to all privileges and immunities of citizens in the several States.

A person charged in any State with treason, felony, or other crime, who shall flee from justice, and be found in another State, shall on demand of the executive authority of the State from which he fled, be delivered up, to be removed to the State having jurisdiction of the crime.

No Person held to service or labor in one State, under the laws thereof, escaping into another, shall, in consequence of any law or regulation therein, be discharged from such service or labor, but shall be delivered up on claim of the party to whom such service or labor may be due.

Section 3 New States may be admitted by the Congress into this Union; but no new State shall be formed or erected within the jurisdiction of any other State; nor any State be formed by the junction of two or more States, or parts of States, without the consent of the legislatures of the States concerned as well as of the Congress.

The Congress shall have power to dispose of and make all needful rules and regulations respecting the territory or other property belonging to the United States; and nothing in this Constitution shall be so construed as to prejudice any claims of the United States, or of any particular State.

Section 4 The United States shall guarantee to every State in this Union a republican form of government, and shall protect each of them against invasion; and on application of the legislature, or of the executive (when the legislature cannot be convened), against domestic violence.

Article V

The Congress, whenever two-thirds of both houses shall deem it necessary, shall propose amendments to this Constitution, or, on the application of the legislatures of two-thirds of the several States, shall call a convention for proposing amendments, which, in either case, shall be valid to all intents and purposes, as part of this Constitution, when ratified by the legislatures of three-fourths of the several States, or by conventions in three-fourths thereof, as the one or the other mode of ratification may be proposed by the Congress; provided *that no amendments which may be made prior to the year one thousand eight hundred and eight shall in any manner affect the first and fourth clauses in the ninth section of the first article*; and that no State, without its consent, shall be deprived of its equal suffrage in the Senate.

Article VI

All debts contracted and engagements entered into, before the adoption of this Constitution, shall be as valid against the United States under this Constitution, as under the Confederation.

This Constitution, and the laws of the United States which shall be made in pursuance thereof; and all treaties made, or which shall be made, under the authority of the United States, shall be the supreme law of the land; and the judges in every State shall be bound thereby, anything in the Constitution or laws of any State to the contrary notwithstanding.

The Senators and Representatives before mentioned, and the members of the several State legislatures, and all executive and judicial officers, both of the United States and of the several States, shall be bound by oath or affirmation to support this Constitution; but no religious test shall ever be required as a qualification to any office or public trust under the United States.

Article VII

The ratification of the conventions of nine States shall be sufficient for the establishment of this Constitution between the States so ratifying the same.

Done in convention by the unanimous consent of the States present, the seventeenth day of September in the year of our Lord one thousand seven hundred and eighty-seven and of the Independence of the United States of America the twelfth. In witness whereof we have hereunto subscribed our names.

GEORGE WASHINGTON
PRESIDENT AND DEPUTY FROM VIRGINIA

New Hampshire
John Langdon
Nicholas Gilman

Massachusetts
Nathaniel Gorham
Rufus King

Connecticut
William Samuel
    Johnson
Roger Sherman

New York
Alexander Hamilton

New Jersey
William Livingston
David Brearley
William Paterson
Jonathan Dayton

Pennsylvania
Benjamin Franklin
Thomas Mifflin
Robert Morris
George Clymer
Thomas FitzSimons
Jared Ingersoll
James Wilson
Gouverneur Morris

Delaware
George Read
Gunning Bedford, Jr.
John Dickinson
Richard Bassett
Jacob Broom

Maryland
James McHenry
Daniel of St. Thomas
    Jenifer
Daniel Carroll

Virginia
John Blair
James Madison, Jr.

North Carolina
William Blount
Richard Dobbs Spaight
Hugh Williamson

South Carolina
John Rutledge
Charles Cotesworth
    Pinckney
Charles Pinckney
Pierce Butler

Georgia
William Few
Abraham Baldwin

AMENDMENTS TO THE CONSTITUTION WITH ANNOTATIONS (including the six unratified amendments)

IN THEIR EFFORT TO GAIN Antifederalists' support for the Constitution, Federalists frequently pointed to the inclusion of Article 5, which provides an orderly method of amending the Constitution. In contrast, the Articles of Confederation, which were universally recognized as seriously flawed, offered no means of amendment. For their part, Antifederalists argued that the amendment process was so "intricate" that one might as easily roll "sixes an hundred times in succession" as change the Constitution.

The system for amendment laid out in the Constitution requires that two-thirds of both houses of Congress agree to a proposed amendment, which must then be ratified by three-quarters of the legislatures of the states. Alternatively, an amendment may be proposed by a convention called by the legislatures of two-thirds of the states. Since 1789, members of Congress have proposed thousands of amendments. Besides the seventeen amendments added since 1789, only the six "unratified" ones included here were approved by two-thirds of both houses and sent to the states for ratification.

Among the many amendments that never made it out of Congress have been proposals to declare dueling, divorce, and interracial marriage unconstitutional as well as proposals to establish a national university, to acknowledge the sovereignty of Jesus

Christ, and to prohibit any person from possessing wealth in excess of $10 million.*

Among the issues facing Americans today that might lead to constitutional amendment are efforts to balance the federal budget, to limit the number of terms elected officials may serve, to limit access to or prohibit abortion, to establish English as the official language of the United States, and to prohibit flag burning. None of these proposed amendments has yet garnered enough support in Congress to be sent to the states for ratification.

Although the first ten amendments to the Constitution are commonly known as the Bill of Rights, only Amendments 1–8 actually provide guarantees of individual rights. Amendments 9 and 10 deal with the structure of power within the constitutional system. The Bill of Rights was promised to appease Antifederalists who refused to ratify the Constitution without guarantees of individual liberties and limitations to federal power. After studying more than two hundred amendments recommended by the ratifying conventions of the states, Federalist James Madison presented a list of seventeen to Congress, which used Madison's list as the foundation for the twelve amendments that were sent

---

*Richard B. Bernstein, *Amending America* (New York: Times Books, 1993), 177–81.

to the states for ratification. Ten of the twelve were adopted in 1791. The first on the list of twelve, known as the Reapportionment Amendment, was never adopted (see page A-15). The second proposed amendment was adopted in 1992 as Amendment 27 (see page A-24).

Amendment I

Congress shall make no law respecting an establishment of religion, or prohibiting the free exercise thereof; or abridging the freedom of speech, or of the press; or the right of the people peaceably to assemble, and to petition the government for a redress of grievances.

♦ ♦ ♦

▶ *The First Amendment is a potent symbol for many Americans. Most are well aware of their rights to free speech, freedom of the press, and freedom of religion and their rights to assemble and to petition, even if they cannot cite the exact words of this amendment.*

The First Amendment guarantee of freedom of religion has two clauses: the "free exercise clause," which allows individuals to practice or not practice any religion, and the "establishment clause," which prevents the federal government from discriminating against or favoring any particular religion. This clause was designed to create what Thomas Jefferson referred to as "a wall of separation between church and state." In the 1960s, the Supreme Court ruled that the First Amendment prohibits prayer (see Engel v. Vitale, online) and Bible reading in public schools.

Although the rights to free speech and freedom of the press are established in the First Amendment, it was not until the twentieth century that the Supreme Court began to explore the full meaning of these guarantees. In 1919, the Court ruled in Schenck v. United States (online) that the government could suppress free expression only where it could cite a "clear and present danger." In a decision that continues to raise controversies, the Court ruled in 1990, in Texas v. Johnson, that flag burning is a form of symbolic speech protected by the First Amendment.

Amendment II

A well-regulated militia being necessary to the security of a free State, the right of the people to keep and bear arms shall not be infringed.

♦ ♦ ♦

▶ *Fear of a standing army under the control of a hostile government made the Second Amendment an important part of the Bill of Rights. Advocates of gun ownership claim that the amendment prevents the government from regulating firearms. Proponents of gun control argue that the amendment is designed only to protect the right of the states to maintain militia units.*

In 1939, the Supreme Court ruled in United States v. Miller that the Second Amendment did not protect the right of an individual to own a sawed-off shotgun, which it argued was not ordinary militia equipment. Since then, the Supreme Court has refused to hear Second Amendment cases, while lower courts have upheld firearms regulations. Several justices currently on the bench seem to favor a narrow interpretation of the Second Amendment, which would allow gun control legislation. The controversy over the impact of the Second Amendment on gun owners and gun control legislation will certainly continue.

Amendment III

No soldier shall, in time of peace, be quartered in any house without the consent of the owner, nor in time of war, but in a manner to be prescribed by law.

♦ ♦ ♦

▶ *The Third Amendment was extremely important to the framers of the Constitution, but today it is nearly forgotten. American colonists were especially outraged that they were forced to quarter British troops in the years before and during the American Revolution. The philosophy of the Third Amendment has been viewed by some justices and scholars as the foundation of the modern constitutional right to privacy. One example of this can be found in Justice William O. Douglas's opinion in Griswold v. Connecticut (online).*

Amendment IV

The right of the people to be secure in their persons, houses, papers, and effects, against unreasonable searches and seizures, shall not be violated, and no warrants shall issue but upon probable cause, supported by oath or affirmation, and particularly describing the place to be searched, and the persons or things to be seized.

♦ ♦ ♦

▶ *In the years before the Revolution, the houses, barns, stores, and warehouses of American colonists were ransacked by British authorities under "writs of assistance" or general warrants. The British, thus empowered, searched for seditious material or smuggled goods that could then be used as evidence against colonists who were charged with a crime only after the items were found. The first part of the Fourth Amendment protects citizens from "unreasonable" searches and seizures.*

The Supreme Court has interpreted this protection as well as the words search and seizure in different ways at different times. At one time, the Court did not recognize electronic eavesdropping as a form of search and seizure, though it does today. At times, an "unreasonable" search has been almost any search carried out without a warrant, but in the two decades before 1969, the Court sometimes sanctioned warrantless searches that it considered reasonable based on "the total atmosphere of the case."

The second part of the Fourth Amendment defines the procedure for issuing a search warrant and states the requirement of "probable cause," which is generally viewed as evidence indicating that a suspect has committed an offense.

The Fourth Amendment has been controversial because the Court has sometimes excluded evidence that has been seized in violation of constitutional standards. The justification is that excluding such evidence deters violations of the amendment, but doing so may allow a guilty person to escape punishment.

Amendment V

No person shall be held to answer for a capital, or otherwise infamous crime, unless on a presentment or indictment of a grand jury, except in cases arising in the land or naval forces, or in the militia, when in actual service in time of war or public danger; nor shall any person be subject for the same offence to be twice put in jeopardy of life or limb; nor shall be compelled in any criminal case to be a witness against himself, nor be deprived of life, liberty, or property, without due process of law; nor shall private property be taken for public use without just compensation.

◆ ◆ ◆

▶ *The Fifth Amendment protects people against government authority in the prosecution of criminal offenses. It prohibits the state, first, from charging a person with a serious crime without a grand jury hearing to decide whether there is sufficient evidence to support the charge and, second, from charging a person with the same crime twice. The best-known aspect of the Fifth Amendment is that it prevents a person from being "compelled . . . to be a witness against himself." The last clause, the "takings clause," limits the power of the government to seize property.*

Although invoking the Fifth Amendment is popularly viewed as a confession of guilt, a person may be innocent yet still fear prosecution. For example, during the Red-baiting era of the late 1940s and 1950s, many people who had participated in legal activities that were associated with the Communist Party claimed the Fifth Amendment privilege rather than testify before the House Un-American Activities Committee because the mood of the times cast those activities in a negative light. Since "taking the Fifth" was viewed as an admission of guilt, those people often lost their jobs or became unemployable. (See chapter 26.) Nonetheless, the right to protect oneself against self-incrimination plays an important role in guarding against the collective power of the state.

Amendment VI

In all criminal prosecutions, the accused shall enjoy the right to a speedy and public trial, by an impartial jury of the State and district wherein the crime shall have been committed, which district shall have been previously ascertained by law, and to be informed of the nature and cause of the accusation; to be confronted with the witnesses against him; to have compulsory process for obtaining witnesses in his favor, and to have the assistance of counsel for his defence.

◆ ◆ ◆

▶ *The original Constitution put few limits on the government's power to investigate, prosecute, and punish crime. This process was of great concern to the early Americans, however, and of the twenty-eight rights specified in the first eight amendments, fifteen have to do with it. Seven rights are specified in the Sixth Amendment. These include the right to a speedy trial, a public trial, a jury trial, a notice of accusation, confrontation by opposing witnesses, testimony by favorable witnesses, and the assistance of counsel.*

Although this amendment originally guaranteed these rights only in cases involving the federal government, the adoption of the Fourteenth Amendment began a process of applying the protections of the Bill of Rights to the states through court cases such as Gideon v. Wainwright *(online).*

Amendment VII

In suits at common law, where the value in controversy shall exceed twenty dollars, the right of trial by jury shall be preserved, and no fact tried by a jury shall be otherwise reexamined in any court of the United States, than according to the rules of the common law.

◆ ◆ ◆

▶ *This amendment guarantees people the same right to a trial by jury as was guaranteed by English common law in 1791. Under common law, in civil trials (those involving money damages) the role of the judge was to settle questions of law and that of the jury was to settle questions of fact. The amendment does not specify the size of the jury or its role in a trial, however. The Supreme Court has generally held that those issues be determined by English common law of 1791, which stated that a jury consists of twelve people, that a trial must be conducted before a judge who instructs the jury on the law and advises it on facts, and that a verdict must be unanimous.*

Amendment VIII

Excessive bail shall not be required, nor excessive fines imposed, nor cruel and unusual punishments inflicted.

♦ ♦ ♦

The language used to guarantee the three rights in this amendment was inspired by the English Bill of Rights of 1689. The Supreme Court has not had a lot to say about "excessive fines." In recent years it has agreed that, despite the provision against "excessive bail," persons who are believed to be dangerous to others can be held without bail even before they have been convicted.

Although opponents of the death penalty have not succeeded in using the Eighth Amendment to achieve the end of capital punishment, the clause regarding "cruel and unusual punishments" has been used to prohibit capital punishment in certain cases (see Furman v. Georgia, online) and to require improved conditions in prisons.

Amendment IX

The enumeration in the Constitution, of certain rights, shall not be construed to deny or disparage others retained by the people.

♦ ♦ ♦

▶ *Some Federalists feared that inclusion of the Bill of Rights in the Constitution would allow later generations of interpreters to claim that the people had surrendered any rights not specifically enumerated there. To guard against this, Madison added language that became the Ninth Amendment. Interest in this heretofore largely ignored amendment revived in 1965 when it was used in a concurring opinion in Griswold v. Connecticut (online). While Justice William O. Douglas called on the Third Amendment to support the right to privacy in deciding that case, Justice Arthur Goldberg, in the concurring opinion, argued that the right to privacy regarding contraception was an unenumerated right that was protected by the Ninth Amendment.*

In 1980, the Court ruled that the right of the press to attend a public trial was protected by the Ninth Amendment. While some scholars argue that modern judges cannot identify the unenumerated rights that the framers were trying to protect, others argue that the Ninth Amendment should be read as providing a constitutional "presumption of liberty" that allows people to act in any way that does not violate the rights of others.

Amendment X

The powers not delegated to the United States by the Constitution, nor prohibited by it to the States, are reserved to the States respectively, or to the people.

♦ ♦ ♦

▶ *The Antifederalists were especially eager to see a "reserved powers clause" explicitly guaranteeing the states control over their internal affairs. Not*

surprisingly, the Tenth Amendment has been a frequent battleground in the struggle over states' rights and federal supremacy. Prior to the Civil War, the Democratic Republican Party and Jacksonian Democrats invoked the Tenth Amendment to prohibit the federal government from making decisions about whether people in individual states could own slaves. The Tenth Amendment was virtually suspended during Reconstruction following the Civil War. In 1883, however, the Supreme Court declared the Civil Rights Act of 1875 unconstitutional on the grounds that it violated the Tenth Amendment. Business interests also called on the amendment to block efforts at federal regulation.

The Court was inconsistent over the next several decades as it attempted to resolve the tension between the restrictions of the Tenth Amendment and the powers the Constitution granted to Congress to regulate interstate commerce and levy taxes. The Court upheld the Pure Food and Drug Act (1906), the Meat Inspection Acts (1906 and 1907), and the White Slave Traffic Act (1910), all of which affected the states, but struck down an act prohibiting interstate shipment of goods produced through child labor. Between 1934 and 1935, a number of New Deal programs created by Franklin D. Roosevelt were declared unconstitutional on the grounds that they violated the Tenth Amendment. (See chapter 24.) As Roosevelt appointees changed the composition of the Court, the Tenth Amendment was declared to have no substantive meaning. Generally, the amendment is held to protect the rights of states to regulate internal matters such as local government, education, commerce, labor, and business, as well as matters involving families such as marriage, divorce, and inheritance within the state.

Unratified Amendment

Reapportionment Amendment (proposed by Congress September 25, 1789, along with the Bill of Rights)

After the first enumeration required by the first article of the Constitution, there shall be one Representative for every thirty thousand, until the number shall amount to one hundred, after which the proportion shall be so regulated by Congress, that there shall be not less than one hundred Representatives, nor less than one Representative for every forty thousand persons, until the number of Representatives shall amount to two hundred; after which the proportion shall be so regulated by Congress, that there shall not be less than two hundred Representatives, nor more than one Representative for every fifty thousand persons.

♦ ♦ ♦

▶ *If the Reapportionment Amendment had passed and remained in effect, the House of Representatives today would have more than 5,000 members rather than 435.*

Amendment XI

[Adopted 1798]

The judicial power of the United States shall not be construed to extend to any suit in law or equity, commenced or prosecuted against one of the United States by citizens of another State, or by citizens or subjects of any foreign state.

♦ ♦ ♦

▶ *In 1793, the Supreme Court ruled in favor of Alexander Chisholm, executor of the estate of a deceased South Carolina merchant. Chisholm was suing the state of Georgia because the merchant had never been paid for provisions he had supplied during the Revolution. Many regarded this Court decision as an error that violated the intent of the Constitution.*

Antifederalists had long feared a federal court system with the power to overrule a state court.

When the Constitution was being drafted, Federalists had assured worried Antifederalists that section 2 of Article 3, which allows federal courts to hear cases "between a State and citizens of another State," did not mean that the federal courts were authorized to hear suits against a state by citizens of another state or a foreign country. Antifederalists and many other Americans feared a powerful federal court system because they worried that it would become like the British courts of this period, which were accountable only to the monarch. Furthermore, Chisholm v. Georgia prompted a series of suits against state governments by creditors and suppliers who had made loans during the war.

In addition, state legislators and Congress feared that the shaky economies of the new states, as well as the country as a whole, would be destroyed, especially if loyalists who had fled to other countries sought reimbursement for land and property that had been seized. The day after the Supreme Court announced its decision, a resolution proposing the Eleventh Amendment, which overturned the decision in Chisholm v. Georgia, *was introduced in the U.S. Senate.*

Amendment XII

[Adopted 1804]

The electors shall meet in their respective States, and vote by ballot for President and Vice-President, one of whom, at least, shall not be an inhabitant of the same State with themselves; they shall name in their ballots the person voted for as President, and in distinct ballots the person voted for as Vice-President, and they shall make distinct lists of all persons voted for as President, and of all persons voted for as Vice-President, and of the number of votes for each, which lists they shall sign and certify, and transmit sealed to the seat of government of the United States, directed to the President of the Senate;—the President of the Senate shall, in the presence of the Senate and House of Representatives, open all the certificates and the votes shall then be counted;—the person having the greatest number of votes for President shall be the President, if such number be a majority of the whole number of electors appointed; and if no person have such majority, then from the persons having the highest numbers not exceeding three on the list of those voted for as President, the House of Representatives shall choose immediately, by ballot, the President. But in choosing the President, the votes shall be taken by States, the representation from each State having one vote; a quorum for this purpose shall consist of a member or members from two-thirds of the States, and a majority of all the States shall be necessary to a choice. And if the House of Representatives shall not choose a President whenever the right of choice shall devolve upon them, before the fourth day of March next following, then the Vice-President shall act as President, as in the case of the death or other constitutional disability of the President.

The person having the greatest number of votes as Vice-President shall be the Vice-President, if such number be a majority of the whole number of electors appointed; and if no person have a majority, then from the two highest numbers on the list the Senate shall choose the Vice-President; a quorum for the purpose shall consist of two-thirds of the whole number of Senators, and a majority of the whole number shall be necessary to a choice. But no person constitutionally ineligible to the office of President shall be eligible to that of Vice-President of the United States.

♦ ♦ ♦

▶ *The framers of the Constitution disliked political parties and assumed that none would ever form. Under the original system, electors chosen by the states would each vote for two candidates. The candidate who won the most votes would become president, while the person who won the second-highest number of votes would become vice president. Rivalries between Federalists and Antifederalists led to the formation of political parties, however, even before George Washington had left office. Though Washington was elected unanimously in 1789 and 1792, the elections of 1796 and 1800 were procedural disasters because of party maneuvering (see chapters 9 and 10). In 1796, Federalist John Adams was chosen as president, and his great rival, the Antifederalist Thomas Jefferson (whose party was called the Republican Party), became his vice president. In 1800, all the electors cast their two votes as one of two party blocs. Jefferson and his fellow Republican nominee, Aaron Burr, were tied with 73 votes each. The contest went to the House of Representatives, which finally elected Jefferson after 36 ballots. The Twelfth Amendment prevents these problems by requiring electors to vote separately for the president and vice president.*

Unratified Amendment

Titles of Nobility Amendment (proposed by Congress May 1, 1810)

If any citizen of the United States shall accept, claim, receive or retain any title of nobility or honor or shall, without the consent of Congress, accept and retain any present, pension, office or emolument of any kind whatever, from any emperor, king, prince or foreign power, such person shall cease to be a citizen of the United States, and shall be incapable of holding any office of trust or profit under them or either of them.

♦ ♦ ♦

▶ *This amendment would have extended Article 1, section 9, clause 8 of the Constitution, which prevents the awarding of titles by the United States and the acceptance of such awards from foreign powers without congressional consent. Historians speculate that general nervousness about the power of the emperor Napoleon, who was at that time extending France's empire throughout Europe, may have prompted the proposal. Though it fell one vote short of ratification, Congress and the American people thought the proposal had been ratified, and it was included in many nineteenth-century editions of the Constitution.*

The Civil War and Reconstruction Amendments (Thirteenth, Fourteenth, and Fifteenth Amendments)

▶ *In the four months between the election of Abraham Lincoln and his inauguration, more than 200 proposed constitutional amendments were presented to Congress as part of a desperate attempt to hold the rapidly dissolving Union together. Most of these were efforts to appease the southern states by protecting the right to own slaves or by disfranchising African Americans through constitutional amendment. None were able to win the votes required from Congress to send them to the states. The relatively innocuous Corwin Amendment seemed to be the only hope for preserving the Union by amending the Constitution.*

The northern victors in the Civil War tried to restructure the Constitution just as the war had restructured the nation. Yet they were often divided in their goals. Some wanted to end slavery; others hoped for social and economic equality regardless of race; others hoped that extending the power of the ballot box to former slaves would help create a new political order. The debates over the Thirteenth, Fourteenth, and Fifteenth Amendments were bitter. Few of those who fought for these changes were satisfied with the amendments themselves; fewer still were satisfied with their interpretation. Although the

amendments put an end to the legal status of slavery, it took nearly a hundred years after the amendments' passage before most of the descendants of former slaves could begin to experience the economic, social, and political equality the amendments had been intended to provide.

Unratified Amendment

Corwin Amendment (proposed by Congress March 2, 1861)

No amendment shall be made to the Constitution which will authorize or give to Congress the power to abolish or interfere, within any State, with the domestic institutions thereof, including that of persons held to labor or service by the laws of said State.

♦ ♦ ♦

▶ *Following the election of Abraham Lincoln, Congress scrambled to try to prevent the secession of the slaveholding states. House member Thomas Corwin of Ohio proposed the "unamendable" amendment in the hope that by protecting slavery where it existed, Congress would keep the southern states in the Union. Lincoln indicated his support for the proposed amendment in his first inaugural address. Only Ohio and Maryland ratified the Corwin Amendment before it was forgotten.*

Amendment XIII
[Adopted 1865]

Section 1 Neither slavery nor involuntary servitude, except as a punishment for crime whereof the party shall have been duly convicted, shall exist within the United States, or any place subject to their jurisdiction.

Section 2 Congress shall have power to enforce this article by appropriate legislation.

♦ ♦ ♦

▶ *Although President Lincoln had abolished slavery in the Confederacy with the Emancipation Proclamation of 1863, abolitionists wanted to rid the entire country of slavery. The Thirteenth Amendment did this in a clear and straightforward manner. In February 1865, when the proposal was approved by the House, the gallery of the House was newly opened to black Americans who had a chance at last to see their government at work. Passage of the proposal was greeted by wild cheers from the gallery as well as tears on the House floor, where congressional representatives openly embraced one another.*

The problem of ratification remained, however. The Union position was that the Confederate states were part of the country of thirty-six states. Therefore, twenty-seven states were needed to ratify the amendment. When Kentucky and Delaware rejected it, backers realized that without approval from at least four former Confederate states, the amendment would fail. Lincoln's successor, President Andrew Johnson, made ratification of the

Thirteenth Amendment a condition for southern states to rejoin the Union. Under those terms, all the former Confederate states except Mississippi accepted the Thirteenth Amendment, and by the end of 1865 the amendment had become part of the Constitution and slavery had been prohibited in the United States.

Amendment XIV
[Adopted 1868]

Section 1 All persons born or naturalized in the United States, and subject to the jurisdiction thereof, are citizens of the United States and of the State wherein they reside. No State shall make or enforce any law which shall abridge the privileges or immunities of citizens of the United States; nor shall any State deprive any person of life, liberty, or property, without due process of law; nor deny to any person within its jurisdiction the equal protection of the laws.

Section 2 Representatives shall be appointed among the several States according to their respective numbers, counting the whole number of persons in each State, excluding Indians not taxed. But when the right to vote at any election for the choice of Electors for President and Vice-President of the United States, Representatives in Congress, the executive and judicial officers of a State, or the members of the legislature thereof, is denied to any of the male inhabitants of such State, being twenty-one years of age and citizens of the United States, or in any way abridged, except for participation in rebellion, or other crime, the basis of representation therein shall be reduced in the proportion which the number of such male citizens shall bear to the whole number of male citizens twenty-one years of age in such State.

Section 3 No person shall be a Senator or Representative in Congress, or Elector of President and Vice-President, or hold any office, civil or military, under the United States, or under any State, who, having previously taken an oath, as a member of Congress, or as an officer of the United States, or as a member of any State legislature, or as an executive or judicial officer of any State, to support the Constitution of the United States, shall have engaged in insurrection or rebellion against the same, or given aid or comfort to the enemies thereof. Congress may, by a vote of two-thirds of each house, remove such disability.

Section 4 The validity of the public debt of the United States, authorized by law, including debts incurred for payment of pensions and bounties for services in suppressing insurrection or rebellion, shall not be questioned. But neither the United States nor any State shall assume or pay any debt or obligation incurred in aid of insurrection or rebellion against the United States, or any claim for the loss or emancipation of any slave; but all such debts, obligations, and claims shall be held illegal and void.

Section 5 The Congress shall have power to enforce, by appropriate legislation, the provisions of this article.

◆ ◆ ◆

▶ *Without Lincoln's leadership in the reconstruction of the nation following the Civil War, it soon became clear that the Thirteenth Amendment needed additional constitutional support. Less than a year after Lincoln's assassination, Andrew Johnson was ready to bring the former Confederate states back into the Union with few changes in their governments or politics. Anxious Republicans drafted the Fourteenth Amendment to prevent that from happening. The most important provisions of this complex amendment made all native-born or naturalized persons American citizens and prohibited states from abridging the "privileges or immunities" of citizens; depriving them of "life, liberty, or property, without due process of law"; and denying them "equal protection of the laws." In essence, it made all ex-slaves citizens and protected the rights of all citizens against violation by their own state governments.*

As occurred in the case of the Thirteenth Amendment, former Confederate states were forced to ratify the amendment as a condition of representation in the House and the Senate. The intentions of the Fourteenth Amendment, and how those intentions should be enforced, have been the most debated point of constitutional history. The terms due process *and* equal protection *have been especially troublesome. Was the amendment designed to outlaw racial segregation? Or was the goal simply to prevent the leaders of the rebellious South from gaining political power?*

The framers of the Fourteenth Amendment hoped Article 2 would produce black voters who would increase the power of the Republican Party. The federal government, however, never used its power to punish states for denying blacks their right to vote. Although the Fourteenth Amendment had an immediate impact in giving black Americans citizenship, it did nothing to protect blacks from the vengeance of whites once Reconstruction ended. In the late nineteenth and early twentieth centuries, section 1 of the Fourteenth Amendment was often used to protect business interests and strike down laws protecting workers on the grounds that the rights of "persons," that is, corporations, were protected by "due process." More recently, the Fourteenth Amendment has been used to justify school desegregation and affirmative action programs, as well as to dismantle such programs.

Amendment XV

[Adopted 1870]

Section 1 The right of citizens of the United States to vote shall not be denied or abridged by the United States or by any State on account of race, color, or previous condition of servitude.

Section 2 The Congress shall have power to enforce this article by appropriate legislation.

♦ ♦ ♦

▶ *The Fifteenth Amendment was the last major piece of Reconstruction legislation. While earlier Reconstruction acts had already required black suffrage in the South, the Fifteenth Amendment extended black voting rights to the entire nation. Some Republicans felt morally obligated to do away with the double standard between North and South since many northern states had stubbornly refused to enfranchise blacks. Others believed that the freedman's ballot required the extra protection of a constitutional amendment to shield it from white counterattack. But partisan advantage also played an important role in the amendment's passage, since Republicans hoped that by giving the ballot to northern blacks, they could lessen their political vulnerability.*

Many women's rights advocates had fought for the amendment. They had felt betrayed by the inclusion of the word "male" in section 2 of the Fourteenth Amendment and were further angered when the proposed Fifteenth Amendment failed to prohibit denial of the right to vote on the grounds of sex as well as "race, color, or previous condition of servitude." In this amendment, for the first time, the federal government claimed the power to regulate the franchise, or vote. It was also the first time the Constitution placed limits on the power of the states to regulate access to the franchise. Although ratified in 1870, the amendment was not enforced until the twentieth century.

The Progressive Amendments (Sixteenth–Nineteenth Amendments)

▶ *No amendments were added to the Constitution between the Civil War and the Progressive Era. America was changing, however, in fundamental ways. The rapid industrialization of the United States after the Civil War led to many social and economic problems. Hundreds of amendments were proposed, but none received enough support in Congress to be sent to the states. Some scholars believe that regional differences and rivalries were so strong during this period that it was almost impossible to gain a consensus on a constitutional amendment. During the Progressive Era, however, the Constitution was amended four times in seven years.*

Amendment XVI

[Adopted 1913]

The Congress shall have power to lay and collect taxes on incomes, from whatever source derived, without apportionment among the several States, and without regard to any census or enumeration.

♦ ♦ ♦

▶ *Until passage of the Sixteenth Amendment, most of the money used to run the federal government came from customs duties and taxes on specific items, such as liquor. During the Civil War, the federal government taxed incomes as an emergency measure. Pressure to enact an income tax came from those who were concerned about the growing gap between rich and poor in the United States. The Populist Party began campaigning for a graduated income tax in 1892, and support continued to grow. By 1909, thirty-three proposed income tax amendments had been presented in Congress, but lobbying by corporate and other special interests had defeated them all. In June 1909, the growing pressure for an income tax, which had been endorsed by Presidents Roosevelt and Taft, finally pushed an amendment through the Senate. The required thirty-six states had ratified the amendment by February 1913.*

Amendment XVII

[Adopted 1913]

Section 1 The Senate of the United States shall be composed of two Senators from each State, elected by the people thereof, for six years; and each Senator shall have one vote. The electors in each State shall have the qualifications requisite for electors of [voters for] the most numerous branch of the State legislatures.

Section 2 When vacancies happen in the representation of any State in the Senate, the executive authority of such State shall issue writs of election to fill such vacancies: Provided, that the Legislature of any State may empower the executive thereof to make temporary appointments until the people fill the vacancies by election as the Legislature may direct.

Section 3 This amendment shall not be so construed as to affect the election or term of any Senator chosen before it becomes valid as part of the Constitution.

♦ ♦ ♦

▶ *The framers of the Constitution saw the members of the House as the representatives of the people and the members of the Senate as the representatives of the states. Originally senators were to be chosen by the state legislators. According to reform advocates, however, the growth of private industry and transportation conglomerates during the Gilded Age had created a network of corruption in which wealth and power were exchanged for influence and votes in the Senate. Senator Nelson Aldrich, who represented Rhode Island in the late nineteenth and early twentieth centuries, for example, was known as "the senator from Standard Oil" because of his open support of special business interests.*

Efforts to amend the Constitution to allow direct election of senators had begun in 1826, but since any proposal had to be approved by the Senate, reform seemed impossible. Progressives tried to gain influence in the Senate by instituting party caucuses and primary elections, which gave citizens the chance to express their choice of a senator who could then be officially elected by the state legislature. By 1910, fourteen of the country's thirty senators received popular votes through a state primary before the state legislature made its selection. Despairing of getting a proposal through the Senate, supporters of a direct election amendment had begun in 1893 to seek a convention of representatives from two-thirds of the states to propose an amendment that could then be ratified. By 1905, thirty-one of forty-five states had endorsed such an amendment. Finally, in 1911, despite extraordinary opposition, a proposed amendment passed the Senate; by 1913, it had been ratified.

Amendment XVIII

[Adopted 1919; repealed 1933 by Amendment XXI]

Section 1 After one year from the ratification of this article the manufacture, sale, or transportation of intoxicating liquors within, the importation thereof into, or the exportation thereof from the United States and all territory subject to the jurisdiction thereof, for beverage purposes, is hereby prohibited.

Section 2 The Congress and the several States shall have concurrent power to enforce this article by appropriate legislation.

Section 3 This article shall be inoperative unless it shall have been ratified as an amendment to the Constitution by the legislatures of the several States, as provided by the Constitution, within seven years from the date of the submission thereof to the States by the Congress.

♦ ♦ ♦

▶ *The Prohibition Party, formed in 1869, began calling for a constitutional amendment to outlaw alcoholic beverages in 1872. A prohibition amendment was first proposed in the Senate in 1876 and was revived eighteen times before 1913. Between 1913 and 1919, another thirty-nine attempts were made to prohibit liquor in the United States through a constitutional amendment. Prohibition became a key element of the progressive agenda as reformers linked alcohol and drunkenness to numerous*

social problems, including the corruption of immigrant voters. While opponents of such an amendment argued that it was undemocratic, supporters claimed that their efforts had widespread public support. The admission of twelve "dry" western states to the Union in the early twentieth century and the spirit of sacrifice during World War I laid the groundwork for passage and ratification of the Eighteenth Amendment in 1919. Opponents added a time limit to the amendment in the hope that they could thus block ratification, but this effort failed. (See also Amendment XXI.)

Amendment XIX

[Adopted 1920]

Section 1 The right of citizens of the United States to vote shall not be denied or abridged by the United States or by any State on account of sex.

Section 2 Congress shall have the power to enforce this article by appropriate legislation.

♦ ♦ ♦

▶ *Advocates of women's rights tried and failed to link woman suffrage to the Fourteenth and Fifteenth Amendments. Nonetheless, the effort for woman suffrage continued. Between 1878 and 1912, at least one and sometimes as many as four proposed amendments were introduced in Congress each year to grant women the right to vote. While over time women won very limited voting rights in some states, at both the state and federal levels opposition to an amendment for woman suffrage remained very strong. President Woodrow Wilson and other officials felt that the federal government should not interfere with the power of the states in this matter. Others worried that granting suffrage to women would encourage ethnic minorities to exercise their own right to vote. And many were concerned that giving women the vote would result in their abandoning traditional gender roles. In 1919, following a protracted and often bitter campaign of protest in which women went on hunger strikes and chained themselves to fences, an amendment was introduced with the backing of President Wilson. It narrowly passed the Senate (after efforts to limit the suffrage to white women failed) and was adopted in 1920 after Tennessee became the thirty-sixth state to ratify it.*

Unratified Amendment

Child Labor Amendment (proposed by Congress June 2, 1924)

Section 1 The Congress shall have power to limit, regulate, and prohibit the labor of persons under eighteen years of age.

Section 2 The power of the several States is unimpaired by this article except that the operation of State laws shall be suspended to the extent necessary to give effect to legislation enacted by Congress.

◆ ◆ ◆

▶ *Throughout the late nineteenth and early twentieth centuries, alarm over the condition of child workers grew. Opponents of child labor argued that children worked in dangerous and unhealthy conditions, that they took jobs from adult workers, that they depressed wages in certain industries, and that states that allowed child labor had an economic advantage over those that did not. Defenders of child labor claimed that children provided needed income in many families, that working at a young age developed character, and that the effort to prohibit the practice constituted an invasion of family privacy.*

In 1916, Congress passed a law that made it illegal to sell goods made by children through interstate commerce. The Supreme Court, however, ruled that the law violated the limits on the power of Congress to regulate interstate commerce. Congress then tried to penalize industries that used child labor by taxing such goods. This measure was also thrown out by the courts. In response, reformers set out to amend the Constitution. The proposed amendment was ratified by twenty-eight states, but by 1925, thirteen states had rejected it. Passage of the Fair Labor Standards Act in 1938, which was upheld by the Supreme Court in 1941, made the amendment irrelevant.

Amendment XX
[Adopted 1933]

Section 1 The terms of the President and Vice-President shall end at noon on the 20th day of January, and the terms of Senators and Representatives at noon on the 3rd day of January, of the years in which such terms would have ended if this article had not been ratified; and the terms of their successors shall then begin.

Section 2 The Congress shall assemble at least once in every year, and such meeting shall begin at noon on the 3rd day of January, unless they shall by law appoint a different day.

Section 3 If, at the time fixed for the beginning of the term of the President, the President-elect shall have died, the Vice-President-elect shall become President. If a President shall not have been chosen before the time fixed for the beginning of his term, or if the President-elect shall have failed to qualify, then the Vice-President-elect shall act as President until a President shall have qualified; and the Congress may by law provide for the case wherein neither a President-elect nor a Vice-President-elect shall have qualified, declaring who shall then act as President, or the manner in which one who is to act shall be selected, and

such person shall act accordingly until a President or Vice-President shall have qualified.

Section 4 The Congress may by law provide for the case of the death of any of the persons from whom the House of Representatives may choose a President whenever the right of choice shall have devolved upon them, and for the case of the death of any of the persons from whom the Senate may choose a Vice-President whenever the right of choice shall have devolved upon them.

Section 5 Sections 1 and 2 shall take effect on the 15th day of October following the ratification of this article.

Section 6 This article shall be inoperative unless it shall have been ratified as an amendment to the Constitution by the Legislatures of three-fourths of the several States within seven years from the date of its submission.

◆ ◆ ◆

▶ *Until 1933, presidents took office on March 4. Since elections are held in early November and electoral votes are counted in mid-December, this meant that more than three months passed between the time a new president was elected and when he took office. Moving the inauguration to January shortened the transition period and allowed Congress to begin its term closer to the time of the president's inauguration. Although this seems like a minor change, an amendment was required because the Constitution specifies terms of office. This amendment also deals with questions of succession in the event that a president- or vice president-elect dies before assuming office. Section 3 also clarifies a method for resolving a deadlock in the electoral college.*

Amendment XXI
[Adopted 1933]

Section 1 The eighteenth article of amendment to the Constitution of the United States is hereby repealed.

Section 2 The transportation or importation into any State, Territory, or Possession of the United States for delivery or use therein of intoxicating liquors, in violation of the laws thereof, is hereby prohibited.

Section 3 This article shall be inoperative unless it shall have been ratified as an amendment to the Constitution by conventions in the several States, as provided in the Constitution, within seven years from the date of the submission thereof to the States by Congress.

◆ ◆ ◆

▶ *Widespread violation of the Volstead Act, the law enacted to enforce prohibition, made the United*

States a nation of lawbreakers. Prohibition caused more problems than it solved by encouraging crime, bribery, and corruption. Further, a coalition of liquor and beer manufacturers, personal liberty advocates, and constitutional scholars joined forces to challenge the amendment. By 1929, thirty proposed repeal amendments had been introduced in Congress, and the Democratic Party made repeal part of its platform in the 1932 presidential campaign. The Twenty-first Amendment was proposed in February 1933 and ratified less than a year later. The failure of the effort to enforce prohibition through a constitutional amendment has often been cited by opponents to subsequent efforts to shape public virtue and private morality.

Amendment XXII
[Adopted 1951]

Section 1 No person shall be elected to the office of the President more than twice, and no person who has held the office of President, or acted as President, for more than two years of a term to which some other person was elected President shall be elected to the office of President more than once. But this article shall not apply to any person holding the office of President when this Article was proposed by the Congress, and shall not prevent any person who may be holding the office of President, or acting as President, during the term within which this Article becomes operative from holding the office of President or acting as President during the remainder of such term.

Section 2 This article shall be inoperative unless it shall have been ratified as an amendment to the Constitution by the legislatures of three-fourths of the several States within seven years from the date of its submission to the States by the Congress.

♦ ♦ ♦

▶ *George Washington's refusal to seek a third term of office set a precedent that stood until 1912, when former president Theodore Roosevelt sought, without success, another term as an independent candidate. Democrat Franklin Roosevelt was the only president to seek and win a fourth term, though he did so amid great controversy. Roosevelt died in April 1945, a few months after the beginning of his fourth term. In 1946, Republicans won control of the House and the Senate, and early in 1947 a proposal for an amendment to limit future presidents to two four-year terms was offered to the states for ratification. Democratic critics of the Twenty-second Amendment charged that it was a partisan posthumous jab at Roosevelt.*

Since the Twenty-second Amendment was adopted, however, the only presidents who might have been able to seek a third term, had it not existed, were Republicans Dwight Eisenhower, Ronald Reagan, and George W. Bush, and Democrat Bill

Clinton. Since 1826, Congress has entertained 160 proposed amendments to limit the president to one six-year term. Such amendments have been backed by fifteen presidents, including Gerald Ford and Jimmy Carter.

Amendment XXIII
[Adopted 1961]

Section 1 The District constituting the seat of Government of the United States shall appoint in such manner as the Congress may direct: A number of electors of President and Vice-President equal to the whole number of Senators and Representatives in Congress to which the District would be entitled if it were a State, but in no event more than the least populous State; they shall be in addition to those appointed by the States, but they shall be considered for the purposes of the election of President and Vice-President, to be electors appointed by a State; and they shall meet in the District and perform such duties as provided by the twelfth article of amendment.

Section 2 The Congress shall have the power to enforce this article by appropriate legislation.

♦ ♦ ♦

▶ *When Washington, D.C., was established as a federal district, no one expected that a significant number of people would make it their permanent and primary residence. A proposal to allow citizens of the district to vote in presidential elections was approved by Congress in June 1960 and was ratified on March 29, 1961.*

Amendment XXIV
[Adopted 1964]

Section 1 The right of citizens of the United States to vote in any primary or other election for President or Vice-President, for electors for President or Vice-President, or for Senator or Representative in Congress, shall not be denied or abridged by the United States or any State by reason of failure to pay any poll tax or other tax.

Section 2 The Congress shall have the power to enforce this article by appropriate legislation.

♦ ♦ ♦

▶ *In the colonial and Revolutionary eras, financial independence was seen as necessary to political independence, and the poll tax was used as a requirement for voting. By the twentieth century, however, the poll tax was used mostly to bar poor people, especially southern blacks, from voting. While conservatives complained that the amendment interfered with states' rights, liberals thought that the amendment did not go far enough because it barred the poll tax only in national elections and not in state or local elections. The amendment was ratified in 1964, however, and two years later, the Supreme Court ruled that poll taxes in state and local elections also violated the equal protection clause of the Fourteenth Amendment.*

Amendment XXV

[Adopted 1967]

Section 1 In case of the removal of the President from office or of his death or resignation, the Vice-President shall become President.

Section 2 Whenever there is a vacancy in the office of the Vice-President, the President shall nominate a Vice-President who shall take office upon confirmation by a majority vote of both Houses of Congress.

Section 3 Whenever the President transmits to the President pro tempore of the Senate and the Speaker of the House of Representatives his written declaration that he is unable to discharge the powers and duties of his office, and until he transmits to them a written declaration to the contrary, such powers and duties shall be discharged by the Vice-President as Acting President.

Section 4 Whenever the Vice-President and a majority of either the principal officers of the executive departments or of such other body as Congress may by law provide, transmit to the President pro tempore of the Senate and the Speaker of the House of Representatives their written declaration that the President is unable to discharge the powers and duties of his office, the Vice-President shall immediately assume the powers and duties of the office as Acting President.

Thereafter, when the President transmits to the President pro tempore of the Senate and the Speaker of the House of Representatives his written declaration that no inability exists, he shall resume the powers and duties of his office unless the Vice-President and a majority of either the principal officers of the executive department[s] or of such other body as Congress may by law provide, transmit within four days to the President pro tempore of the Senate and the Speaker of the House of Representatives their written declaration that the President is unable to discharge the powers and duties of his office. Thereupon Congress shall decide the issue, assembling within forty-eight hours for that purpose if not in session. If the Congress, within twenty-one days after receipt of the latter written declaration, or, if Congress is not in session, within twenty-one days after Congress is required to assemble, determines by two-thirds vote of both Houses that the President is unable to discharge the powers and duties of his office, the Vice-President shall continue to discharge the same as Acting President; otherwise, the President shall resume the powers and duties of his office.

♦ ♦ ♦

▶ *The framers of the Constitution established the office of vice president because someone was needed to preside over the Senate. The first president to die in office was William Henry Harrison, in 1841. Vice President John Tyler had himself sworn in as president, setting a precedent that was followed when seven later presidents died in office. The assassination of President James A. Garfield in 1881 posed a new problem, however. After he was shot, the president was incapacitated for two months before he died; he was unable to lead the country, while his vice president, Chester A. Arthur, was unable to assume leadership. Efforts to resolve questions of succession in the event of a presidential disability thus began with the death of Garfield.*

In 1963, the assassination of President John F. Kennedy galvanized Congress to action. Vice President Lyndon Johnson was a chain smoker with a history of heart trouble. According to the 1947 Presidential Succession Act, the two men who stood in line to succeed him were the seventy-two-year-old Speaker of the House and the eighty-six-year-old president of the Senate. There were serious concerns that any of these men might become incapacitated while serving as chief executive. The first time the Twenty-fifth Amendment was used, however, was not in the case of presidential death or illness, but during the Watergate crisis. When Vice President Spiro T. Agnew was forced to resign following allegations of bribery and tax violations, President Richard M. Nixon appointed House Minority Leader Gerald R. Ford vice president. Ford became president following Nixon's resignation eight months later and named Nelson A. Rockefeller as his vice president. Thus, for more than two years, the two highest offices in the country were held by people who had not been elected to them.

Amendment XXVI

[Adopted 1971]

Section 1 The right of citizens of the United States, who are eighteen years of age or older, to vote shall not be denied or abridged by the United States or by any State on account of age.

Section 2 The Congress shall have power to enforce this article by appropriate legislation.

♦ ♦ ♦

▶ *Efforts to lower the voting age from twenty-one to eighteen began during World War II. Recognizing that those who were old enough to fight a war should have some say in the government policies that involved them in the war, Presidents Eisenhower, Johnson, and Nixon endorsed the idea. In 1970, the combined pressure of the antiwar movement and the demographic pressure of the baby boom generation led to a Voting Rights Act lowering the voting age in federal, state, and local elections.*

In Oregon v. Mitchell *(1970), the state of Oregon challenged the right of Congress to determine the age at which people could vote in state or local elections. The Supreme Court agreed with Oregon. Since the Voting Rights Act was ruled unconstitutional, the Constitution had to be amended to allow passage of a law that would lower the voting age. The amendment was ratified in a little more than three months, making it the most rapidly ratified amendment in U.S. history.*

Unratified Amendment

Equal Rights Amendment (proposed by Congress March 22, 1972; seven-year deadline for ratification extended to June 30, 1982)

Section 1 Equality of rights under the law shall not be denied or abridged by the United States or by any State on account of sex.

Section 2 The Congress shall have the power to enforce, by appropriate legislation, the provisions of this article.

Section 3 This amendment shall take effect two years after the date of ratification.

◆ ◆ ◆

▶ *In 1923, soon after women had won the right to vote, Alice Paul, a leading activist in the woman suffrage movement, proposed an amendment requiring equal treatment of men and women. Opponents of the proposal argued that such an amendment would invalidate laws that protected women and would make women subject to the military draft. After the 1964 Civil Rights Act was adopted, protective workplace legislation was removed anyway.*

The renewal of the women's movement, as a byproduct of the civil rights and antiwar movements, led to a revival of the Equal Rights Amendment (ERA) in Congress. Disagreements over language held up congressional passage of the proposed amendment, but on March 22, 1972, the Senate approved the ERA by a vote of 84 to 8, and it was sent to the states. Six states ratified the amendment within two days, and by the middle of 1973 the amendment seemed well on its way to adoption, with thirty of the needed thirty-eight states having ratified it. In the mid-1970s, however, a powerful "Stop ERA" campaign developed. The campaign portrayed the ERA as a threat to "family values" and traditional relationships between men

and women. Although thirty-five states ultimately ratified the ERA, five of those state legislatures voted to rescind ratification, and the amendment was never adopted.

Unratified Amendment

D.C. Statehood Amendment (proposed by Congress August 22, 1978)

Section 1 For purposes of representation in the Congress, election of the President and Vice-President, and article V of this Constitution, the District constituting the seat of government of the United States shall be treated as though it were a State.

Section 2 The exercise of the rights and powers conferred under this article shall be by the people of the District constituting the seat of government, and as shall be provided by Congress.

Section 3 The twenty-third article of amendment to the Constitution of the United States is hereby repealed.

Section 4 This article shall be inoperative, unless it shall have been ratified as an amendment to the Constitution by the legislatures of three-fourths of the several states within seven years from the date of its submission.

◆ ◆ ◆

▶ *The 1961 ratification of the Twenty-third Amendment, giving residents of the District of Columbia the right to vote for a president and vice president, inspired an effort to give residents of the district full voting rights. In 1966, President Lyndon Johnson appointed a mayor and city council; in 1971, D.C. residents were allowed to name a nonvoting delegate to the House; and in 1981, residents were allowed to elect the mayor and city council. Congress retained the right to overrule laws that might affect commuters, the height of federal buildings, and selection of judges and prosecutors. The district's nonvoting delegate to Congress, Walter Fauntroy, lobbied fiercely for a congressional amendment granting statehood to the district. In 1978, a proposed amendment was approved and sent to the states. A number of states quickly ratified the amendment, but, like the ERA, the D.C. Statehood Amendment ran into trouble.*

Opponents argued that section 2 created a separate category of "nominal" statehood. They argued that the federal district should be eliminated and that the territory should be reabsorbed into the state of Maryland. Although these theoretical arguments were strong, some scholars believe that racist attitudes toward the predominantly black population of the city were also a factor leading to the defeat of the amendment.

Amendment XXVII

[Adopted 1992]

No law, varying the compensation for the services of the Senators and Representatives, shall take effect, until an election of Representatives shall have intervened.

♦ ♦ ♦

▶ *While the Twenty-sixth Amendment was the most rapidly ratified amendment in U.S. history, the Twenty-seventh Amendment had the longest journey to ratification. First proposed by James Madison in 1789 as part of the package that included the Bill of Rights, this amendment had been ratified by only six states by 1791. In 1873, however, it was ratified by Ohio to protest a massive retroactive salary increase by the federal government. Unlike later proposed amendments, this one came with no time limit on ratification.*

In the early 1980s, Gregory D. Watson, a University of Texas economics major, discovered the "lost" amendment and began a single-handed campaign to get state legislators to introduce it for ratification. In 1983, it was accepted by Maine. In 1984, it passed the Colorado legislature. Ratifications trickled in slowly until May 1992, when Michigan and New Jersey became the thirty-eighth and thirty-ninth states, respectively, to ratify. This amendment prevents members of Congress from raising their own salaries without giving voters a chance to vote them out of office before they can benefit from the raises.

PRESIDENTIAL ELECTIONS

Year	Candidates	Parties	Popular Vote	Percentage of Popular Vote	Electoral Vote	Percentage of Voter Participation
1789	**GEORGE WASHINGTON (Va.)***				69	
	John Adams				34	
	Others				35	
1792	**GEORGE WASHINGTON (Va.)**				132	
	John Adams				77	
	George Clinton				50	
	Others				5	
1796	**JOHN ADAMS (Mass.)**	Federalist			71	
	Thomas Jefferson	Democratic-Republican			68	
	Thomas Pinckney	Federalist			59	
	Aaron Burr	Dem.-Rep.			30	
	Others				48	
1800	**THOMAS JEFFERSON (Va.)**	Dem.-Rep.			73	
	Aaron Burr	Dem.-Rep.			73	
	John Adams	Federalist			65	
	C. C. Pinckney	Federalist			64	
	John Jay	Federalist			1	
1804	**THOMAS JEFFERSON (Va.)**	Dem.-Rep.			162	
	C. C. Pinckney	Federalist			14	
1808	**JAMES MADISON (Va.)**	Dem.-Rep.			122	
	C. C. Pinckney	Federalist			47	
	George Clinton	Dem.-Rep.			6	
1812	**JAMES MADISON (Va.)**	Dem.-Rep.			128	
	De Witt Clinton	Federalist			89	
1816	**JAMES MONROE (Va.)**	Dem.-Rep.			183	
	Rufus King	Federalist			34	
1820	**JAMES MONROE (Va.)**	Dem.-Rep.			231	
	John Quincy Adams	Dem.-Rep.			1	
1824	**JOHN Q. ADAMS (Mass.)**	Dem.-Rep.	108,740	30.5	84	26.9
	Andrew Jackson	Dem.-Rep.	153,544	43.1	99	
	William H. Crawford	Dem.-Rep.	46,618	13.1	41	
	Henry Clay	Dem.-Rep.	47,136	13.2	37	
1828	**ANDREW JACKSON (Tenn.)**	Democratic	647,286	56.0	178	57.6
	John Quincy Adams	National Republican	508,064	44.0	83	
1832	**ANDREW JACKSON (Tenn.)**	Democratic	687,502	55.0	219	55.4
	Henry Clay	National Republican	530,189	42.4	49	
	John Floyd	Independent			11	
	William Wirt	Anti-Mason	33,108	2.6	7	

*State of residence when elected president.

Year	Candidates	Parties	Popular Vote	Percentage of Popular Vote	Electoral Vote	Percentage of Voter Participation
1836	**MARTIN VAN BUREN (N.Y.)**	Democratic	765,483	50.9	170	57.8
	W. H. Harrison	Whig			73	
	Hugh L. White	Whig	739,795	49.1	26	
	Daniel Webster	Whig			14	
	W. P. Mangum	Independent			11	
1840	**WILLIAM H. HARRISON (Ohio)**	Whig	1,274,624	53.1	234	78.0
	Martin Van Buren	Democratic	1,127,781	46.9	60	
	J. G. Birney	Liberty	7,069		—	
1844	**JAMES K. POLK (Tenn.)**	Democratic	1,338,464	49.6	170	78.9
	Henry Clay	Whig	1,300,097	48.1	105	
	J. G. Birney	Liberty	62,300	2.3	—	
1848	**ZACHARY TAYLOR (La.)**	Whig	1,360,099	47.4	163	72.7
	Lewis Cass	Democratic	1,220,544	42.5	127	
	Martin Van Buren	Free-Soil	291,263	10.1	—	
1852	**FRANKLIN PIERCE (N.H.)**	Democratic	1,601,117	50.9	254	69.6
	Winfield Scott	Whig	1,385,453	44.1	42	
	John P. Hale	Free-Soil	155,825	5.0	—	
1856	**JAMES BUCHANAN (Pa.)**	Democratic	1,832,995	45.3	174	78.9
	John C. Frémont	Republican	1,339,932	33.1	114	
	Millard Fillmore	American	871,731	21.6	8	
1860	**ABRAHAM LINCOLN (Ill.)**	Republican	1,866,452	39.8	180	81.2
	Stephen A. Douglas	Democratic	1,375,157	29.4	12	
	John C. Breckinridge	Democratic	847,953	18.1	72	
	John Bell	Union	590,631	12.6	39	
1864	**ABRAHAM LINCOLN (Ill.)**	Republican	2,213,665	55.1	212	73.8
	George B. McClellan	Democratic	1,805,237	44.9	21	
1868	**ULYSSES S. GRANT (Ill.)**	Republican	3,012,833	52.7	214	78.1
	Horatio Seymour	Democratic	2,703,249	47.3	80	
1872	**ULYSSES S. GRANT (Ill.)**	Republican	3,597,132	55.6	286	71.3
	Horace Greeley	Democratic; Liberal Republican	2,834,125	43.9	66	
1876	**RUTHERFORD B. HAYES (Ohio)**	Republican	4,036,298	48.0	185	81.8
	Samuel J. Tilden	Democratic	4,288,590	51.0	184	
1880	**JAMES A. GARFIELD (Ohio)**	Republican	4,454,416	48.5	214	79.4
	Winfield S. Hancock	Democratic	4,444,952	48.1	155	
1884	**GROVER CLEVELAND (N.Y.)**	Democratic	4,874,986	48.5	219	77.5
	James G. Blaine	Republican	4,851,981	48.3	182	
1888	**BENJAMIN HARRISON (Ind.)**	Republican	5,439,853	47.9	233	79.3
	Grover Cleveland	Democratic	5,540,309	48.6	168	
1892	**GROVER CLEVELAND (N.Y.)**	Democratic	5,555,426	46.1	277	74.7
	Benjamin Harrison	Republican	5,182,690	43.0	145	
	James B. Weaver	People's	1,029,846	8.5	22	
1896	**WILLIAM McKINLEY (Ohio)**	Republican	7,104,779	51.1	271	79.3
	William J. Bryan	Democratic-People's	6,502,925	47.7	176	
1900	**WILLIAM McKINLEY (Ohio)**	Republican	7,207,923	51.7	292	73.2
	William J. Bryan	Dem.-Populist	6,358,133	45.5	155	
1904	**THEODORE ROOSEVELT (N.Y.)**	Republican	7,623,486	57.9	336	65.2
	Alton B. Parker	Democratic	5,077,911	37.6	140	
	Eugene V. Debs	Socialist	402,283	3.0	—	
1908	**WILLIAM H. TAFT (Ohio)**	Republican	7,678,908	51.6	321	65.4
	William J. Bryan	Democratic	6,409,104	43.1	162	
	Eugene V. Debs	Socialist	420,793	2.8	—	

Year	Candidates	Parties	Popular Vote	Percentage of Popular Vote	Electoral Vote	Percentage of Voter Participation
1912	**WOODROW WILSON (N.J.)**	Democratic	6,293,454	41.9	435	58.8
	Theodore Roosevelt	Progressive	4,119,538	27.4	88	
	William H. Taft	Republican	3,484,980	23.2	8	
	Eugene V. Debs	Socialist	900,672	6.1	—	
1916	**WOODROW WILSON (N.J.)**	Democratic	9,129,606	49.4	277	61.6
	Charles E. Hughes	Republican	8,538,221	46.2	254	
	A. L. Benson	Socialist	585,113	3.2	—	
1920	**WARREN G. HARDING (Ohio)**	Republican	16,143,407	60.5	404	49.2
	James M. Cox	Democratic	9,130,328	34.2	127	
	Eugene V. Debs	Socialist	919,799	3.4	—	
1924	**CALVIN COOLIDGE (Mass.)**	Republican	15,725,016	54.0	382	48.9
	John W. Davis	Democratic	8,386,503	28.8	136	
	Robert M. La Follette	Progressive	4,822,856	16.6	13	
1928	**HERBERT HOOVER (Calif.)**	Republican	21,391,381	57.4	444	56.9
	Alfred E. Smith	Democratic	15,016,443	40.3	87	
	Norman Thomas	Socialist	881,951	2.3	—	
	William Z. Foster	Communist	102,991	0.3	—	
1932	**FRANKLIN D. ROOSEVELT (N.Y.)**	Democratic	22,821,857	57.4	472	56.9
	Herbert Hoover	Republican	15,761,841	39.7	59	
	Norman Thomas	Socialist	881,951	2.2	—	
1936	**FRANKLIN D. ROOSEVELT (N.Y.)**	Democratic	27,751,597	60.8	523	61.0
	Alfred M. Landon	Republican	16,679,583	36.5	8	
	William Lemke	Union	882,479	1.9	—	
1940	**FRANKLIN D. ROOSEVELT (N.Y.)**	Democratic	27,244,160	54.8	449	62.5
	Wendell Willkie	Republican	22,305,198	44.8	82	
1944	**FRANKLIN D. ROOSEVELT (N.Y.)**	Democratic	25,602,504	53.5	432	55.9
	Thomas E. Dewey	Republican	22,006,285	46.0	99	
1948	**HARRY S. TRUMAN (Mo.)**	Democratic	24,105,695	49.5	303	53.0
	Thomas E. Dewey	Republican	21,969,170	45.1	189	
	J. Strom Thurmond	States'-Rights Democratic	1,169,021	2.4	38	
	Henry A. Wallace	Progressive	1,156,103	2.4	—	
1952	**DWIGHT D. EISENHOWER (N.Y.)**	Republican	33,936,252	55.1	442	63.3
	Adlai Stevenson	Democratic	27,314,992	44.4	89	
1956	**DWIGHT D. EISENHOWER (N.Y.)**	Republican	35,575,420	57.6	457	60.6
	Adlai Stevenson	Democratic	26,033,066	42.1	73	
	Other	—	—		1	
1960	**JOHN F. KENNEDY (Mass.)**	Democratic	34,227,096	49.9	303	62.8
	Richard M. Nixon	Republican	34,108,546	49.6	219	
	Other	—	—		15	
1964	**LYNDON B. JOHNSON (Texas)**	Democratic	43,126,506	61.1	486	61.7
	Barry M. Goldwater	Republican	27,176,799	38.5	52	
1968	**RICHARD M. NIXON (N.Y.)**	Republican	31,770,237	43.4	301	60.9
	Hubert H. Humphrey	Democratic	31,270,533	42.7	191	
	George Wallace	American Indep.	9,906,141	13.5	46	
1972	**RICHARD M. NIXON (N.Y.)**	Republican	47,169,911	60.7	520	55.2
	George S. McGovern	Democratic	29,170,383	37.5	17	
	Other	—	—		1	
1976	**JIMMY CARTER (Ga.)**	Democratic	40,830,763	50.0	297	53.5
	Gerald R. Ford	Republican	39,147,793	48.0	240	
	Other	—	1,575,459	2.1	—	
1980	**RONALD REAGAN (Calif.)**	Republican	43,901,812	51.0	489	54.0
	Jimmy Carter	Democratic	35,483,820	41.0	49	
	John B. Anderson	Independent	5,719,722	7.0	—	
	Ed Clark	Libertarian	921,188	1.1	—	

Year	Candidates	Parties	Popular Vote	Percentage of Popular Vote	Electoral Vote	Percentage of Voter Participation
1984	**RONALD REAGAN (Calif.)**	Republican	54,455,075	59.0	525	53.1
	Walter Mondale	Democratic	37,577,185	41.0	13	
1988	**GEORGE H. W. BUSH (Texas)**	Republican	47,946,422	54.0	426	50.2
	Michael S. Dukakis	Democratic	41,016,429	46.0	112	
1992	**WILLIAM J. CLINTON (Ark.)**	Democratic	44,908,254	43.0	370	55.9
	George H. W. Bush	Republican	39,102,282	38.0	168	
	H. Ross Perot	Independent	19,721,433	19.0	—	
1996	**WILLIAM J. CLINTON (Ark.)**	Democratic	47,401,185	49.2	379	49.0
	Robert Dole	Republican	39,197,469	40.7	159	
	H. Ross Perot	Independent	8,085,294	8.4	—	
2000	**GEORGE W. BUSH (Texas)**	Republican	50,456,062	47.8	271	51.2
	Al Gore	Democratic	50,996,862	48.4	267	
	Ralph Nader	Green Party	2,858,843	2.7	—	
	Patrick J. Buchanan	—	438,760	0.4	—	
2004	**GEORGE W. BUSH (Texas)**	Republican	61,872,711	50.7	286	60.3
	John F. Kerry	Democratic	58,894,584	48.3	252	
	Other	—	1,582,185	1.3	—	
2008	**BARACK OBAMA (Illinois)**	Democratic	69,456,897	52.9	365	56.8
	John McCain	Republican	59,934,314	45.7	173	
2012	**BARACK OBAMA (Illinois)**	Democratic	65,899,660	51.1	332	—
	Willard Mitt Romney	Republican	60,932,152	47.2	152	

ADMISSION OF STATES TO THE UNION

State	Date of Admission	State	Date of Admission
Delaware	December 7, 1787	Florida	March 3, 1845
Pennsylvania	December 12, 1787	Texas	December 29, 1845
New Jersey	December 18, 1787	Iowa	December 28, 1846
Georgia	January 2, 1788	Wisconsin	May 29, 1848
Connecticut	January 9, 1788	California	September 9, 1850
Massachusetts	February 6, 1788	Minnesota	May 11, 1858
Maryland	April 28, 1788	Oregon	February 14, 1859
South Carolina	May 23, 1788	Kansas	January 29, 1861
New Hampshire	June 21, 1788	West Virginia	June 19, 1863
Virginia	June 25, 1788	Nevada	October 31, 1864
New York	July 26, 1788	Nebraska	March 1, 1867
North Carolina	November 21, 1789	Colorado	August 1, 1876
Rhode Island	May 29, 1790	North Dakota	November 2, 1889
Vermont	March 4, 1791	South Dakota	November 2, 1889
Kentucky	June 1, 1792	Montana	November 8, 1889
Tennessee	June 1, 1796	Washington	November 11, 1889
Ohio	March 1, 1803	Idaho	July 3, 1890
Louisiana	April 30, 1812	Wyoming	July 10, 1890
Indiana	December 11, 1816	Utah	January 4, 1896
Mississippi	December 10, 1817	Oklahoma	November 16, 1907
Illinois	December 3, 1818	New Mexico	January 6, 1912
Alabama	December 14, 1819	Arizona	February 14, 1912
Maine	March 15, 1820	Alaska	January 3, 1959
Missouri	August 10, 1821	Hawaii	August 21, 1959
Arkansas	June 15, 1836		
Michigan	January 16, 1837		

Population

FROM AN ESTIMATED 4,600 white inhabitants in 1630, the country's population grew to a total of more than 308 million in 2010. It is important to note that the U.S. census, first conducted in 1790 and the source of these figures, counted blacks, both free and slave, but did not include American Indians until 1860. The years 1790 to 1900 saw the most rapid population growth, with an average increase of 25 to 35 percent per decade. In addition to "natural" growth—birthrate exceeding death rate—immigration was also a factor in that rise, especially between 1840 and 1860, 1880 and 1890, and 1900 and 1910. The twentieth century witnessed slower growth, partly a result of 1920s immigration restrictions and a decline in the birthrate, especially during the depression era and the 1960s and 1970s. The U.S. population is expected to pass 340 million by the year 2020.

POPULATION GROWTH, 1630–2010

Year	Population	Percent Increase	Year	Population	Percent Increase
1630	4,600	—	1830	12,866,020	33.5
1640	26,600	473.3	1840	17,069,453	32.7
1650	50,400	89.1	1850	23,191,876	35.9
1660	75,100	49.0	1860	31,443,321	35.6
1670	111,900	49.1	1870	39,818,449	26.6
1680	151,500	35.4	1880	50,155,783	26.0
1690	210,400	38.9	1890	62,947,714	25.5
1700	250,900	19.3	1900	75,994,575	20.7
1710	331,700	32.2	1910	91,972,266	21.0
1720	466,200	40.5	1920	105,710,620	14.9
1730	629,400	35.0	1930	122,775,046	16.1
1740	905,600	43.9	1940	131,669,275	7.2
1750	1,170,800	30.0	1950	150,697,361	14.5
1760	1,593,600	36.1	1960	179,323,175	19.0
1770	2,148,100	34.8	1970	203,302,031	13.4
1780	2,780,400	29.4	1980	226,542,199	11.4
1790	3,929,214	41.3	1990	248,718,302	9.8
1800	5,308,483	35.1	2000	281,422,509	13.1
1810	7,239,881	36.4	2010	308,745,538	9.7
1820	9,638,453	33.1			

SOURCE: *Historical Statistics of the U.S.* (1960), *Historical Statistics of the U.S., Colonial Times to 1970* (1975), *Statistical Abstract of the U.S., 1996* (1996), *Statistical Abstract of the U.S., 2003* (2003), and United States Census (2010).

Major Trends in Immigration

THE QUANTITY AND CHARACTER OF IMMIGRATION to the United States has varied greatly over time. During the first major influx, between 1840 and 1860, newcomers hailed primarily from northern and western Europe. From 1880 to 1915, when rates soared even more dramatically, the profile changed, with 80 percent of the "new immigration" coming from central, eastern, and southern Europe. Following World War I, strict quotas reduced the flow considerably. Note also the significant falloff during the years of the Great Depression and World War II. The sources of immigration during the last half century have changed significantly, with the majority of people coming from Latin America, the Caribbean, and Asia. The latest surge during the 1980s and 1990s brought more immigrants to the United States than in any decade except 1901–1910.

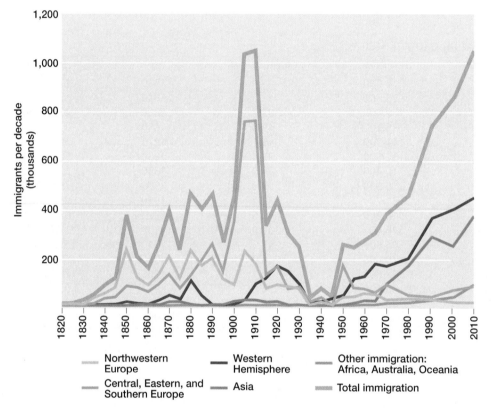

SOURCE: Data from *Historical Statistics of the U.S., Colonial Times to 1970* (1975), *Statistical Abstract of the U.S., 1999* (1999), and *Statistical Abstract of the U.S., 2011* (2011).

Selected Bibliography

Chapter 1

GENERAL WORKS

Robson Bonnichsen and Karen L. Turnmire, *Ice Age Peoples of North America* (1999).

Karen Olsen Bruhns and Karen R. Stothert, *Women in Ancient America* (1999).

Thomas D. Dillehay, *The Settlement of the Americas: A New Prehistory* (2000).

Brian Fagan, *Ancient North America* (2005).

Tim Flannery, *The Eternal Frontier: An Ecological History of North America and Its Peoples* (2001).

J. C. H. King, *First People, First Contacts: Native Peoples of North America* (1999).

Charles C. Mann, *1491: New Revelations of the Americas before Columbus* (2006).

Francis McManamon et al., eds., *Archaeology in America* (2008).

Steven Mithen, *After the Ice: A Global Human History, 20,000–5000 BC* (2003).

Daniel K. Richter, *Before the Revolution: America's Ancient Pasts* (2011).

Christina Snyder, *Slavery in Indian Country: The Changing Face of Captivity in Early America* (2010).

Nicholas Wade, *Before the Dawn: Recovering the Lost History of Our Ancestors* (2006).

NATIVE AMERICAN CULTURES IN TERRITORY OF PRESENT-DAY UNITED STATES

Kenneth M. Ames and Herbert D. G. Maschner, *Peoples of the Northwest Coast: Their Archaeology and Prehistory* (1999).

Sally A. Kitt Chappell, *Cahokia: Mirror of the Cosmos* (2002).

Linda S. Cordell, *Archaeology of the Southwest* (2009).

Richard J. Dent Jr., *Chesapeake Prehistory: Old Traditions, New Directions* (1995).

E. James Dixon, *Bones, Boats, and Bison: Archeology and the First Colonization of Western North America* (1999).

Thomas E. Emerson et al., eds., *Late Woodland Societies: Tradition and Transformation across the Midcontinent* (2008).

Kendrick Frazier, *People of Chaco: A Canyon and Its Cultures* (1999).

George C. Frison, *Prehistoric Hunters of the High Plains* (2nd ed., 1991).

Sarah A. Kerr, *Beyond Chaco: Great Kiva Communities on the Mogollon Rim Frontier* (2001).

Steven A. LeBlanc, *Prehistoric Warfare in the American Southwest* (1999).

Stephen H. Lekson, *The Chaco Meridian: Centers of Political Power in the Ancient Southwest* (1999).

Jerald T. Milanich, *Archaeology of Precolumbian Florida* (1994).

Timothy R. Pauketat, *Cahokia: Ancient America's Greatest City on the Mississippi* (2009).

Jefferson Reid and Stephanie Whittlesley, *The Archaeology of Ancient Arizona* (1997).

Karl H. Schlesier, *Plains Indians, A.D. 500–1500: The Archaeological Past of Historic Groups* (1994).

Lynne Sebastian, *The Chaco Anasazi: Sociopolitical Evolution in the Prehistoric Southwest* (1992).

Lynda Shaffer, *Native Americans before 1492: The Moundbuilding Centers of the Eastern Woodlands* (1992).

Marvin T. Smith, *Coosa: The Rise and Fall of a Southeastern Mississippian Chiefdom* (2000).

Biloine Whiting Young and Melvin L. Fowler, *Cahokia: The Great Native American Metropolis* (1999).

THE MEXICA

David Carrasco, *City of Sacrifice: The Aztec Empire and the Role of Violence in Civilization* (1999).

Michael D. Coe and Rex Koontz, *Mexico: From the Olmecs to the Aztecs* (5th ed., 2002).

Susan Toby Evans, *Ancient Mexico and Central America: Archaeology and Culture History* (2008).

Eduardo Matos Moctezuma and Felipe Solis Olguin, *Aztecs* (2002).

Chapter 2

GENERAL WORKS

J. H. Elliott, *Empires of the Atlantic World: Britain and Spain in America, 1491–1830* (2006).

John L. Kessell, *Spain in the Southwest: A Narrative History of Colonial New Mexico, Arizona, Texas, and California* (2002).

Diarmaid MacCulloch, *Christianity: The First Three Thousand Years* (2009).

David Parrott, *The Business of War: Military Enterprise and Military Revolution in Early Modern Europe* (2013).

William D. Phillips and Carla Rahn Phillips, *The Worlds of Christopher Columbus* (1992).

Daniel K. Richter, *Before the Revolution: America's Ancient Pasts* (2011).

John K. Thornton, *A Cultural History of the Atlantic World, 1250–1820* (2012).

David J. Weber, *The Spanish Frontier in North America* (2009).

EXPLORERS AND EMPIRES

James Horn, *A Kingdom Strange: The Brief and Tragic History of the Lost Colony of Roanoke* (2010).

Henry Arthur Francis Kamen, *Empire: How Spain Became a World Power, 1492–1763* (2004).

Karen Ordahl Kupperman, *Roanoke: The Abandoned Colony* (2nd ed., 2007).

Francesc Relaño, *The Shaping of Africa: Cosmographic Discourse and Cartographic Science in Late Medieval and Early Modern Europe* (2002).

A. J. R. Russell-Wood, *The Portuguese Empire, 1415–1808: A World on the Move* (1998).

Hugh Thomas, *Rivers of Gold: The Rise of the Spanish Empire from Columbus to Magellan* (2004).

EUROPEANS ENCOUNTER THE NEW WORLD

Ricardo Alegria and Jose Arrom, *Taino: Pre-Columbian Art and Culture from the Caribbean* (1998).

Rebecca Catz, *Christopher Columbus and the Portuguese, 1476–1498* (1993).

Noble David Cook, *Born to Die: Disease and New World Conquest, 1492–1650* (1998).

Michael Leroy Oberg, *The Head in Edward Nugent's Hand: Roanoke's Forgotten Indians* (2008).

Anthony Pagden, *Lords of All the World: Ideologies of Empire in Spain, Britain, and France, 1500–1800* (1995).

Irving Rouse, *The Tainos: Rise and Decline of the People Who Greeted Columbus* (1992).

CONQUEST AND NEW SPAIN

Herman L. Bennett, *Africans in Colonial Mexico: Absolutism, Christianity, and Afro-Creole Consciousness, 1570–1640* (2003).

Louise M. Burkhart, *The Slippery Earth: Nahua-Christian Moral Dialogue in Sixteenth-Century Mexico* (1989).

David Ewing Duncan, *Hernando de Soto: A Savage Quest in the Americas* (1995).

Richard Flint and Shirley Cushing Flint, *The Coronado Expedition* (2003).

Serge Gruzinski, *The Conquest of Mexico: The Incorporation of Indian Societies into the Western World, Sixteenth–Eighteenth Centuries* (1993).

Ramón A. Gutiérrez, *When Jesus Came, the Corn Mothers Went Away: Marriage, Sexuality, and Power in New Mexico, 1500–1846* (1991).

Robert H. Jackson, *Race, Caste, and Status: Indians in Colonial Spanish America* (1999).

John L. Kessell, *Pueblos, Spaniards, and the Kingdom of New Mexico* (2010).

Andrew L. Knaut, *The Pueblo Revolt of 1680: Conquest and Resistance in Seventeenth-Century New Mexico* (1995).

Miguel León-Portilla, *Bernardino de Sahagún: First Anthropologist* (2002).

Jerald T. Milanich, *Laboring in the Fields of the Lord: Spanish Missions and Southwestern Indians* (1999).

Matthew Restall, *Seven Myths of the Spanish Conquest* (2004).

Stuart B. Schwartz, *All Can Be Saved: Religious Tolerance and Salvation in the Iberian Atlantic World* (2009).

Charles A. Truxillo, *By the Sword and the Cross: The Historical Evolution of the Catholic World Monarchy in Spain and the New World, 1492–1825* (2001).

Stephanie Gail Wood, *Transcending Conquest: Nahua Views of Spanish Colonial Mexico* (2003).

Chapter 3

CHESAPEAKE SOCIETY

Bernard Bailyn, *The Barbarous Yeas: The Peopling of British North America: The Conflict of Civilizations, 1600-1675* (2012).

Kathleen Brown, *Good Wives, Nasty Wenches, and Anxious Patriarchs: Gender, Race, and Power in Colonial Virginia* (1996).

Alison Games, *The Web of Empire: English Cosmopolitans in the Age of Expansion, 1560–1660* (2009).

April Hatfield, *Atlantic Virginia: Intercolonial Relations in the Seventeenth Century* (2003).

Karen Ordahl Kupperman, *The Jamestown Project* (2010).

Peter C. Mancall, *The Atlantic World and Virginia, 1550–1624* (2007).

Debra Meyers, *Common Whores, Vertuous Women, and Loveing Wives: Free Will Christian Women in Colonial Maryland* (2003).

Marcy Norton, *Sacred Gifts, Profane Pleasures: A History of Tobacco and Chocolate in the Atlantic World* (2010).

Geoffrey Parker, *Global Crisis: War, Climate Change and Catastrophe in the Seventeenth Century* (2013).

Steve Sarson, *British America, 1500–1800: Creating Colonies, Imagining an Empire* (2005).

Terry L. Snyder, *Brabbling Women: Disorderly Speech and the Law in Early Virginia* (2003).

Christopher L. Tomlins, *Freedom Bound: Law, Labor, and Civic Identity in Colonizing English America, 1580–1865* (2010).

Lorena S. Walsh, *Motives of Honor, Pleasure, and Profit: Plantation Management in the Colonial Chesapeake, 1607–1763* (2010).

INDIANS

Alan Gallay, *The Indian Slave Trade: The Rise of the English Empire in the American South, 1670–1717* (2002).

Joseph M. Hall, Jr., *Zamuno's Gifts: Indian European Exchange in the Colonial Southeast* (2012).

Karen Ordahl Kupperman, *Indians and English: Facing Off in Early America* (2000).

Helen C. Rountree, *Pocahontas, Powhatan, Opechancanough: Three Indian Lives Changed by Jamestown* (2005).

Christina Snyder, *Slavery in Indian Country: The Changing Face of Captivity in Early America* (2010).

Jayme A. Sokolow, *The Great Encounter: Native Peoples and European Settlers in the Americas, 1492–1800* (2003).

Margaret Holmes Williamson, *Powhatan Lords of Life and Death: Command and Consent in Seventeenth-Century Virginia* (2003).

SLAVERY AND INDENTURED SERVITUDE

Susan Dwyer Amussen, *Caribbean Exchanges: Slavery and the Transformation of English Society, 1640–1700* (2007).

James F. Brooks, *Captives and Cousins: Slavery, Kinship, and Community in the Southwest Borderlands* (2002).

Tim Hashaw, *The Birth of Black America: The First African Americans and the Pursuit of Freedom at Jamestown* (2007).

Linda M. Heywood and John K. Thornton, *Central Africans, Atlantic Creoles, and the Foundation of the Americas* (2007).

Russell R. Menard, *Migrants, Servants, and Slaves: Unfree Labor in Colonial British America* (2001).

Jerald T. Milanich, *Laboring in the Fields of the Lord: Spanish Missions and Southeastern Indians* (1999).

Edmund S. Morgan, *American Slavery, American Freedom: The Ordeal of Colonial Virginia* (1975).

Jennifer L. Morgan, *Laboring Women: Reproduction and Gender in New World Slavery* (2004).

Simon P. Newman, *A New World of Labor: The Development of Plantation Slavery in the British Atlantic* (2013).

John Ruston Pagan, *Anne Orthwood's Bastard: Sex and Law in Early Virginia* (2003).

CAROLINA SOCIETY AND THE WEST INDIES

Cara Anzilotti, *In the Affairs of the World: Women, Patriarchy, and Power in Colonial South Carolina* (2002).

S. Max Edelson, *Plantation Enterprise in Colonial South Carolina* (2006).

Kirsten Fischer, *Suspect Relations: Sex, Race, and Resistance in Colonial North Carolina* (2002).

Michael Jarvis, *In the Eye of All Trade: Bermuda, Bermudians, and the Maritime Atlantic World, 1680–1783* (2010).

Russell K. Menard, *Sweet Negotiations: Sugar, Slavery, and Plantation Agriculture in Early Barbados* (2006).

Chapter 4

GENERAL WORKS

Virginia DeJohn Anderson, *Creatures of Empire: How Domestic Animals Transformed Early America* (2004).

Bernard Bailyn, *The Barbarous Years: The Peopling of British North America: The Conflict of Civilizations, 1600–1675* (2012).

Colin G. Calloway, *New Worlds for All: Indians, Europeans, and the Remaking of Early America* (1998).

Eric Jay Dolin, *Fur, Fortune, and Empire: The Epic History of the Fur Trade in America* (2010).

David D. Hall, *Worlds of Wonder, Days of Judgment: Popular Religious Belief in Early New England* (1989).

Peter Moogk, *La Nouvelle France: The Making of French Canada—A Cultural History* (2000).

Carla Gardina Pestana, *The English Atlantic in the Age of Revolution, 1640–1661* (2004).

James Pritchard, *In Search of Empire: The French in the Americas, 1670–1730* (2007).

NATIVE AMERICANS

Russell Bourne, *Gods of War, Gods of Peace: How the Meeting of Native and Colonial Religions Shaped Early America* (2002).

Roger M. Carpenter, *The Renewed, the Destroyed, and the Remade: The Three Thought Worlds of the Huron and the Iroquois, 1609–1675* (2004).

Jill Lepore, *The Name of War: King Philip's War and the Origins of American Identity* (1998).

Daniel R. Mandell, *King Philip's War: Colonial Expansion, Native Resistance, and the End of Indian Sovereignty* (2010).

Donna Merwick, *The Shame and the Sorrow: Dutch-Amerindian Encounters in New Netherland* (2006).

Michael Leroy Oberg, *Dominion and Civility: English Imperialism and Native America, 1585–1685* (1999).

Ann Marie Plane, *Colonial Intimacies: Indian Marriages in Early New England* (2000).

NEW ENGLAND

Louise A. Breen, *Transgressing the Bounds: Subversive Enterprises among the Puritan Elite in Massachusetts, 1630–1692* (2001).

Nick Bunker, *Making Haste from Babylon: The Mayflower Pilgrims and Their World* (2010).

James F. Cooper Jr., *Tenacious of Their Liberties: The Congregationalists in Colonial Massachusetts* (1999).

Cornelia Hughes Dayton, *Women before the Bar: Gender, Law, and Society in Connecticut, 1639–1789* (1995).

Lisa M. Gordis, *Opening Scriptures: Bible Reading and Interpretive Authority in Puritan New England* (2003).

David D. Hall, *A Reforming People: Transformation of Public Life in New England* (2013).

Jane Kamensky, *Governing the Tongue: The Politics of Speech in Early New England* (1997).

Eve LaPlante, *American Jezebel: The Uncommon Life of Anne Hutchinson, the Woman Who Defied the Puritans* (2005).

Mary Beth Norton, *In the Devil's Snare: The Salem Witchcraft Crisis of 1692* (2002).

Mark A. Peterson, *The Price of Redemption: The Spiritual Economy of Puritan New England* (1998).

Nathaniel Philbrick, *Mayflower: A Story of Courage, Community, and War* (2006).

Michael P. Winship, *Making Heretics: Militant Protestantism and Free Grace in Massachusetts, 1636–1641* (2002).

MIDDLE COLONIES

Evan Haefeli, *New Netherland and the Dutch Origins of American Religious Liberty* (2012).

Ned C. Landsman, *Crossroads of Empire: The Middle Colonies in British North America* (2010).

Peter C. Mancall, *Fatal Journey: The Final Expedition of Henry Hudson* (2009).

Cathy Matson, *Merchants and Empire: Trading in Colonial New York* (1998).

David E. Narrett, *Inheritance and Family Life in Colonial New York City* (1992).

Russell Shorto, *The Island at the Center of the World: The Epic Story of Dutch Manhattan and the Forgotten Colony That Shaped America* (2004).

Allen Tully, *Forming American Politics: Ideals, Interests, and Institutions in Colonial New York and Pennsylvania* (1994).

Chapter 5

GENERAL WORKS

Jennifer L. Anderson, *Mahogany: The Costs of Luxury in Early America* (2012).

Ira Berlin, *Generations of Captivity: A History of African-American Slaves* (2003).

Holly Brewer, *By Birth or Consent: Children, Law, and the Anglo-American Revolution in Authority* (2005).

Eric Jay Dolin, *Fur, Fortune, and Empire: The Epic History of the Fur Trade in America* (2010).

Kathleen DuVal, *The Native Ground: Indians and Colonists in the Heart of the Continent* (2006).

Patrick Griffin, *The People with No Name: Ireland's Ulster Scots, America's Scots Irish, and the Creation of a British Atlantic World, 1689–1764* (2001).

David Hancock, *Oceans of Wine: Madeira and the Emergence of American Trade and Taste* (2009).

Brendan McConville, *The King's Three Faces: The Rise and Fall of Royal America, 1688–1776* (2007).

Peter Silver, *Our Savage Neighbors: How Indian War Transformed Early America* (2008).

Christina Snyder, *Slavery in Indian Country: The Changing Face of Captivity in Early America* (2012).

Michael Witgen, *An Infinity of Nations: How the Native New World Shaped Early North America* (2013)

NEW ENGLAND

Richard Aquila, *The Iroquois Restoration: Iroquois Diplomacy on the Colonial Frontier, 1701–1754* (1997).

Elaine Forman Crane, *Ebb Tide in New England: Women, Seaports, and Social Change, 1630–1800* (1998).

Phyllis Whitman Hunter, *Purchasing Identity in the Atlantic World: Massachusetts Merchants, 1670–1780* (2001).

George M. Marsden, *Jonathan Edwards: A Life* (2003).

Lisa Norling, *Captain Ahab Had a Wife: New England Women and the Whale Fishery, 1720–1870* (2000).

Daniel Vickers, *Young Men and the Sea: Yankee Seafarers in the Age of Sail* (2005).

MIDDLE COLONIES

Katherine Carté Engel, *Religion and Profit: Moravians in Early America* (2009).

Leslie M. Harris, *In the Shadow of Slavery: African Americans in New York City, 1626–1863* (2003).

Eric Hinderaker, *Elusive Empires: Constructing Colonialism in the Ohio Valley, 1673–1800* (1997).

Jill Lepore, *New York Burning: Liberty, Slavery, and Conspiracy in Eighteenth-Century Manhattan* (2005).

James H. Merrell, *Into the American Woods: Negotiators on the Pennsylvania Frontier* (1999).

Jane T. Merritt, *At the Crossroads: Indians and Empires on a Mid-Atlantic Frontier, 1700–1763* (2003).

Donna Merwick, *The Shame and the Sorrow: Dutch-Amerindian Encounters in New Netherland* (2006).

Simon P. Newman, *Embodied History: The Lives of the Poor in Early Philadelphia* (2003).

David Waldstreicher, *Runaway America: Benjamin Franklin, Slavery, and the American Revolution* (2004).

SOUTHERN COLONIES

Vincent Carretta, *Equiano the African: Biography of a Self-Made Man* (2005).

Steven W. Hackel, *Children of Coyote, Missionaries of Saint Francis: Indian-Spanish Relations in Colonial California, 1769–1850* (2005).

Robert H. Jackson, *Missions and the Frontiers of Spanish America* (2005).

Catherine Kerrison, *Claiming the Pen: Women and Intellectual Life in the Early American South* (2006).

Philip D. Morgan, *Slave Counterpoint: Black Culture in the Eighteenth-Century Chesapeake and Low Country* (1998).

Robert Olwell, Brett Rushforth, *Bonds of Alliance: Indigenous and Atlantic Slaveries in New France* (2012).

Jon F. Sensbach, *Rebecca's Revival: Creating Black Christianity in the Atlantic World* (2005).

Randy Sparks, *The Two Princes of Calabar: An Eighteenth-Century Atlantic Odyssey* (2004).

David J. Weber, *Bárbaros: Spaniards and Their Savages in the Age of Enlightenment* (2005).

Bradford J. Wood, *This Remote Part of the World: Regional Formation in Lower Cape Fear, North Carolina, 1725–1775* (2004).

Chapter 6

GENERAL WORKS

Edward Countryman, *The American Revolution* (2003).

Merrill Jensen, *The Founding of a Nation: A History of the American Revolution, 1763–1776* (2004).

Robert Middlekauff, *The Glorious Cause: The American Revolution, 1763–1789* (2005).

Gordon Wood, *The Radicalism of the American Revolution* (1993).

Alfred F. Young, *Liberty Tree: Ordinary People and the American Revolution* (2006).

Native Americans and the Seven Years' War.

Fred Anderson, *Crucible of War: The Seven Years' War and the Fate of Empire in British North America, 1754–1766* (2001).

Colin G. Calloway, *The Scratch of a Pen: 1763 and the Transformation of America* (2007).

Gregory Evans Dowd, *War under Heaven: Pontiac, the Indian Nations, and the British Empire* (2004).

Eric Hinderaker, *The Two Hendricks: Unraveling a Mohawk Mystery* (2010).

James H. Merrell, *Into the American Woods: Negotiators on the Pennsylvania Frontier* (2000).

Timothy J. Shannon, *Indians and Colonists at the Crossroads of Empire: The Albany Congress of 1754* (2002).

Peter Silver, *Our Savage Neighbors: How Indian War Transformed Early America* (2009).

Richard White, *The Middle Ground: Indians, Empires, and Republics in the Great Lakes Region, 1650–1815* (1991).

The Revolutionary Crisis of the 1760s and 1770s.

Richard Archer, *As If an Enemy's Country: The British Occupation of Boston and the Origins of Revolution* (2010).

Bernard Bailyn, *The Ordeal of Thomas Hutchinson* (1976).

Carol Berkin, *Revolutionary Mothers: Women in the Struggle for America's Independence* (2006).

T. H. Breen, *American Insurgents, American Patriots: The Revolution of the People* (2010).

Benjamin L. Carp, *Defiance of the Patriots: The Boston Tea Party and the Making of America* (2010).

John E. Ferling, *The First of Men: A Life of George Washington* (1988).

David Hackett Fischer, *Paul Revere's Ride* (1995).

Robert A. Gross, *The Minutemen and Their World* (2001).

Joan Gundersen, *To Be Useful to the World: Women in Revolutionary America, 1740–1790* (1996).

Woody Holton, *Forced Founders: Indians, Debtors, Slaves, and the Making of the American Revolution in Virginia* (1999).

Pauline Maier, *From Resistance to Revolution: Colonial Radicals and the Development of American Opposition to Britain, 1765–1776* (1992).

Gary B. Nash, *The Unknown American Revolution: The Unruly Birth of Democracy and the Struggle to Create America* (2006).

Mary Beth Norton, *Liberty's Daughters: The Revolutionary Experience of American Women, 1750–1800* (1996).

Andrew Jackson O'Shaughnessy, *The Men who Lost America: British Leadership, the American Revolution, and the Fate of the Empire* (2013).

Ray Raphael, *The First American Revolution: Before Lexington and Concord* (2002).

William B. Warner, *Protocols of Liberty: Communication Innovation and the American Revolution* (2013).

Alfred F. Young, *The Shoemaker and the Tea Party: Memory and the American Revolution* (2000).

SLAVERY

Ira Berlin, *Many Thousands Gone: The First Two Centuries of Slavery in North America* (2000).

Douglas R. Egerton, *Death or Liberty: African Americans and Revolutionary America* (2009).

Sylvia Frey, *Water from the Rock: Black Resistance in a Revolutionary Age* (1991).

Philip Morgan, *Slave Counterpoint* (1998).

Chapter 7

GENERAL WORKS

Carol Berkin, *Revolutionary Mothers: Women in the Struggle for America's Independence* (2005).

Edward Countryman, *The American Revolution* (1985).

John Fering, *Almost a Miracle: The American Victory in the War of Independence* (2009).

Gary B. Nash, *The Unknown American Revolution: The Unruly Birth of Democracy and the Struggle to Create America* (2005).

Jack Rakove, *Revolutionaries: A New History of the Invention of America* (2010).

Ray Raphael, *A People's History of the American Revolution: How Common People Shaped the Fight for Independence* (2001).

Charles Royster, *A Revolutionary People at War: The Continental Army and American Character, 1775–1783* (1996).

Gordon S. Wood, *The Radicalism of the American Revolution* (1992).

Alfred F. Young, Gary B. Nash, and Ray Raphael, *Revolutionary Founders: Rebels, Radicals, and Reformers in the Making of the Nation* (2011).

THE WARTIME CONFEDERATION AND ITS LEADERS

Ron Chernow, *George Washington: A Life* (2010).

Joseph J. Ellis, *His Excellency: George Washington* (2004).

John E. Ferling, *Setting the World Ablaze: Washington, Adams, Jefferson, and the American Revolution* (2000).

Eric Foner, *Tom Paine and Revolutionary America* (2004).

Edith Gelles, *Portia: The World of Abigail Adams* (1992).

Woody Holton, *Abigail Adams* (2010).

Pauline Maier, *American Scripture: Making the Declaration of Independence* (1997).

Jackson Turner Main, *The Sovereign States, 1775–1783* (1973).

Jack N. Rakove, *The Beginnings of National Politics: An Interpretive History of the Continental Congress* (1979).

Sheila L. Skemp, *The Making of a Patriot: Benjamin Franklin at the Cockpit* (2012).

CAMPAIGNS, BATTLES, AND SOLDIERS

Wayne K. Bodle, *The Valley Forge Winter: Civilians and Soldiers in War* (2004).

W. Jeffrey Bolster, *Black Jacks: African American Seamen in the Age of Sail* (1998).

Edwin G. Burrows, *The Prisoners of New York* (2008).

Colin G. Calloway, *The American Revolution in Indian Country: Crisis and Diversity in Native American Communities* (1995).

E. Wayne Carp, *To Starve the Army at Pleasure: Continental Army Administration and American Political Culture, 1775–1783* (1984).

Elizabeth A. Fenn, *Pox Americana: The Great Smallpox Epidemic of 1775–1782* (2002).

David Hackett Fischer, *Washington's Crossing* (2004).

Joseph R. Fischer, *A Well-Executed Failure: The Sullivan Campaign against the Iroquois, July–September 1779* (1997).

Sylvia Frey, *The British Soldier in America: A Social History of Military Life in the Revolutionary Period* (1965).

Robert Gross, *The Minutemen and Their World* (1976).

Myra Jasanoff, *Liberty's Exiles: American Loyalists in the Revolutionary World* (2012).

Sidney Kaplan and Emma Nogrady Kaplan, *The Black Presence in the Era of the American Revolution* (1989).

Richard M. Ketchum, *Saratoga: Turning Point of America's Revolutionary War* (1997).

David G. Martin, *The Philadelphia Campaign: June 1777–1778* (2003).

James Kirby Martin, *Benedict Arnold, Revolutionary Hero: An American Warrior Reconsidered* (1997).

Holly A. Mayer, *Belonging to the Army: Camp Followers and Community during the American Revolution* (1996).

David McCullough, *1776* (2005).

Alfred F. Young, *Masquerade: The Life and Times of Deborah Sampson, Continental Soldier* (2004).

Chapter 8

GENERAL WORKS

Lance Banning, *The Sacred Fire of Liberty: James Madison and the Founding of the Federal Republic* (1995).

Gary B. Nash, *The Unknown American Revolution: The Unruly Birth of Democracy and the Struggle to Create America* (2006).

Peter S. Onuf and Cathy D. Matson, *A Union of Interests: Political and Economic Thought in Revolutionary America* (1990).

Jack Rakove, *Revolutionaries: A New History of the Invention of America* (2010).

Robert E. Shalhope, *The Roots of Democracy: American Thought and Culture, 1760–1800* (2004).

Alan Taylor, *The Divided Ground: Indians, Settlers, and the Northern Borderland of the American Revolution* (2006).

Gordon Wood, *The Creation of the American Republic, 1776–1787* (1969).

Alfred F. Young, ed., *Beyond the American Revolution: Explorations in the History of American Radicalism* (1993).

THE CONFEDERATION GOVERNMENT AND THE STATES

Daniel M. Friedenberg, *Life, Liberty, and the Pursuit of Land: The Plunder of Early America* (1992).

Marc W. Kruman, *Between Authority and Liberty: State Constitution Making in Revolutionary America* (1997).

Peter S. Onuf, *Statehood and Union: A History of the Northwest Ordinance* (1987).

Charles Rappleye, *Robert Morris, Financier of the American Revolution* (2010).

Jack N. Rakove, *The Beginnings of National Politics: An Interpretive History of the Continental Congress* (1979).

CITIZENSHIP

Ira Berlin, *Many Thousands Gone: The First Two Centuries of Slavery in North America* (1998).

Linda K. Kerber, *Women of the Republic: Intellect and Ideology in Revolutionary America* (1980).

Joanne Pope Melish, *Disowning Slavery: Gradual Emancipation and "Race" in New England, 1780–1860* (1998).

Gary B. Nash and Jean R. Sonderlund, *Freedom by Degrees: Emancipation in Pennsylvania and Its Aftermath* (1991).

Leonard L. Richards, *Shays's Rebellion: The American Revolution's Final Battle* (2002).

Marylynn Salmon, *Women and the Law of Property in Early America* (1986).

Rosemarie Zagarri, *A Woman's Dilemma: Mercy Otis Warren and the American Revolution* (1995).

THE CONSTITUTION AND RATIFICATION

John K. Alexander, *The Selling of the Constitutional Convention: A History of News Coverage* (1990).

Richard Beeman, *Plain, Honest Men: The Making of the American Constitution* (2010).

Carol Berkin, *A Brilliant Solution: Inventing the American Constitution* (2003).

Richard Brookhiser, *Gentleman Revolutionary: Gouverneur Morris, the Rake Who Wrote the Constitution* (2003).

Saul Cornell, *The Other Founders: Anti-Federalism and the Dissenting Tradition in America, 1788–1828* (1999).

Michael Allen Gillespie and Michael Lienesch, eds., *Ratifying the Constitution* (1989).

Woody Holton, *Unruly Americans and the Origins of the Constitution* (2007).

John P. Kaminski and Richard Leffler, *Federalists and Antifederalists: The Debate over the Constitution* (1998).

Leonard W. Levy, *The Establishment Clause: Religion and the First Amendment* (1994).

Pauline Maier, *Ratification: The People Debate the Constitution, 1787–1788* (2011).

Jackson Turner Main, *The Antifederalists: Critics of the Constitution, 1781–1788* (2006).

William Lee Miller, *The First Liberty: Religion and the American Republic* (1986).

Richard B. Morris, *Witnesses at the Creation: Hamilton, Madison, Jay, and the Constitution* (1985).

Jack N. Rakove, *Original Meanings: Politics and Ideas in the Making of the Constitution* (1996).

Chapter 9

POLITICS

Bernard Bailyn, *To Begin the World Anew: The Genius and Ambiguities of the American Founders* (2003).

Ron Chernow, *Alexander Hamilton* (2004).

Ron Chernow, *Washington: A Life* (2010).

Jerry A. Clouse, *The Whiskey Rebellion: Southwestern Pennsylvania's Frontier People Test the American Constitution* (1995).

Stanley Elkins and Eric McKitrick, *The Age of Federalism: The Early American Republic, 1788–1800* (1993).

Joseph J. Ellis, *American Creation: Triumphs and Tragedies in the Founding of the Republic* (2008).

Joseph J. Ellis, *Founding Brothers: The Revolutionary Generation* (2000).

Todd Estes, *The Jay Treaty Debate, Public Opinion, and the Evolution of Early American Political Culture* (2006).

John E. Ferling, *Adams vs. Jefferson: The Tumultuous Election of 1800* (2005).

John E. Ferling, *The Ascent of George Washington: The Hidden Political Genius of an American Icon* (2010).

David P. Geggus, ed., *The Impact of the Haitian Revolution in the Atlantic World* (2002).

David Patrick Geggus and Norman Fiering, eds., *The World of the Haitian Revolution* (2008).

Peter P. Hill, *French Perceptions of the Early American Republic, 1783–1793* (1988).

Ralph Ketcham, *Presidents above Party: The First American Presidency, 1789–1829* (1984).

David McCullough, *John Adams* (2001).

Jeffrey L. Pasley, *The Tyranny of Printers: Newspaper Politics in the Early American Republic* (2001).

Thomas P. Slaughter, *The Whiskey Rebellion: Frontier Epilogue to the American Revolution* (1986).

Larry E. Tise, *The American Counterrevolution: A Retreat from Liberty, 1783–1800* (1999).

Richard J. Twomey, *Jacobins and Jeffersonians: Anglo-American Radicalism in the United States, 1790–1820* (1989).

SOCIETY AND CULTURE

Susan Branson, *These Fiery Frenchified Dames: Women and Political Culture in Early National Philadelphia* (2001).

Richard D. Brown, *Knowledge Is Power: The Diffusion of Information in Early America, 1700–1865* (1989).

Nancy Cott, *The Bonds of Womanhood: Women's Sphere in New England, 1780–1835* (1997).

Joanne B. Freeman, *Affairs of Honor: National Politics in the New Republic* (2001).

Richard R. John, *Spreading the News: The American Postal System from Franklin to Morse* (1996).

Linda Kerber, *Women of the Republic: Intellect and Ideology in Revolutionary America* (1997).

Clare A. Lyons, *Sex among the Rabble: An Intimate History of Gender and Power in the Age of Revolution, Philadelphia, 1730–1830* (2006).

Bruce H. Mann, *Republic of Debtors: Bankruptcy in the Age of American Independence* (2002).

Simon P. Newman, *Parades and the Politics of the Street: Festive Culture in the Early American Republic* (2000).

Sheila L. Skemp, *Judith Sargent Murray: A Brief Biography with Documents* (1998).

David Waldstreicher, *In the Midst of Perpetual Fetes: The Making of American Nationalism, 1776–1820* (1997).

Rosemarie Zagarri, *Revolutionary Backlash: Women and Politics in the Early American Republic* (2007).

INDIANS AND THE FRONTIER

Andrew R. L. Cayton, *Frontier Republic: Ideology and Politics in the Ohio Country, 1780–1825* (1989).

Gregory E. Dowd, *A Spirited Resistance: The North American Indian Struggle for Unity, 1745–1815* (1992).

R. Douglas Hurt, *The Ohio Frontier: Crucible of the Old Northwest, 1720–1830* (1998).

Claudio Saunt, *A New Order of Things: Property, Power, and the Transformation of the Creek Indians, 1733–1816* (1999).

Chapter 10

POLITICS

Andrew Burstein and Nancy Isenberg, *Madison and Jefferson* (2010).

Saul Cornell, *The Other Founders: Anti-Federalism and the Dissenting Tradition in America, 1788–1828* (1999).

Joseph J. Ellis, *American Sphinx: The Character of Thomas Jefferson* (1997).

Joanne B. Freeman, *Affairs of Honor: National Politics in the New Republic* (2001).

Nancy Isenberg, *Fallen Founder: The Life of Aaron Burr* (2008).

Alexander Keyssar, *The Right to Vote: The Contested History of Democracy in the United States* (2000).

Peter J. Kastor, *The Nation's Crucible: The Louisiana Purchase and the Creation of America* (2004).

Edward J. Larson, *A Magnificent Catastrophe: The Tumultuous Election of 1800, America's First Presidential Campaign* (2007).

Jeffrey L. Pasley, Andrew W. Robertson, and David Waldstreicher, *Beyond the Founders: New Approaches to the Political History of the Early American Republic* (2003).

Sean Wilentz, *The Rise of American Democracy: Jefferson to Lincoln* (2005).

Richard Zacks, *The Pirate Coast: Thomas Jefferson, the First Marines, and the Secret Mission of 1805* (2006).

INDIANS, THE WAR OF 1812, AND THE WEST

Stephen E. Ambrose, *Undaunted Courage: Meriwether Lewis, Thomas Jefferson, and the Opening of the American West* (1996).

Carl Benn, *The Iroquois in the War of 1812* (1998).

James F. Brooks, *Captives and Cousins: Slavery, Kinship, and Community in the Southwest Borderlands* (2002).

Kathleen DuVal, *The Native Ground: Indians and Colonists in the Heart of the Continent* (2007).

Albert Furtwangler, *Acts of Discovery: Visions of America in the Lewis and Clark Journals* (1993).

Pekka Hämäläinen, *The Comanche Empire* (2009).

John Sugden, *Tecumseh: A Life* (1997).

Alan Taylor, *The Internal Enemy: Slavery and War in Virginia, 1772–1832* (2013).

Alan Taylor, *The Civil War of 1812: American Citizens, British Subjects, Irish Rebels, and Indian Allies* (2010).

Richard White, *The Middle Ground: Indians, Empires, and Republics in the Great Lakes Region, 1650–1815* (1991).

SLAVERY

Douglas Egerton, *Gabriel's Rebellion* (1993).

Annette Gordon-Reed, *The Hemingses of Monticello: An American Family* (2009).

James Oliver Horton and Lois E. Horton, *In Hope of Liberty: Culture, Community, and Protest among Northern Free Blacks, 1700–1860* (1997).

Gary B. Nash, *Forging Freedom: The Formation of Philadelphia's Black Community, 1720–1840* (1988).

Shane White, *Somewhat More Independent: The End of Slavery in New York City, 1710–1810* (1991).

WOMEN, MARRIAGE, AND RELIGION

Catherine Allgor, *Parlor Politics: In Which the Ladies of Washington Help Build a City and a Government* (2000).

Norma Basch, *Framing American Divorce: From the Revolutionary Generation to the Victorians* (1999).

Norma Basch, *In the Eyes of the Law: Women, Marriage, and Property in Nineteenth-Century New York* (1982).

Catherine A. Brekus, *Strangers and Pilgrims: Female Preaching in America, 1740–1845* (1998).

Nancy Cott, *Public Vows: A History of Marriage and the Nation* (2001).

Susan Juster, *Disorderly Women: Sexual Politics and Evangelicalism in Revolutionary New England* (1994).

Mary Kelley, *Learning to Stand and Speak: Women, Education, and Public Life in America's Republic* (2006).

Susan E. Klepp, *Revolutionary Conceptions: Women, Fertility, and Family Limitation in America, 1760–1820* (2009).

Mary Beth Sievens, *Stray Wives: Marital Conflict in Early National New England* (2005).

Chapter 11
THE MARKET REVOLUTION

Edward J. Balleisen, *Navigating Failure: Bankruptcy and Commercial Society in Antebellum America* (2001).

Mary H. Blewett, *Men, Women, and Work: Class, Gender, and Protest in the New England Shoe Industry, 1780–1910* (1988).

Jeanne Boydston, *Home and Work: Housework, Wages, and the Ideology of Labor in the Early Republic* (1990).

Thomas Dublin, *Transforming Women's Work: New England Lives in the Industrial Revolution* (1994).

John Lauritz Larson, *The Market Revolution in America: Liberty, Ambition, and the Eclipse of the Common Good* (2009).

Stephen Mihm, *A Nation of Counterfeiters: Capitalists, Con Men, and the Making of the United States* (2009).

Seth Rockman, *Scraping By: Wage Labor, Slavery, and Survival in Early Baltimore* (2008).

Charles G. Sellers, *The Market Revolution: Jacksonian America, 1815–1846* (1991).

Carol Sheriff, *The Artificial River: The Erie Canal and the Paradox of Progress, 1817–1862* (1996).

POLITICS

Andrew Burstein, *The Passions of Andrew Jackson* (2003).

John Ehle, *Trail of Tears: The Rise and Fall of the Cherokee Nation* (1997).

Daniel Walker Howe, *What Hath God Wrought: The Transformation of America, 1815–1845* (2009).

Jon Meacham, *American Lion: Andrew Jackson in the White House* (2009).

Sean Michael O'Brien, *In Bitterness and in Tears: Andrew Jackson's Destruction of the Creeks and Seminoles* (2003).

Theda Perdue, *Cherokee Women: Gender and Culture Change, 1700–1835* (1998).

Merrill D. Peterson, *The Great Triumvirate: Webster, Clay, and Calhoun* (1987).

Sean Wilentz, *The Rise of American Democracy, Jefferson to Lincoln* (2005).

CULTURE, RELIGION, AND REFORM

Bruce Dorsey, *Reforming Men and Women: Gender in the Antebellum City* (2002).

Lori D. Ginzberg, *Women and the Work of Benevolence: Morality, Politics, and Class in the Nineteenth-Century United States* (1990).

Nathan O. Hatch, *The Democratization of American Christianity* (1991).

Julie Roy Jeffrey, *The Great Silent Army of Abolitionism: Ordinary Women in the Antislavery Movement* (1998).

Richard R. John, *Spreading the News: The American Postal System from Franklin to Morse* (1995).

Catherine E. Kelly, *In the New England Fashion: Reshaping Women's Lives in the Nineteenth Century* (1999).

Bruce Laurie, *Beyond Garrison: Antislavery and Social Reform* (2005).

Gerda Lerner, *The Grimké Sisters from South Carolina: Pioneers for Women's Rights and Abolition* (2009).

Richard S. Newman, *The Transformation of American Abolitionism: Fighting Slavery in the Early Republic* (2002).

Mark Perry, *Lift Up Thy Voice: The Grimké Family's Journey from Slaveholders to Civil Rights Leaders* (2002).

Alisse Portnoy, *Their Right to Speak: Women's Activism in the Indian and Slave Debates* (2005).

Patrick Rael, *Black Identity and Black Protest in the Antebellum North* (2002).

Stacey M. Robertson, *Hearts Beating for Liberty: Women Abolitionists in the Old Northwest* (2010).

Scott A. Sandage, *Born Losers: A History of Failure in America* (2005).

Kathryn Kish Sklar and James Brewer Stewart, *Women's Rights and Transatlantic Slavery in the Era of Emancipation* (2007).

Richard B. Stott, *Jolly Fellows: Male Milieus in Mid-Nineteenth Century America* (2009).

Daniel S. Wright, *"The First of Causes to Our Sex": The Female Moral Reform Movement in the Antebellum Northeast, 1834–1848* (2006).

Ronald J. Zboray, *Literary Dollars and Social Sense: A People's History of the Mass Market Book* (2005).

Chapter 12

THE ECONOMY AND FREE LABOR

Jeanne Boydston, *Home and Work: Housework, Wages, and the Ideology of Labor in the Early Republic* (1990).

J. Matthew Gallman, *Receiving Erin's Children: Philadelphia, Liverpool, and the Irish Famine Migration, 1854–1855* (2000).

Jonathan A. Glickstein, *Concepts of Free Labor in the Antebellum United States* (1991).

Donald R. Hoke, *Ingenious Yankees: The Rise of the American System of Manufactures in the Private Sector* (1990).

Jonathan Hughes and Louis P. Cain, *American Economic History* (2011).

Robert A. Margo, *Wages and Labor Markets in the United States, 1820–1860* (2000).

David R. Meyer, *The Roots of American Industrialization* (2003).

Scott A. Sandage, *Born Losers: A History of Failure in America* (2005).

Kenneth J. Winkle, *The Young Eagle: The Rise of Abraham Lincoln* (2001).

WESTWARD EXPANSION AND THE MEXICAN-AMERICAN WAR

Gary Anderson, *The Conquest of Texas: Ethnic Cleansing in the Promised Land, 1820–1875* (2005).

Juliana Barr, *Peace Came in the Form of a Woman: Indians and Spaniards in the Texas Borderlands* (2007).

Peter J. Blodgett, *Land of Golden Dreams: California in the Gold Rush Decade, 1848–1858* (1999).

H. W. Brand, *Lone Star Nation* (2004).

Richard L. Bushman, *Joseph Smith: Rough Stone Rolling* (2005).

David C. Clary, *Eagles and Empire: The United States, Mexico, and the Struggle for a Continent* (2009).

Christopher Corbett, *The Poker Bride: The First Chinese in the Wild West* (2009).

David Dary, *The Oregon Trail: An American Saga* (2004).

Brian DeLay, *War of a Thousand Deserts: Indian Raids and the U.S.-Mexican War* (2008).

Jared Farmer, *On Zion's Mount: Mormons, Indians, and the American Landscape* (2008).

Paul W. Foos, *A Short, Offhand, Killing Affair: Soldiers and Social Conflict during the Mexican-American War* (2002).

Sarah Barringer Gordon, *The Mormon Question: Polygamy and Constitutional Conflict in Nineteenth-Century America* (2002).

Amy S. Greenberg, *Manifest Manhood and the Antebellum American Empire* (2005).

———*A Wicked War: Polk, Clay, Lincoln and the 1846 U.S. Invasion of Mexico* (2013).

Timothy J. Henderson, *A Glorious Defeat: Mexico and Its War with the United States* (2007).

Albert Hurtado, *John Sutter: A Life on the North American Frontier* (2006).

Benjamin Heber Johnson, *Revolution in Texas: How a Forgotten Rebellion and Its Bloody Suppression Turned Mexicans into Americans* (2003).

Susan Lee Johnson, *Roaring Camp: The Social World of the California Gold Rush* (2000).

Kent G. Lightfoot, *Indians, Missionaries, and Merchants: The Legacy of Colonial Encounters on the California Frontier* (2005).

Robert W. Merry, *A Country of Vast Designs: James K. Polk, the Mexican War, and the Conquest of the American Continent* (2009).

Gregory H. Nobles, *American Frontiers: Cultural Encounters and Continental Conquest* (1997).

Andres Resendez, *Changing National Identities at the Frontier: Texas and New Mexico, 1800–1850* (2005).

Malcolm Rohrbough, *Days of Gold: The California Gold Rush and the American Nation* (1997).

James A. Sandos, *Converting California: Indians and Franciscans in the Missions* (2004).

Virginia Scharff and Carolyn Brucken, *Home Lands: How Women Made the West* (2010).

Joel H. Sibley, *Storm over Texas: The Annexation Controversy and the Road to Civil War* (2005).

Michael L. Tate, *Indians and Emigrants: Encounters on the Overland Trail* (2006).

John G. Turner, *Brigham Young: Pioneer Prophet* (2012).

Richard White, *"It's Your Misfortune and None of My Own": A New History of the American West* (1993).

Richard Bruce Winders, *Mr. Polk's Army: The American Military Experience in the Mexican War* (1997).

Steven E. Woodworth, *Manifest Destinies: America's Westward Expansion and the Road to Civil War* (2010).

ANTEBELLUM CULTURE AND REFORM

Bruce Dorsey, *Reforming Men and Women: Gender in the Antebellum City* (2002).

Lori D. Ginzberg, *Elizabeth Cady Stanton: An American Life* (2009).

Bruce Laurie, *Beyond Garrison: Antislavery and Social Reform* (2005).

Sally McMillen, *Seneca Falls and the Origins of the Women's Rights Movement* (2008).

Patrick Rael, *Black Identity and Black Protest in the Antebellum North* (2002).

Susan M. Ryan, *The Grammar of Good Intentions: Race and the Antebellum Culture of Benevolence* (2003).

Beth A. Salerno, *Sister Societies: Women's Antislavery Organizations in Antebellum America* (2005).

Susan Zaeske, *Signatures of Citizenship: Petitioning, Antislavery, and Women's Political Identity* (2003).

Chapter 13
SLAVEHOLDERS AND THE ECONOMY

Edward E. Baptist, *Creating an Old South: Middle Florida's Plantation Frontier before the Civil War* (2002).

David L. Carlton and Peter A. Coclanis, *The South, the Nation, and the World: Perspectives on Southern Economic Development* (2003).

Steven Deyle, *Carry Me Back: The Domestic Slave Trade in American Life* (2005).

Richard Follett, *The Sugar Masters: Planters and Slaves in Louisiana's Cane World, 1820–1860* (2005).

Walter Johnson, *River of Dark Dreams: Slavery and Empire in the Cotton South* (2013).

Aaron W. Marrs, *Railroads in the Old South: Pursuing Progress in a Slave Society* (2009).

Jonathan Martin, *Divided Mastery: Slave Hiring in the American South* (2004).

James David Miller, *South by Southwest: Planter Emigration and Identity in the Slave South* (2002).

Gavin Wright, *Slavery and American Economic Development* (2006).

SLAVES, SLAVERY, AND RACE RELATIONS

Ira Berlin, *Generations of Captivity: A History of African-American Slaves* (2003).

Thomas C. Buchanan, *Black Life on the Mississippi: Slaves, Free Blacks, and the Western Steamboat World* (2004).

Diane Mutti Burke, *On Slavery's Border: Missouri's Small-Slaveholding Households, 1815–1865* (2011).

Stephanie M. H. Camp, *Closer to Freedom: Enslaved Women and Everyday Resistance in the Plantation South* (2004).

Erskine Clarke, *Dwelling Place: A Plantation Epic* (2005).

Sylvia R. Frey and Betty Wood, *Come Shouting to Zion: African American Protestantism in the American South and British Caribbean to 1830* (1998).

Sharla Fett, *Working Cures: Healing, Health, and Power on Southern Slave Plantations* (2002).

Kenneth S. Greenberg, ed., *Nat Turner: A Slave Rebellion in History and Memory* (2003).

Eugene D. Genovese, *Roll, Jordan, Roll: The World the Slave Made* (1974).

Kenneth S. Greenberg, ed., *Nat Turner: A Slave Rebellion in History and Memory* (2002).

Gwendolyn Midlo Hall, *Slavery and African Ethnicities in the Americas: Restoring the Links* (2005).

Anthony E. Kaye, *Joining Places: Slave Neighborhoods in the Old South* (2007).

Tiya Miles, *Ties that Bind: The Story of an Afro-Cherokee Family in Slavery and Freedom* (2005).

Sydney Nathans, *To Free a Family: The Journey of Mary Walker* (2012).

Dylan C. Penningroth, *The Claims of Kinfolk: African American Property and Community in the Nineteenth-Century South* (2003).

Larry Eugene Rivers, *Rebels and Runaways: Slave Resistance in Nineteenth-Century Florida* (2012).

Brenda E. Stevenson, *Life in Black and White: Family and Community in the Slave South* (1996).

Leonard Todd, *Carolina Clay: The Life and Legend of the Slave Potter Dave* (2008).

SOCIETY AND CULTURE

Ira Berlin, *Slaves without Masters: The Free Negro in the Antebellum South* (1974).

Charles C. Bolton and Scott P. Culclasure, eds., *The Confessions of Edward Isham: A Poor White Life of the Old South* (1998).

Christine Jacobson Carter, *Southern Single Blessedness: Unmarried Women in the Urban South, 1800–1865* (2006).

Laura F. Edwards, *The People and Their Peace: Legal Culture and the Transformation of Inequality in the Post-Revolutionary South* (2009).

Craig T. Friend and Lorri Glover, eds., *Southern Manhood: Perspectives on Masculinity in the Old South* (2004).

Steven Hahn, *The Roots of Southern Populism: Yeoman Farmers and the Transformation of the Georgia Upcountry, 1850–1890* (1983).

Christine Leigh Heyrman, *Southern Cross: The Beginnings of the Bible Belt* (1997).

Charles F. Irons, *The Origins of Proslavery Christianity: White and Black Evangelicals in Colonial and Antebellum Virginia* (2008).

Anya Jabour, *Scarlett's Sisters: Young Women in the Old South* (2007).

Michael P. Johnson and James L. Roark, *Black Masters: A Free Family of Color in the Old South* (1984).

Stephanie McCurry, *Masters of Small Worlds: Yeoman Households, Gender Relations, and the Political Culture of the Antebellum South* (1995).

Glenn McNair, *Criminal Injustice: Slaves and Free Blacks in Georgia's Criminal Justice System* (2009).

Seth Rockman, *Scraping By: Wage Labor, Slavery, and Survival in Early Baltimore* (2009).

Adam Rothman, *Slave Country: American Expansion and the Deep South* (2005).

Joshua D. Rothman, *Notorious in the Neighborhood: Sex and Families across the Color Line in Virginia, 1787–1861* (2002).

Loren Schweninger, *Families in Crisis in the Old South: Divorce, Slavery, and the Law* (2012).

Jonathan Daniel Wells, *Origins of the Southern Middle Class, 1800–1861* (2004).

Eva Sheppard Wolf, *Almost Free: A Story about Family and Race in Antebellum Virginia* (2012).

Bertram Wyatt-Brown, *Southern Honor: Ethics and Behavior in the Old South* (1982).

Jeffrey Robert Young, *Domesticating Slavery: The Master Class in Georgia and South Carolina, 1670–1837* (1999).

POLITICS AND POLITICAL CULTURE

Anthony Gene Carey, *Parties, Slavery, and the Union in Antebellum Georgia* (1997).

William J. Cooper Jr., *Liberty and Slavery: Southern Politics to 1860* (1983).

Lacy K. Ford Jr., *Deliver Us from Evil: The Slavery Question in the Old South* (2009).

Michael Perman, *Pursuit of Unity: A Political History of the American South* (2009).

Elizabeth R. Varon, *We Mean to Be Counted: White Women and Politics in Antebellum Virginia* (1998).

Peter Wallenstein, *From Slave South to New South: Public Policy in Nineteenth-Century Georgia* (1987).

Chapter 14

GENERAL WORKS

Don E. Fehrenbacher, *The Slaveholding Republic: An Account of the United States Government's Relations to Slavery* (2001).

Michael Holt, *Fate of Their Country: Politicians, Slavery Extension, and the Coming of the Civil War* (2004).

Bruce C. Levine, *Half Slave and Half Free: The Roots of the Civil War* (1992).

James M. McPherson, *Ordeal by Fire: The Civil War and Reconstruction* (1982).

David M. Potter, *The Impending Crisis: America Before the Civil War, 1848–1861* (2011).

Mark E. Neely, *Boundaries of American Political Culture in the Civil War Era* (2005).

Eric H. Walther, *The Shattering of the Union: America in the 1850s* (2004).

Sean Wilentz, *The Rise of American Democracy: Jefferson to Lincoln* (2005).

NORTHERN SECTIONALISM

Tom Chaffin, *Pathfinder: John Charles Frémont and the Course of American Empire* (2002).

Rodney O. Davis and Douglas L. Wilson, eds., *The Lincoln-Douglas Debates* (2008).

Eric Foner, *Free Labor, Free Soil, Free Men: The Ideology of the Republican Party before the Civil War* (1970).

William E. Gienapp, *The Origins of the Republican Party, 1852–1856* (1987).

R. Blakeslee Gilpin, *John Brown Still Lives! America's Long Reckoning with Violence, Equality, and Change* (2011).

Susan-Mary Grant, *North over South: Northern Nationalism and American Identity in the Antebellum Era* (2000).

David Grimsted, *American Mobbing, 1828–1865: Toward Civil War* (1998).

Joan D. Hedrick, *Harriet Beecher Stowe: A Life* (1994).

Pamela Herr, *Jessie Benton Frémont: A Biography* (1987).

Nancy Isenberg, *Sex and Citizenship in Antebellum America* (1998).

David S. Reynolds, *John Brown, Abolitionist: The Man Who Killed Slavery, Sparked the Civil War, and Seeded Civil Rights* (2005).

Leonard L. Richards, *The California Gold Rush and the Coming of the Civil War* (2007).

Brian Schoen, *The Fragile Fabric of Union: Cotton Federal Politics, and the Global Origins of the Civil War* (2009).

James Brewer Stewart, *Wendell Phillips, Liberty's Hero* (1986).

Wendy Hamand Venet, *Neither Ballots nor Bullets: Women Abolitionists and the Civil War* (1991).

Douglas L. Wilson, *Honor's Voice: The Transformation of Abraham Lincoln* (1998).

Kenneth J. Winkle, *The Young Eagle: The Rise of Abraham Lincoln* (2001).

SOUTHERN SECTIONALISM

Robert E. Bonner, *Mastering America: Southern Slaveholders and the Crisis of American Nationhood* (2009).

William J. Cooper Jr., *The South and the Politics of Slavery, 1828–1856* (1978).

John Patrick Daly, *When Slavery Was Called Freedom: Evangelicalism, Proslavery, and the Causes of the Civil War* (2002).

Lacy K. Ford Jr., *Origins of Southern Radicalism: The South Carolina Upcountry, 1800–1860* (1988).

William W. Freehling, *The Road to Disunion*, 2 vols. (1990-2007).

Matthew Pratt Guterl, *American Mediterranean: Southern Slaveholders in the Age of Emancipation* (2008).

David S. Heidler and Jeanne T. Heidler, *Henry Clay: The Essential American* (2010).

William A. Link, *Roots of Secession: Slavery and Politics in Antebellum Virginia* (2002).

Robert E. May, *Manifest Destiny's Underworld: Filibustering in Antebellum America* (2002).

Christopher J. Olsen, *Political Culture and Secession in Mississippi: Masculinity, Honor, and the Antiparty Tradition, 1830–1860* (2002).

Edward Rugemer, *The Problem of Emancipation: The Caribbean Roots of the American Civil War* (2008).

Manisha Sinha, *The Counterrevolution of Slavery: Politics and Ideology in Antebellum South Carolina* (2000).

Mitchell Snay, *Gospel of Disunion: Religion and Separatism in the Antebellum South* (1993).

SECESSION

Shearer Davis Bowman, *At the Precipice: Americans North and South during the Secession Crisis* (2010).

Daniel Crofts, *Reluctant Confederates: Upper South Unionists in the Secession Crisis* (1989).

Charles B. Dew, *Apostles of Disunion: Southern Secession Commissioners and the Causes of the Civil War* (2001).

Michael P. Johnson, *Toward a Patriarchal Republic: The Secession of Georgia* (1977).

Russell McClintock, *Lincoln and the Decision for War: The Northern Response to Secession* (2008).

David M. Potter, *Lincoln and His Party in the Secession Crisis* (1942).

Lorman A. Ratner and Dwight L. Teeter Jr., *Fanatics and Fire-Eaters: Newspapers and the Coming of the Civil War* (2003).

Chapter 15

GENERAL WORKS

Orville Vernon Burton, *The Age of Lincoln* (2007).

Allen C. Guelzo, *A New History of the Civil War and Reconstruction* (2012).

James M. McPherson, *The Battle Cry of Freedom: The Civil War Era* (1988).

Scott Nelson and Carol Sheriff, *A People at War: Civilians and Soldiers in America's Civil War* (2007).

Adam I. P. Smith, *The American Civil War* (2007).

MILITARY HISTORY

Michael J. Bennett, *Union Jacks: Yankee Sailors in the Civil War* (2004).

Mark Grimsley, *The Hard Hand of War: Union Military Policy toward Southern Civilians, 1861–1865* (1995).

Joseph T. Glatthaar, *General Lee's Army: From Victory to Collapse* (2008).

Chandra Manning, *What This Cruel War Was Over: Soldiers, Slavery, and the Civil War* (2007).

James M. McPherson, *Tried by War: Abraham Lincoln as Commander in Chief* (2008).

Mark E. Neely Jr., *The Civil War and the Limits of Destruction* (2007).

Brooks D. Simpson, *Ulysses S. Grant: Triumph over Adversity, 1822–1865* (2000).

Donald Stoker, *The Grand Design: Strategy and the U.S. Civil War* (2010).

Daniel E. Sutherland, *A Savage Conflict: The Decisive Role of Guerrillas in the American Civil War* (2009).

William G. Thomas, *The Iron Way: Railroads, the Civil War, and the Making of Modern America* (2011).

Joan Waugh, *U.S. Grant: American Hero, American Myth* (2009).

Russell F. Weigley, *A Great Civil War: A Military and Political History, 1861–1865* (2000).

John Fabian Witt, *Lincoln's Code: The Laws of War* (2012)

THE NORTH AND SOUTH AT WAR

Stephen V. Ash, *When the Yankees Came: Conflict and Chaos in the Occupied South, 1861–1865* (1995).

Iver Bernstein, *The New York City Draft Riots: Their Significance for American Society and Politics in the Age of the Civil War* (1990).

William A. Blair, *Virginia's Private War: Feeding Body and Soul in the Confederacy, 1861–1865* (1998).

Victoria E. Bynum, *The Long Shadow of the Civil War: Southern Dissent and Its Legacies* (2010).

William J. Cooper, *Jefferson Davis, American* (2000).

Alice Fahs, *The Imagined Civil War: Popular Literature of the North and South, 1861–1865* (2001).

Drew Gilpin Faust, *This Republic of Suffering: Death and the American Civil War* (2008).

William W. Freehling, *The South vs. the South: How Anti-Confederate Southerners Shaped the Course of the Civil War* (2001).

Gary W. Gallagher, *The Confederate War* (1997).

Judith Ann Giesberg, *Civil War Sisterhood: The U.S. Sanitary Commission and Women's Politics in Transition* (2000).

William C. Harris, *Lincoln and the Border States: Preserving the Union* (2012).

Libra R. Hilde, *Worth a Dozen Men: Women and Nursing in the Civil War South* (2012).

Jacqueline Jones, *Saving Savannah: The City and the Civil War* (2008).

Bruce Levine, *The Fall of the House of Dixie: The Civil War and the Social Revolution that Transformed the South* (2013).

Stephanie McCurry, *Confederate Reckoning: Power and Politics in the Civil War* (2010).

Mark E. Neely Jr., *The Fate of Liberty: Abraham Lincoln and Civil Liberties* (1991).

Megan Kate Nelson, *Ruin Nation: Destruction and the American Civil War* (2012).

Mark A. Noll, *The Civil War as a Theological Crisis* (2006).

George C. Rable, *God's Almost Chosen People: A Religious History of the American Civil War* (2010).

Heather Cox Richardson, *The Greatest Nation of the Earth: Republican Economic Policies during the Civil War* (1997).

James L. Roark, *Masters without Slaves: Southern Planters in the Civil War and Reconstruction* (1977).

Anne Sarah Rubin, *A Shattered Nation: The Rise and Fall of the Confederacy, 1861–1868* (2005).

Mark S. Schantz, *Awaiting the Heavenly Country: The Civil War and America's Culture of Death* (2008).

Nina Silber, *Daughters of the Union: Northern Women Fight the Civil War* (2006).

Walter Stahr, *Seward: Lincoln's Indispensable Man* (2012).

Yael A. Sternhell, *Routes of War: The World of Movement in the Confederate South* (2012).

Margaret M. Storey, *Loyalty and Loss: Alabama's Unionists in the Civil War and Reconstruction* (2004).

Harry S. Stout, *Upon the Altar of the Nation: A Moral History of the American Civil War* (2006).

Amy Murrell Taylor, *The Divided Family in Civil War America* (2005).

Jennifer L. Weber, *Copperheads: The Rise and Fall of Lincoln's Opponents in the North* (2008).

THE STRUGGLE FOR FREEDOM

Ira Berlin et al., eds., *Freedom: A Documentary History of Emancipation, 1861–1867,* 5 vols. (1982–2008).

Eric Foner, *The Fiery Trial: Abraham Lincoln and American Slavery* (2010).

Joseph T. Glatthaar, *Forged in Battle: The Civil War Alliance of Black Soldiers and White Officers* (1990).

William B. Gould IV, ed., *Diary of a Contraband: The Civil War Passage of a Black Sailor* (2002).

Allen C. Guelzo, *Lincoln's Emancipation Proclamation: The End of Slavery in America* (2004).

Steven Hahn, *The Political Worlds of Slavery and Freedom* (2009).

Bruce Levine, *Confederate Emancipation: Southern Plans to Free and Arm Slaves during the Civil War* (2006).

William S. McFeely, *Frederick Douglass* (1991).

James Oakes, *The Radical and the Republican: Frederick Douglass, Abraham Lincoln, and the Triumph of Antislavery Politics* (2007).

Chapter 16

GENERAL WORKS

Thomas J. Brown, ed., *Reconstructions: New Perspectives on the Postbellum United States* (2006).

Michael W. Fitzgerald, *Splendid Failure: Postwar Reconstruction in the American South* (2007).

Eric Foner, *Reconstruction: America's Unfinished Revolution* (1988).

James M. McPherson, *Ordeal by Fire: The Civil War and Reconstruction* (3rd ed., 2000).

THE MEANING OF FREEDOM

Ira Berlin et al., eds., *Freedom: A Documentary History of Emancipation, 1861–1867*, 5 vols. (1982–2008).

Ronald E. Butchart, *Schooling the Freed People: Teaching, Learning, and the Struggle for Black Freedom, 1861–1876* (2010).

Jim Downs, *Sick for Freedom: African-American Illness and Suffering during the Civil War and Reconstruction* (2012).

John Hope Franklin and Loren Schweninger, *In Search of the Promised Land: A Slave Family in the Old South* (2006).

Thavolia Glymph, *Out of the House of Bondage: The Transformation of the Plantation Household* (2008).

Steven Hahn, *A Nation under Our Feet: Black Political Struggles in the Rural South, from Slavery to the Great Migration* (2003).

Leon F. Litwack, *Been in the Storm So Long: The Aftermath of Slavery* (1979).

Susan Eva O'Donovan, *Becoming Free in the Cotton South* (2007).

Joshua Paddison, *American Heathens: Religion, Race, and Reconstruction in California* (2012).

Howard N. Rabinowitz, *Race Relations in the Urban South, 1865–1890* (1978).

Roger L. Ransom and Richard Sutch, *One Kind of Freedom: The Economic Consequences of Emancipation* (1977).

Leslie Schwalm, *A Hard Fight for We: Women's Transition from Slavery to Freedom in South Carolina* (1997).

Loren Schweninger, *James T. Rapier and Reconstruction* (1978).

Rebecca J. Scott, *Degrees of Freedom: Louisiana and Cuba after Slavery* (2005).

Clarence E. Walker, *A Rock in a Weary Land: The African Methodist Episcopal Church during the Civil War and Reconstruction* (1982).

THE POLITICS OF RECONSTRUCTION

Richard F. Bensel, *Yankee Leviathan: The Origins of Central State Authority in America, 1859–1877* (1990).

Philip Dray, *Capitol Men: The Epic Story of Reconstruction Through the Lives of the First Black Congressmen* (2008).

Ellen Carol DuBois, *Feminism and Suffrage: The Emergence of an Independent Women's Movement in America, 1848–1869* (1978).

Laura Edwards, *Gendered Strife and Confusion: The Political Culture of Reconstruction* (1997).

James K. Hogue, *Uncivil War: Five New Orleans Street Battles and the Rise and Fall of Radical Reconstruction* (2006).

Richard L. Hume and Jerry B. Gough, *Blacks, Carpetbaggers, and Scalawags: The Constitutional Conventions of Radical Reconstruction* (2008).

Heather Cox Richardson, *The Death of Reconstruction: Race, Labor, and Politics in the Post–Civil War North, 1865–1901* (2001).

Leslie A. Schwalm, *Emancipation's Diaspora: Race and Reconstruction in the Upper Midwest* (2009).

Brooks D. Simpson, *The Reconstruction Presidents* (1998).

Mark Wahlgren Summers, *A Dangerous Stir: Fear, Paranoia, and the Making of Reconstruction* (2009).

Michael Vorenberg, *Final Freedom: The Civil War, the Abolition of Slavery, and the Thirteenth Amendment* (2001).

C. Vann Woodward, *Reunion and Reaction: The Compromise of 1877 and the End of Reconstruction* (1951).

THE STRUGGLE IN THE SOUTH

James Alex Baggett, *The Scalawags: Southern Dissenters in the Civil War and Reconstruction* (2003).

Nancy D. Bercaw, *Gendered Freedoms: Race, Rights, and the Politics of Household in the Delta, 1861–1875* (2003).

Stephen Budiansky, *The Bloody Shirt: Terror After the Civil War* (2008).

Jane Turner Censer, *The Reconstruction of White Southern Womanhood, 1865–1895* (2003).

Paul A. Cimbala, *Under the Guardianship of the Nation: The Freedmen's Bureau and the Reconstruction of Georgia, 1865–1870* (1997).

Jane E. Dailey, *Before Jim Crow: The Politics of Race in Post-emancipation Virginia* (2000).

Sarah E. Gardner, *Blood and Irony: Southern White Women's Narratives of the Civil War, 1861–1937* (2004).

Carole Faulkner, *Women's Radical Reconstruction: The Freedmen's Aid Movement* (2004).

Moon-Ho Jung, *Coolies and Cane: Race, Labor, and Sugar in the Age of Emancipation* (2006).

Stephen Kantrowitz, *Ben Tillman and the Reconstruction of White Supremacy* (2000).

Charles Lane, *The Day Freedom Died: The Colfax Massacre, the Supreme Court, and the Betrayal of Reconstruction* (2008).

Amy Feely Morsman, *The Big House After Slavery: Virginian Plantation Families and Their Postbellum Domestic Experiences* (2010).

George C. Rable, *But There Was No Peace: The Role of Violence in the Politics of Reconstruction* (1984).

James L. Roark, *Masters without Slaves: Southern Planters in the Civil War and Reconstruction* (1977).

Hannah Rosen, *Terror in the Heart of Freedom: Citizenship, Sexual Violence, and the Meaning of Race in the Postemancipation South* (2009).

Hyman Rubin III, *South Carolina Scalawags* (2006).

Christopher M. Span, *From Cotton Field to Schoolhouse: African American Education in Mississippi, 1862–1875* (2009).

Peter Wallenstein, *From Slave South to New South: Public Policy in Nineteenth-Century Georgia* (1987).

Glossary

Acoma pueblo revolt Revolt against the Spaniards by Indians living at the Acoma pueblo in 1599. Juan de Oñate violently suppressed the uprising, but the Indians revolted again later that year, after which many Spanish settlers returned to Mexico.

Agent Orange Herbicide used extensively during the Vietnam War to destroy the Vietcong's jungle hideouts and food supply. Its use was later linked to a wide range of illnesses that veterans and the Vietnamese suffered after the war, including birth defects, cancer, and skin disorders.

Agricultural Adjustment Act (AAA) New Deal legislation passed in May 1933 aimed at cutting agricultural production and raising crop prices and, consequently, farmers' income. Through the "domestic allotment plan," the AAA paid farmers to not grow crops.

Algonquian Indians People who inhabited the coastal plain of present-day Virginia, near the Chesapeake Bay, when English colonists first settled the region.

Alien and Sedition Acts 1798 laws passed to suppress political dissent. The Sedition Act criminalized conspiracy and criticism of government leaders. The two Alien Acts extended the waiting period for citizenship and empowered the president to deport or imprison without trial any foreigner deemed a danger.

American Colonization Society An organization dedicated to sending freed slaves and other black Americans to Liberia in West Africa. Although some African Americans cooperated with the movement, others campaigned against segregation and discrimination.

American Expeditionary Force (AEF) American armed forces under the command of General John Pershing who fought under a separate American command in Europe during World War I. They helped defeat Germany when they entered the conflict in full force in 1918.

American Federation of Labor (AFL) Organization created by Samuel Gompers in 1886 that coordinated the activities of craft unions throughout the United States. The AFL worked to achieve immediate benefits for skilled workers. Its narrow goals for unionism became popular after the Haymarket bombing.

American Indian Movement (AIM) Organization established in 1968 to address the problems Indians faced in American cities, including poverty and police harassment. AIM organized Indians to end relocation and termination policies and to win greater control over their cultures and communities.

American system The practice of manufacturing and then assembling interchangeable parts. A system that spread quickly across American industries, the use of standardized parts allowed American manufacturers to employ cheap unskilled workers.

American Temperance Society Organization founded in 1826 by Lyman Beecher that linked drinking with poverty, idleness, ill-health, and violence. Temperance lecturers traveled the country gaining converts to the cause. The temperance movement had considerable success, contributing to a sharp drop in American alcohol consumption.

Americans with Disabilities Act (ADA) Legislation signed by President George H. W. Bush in 1990 that banned discrimination against the disabled. The law also required handicapped accessibility in public facilities and private businesses.

Antifederalists Opponents of ratification of the Constitution. Antifederalists feared that a powerful and distant central government would be out of touch with the needs of citizens. They also complained that the Constitution failed to guarantee individual liberties in a bill of rights.

antinomians Individuals who believed that Christians could be saved by faith alone and did not need to act in accordance with God's law as set forth in the Bible. Puritan leaders considered this belief to be a heresy.

Apollo program Project initiated by John F. Kennedy in 1961 to surpass the Soviet Union in space exploration and send a man to the moon.

appeasement British strategy aimed at avoiding a war with Germany in the late 1930s by not objecting to Hitler's policy of territorial expansion.

Archaic Indians Hunting and gathering peoples that descended from Paleo-Indians and dominated the Americas from 10,000 BP to between 4000 and 3000 BP, approximately.

Articles of Confederation The written document defining the structure of the government from 1781 to 1788 under which the union was a confederation of equal states, with no executive and limited powers, existing mainly to foster a common defense.

baby boom The surge in the American birthrate between 1945 and 1965, which peaked in 1957 with 4.3 million births. The baby boom both reflected and promoted Americans' postwar prosperity.

Bacon's Rebellion An unsuccessful rebellion against the colonial government in 1676, led by frontier settler Nathaniel Bacon, that arose when increased violence between Indians and colonists pushing westward was met with government refusal to protect settlers or allow them to settle Indian lands.

Barbados Colonized in the 1630s, this island in the British West Indies became an enormous sugar producer and a source of wealth for England. The island's African slaves quickly became a majority of the island's population despite the deadliness of their work.

battle of Antietam Battle fought in Maryland on September 17, 1862, between the Union forces of George McClellan and Confederate troops of Robert E. Lee. The battle, a Union victory that left 6,000 dead and 17,000 wounded, was the bloodiest day of the war.

battle of Bull Run (Manassas) First major battle of the Civil War, fought at a railroad junction in northern Virginia on July 21, 1861. The Union suffered a sobering defeat, while the Confederates felt affirmed in their superiority and the inevitability of Confederate nationhood.

battle of Bunker Hill Second battle of the Revolutionary War, on June 16, 1775, involving a massive British attack on New England militia units on a hill facing Boston. The militiamen finally yielded the hill, but not before inflicting heavy casualties on the British.

battle of Gettysburg Battle fought at Gettysburg, Pennsylvania (July 1–3, 1863), between Union forces under General Meade and Confederate forces under General Lee. The Union emerged victorious, and Lee lost more than one-third of his men. Together with Vicksburg, Gettysburg marked a major turning point in the Civil War.

Battle of the Little Big Horn 1876 battle begun when American cavalry under George Armstrong Custer attacked an encampment of Indians who refused to remove to a reservation. Indian warriors led by Crazy Horse and Sitting Bull annihilated the American soldiers, but their victory was short-lived.

battle of Long Island First major engagement of the new Continental army, defending against 45,000 British troops newly arrived on western Long Island (today Brooklyn). The Continentals retreated, with high casualties and many taken prisoner.

Battle of Midway June 3–6, 1942, naval battle in the Central Pacific in which American forces surprised and defeated the Japanese who had been massing an invasion force aimed at Midway Island. The battle put the Japanese at a disadvantage for the rest of the war.

battle of New Orleans The final battle in the War of 1812, fought and won by General Andrew Jackson and his militiamen against the much larger British army in New Orleans. The celebrated battle made no difference since the peace had already been negotiated.

battle of Oriskany A punishing defeat for Americans in a ravine named Oriskany near Fort Stanwix in New York in August 1777. German American militiamen aided by allied Oneida warriors were ambushed by Mohawk and Seneca Indians, and 500 on the revolutionary side were killed.

battle of Saratoga A multistage battle in New York ending with the decisive defeat and surrender of British general John Burgoyne on October 17, 1777. France was convinced by this victory to throw its official support to the American side in the war.

battle of Shiloh Battle at Shiloh Church, Tennessee, on April 6–7, 1862, between Albert Sidney Johnston's Confederate forces and Ulysses S. Grant's Union army. The Union army ultimately prevailed, though at great cost to both sides. Shiloh ruined the Confederacy's bid to control the war in the West.

battle of Tippecanoe An attack on Shawnee Indians at Prophetstown on the Tippecanoe River in 1811 by American forces headed by William Henry Harrison, Indiana's territorial governor. The Prophet Tenskwatawa fled with his followers. Tecumseh, his brother, deepened his resolve to make war on the United States.

battle of Yorktown October 1781 battle that sealed American victory in the Revolutionary War. American troops and a French fleet trapped the British army under the command of General Charles Cornwallis at Yorktown, Virginia.

Bay of Pigs Failed U.S.-sponsored invasion of Cuba by anti-Castro forces in 1961 who planned to overthrow Fidel Castro's government. The disaster humiliated Kennedy and the United States. It alienated Latin Americans who saw the invasion as another example of Yankee imperialism.

Beringia The land bridge between Siberia and Alaska that was exposed by the Wisconsin glaciation, allowing people to migrate into the Western Hemisphere.

Berlin Wall Structure erected by East Germany in 1961 to stop the massive exodus of East Germans into West Berlin, which was an embarrassment to the Communists.

Bill of Rights The first ten amendments to the Constitution, officially ratified by 1791. The First through Eighth Amendments dealt with individual liberties, and the Ninth and Tenth concerned the boundary between federal and state authority.

birth control movement Movement launched in 1915 by Margaret Sanger in New York's Lower East Side. Birth control advocates hoped contraception would alter social and political power relationships by reducing the numbers of the working class to induce higher wages and by limiting the supply of soldiers to end wars.

black codes Laws passed by state governments in the South in 1865 that sought to keep ex-slaves subordinate to whites. At the core of the black codes lay the desire to force freedmen back to the plantations.

Black Death A disease that in the mid-fourteenth century killed about a third of the European population and left a legacy of increased food and resources for the survivors as well as a sense of a world in precarious balance.

Black Hills Mountains in western South Dakota and northeast Wyoming that are sacred to the Lakota Sioux. In the 1868 Treaty of Fort Laramie, the United States guaranteed Indians control of the Black Hills but broke its promise after gold was discovered there in 1874.

black power movement Movement of the 1960s and 1970s that emphasized black racial pride and autonomy. Black power advocates encouraged African Americans to assert community control, and some within the movement also rejected the ethos of nonviolence.

"Bleeding Kansas" Term for the bloody struggle between proslavery and antislavery factions in Kansas following its organization in the fall of 1854. Corrupt election tactics led to a proslavery victory, but free-soil Kansans established a rival territorial government, and violence quickly ensued.

Bolshevik Russian revolutionary. Bolsheviks forced Czar Nicholas II to abdicate and seized power in Russia in 1917. In a separate peace with Germany, the Bolshevik government withdrew Russia from World War I.

Bonus Marchers World War I veterans who marched on Washington, D.C., in 1932 to lobby for immediate payment of the pension ("bonus") promised them in 1924. President Herbert Hoover believed the bonuses would bankrupt the government and sent the U.S. Army to evict the veterans from the city.

bossism Pattern of urban political organization that arose in the late nineteenth century in which an often corrupt "boss" maintains an inordinate level of power through command of a political machine that distributes services to its constituents.

Boston Massacre March 1770 incident in Boston in which British soldiers fired on an American crowd, killing five. The Boston Massacre became a rallying point for colonists who increasingly saw the British government as tyrannical and illegitimate.

Boxer uprising Uprising in China led by the Boxers, an antiforeign society, in which 30,000 Chinese converts and 250 foreign Christians were killed. An international force rescued foreigners in Beijing, and European powers imposed the humiliating Boxer Protocol on China in 1901.

Brown v. Board of Education 1954 Supreme Court ruling that overturned the "separate but equal" precedent established in *Plessy v. Ferguson* in 1896. The Court declared that separate educational facilities were inherently unequal and thus violated the Fourteenth Amendment.

burial mounds Earthen mounds constructed by ancient American peoples, especially throughout the gigantic drainage of the Ohio and Mississippi rivers, after about 2500 BP and often used to bury important leaders and to enact major ceremonies.

Cahokia The largest ceremonial site in ancient North America located on the eastern bank of the Mississippi River across from present-day St. Louis where thousands of inhabitants built hundreds of earthen mounds between about AD 700 and AD 1400.

California gold rush Mining rush initiated by James Marshall's discovery of gold in the foothills of the Sierra Nevada in 1848. The hope of striking it rich drew over 250,000 aspiring miners to California between 1849 and 1852 and accelerated the push for statehood.

Calvinism Christian doctrine of Swiss Protestant theologian John Calvin. Its chief tenet was predestination, the idea that God had determined which human souls would receive eternal salvation. Despite this, Calvinism promoted strict discipline in daily and religious life.

Camp David accords Agreements between Egypt and Israel reached at the 1979 talks hosted by President Carter at Camp David. In the accords, Egypt became the first Arab state to recognize Israel, and Israel agreed to gradual withdrawal from the Sinai Peninsula.

Carlisle Indian School Institution established in Pennsylvania in 1879 to educate and assimilate American Indians. It pioneered the "outing system," in which Indian students were sent to live with white families in order to accelerate acculturation.

carpetbaggers Southerners' pejorative term for northern migrants who sought opportunity in the South after the Civil War. Northern migrants formed an important part of the southern Republican Party.

Central Intelligence Agency (CIA) Agency created by the National Security Act of 1947 to expand the government's espionage capacities and ability to thwart communism through covert activities, including propaganda, sabotage, economic warfare, and support for anti-Communist forces around the world.

Chicano movement Mobilization of Mexican Americans in the 1960s and 1970s to fight for civil rights, economic justice, and political power and to combat police brutality. Most notably, the movement worked to improve the lives of migrant farmworkers and to end discrimination in employment and education.

chiefdom Hierarchical social organization headed by a chief. Archaeologists posit that the Woodland cultures were organized into chiefdoms because the construction of their characteristic burial mounds likely required one person having command over the labor of others.

Chinese Exclusion Act 1882 law that effectively barred Chinese immigration and set a precedent for further immigration restrictions. The Chinese population in America dropped sharply as a result of the passage of the act, which was fueled by racial and cultural animosities.

chivalry The South's romantic ideal of male-female relationships. Chivalry's underlying assumptions about the weakness of white women and the protective authority of men resembled the paternalistic defense of slavery.

Civil Rights Act of 1866 Legislation passed by Congress in 1866 that nullified the black codes and affirmed that black Americans should have equal benefit of the law. This expansion of black rights and federal authority drew a veto from President Johnson, which Congress later overrode.

Civil Rights Act of 1964 Law that responded to demands of the civil rights movement by making discrimination in employment, education, and public accommodations illegal. It was the strongest such measure since Reconstruction and included a ban on sex discrimination in employment.

civil service reform Effort in the 1880s to end the spoils system and reduce government corruption. The Pendleton Civil Service Act of 1883 created the Civil Service Commission to award government jobs under a merit system that required examinations for office and made it impossible to remove jobholders for political reasons.

Civilian Conservation Corps (CCC) Federal relief program established in March 1933 that provided assistance in the form of jobs to millions of unemployed young men and a handful of women. CCC workers worked on conservation projects throughout the nation.

Clean Air Act of 1990 Environmental legislation signed by President George H. W. Bush. The legislation was the strongest and most comprehensive environmental law in the nation's history.

Clovis point Distinctively shaped spearhead used by Paleo-Indians and named for the place in New Mexico where the points were first excavated.

Coercive (Intolerable) Acts Four British acts of 1774 meant to punish Massachusetts for the destruction of three shiploads of tea. Known in America as the Intolerable Acts, they led to open rebellion in the northern colonies.

Cold War Term given to the tense and hostile relationship between the United States and the Soviet Union from 1947 to 1989. The term *cold* was apt because the hostility stopped short of direct armed conflict.

Columbian exchange The transatlantic exchange of goods, people, and ideas that began when Columbus arrived in the Caribbean, ending the age-old separation of the hemispheres.

Comanchería Indian empire based on trade in horses, hides, guns, and captives that stretched from the Canadian plains to Mexico in the eighteenth century. By 1865, fewer than five thousand Comanches lived in the empire, which ranged from west Texas north to Oklahoma.

Committee for Industrial Organization (CIO) Coalition (later called Congress of Industrial Organizations) of mostly unskilled workers formed in 1935 that mobilized massive union organizing drives in major industries. By 1941, through the CIO-affiliated United Auto Workers, organizers had overcome violent resistance to unionize the entire automobile industry.

committees of correspondence A communications network established among towns in Massachusetts and also among colonial capital towns in 1772–1773 to provide for rapid dissemination of news about important political developments. These committees politicized ordinary townspeople, sparking a revolutionary language of rights and duties.

Common Sense Pamphlet written by Thomas Paine in 1776 that laid out the case for independence. In it, Paine rejected monarchy, advocating its replacement with republican government based on the consent of the people. The pamphlet influenced public opinion throughout the colonies.

Compromise of 1850 Laws passed in 1850 meant to resolve the dispute over the spread of slavery in the territories. Key elements included the admission of California as a free state and the Fugitive Slave Act. The Compromise soon unraveled.

Compromise of 1877 Informal agreement in which Democrats agreed not to block Hayes's inauguration and to deal fairly with freedmen, and Hayes vowed not to use the army to uphold the remaining Republican regimes in the South and to provide the South with substantial federal subsidies for railroads. The Compromise brought the Reconstruction era to an end.

Comstock Lode Silver ore deposit discovered in 1859 in Nevada. Discovery of the Comstock Lode touched off a mining rush that brought a diverse population into the region and led to the establishment of a number of boomtowns, including Virginia City, Nevada.

Confederate States of America Government formed by Lower South states on February 7, 1861, following their secession from the Union. Secessionists argued that the election of a Republican to the presidency imperiled slavery and the South no longer had political protection within the Union.

conquistadors Term, literally meaning "conqueror," that refers to the Spanish explorers and soldiers who conquered lands in the New World.

containment The post–World War II foreign policy strategy that committed the United States to resisting the influence and expansion of the Soviet Union and communism. The strategy of containment shaped American foreign policy throughout the Cold War.

Continental army The army created in June 1775 by the Second Continental Congress to oppose the British. Virginian George Washington, commander in chief, had the task of turning local militias and untrained volunteers into a disciplined army.

contraband of war General Benjamin F. Butler's term for runaway slaves, who were considered confiscated property of war, not fugitives, and put to work in the Union army. This policy proved to be a step on the road to emancipation.

cotton kingdom Term for the South that reflected the dominance of cotton in the southern economy. Cotton was particularly important in the tier of states from South Carolina west to Texas. Cotton cultivation was the key factor in the growth of slavery.

court-packing plan Law proposed by Franklin Roosevelt to add one new Supreme Court justice for each existing judge who was over the age of seventy. Roosevelt wanted to pack the Court with up to six New Dealers who could protect New Deal legislation, but the Senate defeated the bill in 1937.

Coxey's army Unemployed men who marched to Washington, D.C., in 1894 to urge Congress to enact a public works program to end unemployment. Jacob S. Coxey of Ohio led the most publicized contingent. The movement failed to force federal relief legislation.

Creek War Part of the War of 1812 involving the Creek nation in Mississippi Territory and Tennessee militiamen. General Andrew Jackson's forces gained victory at the Battle of Horseshoe Bend in 1814, forcing the Creeks to sign away much of their land.

creoles Children born to Spanish parents in the New World who, with the *peninsulares*, made up the tiny portion of the population at the top of the colonial social hierarchy.

Cripple Creek miners' strike of 1894 Strike led by the Western Federation of Miners in response to an attempt to lengthen their workday to ten hours. With the support of local businessmen and the Populist governor of Colorado, the miners successfully maintained an eight-hour day.

Cuban missile crisis 1962 nuclear standoff between the Soviet Union and the United States when the Soviets attempted to deploy nuclear missiles in Cuba. In a negotiated settlement, the Soviet Union agreed to remove its missiles from Cuba, and the United States agreed to remove its missiles from Turkey.

Cuban revolution Uprising led by Fidel Castro that drove out U.S.-supported dictator Fulgencio Batista and eventually allied Cuba with the Soviet Union.

cult of domesticity Nineteenth-century belief that women's place was in the home, where they should create havens for their families. This sentimentalized ideal led to an increase in the hiring of domestic servants and freed white middle-class women to spend time in pursuits outside the home.

Dawes Allotment Act 1887 law that divided up reservations and allotted parcels of land to individual Indians as private property. In the end, the American government sold almost two-thirds of "surplus" Indian land to white settlers. The Dawes Act dealt a crippling blow to traditional tribal culture.

D Day June 6, 1944, the date of the Allied invasion of northern France. D Day was the largest amphibious assault in world history. The invasion opened a second front against the Germans and moved the Allies closer to victory in Europe.

Declaration of Independence A document containing philosophical principles and a list of grievances that declared separation from Britain. Adopted by the Second Continental Congress on July 4, 1776, it ended a period of intense debate with moderates still hoping to reconcile with Britain.

Declaratory Act 1766 law issued by Parliament to assert Parliament's unassailable right to legislate for its British colonies "in all cases whatsoever," putting Americans on notice that the simultaneous repeal of the Stamp Act changed nothing in the imperial powers of Britain.

Democrats Political party that evolved out of the Democratic Republicans after 1834. Strongest in the South and West, the Democrats embraced Andrew

Jackson's vision of limited government, expanded political participation for white men, and the promotion of an ethic of individualism.

détente Term given to the easing of conflict between the United States and the Soviet Union during the Nixon administration by focusing on issues of common concern, such as arms control and trade.

domino theory Theory of containment articulated by President Eisenhower in the context of Vietnam. He warned that the fall of a non-Communist government to communism would trigger the spread of communism to neighboring countries.

Double V campaign World War II campaign in America to attack racism at home and abroad. The campaign pushed the federal government to require defense contractors to integrate their workforces. In response, Franklin Roosevelt authorized a committee to investigate and prevent racial discrimination in employment.

***Dred Scott* decision** 1857 Supreme Court decision that ruled the Missouri Compromise unconstitutional. The Court ruled against slave Dred Scott, who claimed travels with his master into free states made him and his family free. The decision also denied the federal government the right to exclude slavery in the territories and declared that African Americans were not citizens.

Earned Income Tax Credit (EITC) Federal antipoverty program initiated in 1975 that assisted the working poor by giving tax breaks to low-income, fulltime workers or a subsidy to those who owed no taxes. President Clinton pushed through a significant increase in the program in 1993.

Economic Recovery Tax Act Legislation passed by Congress in 1981 that authorized the largest reduction in taxes in the nation's history. The tax cuts benefited affluent Americans disproportionately and widened the distribution of American wealth in favor of the rich.

Eighteenth Amendment (prohibition) Amendment banning the manufacture, transportation, and sale of alcohol. Congress passed the amendment in December 1917, and it was ratified in January 1920. World War I provided a huge boost to the crusade to ban alcohol.

Eisenhower Doctrine President Eisenhower's 1957 declaration that the United States would actively combat communism in the Middle East. Following this doctrine, Congress approved the policy, and Eisenhower sent aid to Jordan in 1957 and troops to Lebanon in 1958.

Ellis Island Immigration facility opened in 1892 in New York harbor that processed new immigrants coming into New York City. In the late nineteenth century, some 75 percent of European immigrants to America came through New York.

Emancipation Proclamation President Lincoln's proclamation issued on January 1, 1863, declaring all slaves in Confederate-controlled territory free. The proclamation made the Civil War a war to free slaves though its limitations—exemptions for loyal border states and Union-occupied areas of the Confederacy—made some ridicule the act.

Embargo Act of 1807 Act of Congress that prohibited U.S. ships from traveling to foreign ports and effectively banned overseas trade in an attempt to deter Britain from halting U.S. ships at sea. The embargo caused grave hardships for Americans engaged in overseas commerce.

encomienda A system for governing used during the Reconquest and in New Spain. It allowed the Spanish *encomendero*, or "owner" of a town, to collect tribute from the town in return for providing law and order and encouraging "his" Indians to convert to Christianity.

English Reformation Reform effort initiated by King Henry VIII that included banning the Catholic Church and declaring the English monarch head of the new Church of England but little change in doctrine. Henry's primary concern was consolidating his political power.

Enlightenment An eighteenth-century philosophical movement that emphasized the use of reason to reevaluate previously accepted doctrines and traditions. Enlightenment ideas encouraged examination of the world and independence of mind.

Environmental Protection Agency (EPA) Federal agency created by President Nixon in 1970 to enforce environmental laws, conduct environmental research, and reduce human health and environmental risks from pollutants.

Equal Rights Amendment (ERA) Constitutional amendment passed by Congress in 1972 requiring equal treatment of men and women under federal and state law. Facing fierce opposition from the New Right and the Republican Party, the ERA was defeated as time ran out for state ratification in 1982.

Erie Canal Canal finished in 1825, covering 350 miles between Albany and Buffalo and linking the port of New York City with the entire Great Lakes region. The canal turned New York City into the country's premier commercial city.

family economy Economic contributions of multiple members of a household that were necessary to the survival of the family. From the late nineteenth century into the twentieth, many working-class families depended on the wages of all family members, regardless of sex or age.

Farmers' Alliance Movement to form local organizations to advance farmers' collective interests that gained wide popularity in the 1880s. Over time, farmers' groups consolidated into the Northwestern Farmers' Alliance and the Southern Farmers' Alliance. In 1892, the Farmers' Alliance gave birth to the People's Party.

Federal Deposit Insurance Corporation (FDIC) Regulatory body established by the Glass-Steagall Banking Act that guaranteed the federal government would reimburse bank depositors if their banks failed. This key feature of the New Deal restored depositors' confidence in the banking system during the Great Depression.

Federalists One of the two dominant political groups that emerged in the 1790s. Federalist leaders supported Britain in foreign policy and commercial interests at home. Prominent Federalists included George Washington, Alexander Hamilton, and John Adams.

feme covert Legal doctrine grounded in British common law that held that a wife's civic life was subsumed by her husband's. Married women lacked independence to own property, make contracts, or keep wages earned. The doctrine shaped women's status in the early Republic.

Fifteenth Amendment Constitutional amendment passed in February 1869 prohibiting states from depriving any citizen of the right to vote because of "race, color, or previous condition of servitude." It extended black suffrage nationwide. Woman suffrage advocates were disappointed the amendment failed to extend voting rights to women.

finance capitalism Investment sponsored by banks and bankers that typified the American business scene at the end of the nineteenth century. After the panic of 1893, bankers stepped in and reorganized major industries to stabilize them, leaving power concentrated in the hands of a few influential capitalists.

fireside chats Series of informal radio addresses Franklin Roosevelt made to the nation in which he explained New Deal initiatives. The chats helped bolster Roosevelt's popularity and secured popular support for his reforms.

First Continental Congress September 1774 gathering of colonial delegates in Philadelphia to discuss the crisis precipitated by the Coercive Acts. The congress produced a declaration of rights and an agreement to impose a limited boycott of trade with Britain.

first transcontinental railroad Railroad completed in 1869 that was the first to span the North American continent. Built in large part by Chinese laborers, this railroad and others opened access to new areas, fueled land speculation, and actively recruited settlers.

Five-Power Naval Treaty of 1922 Treaty that committed Britain, France, Japan, Italy, and the United States to a proportional reduction of naval forces, producing the world's greatest success in disarmament up to that time. Republicans orchestrated its development at the 1921 Washington Disarmament Conference.

Fort Sumter Union fort on an island at the entrance to Charleston harbor in South Carolina. After Confederate leaders learned President Lincoln intended to resupply Fort Sumter, Confederate forces attacked the fort on April 12, 1861, thus marking the start of the Civil War.

Fourteen Points Woodrow Wilson's plan, proposed in 1918, to create a new democratic world order with lasting peace. Wilson's plan affirmed basic liberal ideals, supported the right to self-determination, and called for the creation of a League of Nations. Wilson compromised on his plan at the 1919 Paris peace conference, and the U.S. Senate refused to ratify the resulting treaty.

Fourteenth Amendment Constitutional amendment passed in 1866 that made all native-born or naturalized persons U.S. citizens and prohibited states from abridging the rights of national citizens. The amendment hoped to provide guarantee of equality before the law for black citizens.

free black An African American who was not enslaved. Southern whites worried about the increasing numbers of free blacks. In the 1820s and 1830s, state legislatures stemmed the growth of the free black population and shrank the liberty of free blacks.

free labor Term referring to work conducted free from constraint and according to the laborer's own inclinations and will. The ideal of free labor lay at the heart of the North's argument that slavery should not be extended into the western territories.

free silver Term used in the late nineteenth century by those who advocated minting silver dollars in addition to supporting the gold standard and the paper currency backed by gold. Western silver barons and poor farmers from the West and South hoped this would result in inflation, effectively providing them with debt relief.

Freedmen's Bureau Government organization created in March 1865 to distribute food and clothing to destitute Southerners and to ease the transition of slaves to free persons. Early efforts by the Freedmen's Bureau to distribute land to the newly freed blacks were later overturned by President Johnson.

Fugitive Slave Act A law included in the Compromise of 1850 to help attract southern support for the legislative package. Its strict provisions for capturing runaway slaves provoked outrage in the North and intensified antislavery sentiment in the region.

Ghost Dance Religion founded in 1889 by Paiute shaman Wovoka that combined elements of Christianity and traditional Indian religion and served as a nonviolent form of resistance for Indians in the late nineteenth century. The Ghost Dance frightened whites and was violently suppressed.

GI Bill of Rights Legislation passed in 1944 authorizing the government to provide World War II veterans with funds for education, housing, and health care, as well as loans to start businesses and buy homes.

Gilded Age A period of enormous economic growth and ostentatious displays of wealth during the last quarter of the nineteenth century. Industrialization dramatically changed U.S. society and created a newly dominant group of rich entrepreneurs and an impoverished working class.

global migration Movement of populations across large distances such as oceans and continents. In the late nineteenth century, large-scale immigration from southern and eastern Europe into the United States contributed to the growth of cities and changes in American demographics.

good neighbor policy Foreign policy announced by Franklin Roosevelt in 1933 that promised the United States would not interfere in the internal or external affairs of another country, thereby ending U.S. military interventions in Latin America.

gospel of wealth The idea that the financially successful should use their wisdom, experience, and wealth as stewards for the poor. Andrew Carnegie promoted this view in an 1889 essay in which he maintained that the wealthy should serve as stewards for society as a whole.

gradual emancipation A law passed in five northern states that balanced civil rights against property rights by providing a multistage process for freeing slaves, distinguishing persons already alive from those not yet born and providing benchmark dates when freedom would arrive for each group.

Great Awakening Wave of revivals that began in Massachusetts and spread through the colonies in the 1730s and 1740s. The movement emphasized vital religious faith and personal choice. It was characterized by large, open-air meetings at which emotional sermons were given by itinerant preachers.

Great Railroad Strike A violent multicity strike that began in 1877 with West Virginia railroad brakemen who protested against sharp wage reductions and quickly spread to include roughly 600,000 workers. President Rutherford B. Hayes used federal troops to break the strike. Despite the strike's failure, union membership surged.

Gulf of Tonkin Resolution Resolution passed by Congress in 1964 in the wake of a naval confrontation in the Gulf of Tonkin. It gave the president virtually unlimited authority in conducting the Vietnam War. The Senate terminated the resolution following outrage over the U.S. invasion of Cambodia in 1970.

Haitian Revolution The 1791–1804 conflict involving diverse Haitian participants and armies from three

European countries. At its end, Haiti became a free, independent, black-run country. The Haitian Revolution fueled fears of slave insurrections in the United States.

Halfway Covenant A Puritan compromise established in Massachusetts in 1662 that allowed the unconverted children of the "visible saints" to become "halfway" members of the church and baptize their own children even though they were not full members of the church themselves.

Hartford Convention A secret meeting of New England Federalist politicians held in late 1814 to discuss constitutional changes to reduce the South's political power and thus help block policies that injured northern commercial interests.

Haymarket bombing May 4, 1886, conflict in which both workers and policemen were killed or wounded during a labor demonstration in Chicago. The violence began when someone threw a bomb into the ranks of police at the gathering. The incident created a backlash against labor activism.

headright Fifty acres of free land granted by the Virginia Company to planters for each indentured servant they purchased.

Helsinki accords 1975 agreement signed by U.S., Canadian, Soviet, and European leaders, recognizing the post–World War II borders in Europe and pledging the signatories to respect human rights and fundamental freedoms.

Hernandez v. Texas 1954 Supreme Court decision that found that the systematic exclusion of Mexican Americans from juries violated the constitutional guarantee of equal protection.

Holocaust German effort during World War II to murder Europe's Jews, along with other groups the Nazis deemed "undesirable." Despite reports of the ongoing genocide, the Allies did almost nothing to interfere. In all, some 11 million people were killed in the Holocaust, most of them Jews.

Homestead Act of 1862 Act that promised 160 acres in the trans-Mississippi West free to any citizen or prospective citizen who settled on the land for five years. The act spurred American settlement of the West. Altogether, nearly one-tenth of the United States was granted to settlers.

Homestead lockout 1892 lockout of workers at the Homestead, Pennsylvania, steel mill after Andrew Carnegie refused to renew the union contract and workers prepared to strike. Union supporters attacked the Pinkerton National Detective Agency guards hired to protect the mill, but the National Guard soon broke the strike.

House of Burgesses Organ of government in colonial Virginia made up of an assembly of representatives elected by the colony's male inhabitants. It was established by the Virginia Company and continued by the crown after Virginia was made a royal colony.

House Un-American Activities Committee (HUAC) Congressional committee especially prominent during the early years of the Cold War that investigated Americans who might be disloyal to the government or might have associated with Communists or other radicals. It was one of the key institutions that promoted the second Red scare.

Housing Act of 1949 Law authorizing the construction of 810,000 units of government housing. This landmark effort marked the first significant commitment of the federal government to meet the housing needs of the poor.

hunter-gatherer A way of life that involved hunting game and gathering food from naturally occurring sources, as opposed to engaging in agriculture and animal husbandry. Archaic Indians and their descendants survived in North America for centuries as hunter-gatherers.

Immigration and Nationality Act of 1965 Legislation passed during Lyndon Johnson's administration abolishing discriminatory immigration quotas based on national origins. Although it did limit the number of immigrants, including those from Latin America for the first time, it facilitated a surge in immigration later in the century.

impressment A British naval practice of seizing sailors on American ships under the claim they were deserters from the British navy. Some 2,500 British and American men were taken by force into service, a grievance that helped propel the United States to declare war on Britain in 1812.

Incan empire A region under the control of the Incas and their emperor, Atahualpa, that stretched along the western coast of South America and contained more than nine million people and a wealth in gold and silver.

indentured servants Poor immigrants who signed contracts known as indentures, in which they committed to four to seven years of labor in North America in exchange for transportation from England, as well as food and shelter after they arrived in the colony.

Indian Removal Act of 1830 Act that directed the mandatory relocation of eastern tribes to territory west of the Mississippi. Jackson insisted his goal was to save the Indians. Indians resisted the controversial act, but in the end most were forced to comply.

Industrial Workers of the World (IWW) Umbrella union and radical political group founded in 1905 that was dedicated to organizing unskilled workers to oppose capitalism. Nicknamed the Wobblies, it advocated direct action by workers, including sabotage and general strikes, in hopes of triggering a widespread workers' uprising.

intermediate-range nuclear forces (INF) agreement Nuclear disarmament agreement reached between the United States and the Soviet Union in 1987, signifying a major thaw in the Cold War. The treaty eliminated all short- and medium-range missiles from Europe and provided for on-site inspection for the first time.

internment camps Makeshift prison camps, to which Americans of Japanese descent were sent as a result of Roosevelt's Executive Order 9066, issued in February 1942. In 1944, the Supreme Court upheld this blatant violation of constitutional rights as a "military necessity."

Interstate Commerce Commission (ICC) Federal regulatory agency designed to oversee the railroad industry. Congress created it through the 1887 Interstate Commerce Act after the Supreme Court decision in *Wabash v. Illinois* (1886) effectively denied states the right to regulate railroads. The ICC proved weak and did not immediately pose a threat to the industry.

Interstate Highway and Defense System Act of 1956 Law authorizing the construction of a national highway system. Promoted as essential to national defense and an impetus to economic growth, the national highway system accelerated the movement of people and goods and changed the nature of American communities.

Iran-Contra scandal Reagan administration scandal that involved the sale of arms to Iran in exchange for Iran's help securing the release of hostages held in Lebanon and the redirection of the sale's proceeds to finance the Nicaraguan Contras who wanted to unseat an elected government.

Iran hostage crisis Crisis that began in 1979 after the deposed shah of Iran was allowed into the United States following the Iranian revolution. Iranians broke into the U.S. Embassy in Teheran and took sixty-six Americans hostage, imprisoning most of them for more than a year.

Iraq War War launched by the United States, Britain, and several smaller countries in March 2003 against the government of Iraqi dictator Saddam Hussein. It was based on claims (subsequently refuted) that Hussein's government had links to Al Qaeda, harbored terrorists, and possessed weapons of mass destruction.

iron curtain Metaphor coined by Winston Churchill in 1946 to demark the line dividing Soviet-controlled countries in Eastern Europe from democratic nations in Western Europe following World War II.

Jamestown The first permanent English settlement in North America, established in 1607 by colonists sponsored by the Virginia Company.

Jay Treaty 1795 treaty between the United States and Britain, negotiated by John Jay. It secured limited trading rights in the West Indies but failed to ensure timely removal of British forces from western forts and reimbursement for slaves removed by the British after the Revolution.

Jim Crow System of racial segregation in the South lasting from after the Civil War into the twentieth century. Jim Crow laws segregated African Americans in public facilities such as trains and streetcars, curtailed their voting rights, and denied other basic civil rights.

Johnson-Reed Act 1924 law that severely restricted immigration to the United States to no more than 161,000 a year with quotas for each European nation. The racist restrictions were designed to staunch the flow of immigrants from southern and eastern Europe and Asia.

Kansas-Nebraska Act 1854 law that divided Indian territory into Kansas and Nebraska, repealed the Missouri Compromise, and left the new territories to decide the issue of slavery on the basis of popular sovereignty. The law led to bloody fighting in Kansas.

King Cotton diplomacy Confederate diplomatic strategy built on the hope that European nations starving for cotton would break the Union blockade and recognize the Confederacy. This strategy failed as Europeans held stores of surplus cotton and developed new sources outside the South.

King Philip's War War begun by Metacomet (King Philip), in which the Wampanoag Indians attacked colonial settlements in western Massachusetts in 1675. Colonists responded by attacking the Wampanoag and other tribes they believed conspired with them. The colonists prevailed in the brutal war.

Knights of Labor The first mass organization of America's working class. Founded in 1869, the Knights of Labor attempted to bridge the boundaries of ethnicity, gender, ideology, race, and occupation to build a "universal brotherhood" of all workers.

Korean War Conflict between North Korean forces supported by China and the Soviet Union and South Korean and U.S.-led United Nations forces over control of South Korea. Lasting from 1950 to 1953, the war represented the first time that the United States went to war to implement containment.

Ku Klux Klan Secret society that first thwarted black freedom after the Civil War as a paramilitary organization supporting Democrats. It was reborn in 1915 to fight against perceived threats posed by blacks, immigrants, radicals, feminists, Catholics, and Jews. The new Klan spread well beyond the South in the 1920s.

Ladies Association A women's organization in Philadelphia that collected substantial money donations in 1780 to reward Continental soldiers for their service. A woman leader authored a declaration, "The Sentiments of an American Woman," to justify women's unexpected entry into political life.

League of Nations International organization proposed in Woodrow Wilson's Fourteen Points designed to secure political independence and territorial integrity for all states and thus ensure enduring peace. The U.S. Senate refused to ratify the Treaty of Versailles, and the United States never became a member.

Lend-Lease Act Legislation in 1941 that enabled Britain to obtain arms from the United States without cash but with the promise to reimburse the United States when the war ended. The act reflected Roosevelt's desire to assist the British in any way possible, short of war.

Lewis and Clark expedition 1804–1806 expedition led by Meriwether Lewis and William Clark that explored the trans-Mississippi West for the U.S. government. The expedition's mission was scientific, political, and geographic.

Lincoln-Douglas debates Series of debates on the issue of slavery and freedom between Democrat Stephen Douglas and Republican Abraham Lincoln, held as part of the 1858 Illinois senatorial race. Douglas won the election, but the debates helped catapult Lincoln to national attention.

Lone Star Republic Independent republic, also known as the Republic of Texas, that was established by a rebellion of Texans against Mexican rule. The victory at San Jacinto in April 1836 helped ensure the region's independence and recognition by the United States.

Louisiana Purchase 1803 purchase of French territory west of the Mississippi River that stretched from the Gulf of Mexico to Canada. The Louisiana Purchase nearly doubled the size of the United States and opened the way for future American expansion west.

Lowell mills Water-powered textile mills constructed along the Merrimack River in Lowell, Massachusetts, that pioneered the extensive use of female laborers. By 1836, the eight mills there employed more than five thousand young women, living in boardinghouses under close supervision.

loyalists Colonists who remained loyal to Britain during the Revolutionary War, probably numbering around one-fifth of the population in 1776. Colonists remained loyal to Britain for many reasons, and loyalists could be found in every region of the country.

Lusitania British passenger liner torpedoed by a German U-boat on May 7, 1915. The attack killed 1,198 passengers, including 128 Americans. The incident challenged American neutrality during World War I and moved the United States on a path toward entering the war.

Manhattan Project Top-secret project authorized by Franklin Roosevelt in 1942 to develop an atomic bomb ahead of the Germans. The thousands of Americans who worked on the project at Los Alamos, New Mexico, succeeded in producing a successful atomic bomb by July 1945.

manifest destiny Term coined in 1845 by journalist John L. O'Sullivan to justify American expansion. O'Sullivan claimed that it was the nation's "manifest destiny" to transport its values and civilization westward. Manifest destiny framed the American conquest of the West as part of a divine plan.

Marbury v. Madison 1803 Supreme Court case that established the concept of judicial review in finding that parts of the Judiciary Act of 1789 were in conflict with the Constitution. The Supreme Court assumed legal authority to overrule acts of other branches of the government.

Marshall Plan Aid program begun in 1948 to help European economies recover from World War II. Between 1948 and 1953, the United States provided $13 billion to seventeen Western European nations in a project that helped its own economy as well.

Mason-Dixon line A surveyor's mark that had established the boundary between Maryland and Pennsylvania in colonial times. By the 1830s, the boundary divided the free North and the slave South.

mechanical reapers Tools usually powered by horses or oxen that enabled farmers to harvest twelve acres of wheat a day, compared to the two or three acres a day possible with manual harvesting methods.

Medicare and Medicaid Social programs enacted as part of Lyndon Johnson's Great Society. Medicare provided the elderly with universal compulsory medical insurance financed primarily by Social Security taxes. Medicaid authorized federal grants to supplement state-paid medical care for poor people of all ages.

Mexica An empire that stretched from coast to coast across central Mexico and encompassed as many as 25 million people. Their culture was characterized by steep hierarchy and devotion to the war god Huitzilopochtli.

Middle Passage The crossing of the Atlantic by slave ships traveling from West Africa to the Americas. Slaves were crowded together in extremely unhealthful circumstances, and mortality rates were high.

military-industrial complex A term President Eisenhower used to refer to the military establishment and defense contractors who, he warned, exercised undue influence in city, state, and federal government.

Military Reconstruction Act Congressional act of March 1867 that initiated military rule of the South. Congressional reconstruction divided the ten unreconstructed Confederate states into five military districts, each under the direction of a Union general. It also established the procedure by which unreconstructed states could reenter the Union.

miscegenation Interracial sex. Proslavery spokesmen played on the fears of whites when they suggested that giving blacks equal rights would lead to miscegenation. In reality, slavery led to considerable sexual abuse of black women by their white masters.

Missouri Compromise 1820 congressional compromise engineered by Henry Clay that paired Missouri's entrance into the Union as a slave state with Maine's as a free state. The compromise also established Missouri's southern border as the permanent line dividing slave from free states.

Monroe Doctrine President James Monroe's 1823 declaration that the Western Hemisphere was closed to further colonization or interference by European powers. In exchange, Monroe pledged that the United States would not become involved in European struggles. The United States strengthened the doctrine during the late nineteenth century.

Montgomery bus boycott Yearlong boycott of Montgomery's segregated bus system in 1955–1956 by the city's African American population. The boycott brought Martin Luther King Jr. to national prominence and ended in victory when the Supreme Court declared segregated transportation unconstitutional.

Mormons Members of the Church of Jesus Christ of Latter-Day Saints founded by Joseph Smith in 1830. Most Americans deemed the Mormons heretics. After Smith's death at the hands of an angry mob in 1844, Brigham Young moved the people to Utah in 1846.

muckraking Early-twentieth-century style of journalism that exposed the corruption of big business and government. Theodore Roosevelt coined the term after a character in Pilgrim's Progress who was too busy raking muck to notice higher things.

mutually assured destruction (MAD) Term for the standoff between the United States and Soviet Union based on the assumption that a nuclear first strike by either nation would result in massive retaliation and mutual destruction for each. Despite this, both countries pursued an ever-escalating arms race.

National American Woman Suffrage Association (NAWSA) Organization formed in 1890 that united the National Woman Suffrage Association and the American Woman Suffrage Association. The NAWSA pursued state-level campaigns to gain the vote for women. With successes in Idaho, Colorado, and Utah, woman suffrage had become more accepted by the 1890s.

National Energy Act of 1978 Legislation that penalized manufacturers of gas-guzzling automobiles and provided additional incentives for energy conservation and development of alternative fuels, such as wind and solar power. The act fell short of the long-term, comprehensive program that President Carter advocated.

National Organization for Women (NOW) Women's civil rights organization formed in 1966. Initially, NOW focused on eliminating gender discrimination in public institutions and the workplace, but by the 1970s it also embraced many of the issues raised by more radical feminists.

National Recovery Administration (NRA) Federal agency established in June 1933 to promote industrial recovery. It encouraged industrialists to voluntarily adopt codes that defined fair working conditions, set prices, and minimized competition. In practice, large corporations developed codes that served primarily their own interests rather than those of workers or the economy.

natural increase Growth of population through reproduction, as opposed to immigration. In the eighteenth century, natural increase accounted for about three-fourths of the American colonies' population growth.

Navigation Acts English laws passed in the 1650s and 1660s requiring that English colonial goods be shipped through English ports on English ships in order to benefit English merchants, shippers, and seamen.

neutrality acts Legislation passed in 1935 and 1937 that sought to avoid entanglement in foreign wars while protecting trade. It prohibited selling arms to nations at war and required nations to pay cash for nonmilitary goods and to transport them in their own ships.

New (Christian) Right Politically active religious conservatives who became particularly prominent in the 1980s. The New Right criticized feminism, opposed abortion and homosexuality, and promoted a larger role for religion in public life, "family values," and military preparedness.

New Deal coalition Political coalition that supported Franklin D. Roosevelt's New Deal and the Democratic Party, including farmers, factory workers, immigrants, city folk, women, African Americans, and progressive intellectuals. The coalition dominated American politics during and long after Roosevelt's presidency.

"The New Freedom" Woodrow Wilson's 1912 campaign slogan, which reflected his belief in limited government and states' rights. Wilson promised to use antitrust legislation to eliminate big corporations and to improve opportunities for small businesses and farmers.

"The New Nationalism" Theodore Roosevelt's 1912 campaign slogan, which reflected his commitment to federal planning and regulation. Roosevelt wanted to use the federal government to act as a "steward for the people" to regulate giant corporations.

New Jersey Plan Alternative plan drafted by delegates from small states, retaining the confederation's single-house congress with one vote per state. It shared with the Virginia Plan enhanced congressional powers, including the right to tax, regulate trade, and use force to stop popular uprisings.

New Negro Term referring to African Americans who challenged American racial hierarchy through the arts. The New Negro emerged in New York City in the 1920s in what became known as the Harlem Renaissance, which produced dazzling literary, musical, and artistic talent.

new Negroes Term given to newly arrived African slaves in the colonies. Planters usually maintained only a small number of recent arrivals among their slaves at any given time in order to accelerate their acculturation to their new circumstances.

New Netherland Dutch colony on Manhattan Island. New Amsterdam was its capital and colony headquarters.

New Spain Land in the New World held by the Spanish crown. Spain pioneered techniques of using New World colonies to strengthen the kingdom in Europe and would become a model for other European nations.

new woman Alternative image of womanhood that came into the American mainstream in the 1920s. The mass media frequently portrayed young, college-educated women who drank, smoked, and wore skimpy dresses. New women also challenged American convictions about separate spheres for women and men and the sexual double standard.

New York City draft riots Four days of rioting in New York City in July 1863 triggered by efforts to enforce the military draft. Democratic Irish workingmen, suffering economic hardship, infuriated by the draft, and opposed to emancipation, killed at least 105 people, most of them black.

New York Female Moral Reform Society An organization of religious women inspired by the Second Great Awakening to eradicate sexual sin and male licentiousness. Formed in 1833, it spread to hundreds of auxiliaries and worked to curb male licentiousness, prostitution, and seduction.

Newburgh Conspiracy A bogus threatened coup staged by Continental army officers and leaders in the congress in 1782–1783, who hoped that a forceful demand for military back pay and pensions would create pressure for stronger taxation powers. General Washington defused the threat.

Nineteenth Amendment (woman suffrage) Amendment granting women the vote. Congress passed the amendment in 1919, and it was ratified in August 1920. Like proponents of prohibition, the advocates of woman suffrage triumphed by linking their cause to the war.

No Child Left Behind Act 2002 legislation championed by President George W. Bush that expanded the role of the federal government in public education. The law required every school to meet annual testing standards, penalized failing schools, and allowed parents to transfer their children out of such schools.

North American Free Trade Agreement (NAFTA) 1993 treaty that eliminated all tariffs and trade barriers among the United States, Canada, and Mexico. NAFTA was supported by President Clinton, a minority of Democrats, and a majority of Republicans.

North Atlantic Treaty Organization (NATO) Military alliance formed in 1949 among the United States, Canada, and Western European nations to counter any possible Soviet threat. It represented an unprecedented commitment by the United States to go to war if any of its allies were attacked.

Northwest Ordinance Land act of 1787 that established a three-stage process by which settled territories would become states. It also banned slavery in the Northwest Territory. The ordinance guaranteed that western lands with white population would not become colonial dependencies.

NSC 68 Top-secret government report of April 1950 warning that national survival required a massive military buildup. The Korean War brought nearly all of the expansion called for in the report, and by 1952 defense spending claimed nearly 70 percent of the federal budget.

nullification Theory asserting that states could nullify acts of Congress that exceeded congressional powers. South Carolina advanced the theory of nullification in 1828 in response to an unfavorable federal tariff. A show of force by Andrew Jackson, combined with tariff revisions, ended the crisis.

Oneida community Utopian community organized by John Humphrey Noyes in New York in 1848. Noyes's opposition to private property led him to denounce marriage as the root of the problem. The community embraced sexual and economic communalism, to the dismay of its mainstream neighbors.

Open Door policy Policy successfully insisted upon by Secretary of State John Hay in 1899–1900 recommending that the major powers of the United States, Britain, Japan, Germany, France, and Russia should all have access to trade with China and that Chinese sovereignty be maintained.

Oregon Trail Route from Independence, Missouri, to Oregon traveled by American settlers starting in the late 1830s. Disease and accidents caused many more deaths along the trail than did Indian attacks, which migrants feared.

Paleo-Indians Archaeologists' term for the first migrants into North America and their descendants who spread across the Americas between 15,000 BP and 13,500 BP, approximately.

Panama Canal treaty 1977 agreement that returned control of the Panama Canal from the United States to Panama in 2000. To pass the treaty, President Carter overcame stiff opposition in the Senate from conservatives who regarded control of the canal as vital to America's interests.

panic of 1837 First major economic crisis of the United States that led to several years of hard times from 1837 to 1841. Sudden bankruptcies, contraction of credit, and runs on banks worked hardships nationwide. Causes were multiple and global and not well understood.

partible inheritance System of inheritance in which land was divided equally among sons. By the eighteenth century, this practice in Massachusetts had subdivided plots of land into units too small for subsistence, forcing children to move away to find sufficient farmland.

paternalism The theory of slavery that emphasized reciprocal duties and obligations between masters and their slaves, with slaves providing labor and obedience and masters providing basic care and direction. Whites employed the concept of paternalism to deny that the slave system was brutal and exploitative.

Patient Protection and Affordable Care Act Sweeping 2010 health care reform bill that established nearly universal health insurance by providing subsidies and compelling larger businesses to offer coverage to employees. Championed by President Obama, it also imposed new regulations on insurance companies and contained provisions to limit health care costs.

Peace Corps Program launched by President Kennedy in 1961 through which young American volunteers helped with education, health, and other projects in developing countries around the world. More than 60,000 volunteers had served by the mid-1970s.

Pennsylvania Dutch Name given by other colonists to German immigrants to the middle colonies; an English corruption of the German term Deutsch. Germans were the largest contingent of migrants from continental Europe to the middle colonies in the eighteenth century.

Pentagon Papers Secret government documents published in 1971 containing an internal study of the Vietnam War. The documents further disillusioned the public by revealing that officials harbored pessimism about the war even as they made rosy public pronouncements about its progress.

People's Party (Populist Party) Political party formed in 1892 by the Farmers' Alliance to advance the goals of the Populist movement. Populists sought economic democracy, promoting land, electoral, banking, and monetary reform. Republican victory in the presidential election of 1896 effectively destroyed the People's Party.

Persian Gulf War 1991 war between Iraq and a U.S.-led international coalition. The war was sparked by the 1990 Iraqi invasion of Kuwait. A forty-day bombing campaign against Iraq followed by coalition troops storming into Kuwait brought a quick coalition victory.

Personal Responsibility and Work Opportunity Reconciliation Act Legislation signed by President Clinton in 1996 that replaced Aid to Families with Dependent Children with Temporary Assistance for Needy Families. It provided grants to the states to assist the poor and limited welfare payments to two years, with a lifetime maximum of five years.

plantation Large farm worked by twenty or more slaves. Although small farms were more numerous, plantations produced more than 75 percent of the South's export crops.

plantation belt Flatlands that spread from South Carolina to east Texas and were dominated by large plantations.

planter A substantial landowner who tilled his estate with twenty or more slaves. Planters dominated the social and political world of the South. Their values and ideology influenced the values of all southern whites.

Plessy v. Ferguson 1896 Supreme Court ruling that upheld the legality of racial segregation. According to the ruling, blacks could be segregated in separate schools, restrooms, and other facilities as long as the facilities were "equal" to those provided for whites.

Pontiac's Rebellion A coordinated uprising of Native American tribes in 1763 in the Northwest after the end of the Seven Years' War. The rebellion heightened Britain's determination to create a boundary between Americans and Indians, embodied in the Proclamation of 1763.

popular sovereignty The idea that government is subject to the will of the people. Applied to the territories, popular sovereignty meant that the residents of a territory should determine, through their legislatures, whether to allow slavery.

predestination Doctrine stating that God determined whether individuals were destined for salvation or damnation before their birth. According to the doctrine, nothing an individual did during his or her lifetime could affect that person's fate.

presidios Spanish forts built to block Russian advance into California.

progressivism A reform movement that often advocated government activism to mitigate the problems created by urban industrialism. Progressivism reached its peak in 1912 with the creation of the Progressive Party. The term *progressivism* has come to mean any general effort advocating for social welfare programs.

prohibition The ban on the manufacture and sale of alcohol that went into effect in January 1920 with the Eighteenth Amendment. Prohibition proved almost impossible to enforce. By the end of the 1920s, most Americans wished it to end, and it was finally repealed in 1933.

Protestant Reformation The reform movement that began in 1517 with Martin Luther's critiques of the Roman Catholic Church, which precipitated an enduring schism that divided Protestants from Catholics.

Pueblo Bonito The largest residential and ceremonial site, containing more than 600 rooms and thirty-five kivas, in the major Anasazi cultural center of Chaco Canyon in present-day New Mexico.

Pueblo Revolt An effective revolt of Pueblo Indians in New Mexico, under the leadership of Popé, against the Spaniards in 1680. Particularly targeting symbols of Christianity, they succeeded in killing two-thirds of

Spanish missionaries and driving the Spaniards out of New Mexico.

pueblos Multiunit dwellings, storage spaces, and ceremonial centers—often termed kivas—built by ancient Americans in the Southwest for centuries around AD 1000.

Pullman boycott Nationwide railroad workers' boycott of trains carrying Pullman cars in 1894 after Pullman workers, suffering radically reduced wages, joined the American Railway Union (ARU) and union leaders were fired in response. The boycott ended after the U.S. Army fired on strikers and ARU leader Eugene Debs was jailed.

Puritan Revolution English civil war that arose out of disputes between King Charles I and Parliament, which was dominated by Puritans. The conflict began in 1642 and ended with the execution of Charles I in 1649, resulting in Puritan rule in England until 1660.

Puritans Dissenters from the Church of England who wanted a genuine Reformation rather than the partial Reformation sought by Henry VIII. The Puritans' religious principles emphasized the importance of an individual's relationship with God developed through Bible study, prayer, and introspection.

Quakers Epithet for members of the Society of Friends. Their belief that God spoke directly to each individual through an "inner light" and that neither ministers nor the Bible was essential to discovering God's Word put them in conflict with orthodox Puritans.

Reconquest The centuries-long drive to expel Muslims from the Iberian Peninsula undertaken by the Christian kingdoms of Spain and Portugal. The military victories of the Reconquest helped the Portuguese gain greater access to sea routes.

Reconstruction Finance Corporation (RFC) Federal agency established by Herbert Hoover in 1932 to help American industry by lending government funds to endangered banks and corporations, which Hoover hoped would benefit people at the bottom through trickle-down economics. In practice, this provided little help to the poor.

Red scare The widespread fear of internal subversion and Communist revolution that swept the United States in 1919 and resulted in suppression of dissent. Labor unrest, postwar recession, the difficult peacetime readjustment, and the Soviet establishment of the Comintern all contributed to the scare.

Redeemers Name taken by southern Democrats who harnessed white rage in order to overthrow Republican rule and black political power and thus, they believed, save southern civilization.

redemptioners A variant of indentured servants. In this system, a captain agreed to provide passage to Philadelphia, where redemptioners would obtain money to pay for their transportation, usually by selling themselves as servants.

reform Darwinism Sociological theory developed in the 1880s that argued humans could speed up evolution by altering their environment. A challenge to the laissez-faire approach of social Darwinism, reform Darwinism insisted the liberal state should play an active role in solving social problems.

Report on Manufactures A proposal by Treasury Secretary Alexander Hamilton in 1791 calling for the federal government to encourage domestic manufacturers with subsidies while imposing tariffs on foreign imports. Congress initially rejected the measure.

Report on Public Credit Hamilton's January 1790 report recommending that the national debt be funded—but not repaid immediately—at full value. Hamilton's goal was to make the new country creditworthy, not debt-free. Critics of his plan complained that it would benefit speculators.

republicanism A social philosophy that embraced representative institutions (as opposed to monarchy), a citizenry attuned to civic values above private interests, and a virtuous community in which individuals work to promote the public good.

Republican Party Antislavery party formed in 1854 following passage of the Kansas-Nebraska Act. The Republicans attempted to unite all those who opposed the extension of slavery into any territory of the United States.

Republicans One of the two dominant political groups that emerged in the 1790s. Republicans supported the revolutionaries in France and worried about monarchical Federalists at home. Prominent Republicans included Thomas Jefferson and James Madison.

reservations Land given by the federal government to American Indians beginning in the 1860s in an attempt to reduce tensions between Indians and western settlers. On reservations, Indians subsisted on meager government rations and faced a life of poverty and starvation.

rock and roll A music genre created from country music and black rhythm and blues that emerged in the 1950s and captivated American youth.

Roe v. Wade 1973 Supreme Court ruling that the Constitution protects the right to abortion, which states cannot prohibit in the early stages of pregnancy. The decision galvanized social conservatives and made abortion a controversial policy issue for decades to come.

Roosevelt Corollary Theodore Roosevelt's 1904 follow-up to the Monroe Doctrine in which he declared the United States had the right to intervene in Latin America to stop "brutal wrongdoing" and protect American interests. The corollary warned European powers to keep out of the Western Hemisphere.

royal colony A colony ruled by a king or queen and governed by officials appointed to serve the monarchy and represent its interests.

scalawag A derogatory term that Southerners applied to southern white Republicans, who were seen as traitors to the South. Most were yeoman farmers.

Schenck v. United States 1919 Supreme Court decision that established a "clear and present danger" test for restricting free speech. The Court upheld the conviction of socialist Charles Schenck for urging resistance to the draft during wartime.

Scopes trial 1925 trial of John Scopes, a biology teacher in Dayton, Tennessee, for violating his state's ban on teaching evolution. The trial created a nationwide media frenzy and came to be seen as a showdown between urban and rural values.

Scottsboro Boys Nine African American youths who were arrested for the alleged rape of two white women in Scottsboro, Alabama, in 1931. After an all-white jury sentenced the young men to death, the Communist Party took action that saved them from the electric chair.

Scots-Irish Protestant immigrants from northern Ireland, Scotland, and northern England. Deteriorating economic conditions in their European homelands contributed to increasing migration to the colonies in the eighteenth century.

second Bank of the United States National bank with multiple branches chartered in 1816 for twenty years. Intended to help regulate the economy, the bank became a major issue in Andrew Jackson's reelection campaign in 1832, framed in political rhetoric about aristocracy versus democracy.

Second Continental Congress Legislative body that governed the United States from May 1775 through the war's duration. It established an army, created its own money, and declared independence once all hope for a peaceful reconciliation with Britain was gone.

Second Great Awakening Unprecedented religious revival in the 1820s and 1830s that promised access to salvation. The Second Great Awakening proved to be a major impetus for reform movements of the era, inspiring efforts to combat drinking, sexual sin, and slavery.

Selective Service Act Law enacted in 1940 requiring all men who would be eligible for a military draft to register in preparation for the possibility of a future conflict. The act also prohibited discrimination based on "race or color."

Seneca Falls Declaration of Sentiments Declaration issued in 1848 at the first national woman's rights convention in the United States, which was held in Seneca Falls, New York. The document adopted the style of the Declaration of Independence and demanded equal rights for women, including the franchise.

Separatists People who sought withdrawal from the Church of England. The Pilgrims were Separatists.

settlement houses Settlements established in poor neighborhoods beginning in the 1880s. Reformers like Jane Addams and Lillian Wald believed that only by living among the poor could they help bridge the growing class divide. College-educated women formed the backbone of the settlement house movement.

Seven Years' War War (1754–1762) between Britain and France that ended with British domination of North America; known in America as the French and Indian War. Its high expense laid the foundation for conflict that would lead to the American Revolution.

sharecropping Labor system that emerged in the South during reconstruction. Under this system, planters divided their plantations into small farms that freedmen rented, paying with a share of each year's crop. Sharecropping gave blacks some freedom, but they remained dependent on white landlords and country merchants.

Shays's Rebellion Uprising (1786–1787) led by farmers centered in western Massachusetts. Dissidents protested taxation policies of the eastern elites who controlled the state's government. Shays's Rebellion caused leaders throughout the country to worry about the confederation's ability to handle civil disorder.

Sherman Antitrust Act 1890 act that outlawed pools and trusts, ruling that businesses could no longer enter into agreements to restrict competition. Government inaction, combined with the Supreme Court's narrow reading of the act in the *United States v. E. C. Knight Company* decision, undermined the law's effectiveness.

Sherman's March to the Sea Military campaign from September through December 1864 in which Union forces under General Sherman marched from Atlanta, Georgia, to the coast at Savannah. Carving a path of destruction as it progressed, Sherman's army aimed at destroying white Southerner's will to continue the war.

siege of Vicksburg Six-week siege by General Grant intended to starve out Vicksburg. On July 4, 1863, the 30,000 Confederate troops holding the city surrendered. The victory gave the Union control of the Mississippi River and, together with Gettysburg, marked a major turning point of the war.

Six-Day War 1967 conflict between Israel and the Arab nations of Egypt, Syria, and Jordan. Israel attacked Egypt after Egypt had massed troops on its border and cut off the sea passage to Israel's southern port. Israel won a stunning victory, seizing territory that amounted to twice its original size.

slave codes Laws enacted in southern states in the 1820s and 1830s that required the total submission of slaves. Attacks by antislavery activists and by slaves convinced southern legislators that they had to do everything in their power to strengthen the institution.

slavery Coerced labor. African slavery became the most important form of coerced labor in the New World in the seventeenth century.

social Darwinism A social theory popularized in the late nineteenth century by Herbert Spencer and William Graham Sumner. Proponents believed only relentless competition could produce social progress and wealth was a sign of "fitness" and poverty a sign of "unfitness" for survival.

social gospel A vision of Christianity that saw its mission not simply to reform individuals but to reform society. Emerging in the early twentieth century, it offered a powerful corrective to social Darwinism and the gospel of wealth, which fostered the belief that riches signaled divine favor.

Social Security A New Deal program created in August 1935 that was designed to provide a modest income for elderly people. The act also created unemployment insurance with modest benefits. Social Security provoked sharp opposition from conservatives and the wealthy.

Socialist Party Political party formed in 1900 that advocated cooperation over competition and promoted the breakdown of capitalism. Its members, who were largely middle-class and native-born, saw both the Republican and the Democratic parties as hopelessly beholden to capitalism.

Spanish-American War 1898 war between Spain and the United States that began as an effort to free Cuba from Spain's colonial rule. This popular war left the United States an imperial power in control of Cuba and colonies in Puerto Rico, Guam, and the Philippines.

spoils system System in which politicians doled out government positions to their loyal supporters. This patronage system led to widespread corruption during the Gilded Age.

Stamp Act 1765 British law imposing a tax on all paper used for official documents, for the purpose of raising revenue. Widespread resistance to the Stamp Act led to its repeal in 1766.

Strategic Arms Limitation Talks (SALT) Negotiations begun in 1969 that produced an agreement between the United States and the Soviet Union in 1972, limiting antiballistic missiles (ABMs) to two each. The treaty prevented either nation from building an ABM system defense so secure against a nuclear attack that it would risk a first strike.

Strategic Defense Initiative (SDI) Project launched by President Reagan to deploy lasers in space that would prevent enemy missiles from reaching their targets. Critics protested that it violated the 1972 Antiballistic Missile Treaty. The project cost billions of dollars without producing a working system.

Stono Rebellion Slave uprising in Stono, South Carolina, in 1739 in which a group of slaves armed themselves, plundered six plantations, and killed more than twenty whites. Whites quickly suppressed the rebellion.

Sugar (Revenue) Act 1764 British law that decreased the duty on French molasses, making it more attractive for shippers to obey the law, and at the same time raised penalties for smuggling. The Sugar Act regulated trade but was also intended to raise revenue.

Sun Belt Name applied to the West, Southwest, and parts of the South, which grew rapidly after World War II as a center of defense industries and non-unionized labor.

supply-side economics Economic theory that justified the Reagan administration's large tax cuts on the grounds that they would encourage investment and production (supply) and stimulate consumption (demand) because individuals could keep more of their earnings. Reagan's supply-side economics created a massive federal budget deficit.

sweatshop A small room used for clothing piecework beginning in the late nineteenth century. As mechanization transformed the garment industry with the introduction of foot-pedaled sewing machines and mechanical cloth-cutting knives, independent tailors were replaced with sweatshop workers hired by contractors to sew pieces into clothing.

Taft-Hartley Act Law passed by the Republicancontrolled Congress in 1947 that amended the Wagner Act and placed restrictions on organized labor that made it more difficult for unions to organize workers.

Tainos The Indians who inhabited San Salvador and many Caribbean islands and who were the first people Columbus encountered after making landfall in the New World.

task system A system of labor in which a slave was assigned a daily task to complete and allowed to do as he wished upon its completion. This system offered more freedom than the carefully supervised gang-labor system.

Tea Act of 1773 British act that lowered the existing tax on tea to entice boycotting Americans to buy it. Resistance to the Tea Act led to the passage of the Coercive Acts and imposition of military rule in Massachusetts.

Teapot Dome Nickname for scandal in which Interior Secretary Albert Fall accepted $400,000 in bribes for leasing oil reserves on public land in Teapot Dome, Wyoming. It was part of a larger pattern of corruption that marred Warren G. Harding's presidency.

Tet Offensive Major campaign of attacks launched throughout South Vietnam in early 1968 by the North Vietnamese and Vietcong. A major turning point in the war, it exposed the credibility gap between official statements and the war's reality, and it shook Americans' confidence in the government.

three-fifths clause Clause in the Constitution that stipulated that all free persons plus "three-fifths of all other Persons" would constitute the numerical base for apportioning both representation and taxation. The clause tacitly acknowledged the existence of slavery in the United States.

Townshend duties British law that established new duties on tea, glass, lead, paper, and painters' colors imported into the colonies. The Townshend duties led to boycotts and heightened tensions between Britain and the American colonies.

Trail of Tears Forced westward journey of Cherokees from their lands in Georgia to present-day Oklahoma in 1838. Despite favorable legal action, the Cherokees endured a grueling 1,200-mile march overseen by federal troops. Nearly a quarter of the Cherokees died en route.

Treaty of Fort Stanwix 1784 treaty with the Iroquois Confederacy that established the primacy of the American confederation (and not states) to negotiate with Indians and resulted in large land cessions in the Ohio Country (northwestern Pennsylvania). Tribes not present at Fort Stanwix disavowed the treaty.

Treaty of Greenville 1795 treaty between the United States and various Indian tribes in Ohio. The United States gave the tribes treaty goods valued at $25,000. In exchange, the Indians ceded most of Ohio to the Americans. The treaty brought only temporary peace to the region.

Treaty of Guadalupe Hidalgo February 1848 treaty that ended the Mexican-American War. Mexico gave up all claims to Texas north of the Rio Grande and ceded New Mexico and California to the United States. The United States agreed to pay Mexico $15 million and to assume American claims against Mexico.

Treaty (Peace) of Paris, 1783 September 3, 1783, treaty that ended the Revolutionary War. The treaty acknowledged America's independence, set its boundaries, and promised the quick withdrawal of British troops from American soil. It failed to recognize Indians as players in the conflict.

Treaty of Tordesillas The treaty negotiated in 1494 to delineate land claims in the New World. The treaty drew an imaginary line west of the Canary Islands; land discovered west of the line belonged to Spain, and land to the east belonged to Portugal.

tribute The goods the Mexica collected from conquered peoples, from basic food products to candidates for human sacrifice. Tribute engendered resentment among the Mexica's subjects, creating a vulnerability the Spaniards would later exploit.

Triple Alliance Early-twentieth-century alliance between Germany, Austria-Hungary, and Italy, formed as part of a complex network of military and diplomatic agreements intended to prevent war in Europe by balancing power. In actuality, such alliances made largescale conflict more likely.

Triple Entente Early-twentieth-century alliance between Great Britain, France, and Russia, which was formed as part of a complex network of military and diplomatic agreements intended to prevent war in Europe by balancing power. In actuality, such alliances made large-scale conflict more likely.

Truman Doctrine President Harry S. Truman's commitment to "support free peoples who are resisting attempted subjugation by armed minorities or outside pressures." First applied to Greece and Turkey in 1947, it became the justification for U.S. intervention into many countries during the Cold War.

trust A system in which corporations give shares of their stock to trustees who hold the stocks "in trust" for their stockholders, thereby coordinating the industry to ensure profits to the participating corporations and curb competition.

"typewriters" Women who were hired by businesses in the decades after the Civil War to keep records and conduct correspondence, often using equipment such as typewriters. Secretarial work constituted one of the very few areas where middle-class women could use their literacy for wages.

Uncle Tom's Cabin Enormously popular antislavery novel written by Harriet Beecher Stowe and published in 1852. It helped to solidify northern sentiment against slavery and to confirm white Southerners' sense that no sympathy remained for them in the free states.

underconsumption New Dealers' belief that the root cause of the country's economic paralysis was that factories and farms produced more than they could sell, causing factories to lay off workers and farmers to lose money. The only way to increase consumption, they believed, was to provide jobs that put wages in consumers' pockets.

underground railroad Network consisting mainly of black homes, black churches, and black neighborhoods that helped slaves escape to the North by supplying shelter, food, and general assistance.

Union blockade The United States' use of its navy to patrol the southern coastline to restrict Confederate access to supplies. Over time, the blockade became increasingly effective and succeeded in depriving the Confederacy of vital supplies.

United States Constitution The document written in 1787 and subsequently ratified by the original thirteen states that laid out the governing structure of the United States in separate legislative, executive, and judicial branches.

upcountry The hills and mountains of the South whose higher elevation, colder climate, rugged terrain, and poor transportation made the region less hospitable than the flatlands to slavery and large plantations.

USA Patriot Act 2001 law that gave the government new powers to monitor suspected terrorists and their associates, including the ability to access personal information. Critics charged that it represented an unwarranted abridgment of civil rights.

Versailles treaty Treaty signed on June 28, 1919, that ended World War I. The agreement redrew the map of the world and assigned Germany sole responsibility for the war and saddled it with a debt of $33 billion in war damages. Many Germans felt betrayed by the treaty.

Virginia and Kentucky Resolutions 1798 resolutions condemning the Alien and Sedition Acts submitted to the federal government by the Virginia and Kentucky state legislatures. The resolutions tested the idea that state legislatures could judge the constitutionality of federal laws and nullify them.

Virginia Company A joint-stock company organized by London investors in 1606 that received a land grant from King James I in order to establish English colonies in North America. Investors hoped to enrich themselves and strengthen England economically and politically.

Virginia Plan Plan drafted by James Madison, presented at the opening of the Philadelphia constitutional convention. Designed as a powerful three-branch government, with representation in both houses of the congress to be tied to population, this plan eclipsed the voice of small states in national government.

virtual representation The theory that all British subjects were represented in Parliament, whether they had elected representatives in that body or not. American colonists rejected the theory of virtual representation, arguing that only direct representatives had the right to tax the colonists.

visible saints Puritans who had passed the tests of conversion and church membership and were therefore thought to be among God's elect.

Voting Rights Act of 1965 Law passed during Lyndon Johnson's administration that empowered the federal government to intervene to ensure minorities access to the voting booth. As a result of the act, black voting and officeholding in the South shot up, initiating a major transformation in southern politics.

Wagner Act 1935 law that guaranteed industrial workers the right to organize into unions; also known as the National Labor Relations Act. Following passage of the act, union membership skyrocketed to 30 percent of the workforce, the highest in American history.

War Hawks Young men newly elected to the Congress of 1811 who were eager for war against Britain in order to end impressments, fight Indians, and expand into neighboring British territory. Leaders included Henry Clay of Kentucky and John C. Calhoun of South Carolina.

War on Poverty President Lyndon Johnson's efforts, organized through the Office of Economic Opportunity, to ameliorate poverty primarily through education and training as well as by including the poor in decision making.

Warren Court The Supreme Court under Chief Justice Earl Warren (1953–1969), which expanded the Constitution's promise of equality and civil rights. It issued landmark decisions in the areas of civil rights, criminal rights, reproductive freedom, and separation of church and state.

Watergate Term referring to the 1972 break-in at Democratic Party headquarters in the Watergate complex in Washington, D.C., by men working for President Nixon's reelection, along with Nixon's efforts to cover it up. The Watergate scandal led to President Nixon's resignation.

welfare capitalism Industrial programs for workers that became popular in the 1920s. Some businesses improved safety and sanitation inside factories. They also instituted paid vacations and pension plans. This encouraged loyalty to companies rather than to independent labor unions.

Whigs Political party that evolved out of the National Republicans after 1834. With a Northeast power base, the Whigs supported federal action to promote commercial development and generally looked favorably on the reform movements associated with the Second Great Awakening.

Whiskey Rebellion July 1794 uprising by farmers in western Pennsylvania in response to enforcement of an unpopular excise tax on whiskey. The federal government responded with a military presence that caused dissidents to disperse before blood was shed.

Wilmot Proviso Proposal put forward by Representative David Wilmot of Pennsylvania in August 1846 to ban slavery in territory acquired from the Mexican-American War. The proviso enjoyed widespread support in the North, but Southerners saw it as an attack on their interests.

Woman's Christian Temperance Union (WCTU) All-women organization founded in 1874 to advocate for total abstinence from alcohol. The WCTU provided important political training for women, which many used in the suffrage movement.

Works Progress Administration (WPA) Federal New Deal program established in 1935 that provided government-funded public works jobs to millions of unemployed Americans during the Great Depression, in areas ranging from construction to the arts.

World Trade Organization (WTO) International economic body established in 1994 through the General Agreement on Tariffs and Trade to enforce substantial tariff and import quota reductions. Many corporations welcomed these trade barrier reductions, but critics linked them to job loss and the weakening of unions.

World's Columbian Exposition World's fair held in Chicago in 1893 that attracted millions of visitors. The elaborately designed pavilions of the "White City" included exhibits of technological innovation and of cultural exoticism. They embodied an urban ideal that contrasted with the realities of Chicago life.

Wounded Knee 1890 massacre of Sioux Indians by American cavalry at Wounded Knee Creek, South Dakota. Sent to suppress the Ghost Dance, the soldiers opened fire on the Sioux as they attempted to surrender. More than two hundred Sioux men, women, and children were killed.

XYZ affair 1797 incident in which American negotiators in France were rebuffed for refusing to pay a substantial bribe. The incident led the United States into an undeclared war with France, known as the Quasi-War, which intensified antagonism between Federalists and Republicans.

yellow journalism Term first given to sensationalistic newspaper reporting and cartoon images rendered in yellow. A circulation war between two New York City papers provoked the yellow journalism tactics that fueled popular support for the Spanish-American War in 1898.

yeomen Farmers who owned and worked on their own small plots of land. Yeomen living within the plantation belt were more dependent on planters than were yeomen in the upcountry, where small farmers dominated.

Acknowledgments

CHAPTER 5

Father Luís Jayme Describes Conditions at Mission San Diego de Alcalá, 1772:
CREDIT LINE:
From Maynard Geiger, trans. and ed., The Letter of Luís Jayme, O.F.M.: San Diego, October 17, 1772 (Los Angeles, 1970), 38–42. Reprinted by permission of the Academy of American Franciscan History

Father Junípero Serra Describes the Indian Revolt at Mission San Diego de Alcalá, 1775
CREDIT LINE:
From Antonine Tibesar, O.F.M., ed., The Writings of Junípero Serra (Washington, D.C., 1956), 2:401–7. Reprinted by permission of the American Academy of Franciscan History

CHAPTER 9

Abigail Adams Complains of Sedition, 1798
CREDIT LINE:
New Letters of Abigail Adams, 1788–1801, edited by Stewart Mitchell, pp. 165, 167, 172, 179, 193, 196. Copyright © 1974 by The American Antiquarian Society. Reprinted by permission of Houghton Mifflin Company. All rights reserved.

Matthew Lyon Criticizes John Adams, 1798
CREDIT LINE:
Matthew Lyon, Essay in Spooner's Vermont Journal, July 31, 1798, p. 1-2. America's Historical Newspapers, Reprinted with permission of Newsbank and American Antiquarian Society.

Index

Sullivan, John, 185
Sumner, Charles, 329, 376, 389–390, 436, 445, 446
Sumter, Fort, attack on, 401–402, 402(i)
Sunday laws, 221(b)
Sunday Schools, 300
Sun Falcon (Cahokia), 1, 2
Supreme Court (U.S.)
    Cherokee removal and, 295
    on Colfax massacre attackers, 458
    government appointments and, 259
    Jay on, 228
    Reconstruction and, 457
    on slavery in territories, 390, 390(i), 391
Surgery, in Civil War, 428(b), 429(i)
Surplus (financial), 297
Susan Constant (ship), 53
Sutter's Creek, 324(m), 334(b)
Sweden, settlers from, 94
Syphilis, 34

Taino people, 31, 31(i)
Tallmadge amendments, 275–276
Tanaghrisson (Mingo Indians), 139
Taney, Roger B., 390
Tariffs
    of Abominations (1828), 293, 296
    Force Bill and, 296
    reduction of, 296
    revenue from, 258, 265
    as trade barriers, 315
Task system, 121
Taxation. *See also* Duties
    Albany Plan of Union and, 140
    under Articles of Confederation, 197–198, 207
    Civil War and, 405, 419, 421
    in colonies, 131, 135–136, 145–146
    Constitution on, 217
    external and internal, 147
    Grenville duties and, 145–146
    on imports, 67
    Jefferson and, 258
    on land, 368
    protests against, 212–213, 214(i)
    after Revolution, 212–213
    on slaves, 367
    in South, 367–368, 451, 458
    in Spain, 47
    Stamp Act and, 146–150
    of tobacco, 67, 70
    Townshend duties and, 151
    of whiskey, 235–236, 236(i)
    yeomen and, 367–368
Taxation without representation, 146, 151, 160
Taylor, Walter H., 430(i)
Taylor, Zachary, 377
    election of 1848 and, 375, 376, 376(m), 384(m), 385
    free soil and, 376
    in Mexican American War, 330–331, 332
Tea
    protests against British, 154–155
    sugar and, 145(i)
Tea Act (1773), 136, 154–155
Teachers
    in black schools, Klan and, 450(b)
    women and, 299, 317
Technology. *See also* Weapons
    agricultural, 422
    exploration and, 28
    military, 35

Tecumseh (Shawnee Indians), 254(i)
    confederacy of, 253, 254, 265, 266, 268, 295
    death of, 268, 270
    on sale of land, 266–267
    Tippecanoe and, 267
Tejanos, 327, 328(i)
Telegraph, 315, 315(i), 316, 422
Temperance
    movement, 298, 300–301, 301(i)
    "pledge" about, 301, 301(i)
    women and, 301
Tenant farmers, in South, 122
Tennent, William, 127
Tennessee, 436, 445
    Civil War in, 409
    Democrats in, 458
    secession and, 401, 402, 403(m)
Tennessee River region, in Civil War, 407(m), 410
Tenochtitlán, 22, 35, 35(i), 36
Tenskwatawa (Prophet, Shawnee Indians), 253, 254, 266, 267, 270
Tenth Amendment, 229
Tenure of Office Act (1867), 447
Teosinte, 12(b)
Term lengths, in Congress, 216
Territories. *See also* Indian Territory; Northwest Territory
    slavery in, 413
Terrorism
    by Klan, 450–451(b)
    southern Democratic party and, 458, 459(i)
Teton Sioux Indians, 19
Texas
    border with Mexico, 327(m)
    immigrants in, 319
    Lone Star Republic in, 327(m), 328
    migration to, 346
    Redeemers in, 459
    Republic of, 327(m), 329
    secession of, 396, 396(m), 401
    as slave state, 382(m)
    U.S. claims to, 277
Texas War for Independence (1836), 327–328, 328(m)
Texcoco, Lake, 22
Textiles and textile industry
    cotton textile industry (ca. 1840) and, 286, 286(m)
    in Lowell, 286
    mechanization in, 286(i)
    after Revolution, 232
    sample book for, 105(i)
    in South, 352
    strikes in, 287
    women workers in, 286, 286(i), 287, 288–289(b)
Thames, Battle of the (1813), 268
Thanksgiving, feast of, 82
Thayendanegea (Joseph Brant). *See* Brant, Joseph
Thirteenth Amendment, 441
Thomas, Lorenzo, 438(b)
Thomson, Charles, 201(i)
Three-fifths clause, 216, 269, 275
Ticonderoga, Fort, British capture of, 142
Tilden, Samuel J., 459–460, 460(m)
Tippecanoe
    Battle of (1811), 267, 267(m)
    Tecumseh and, 267
Title, of President, 227
Tlaxcala and Tlaxcalan people, 35
Tobacco and tobacco industry, 34, 57–60, 57–66, 350, 351(m)

in Chesapeake region, 57–66, 57(i)
    cutter for, 58(i)
    in English colonies, 52
    European consumers and, 58–59(b)
    price decline in, 289
    regulation of commerce and, 222(i)
    in South, 350, 351(m)
    in southern colonies, 117–118, 122
    taxation of, 67, 70
    trade in, 265
    wrapper from, 75(i)
Todd, Dolley Payne. *See* Madison, Dolley
Toleration. *See* Religious toleration
Tools
    of ancient Americans, 5(i)
    at Chaco Canyon, 17(i)
Toombs, Robert, 376, 393, 402
Tordesillas, Treaty of (1494), 31, 39(m), 53
Tories, loyalists as, 177
Toronto, in War of 1812, 267, 268(m)
Touro synagogue, 221(i)
Town meetings, in New England, 86–87
Townshend, Charles, 150–151
Townshend Acts, 150–154
Townshend duties, 151, 154
Trade. *See also* Commerce; Ships and shipping; Slave trade; Transportation
    Articles of Confederation on, 214
    with Asia, 323
    in borderlands, 127–129
    boycott of British, 151–153, 159–160
    China, 323
    during Civil War, 411–412
    Constitution on, 216
    Embargo Act (1807) and, 265
    European, 28(m)
    expansion of (1870–1910), 290, 309
    French forts and, 137
    Hopewell, 15
    with Indians, 261, 262–263(b), 264
    Mediterranean, 27–28
    Navigation Acts and, 67
    in New England, 89, 108, 267
    in Pacific Northwest, 20, 261
    in Philadelphia, 115–116
    Portugal and, 30
    regulation of, 97–98, 198
    along Sante Fe Trail, 327
    transatlantic, 302(b), 347
    in Virginia, 56(i)
    of Woodland cultures, 11
Trail(s), to West, 324–325, 324(m), 325(i), 325(m)
Trail of Tears, 294(m), 295, 295(i)
Traitors, in Revolution, 178–179, 189(i)
Transcendentalism, 337, 338
Transcontinental railroad, 323, 382, 422, 431
Transportation. *See also* specific types
    improvements in, 283–285, 284(m), 315, 316
    after Revolution, 232–233
    routes of (1840), 284(m)
    segregation of, 457
Travel, after Revolution, 232–233, 233(m)
Travis, Joseph, 343
Travis, William B., 327
Treason. *See also* Traitors
    Declaration of Independence and, 171
    in Revolutionary War, 188–189
Treasury Department, 228, 246
    Hamilton and, 225–226, 246
    Jefferson and, 258–259

ATLAS OF THE TERRITORIAL GROWTH OF THE UNITED STATES

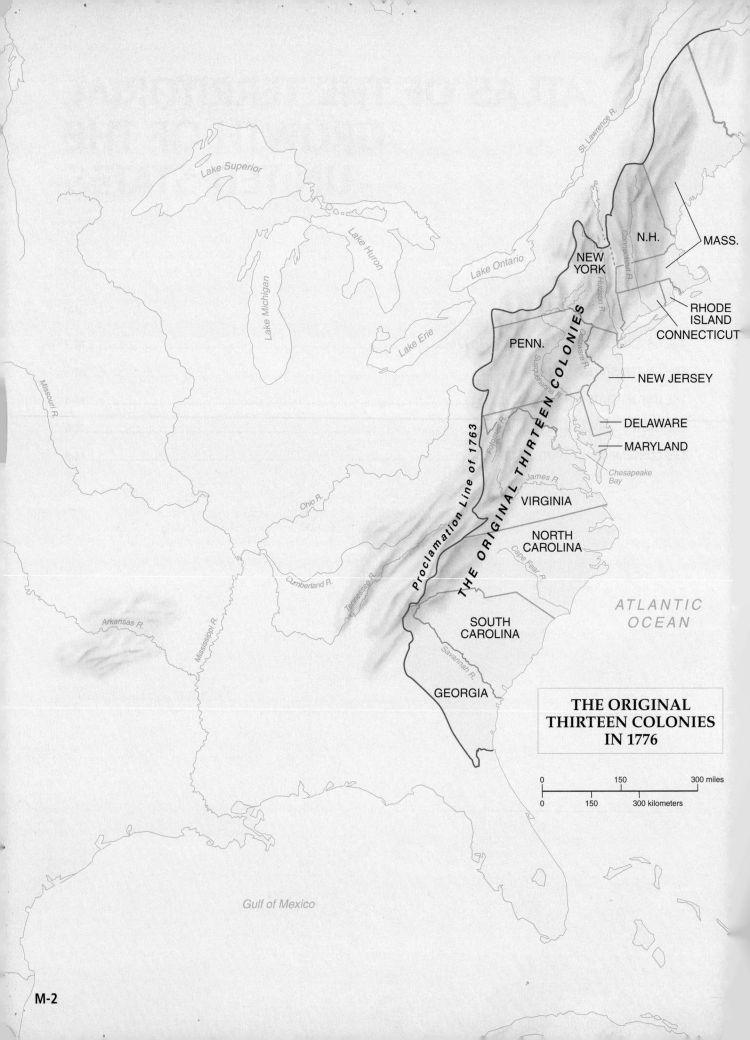

Lake Superior

Lake Huron

Lake Michigan

Lake Ontario

Lake Erie

St. Lawrence R.

N.H.

MASS.

NEW YORK

Connecticut R.

Hudson R.

RHODE ISLAND

CONNECTICUT

PENN.

Delaware R.

Susquehanna R.

NEW JERSEY

DELAWARE

MARYLAND

THE ORIGINAL THIRTEEN COLONIES

Proclamation Line of 1763

Potomac R.

Chesapeake Bay

James R.

VIRGINIA

Ohio R.

NORTH CAROLINA

Cumberland R.

Tennessee R.

Cape Fear R.

ATLANTIC OCEAN

SOUTH CAROLINA

Arkansas R.

Mississippi R.

Savannah R.

GEORGIA

Missouri R.

THE ORIGINAL THIRTEEN COLONIES IN 1776

0   150   300 miles

0   150   300 kilometers

Gulf of Mexico

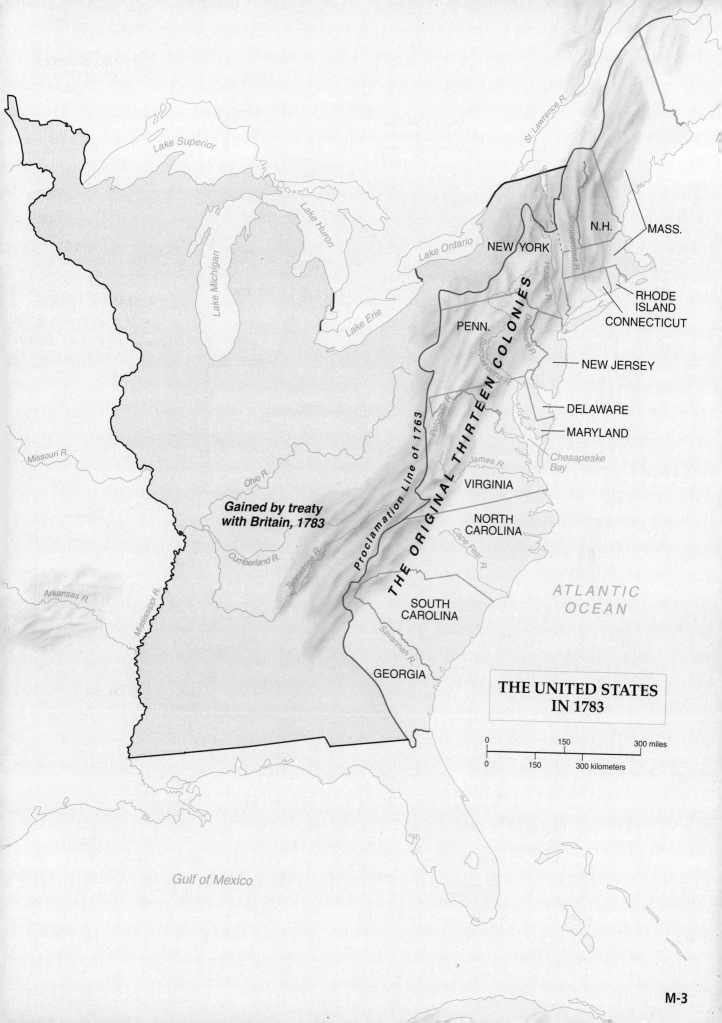

Lake Superior

Lake Huron

Lake Michigan

Lake Ontario

Lake Erie

St. Lawrence R.

N.H.

MASS.

NEW YORK

RHODE ISLAND

CONNECTICUT

Connecticut R.

Hudson R.

PENN.

Delaware R.

Susquehanna R.

NEW JERSEY

DELAWARE

MARYLAND

Missouri R.

Ohio R.

**Gained by treaty
with Britain, 1783**

Proclamation Line of 1763

THE ORIGINAL THIRTEEN COLONIES

Potomac R.

James R.

Chesapeake Bay

VIRGINIA

NORTH CAROLINA

Cape Fear R.

Cumberland R.

Tennessee R.

Arkansas R.

Mississippi R.

SOUTH CAROLINA

Savannah R.

ATLANTIC OCEAN

GEORGIA

**THE UNITED STATES
IN 1783**

0   150   300 miles

0   150   300 kilometers

Gulf of Mexico

M-3

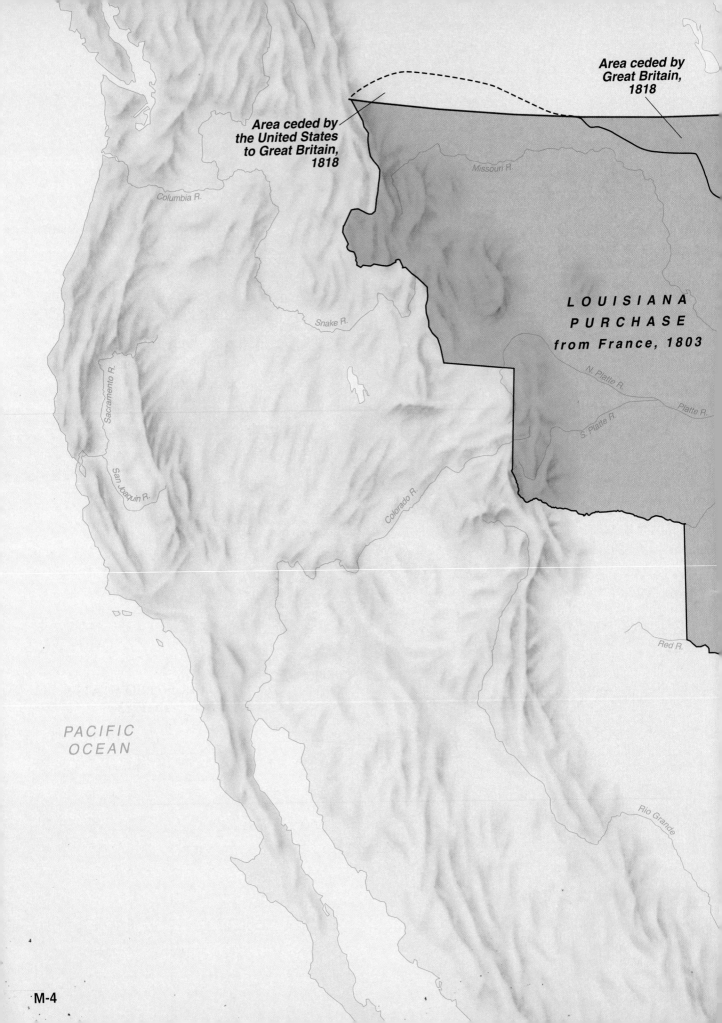

Area ceded by
Great Britain,
1818

Area ceded by
the United States
to Great Britain,
1818

Missouri R.

Columbia R.

Snake R.

**LOUISIANA
PURCHASE**
from France, 1803

N. Platte R.

Platte R.

S. Platte R.

Sacramento R.

San Joaquin R.

Colorado R.

Red R.

**PACIFIC
OCEAN**

Rio Grande

M-4

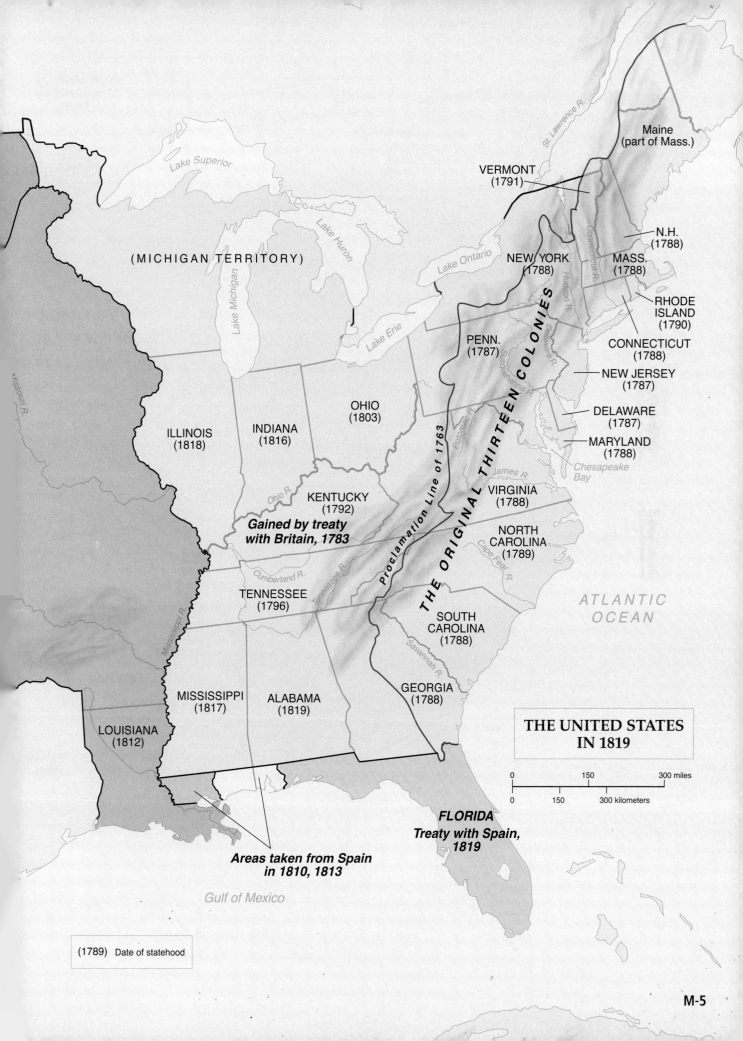

Lake Superior

Lake Huron

Lake Michigan

(MICHIGAN TERRITORY)

Lake Erie

Lake Ontario

St. Lawrence R.

Maine
(part of Mass.)

VERMONT
(1791)

Connecticut R.

N.H.
(1788)

NEW YORK
(1788)

MASS.
(1788)

Hudson R.

RHODE
ISLAND
(1790)

PENN.
(1787)

Delaware R.

CONNECTICUT
(1788)

NEW JERSEY
(1787)

Susquehanna R.

DELAWARE
(1787)

OHIO
(1803)

Potomac R.

MARYLAND
(1788)

ILLINOIS
(1818)

INDIANA
(1816)

Chesapeake
Bay

James R.

Ohio R.

KENTUCKY
(1792)

VIRGINIA
(1788)

**Gained by treaty
with Britain, 1783**

NORTH
CAROLINA
(1789)

Cape Fear R.

Cumberland R.

Tennessee R.

Proclamation Line of 1763

THE ORIGINAL THIRTEEN COLONIES

TENNESSEE
(1796)

SOUTH
CAROLINA
(1788)

ATLANTIC
OCEAN

Mississippi R.

MISSISSIPPI
(1817)

ALABAMA
(1819)

Savannah R.

GEORGIA
(1788)

Missouri R.

LOUISIANA
(1812)

THE UNITED STATES
IN 1819

| 0 | 150 | 300 miles |
| 0 | 150 | 300 kilometers |

FLORIDA
**Treaty with Spain,
1819**

**Areas taken from Spain
in 1810, 1813**

Gulf of Mexico

(1789)   Date of statehood

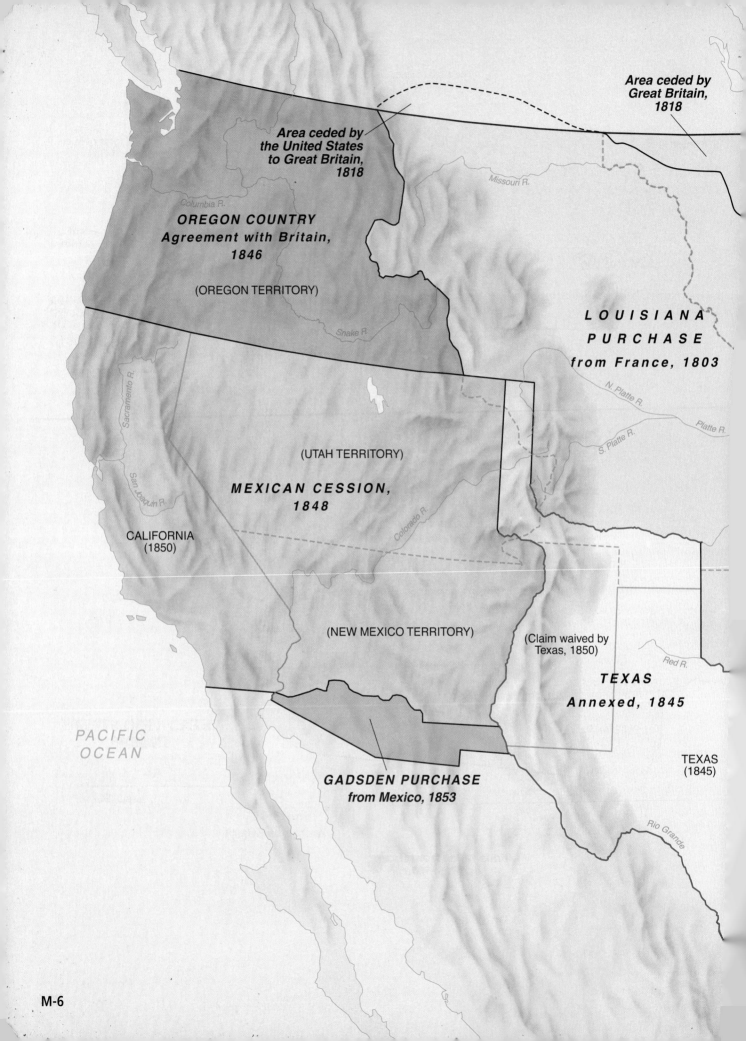

Area ceded by
Great Britain,
1818

Area ceded by
the United States
to Great Britain,
1818

OREGON COUNTRY
Agreement with Britain,
1846

(OREGON TERRITORY)

Columbia R.

Missouri R.

L O U I S I A N A
P U R C H A S E
from France, 1803

Snake R.

N. Platte R.

Platte R.

S. Platte R.

(UTAH TERRITORY)

MEXICAN CESSION,
1848

Sacramento R.

San Joaquin R.

Colorado R.

CALIFORNIA
(1850)

(NEW MEXICO TERRITORY)

(Claim waived by
Texas, 1850)

Red R.

TEXAS
Annexed, 1845

TEXAS
(1845)

PACIFIC
OCEAN

GADSDEN PURCHASE
from Mexico, 1853

Rio Grande

M-6

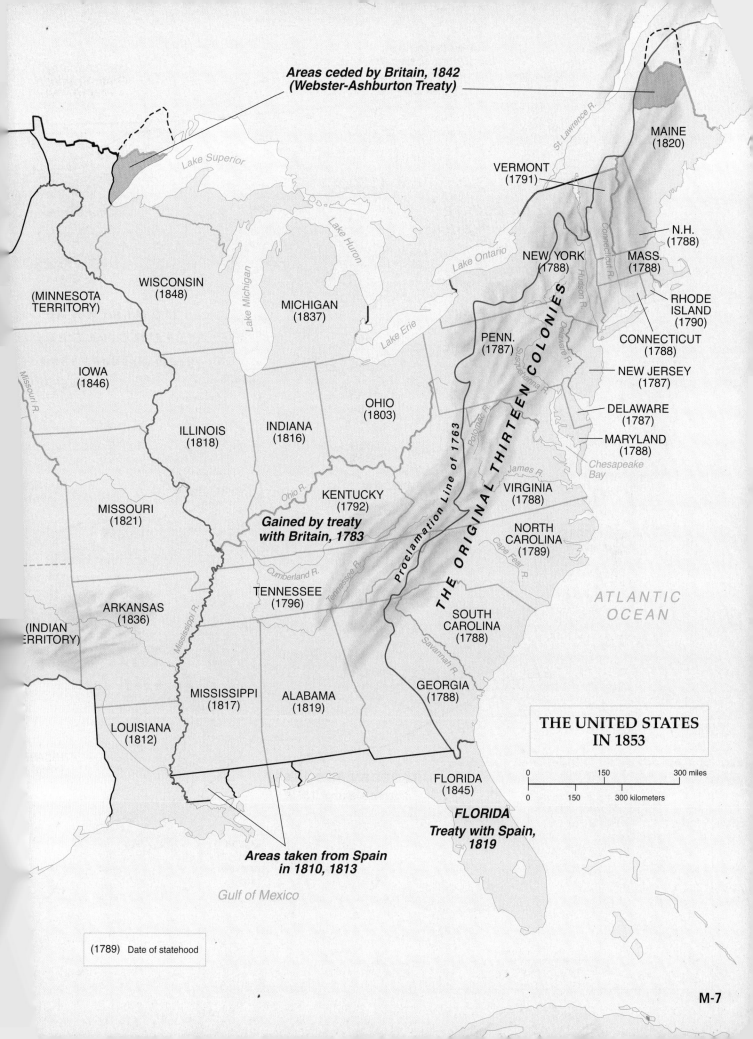

Areas ceded by Britain, 1842
(Webster-Ashburton Treaty)

St. Lawrence R.

MAINE
(1820)

VERMONT
(1791)

N.H.
(1788)

Lake Superior

NEW YORK
(1788)

Connecticut R.

MASS.
(1788)

Lake Ontario

Hudson R.

RHODE
ISLAND
(1790)

(MINNESOTA
TERRITORY)

WISCONSIN
(1848)

Lake Huron

MICHIGAN
(1837)

CONNECTICUT
(1788)

Lake Michigan

Lake Erie

PENN.
(1787)

Delaware R.

NEW JERSEY
(1787)

DELAWARE
(1787)

Susquehanna R.

IOWA
(1846)

OHIO
(1803)

MARYLAND
(1788)

Chesapeake
Bay

Missouri R.

ILLINOIS
(1818)

INDIANA
(1816)

THE ORIGINAL THIRTEEN COLONIES

Potomac R.

James R.

VIRGINIA
(1788)

Ohio R.

KENTUCKY
(1792)

Proclamation Line of 1763

*Gained by treaty
with Britain, 1783*

NORTH
CAROLINA
(1789)

MISSOURI
(1821)

Cape Fear R.

Cumberland R.

Tennessee R.

TENNESSEE
(1796)

ATLANTIC
OCEAN

ARKANSAS
(1836)

SOUTH
CAROLINA
(1788)

(INDIAN
TERRITORY)

Savannah R.

Mississippi R.

MISSISSIPPI
(1817)

ALABAMA
(1819)

GEORGIA
(1788)

THE UNITED STATES
IN 1853

LOUISIANA
(1812)

FLORIDA
(1845)

| 0 | | 150 | | 300 miles |

| 0 | 150 | | 300 kilometers | |

*FLORIDA
Treaty with Spain,
1819*

*Areas taken from Spain
in 1810, 1813*

Gulf of Mexico

(1789)   Date of statehood

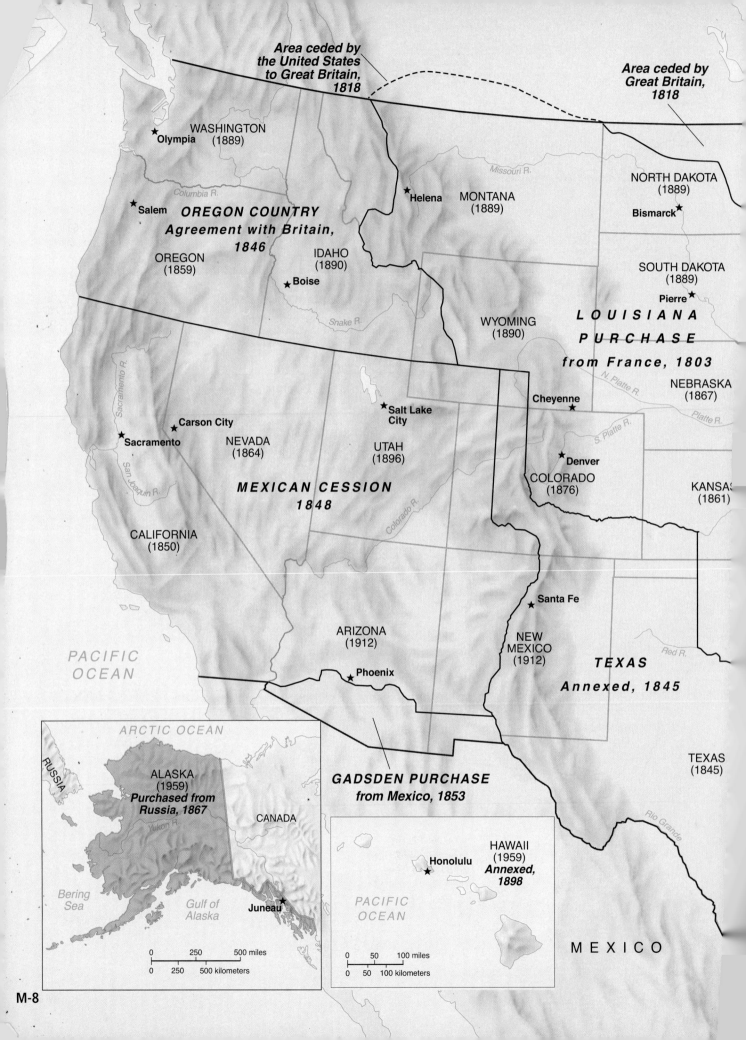

Area ceded by the United States to Great Britain, 1818

Area ceded by Great Britain, 1818

WASHINGTON
(1889)
★ Olympia

Missouri R.

★ Helena
MONTANA
(1889)

NORTH DAKOTA
(1889)
Bismarck ★

Columbia R.

★ Salem
OREGON COUNTRY
Agreement with Britain,
1846

OREGON
(1859)

IDAHO
(1890)
★ Boise

Snake R.

SOUTH DAKOTA
(1889)
Pierre ★

WYOMING
(1890)

L O U I S I A N A
P U R C H A S E
from France, 1803

Cheyenne
★

N. Platte R.
NEBRASKA
(1867)
S. Platte R.
Platte R.

★ Salt Lake City

★ Carson City

★ Sacramento
NEVADA
(1864)

UTAH
(1896)

★ Denver
COLORADO
(1876)

KANSAS
(1861)

Sacramento R.

San Joaquin R.

MEXICAN CESSION
1848

Colorado R.

CALIFORNIA
(1850)

PACIFIC
OCEAN

ARIZONA
(1912)

★ Santa Fe

NEW
MEXICO
(1912)

T E X A S
Annexed, 1845

Red R.

★ Phoenix

GADSDEN PURCHASE
from Mexico, 1853

TEXAS
(1845)

Rio Grande

ARCTIC OCEAN

RUSSIA

ALASKA
(1959)
Purchased from
Russia, 1867

CANADA

Yukon R.

Bering
Sea

Gulf of
Alaska

Juneau ★

0   250   500 miles
0 250   500 kilometers

Honolulu
★

HAWAII
(1959)
Annexed,
1898

PACIFIC
OCEAN

0   50   100 miles
0 50 100 kilometers

M E X I C O

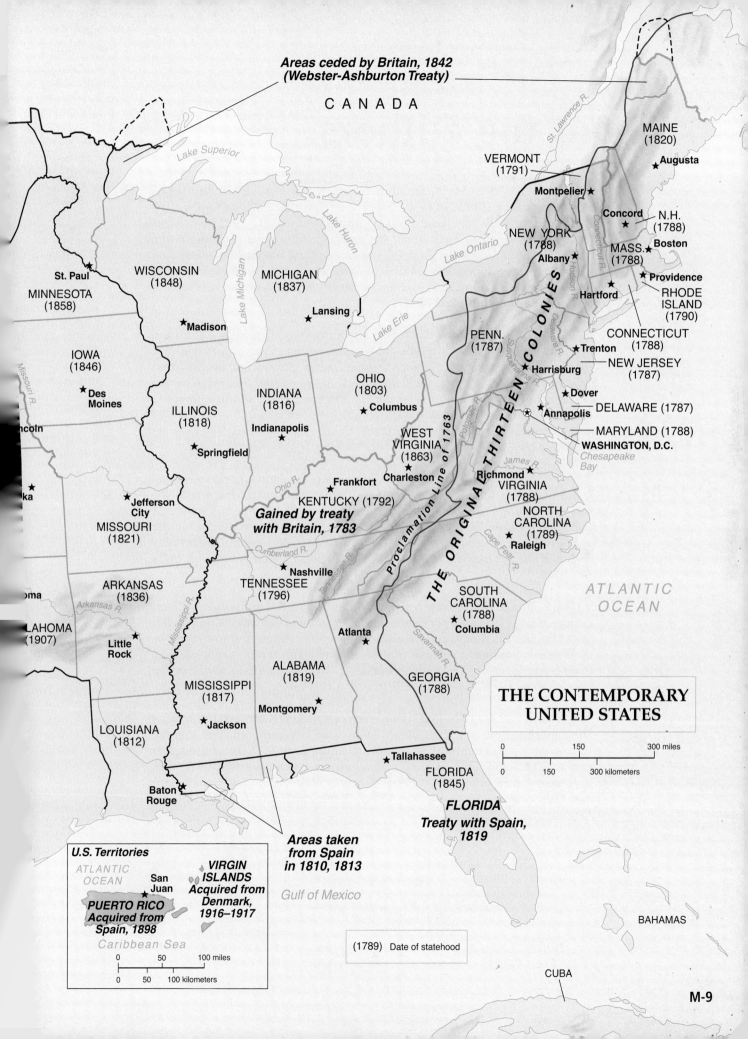

Areas ceded by Britain, 1842
(Webster-Ashburton Treaty)

CANADA

Lake Superior

Lake Huron

Lake Michigan

St. Lawrence R.

MAINE
(1820)
★ Augusta

VERMONT
(1791)
Montpelier ★

Concord ★
N.H.
(1788)

NEW YORK
(1788)
Albany ★

MASS.
(1788)
★ Boston

Connecticut R.

Hudson R.

Hartford ★

★ Providence
RHODE
ISLAND
(1790)

MINNESOTA
(1858)
St. Paul ★

WISCONSIN
(1848)

MICHIGAN
(1837)
Lansing ★

Lake Ontario

Lake Erie

★ Madison

IOWA
(1846)
★ Des
Moines

ILLINOIS
(1818)
★ Springfield

INDIANA
(1816)
Indianapolis ★

OHIO
(1803)
★ Columbus

PENN.
(1787)

Delaware R.

Susquehanna R.

Harrisburg ★

CONNECTICUT
(1788)

★ Trenton
NEW JERSEY
(1787)

★ Dover
DELAWARE (1787)

WEST
VIRGINIA
(1863)
Charleston ★

★ Annapolis
MARYLAND (1788)
WASHINGTON, D.C.

*Chesapeake
Bay*

ncoln

★ Jefferson
City

MISSOURI
(1821)

Ohio R.

Frankfort ★

KENTUCKY (1792)
**Gained by treaty
with Britain, 1783**

Cumberland R.

Potomac R.

James R.

Richmond ★
VIRGINIA
(1788)

Proclamation Line of 1763

THE ORIGINAL THIRTEEN COLONIES

ka

★ Jefferson
City

Tennessee R.

Arkansas R.

Mississippi R.

ARKANSAS
(1836)
Little
Rock ★

LAHOMA
(1907)

oma

Nashville ★
TENNESSEE
(1796)

Atlanta ★

NORTH
CAROLINA
(1789)
Raleigh ★

Cape Fear R.

SOUTH
CAROLINA
(1788)
★ Columbia

ATLANTIC
OCEAN

ALABAMA
(1819)
Montgomery ★

MISSISSIPPI
(1817)
★ Jackson

Savannah R.

GEORGIA
(1788)

**THE CONTEMPORARY
UNITED STATES**

LOUISIANA
(1812)

Baton
Rouge ★

**Areas taken
from Spain
in 1810, 1813**

★ Tallahassee
FLORIDA
(1845)

**FLORIDA
Treaty with Spain,
1819**

0   150   300 miles
0   150   300 kilometers

Gulf of Mexico

U.S. Territories

*ATLANTIC
OCEAN*

San
Juan ★

*VIRGIN
ISLANDS
Acquired from
Denmark,
1916–1917*

**PUERTO RICO
Acquired from
Spain, 1898**

Caribbean Sea

0   50   100 miles
0   50   100 kilometers

(1789)   Date of statehood

BAHAMAS

CUBA

M-9

About the authors

JAMES L. ROARK (Ph.D., Stanford University) is Samuel Candler Dobbs Professor of American History at Emory University. In 1993, he received the Emory Williams Distinguished Teaching Award, and in 2001–2002 he was Pitt Professor of American Institutions at Cambridge University. He has written *Masters without Slaves: Southern Planters in the Civil War and Reconstruction* and with Michael P. Johnson coauthored *Black Masters: A Free Family of Color in the Old South* and coedited *No Chariot Let Down: Charleston's Free People of Color on the Eve of the Civil War*.

MICHAEL P. JOHNSON (Ph.D., Stanford University) is professor of history at Johns Hopkins University. His publications include *Toward a Patriarchal Republic: The Secession of Georgia; Abraham Lincoln, Slavery, and the Civil War: Selected Speeches and Writings;* and *Reading the American Past: Selected Historical Documents,* the documents reader for *The American Promise*. With James L. Roark he has coauthored *Black Masters: A Free Family of Color in the Old South* and coedited *No Chariot Let Down: Charleston's Free People of Color on the Eve of the Civil War.*

PATRICIA CLINE COHEN (Ph.D., University of California, Berkeley) is professor of history at the University of California, Santa Barbara, where she received the Distinguished Teaching Award in 2005–2006. She has written *A Calculating People: The Spread of Numeracy in Early America* and *The Murder of Helen Jewett: The Life and Death of a Prostitute in Nineteenth-Century New York,* and she has coauthored *The Flash Press: Sporting Male Weeklies in 1840s New York.*

SARAH STAGE (Ph.D., Yale University) has taught U.S. history at Williams College and the University of California, Riverside, and she was visiting professor at Beijing University and Szechuan University. Currently she is professor of Women's Studies at Arizona State University. Her books include *Female Complaints: Lydia Pinkham and the Business of Women's Medicine* and *Rethinking Home Economics: Women and the History of a Profession.*

SUSAN M. HARTMANN (Ph.D., University of Missouri) is Arts and Humanities Distinguished Professor of History at Ohio State University. In 1995 she won the university's Exemplary Faculty Award in the College of Humanities. Her publications include *Truman and the 80th Congress; The Home Front and Beyond: American Women in the 1940s; From Margin to Mainstream: American Women and Politics since 1960;* and *The Other Feminists: Activists in the Liberal Establishment.*